INSTRUCTIONAL-DESIGN THEORIES AND MODELS:
An Overview of their Current Status

INSTRUCTIONAL-DESIGN THEORIES AND MODELS:
An Overview of their Current Status

Edited by
Charles M. Reigeluth
Syracuse University

LAWRENCE ERLBAUM ASSOCIATES, PUBLISHERS
1983   Hillsdale, New Jersey   London

Lawrence Erlbaum Associates, Inc., Publishers
365 Broadway
Hillsdale, New Jersey 07642

Library of Congress Cataloging in Publication Data
Main entry under title:

Instructional-design theories and models.

Bibliography: p.
Includes index.
1. Lesson planning. 2. Curriculum planning.
3. Learning, Psychology of. I. Reigeluth, Charles M.
LB1025.2.I646   1983   371.3   83-14185
ISBN 0-89859-275-5

Printed in the United States of America
Thirteenth Printing

Contents

About This Book   xi

Suggestions for Reading This Book   xiii

Foreword   xv
   David R. Krathwohl

UNIT I
INSTRUCTION: WHAT THE DISCIPLINE IS LIKE

1. **Instructional Design: What Is It and Why Is It?**
    Charles M. Reigeluth   3

       Purpose of This Chapter   4
       Why Instructional Design?   5
       How Does Instructional Design Relate
         to Education   6
       What is Instructional Design Like?   12
       How Should You Read This Book?   25
       History of Instructional-Design Theory   27
       Advanced Topics   30

2. **A Metatheory of Instruction: A Framework for Analyzing and Evaluating Instructional Theories and Models**
    George L. Gropper   *37*

> Introduction   38
> A Proposal for a Metatheory of Instruction   39
> Characteristics of Instructional Theories
>   and Models   48
> Summary   52

3. **Descriptive and Prescriptive Theories of Learning and Instruction: An Analysis of Their Relationships and Interactions**
    Lev N. Landa   *55*

> Instructional Processes As A Particular Case of
>   Control (Management) Processes   56
> Descriptive Theories, Prescriptive Theories, and
>   Programs of Instruction   59
> Learning Theories and Programs: Their
>   Relationships With Instructional Theories
>   and Programs   62
> Can Instructional Theories and Programs Be
>   Derived From Learning Theories and
>   Programs?   65
> Regularities of Learning and Instructional
>   Practice   67
> Two Objectives of Instruction   67
> Summary   68

UNIT II
MODELS AND THEORIES OF INSTRUCTION

4. **Contributions of Gagné and Briggs to a Prescriptive Model of Instruction**
    Dennis T. Aronson and Leslie J. Briggs   *75*

> Learning-Theory Background   81
> Selecting Instructional Objectives and
>   Sequencing Instruction   85
> Instructional Events   89
> Instructional Media   93
> Conclusion   97
> Glossary   97

5. **A Behavioral Approach to Instructional Prescription**
    George L. Gropper   101

        Introduction   106
        Conditions   112
        Treatments   124
        Matching Treatments and Conditions   144
        Multiple Objectives   155
        Summary   159

6. **The Algo-Heuristic Theory of Instruction**
    Lev N. Landa   163

        What is the Algo-Heuristic Theory of
            Instruction About?   166
        Building and Testing Models of Unobservable
            Cognitive Processes   172
        Algo-Heuristic Prescriptions as a Means of
            Increasing the Efficiency of Instruction   178
        Some Shortcomings of Conventional
            Instruction   180
        Additional Definitions   186
        Some Methods of the Management and
            Development of Algo-Heuristic
            Processes   190
        An Integrated Model of Instruction   204
        Concluding Remarks and Summary   207

7. **Instructional Strategies Based on the Structural Learning
    Theory**
    Joseph M. Scandura   213

        Introduction   216
        A Prototypic Instructional Strategy Based on
            the Structural Learning Theory   217
        Essentials of Instructional Theory   224
        Overview of the Structural Learning
            Theory   227

8. **A Cognitive Theory of Inquiry Teaching**
    Allan Collins and Albert L. Stevens   247

        Introduction   250
        The Theory   257
        Conclusion   276

9. Component Display Theory
M. David Merrill   279

Introduction   282
The Performance-Content Matrix   285
Presentation Forms   305
Performance-PPF Consistency   311
Content-PPF Consistency   313
Adequacy Rules   320
Learner Control   327
Student Conscious Cognitive Processing   328
Training Materials for CDT   330
Research Support for CDT   330

10. The Elaboration Theory of Instruction
Charles M. Reigeluth and Faith S. Stein   335

Introduction   338
An Analogy   340
Strategy Components   342
The Elaboration Model   364
Variations of the Model   368
Using the Elaboration Theory   370
Support for Validity   372
Conclusion   379

11. Motivational Design of Instruction
John M. Keller   383

Introduction   386
Problems in the Study of Motivation   387
Motivation and Learning   390
Motivational-Design Model   395
Interest   398
Relevance   406
Expectancy   415
Outcomes   422
Conclusions   429

UNIT III
COMMENTARY

12. **Is Instructional Theory Alive and Well?**
  Glenn E. Snelbecker   *437*

      Actual and Potential Audiences   440
      Historical and Contemporary Perspectives   442
      Observations About the Total Group of
          Theories   452
      Observations About Individual
          Theories   456
      Conclusions: Status of Instructional Theory
          and Implications for Users   468

Concluding Remarks   473

Author Index   477
Subject Index   483

About This Book

This book is dedictated to increasing our knowledge about how to improve instruction. It is founded on the premise that the process of learning can be made easier and more enjoyable. During the past twenty-five years, a young discipline has developed to so improve instruction. This discipline about *Instruction* has produced a growing knowledge base about methods of instruction and their effects for different kinds of goals, content, and learners. Because it is a very new discipline, the knowledge that has been generated so far has tended to be piecemeal, and instructional researchers have tended to develop independent "knowledge bases." Moreover, different researchers often use different terms to refer to the same phenomenon, and they often use the same term to refer to different phenomena. The result has been somewhat chaotic.

The major purpose of this book is to encourage the building of a *common knowledge base* that integrates the independent and piecemeal "knowledge bases" that presently characterize the discipline. Unit I discusses the nature of the discipline, especially the nature of the knowledge it generates. Unit II summarizes some of the most comprehensive "knowledge bases" that presently characterize the discipline. It shows that, rather than conflicting and competing with each other, these "knowledge bases"—theories and models—tend to either duplicate or complement each other. Several of these theories represent efforts to integrate independent and piecemeal "knowledge bases" into a common knowledge base, mainly in the form of *optimal models of instruction* which are prescribed on the basis of kind of goals, content, and/or learners. It should be noted that this unit summarizes but a sampling of instructional design theories and models—it is by no means a complete representation of work that has been done. Finally, Unit III presents a discussion about the preceding chapters.

At the time that this book is going to press, a companion volume is nearing completion. It is also edited by myself, and is entitled *Instructional Theories in Action: Lessons Illustrating Selected Theories and Models.* In that book, each of the theories in this book is illustrated in a Lesson, and all lessons teach the same objectives in order to facilitate comparison of the theories and models. Each lesson is followed by commentary that relates specific aspects of the lesson design to specific prescriptions in the theory or model. With only one exception (the Gagné-Briggs theory), the lesson and commentary are authored by the original theorist. The six objectives that comprise each lesson represent a variety of intellectual skills and verbal information. That book complements this one nicely by (1) facilitating the understanding of each theory or model through a concrete representation of it and (2) facilitating the comparison and integration of the theories and models through a clear indication of what unique and valuable contributions each makes to the design of a variety of objectives.

One can envision a time when there will be a variety of different models of instruction, each prescribing the best available methods for achieving a different kind of learning goal under different kinds of conditions. One can also envision researchers all over the world building upon this common knowledge base, continually improving and refining those models. It is my hope that this book will contribute in some small way to forming that common knowledge base.

Charles M. Reigeluth
Syracuse University

Suggestions for Reading
This Book

For use by people who are relatively unfamiliar with the discipline of instructional design (including use as a text in graduate level course), it is suggested that something similar to the following order be used:

Chapter 1, pp. 1–13
Chapters 4 and 8
Review of Chapter 1 (pp. 1–13) in relation to Chapters 4 and 8
Chapter 1 (remainder)
Chapters 2 and 3 +
Review of Chapters 4 and 8 in relation to Chapters 1–3
Chapters 5–7*
Chapters 9–11
Chapter 12

Alternatively, it may be desirable to use a sequence that begins with the most comprehensive of the detailed theories:

Chapter 1, pp. 1–13
Chapters 9–11
Review of Chapter 1 (pp. 1–13) in relation to Chapters 9–11
Chapter 1 (remainder)
Chapters 2 and 3 +
Review of Chapters 9–11 in relation to Chapters 1–3
Chapters 4 and 8
Chapters 5–7
Chapter 12

---

*One or more of these, as time permits
+ If time permits

In either case, we strongly recommend for graduate courses that students be required to develop a small piece of instruction according to the specifications of at least one of the first two theories they study.

Foreword

David R. Krathwohl
Syracuse University

A fast-moving New York executive was weaving his way through the stream of pedestrians, pushing the pace. Suddenly he stepped aside from the line of traffic, stopped, and his face relaxed. Curious, I asked about the change. His reply: "I suddenly asked myself what I was doing, how I got here, and where I was going in such a hurry." We need to copy that behavior in knowledge development as well. It is important to examine the bases out of which a field of knowledge developed, the theories of the field that have operated with some success, and how current work can be consolidated into new models pointing the way to further development. That is what Dr. Reigeluth and his authors have attempted with respect to the field of instructional design.

Instructional design? Is that not pretty presumptuous? Can we really claim to have a base for solidly designing instruction? It seems only a short time ago that learning theorists were telling us that they did not think they had anything substantial to tell us about the pratice of instruction. Of course, shortly after that, such modesty faded when behavioristic psychology was translated into teaching machines and into programmed learning. Education was to be revolutionized. But that has not happened. Though the tantalizing promise of these ideas remains, both teaching machines and programmed instruction have yet to achieve substantial educational roles. This suggests that there is much yet to be learned about instructional design. New and more fully developed formulations of theory into practice are needed. Such efforts are found in this volume in the chapters of Aronson and Briggs, Gropper, Landa, and Scandura. Some practitioners may need to translate some of the terms; physical educators will recognize Landa's *snowball technique* as their method of progressive parts. But the effort is made to move to a level where there is a sufficient translation of the abstract to make instructional design practical at some level.

Proceeding from the abstract to the practical dominates the models presented, but going from practice to theory also has its advantages. It can give a grounded base that is close to reality. A rapid pace has also characterized research on teaching with the adaptation of the work of Bales by Flanders and others. It captured important aspects of the teacher's behavior that were found to be correlated with achievement. For the first time, this gave empirical evidence that we could identify and track a teacher's behaviors, tactics, and strategies, and formulate them into theories of what made a difference in instruction. This orientation from practice to theory underlies the chapter by Collins and Stevens. It is important that both approaches, theory to practice and vice versa, are represented.

Do these formulations provide a solid base on which to advance? Are the future directions suggested by Merrill and Reigeluth the best ones? It is too early to tell. The fact that both Merrill's and Reigeluth's formulations grew out of their experience with TICCIT, an NSF-supported, computer-assisted instruction project that emphasized the development of instructional materials and software rather than hardware, suggests that they have an undergirding foundation for both validity and practicality. But, attempts such as this are important in their own right to help us see how far we have come and to suggest how to extend the state of the art.

Claiming to set forth a general model for instructional design when leaders in the field like Cronbach (1975) are raising questions as to whether there are *any* significant principles of psychology that are not situationally specific may seem daring and presumptuous. But in the discussion, critique, refinement, and challenge to empirical validation of such models comes the test of Cronbach's and others' pessimism, and, if ever, the pressing back of limitations on the possible. This volume should stimulate such testing, and, it is hoped, extend the possible.

ACKNOWLEDGMENTS

The author is very grateful to the Spencer Foundation and to Syracuse University for, respectively, funds and a leave, which made the year at the center possible.

REFERENCE

Cronbach, L. J. Beyond the two disciplines of scientific psychology. *American Psychologist,* 1975, *30,* 116–127.

This book is dedicated to Dave Merrill, whose creativity, objectivity, pragmatism, and dedication to the search for understanding have profoundly influenced my professional life.

INSTRUCTIONAL-DESIGN THEORIES AND MODELS:
An Overview of their Current Status

Unit I
INSTRUCTION: WHAT THE DISCIPLINE IS LIKE

This Unit does not describe any instructional design theories or models; rather it discusses ideas that will help the reader to understand, analyze, and/or evaluate such theories and models.

Chapter 1 focuses primarily on ideas that will facilitate an *understanding* of the theories and models presented in Unit II. At the end of the Chapter, these ideas are synthesized in the form of some specific guidelines to follow as you read each of the chapters in Unit II.

Chapter 2 focuses primarily on ideas that will facilitate the *evaluation* of theories and models of instruction. It presents a "metatheory" that can be used to quantitatively compare two or more theories or models.

Finally, Chapter 3 discusses some of the most important characteristics of instructional theories and models and contrasts them with related characteristics of learning theory and educational practice. The insights it provides will be very useful for a subsequent understanding and analysis of the chapters in Unit II.

1 Instructional Design: What Is It And Why Is It?

Charles M. Reigeluth
Syracuse University

CONTENTS

Purpose Of This Chapter 4
Why Instructional Design? 5
  Inadequacies Of Instruction In Public Schools 5
  Instructional Needs In Other Contexts 6
How Does Instructional Design Relate To Education? 6
  Instruction 7
    Instructional Design 7
    Instructional Development 8
    Instructional Implementation 8
    Instructional Management 8
    Instructional Evaluation 9
    Summary 9
  Interrelationships Among These Disciplines 9
What Is Instructional Design Like? 12
  Concepts (Classification Schemes) 12
  Principles 14
  A Theoretical Framework 14
  An Extension Of The Theoretical Framework 18
    Instructional Methods 18
    Instructional Outcomes 20
    Instructional Conditions 20
  Models And Theories 21
  Descriptive Vs. Prescriptive Principles And Theories 21
  Things Often Confused With Instructional Design 23
  Criteria For Evaluating Instructional Design Theory 24

How Should You Read This Book?   25
History Of Instructional-Design Theory   27
    Contributions Of Others   27
    Some Other Important Contributors To Instructional Design   28
Advanced Topics   30
    How Do You Build Instructional-Design Theory?   30
    Controversy Over Instructional-Design Theory   31

FOREWORD

This chapter discusses why the discipline of instructional design is important, how the discipline relates to the field of education in general, and what the discipline is about. It is argued that instructional design can do much to improve the quality of instruction in public schools, industry, government, and many other contexts. It is shown that instructional design deals with but one aspect of education, and its relationship to some other aspects is discussed.

But most importantly, this chapter is intended to make it *easier* for you to understand and evaluate the instructional theories and models that are presented in Unit II of this book. It discusses such things as concepts, principles, strategies, models, and theories of instruction; it discusses classification schemes; it presents a theoretical framework to facilitate the understanding of theories and models; and it presents a set of criteria for evaluating instructional-design theories. Because all of these topics are intended to facilitate the understanding of subsequent chapters, they are followed by some specific guidelines to follow as you read each of those chapters. Finally, this chapter briefly mentions some of the important contributors to the discipline who are not represented in this book.

C. M. R.

Instructional design is a discipline that is concerned with understanding and improving one aspect of education: the process of instruction. The purpose of any design activity is to devise optimal means to achieve desired ends. Therefore, the discipline of instructional design is concerned primarily with prescribing optimal methods of instruction to bring about desired changes in student knowledge and skills.

PURPOSE OF THIS CHAPTER

The purpose of this introductory chapter is to make it easier for you to read, understand, and evaluate models and theories of instructional design.

The first two sections describe why instructional design is important and how it relates to other aspects of education. The next section helps you to understand and evaluate the following chapters by: (1) clarifying what are the major components of the discipline of instructional design (e.g., what is a theory versus what is a model); (2) presenting a theoretical framework that serves as a "schema" or template for interpreting and understanding the following chapters; (3) identifying other disciplines that are sometimes confused with instructional design (e.g., learning theory and instructional development); and (4) presenting a set of criteria for evaluating instructional-design theories.

The next section presents procedural guidelines for analyzing the chapters in Unit II of this book. The purpose of the following section is to pay tribute to the three great pioneers who founded instructional design as a discipline. Then a brief reference is made to some other important contributors to the discipline. And finally, several advanced topics are discussed.

WHY INSTRUCTIONAL DESIGN?

What is the point in spending a considerable amount of effort and resources to develop knowledge about methods of instruction? Simply put, it is an effective way to alleviate many pressing problems in education. In his presidential address to the American Psychological Association in 1899, John Dewey (1900) called for the development of a "linking science" between learning theory and educational practice. Ralph Tyler has also stated the need for such a body of knowledge. He has described it as playing a sort of *middleman* role (see, for example, Tyler, 1978). Instructional design is this linking science—a body of knowledge that prescribes instructional actions to optimize desired instructional outcomes, such as achievement and affect.

INADEQUACIES OF INSTRUCTION IN PUBLIC SCHOOLS

But do we need such a linking science? Why do we need to know more about instruction? There is a growing concern that public education is not what it should be and could be. The accountability movement is an indication of increasing concern that instruction is inadequate in many public schools. Many students develop a poor conception of their own learning ability (and hence an often devastating self-image) because of frequent failure to learn what was "taught" (see, for example, Bloom, 1972; deCharms, 1968, 1976; Lynch, 1978). Statistics show that the number and proportion of high-school dropouts has been steadily rising since 1967 (Grant & Lind, 1978). Students seem to be more turned off to learning than ever— precisely when learning is becoming increasingly important to cope in a rapidly changing technological society (see, for example, Toffler, 1970). And the increasing cost of public education is raising concern for more cost-effective methods of educating our children. All of these factors and more are evidence of our need for better methods of instruction in public education.

But there is another, more important reason for learning about instruction. Children have important educational needs besides intellectual ones. Because our methods of instruction are generally ineffective, educators have not been able to devote much time and effort to the whole child. If we can develop highly effective instructional resources (whether in books or in computers), then we can free some (more) of the teacher's time to work on the social, psychological, emotional, and moral development of our children. The field of instruction can also show us how to improve the development of our children in those areas.

It is likely that our schools of the future will entail a vastly different role for teachers: Rather than having primary responsibility for a subject, the future teacher will have primary responsibility for a number of children. The teacher will become an advisor, a motivator, and someone whose major interest is the child—the whole child. The teacher will be liberated from the more routine, boring aspects of his or her profession by well-designed instructional resources (including the effective use of lay tutors), by better testing methods, and by better record-keeping systems. But such improvements in education cannot occur before we improve our knowledge about how to design more effective, efficient, and appealing methods of instruction (nor before we improve our knowledge in such areas as computer-assisted testing and computer-managed instruction).

Instructional Needs in Other Contexts

The need for better methods of instruction does not begin and end with public education. Adult (or continuing) education and distance learning (e.g., correspondence schools) need better methods of instruction to prevent attrition. Businesses and the military need better methods to reduce the amount of money and employee time needed for job training. The medical profession needs better methods of instruction for effective patient education and for professional training. Special education needs better methods of instruction to help teachers cope with mentally and physically handicapped children. The list goes on and on.

All indications are that, as our technological society increases its rate of change, education will become increasingly important, and there will be an increasing need to make our methods of instruction more effective, efficient, and appealing in a wide variety of contexts besides public education. We believe that our present point in the history of education is similar to the point at which agriculture was at the time that McCormack was developing the first automatic reaper. A knowledge base on instructional design is necessary to effect the change.

HOW DOES INSTRUCTIONAL DESIGN RELATE TO EDUCATION?

To understand what instructional design is, it is helpful to look at how it relates to other areas of inquiry within education. On the most general level, the field of education can be viewed as being comprised of knowledge about curriculum, counseling, administration, and evaluation, as well as instruction (Beauchamp, 1968). Although there is some overlap, the primary difference between curriculum and instruction as areas of inquiry is that curriculum is concerned primarily with *what* to teach, whereas instruction is concerned primarily with *how* to teach it (Snelbecker, 1974). In this book we are concerned exclusively with the area of instruction.

Instruction

But how does instructional *design* relate to other disciplines within the area of instruction? On the most general level, the area of instruction can be viewed as being comprised of five major activities: design, development, implementation, management, and evaluation (see Fig. 1.1). Each of these five areas within instruction is a *professional activity* done by people who are concerned with instruction. But there is also a *discipline* associated with each—an area of inquiry that is concerned with understanding and improving the means to perform each activity with optimal results. Following is a brief description of these five major disciplines of instruction. Then the major interrelationships among these five disciplines are briefly discussed.

Instructional Design

Instructional design is concerned with understanding, improving, and applying methods of instruction. As a *professional activity* done by teachers and instructional developers, it is the process of deciding what methods of instruction are best for bringing about desired changes in student knowledge and skills for a specific course content and a specific student population. The result of instructional design as a professional activity is an "architect's blueprint" for what the instruction should be like. This "blueprint" is a prescription as to what methods of instruction should be used when for that course content and those students.

On the other side of the coin, instructional design as a *discipline* is concerned with producing knowledge about optimal "blueprints"—knowledge about diverse methods of instruction, optimal combinations of methods (i.e., whole models), and situations in which each of those instructional models is optimal. Some excellent work has been and is being done in this area, and that work is the focus of this book. More is said about this shortly.

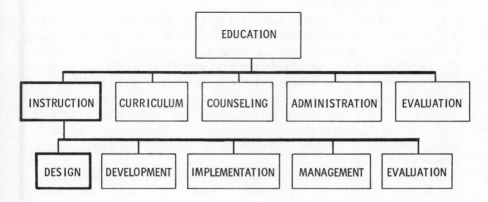

FIG. 1.1 Instructional design's relationship to other areas of inquiry within education.

Instructional Development

Instructional development is concerned with understanding, improving, and applying methods of creating instruction. As a *professional activity,* it is like constructing a building from the architect's blueprint—it is the process of prescribing and using optimal procedures for creating new instruction in a given situation. The result of instructional development as a professional activity is ready-to-use instructional resources, lecture notes, and/or lesson plans (like a ready-to-use building).

On the other side of the development coin, the *discipline* is concerned with producing knowledge about diverse development procedures, optimal combinations of procedures (i.e., whole models), and situations in which each of those development models is optimal. Such models are beyond the scope of this book. The reader is referred to Gustafson (1981) for an excellent review of such models.

Instructional Implementation

Instructional implementation is concerned with understanding, improving, and applying methods of putting some developed instruction into use. As a *professional activity,* it is like a renter's adapting his or her floor of the building to his or her needs and adapting his or her planned operations to the building's constraints. It is the process of prescribing and using optimal procedures for adapting a specific instructional program and/or the instructional institution in which that program is being implemented, so as to enable optimal outcomes from that program in that institution. The result of instructional implementation as a professional activity is an instructional program and/or an institution that has been modified in such a way as to result in the optimal effectiveness of that program.

The *discipline* of instructional implementation is concerned with producing knowledge about diverse implementation procedures, optimal combinations of procedures (i.e., whole models), and situations in which each of those implementation models is optimal. Such models are beyond the scope of this book.

Instructional Management

Instructional management is concerned with understanding, improving, and applying methods of managing the use of an implemented instructional program. It is much narrower than educational administration (mentioned previously) in that it deals only with managing a single instructional program within an institution. As a *professional activity,* it is like maintaining and operating the building—it is the process of prescribing and using optimal time-lines, data-gathering techniques (for data on student progress and on program weaknesses), grading procedures, program revisions and update procedures, and so on. The result of instructional management as a professional activity is the use and maintenance of an implemented instructional program.

The *discipline* of instructional management is concerned with producing knowledge about diverse management procedures, optimal combinations of procedures (i.e., whole models), and situations in which each of those management models is optimal. Such models are beyond the scope of this book.

Instructional Evaluation

Instructional evaluation is concerned with understanding, improving, and applying methods of assessing the effectiveness and efficiency of all of the aforementioned activities: how well an instructional program was designed, how well it was developed, how well it was implemented, and how well it is being managed. It is much narrower than educational evaluation, policy evaluation, and the evaluation of other noninstructional aspects of education. As a *professional activity,* it is like a consultant's giving advice about how the renter can better utilize the building to meet his or her needs. It is the process of prescribing and using optimal techniques for identifying weaknesses. The result of instructional evaluation as a professional activity is a description of weaknesses, consequences, and/or recommendations for improvements.

The *discipline* of instructional evaluation is concerned with producing knowledge about diverse evaluation techniques, optimal combinations of techniques (i.e., whole models), and situations in which each of those evaluation models is optimal. Such models are also beyond the scope of this book.

Summary

In summary, instructional design is concerned with optimizing the process of *instructing.* Instructional development is concerned with optimizing the process of developing the instruction. Instructional implementation is concerned with optimizing the process of implementing the instruction. Instructional management is concerned with optimizing the process of managing the instruction. And instructional evaluation is concerned with optimizing the process of evaluating the instruction.

Interrelationships Among These Disciplines

These five disciplines in instruction are interrelated and interdependent in many ways. For instance, we mentioned earlier that the activity of instructional *evaluation* may deal with evaluating the design, the development, the implementation, and/or the management of an instructional program. Evaluation also draws upon each of the other four disciplines for empirically verified principles and procedures as a sound basis both for identifying specific weaknesses (e.g., see Cronbach, 1963, on "intrinsic evaluation") and for prescribing effective ways to eliminate those weaknesses (e.g., see Merrill, Reigeluth, & Faust, 1979; Reigeluth & Sari, 1980). Also, the activity of instructional *development* is often viewed as encompassing design, implementation, and formative evaluation activities (although in such a view there is still something distinct that happens between design and implementation, and this activity is also what is sometimes referred to as development).

The interactions and interdependencies that are of most interest to us are those involving instructional *design* (see Fig. 1.2). Because design is usually viewed as a part of the development process (broadly defined), design theories and models are usually viewed as an essential component of *development* models. Design is also an important input for the *implementation* process because different kinds of

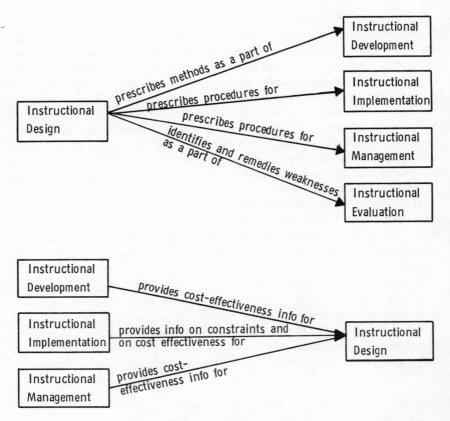

FIG. 1.2   Instructional design as an input for other disciplines in instruction (top), and the other disciplines as inputs for instructional design (bottom).

instructional designs may require different procedures for implementing the instructional program. Thirdly, design is an important input for the *management* process because the best way to manage an instructional program may be different for different kinds of instructional designs. And finally, design is an important input for the *evaluation* process for reasons mentioned previously: instructional design's empirically verified principles are a sound basis for both identifying and remedying weaknesses in an instructional system.

But design is not just an input for other processes; it is also dependent on other processes (see Fig. 1.2). *Implementation* should usually have the greatest impact on instructional design. Design must take into account implementation needs whenever possible because innovative programs of instruction are usually very poorly implemented in existing institutions (e.g., see Cooley & Lohnes, 1976). In a recent evaluation study of the follow-through program, it was found that many "experimental" classrooms did not use individualized teaching methods even though they were supposed to (Cooley & Leinhardt, 1980). The indication is that, because teachers and administrative systems are accustomed to carrying out and supporting instruction in a "usual" way, instructional-design innovations that require substantial changes in the "usual" way often are not implemented. The discipline of instructional implementation may indicate that some designs are incompatible with some characteristics of an existing institution. For instance, it is likely that classrooms with all desks facing forward and attached to the floor are incompatible with designs that call for active classroom discussion among students; and an institution that requires each course to be completed in one term or semester is probably incompatible with a design that is based on self-pacing and mastery learning. If such institution characteristics cannot be changed by the implementers, they become important inputs into the design process in that they constrain the selection of methods. The disciplines of instructional implementation and instructional design should interact to provide the key as to which institution characteristics significantly constrain which instructional methods and which institution characteristics it is possible to change.

Design is also dependent on *development* for important cost-effectiveness information on the design process—some designs may be more expensive to develop than they are worth. The disciplines of *implementation* and *management* may provide similar cost-effectiveness information—some designs may be more expensive to implement or to manage than they are worth. *Evaluation* has no direct input into instructional-design models and theory, but it does provide a basis for validating and/or revising instructional-design prescriptions. For example, a program may have been designed according to a set of instructional-design prescriptions. An evaluation of that program might identify certain weaknesses that require revision of those prescriptions. On the other hand, it might find no weaknesses in the instruction itself, in which case the prescriptions would be validated to some extent.

One final distinction of interest on this subject is that each of the just-described disciplines has *models* that are used by practitioners and processes that are used on those models. The models are of the five kinds previously described: design, development, implementation, management, and evaluation. To confuse the issue, the processes that are applied to each of those kinds of models are: design, development, implementation, management, and evaluation. For example, instructional-design models can be designed, developed, implemented, managed, and evaluated. Such is the case for the four other kinds of models, too.

Having now looked at why instructional design is important and how it relates to other disciplines within education, let us move on to what instructional-design theories and models are and some useful background knowledge for understanding and evaluating them.

WHAT IS INSTRUCTIONAL DESIGN LIKE?

This section of this chapter is intended to help you understand and evaluate the instructional theories and models presented in Unit II of this book. It discusses such topics as concepts, principles, strategies, models, and theories of instruction; it discusses conceptual and theoretical frameworks; and it presents a set of criteria for evaluating instructional-design theories.

The discipline of instructional design (which is often called instructional science) is concerned with producing knowledge about optimal "blueprints"—knowledge about what methods of instruction will optimize different kinds of desired outcomes. This knowledge has two components: concepts and principles. *Concepts* are human-made and hence are arbitrary, whereas *principles* exist naturally and hence are discovered. Concepts are categories of phenomena (such as "trees" or quadratic equations" or "sonnets"), whereas principles show change relationships—they show how one change (or action) is related to another change (or action)—usually by describing causes and effects (such as "the law of supply and demand" or "the law of gravity" or "the pendulum principle").[1]

Concepts (Classification Schemes)

When we say that concepts are human-made and arbitrary, we mean that phenomena can be conceptualized (i.e., grouped or categorized) in *many alternative ways*. Trees can be classified according to their age (e.g., saplings), their leaves (e.g., deciduous), their genus (e.g., oak), their climate (e.g., tropical), or many other characteristics; and each of these categories cuts across a number of other categories (e.g., saplings may be oaks, maples, etc.; seedlings may be oaks, maples, etc., and so on). In a similar way, the instructional world can be conceptualized in different ways. Methods of instruction can be classified according to the subject matter on which they are used (e.g., methods for teaching mathematics), the students with whom they are used (e.g., methods for special education), the philosophical orientation with which they are associated (e.g., behaviorist methods), or many other characteristics.

Practically all classification schemes will improve our understanding of instructional phenomena, but concepts are not the kind of knowledge for which instructional scientists are looking, except as a stepping stone. Instructional scientists want to determine *when* different methods should be used—they want to discover principles of instruction—so that they can prescribe optimal methods. But not all classification schemes are equally useful for forming highly reliable and broadly applicable principles (see Fig. 1.3). Some classifications of trees and diseases will

---

[1] All principles show "change" relationships: They show that one change is related to another. However, not all change relationships are causal relationship—for instance, they may be correlational (non-directional).

Classification Schemes

- are arbitrary
- may categorize phenomena in many alternative ways
- have different degrees of predictive usefulness
    - due to the way that the phenomena are categorized
    - due to the level of generality of the categories.

FIG. 1.3 Characteristics of classification schemes.

have little value for predicting which trees are likely to come down with which diseases (e.g., classes of trees based on their ages), whereas other classifications will have high predictive value (e.g., genus—only elms are attacked by Dutch Elm disease). The same is true of classes of instructional phenomena: Some will have high *predictive usefulness* and some will not. The challenge to our discipline is to find out which ones are the most useful.

Besides the grouping of phenomena (in ways that may or may not be useful), another factor that will influence the predictive usefulness of a classification scheme is the *level of generality* of the concepts, especially of the methods. Many methods that have been investigated in the past are not very useful because they are too general (and often too loosely defined). For instance, "lecture" versus "discussion group," "inductive" versus "deductive," and "discovery" versus "expository" often vary more within each category than between categories. If progress is to be made in improving our methods of instruction, then it is essential to break down such general methods into more elemental *strategy components*—which are more precise and clearly defined—and to build one's models and theories with those more precise, clearly defined, elemental, building blocks. (Strategy components include such parts of methods as definitions, examples, and practice; but even more elemental characteristics of each of these can also be identified, such as visual versus verbal representations of each, formating of each, ways in which the examples can differ from each other, and many more. See Chapter 9 for more information about and examples of these strategy components.)

As you proceed to analyze the instructional models and theories presented in the remainder of this book, keep in mind that concepts are arbitrary, that categories of phenomena (such as methods and the conditions under which those methods are used) will vary from one model or theory to another, that some categorization schemes may be too general to be useful, whereas others, although precise enough, may just group phenomena in a way that is not useful, and that classification schemes (concepts) can ultimately only be evaluated on the basis of their predictive usefulness—the reliability of the cause-and-effect relationships into which they enter (see Fig. 1.3). (Categorization schemes can be evaluated on the basis of a number of internal characteristics, such as whether or not every phenomenon fits into one, and only one, category of a single scheme. However, for our purposes, such internal characteristics are of minor importance in relation to their predictive usefulness.)

Principles

A principle describes a relationship between two actions or changes. This relationship may be *correlational*, in which case it does not state which action influences the other, or it may be *causal*, in which case it does state which action influences the other (see Fig. 1.4). It also may be *deterministic*, in which case the cause always has the stated effect, or it may be *probabilistic*, in which case the cause sometimes (or often) has the stated effect. Finally, the term *principle* is used here regardless of the degree of certainty of the relationship. Hence, it includes everything from pure conjecture or hypothesis (having little or no evidence for its truthfulness) to scientific law (having much evidence for its truthfulness).

A Theoretical Framework

Several people who have written about the process of theory construction have advocated the use of paradigms or metatheories as useful for providing a framework within which to build one's theory (e.g., Snelbecker, 1974; Snow, 1971), and such frameworks can be very useful for both understanding and evaluating a theory or model as well. A *paradigm*, according to Snelbecker (1974), is "a basic building block or basic theme which occurs frequently in articulation of the theory or model [p. 33]." A *metatheory*, according to Snow (1971), "provides a kind of syntax or grammatical structure within which a particular theory can be developed and stated [p. 80]." For our purposes, we use the term *framework* as synonymous with both paradigm and metatheory. We propose that the following framework (from Reigeluth & Merrill, 1978, 1979) is a particularly useful one for understanding and analyzing instructional theories and models.

In contrast to Glaser's (1965, 1976) four components of a *psychology* of instruction (analyzing the subject matter, diagnosing preinstructional behavior, carrying out the instructional process, and measuring learning outcomes), Reigeluth and Merrill (1978, 1979) have proposed that there are three major components of a *theory* of instruction: methods, conditions, and outcomes. Instructional *methods* are the different ways to achieve different outcomes under different conditions. An instructional designer or educator must be able to manipulate them in order for them to be method variables. Instructional *conditions* are defined as factors that influence the effects of methods and are therefore important for prescribing methods. Hence, conditions are variables that both (1) interact with methods to influence their relative effectiveness and (2) cannot be manipulated in a given situation (i.e., they are beyond the control of the instructional designer or educator).[2]

---

[2]Instructional conditions are not the same as *conditions of learning* (Gagné, 1977, and Chapter 4 of this book). Conditions of learning may be factors internal or external to the learner. *Internal conditions of learning* include such things as mastery of prerequisite skills and knowledge. Any internal conditions

Instructional *outcomes* are the various effects that provide a measure of the value of alternative methods under different conditions. Outcomes may be actual or desired. *Actual* outcomes are the real-life results of using specific methods under specific conditions, whereas *desired* outcomes are goals, which often influence what methods should be selected.

The identification of instructional conditions, methods, and outcomes as the three major components of principles and theories of instruction is akin to the distinction drawn by Herbert Simon. Simon (1969) has stated that all design sciences have three major components: (1) alternative goals or requirements; (2) possibilities for action; and (3) fixed parameters or constraints. He has also stated that these three components provide a framework for devising functional prescriptions for goal attainment. These three major components are equivalent to instructional outcomes, methods, and conditions, respectively. And the functional prescriptions for goal attainment are prescriptive principles and theories of instruction.

It should also be noted that the notion of ATI (Aptitude-Treatment Interaction; see, for example, Cronbach & Snow, 1977) is a special case of the conditions–methods–outcomes framework. "Aptitude" in this context means "student characteristic," and "treatment" is synonymous with method. Hence, the term *ATI* refers to prescribing methods on the basis of student characteristics. (Note that ATI is a metatheory, not a theory of instruction, and hence it is not included in this book.) The major problem with the ATI metatheory is that it ignores other important kinds of condition variables that are necessary to prescribe optimal methods of instruction.

Conditions and methods are not fixed categories. Something that is a method variable in one school (because the teacher can change it) may be a condition variable in another school (because the teacher cannot change it). For example, "medium of instruction" may be a method variable in School A because the teacher has a choice of lecture, discussion, or film for presenting instruction on a topic. On the other hand, "medium of instruction" may be a condition variable in School B because lecture is the only available way of presenting the instruction—films are not available and the class is too large for discussion.

If a "method" cannot be changed in a given situation, then it is no longer a method: It is a condition (assuming that it interacts with methods). And, if a "condition" can be *manipulated* in a given situation (e.g., being able to select only students who are highly motivated, as opposed to being forced to take students who are at all levels of motivation), it has become a method—assuming that it influences outcomes. Also, "conditions" that do not *interact with methods* (e.g., the color of the ceiling) are not considered as conditions even if they influence outcomes, because they have no value for deciding when to use different methods.

---

of learning that interact with methods of instruction are instructional conditions. *External conditions of learning* include such things as examples and generalities. Because they can be manipulated by an instructional designer or teacher, they are instructional methods. Internal and external conditions of learning are discussed in some detail in Chapter 4.

KINDS OF PRINCIPLES

CORRELATIONAL:
non-directional relationship

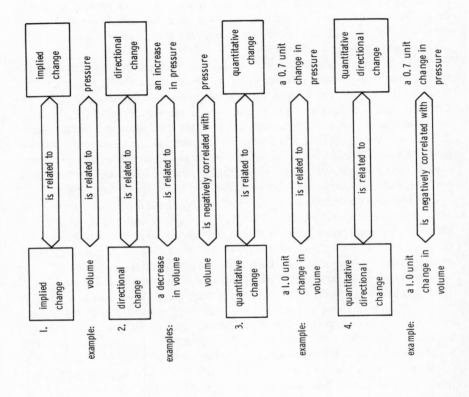

1. implied change — is related to → implied change

example: volume — is related to → pressure

2. directional change — is related to → directional change

examples: a decrease in volume — is related to → an increase in pressure

volume — is negatively correlated with → pressure

3. quantitative change — is related to → quantitative change

example: a 1.0 unit change in volume — is related to → a 0.7 unit change in pressure

4. quantitative directional change — is related to → quantitative directional change

example: a 1.0 unit change in volume — is negatively correlated with → a 0.7 unit change in pressure

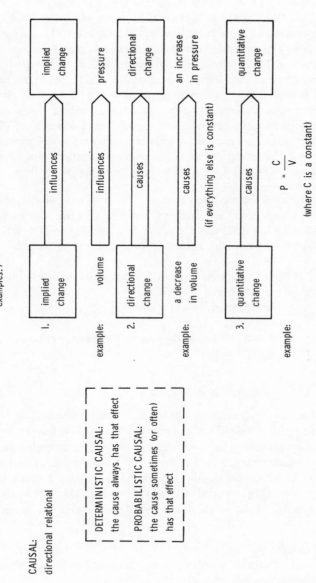

(NOTE: These are all non-directional or bi-directional because we don't know which influences which in any of the above examples.)

CAUSAL:
directional relational

DETERMINISTIC CAUSAL:
the cause always has that effect

PROBABILISTIC CAUSAL:
the cause sometimes (or often) has that effect

1. implied change → influences → implied change

example: volume → influences → pressure

2. directional change → causes → directional change

example: a decrease in volume → causes → an increase in pressure
(if everything else is constant)

3. quantitative change → causes → quantitative change

example: $P = \dfrac{C}{V}$
(where C is a constant)

FIG. 1.4 Two major kinds of principles and varieties of each.

17

For example, in instructional design there is a concept called "alternative representation," which is a different way of communicating something that has already been said or shown. It might be a paraphrase of an earlier statement, or it might be a diagram that says the same thing visually as was just said verbally. In any instruction, you can classify parts of that instruction as to whether or not each is an alternative representation. Now, in instructional design there is also a *principle* that goes by the same name (alternative representation): If what is being taught is relatively difficult for the student (a condition), then you should use an alternative representation (a method variable) if you want the student to be able to acquire and retain the knowledge better (the desired outcome). It is useful to think of all principles of instruction as having a method variable (e.g., alternative representation), at least one outcome variable (e.g., better acquisition and retention), and often one or more condition variables that delimit the validity of the principle (e.g., only for relatively difficult content).

A principle is fundamentally the same in all disciplines—it can always be expressed in the same conditions–methods–outcomes format. For example, in physics, the following is a statement of a principle whose degree of certainty (i.e., validation through experimentation) places it in the category of "law":

Conditions: If there is no wind resistance and you are relatively close to the surface of the earth, . . .

Method: . . . dropping any object . . .
     . . . will cause . . .

Outcome: . . . it to accelerate at the rate of 9.8 meters per second squared (9.8 m/sec^2).

An Extension of the Theoretical Framework

Instructional models and theories should be as comprehensive as possible. This means that they should include all kinds of method variables that have an important influence on outcomes. Reigeluth and Merrill (1979) have extended the conditions–methods–outcomes framework in an attempt to identify all of the important kinds of method variables that should be included in a comprehensive model or theory of instruction. This extended framework (see Fig. 1.5) should also prove very helpful for analyzing the instructional models and theories that appear in Unit II of this book.

Instructional Methods

First, instructional-method variables (for instructional design) are classified as three types: organizational, delivery, and management.

Organizational-strategy variables are elemental methods for organizing the subject-matter content that has been selected for instruction. They include such

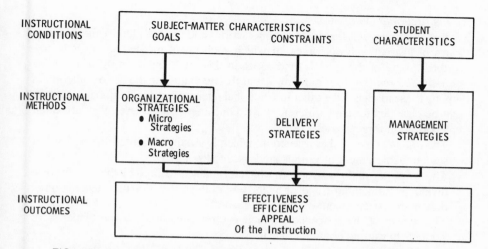

FIG. 1.5 A framework showing classes of instructional-method variables and the major condition variables that influence each. The classes of condition variables are *not* a complete list. Rather, they represent the conditions that are likely to have the strongest influence on each class of method variables.

things as use of examples and diagrams, sequence of content, and formating. (For more detail refer to the following list.)

Delivery-strategy variables are elemental methods for conveying the instruction to the learner and/or for receiving and responding to input from the learner. Media, teachers, and textbooks (and their characteristics) are the major part of delivery-strategy concerns.

Management-strategy variables are elemental methods for making decisions about which organizational- and delivery-strategy components to use when, during the instructional process. They include such concerns as how to individualize the instruction and when to schedule the instructional resources.

It is also useful to further conceptualize organizational strategies as being of two kinds: micro strategies and macro strategies.

Micro-strategy variables are elemental methods for organizing the instruction on a *single* idea (i.e., a single concept, principle, etc.). They include such strategy components as definition, example, practice, and alternative representation. (See Chapter 9 for additional examples of micro-strategy variables.)

Macro-strategy variables are elemental methods for organizing those aspects of instruction that relate to *more than one* idea, such as sequencing, synthesizing, and summarizing (previewing and reviewing) the ideas that are taught. (See Chapter 10 for more specific examples of macro-strategy variables.)

Instructional-design theories and models must take all of the just-described types of instructional strategies into consideration in order to be broadly useful.

Instructional Outcomes

It is also important that instructional theories and models identify the different kinds of instructional outcomes for which each set of method variables is prescribed. Some of the models or theories in this book are intended to optimize entirely *different kinds* of outcomes, and this accounts for the major differences among those models. Like other instructional phenomena, instructional outcomes can be classified in many different ways. On a very general level, they are often categorized in three classes:

The *effectiveness* of the instruction, which is usually measured by the level of student achievement of various kinds (see following);

The *efficiency* of the instruction, which is usually measured by the effectiveness divided by student time and/or by the cost of the instruction (e.g., teacher time, design and development expenses, etc.), and

The *appeal* of the instruction, which is often measured by the tendency of students to want to continue to learn.

(Notice that instructional outcomes focus on the instruction rather than on the learner; learner outcomes are but one aspect of instructional outcomes.)

The *effectiveness* of the instruction can then be broken down into various kinds of student achievement, from such *generic* knowledge as the ability to solve problems, being able to discover relationships, and being able to reason logically, to such *content-specific* knowledge as being able to recall a certain fact, being able to classify examples of a specific concept, and being able to follow a specific procedure. As you read the instructional theories and models in this book, be sure to identify and keep in mind the kind(s) of outcomes that each is intended to optimize.

Also, it is useful to know that *methods* of instruction can be classified and labeled by the kind of *outcome* towards which they contribute. For example, strategy components that are intended primarily to increase the appeal of the instruction are usually called *motivational-strategy components*. Of course, different motivational-strategy components may be further classified as organizational-, delivery-, or management-strategy components. Chapter 11 of this book is dedicated solely to this fledgling yet extremely important part of instructional-design theory.

Instructional Conditions

In addition to identifying and classifying precise method and outcome variables, it is important that instructional theories and models specify the conditions under which each set of method variables should or should not be used. For example, a certain strategy component may be very important for desired outcomes if students are poorly motivated but it may be detrimental for those desired outcomes for students who are already highly motivated. Figure 1.5 shows the major classes of condition variables that are likely to have the strongest influence on each class of method variables. But other condition variables are likely to be important, too, and many condition variables are likely to have an important influence on more than one class of method variables.

Models and Theories

Instructional scientists are not just interested in knowing that one method variable has better results than any other under given conditions—we are not just interested in single strategy components and isolated principles of instruction. What instructional designers and teachers need to know is what *complete set* of strategy components has better results (for desired outcomes) than any other set under given conditions: We are interested in complete models and theories of instruction.

People use the term *model* in many different ways. However, what is referred to as an instructional model (not to be confused with *instructional development model*; see following discussion) is usually an integrated set of strategy components, such as: the particular way the content ideas are sequenced, the use of overviews and summaries, the use of examples, the use of practice, and the use of different strategies for motivating the students. An architect's blueprint should show what many different aspects (preferably all different aspects) of the building are to be like. So also should an instructional model show what *many* different aspects (preferably *all* aspects) of the instruction are to be like in order to best achieve the desired outcomes under the anticipated conditions. Hence, an instructional model is merely a *set of strategy components*; it is a complete *method* with all of its parts (elementary components) described in detail.

Instructional models may be *fixed*—that is, they prescribe the same method variables regardless of what the student does (see, for example, Chapter 4)— or they may be *adaptive*—that is, they prescribe different method variables depending on student actions or responses (see, for example, Chapter 8).

People also use the term *theory* in different ways. But an instructional-design theory (often referred to simply as an instructional theory) is usually thought of as a *set of principles* that are systematically integrated and are a means to explain and predict instructional phenomena. Just as conditions and outcomes are integral parts of a principle, so also are conditions and outcomes integral parts of a theory. In fact, a theory is to a model what a principle is to a single method variable; and hence a theory is to a principle what a model is to a single method variable:

$$\frac{\text{theory}}{\text{model}} = \frac{\text{principle}}{\text{method variable}} \qquad \frac{\text{theory}}{\text{principle}} = \frac{\text{model}}{\text{method variable}}$$

This means that a theory can be viewed as a set of statements that take the form conditions–model–outcomes, just as a principle takes the form conditions–method–outcome. These distinctions are valuable to keep in mind for understanding and analyzing subsequent chapters, and they are further clarified in the next section.

Descriptive versus Prescriptive Principles and Theories

Instructional design is a prescriptive science (Glaser, 1976; Reigeluth, Bunderson, & Merrill, 1978; Simon, 1969; Snelbecker, 1974) because its primary purpose is

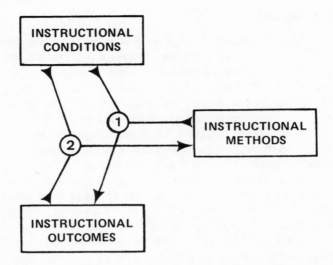

1. For descriptive theories, the condition variables and the method variables are independent variables and their parameters may interact to produce fairly consistent effects on the outcome variables, which are dependent variables.

2. For prescriptive theories, the desired outcomes and the conditions are independent variables that may also interact and their parameters are used to prescribe good methods of instruction, which are dependent variables.

FIG. 1.6 Three categories of instructional variables, and two sets of interrelationships among those categories.

to *prescribe* optimal methods of instruction. (In this sense, it is very different from learning science, whose primary purpose is to describe the processes of learning.) But principles and theories of instructional design may be stated in either a descriptive or prescriptive form (see Fig. 1.6). *Descriptive* principles and theories take sets of conditions and methods as givens (constants) and describe the likely outcomes as the variables of interest. In contrast, *prescriptive* principles and theories use sets of conditions and desired outcomes as givens and prescribe the best methods as the variables of interest. This distinction between descriptive and prescriptive principles and theories is summarized in Fig. 1.6.*

Prescriptive principles and theories are goal oriented, whereas descriptive ones are goal free (the former is intended to achieve a goal, whereas the latter is intended

---

*Editor's note: For more about the distinction between descriptive and prescriptive theory, see Chapter 2, p. 51, and Chapter 3, p. 59.

to describe the outcomes); and prescriptive principles have optimal methods as the variables of interest, whereas descriptive ones have outcomes as the variable of interest. Also the outcomes in prescriptive principles and theories are desired outcomes, whereas in descriptive principles and theories they are actual outcomes (usually in a probabilistic sense—that is, they are likely outcomes) and may or may not be desirable. A prescriptive theory is concerned with prescribing whole models that will be "optimal" for given sets of conditions and desired outcomes. A descriptive theory, on the other hand, is concerned with merely describing the likely outcomes of using whole models under different sets of conditions.

Hence a theory is: (1) a set of *models*; and (2a) in the case of a prescriptive theory, a set of *prescriptions* as to which model will optimize given desired outcomes under given conditions; or (2b) in the case of a descriptive theory, a set of *descriptions* as to which outcomes occur under given conditions for a given model.

Things Often Confused with Instructional Design

There are two things that are often confused with instructional design: learning theory and instructional development. The major difference between a theory of instructional design and a theory of *learning* is that the former focuses on methods of instruction, whereas the latter focuses on the learning process. Instructional-design theory is concerned with what the teacher does, whereas learning theory is concerned with what happens to the learner. Like instructional theory, learning theory may be descriptive or prescriptive. But prescriptive learning theory is *not* instructional theory.* Note the following example:

Prescriptive principle of learning	To increase long-term retention, ensure that knowledge is organized into stable cognitive structures.
Prescriptive principle of instruction	To increase long-term retention, begin instruction with an overview that epitomizes the content rather than summarizes it. Then gradually elaborate on each aspect of that overview, one level at a time, constantly relating each elaboration to the overview.

Instructional-design theory must include specific instructional *method* variables. If it does not, it is not. This is important because much of what is called instructional theory is really learning theory. Instructional-design theory is relatively easy to apply in the classroom because it spells out methods of instruction. Learning theory is usually difficult to apply in the classroom because it does not spell out methods of instruction; at best it spells out "conditions of learning" (Gagné [1977] and Chapter 4 of this book), for which a teacher must then develop his or her own methods of instruction.

---

*Editor's note: For more about this distinction, see Chapter 3, p. 62.

Instructional-design models are also often confused with instructional-*development models*. The major difference here is that the former indicate *what* the instruction should be like, whereas development models indicate *how* to make it that way. Instructional-design models are "blueprints" of the instruction itself, whereas development models describe the steps that developers should follow in order to make the instruction. This is a very real and important difference.

Criteria for Evaluating Instructional-Design Theory

There are two important aspects to evaluating instructional-design theory: whether it is and how good it is. *Whether it is* an instructional-design theory depends on two things: (1) whether it is *instructional* rather than learning; and (2) whether it is a *theory* rather than a model or a list of propositions. To be an *instructional*-design theory, its focus must be on methods of instruction—specific ways to manipulate the instructional environment—rather than on learning processes. Knowledge of learning processes may be useful in developing an instructional theory, but it does not constitute any part of an instructional theory.

To be an instructional-design *theory* it must include three things: (1) one or more instructional *models*; (2) a set of *conditions* under which each model should be used; and (3) the *outcomes* (desired or actual) for each model under each set of conditions. A descriptive instructional theory describes the *actual* outcomes that result from using each model under each set of conditions. A prescriptive instructional theory prescribes the models that should be used to achieve *desired* outcomes under different conditions. Hence a theory can be viewed either as an integrated set of principles or as a set of models that are related to conditions and outcomes.

How good it is as an instructional-design theory is the second important aspect to evaluating it. The Association for Supervision and Curriculum Development (ASCD) formed a commission on instructional theory in 1964. This commission established criteria for evaluating theories of instruction (Gordon, 1968). The following are its criteria that we believe are most valuable for judging "how good it is": (1) it should have internal consistency (i.e., it should not contradict itself); (2) its boundaries and limitations should be explicit; and (3) it should not be contradicted by empirical data (although we caution that apparent contradictions may disappear in the light of reinterpretation of such data).

To these criteria we add Snelbecker's (1974) criterion of (4) parsimony: It should be simple—the fewer the variables, the better. Also we add Snow's (1971) criterion of (5) usefulness: "The primary criterion for the evaluation of theory is usefulness, not truthfulness [p. 103]." This is reminiscent of Hebb (1969): "A good theory is one that holds together long enough to get you to a better theory [p. 27]." Snow (1971) states that theory should be useful for organizing existing data meaningfully and for producing useful hypotheses.

A. Whether it is:
    1. Instructional rather than learning.
    2. Theory rather than model or list.

B. How good it is:
    1. Internal consistency.
    2. Explicit boundaries and limitations.
    3. Not contradicted by data.
    4. Parsimony (i.e., simplicity).
    5. Usefulness.
    6. Comprehensiveness (number of relevant classes of methods).
    7. Optimality.
    8. Breadth of applicability (percent of conditions).

FIG. 1.7   Criteria for evaluating theories of instruction.

In addition to these criteria for evaluating "how good it is," we propose the following. (6) Comprehensiveness: For how much of the total variance does it account? This may be influenced to a large extent by the number of classes of method variables that it includes: organizational/delivery/management, effectiveness/efficiency/appeal, and so on. (7) Optimality (which is related to usefulness): It is not enough to be valid, is it better than anything else available? In the case of a prescriptive theory, does it present the best models for achieving desired outcomes under given conditions? In the case of descriptive theory, do the models have the best outcomes for the given conditions?[3] (8) Breadth of applicability: For what percent of conditions is it optimal?

All of these criteria are summarized in Fig. 1.7. For more about evaluating instructional-design theory, see Chapter 2.

HOW SHOULD YOU READ THIS BOOK?

The following suggestions may be helpful for understanding and evaluating the theories and models that are described in this book. As you read each chapter, do the following:

1. Search for and label conditions, methods, and outcomes.

— Put a C, M, or O in the margin by each.

— Remember that the classifications are *arbitrary* and hence vary from one chapter to another. (Caution: Sometimes the same lable is used with different

---

[3]In descriptive theories, "optimality" would be replaced by "precision": Does it merely indicate that a relationship exists, or does it state the directionality of the (causal) relationship, or does it quantify the relationship, or does it quantify the directional relationship?

meanings by different theorists, and sometimes different lables are used for the same concept by different theorists.)

— Remember that the methods must be methods of *instruction*, not methods of developing or designing instruction.

2. Search for and flag all principles of instruction.

— Remember that they must be principles of *instruction* rather than of learning— each must include a specific method variable.

— Remember that they are more useful if they are stated in a *prescriptive* way rather than a descriptive way.

3. Evaluate the classification scheme.

— Remember that *predictive value* is the criterion of importance—the reliability of the cause-and-effect relationships into which they enter.

— Remember that predictive value can be low for two reasons:

- The methods are *too general*—too much within-method variation.
- Phenomena are *categorized* in a poor way.

4. Search for instructional models.

— Remember that each of these is a "blueprint" of what the instruction should be like.

5. Evaluate each instructional model for:

a. Comprehensiveness.

— Remember that this is determined by the percent of total variation that can be accounted for. It can be estimated by considering whether or not the model includes strategy components from all major classes of methods—organizational (both micro and macro), delivery, and management. Boundaries and limitations should be spelled out by the theorist.

b. Optimality or Usefulness.

— Try to decide whether or not any other model could do a better job of achieving the desired outcomes under the specified conditions. If the model is not optimal, try to assess whether or not any parts or aspects of the model are novel and thereby represent a useful advance that should be integrated into the better model.

c. Breadth of Application.

— Remember that this is determined partly by the number of conditions under which the model is optimal and partly by the number of desired outcomes for which it is optimal.

6. Search for instructional theories.

— Remember to look for conditions–models–outcomes. This means that there must be:

- more than one model and
- a basis (i.e., conditions and/or desired outcomes) for prescribing which model to use when.

7. Evaluate the theory (if any).

— Remember these major criteria:

- Comprehensiveness (same as 5a).

• Optimality or usefulness (same as 5b, except that the *bases* for prescribing each model may also represent useful advances that should be integrated into a better theory).

• Breadth of application (same as 5c, except that you should consider the breadth of all the models collectively rather than consider the breadth of each individual model).

• Parsimony: Is its degree of complexity warranted? Is it cost effective?

HISTORY OF INSTRUCTIONAL-DESIGN THEORY*

Aspects of instructional design have developed out of two major areas: (1) psychology, or more specifically, learning theory; and (2) media and communications. However, the media/communications tradition's contributions to instructional design have been in the form of isolated strategies and principles rather than integrated models and theories (see, for example, Fleming & Levie, 1977). The major portion of instructional design's antecedents comes from the learning-theory tradition, and all of the theories and models described in this book have grown out of that tradition.

Instructional design's conception can be primarily attributed to John Dewey and Robert Thorndike, but its birth as a discipline must be credited to B. F. Skinner, Jerome Bruner, and David Ausubel. More than anyone else, *Skinner* motivated the scientific investigation of instruction as something different from the scientific investigation of learning, and he integrated strategy components and principles into the first real empirically tested model of instruction (Skinner, 1954, 1965). In contrast to Skinner's behavioral orientation to instructional design (whose initial conception can be traced back to Thorndike), both Bruner and Ausubel developed cognitive orientations (whose initial conceptions can be traced back to Dewey). *Bruner* developed a model of instruction based on discovery methods and stages of intellectual development (Bruner, 1960), and he was among the first to talk about forming a "theory of instruction" (Bruner, 1966). On the other hand, *Ausubel* developed a model of instruction based on expository methods and cognitive structures (i.e., the way knowledge is organized within one's memory). He also developed a theory of learning, from which he derived most of his instructional-design model (Ausubel, 1968).

Contributions of Others

In addition to the three pioneers just discussed, many other people have had important roles in the history of instructional design. Stimulated by Bruner's work on instructional theories, the Association for Supervision and Curriculum Develop-

---

*Editor's note: For more about the history of instructional theory, see Chapter 12 of this book; Merrill, Kowallis, and Wilson (1981); and Snelbecker (1974).

ment (ASCD) formed a commission in 1964 (Snelbecker, 1974) "to delineate scientifically based instructional theories from the more intuitively based and somewhat speculative 'theorizing' which had been so characteristic of education previously [p. 141]." This commission did much to focus attention on the need for "scientifically based" instructional theories, and it provided guidelines as to the chracteristics of such theories in the form of its *Criteria for Evaluating Theories of Instruction* (Gordon, 1968).

Robert Glaser also contributed much to the early development of the discipline. Not only did he contribute to the development of the "ruleg" (rule-example) model of instruction (Evans, Homme, & Glaser, 1962), but he also contributed on an even higher level by: (1) collecting much of the relevant work of that time into edited volumes (Lumsdaine & Glaser, 1960; Glaser, 1965); and (2) describing and drawing attention to areas that were particularly in need of investigation—his "four components of a psychology of instruction" (Glaser, 1965).

Robert Gagné is another important early contributor to instructional design. His early work on a number of models of instruction and a basis for prescribing each (see Chapter 4) helped to establish the discipline and to attract talented people to it.

Perhaps the most complete of the early models of instruction was that developed by Maria Montessori (1958, 1964). However, her valuable contributions have largely been overlooked by the mainstream of instructional design literature.

There are many other people who contributed in important ways to the early development of the discipline (i.e., during the 1960s). Some of them are mentioned next.

Some other Important Contributors to Instructional Design

In addition to the people just mentioned and the eight theorists described in the remainder of this book, there are many other people who have made important contributions to instructional design. The following is a very brief summary of some of the work of some of these people. This is not intended to be a comprehensive list of such people and their contributions; rather it is intended to be illustrative of the tremendous efforts that many people have contributed to the development of knowledge about better methods of instruction.

Richard C. Anderson has, among other things, confirmed and extended Ausubel's notion that providing learners with higher-level schemata or subsuming knowledge structures makes available a framework for comprehending discourse and increases the ease of learning and retention of such content and structures (see, for example, Anderson, Spiro, & Anderson, 1978; Anderson, Spiro, & Montague, 1977).

Richard C. Atkinson's contributions to the field include his work in the development of a "decision-theoretic model of instruction" (Atkinson, 1972a), in the design of models for computer-assisted instruction (Atkinson & Wilson, 1968), and in the development and validation of strategies for using mnemonics in the teaching of foreign languages (Atkinson, 1972b).

J. H. Block (1971) has done much work in the area of mastery learning, which is primarily a set of management strategies.

C. Victor Bunderson's (1979–80) work has focused on uses of computers in instruction. He was the major force behind the TICCIT System and its learner-control capabilties (a form of management strategy), and he is now in the forefront of videodisc applications in education (see, for example, Bunderson, 1979–80).

Crowder (1960, 1962) helped make considerable advances in the programmed instruction model of instruction by simultaneously relaxing its errorless-learning requirement and introducing branching sequences in the instruction. Thus, student errors provided the basis for individualizing the instruction.

Ivor K. Davies (1972, 1980; Hartley & Davies, 1976) has made important contributions in the area of instructional strategies.

Vernon Gerlach and Donald P. Ely (1971, 1980) have developed strategies for selecting and incorporating media within instruction, among other things.

Thomas Gilbert (1962, 1978) extended the programmed instruction model of instruction to what he calls "mathetics." One of his best-known contributions is the sequencing strategy referred to as "backward chaining."

Horn's (1976) major contribution to instructional design is prescriptions for formating instruction in such a way as to facilitate skipping over blocks of information and locating desired blocks of information.

Herbert Klausmeier has developed aspects of models for teaching concept classification, especially in the selection of examples (see, for example, Klausmeier, 1971; Klausmeier, Ghatala, & Frayer, 1974).

Raymond Kulhavy has been strongly involved in identifying and validating strategies for providing feedback for practice (see, for example, Kulhavy, 1977).

Susan Markle's work in the development of models for teaching concept classification includes the specification of strategies for preventing or remediating specific types of errors in concept-classification tasks (Markle & Tiemann, 1969). She also made important contributions to the earlier programmed instruction model (Markle, 1969).

R. J. Menges (see, for example, Menges & McGaghie, 1974) has worked in the area of group-interaction learning outcomes and instructional strategies.

Joseph Novak (1977) has applied Ausubelian assimilation theory principles to the design of models for teaching elementary science and math courses.

David R. Olson's (1974) work has been in the development of descriptive and prescriptive models of the developmental acquisition of language and critical thinking skills, building on Bruner's work.

Gordon Pask (1975, 1976) has developed a "conversation theory" whereby important cognitive operations can be identified, interrelated, and reduced to manageable units for purposes of planning the instructional "conversation." One of

Pask's greater contributions is his emphasis on teaching relationships within the content.

James Popham and Eva Baker (1970) have developed a general model of instruction that helped to integrate and disseminate current ideas about instructional design.

Lauren Resnick's (1963, 1973, 1976) work has focused primarily on the development of strategies for instruction in reading and mathematics, with particularly important contributions to development of the information-processing approach to task analysis.

Richard Snow (Cronback & Snow, 1977; Snow, 1977) has made major contributions to existing knowledge about the effects of individual aptitudes in the selection of appropriate instructional strategies.

Patrick Suppes' work (1965, 1975) has been concerned with the development and utilization of instructional strategies for computer-assisted instruction.

Among Donald Tosti's contributions to the field are his work with reinforcement strategies and management strategies (Tosti & Ball, 1969).

We would like to emphasize that this is but a sampling of the people who have made important contributions to the development of strategies, principles, models, and/or theories of instruction. It is also but a small indication of the total contributions that these people have made. Also, we have omitted any reference to the aforementioned people's (and other people's) contributions to such areas as learning theory and instructional-development procedures. For a more substantive review of these and other people's contributions to the more broadly defined field of instruction and learning, we strongly recommend Merrill, Kowallis, and Wilson (1981).

ADVANCED TOPICS

How Do You Build Instructional-Design Theory?

There are many different procedures for theory construction, but we have found one particular general procedure to be especially valuable. The stages in this procedure correspond roughly to what Snow (1971) referred to as different levels of theory. We propose that it is more valuable to view them as stages in a theory-construction procedure than as different levels of theory.

1. *Develop formative hypotheses* about instructional design on the basis of data, experience, intuition, and/or logic. These hypotheses may be fairly narrow and local (the start of a basically inductive—or bottom-up—approach to theory construction) or fairly broad and comprehensive (the start of a basically deductive—or top-down—approach to theory construction). This corresponds to Snow's F-theory.

2. *Develop a taxonomy* of variables related to instructional design. This stage entails identifying, describing, and classifying variables that may be of importance

to instructional-design theory. (Many of those variables are indicated by the formative hypotheses.) It is usually best to start with a clear description of desired outcomes. Then generate as many methods as you can for achieving those outcomes. Finally, identify different conditions that will influence which methods will work best. This stage also entails the analysis of the method variables into fairly elementary units. These activities correspond to Snow's D-theory and E-theory, respectively. This stage is an extremely important one in the process of theory construction.

3. *Derive principles* of instructional design. These principles usually describe cause-and-effect relationships among the variables identified in stage 2, and many of them are derived from the formative hypotheses developed in stage 1. This stage relies heavily on experience, intuition, and logic for postulating the principles and on empirical research for testing them. The empirical research has traditionally used the controlled experimental study. No attempt is made to interrelate the principles during this stage. This stage does not correspond to any of Snow's levels.

4. *Develop models and theories* of instructional design. Theories can be developed by integrating strategy components into models that are likely to be optimal for different sets of conditions and outcomes. Here there is an emphasis on empirical research, but the methodology is very different than that for deriving and testing principles. Stepwise multiple regression can be used to rankorder the contribution of each strategy component to the instructional outcomes, when adjusted for all strategy components that contribute more. In this manner, "optimal" models of varying degrees of richness can be derived. This may be the most promising of several approaches to developing optimal prescriptive theories. This stage probably comes closest to Snow's B-theory.

Inductive and deductive approaches. Stages 3 and 4 are used as described earlier in an inductive approach to theory construction. For a deductive approach, stage 4 would precede stage 3 and would entail an intuitive or logical derivation of a theory rather than an empirical derivation. Stage 3 would then be done as a process of working out the details of the theory.

Contrary to implication, the just-described stages are not followed in strictly linear fashion. Rather, it is an interactive process entailing much recycling through the stages and much simultaneous activity on different stages. For example, the taxonomy (stage 2) may be revised as empirical research on principles of instructional design (stage 3) reveals the need for changes. Hence, it would be very rare to find either a purely inductive or a purely deductive approach to theory construction.

Controversy over Instructional-Design Theory

There has been some controversy over the useful breadth of instructional-design theory. Richard Snow is well known for his work on individual differences under the rubric of *ATI*, or aptitude-treatment interactions (see, for example, Cronbach

& Snow, 1977). ATI is a metatheory that in effect states that theories of instruction should prescribe methods (called *treatments*) on the basis of student characteristics (called *aptitudes*), because the effectiveness of those methods varies depending on student characteristics. Snow (1977) has stated that ATI (aptitude-treatment interaction) "makes general theory impossible [p. 12]"—that instructional-design theories must be *narrow and local* to be of value. On the other hand, Scandura (1977) represented the view of many when he stated that instructional-design theories must be *broad and comprehensive* to be useful. We believe this controversy can be reconciled with the help of the conditions–methods–outcomes framework described earlier.

The major source of the difference in opinion over the useful breadth of instructional-design theory can be traced to different definitions of such theory by Snow and Scandura. In reference to Fig. 1.5, Scandura includes only *organizational* strategies, whereas Snow puts heavy emphasis on *management* strategies and relatively little emphasis on organizational strategies. This difference in definition is crucial because research literature indicates relatively little ATI with organizational strategies but very strong ATI with management strategies (hence the configuration of student characteristics in the conditions section of Fig. 1.5).

A useful distinction in the discussion of student characteristics is trait versus state. *Traits* are student characteristics that are relatively constant over time, such as cognitive styles and those kinds of abilities that are measured by IQ tests, whereas *states* are student characteristics that tend to vary during individual learning experiences, such as level of content-specific knowledge.

We believe, as Scandura maintained, that broad and comprehensive instructional-design models and theory can be developed in the area of organizational strategies. Many strategy components have been shown to help students with *all kinds* of traits to learn. For example, matched nonexamples can help students of all traits to learn concept classification. And several quasimodels have also been shown to help all kinds of students to learn (e.g., see Bloom, 1968; Robin, 1976; Schutz, 1979). We believe that such theory can be and will be developed in the area of delivery strategies also. But questions as to which organizational strategy components should be provided when and for how long (which are properly classified as instructional-management decisions) are highly sensitive to student states, and such decisions about the use of organizational strategies will vary considerably over time as a student's understanding develops and misconceptions arise and are dispelled. Hence, broad and comprehensive theory is considerably easier to develop in the area of organizational strategies than in the area of management strategies.

Nevertheless, the difficulty in developing broad and comprehensive theory in the area of management strategies may be attributable to what Snow (1971) refers to as inadequate metatheory:

> The need for new metatheory arises out of the inadequacy of existing metatheory. When hypotheses too frequently fail to be confirmed, when results of investigations are insignificant or inconsistent, and when findings with theoretical or practical value

appear too seldomly, a field of research becomes ripe for the emergence of new metatheories [p. 97].

It may be time for the ATI metatheory for management strategies to give way to new metatheories.

One emerging alternative that shows great promise is the "learner-control" metatheory (Merrill, 1975, 1979, 1980; Reigeluth, 1979), which emphasizes training the learner to make the decisions about which strategy components to study when and for how long. Learner control appears to be equally useful for accommodating individual differences due to either trait or state. For example, rather than presenting "visual" instruction to some students and "verbal" instruction to others, learner control prescribes making both representations available to all students, along with some brief training about what to pick and choose when, rather than studying everything. (It is also likely that the vast majority of students are not strictly verbal or strictly visual and can therefore benefit from having both whenever the content is a bit difficult.) For more about learner control, see Chapter 9. This metatheory is attractive not only for its potential for the construction of a highly *useful, broad,* and *comprehensive* theory, but also for its potential for the construction of theory that can be easily and economically *implemented* in the design of instruction.

Hence, ATI is but one approach to the question of individual differences as a basis for prescribing instruction. But strategies are only one aspect of instruction to be prescribed. Another approach to individualizing instruction is that the *initial state* of the learner is an important basis for prescription of *content* as well as strategy. There is considerable evidence that learner control over content is not always advisable. For example, Brown and Burton (1978) indicate that different learners make errors in certain arithmetic problems because of relatively unique "bugs" in the steps they follow. A student may have difficulty in selecting the content that will correct his or her unique "bug." Therefore, student state is an important condition variable for the selection of some content, and management strategies other than learner control are important for the selection of some content on the basis of student state. However, this does not mean that learners should never have control over the selection of any content. For more about learner control over the selection of content, see Chapter 10.

ACKNOWLEDGMENT

I appreciate the comments of William Montague on the early versions of this chapter.

REFERENCES

Anderson, R. C., Spiro, R. J., & Anderson, M. C. Schemata as scaffolding for the representation of information in connected discourse. *American Educational Research Journal,* 1978, *15,* 433–440.

Anderson, R. C., Spiro, R. J., & Montague, W. E. *Schooling and the acquisition of knowledge.* Hillsdale, N.J.: Lawrence Erlbaum Associates, 1977.

Atkinson, R. C. Ingredients for a theory of instruction. *American Psychologist,* 1972, *27,* 921–931. (a)

Atkinson, R. C. Optimizing the learning of a second-language vocabulary. *Journal of Educational Psychology,* 1972, *96,* 124–129. (b)

Atkinson, R. C., & Wilson, H.A. Computer-assisted instruction. *Science,* 1968, *162,* 73–77.

Ausubel, David P. *Educational psychology: A cognitive view.* New York: Rhinehart & Winston, 1968.

Beauchamp, G. A. *Curriculum theory* (2nd Ed.). Wilmette, IL: Kegg Press, 1968.

Block, J. H. *Mastery learning: Theory and practice.* New York: Rinehart & Winston, 1971.

Bloom, B. S. Learning for mastery. *Evaluation Comment,* 1968, *1,* 1–12.

Bloom, B. S. Innocence in education. *School Review,* 1972, *80,* 1–20.

Brown, J. S., & Burton, R. R. Diagnostic models for procedural bugs in basis mathematical skills. *Cognitive Science,* 1978, *2,* 155–192.

Bruner, J. S. *The process of education.* New York: Random House, 1960.

Bruner, J. S. *Toward a theory of instruction.* New York: W.W. Norton, 1966.

Bunderson, C. V. Instructional strategies for videodisc coursevare: One McGraw-Hill disc. *Journal of Educational Technology Systems,* 1979–80, *8,* 207–210.

Cooley, W., & Leinhardt, G. Instructional dimensions study. *Educational Evaluation and Policy Analysis,* 1980, *2*(1), 7–25.

Cooley, W. W., & Lohnes, P. R. *Evaluation research in education.* New York: Irvington Publishers, 1976.

Cronbach, L. J. Course improvement through evaluation. *Teachers College Record,* 1963, *64,* 672–683.

Cronbach, L. J., & Snow, R. E. *Aptitudes and instructional methods: A handbook for research on interactions.* New York: Irvington, 1977.

Crowder, N. A. Automatic tutoring by intrinsic programming. In A. Lumsdaine & R. Glaser (Eds.), *Teaching machines and programmed learning.* Washington, D.C.: National Education Association, 1960.

Crowder, N. A. The rationale of intrinsic programming. *Programmed Instruction,* April 1962, *1,* 3–6.

Davies, I. K. Presentation strategies. In J. Hartley (Eds.), *Strategies for programmed instruction.* London: 1972.

Davies, I. K. *Instructional technique.* New York: McGraw-Hill, 1980.

deCharms, R. *Personal causation.* New York: Academic Press, 1968.

deCharms, R. *Enhancing motivation change in the classroom.* New York: Irvington Publishers, 1976.

Dewey, J. Psychology and social practice. *The Psychological Review,* 1900, *7,* 105–124.

Evans, J. L., Homme, L. E., & Glaser, R. The ruleg system for the construction of programmed verbal learning sequences. *Journal of Educational Research,* 1962, *55,* 513–518.

Fleming, M., & Levie, W. M. *Instructional message design: Principles from the behavioral sciences.* Englewood Cliffs, N. J.: Educational Technology Publications, 1977.

Gagné, R. M. *The conditions of learning* (3rd ed.). New York: Holt, Rinehart & Winston, 1977.

Gerlach, V. S., & Ely, D. P. *Teaching and media: A systematic approach.* Englewood Cliffs, N.J.: Prentice-Hall, 1971 (1st ed.), 1980 (2nd ed.).

Gilbert, T. F. Mathetics: The technology of education. *Journal of Mathetics,* 1962, 7–73.

Gilbert, T. F. *Human competence: Engineering worthy performance.* New York: McGraw-Hill, 1979.

Glaser, R. Toward a behavioral science base for instructional design. In R. Glaser (Ed.)., *Teaching machines and programmed learning, II.* Washington, D.C.: National Education Association, 1965.

Glaser, R. Components of a psychology of instruction: Toward a science of design. *Review of Educational Research,* 1976, *46,* 1–24.

Gordon I. J. (Ed.). *Criteria for theories of instruction.* Washington, D.C.: Association for Supervision and Curriculum Development, 1968.

Grant, W. V., & Lind, C. G. *Digest of educational statistics 1977-78.* Washington, D.C.: National Center for Education Statistics, 1978.

Gustafson, K. *Survey of instructional development models: ERIC information analysis product.* Syracuse, NY: ERIC Clearinghouse on Information Resources, 1981.

Hartley, J., & Davies, I. K. Preinstructional strategies: The role of pretests, behavioral objectives, overviews, and advance organizers. *Review of Educational Research,* 1976, *46,* 239–265.

Hebb, D. O. Interviewed by Elizabeth Hall in *Psychology Today,* 1969, *3*(6), 20–28.

Horn, Robert E. *How to write information mapping.* Lexington, Mass.: Information Resources, 1976.

Klausmeier, H. J. Cognitive operations in concept learning. *Educational Psychologist,* 1971 *9,* 3–8.

Klausmeier, H. J., Ghatala, E. S., & Frayer, D. A. *Conceptual learning and development: A cognitive view.* New York: Academic Press, 1974.

Kulhavy, R. W. Feedback in written instruction. *Review of Educational Research,* 1977, *47,* 211–232.

Lumsdaine, A., & Glaser, R. *Teaching machines and programmed learning.* Washington, D.C.: Dept. of Audiovisual Instruction, National Education Assoc., 1960.

Lynch, M. D. *Self-concept development in childhood.* Paper presented at the National Symposium on Self-concept, Boston, September, 1978.

Markle, S. M. *Good frames and bad* (2nd ed.). New York: Wiley, 1969.

Markle, S. M., & Tiemann, P. W. *Really understanding concepts.* Chicago: Tiemann Associates, 1969.

Menges, R., & McGaghie, W. Learning in group settings: Toward classification of outcomes. *Educational Technology,* November 1974, *14,* 56.

Merrill, M. D. Learner control: Beyond aptitude-treatment interactions. *A. V. Communication Review,* 1975, *23,* 217–226.

Merrill, M. D. *Learner-controlled instructional strategies: An empirical investigation.* Final report on NSF Grant No. SED 76–01650, February 15, 1979.

Merrill, M. D. Learner control in computer based learning. *Computers and Education,* 1980, *4,* 77–95.

Merrill, M. D., Kowallis, T., & Wilson, B. G. Instructional design in transition. In F. Farley, & N. Gordon (Eds.), *Psychology and education; The state of the union.* Berkeley, CA: McCutchan, 1981.

Merrill, M. D., Reigeluth, C. M., & Faust, G. W. The instructional quality profile: A curriculum evaluation and design tool. In H. F. O'Neill, Jr. (Ed.), *Procedures for instructional systems development.* New York: Academic Press, 1979.

Montessori, M. *Pedagogie scientifique* (5th Ed.), Desclee de Brouwer, 1958.

Montessori, M. *The Montessori method.* New York: Schocken Books, 1964.

Novak, J. *A theory of education.* Ithaca, N.Y.: Cornell University Press, 1977.

Olson, D. R. *Media and symbols: The forms of expression, communication, and education.* Chicago: National Society for the Study of Education, Distributed by University of Chicago Press, 1974.

Pask, G. *Conversation, cognition, and learning.* Amsterdam: Elsevier, 1975.

Pask, G. *Conversation theory: Applications in education and epistemology.* Amsterdam: Elsevier, 1976.

Popham, W. J., & Baker, E. L. *Planning an instructional sequence.* Englewood Cliffs, N.J.: Prentice-Hall, 1970.

Reigeluth, C. M. TICCIT to the future: Advances in instructional theory for CAI. *Journal of Computer-Based Instruction,* 1979, *6*(2), 40–46.

Reigeluth, C. M., Bunderson, C. V., & Merrill, M. D. What is the design science of instruction? *Journal of Instructional Development* 1978, *61*(2), 11–16.

Reigeluth, C. M., & Merrill, M. D. A knowledge base for improving our methods of instruction. *Educational Psychologist,* 1978, *13,* 57–70.

Reigeluth, C. M. & Merrill, M. D. Classes of instructional variables. *Educational Technology,* March, 1979, 5–24.

Reigeluth, C. M., & Sari, F. From better tests to better texts: Instructional design models for writing better textbooks. *NSPI Journal,* 1980, *19*(8), 4–9.

Resnick, L. B. Programmed instruction and the teaching of complex intellectual skills: Problems and prospects. *Harvard Educational Review,* 1963, *33,* 439–471.

Resnick, L. B. Issues in the study of learning hierarchies. In L. R. Resnick (Ed.), Hierarchies in children's learning: A symposium. *Instructional Science,* 1973, *2,* 312–323.

Resnick, L. B. Task analysis in instructional design: Some cases from mathematics. In D. Klahr (Ed.), *Cognition and instruction.* New York: Wiley, 1976.

Robin, A. L. Behavioral instruction in the college classroom. *Review of Educational Research,* Summer 1976 *46*(3), 313–354.

Scandura, J. M. Systems/cybernetic/structural approach to instructional theory: A synthesis. In J. M. Scandura, *Recent advances in instructional theory 1,* A symposium presented at the annual convention of the American Educational Research Association, New York, 1977.

Schutz, R. E. Learning about the costs and instruction about the benefits of research and development in education. *Educational Researchers,* April 1979, 3–7.

Simon, H. A. *Sciences of the artificial.* Cambridge, Mass.: MIT Press, 1969.

Skinner, B. F. The science of learning and the art of teaching. *Harvard Educational Review,* 1954, *24*(2), 86–97.

Skinner, B. F. Reflections on a decade of teaching machines. In R. Glaser (Ed.), *Teaching machines and programmed learning, II.* Washington, D.C.: National Education Association, 1965.

Snelbecker, G. E. *Learning theory, instructional theory, and psychoeducational design.* New York: McGraw Hill, 1974.

Snow, R. E. Theory construction for research on teaching. In R. M. W. Travers (Ed.), *Second handbook of research on teaching.* Chicago: Rand McNally, 1971.

Snow, R. E. The place of individual differences in instructional theory. *Educational Researcher,* November 1977, 11–15.

Suppes, P. Computer based mathematics instruction. *Bulletin of the International Study Group for Mathematics Learning,* 1965, *3,* all. Also in R. Taylor (Ed.), *The computer in the school: Tutor, tool, tutee.* New York: Teachers College Press, 1980.

Suppes, P. Impact of computers on curriculum in the schools and universities. In Lecarme & Lewis (Eds.), *Computers in education.* Amsterdam: IFIP, 1975. Also in R. Taylor (Ed.), *The computer in the school: Tutor, tool, tutee.* New York: Teachers College Press, 1980.

Toffler, A. *Future shock.* New York: Random House, 1970.

Tosti, D. T., & Ball, J. R. A behavioural approach to instructional design and media selection. *A. V. Communication Review,* 1969, *17,* 5–25.

Tyler, R. W. How schools utilize educational research and development. In R. Glaser (Ed.), *Research and development and school change.* Hillsdale, N.J.: Lawrence Erlbaum Associates, 1978.

2

A Metatheory of Instruction: A Framework for Analyzing and Evaluating Instructional Theories and Models

George L. Gropper
Digital Equipment Corporation[1]

CONTENTS

Introduction 38
A Proposal For A Metatheory Of Instruction 39
    Overview 39
    A Rationale 40
    Parameters For The Metatheory Of Instruction 43
    A Proposed Quantitative Function Relating
        Instruction And Achievement 44
    Interpreting The Function 45
    Using The Function 45
    Research Suggestions 46
Characteristics Of Instructional Theories And Models 48
    Differential Analysis Of Learning Requirements 48
    Quantification Of Conditions And Treatments 49
    Compatibility With A Theory Of Learning 50
    Linkages Among Learning Theory, Instructional
        Theory, And An Instructional Model 50
Summary 52

---

[1]The views expressed here do not necessarily reflect those of the Digital Equipment Corporation.

FOREWORD

This chapter presents a *metatheory* for evaluating and comparing instructional-design theories and models. The metatheory provides guidelines for quantitatively assessing the *predictive usefulness* criterion that was briefly described in Chapter 1. On the one hand, it calls for the identification of *learning requirements* for each objective and the quantification of *obstacles* to their being met (based on both learner and subject-matter characteristics). On the other hand, it calls for the identification of the kinds of *attention* (strategy components) that overcome each type of obstacle and the identification of the *degree of attention* that is appropriate for the severity of each obstacle. This metatheory is clearly appropriate for evaluating all models and theories of instruction, regardless of whether they have a cognitive orientation or a behavioral orientation.

The emphasis of this chapter is on the *comparison* of competing models and theories for purposes of eliminating the losers. In contrast, the thesis of this book is that we need to *integrate* existing knowledge into a common knowledge base. Unit II shows that, when two different models or theories address the same objective, their commonalities far outnumber their differences, and hence that integration will be more useful than elimination. However, Gropper's metatheory is likely to prove extremely useful for *improving* any given model or theory of instruction (e.g., by indicating obstacles that had been overlooked), and it may provide guidance as to how to integrate two or more models or theories (e.g., by indicating which parts of which are better for overcoming each different kind of obstacle). Hence, this metatheory may represent an important contribution to the discipline in that it may facilitate the process of integrating our existing knowledge into comprehensive models of instruction and may help to further improve those models.

C. M. R.

INTRODUCTION

Does the appearance of this sizable volume on instructional theory argue for the health of a discipline some would like to call a "science"? Here are eight disparate approaches to the explanation, prediction, or applied promotion of student achievement. It is unclear how many other volumes would be necessary to accommodate other instructional theories that fill the literature—all attempting to do the same. There is no collegial, or even competitive, building of a *common knowledge base* with individuals making incremental contributions to it. Instead, there appear to be as many *knowledge bases* as there are contributors to the discipline. If other disciplines serve as a guide, this diversity does *not* argue for the maturity or sophistication of *instructional theory*.

Movement towards greater disciplinary maturity will require some hardheaded weeding out of the weak and long-term nurturance of a promising few. For that purpose there will have to be *criteria for identifying and evaluating* theory and model characteristics. There will also have to be a bottom line. What will be needed is a means of assessing how well theories predict and how well models produce achievement.

This chapter describes a *metatheory*, or a theory about theories, that can be used in an examination and assessment of instructional theories and models.* The ultimate aim in formulating it is to contribute to a more disciplined *instructional science*. The metatheory does this by providing a means of identifying those theories that are predictive of, and those models that are productive of, achievement—in quantitative terms.

A PROPOSAL FOR A METATHEORY OF INSTRUCTION

Overview

The formulation of the proposed metatheory is based on a number of interrelated assumptions. Effective instruction for any objective is assumed to depend on a comprehensive identification of its *learning requirements* and of *obstacles* to their being met.** Learning to perform effectively may require: the recall of information on a delayed basis; the transfer of skills to new situations; the encoding and decoding of information, and so on. Obstacles to meeting learning requirements may consist of: learner developmental nonreadiness; limits on short-term or long-term memory; stimulus similarity making discriminations difficult; competition between existing habits and new ones, and so on. Together all of an objective's learning requirements and the obstacles to their being met constitute the population of *conditions* that instructional treatments for that objective will have to accommodate. The accurate and comprehensive identification of this population of conditions is a precursor to and a prerequisite for an appropriate prescription of treatments.

The metatheory deemphasizes the importance of attempting to differentiate among *types of treatments* that can be used to accommodate conditions requiring treatment. Even though considerable importance is being attached to achieving a high degree of differentiation among conditions to be treated, proliferation of treatment *types* is considered unnecessary. The specifics of "how" conditions are treated are considered less important than "whether" they are identified in a valid and reliable way and are then, at a minimum, treated.

Dealing with conditions in an *optimal* way does not depend on the selection of treatments that can provide an appropriate *type* of attention. Rather, it depends on the selection of treatments that can provide an appropriate *amount* of attention. Effective instruction for an objective is assumed to depend on the delivery of an appropriate *degree* of attention for *each* condition requiring attention. The appropriate treatments that are of consequence and are capable of delivering relevant

---

*Editor's note: See also Chapter 1, pp. 14–20, for a discussion and presentation of metatheory.

**Editor's note: As you see in later chapters, this is an important aspect of all of the instructional models and theories presented in this book, regardless of whether they are considered to have a behavioral orientation or a cognitive orientation.

attention are limited in number. These limited few can be manipulated to provide differential *amounts* of attention for conditions having varying needs.

These priorities are based on the speculation that considerably more of the variance associated with effective instruction will be accounted for by differentiating among types of *conditions* that demand and receive attention than by differentiating among types of *treatments* that provide it.

A Rationale

A paper delivered at a 1976 American Educational Research (AERA) symposium on instructional theory described a partial move towards the position being taken in this chapter (Gropper, 1976). The following excerpt (slightly edited) illustrates the position taken at that time:

> A theory of instruction should also tell us about differences in treatments in keeping with variations in requirements. Learning theory in contrast has typically sought to identify invariant relationships. The research it has inspired has asked questions beginning with "whether to" rather than with "when to" and "when not to". Atheoretic educational research has typically also neglected these "when to" questions. There are a number of instructional variables, some of them seemingly sacred, about which I would like to propose that we not ask "whether" they belong in our instructional armory. I would propose that we ask instead "when should they be used"; "when might it not be necessary to use them"; and "when should they not be used [p. 9]

The recommendation of a closer analysis of "when to" represented an emphasis on a more detailed look at subject matter and learner characteristics. However, there still remained a preoccupation with a need for differential treatment types to accommodate those characteristics.

What is being stressed now is the importance of an even more detailed analysis of conditions. Further, it is important to recognize that there are only a *limited number* of treatment types that bear the burden of effectively providing attention for those conditions. They include such treatments as telling learners how to do something and providing them with examples of and principles governing that performance. These treatments are applicable to any type of condition requiring attention. Therefore, the accommodation of conditions does not require the creation of treatment types specifically suited to them. It can be effectively (and parsimoniously) accomplished by manipulating the *properties* of a few treatment types to produce varying and appropriate levels of attention for those conditions.*

This current stance results from reflection on: the author's *personal experience* in developing instructional materials, the characteristic *practices* of teachers and materials developers, and the kinds of *research results* that fill the literature.

---

*Editor's note: This is very similar to Merrill's call for varying the amount and kind of "secondary" components that enrich and make up a very few "primary" strategy components (see Chapter 9).

Personal experience.   The author's personal experience in developing instructional materials and using them with learners in one-on-one situations has led to a not-very-surprising conclusion. The more *detail* instruction goes into, the more certain learner mastery becomes. It is this experience that suggests a somewhat less obvious conclusion. In order to determine *what it is* the greater detail should cover, the analysis of "conditions" must be as detailed as possible (see the later section *Differential Analysis of Learning Requirements*).

Developer Practice.   The number of treatment types that it makes sense to examine for clues as to what makes instruction effective is rather small. What are the options? Whether they teach facts, concepts, procedures, or problem solving, developers and teachers and researchers alike have available to them (and in actual practice usually rely on) three principle treatment types: telling learners what to do; providing them with examples; and identifying for them principles that govern the performance to be learned.

Instructional presentations* usually identify for learners the "what" and "how" of the performance expected of them. They are told explicitly *what to do* and *how to do it*. If learners are expected to define a concept, for example to define *positivism*, they are provided with an appropriate definition. Or, if they are expected to follow a procedural algorithm, as in differentiating a function in calculus, the procedural steps are spelled out for them. Additionally, *examples* of the expected performance are provided. A presentation may provide an example of a concept that is to be defined or of a procedural routine that is to be carried out. Finally, presentations provide learners with *principles* to guide the performance to be learned. For example, student teachers learning to use contingency management techniques (rule following) may be cautioned to deliver reinforcement only after an increase (over the previously reinforced episode) in the duration of student attention to work.

Together the three treatment types—what to do, examples, and principles—are capable of accommodating the specific, if differential, requirements of any type of objective. The treatments that are developed for and are most frequently applied to objectives encountered in school or training environments are essentially variants of these three. With minor differences in the emphasis that may be given to any particular one of them, all three appear to be applicable to any of the performance categories in any of the published learning/performance taxonomies.

Research Results.   Research on "treatments" has not produced a profusion of statistically significant results. Nor are those that have been produced impressively robust. There have been studies on the effects created by the introduction of

---

*Editor's note: The following are *all* used for expository (or explicit) approaches. A discovery approach such as that of Collins and Stevens (Chapter 8) would seldom use the first and third treatment types. But this does not in any way limit the usefulness of the more general metatheory (see Fig. 2.1) to expository approaches.

advanced organizers. There have been studies that have varied the order in which rule and example are presented. There have been studies in which words and pictures have been contrasted. The inability of many studies of this general type to produce differences that are statistically significant or that are of more than arguable practical importance invites speculation about causes. It is possible that the treatments studied either have been poorly chosen, have been poorly implemented, or (for lack of sufficient experimental controls) have been *interchangeable variants* of one another. The latter conclusion is advanced here.

It is assumed here that the three major treatment types (what to do, examples, and principles) account for a major portion of the variance associated with effective instruction. They are capable of effectively accommodating the key learning requirements (and their obstacles) that characterize objectives. The three are usually employed in all research on treatment parameters. However, they are not always the conscious object of that research. But, they (or indistinguishable or inconsequential variants of them) usually find their way into *both* experimental and control conditions. For example, a study on advanced organizers may introduce some form of advanced organizer into one condition and withhold it from another. But both conditions are likely to employ one or more of the three major treatment types. If one condition contains them, another is likely to contain an identical counterpart or a minimally different but functionally equivalent version of it.

If experimental and control conditions *both* contain the major three treatment types (which can be expected to produce sizable effects), does it make sense to expect that the introduction into one condition (and not into the other) of advanced organizers, or of a particular order for rule and example, or of negative instances— to pick just a few examples—will be capable of producing still further sizable effects? In some instances the room for further improvement may be marginal. In others the nonmajor treatments that are introduced may not be capable of effectively addressing the *specific* conditions that require attention. Although such treatments may have a contribution to make, their effects can be obscured by the presence in both experimental and control conditions of the major three.

It is this sharing by experimental and control conditions of the same major treatment types that may account for much of the "no differences" reported in the literature. More importantly, it may also account for effects that turn out to be statistically significant but that may be of insufficient magnitude to warrant their practical application.

It is this inspection and analysis of personal experience, developer practice, and research practice and its results that has led to the speculations and hypotheses on which the metatheory proposed in this chapter is based. It is hypothesized that *a few treatment types* are universally applicable and can be varied to provide differential *amounts* of attention to match differential needs created by subject matter and learner characteristics. It is further hypothesized that it will be through an emphasis on *identifying these differential needs*—in painstaking detail—that the most impressive bottom line will result.

Parameters for the Metatheory of Instruction

Because the metatheory being proposed espouses no particular prescriptive orientation (behavioral, cognitive, or humanistic) and is expressed in quantitative terms, its availability makes possible an analysis of, and an empirical comparative evaluation of, competing instructional theories and models. They can be analyzed and compared for: the depth and comprehensiveness with which they identify and analyze *learning requirements* and the *obstacles* to their being met (conditions); the extent to which they are able to *quantify the severity* of (learning difficulties posed by) these conditions; the explicitness of the criteria that they employ to define and *quantify levels of attention* that can be given to conditions requiring attention; and the explicitness of their *criteria for matching* estimated condition severity and attention level. And, most important of all, instructional theories and models can be evaluated for their capacity to *predict and produce achievement*.

The parameters that enter into the proposed metatheory describe both conditions and treatments.

Conditions.   It is postulated that for each *objective* to be learned there is a population of true *learning requirements*. Instructional theories and models are likely to differ in the comprehensiveness with which the learning requirements that they identify sample this population. It is likely to make a difference whether an objective is analyzed for information processing, memory storage and retrieval, or "behavioral" skill requirements. Obtained and "true" characterization of an objective will differ both with respect to the content and the number of relevant learning requirement that are identified.

It is also postulated that for each *learning requirement* there is a population of true *obstacles* to its being met. Some of these obstacles derive from subject-matter characteristics, some from target-audience characteristics, and some from the interaction between the two. Each learning requirement has a true *difficulty level* imposed by those obstacles. Instructional theories and models are likely to identify those obstacles with differing degrees of comprehensiveness and to estimate their difficulty levels with differing degrees of accuracy.

Based on these considerations, two parameters are proposed for the characterization of the conditions applicable to an objective: (1) the *number of conditions* (learning requirements plus obstacles) associated with an objective; and (2) the *difficulty level* posed by each condition. Because instructional theories and models differ with respect to what they consider to be relevant conditions, they are likely to differ with respect to the estimate they make of both the number and the severity of the conditions associated with a given objective. As a consequence, they are also likely to differ with respect to both the relevance and accuracy with which they determine the level of attention required by an objective characterized by those conditions.

Treatments.   It is possible to define *levels of attention* provided by treatments in a number of ways. Levels can be defined in terms of: the *amount and kind of* information provided; the *frequency* with which identical information is repeated; the *amount of variety* (in information) that is provided; or the *duration* during practice for which students have such assistance available. Levels of attention can also be defined in terms of combinations of the three types of major treatments (and *their* levels). For example, using all three treatment types would be assumed to provide more attention than just one or two types. The use of other more specialized and less frequently used treatment tyupes can be still another way to define heightened levels of attention. By these various means, levels of attention can be manipulated to match the anticipated difficulty posed by each identified *condition*.

Two parameters are proposed for the characterization of treatments that are to be provided for each condition. They are: (1) the *presence or absence* of a treatment providing attention for a condition; and (2) an estimate of the *degree of attention* judged necessary (and then delivered) to address that condition. Orientations are likely to differ with respect to how closely obtained and "true" levels of (required) attention coincide.

A Proposed Quantitative Function
Relating Instruction and Achievement

The parameters to be related herein quantitatively describe both conditions and treatments. For the *analysis* of a subject-matter objective, they include: (1) the *number* of conditions potentially obstructing its mastery; and (2) the estimated *level of* (learning) *difficulty* posed by each condition.

In the proposed function (see Fig. 2.1), the letter c represents each *condition* that may require attention. The letter a represents an estimate of the degree of difficulty it will pose (and therefore the degree of attention it will require). When a learning requirment has been met by a particularly target audience (e.g., when the audience already has a particular skill in its repertoire and, therefore, there is no condition requiring attention), the letter a is set to zero (0). Otherwise, it is set to 1 to . . . n to reflect conditions of varying severity.

For the *prescription* of treatments, the proposed parameters are: (1) the *number of conditions* for which a treatment is delivered; and (2) the *level of attention* each treatment is to provide. In the proposed function, the letter t represents the targeting of a *treatment* for a condition, the letter b the level of attention it is to provide. The letter b set to zero (0) indicates that no treatment is to be provided (when none is required).

The proposed function relates instruction and achievement. Letting the letter A represent *achievement* and the letter I *instruction*, it is hypothesized that A is a function of I. I is defined as the sum of all the ratios t/c, or treatment over condition, with both numerator and denominator weighted. With A (achievement) plotted along the ordinate and the sum of the ratios represented by I (instruction) plotted on the abscissa, it is hypothesized that A should be a rising function of I.

(1) $A = f \underline{/\ I\ /}$ A = Achievement
                                          I = Instruction

(2) $$I = \sum \frac{b_1 t_1}{a_1 c_1} + \frac{b_2 t_2}{a_2 c_2} + \frac{b_3 t_3}{a_3 c_3} + \ldots \ldots \frac{b_n t_n}{a_n c_n}$$

t = delivery of a treatment for an identified problem;
b = degree of attention provided by the treatment;

c = the presence of a problem;
a = estimate of the degree of difficulty posed by the problem

FIG. 2.1   A hypothesized function relating instruction and achievement.

Interpreting the Function

Effective instruction, measured by levels of student achievement attained, is hypothesized to be a function of: the accurate and comprehensive identification of the presence of learning requirements and obstacles to their being met (conditions); the accurate assignment of weights to those conditions; the provision of a treatment for each identified condition; and the assignment of an appropriate weight to that treatment (indicating an appropriate level of attention to be given to it). The more accurate the identification of *conditions* is, and the more accurate their (severity) *weighting* is, and the larger the percentage of *conditions treated,* and the more accurate treatment *weighting* is, then the higher are the levels of student achievement to be expected.

Achievement cannot suffer from an overestimate of either the number of conditions to be treated or the degree of attention they are to receive.* Only the *efficiency* of instruction can be so affected. An underestimate, on the other hand, will negatively affect both the effectiveness and the efficiency of instruction. Consider the inefficiency of providing added attention at a later time—as remediation.

Using the Function

Diverse instructional theories and models can be analyzed by means of the proposed function. They can be examined for what it is (for any given objective) that they choose to identify as *conditions*, for which of those conditions they choose to

---

*Editor's note: As Chapter 11 indicates, this may not always be true.

provide *attention*, and *how much* attention they choose to provide for them. Most significantly, instructional theories and models can also be compared for the correlations between *achievement* and instruction that they produce. To make such comparisons possible, each theory or model has to be prepared to identify: its referents for *c* in the function; criteria for assigning values to *a* to indicate severity; criteria for *defining* levels of attention (*t*); criteria for assigning values to *b* that indicate the level of attention to be given to a condition; and criteria for matching attention levels with condition severity.

The need for accurate and comprehensive identification of conditions and treatments and their weighting, as envisioned here, would place a heavy burden on practitioners doing development. They would have to attend in a highly systematic, analytic, and quantitative way to the requirements of each objective, of each audience (possibly of each individual learner), and to the attention to be given to them. At its ultimate level of precision, it is an approach that may be too onerous for all but critical, core curricula.

Whether *development* efforts attempt to approach such precision will depend on empirical research results demonstrating that it leads to more robust effects than are typically found. Onerous or not, it represents a move away from reliance on the *qualitative* analysis of conditions and prescription of treatments that now characterize the instructional-design field. It may be premature to do so, but an eventual move towards *quantitative* analysis, whether in the way suggested here or in some other way, is a prerequisite for evolution and progress towards a more exact *instructional science*.

Whether or not it is used in *development*, quantitative analysis (of some sort) is a must for *research* in the discipline. It is a must for the resolution of competition between instructional theories and models and for being able to identify those that effectively predict (in descriptive research) or produce (in prescriptive research) achievement. In subsequent *applications* of those theories and models diminished rigor (i.e., reliance on less complex and less time-consuming qualitative analysis) is a reasonable possibility. That can occur only after research has demonstrably shown the way. For that, quantification is necessary.

Research Suggestions

The principal hypothesis offered here is that the sum of the treatment/condition ratios represented by *I* will account for a major portion of the variance associated with effective instruction (in any orientation). Three interrelated lines of research suggest themselves to provide data bearing on this hypothesis: (1) research on the *reliability* with which conditions can be identified and with which both conditions and treatments can be weighted; (2) research demonstrating in general the *predictive power* of the function previously described; and (3) a *comparative study* of the predictive power of two or more competing instructional theories or models.

Reliability. Of primary interest is the predictive validity of the proposed function and how differing theories and models fare at predicting achievement. A prerequisite for the conduct of either line of research is an assessment of the reliability with which conditions are identified (in any theory or model), with which both condition severity and treatment level are weighted, and with which condition severity level and attention level are matched. Applied procedures for performing these tasks need to be identified, and the consistency with which independent developers apply them needs to be assessed.

Predictive Validity. In research on the predictive validity of the proposed function, conducted solely within the framework of any one theory or model, experimental variation in the number of c's and t's and the weights assigned to them should lead to predictable changes in correlations between I (instruction) and A (achievement). Manipulating the extend of the *match* between condition severity and attention level (that is provided) should also lead to predictable results. For example, one or more conditions at a *fixed* severity level could be treated with varying degrees of attention—starting with no attention at all. Achievement should rise as a function of the number of conditions treated and as a function of the closeness of the match between need and levels of attention delivered.

Of major interest would be comparisons between zero attention to identified conditions (of whatever severity) and the mere delivery of some attention to those conditions—however poorly conceived or implemented. Findings favoring the latter approach would bolster the central assumption of this chapter that highly differentiated identification of conditions (and delivery of attention to them) is more necessary for high levels of achievement than a comparable differentiation among treatment types.

Comparative Studies. The use of the t/c (treatment over condition) ratios in experimental comparisons or in comparisons of different theories and models makes possible one methodological convenience. Each ratio is a pure number. The letter t given a value of 1 indicates that a treatment (of whatever type) is provided for a condition. The letter c, also assigned the value 1, indicates the presence of a condition (of whatever type) requiring attention. Variation from objective to objective or from one theory or model to another in dealing with a given objective arises only from the number of t/c ratios appearing in the function and from the weights, a and b, assigned to t and c respectively. Weights from $1 \ldots n$ indicate estimated levels of condition severity (however defined) and of attention (however defined) delivered.

Any measurement involving the function will be free of a major methodological problem that typically besets education research. Because only pure numbers are involved, different theories or models can be compared directly (for teaching the same objective) without being vulnerable to an "apples and oranges" criticism. Thus, Collins could be directly compared with Gagné and Briggs, with Landa, with Scandura, or even with Gropper.

The relationship between *I* and *A* should hold up no matter what orientation is adopted and no matter what *c* and *t* are selected to stand for. Differences among theories and models in the *magnitude* of the relationship that they are able to produce should be a function of the relevance or validity of what they choose to call a *c*, the comprehensiveness and reliability with which they identify the *c*'s for any objective, and the accuracy and reliability with which they estimate the degree to which any given *c* represents an obstacle to learning. Differences among theories and models should also depend, on the treatment side, on the relevance of attention levels chosen (to deal with identified conditions) and the reliability with which they are chosen and implemented.

Except for a few metaanalyses performed recently, education has seen few comparative evaluations. The availability of the proposed quantitative function makes possible a direct comparison of competing instructional theories and models. Instructional design might mature more rapidly as a field if a rigorous selection process (of the general type proposed here) were applied to it and if a few healthy survivors received collective, collegial, and (most important) cumulative attention.*

CHARACTERISTICS OF INSTRUCTIONAL THEORIES AND MODELS

What characteristics of instructional theories and models might affect their showing when they are measured against the bottom line—predicting and producing achievement? Four suggest themselves: (1) a capacity for a highly differential *analysis* of learning requirements and obstacles to their being met (conditions); (2) a capacity for *quantifying* the parameters that describe conditions and treatments; (3) *compatibility* with a theory of learning; and (4) explicit *linkage* of learning theory, instructional theory, and an instructional model.

Differential Analysis of Learning Requirements

Instructional theories and models differ with respect to how fine grained and comprehensive their analyses of subject-matter characteristics are. The type of taxonomy they use to analyze objectives places limits on how fine grained and comprehensive their analyses can be. Taxonomies described in the literature fall into two general camps (Gropper, 1974). On the one hand, there are those taxonomies that are used to classify an objective as an intact whole. Others are used to dissect and minutely examine an objective for its *constituent parts*. These differences in approach have implications for how accommodating "prescriptions" can be.

---

*Editor's note: This thesis is to some extent in conflict with the major thesis of this book: the need to *integrate* existing knowledge into a common knowledge base. Unit II proposes that, when two different theories or models address the same objective, their similarities far outnumber their differences, and hence that integration will be more useful than elimination. However, Gropper's metatheory may prove extremely useful for *improving* any given model or theory of instruction and may provide guidance as to how to integrate two or more models or theories.

Intact classification of objectives.   After identifying its skill or performance requirements, some theorists assign an objective to *one* of the several categories that comprise an instructional-design taxonomy (Bloom, 1956; Gagné & Briggs, 1974; Merrill, this volume). Examples of categories that are used in this type of classification include: recalling facts, defining concepts, giving explanations, following rules, or solving problems. An objective like "integrating a polynomial function" would be categorized as "rule following."

Although the categories used for this purpose may differ from one orientation to another, the orientations share a common approach: the intact categorization of an objective. As long as any instance of an objective meets the skill or performance criteria that define one of the categories of any taxonomy, it is assigned (intact) to that category. A prescription for that objective is then made on the basis of the category to which it has been assigned.

Dissection of Objectives.   Using a second type of performance taxonomy, other theorists dissect and analyze an objective for its distinctive, constituent parts. Representative of this approach are those behavioral models that analyze objectives for the discriminations, generalizations, and associations that make up a total chain (Gilbert, 1962; Gropper, 1974 and Chapter 5, this volume; Mechner, 1967). Each objective is analyzed for its specific *mix* of these constituent skills. In its most complete application, behavioral analysis would identify for that objective all the stimulus–response links that make up a total chain. And, the discriminations, generalizations, and associations for each link in the chain would be described—in fine-grained detail.

Intact classification allows an identification of only the *common requirements* that objectives of the same general type share. An analysis of constituent skills makes it possible to go beyond that. It makes it possible to look at learning requirements and to identify potential obstacles to meeting these learning requirements—in considerably more detail. By using this approach, any two objectives that belong to the same general category (e.g., any two objectives that might be classified as "rule following") can be revealed to possess *unique* as well as common requirements. It is revelations of this sort that lead to prescriptions that can accommodate both types of requirements.

The type of analytic tools that an instructional theory or model employs determines how fine grained the analysis of an objective can be. If attention to *detail* does account for a major part of the variance associated with effective instruction, as hypothesized in this chapter, then the choice of tools to be used in analyzing objectives is critical.

Quantification of Conditions and Treatments

The capacity of an instructional theory or model to quantify *conditions* that make it easy or difficult to learn objectives is also critical. It is clearly advantageous to be able to do more than simply identify conditions that may make it difficult to learn an objective. It is useful to know "how difficult" they will make it. For example, in the teaching of concepts it is well known that similarity between example and non-example complicates the discrimination between them. The availability of a metric for identifying degrees of similarity could aid in an estimate of how difficult the discrimination might be. The capacity to quantify *levels* of condition variables accurately, in effect, makes for an even more fine-grained analysis of an objective. Having such a capacity contributes to the power of a theory to predict or of a model to produce achievement.

Also relevant to the potential success of a theory or model is a capacity to characterize the *levels of attention* that can be provided by individual treatments, variants of them, or combinations of them—in quantitative terms. Accurate and relevant matching of condition severity and treatment level depends on it.

Compatibility with a Theory of Learning

A frequently cited desideratum for a theory of instruction is its compatibility with a theory of learning. If the proposed metatheory is on target in its emphasis on *learning requirements and obstacles to their being met,* then "compatibility" is the wrong word. An instructional theory needs to *build on* a theory of learning. That dependence becomes increasingly more pronounced the more explicitly and comprehensively a theory of learning identifies: (1) types of learning requirements that characterize objectives; (2) parameters (characterizing subject matter or learners) that affect how easy or difficult it might be to meet them; and (3) not least, parameters that characterize conditions under which learning per se takes place. These parameters enter into the issues with which an instructional theory must intimately deal. Thus, compatibility between the two types of theory is a minimal requirement.*

Linkages among Learning Theory,
Instructional Theory, and an Instructional Model

The parameters and relationships among them that are identified in a theory of learning are also available as elements for a theory of instruction. They serve as a foundation for the compatibility between the two types of theory. If an instructional model, in turn, accurately translates the instructional theory, applied practice can also be made compatible with theory. The sharing of a *common vocabulary* is what makes for consistency among learning theory, instructional theory, and an instructional model.** What differentiates among the three are the distinctive and differ-

---

*Editor's note: An inductively derived instructional theory need not *build on* any theory of learning, but it is likely to be *compatible with* at least one theory (and probably with parts of several theories) of learning.

**Editor's note: Alternatively, consistency might be viewed as something that occurs on a deeper, more meaningful (semantic) level at which the vocabulary (syntax) is irrelevant.

ing goals towards which that vocabulary is shaped. The words stay the same; the rhetoric changes.

Descriptive and Prescriptive Research. The internal coherence that a learning theory, an instructional theory, and an instructional model exhibit is a worthwhile goal in itself. It is also a prerequisite for demonstrating their external validity (see Fig. 2.2). Research results and applied results could not be readily fed back either to theory or to an instructional model unless there were such internal consistency. Similarly, it is that same internal consistency that permits theoretical propositions, already in place or reformulated, to work their way back into further research and into further practice. Ultimately, the goal of upgraded practice depends on the reciprocal goal of upgraded theory. It is reciprocity of this sort for which a common language is necessary. Its reward is analytic and systematic change in both practice and theory.

A *descriptive* instructional theory is meant to identify specific types of treatments that can, under specific types of conditions, bring about specific types of changes in performance. It leads to research whose major function is to assess the soundness of its descriptions of relationships among these parameters. It is the results of such research that indicate whether and how descriptions need to be modified.

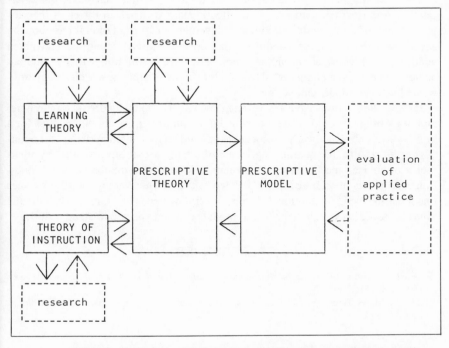

FIG. 2.2   Interrelationships among theory, research, and practice.

When a *prescriptive* instructional theory, mediated through an instructional model, becomes a more explicit guide to practice, its prescriptions are the subject of applied evaluation. The evaluation of instructional materials can serve as a guide to the modification of the instructional model that guided their development. Applied evaluation can also contribute to the modification of the instructional (prescriptive) theory allied to that instructional model.*

Only through its capacity to change can any given instructional theory (prescriptive or descriptive) expect to do well in a competition with other instructional theories.

SUMMARY

A metatheory for analyzing instructional theories and models has been proposed. It calls for an inspection of the approach a theory adopts for identifying learning requirements, obstacles to their being met, and criteria for quantifying the severity of those obstacles. It also calls for an inspection of the approach a theory adopts for determining how much attention should be devoted to learning requirements and obstacles of varying severity (conditions), and for identifying ways to quantify the levels of attention that the treatments it prescribes are to provide.

These parameters are related to one another in a quantitative function that permits an empirical comparison of the effectiveness with which different theories predict and different models produce achievement. Its formulation is based on the assumption that the more conditions that are (accurately) identified and given adequate degrees of attention, the more effective instruction will be. Student achievement is the recommended bottom line for evaluating how well any instructional theory or model can do this.

If these suppositions have any validity, then instructional theorists, researchers, and practitioners would do well to concentrate on principles and techniques for a highly differential analysis of subject-matter and learner characteristics, for quantifying its results, for quantifying levels of attention that are provided by treatments of choice, and for using decision criteria to govern the matching of conditions and levels of attention to be devoted to them. These are the kinds of issues that a hardheaded "instructional-design" discipline needs to address. They are the kinds of issues on which theories and models can be expected to stand or fall.

REFERENCES

Bloom, B. S., (Ed.). *Taxonomy of educational objectives, Handbook I: Cognitive domain*. New York: David McKay, 1956.

Gagné, R. M., & Briggs, L. J. *Principles of instructional design*. New York: Holt, Rinehart & Winston, 1974.

---

*Editor's note: For more about the distinction between descriptive and prescriptive theory, see Chapter 1, p. 21, and Chapter 3, p. 59.

Gilbert, T.F. Mathetics: The technology of education. *Journal of Mathetics,* 1962, *11,* 7–73.

Gropper, G. L. *Instructional strategies*. Englewood Cliffs, N.J.: Educational Technology Publications, 1974.

Gropper, G. L. What should a theory of instruction concern itself with? *Educational Technology,* 1976, *16*(10), 7–12.

Mechner, F. Behavioral analysis and instructional sequencing. In P. C. Lange (Ed.), *Programmed instruction*. Chicago: NSSE, 1967.

Merrill, M.D. Content and instructional analysis for cognitive transfer tasks. *Audio-Visual Communication Review,* 1973, *21*(4), 109–125.

3

Descriptive and Prescriptive Theories of Learning and Instruction: An Analysis of their Relationships and Interactions

Lev N. Landa
The Institute for Advanced Algo-Heuristic Studies, New York

CONTENTS

Instructional Processes As A Particular Case Of Control
    (Management) Processes   56
    Control Processes   56
    Instructional Processes   58
Descriptive Theories, Prescriptive Theories, And
    Programs Of Instruction   59
    Descriptive Theories   59
    Prescriptive Theories   60
    Instructional Programs   61
Learning Theories And Programs: Their Relationship
    With Instructional Theories And Programs   62
Can Instructional Theories And Programs Be Derived From
    Learning Theories And Programs?   65
Regularities Of Learning And Instructional Practice   67
Two Objectives Of Instruction   67
Summary   68

FOREWORD

This chapter discusses with considerable detail and clarity the distinctions between learning theory and instructional theory; between prescriptive theory, descriptive theory, and practice; and the relationships among all of these. Because a clear recog-

---

[1] The approach presented in this section has been set forth in more detail in Landa, 1962, 1976, and 1977. (On cybernetic analysis of instructional processes, see also, for example, Bung, 1971; Bussman, 1971; Couffignal, 1965; Cube, 1964; Frank, 1969; Knochel, 1966; Kopstein, 1977; Lewis & Pask, 1965; Meyer, 1965; Pask, 1975; Smith & Smith, 1966; Stolurow, 1961, 1965a, 1965b; Tracz & Dunlop, 1977.)

nition of these differences is important to both understanding and advancing our knowledge about instruction, this chapter is an important one. Also, the process of instruction is described as a special case of "cybernetic control processes," which are mechanisms (such as a household thermostat) that provide feedback that allows a system to adjust to certain conditions. This Systems-Theory comparison facilitates the analysis and understanding of the instructional process. Many of the ideas presented herein are closely related to Landa's instructional model (see Chapter 6).

C. M. R.

INSTRUCTIONAL PROCESSES AS A PARTICULAR CASE OF CONTROL (MANAGEMENT) PROCESSES

Control Processes

An instructional process can be viewed as a particular case of control processes in the cybernetic sense of the word (Landa, 1976). According to cybernetics, each process of an organized activity represents a series of some *agent's actions* directed at some *object(s)* and aimed at attaining a specified *goal* under given *conditions*. Generally, the agent's actions bring about certain changes in the object, transforming it from some initial state into some final state. The desired final state is a goal. As far as conditions are concerned, they are multiple, and the initial state of this object is just one of them. Among others are the inherent characteristics of the object's nature (internal conditions) and external circumstances influencing the process of transition from the initial to the final state (external conditions).

All the notions used in the preceding description are *relative*. For example, one desired state of the object may represent a final goal with respect to one activity and a subgoal with respect to another. Moreover, a state that emerges as a final goal for one activity may turn into an initial internal condition for achieving a subsequent goal.[2]

Each goal itself may be simple (unitary) or complex (multiple), the latter consisting of a set of component goals. The final goal (or state to be achieved) often represents a set of component goals (or states).[3]

In order to achieve a goal (i.e., bring about a desired transformation of an object's state), the agent should know such things as the nature of the object, the characteristics of its states, the laws of their transition from one to another, and the dependence of the transition on certain external and internal conditions. The agent has to know what actions should be performed on the basis of the given or known

---

[2]In other words, one and the same state of an object may appear as a final goal, as a subgoal, or as an internal condition, depending on the context in which we view it.

[3]There are a lot of publications now on this and related problems (see, for example, Bloom, 1956; Gagné, 1965, 1974; Kopstein, 1977; Mager, 1975; Markle, 1978; Merrill & Tennyson, 1977; Popham & Baker, 1970; Resnick, 1973; Scandura, 1977; White & Gagné, 1974).

information in order to carry out the transformation. In other words, the agent has to have a *program of transformation* that represents a prescription as to what should be done in order to transform a given object from a given state into a desired state under given internal and external conditions. Each *prescription* consists of a set of instructions (rules, directions, commands). In the simplest case the prescription may consist of a single instruction (rule, etc.).

The agent may receive a prescription *from outside* or may develop it *on its own*. The agent may *know* all the actions to be performed before starting the transformation process, or it may *compose the prescription* piecemeal in the very course of the transformation process, each next instruction being devised after a preceding one has been accomplished. A program of actions accepted at the outset of the transformation process may be *followed meticulously* by the agent in the course of transformation or it may be *changed* on the basis of the feedback received during its carrying out. There may even exist programs for changing programs (i.e., programs of *higher order*). Moreover, each program, whether of the first or higher order, may be *effective* or *ineffective* (i.e., may lead or not lead to the achievement of the goals) and *efficient* or *inefficient* or *moderately efficient* (i.e., may lead to the goal with different expenditures of time and resources). It may have some other characteristics as well.

When the agent is a person, quite specific characteristics of programs, actions, and their relationships may take place. A person may *not be aware* of a prescription to follow in the course of an action, but may have a command of a series of actions (operations) and be able to perform them in order to achieve the goal. If we refer to a prescription as an *algorithm* and to a set of actions by which the transformation is carried out as an *algorithmic process*, then one can say that the agent may not know the algorithm but due to having a command of operations, the agent may be able to perform an algorithmic process and achieve a defined goal.[4] We call this an *according-to-rule-process* (Landa, 1976, 1977) and it stands in contrast to a *guided-by-rule process*, for which a performer knows and is guided by a rule, although the objective results of both processes may be the same.

In the case of according-to-rule processes, a program of actions may not exist in a performer's head, but he or she may still be able to perform the process and achieve the goal. The reverse is also possible. A person may know an algorithm but may not be able to perform algorithmic processes (operations) and achieve his or her goal (just as one can know how to swim, but not be able to swim).

A characteristic feature of a person's executing some goal-directed activity is that the program may be of a nonalgorithmic, and in a particular case heuristic, nature. The difference between algorithmic and nonalgorithmic programs (or prescriptions) is that the first determine the corresponding operations unambiguously

---

[4]We see later that programs and processes can be not only of algorithmic but also of nonalgorithmic (in particular, heuristic) nature as well. But with regard to the problem we are discussing, this is not important. What has been said about algorithms and processes is true also of nonalgorithmic ones.

and completely, whereas the second do not. For example, to facilitate a problem solver's search for a solution, the instruction "find an analogous problem" is nonalgorithmic, whereas the instruction "check whether the given number ends in 5" is algorithmic.

This understanding of differences between algorithmic and nonalgorithmic prescriptions or programs differs from that deveveloped in so-called heuristic programming by Newell, Shaw, and some others (cf. Feigenbaum & Feldman, 1963). The distinctions between algorithmic and heuristic programs reflected in this understanding are, however, very important from many points of view (for more details about these distinctions, see Chapters 5 and 6 in Landa, 1976).

Just as a person performing a goal-oriented activity may execute an algorithmic process without a knowledge of its corresponding algorithm, so may he or she perform a nonalgorithmic process without a knowledge of its corresponding nonalgorithmic program.

Instructional Processes

If we move to instructional processes, we see that everything that has been said about goal-directed activity in general is true of instructional activity. An instructional agent (a live teacher or other instructional resource) directs its (or his or her—we just use "it" for simplicity) *actions** at an object or objects (a student or a group of students). These actions are aimed at obtaining specified *goals*** (developing in students certain psychological and behavioral characteristics) under certain internal and external *conditions.****

In order to achieve its goal, a teaching agent may know or devise a program of teaching actions that may be of an algorithmic or nonalgorithmic nature. It may also not be aware of this or that certain program, but have a command of a set of teaching actions that bring about the desired transformations of the students' psychological and behavioral characteristics. (If a program is bad or inadequate, the teaching actions may bring about undesired transformations and develop undesired characteristics in the students.)

Specific features of instructional processes, in contrast to other transformation processes, include the specific nature of the *objects* to be transformed (a live human with specific needs and motives and such abilities as setting one's own goals and regulating himself or herself, etc.), the specific nature of the *characteristics* to be transformed (psychological and behavioral ones), and the specific nature of the *goals* to be achieved.

---

*Editor's note: These were referred to as *methods* in Chapter 1.

**Editor's note: These were referred to as *outcomes* in Chapter 1.

***Editor's note: These were referred to as *conditions* in Chapter 1.

DESCRIPTIVE THEORIES, PRESCRIPTIVE THEORIES, AND PROGRAMS OF INSTRUCTION

It is evident that in order to be able to carry out any instructional activity to achieve a goal, a teacher[5] should know a prescription (algorithmic or nonalgorithmic) for this activity and/or have a command of a system of instructional actions that would lead to the achievement of the goal. In the following discussion, we refer to the knowledge of a prescription as a knowledge of an *instructional program* and the command of actions as a command of an *instructional process*. We remind you that one may know an instructional process to be performed in order to achieve some goal (i.e., have a command of these actions and be able to execute them) without being aware of a prescription (program) that underlies the instructional process and that, if necessary, elicits the actions.

Descriptive Theories

What are the sources of a teacher's knowledge of instructional programs and/or processes? The first of them (historically and often ontologically) is one's own and other teachers' *practical experiences* of what happens (or what outcomes appear) if one performs some instructional actions under certain conditions. This experience leads to a discovery of connections of the type:

If an instructional action A was applied to a condition a, *then* an outcome α appears, where A may be a composite action consisting of a number of constituent actions. A_1. $A_2, \ldots, A_m$, a may be composite condition consisting of a set of conditions a_1, $a_2, \ldots, a_n$, and α may be a composite outcome consisting of a set of outcomes $\alpha_1, \alpha_2, \ldots, \alpha_a$.

When teachers or instructional theorists become well aware of these connections and state them in the form of "if a and A, then α" statements, these statements become *descriptive propositions*. After being verified and organized in some system, this system of propositions forms a *descriptive instructional theory*. In principle, the logic of a descriptive instructional theory does not differ from the logic of descriptive theories in mathematics, physics, biology, medicine, and many other disciplines— all of them representing propositions about what will happen with some object, or phenomenon, or its attributes, their relationships, and so on, if there are such conditions and/or influences on the object under these conditions.

A proposition of physics may serve as an example: If there is water in its "normal" liquid state (condition a) and this water is heated up to $100°\,C$ (action A), then the water will transform itself into vapor (outcome α). In symbolic logic notation:

---

[5]For the purpose of convenience, we would prefer to use this more natural term instead of the more general but, at the same time, more cumbersome term *teaching agent*.

$$a \,\&\, A \to \alpha,$$

where symbol & stands for the logical connective *and* and symbol $\to$ stands for the logical connective "if . . . , then".

Prescriptive Theories

A descriptive theory may represent hundreds of propositions of this type that allow us to predict what will happen to some phenomenon if a certain action occurs. However, if conditions are changed in order to be able not just to passively predict what will happen with the phenomenon under certain conditions, but to actively elicit or produce desired outcomes, descriptive theory is not enough. We have to have a different set of propositions that would point out to us what *should be done* with a phenomenon in order to elicit or produce desired outcomes. An organized set of such propositions would constitute a *prescriptive theory.**

But not only do the two types of theories differ. The two types of propositions—descriptive and prescriptive—are also different in an important way. Whereas the propositions of a descriptive theory have an "if . . . , then" logical structure (if *a & A,* then α), propositions of a prescriptive theory have an "in order to . . . , do this" structure (*in order* to obtain α under conditions *a,* perform *A*).

It is easy to notice that the *passive* "if . . . , then" propositions of the descriptive theory convert themselves into *active* "in order to . . . , do this" rules that prescribe what should be done in order to obtain a desired outcome. Hence, it may seem that it is simple to derive a prescriptive theory of instruction from a descriptive one: that it is enough to restructure *a, A* and α to convert each descriptive "if . . . , then" proposition into a prescriptive "in order to . . . , do this" proposition. A simple example shows that this is not so.

Suppose we have a descriptive proposition: "If a student repeats a statement many times, he or she memorizes it better." This is a 100 percent true proposition. Let us convert it into a prescriptive proposition: "In order to memorize a statement better, one has to repeat it many times." This proposition is not as true as the first one because the state of "memorized" is determined by many factors, not just repetition. For example, for a particular student to memorize a statement, it may be more important to understand it rather than just mechanically repeat it. Some students, due to the specific characteristics of their memory, the personal significance of the proposition for them, and some other factors, may not need to repeat it at all.

The impossibility of building a prescriptive theory from a descriptive one just by converting "if . . . , then" propositions into "in order to . . . , do this" propositions becomes especially evident from the next example. It is true that "if a student can reformulate a statement in his or her own words, then he or she understands it correctly." In a prescriptive form, this statement would look like this: "In

---

*Editor's note: For more about the distinction between descriptive and prescriptive theory, see Chapter 1, p. 21, and Chapter 2, p. 51.

order for a student to understand a statement, it is necessary for him or her to restate it in his or her own words." This proposition is incorrect. Restatement may help to understand a statement, but it is not a necessary condition for comprehension. Comprehension may arise without the restatement, and there may be many causes of inability to comprehend a statement (for example, lack of knowledge of meanings of some words, wrong or incomplete concepts activated by perception of the words, failure to grasp the syntactical structure of the statement, and some others). It is evident that it would be wrong if, in the case of a student's failure to understand a statement, the teacher would be given an instruction or rule: "Urge the student to restate the statement." A correct and helpful rule would be: "Diagnose the psychological reason for the student's failure to understand the statement. If the reason was a, then use method A, if b, use method B, and so on." (Both the reasons and the instructional methods can and should be specified.)

As we see, a simple conversion of a correct descriptive proposition into a prescriptive one may not lead to a correct prescriptive proposition. Even if we had a coherent and complete descriptive theory of instruction, there is no way to automatically convert it into a prescriptive theory of instruction.

Instructional Programs

Let us move to the next problem and suppose that we have built, or just have, a coherent and complete prescriptive theory of instruction. The question is this: Is it sufficient to have such a theory in order to automatically proceed to a *program* of instruction? The answer is no. Even if we had a coherent and comprehensive prescriptive theory of instruction, a teacher would not be able to solve his or her particular instructional problems by simply knowing a set of propositions of the theory. (The instructional process may be viewed as solving a series of specific instructional problems.)

All the instructional problems—that is, which proposition out of all the known propositions to choose, how to chain them, and how to apply them—would arise here. That is why, in order to teach effectively (and to teach at all), a teacher should be provided either with a set of programs for solving particular instructional problems or with a method as to how to independently develop an instructional program (algorithmic or nonalgorithmic) on the basis of known descriptive and prescriptive instructional theories.[6]*

---

[6]A necessity to pass from a theory (even prescriptive) to a program for solving individual problems explains why the knowledge of an instructional theory in itself (even if it were comprehensive and coherent) does not provide a teacher with an ability to teach. The latter ability is based on a knowledge of programs for solving particular problems (or classes of problems) or the ability to pass from theoretical propositions to programs and be guided by them.

*Editor's note: The relationship between a specific instructional *program* and a prescriptive instructional *theory* (or model) is similar to the relationship between an *example* of a procedure and a *statement* (or generality) of the procedure. The instructional theory is general and is used to generate the unique instructional program for the specific subject matter, students, and so on.

The fact that a descriptive instructional theory, a prescriptive instructional theory, and an instructional program are different things or "objects" implies that there should be different methods of their creation and different theories underlying these methods. Theories about how to design instructional theories represent instructional *metatheories.** Theories about designing instructional programs are *theories of instructional design.* Because theories of how to design instructional programs do not specify programs of designing instructional programs, there exist programs for designing instructional programs—that is, *metaprograms* or programs of higher order.** Teaching teachers and student teachers these metatheories and metaprograms is an important task in teacher training that may increase the efficiency of teacher education.

The preceding description might produce an impression that a prescriptive instructional theory may be developed *only* on the basis of a descriptive instructional theory (although it cannot just be deduced from it), and that an instructional program can be developed *only* on the basis of a prescriptive instructional theory (although it also cannot just be deduced from it). This is, however, not quite true, although this way of developing a prescriptive instructional theory and an instructional program would be theoretically founded and preferable. Another way of developing both prescriptive instructional theories and programs is empirical or experimental, whereby propositions of a prescriptive instructional theory are "deduced" from instructional experience and/or experiment.***

LEARNING THEORIES AND PROGRAMS: THEIR RELATIONSHIPS WITH INSTRUCTIONAL THEORIES AND PROGRAMS

Until now we have considered relationships between descriptive and prescriptive instructional theories and instructional programs. What are the relationships between instructional theories and programs, on the one hand, and learning theories and programs, on the other?

The major difference between them is that instructional theories and programs deal with relationships between *teachers'*—or teaching—actions as causes and students' psychological and/or behavioral processes as effects (outcomes), whereas learning theories and programs deal with relationships between *learners'*—or learning—actions as causes and psychological or behavioral processes as effects (outcomes).**** In other words, if instructional theories deal with relationships

---

*Editor's note: See, for example, the conditions—methods—outcomes framework in Chapter 1 and Gropper's metatheory in Chapter 2.

**Editor's note: These were referred to as *instructional-development procedures* in Chapter 1.

***Editor's note: This is the same as the *deductive* and *inductive* approaches to theory construction discussed in Chapter 1.

****Editor's note: For more about the distinction between instructional theory and learning theory, see Chapter 1, p. 23.

between teachers' actions and learners' psychological or behavioral processes, learning theories deal with relationships between learners' actions and learners' psychological or behavioral processes—that is, with relationships of phenomena *inside* a learner. It is another matter that learners' actions may in turn be the results of the teachers' actions; but, first, it is not always the case and, second, relationships of processes inside a learner may be to some extent theoretically abstracted from the scientific analysis of instructional (external) causes that bring about psychological (internal) causes, producing certain psychological or behavioral effects. This question is considered in more detail later.

Like instructional theories, learning theories may be divided into descriptive and prescriptive, and like instructional programs there may exist—and do exist—learning programs. The subject of learning theories and programs and the type of propositions they deal with may be generally represented as follows:

Descriptive learning theories: If a learner performs a learning action A, then it leads to or produces, under certain defined conditions a, psychological or behavioral process α.

For example, if a learner analyzes a text more thoroughly, he or she understands it better.

Prescriptive learning theories: In order for a learner to come to a psychological or behavioral process α, he or she, under certain conditions a, should perform learning action A.

For example, in order to better memorize a text, it is sufficient (but perhaps not necessary) to repeat it several times.

Learning programs: In order for a learner to come to a psychological and/or behavioral process (outcome) α, it is necessary (or may be sufficient) to perform a learning action A. If this action led to psychological or behavioral outcome β, then it is necessary (or may be sufficient) to perform a learning action B. If this action led to a psychological or behavioral outcome Ω, then it is necessary (or sufficient) to perform learning action C. This process is repeated until the target psychological or behavioral outcome has been reached. Like instructional programs, learninig programs may be algorithmic and nonalgorithmic.

We dwelled upon the differences between the subjects of instructional theories and programs, on the one hand, and learning theories and programs, on the other. Before looking into their connections in more detail, let us regard the difference between theories of learning psychology and those of general psychology. Both types of theories deal with lawful inner connections between psychological processes (or psychological and behavioral, behavioral and psychological, etc.).[7] At

---

[7]For stylistic convenience, we speak about connections between psychological processes, keeping in mind that the connections may be between inner psychological and external behavioral processes, and vice versa.

first glance it seems that there is no difference between, say, a descriptive learning-psychology proposition and a descriptive general-psychology proposition. Actually, this is not so, although in many cases the difference may be relative.

The grounds for difference between propositions of a learning theory and those of general-psychology theory lie in the concept of *learning operation*. Operations—motor and cognitive—represent some of the major components of psychological activity. In contrast to knowledge, which is a *representation* of the outer and/or inner world in the form of images, concepts, or propositions, operations are *actions* directed at *transformation* of objects: Motor operations transform material objects, cognitive operations transform their internal psychological representations (images, concepts, or propositions).[8] Goal-directed psychological activity is not possible without execution of cognitive operations. (Responsive psychological activity may be carried out on the basis of associations, which may not include active transformative cognitive operations, or their role may be minimal.)

Cognitive processes (and operations as their components) and learning processes (and operations as their components) are, however, not synonymous. When a person performs some operation (say, on a sentence) in order just to understand it, his or her operations are cognitive, but not learning. But when the person performs the same operations on a text in order to learn it (i.e., when some cognitive operations function as a means of learning), then they become learning operations. Thus, all learning operations are cognitive or motor but not all motor and cognitive operations are learning.

As we mentioned earlier, this difference between learning and cognitive operations is relative, and one and the same operation may emerge in different roles and turn from one into another. For example, some set of operations that may emerge first as learning may later, after having been mastered, become an internal mechanism of psychological activity not aimed at learning. On the other hand, some cognitive nonlearning operations may be purposefully used as means of learning and, in this case, appear as learning operations. There also exist specific learning operations that are used just for purposes of learning.

It can be said, consequently, that *psychological learning theories* deal both with specific learning operations (processes) and nonspecific cognitive operations used as a means of learning, whereas *theories of general psychology* deal with cognitive processes when operations involved are not specific learning operations or are not used as means of learning. What has been said may be put otherwise: General psychology deals with the psychological performance that does not consist of specific learning operations or with nonspecific learning operations that are used as means

---

[8]Cognitive operations are a particular case of inner psychological operations that may be directed at transformation of needs, motives, character traits, and so on. Psychological operations is a generic concept in relation to cognitive operation. Important in our context is that any operation, in contrast to knowledge, is a transformation of something and is not just its mental or inner representation.

of learning, whereas learning psychology deals either with specific learning operations or nonspecific ones used for learning purposes.

The subject of learning theories is the lawful connections between learning operations and their psychological outcomes; *descriptive learning theories* deal with "if . . . , then" propositions stating what happens psychologically if such and such learning actions are performed, and *prescriptive learning theories* prescribe what learning operations should be performed (as necessary, sufficient, or both) in order for a certain psychological process to happen.

Remember that prescriptive instructional theories cannot be automatically derived from descriptive instructional theories, and prescriptive instructional programs from prescriptive instructional theories. This is true also of prescriptive learning theories with regard to descriptive learning theories, as well as learning programs with regard to prescriptive learning theories. The reasons why prescriptive learning theories cannot be automatically derived from descriptive learning theories and learning programs from prescriptive learning theories are exactly the same. Therefore, there is no point in discussing this issue separately and again.

CAN INSTRUCTIONAL THEORIES AND PROGRAMS BE DERIVED FROM LEARNING THEORIES AND PROGRAMS?

Until now we have separately considered relationships within different types of instructional theories (as well as these theories and instructional programs) and within different types of learning theories (as well as these theories and learning programs). We also showed that the principal difference between both groups of theories and programs consists in their subjects: The first reflect relationships between teachers' instructional action and learners' resulting psychological processes, the second, between learners' actions and their resulting psychological processes. Important was the fact that within each group of theories and programs, each particular kind of theory or program is not automatically derivable from another one.

The question arises whether instructional theories may be *derived* from learning theories. If it is not possible to directly derive, say, a prescriptive instructional theory from a descriptive one, maybe it is possible to directly derive a prescriptive instructional program from a learning program?

At first glance, it seems that it is possible and true. Actually, it is not so. Suppose, for example, that a descriptive learning theory says that if a person better understands a text, then he or she remembers it more easily. (Or: In order to more easily memorize the text, it is important to better understand it.) From this seems to follow a prescriptive instructional rule: In order for a learner to better memorize the text, it is necessary (or sufficient) to teach him or her how to understand it (or bring him or her to understanding it). This derived prescriptive instructional proposition is not, however, completely true and comprehensive. Of course, in order to secure that a learner memorizes a text better, it is important to make sure that he or she understands it or to teach him or her how to understand it. But understanding is just *one* of the conditions leading to better memorizing, and to secure (or teach) the understanding is *not sufficient* for gaining the best results in memorization. Other factors not mentioned in *these* propositions of learning theory (both descriptive and prescriptive) should be taken into account. They are stated in other propositions of a learning theory (if it is complete). But the learning theory does not tell anything about which of its propositions should be taken into account and combined (and precisely how combined) in order to state an effective prescriptive instructional proposition.

There is one more important circumstance. Let us suppose that comprehension had been the only factor affecting better memorization. In this case, a prescriptive proposition of an instructional theory might be derived directly from a proposition of a learning theory. However, this is not true with regard to instructional programs, because neither a proposition of a learning theory, nor a corresponding proposition of an instructional theory, says anything about how to secure comprehension or develop an ability (or skill) to comprehend.

Maybe, then, an instructional program can be derived from a learning program—that is, from a knowledge as to what learners do in order to comprehend the text. This information is very important for building an instructional program but, first of all, different learners may perform different processes to understand a text, and from these processes themselves or their describing programs, it is not clear which of them should be used as a basis of instruction or as a sources for an instructional program—for teaching each particular student. Specific operations for the selection and evaluation of learners' programs themselves should be performed by an instructor or instructional designer to this end, and these operations are not indicated in any of learning programs themselves. On the other hand, the just-mentioned problem of how to shape operations that are known to be prerequisite for achieving the desired outcome remains. Even if there existed a single possible program of learner activity, sufficient and necessary for attaining a specified goal, and even if we knew the precise algorithms of this activity (in order to achieve a, it is sufficient and necessary to perform operations $A, B, C, \ldots, N$), we might not know how to teach these operations, because the methods of shaping the operations are not contained in propositions stating the dependence of achieving the goal on the performance of given operations.

Thus, the information provided by learning theories (both descriptive and prescriptive) and learning programs is necessary for building an instructional theory and instructional program, but not sufficient.* Instructional theories and programs cannot be directly and automatically derived from learning theories and programs.

---

*Editor's note: Again, this just refers to a deductive approach to theory construction. An inductive approach does not depend in any way on learning theory or learning programs.

REGULARITIES OF LEARNING AND INSTRUCTIONAL PRACTICE

There is one more reason why theories and programs of instruction cannot be directly derived from theories and programs of learning. In many psychological and pedagogical theories, regularities of learning are viewed as inherent and independent (at least considerably) of instructional influences. This led to a problem of bringing instruction in accordance with the inherent laws of learning, which themselves are supposedly determined internally by physiological and/or biological laws.

However, some components or aspects of learning are actually determined by the nature and mode of instruction that a person received and receives. Moreover, physiological and biological factors and laws themselves manifest themselves primarily through psychological factors and laws, which always represent results of interaction between physiologico–biological, instructional, and environmental factors. Each learning outcome is a function of multiple influences interacting with each other. According to many psychologists, there are no pure, inherent regularities of learning, independent of the nature and mode of instruction. The latter are a partial function of regularities of learning, as learning regularities are a partial function of instruction. The dialectics of the situations are that the development of instructional strategies should draw upon information about regularities of learning (although they cannot be derived directly from them), whereas regularities of learning themselves are determined to a grater or lesser extend by instructional methods and strategies that have been and are applied in the process of instruction.

TWO OBJECTIVES OF INSTRUCTION

As was mentioned earlier, prescriptive theories of learning deal with connections (regularities) of the type: "In order to originate, under certain conditions a, psychological processes α, it is necessary (or sufficient) to perform learning operations A," whereas prescriptive theories of instruction deal with connections (regularities) of the type: "In order to originate, under certain conditions a, psychological processes α, it is necessary (or sufficient) to perform teaching operations A." It is important to note that teaching operations may be directed at originating resulting psychological/behavioral *processes* α *or learning operations* A able, then, to generate processes α, where "or" is not exclusive.

It is evident that instruction in the second case would be aimed at teaching a learning operation (a skill to learn), which would lead to independent acquisition of the knowledge and performance skill, whereas in the first case teaching would be aimed at direct development from outside of knowledge and skills, without teaching the students how, through independent learning operations, to arrive at this knowledge and skills on their own.* Different educational values of these

---

*Editor's note: This is a very important distinction, because different methods are required depending on which type of objective is in effect (see Chapter 4, p. 84, Chapter 6, p. 194, and Chapter 8, p. 258.

approaches are evident. The first develops particular knowledge and skills without developing the ability to learn—that is, to independently acquire them—whereas the second develops this educationally more valuable ability to independently acquire knowledge and skills, which leads to developing self-regulating and self-control psychological mechanisms. In the second case, methods of external instruction convert themselves, if specially organized, into methods of self-instruction, which represent in turn nothing other than conscious methods of learning and cognitive activity.

SUMMARY

In this chapter we have examined some theoretical problems concerning relationships between descriptive and prescriptive theories of learning and instruction, as well as learning and instruction programs. Analysis of methods of building effective and efficient learning and instructional programs that virtually determine the effectiveness and efficiency of real learning and instructional processes is a special task requiring special consideration.

REFERENCES

Bloom, B. S. (Ed.) *Taxonomy of educational objectives: The classification of educational goals. Handbook I. Cognitive domain.* New York: McKay, 1956.
Bung, K. A cybernetic approach to programmed language instruction. *Educational Media International,* 1971, 4.
Bussman, H. *Zur Kybernetik des Lernprozesses.* Düsseldorf: Pädagogischer Verlag Schwann, 1971.
Couffignal, L. La pédagogie cybernétique. *L'Éducation Nationale,* 1965, 15−16.
Cube, F. *Kybernetische Grundlagen des Lernens und Lehrens.* Stuttgart: Ernst Klett, 1964.
Feigenbaum, E. A., & Feldman, J. *Computers and thought.* New York: McGraw Hill, 1963.
Frank, H. *Kybernetische Grundlagen der Pädagogik.* Baden-Baden: Agis-Verlag, 1969.
Gagné, R. The analysis of instructional objectives for the design of instruction. In R. Glaser (Ed.), *Teaching machines and programmed learning,* II. Washington, D.C.: NEA, 1965.
Gagné, R. Task analysis—Its relation to content analysis. *Educational Psychologist,* 1974, *11,* 11−18.
Knöchel, W. *Grundlagenprobleme der Pädagogik in kybernetischer Sicht.* Berlin: Volk und Wissen Volkseigener Verlag, 1966.
Kopstein, F. F. (Ed.) Cybernetics and education. *Educational Technology,* 1977, *17*(10), 7−58.
Landa, L. N. On the cybernetic approach to the theory of instruction. *Problems of Phylosophy,* 1962,9 (in Russian). English translation: JPRS: 17,896, March 1963, OTS:63-21133.
Landa, L. N. *Instructional regulation and control: Cybernetics, algorithmization, and heuristics in education.* Englewood Cliffs, N.J.: Educational Technology Publications, 1976.
Landa, L. N. Cybernetics methods in education. *Educational Technology,* 1977, *10.*
Lewis, B. N., & Pask, G. The theory and practice of adaptive systems. In R. Glaser (Ed.), *Teaching machines and programmed learning,* II. Washington, D.C.: NEA, 1965.
Mager, R. *Preparing instructional objectives.* Belmont, CA: Fearon Publishers, 1975.
Markle, S. *Designs for instructional designers.* Champain, Ill: Stipes Publishing, 1978.
Merrill, M. D., & Tennyson, R. D. *Teaching concepts: An instructional design guide.* Englewood Cliffs, N.J.: Educational Technology Publications, 1977.
Meyer, G. *Kybernetik und Unterrichtsprozess.* Berlin: Volk und Wissen Volkseigener Verlag, 1965.

Pask, G. *The cybernetics of human learning and performance.* London: Hutchinson Educational, 1975.

Popham, W. J. & Baker, E. L. *Systematic instruction.* Englewood Cliffs, N.J.: Prentice-Hall, 1970.

Resnick, L. B. Issues in the study of learning hierarchies. *Instructional Science,* 1973, *2,* 312–323.

Scandura, J. M. Systems/cybernetic/structural approach to instructional theory: A synthesis. In J. M. Scandura, *Recent advances in instructional theory, I.* A symposium presented at the annual convention of the American Educational Research Association, New York, 1977.

Smith, K., & Smith, M. *Cybernetic principles of learning and educational design.* New York: Holt, Rinehart and Winston, 1966.

Stolurow, L. M. *Teaching by machine.* Washington, D.C., 1961.

Stolurow, L. M. A model and cybernetic system for research on the teaching-learning process. *Programmed Learning,* 1965, 10. (a)

Stolurow, L. M. Model of the master teacher or master the teaching model. In J. D. Krumboltz (Ed.), *Learning and educational process.* Chicago, Ill: Rand McNally, 1965. (b)

Tracz, G., & Dunlop, D. Cybernetic view of primary and secondary education system in Ontario. *Educational Technology,* 1977, *17*(10), 41–44.

White, R.T., & Gagné, R. M. Past and future research on learning hierarchies. *Educational Psychologist,* 1974, 11, 19–28.

Unit II
MODELS AND THEORIES OF INSTRUCTION

This unit describes integrative models and theories of instruction. Most of the chapters describe a prescriptive instructional theory—that is, a set of models and a basis for prescribing which model to use when. Each model integrates a fairly substantial number of strategy components by indicating such things as which components should be used together and the order in which those components should be offered to the student. For example, Merrill's Component Display Theory (Chapter 9) prescribes the use of a generality (e.g., the definition of a concept), instances (e.g., examples of the concept), and practice (e.g., experience in classifying new instances as to whether or not they are examples of the concept), as well as prescriptions for the optimal characteristics that each of these components should have. To the extent that these prescriptions incorporate the knowledge generated by different researchers from different theoretical orientations, they represent an integrative model of instruction.

Some models and theories in this unit appear to make *no attempt to integrate* the work of other theorists and researchers. Other theories attempt only to integrate the work of theorists or researchers who are within a *relatively narrow part* of the entire discipline (e.g., only the work of behaviorist researchers and theorists or only that of cognitive researchers and theorists). Finally, some theories have attempted to integrate the work of a *broad spectrum* of researchers and theorists.

It should be noted that this unit is not an extensive representation of the existing models and theories of instruction: Many have been left out due to space limitations. Our intention has been to include the most comprehensive yet substantive ones that are still under development, but even here we may not have been aware of some models or theories that we would otherwise have included. For descriptions of some that we have not included here, see Snelbecker's *Learning Theory, Instructional Theory, and Psychoeducational Design* and Joyce and Weil's *Teaching Models*. In addition, we would like to point out Markle's excellent work on how to teach concepts.

It becomes apparent as you read the chapters in this unit that different models and theories are designed to achieve *different kinds of goals*, such as the acquisition of verbal information or the mastery of cognitive strategies. In fact, this may account for the *major differences* among most of the models, especially between cognitively oriented and behaviorally oriented ones. Discounting for the differences in goals among the various models and theories in this unit, there are great similarities among those models and theories, even though they might be from different theoretical orientations. Footnotes have been used to draw attention to some of those similarities.

The chapters in this unit are arranged in roughly the order in which the models' and theories' major development occurred, which means that behaviorally oriented ones tend to come first, followed by cognitively oriented ones, and finally by multi perspectived ones. The highly integrative Gagné–Briggs theory is the major exception to the rule.

In Chapter 1 we distinguished between *micro* strategies, which are methods for teaching a single idea, and *macro* strategies, which are methods that relate to teaching a number of ideas. Although most of the chapters in this unit describe both kinds of strategies to some extent, all tend to focus mainly on *one* of the two. The Landa, Scandura, and Reigeluth–Stein chapters all tend to emphasize macro strategies (primarily the selection and sequencing of content), whereas the Gropper, Collins–Stevens, and Merrill chapters tend to focus mainly on micro strategies (e.g., ways to facilitate the acquisition of a single concept or principle). For an overview of some of the major characteristics of each model or theory, see the foreword at the beginning of each chapter.

A recurring theme of this book is the need to draw from work in *all* theoretical orientations. We need a knowledge base that can prescribe optimal methods for achieving the full range of desired outcomes (i.e., goals) under different conditions (e.g., for different types of content, students, and constraints). Cognitively oriented instructional theories and models have tended to focus on optimal methods for achieving certain kinds of goals (such as "learning how to discover") whereas behaviorally oriented ones have tended to focus on optimal methods for achieving other kinds of goals (usually content-specific associations, generalizations, and discriminations). Hence, a prescriptive instructional theory must (in order to be truly comprehensive) be able to prescribe *both* kinds of instructional methods (plus humanistic ones such as Rogers'), depending on the desired outcomes.

However, there is also an area of overlap between different orientations—where they both prescribe methods for achieving the same kinds of goals. To what extent can method components from one orientation be integrated with method components from another? Some people have argued that a theorist must operate within a single theoretical perspective (e.g., behavioral, cognitive, or humanistic), but others have disagreed. Perhaps a single perspective is best for generating descriptive theory, whereas a multiperspectived approach is best for generating the most useful prescriptive theory (see Chapter 12 for a discussion of this issue). As instructional researchers, theorists, and developers who are *objectively* searching for the best methods for achieving desired outcomes, we must approach this important question with a truly open mind. It is hoped that a careful analysis of the chapters in this unit will help reveal the answer.

4 Contributions of Gagné and Briggs to a Prescriptive Model of Instruction

Dennis T. Aronson
Aronson Communications
St. Albans, W. Virginia

Leslie J. Briggs
Florida State University

Dennis T. Aronson

Dennis Aronson earned his bachelor's degree in history at Pomona College in Claremont, California and his master's in education at the American University of Beirut in Lebanon. He took his doctorate in instructional design and development at the Florida State University.

Dr. Aronson's teaching experience includes service in Afghanistan as a Peace Corps Volunteer English teacher and in Saudi Arabia as an instructor for Saudi Arabian Airlines. He was on the faculty of the American University of Beirut, where he developed and taught courses on methods of teaching English as a foreign language.

More recently Dr. Aronson was on the faculty of the West Virginia College of Graduate Studies, where he developed and taught courses in the area of instructional technology.

Dr. Aronson now has his own firm, Aronson Communications, specializing in instructional design and audiovisual production. He has developed education and training materials for the West Virginia Department of Education, the West Virginia College of Graduate Studies, and other organizations in West Virginia.

While at Florida State University, Dr. Aronson worked closely with Dr. Leslie Briggs, who was his doctoral advisor, and Dr. Robert Gagné, for whom he was a teaching assistant.

Leslie J. Briggs

Leslie J. Briggs received his Ph.D. degree in psychology from Ohio State University in 1948, after serving three years during World War II as a classification specialist in the Army. From 1948–51 he served as assistant professor of psychology at the University of Hawaii.

His career as an instructional designer began in the Air Force Personnel and Training Research Center at Lowry Air Force Base, Colorado, where he designed training devices and training programs, and conducted research in motivation, morale, and training methods, from 1951–57. From 1957–59 he designed training plans for maintenance of electronic systems for Hughes Aircraft Company.

From 1959–67 he served as director of the Instructional Methods Program at the American Institutes for Research in Palo Alto, California, where he published the first of a series of monographs on the design of instruction.

In 1968 he became professor of instructional systems design in the Department now called Educational Research, Development, and Foundations, at Florida State University. In that position, he has taught instructional design courses, continued writing monographs and textbooks in instructional design, and has directed doctoral dissertations in that area.

Dr. Briggs' research has typically grown out of problems encountered during the development of training programs. For example, in the Air Force, he first designed and evaluated training devices and programs, then conducted basic research in variables accounting for their effectiveness. Based on Air Force experience in forecasting training requirements for weapon systems of the future, he became interested in the study of futurism as a way of orienting instructional design efforts to educational objectives and media expected to be appropriate for activities in a future society. His present interest is in helping assure that instructional design models are applied to meet future needs, employing the media of the future.

Robert M. Gagné

Robert M. Gagné is a Professor of Educational Research in the College of Education, Florida State University. He received his undergraduate education at Yale University, and his doctoral degree in experimental psychology from Brown University in 1940. His college teaching career began at Connecticut College for Women. During World War II, he served as an Aviation Psychologist, engaged in the development of tests of motor and perceptual functions in the classification of aircrew.

He returned to college teaching at Pennsylvania State University and again at Connecticut College, where he also carried out a research project on the learning and transfer of skills. For eight years thereafter, he held positions as Technical Director in two Air Force Laboratories engaged in research programs dealing with learning and methods of technical training.

From 1958 to 1962, Dr. Gagné was Professor of Psychology at Princeton University, where he carried out a series of studies of the acquisition of knowledge and of mathematics learning. From 1962–65, he was the Director of Research of the American Institutes for Research. His writings during this period dealt particularly with methods of instruction, problem-solving, and the conditions of learning. From 1966–69, he was a Professor in the

Department of Education, University of California, Berkeley, in the field of educational psychology. He directed the effort of establishing a regional educational laboratory, managed a program of graduate training in educational research, and continued his research on the learning of school subjects. At Florida State, he has completed research on learning hierarchies related to school instruction, communication skills in object description, and a study of research and development objectives derived from school needs. Current projects deal with scientific literacy in adults, and with effects of learning elaborations on retention of rules.

His publications include more than a hundred articles on human learning and instruction in scholarly journals. He has written five major books, including *The Conditions of Learning,* 3rd Ed., Holt, Rinehart and Winston, 1977; and (with Briggs) *Principles of Instructional Design,* 2nd ed., Holt, Rinehart and Winston, 1979.

CONTENTS

Learning-Theory Background   81
   Varieties Of Learning   81
   Conditions Of Learning   82
   Subcategories Of Intellectual Skills   84
Selecting Instructional Objectives And Sequencing
     Instruction   85
   Prerequisites   85
   Learning Hierarchies For Intellectual Skills   86
   Selecting Objectives For Intellectual-Skill Outcomes   87
   Sequencing Instruction   87
     Entry Level   88
   Sequencing Instruction In Other Domains   88
Instructional Events   89
   Definition   89
   Differential Effects   93
Instructional Media   93
   Instructional Events And Media   96
   Learner Characteristics And Media   96
Conclusion   97
Glossary   97

FOREWORD

The Gagné–Briggs models of instruction represented an extremely important contribution to the then-embryonic discipline of instruction for two major reasons: (1) although the models have continued to evolve over the past 15 years, they are the *oldest* models described in this book; and (2) they represent the first major attempt to integrate a wide range of knowledge about learning and instruction into an instructional theory. Ironically, Gagné's and Briggs' work has not been touted as instructional theory. In fact, much of Gagné's work properly comes under the rubric of learning theory (see, for example, Gagné, 1977), and much of Briggs' work belongs under the rubric of instructional development procedures (see, for example, Briggs, 1970). Nevertheless, the contributions of both to instructional theory—that is, to prescriptions as to what the instruction should be like—are considerable and very important.

One of the most outstanding features of the Gagné–Briggs models of instruction is their *breadth of applicability*. They include a model for teaching attitudes and a model for teaching motor skills, as well as three models in the cognitive domain. As is natural for such a broad undertaking, some sacrifice in depth has been necessary: None of the five models has been developed to the level of detail of guidance that is represented in the other theories and models described in this unit. But the breadth represented in this instructional theory helps to provide a framework for viewing many of the other theories: Those theories can be viewed as providing more detail about a specific part or parts of the Gagné–Briggs theory. Also, the attitudinal and psychomotor models represent significant advances in important domains that have received relatively little attention from instructional theorists. The same was true for all five models when they were first developed. This theory's breadth is also reflected in its specific provision for the use of motivational strategies for instruction in the cognitive domain (it comes under one of the nine *events of instruction*). Although that provision is extremely general and hence not as useful as we would like (especially when compared to Chapter 11 of this book), it is often entirely ignored in the other models and theories of instruction.

Perhaps the most widely used of the Gagné–Briggs models is the model for teaching "intellectual skills." The three major components of this model are: (1) the *selection* of content that represents *learning prerequisites* for each course objective (a macro strategy); (2) the *sequencing* of course content such that prerequisites are always taught before the skills for which they are prerequisite (also a macro strategy); and (3) the prescription of nine *events of instruction* for teaching each objective (a set of micro strategies), including the prescription of *media* for teaching each objective (a set of delivery strategies).

C. M. R.

Contributions of Gagné and Briggs to a Prescriptive Model of Instruction

The work of Robert Gagné and Leslie Briggs has contributed greatly in answering three questions:

1. What is known about human learning that is relevant for instruction?
2. How can that body of knowledge be organized for application by designers of instruction?
3. What procedures should be followed in applying knowledge of human learning to the design of instruction?

The purpose of this chapter is to focus on the second question concerning instructional design.

It is assumed that most readers of this book are not familiar with the work of Gagné and Briggs; therefore, this chapter provides an introduction to aspects of their work that are pertinent to this book. The reader can find more detailed information in the various books written by the two men (Briggs, 1970, 1972, 1977; Gagné, 1970, 1974, 1977; Gagné & Briggs, 1979).

In order to understand the work of Gagné and Briggs, it is necessary for the reader to learn the precise, explicit terminology that they use. To assist the reader, critical concepts are printed in italics and defined. Sometimes the definition appears in the text. When the definition does not appear in the text, the reader may wish to refer to the glossary at the end of the chapter where the key terms are defined.

With respect to organization, this chapter first provides a learning-theory background by discussing Gagné's system for classifying objectives according to the types of *learning outcomes* involved and the different sets of *conditions* that are required for the various types of learning to occur. Second, the chapter discusses the bases for selecting and sequencing objectives for instruction. Third, the chapter explains the concept of *instructional events,* and it shows how these events can be used for determining prescriptions to facilitate different types of learning. Fourth, the chapter discusses prescriptions for selecting and using *instructional media.*

LEARNING-THEORY BACKGROUND

Varieties of Learning

Gagné has classified human learning into five categories or domains: verbal information, attitudes, intellectual skills, motor skills, and cognitive strategies (see Table 4.1). These categories are important for instructional theory because each is hypothesized to require different types of instruction. It is important to grasp the basis upon which Gagné has made this classification.

For Gagné, learning occurs when an individual acquires a particular capability to do something. Because the *learned capability* is not in itself observable, it is from the learner's behavior (which is observable) that one can infer that a particular capability has been learned. Gagné emphasizes that different learned capabilities result in correspondingly different *outcomes*. When these outcomes are anticipated and planned for, they are stated as instructional objectives.

The capability that one acquires when learning *verbal information* (e.g., a spouse's birthday) is stating the information. On the other hand, the capability that one acquires in learning an *attitude* is choosing to act in one way or another (e.g., bringing flowers home on wife's birthday). When a person has learned a concept, which is one type of *intellectual skill*, the person has the capability to correctly identify or classify any previously unencountered example of the concept (e.g., properly classifying different kinds of flowers). When a *motor skill* has been acquired, the capability is being able to execute properly and smoothly all the subskills in a correct sequence (e.g., serving a tennis ball). Finally, a person who has the capability to originate a novel solution to a problem or who is able to devise a

TABLE 4.1
Five Varieties of Learning

Learned Capability	*Performance*
Intellectual skill	Using concepts and rules to solve problems; responding to classes of stimuli as distinct from recalling specific examples
Motor skill	Executing bodily movements smoothly and in proper sequence
Verbal information	Stating information
Cognitive strategy	Originating novel solutions to problems; utilizing various means for controlling one's thinking/learning processes
Attitude	Choosing to behave in a particular way

personal system for remembering information or attending to a task is showing that he or she has learned a *cognitive strategy*.

Conditions of Learning

One reason for using a taxonomy to classify learning outcomes into different categories is that the different categories of outcomes involve entirely different classes of performance (as summarized in Table 4.1).

There is another important reason for classifying outcomes according to types of learner capability. Gagné explains that different sets of conditions* must be established and/or provided for the various types of outcomes to occur. There are two kinds of conditions: internal and external. *Internal conditions* refer to acquisition and storage of prior capabilities that the learner has acquired that are either essential to or supportive of subsequent learning. *External conditions* refer to various ways that instructional events outside the learner function to activate and support the internal processes of learning. Both these concepts—internal and external conditions of learning—are discussed further as the various types of learning are discussed. The important point to grasp at this time is that the various types of learning are distinguished from one another by the fact that different sets of conditions are needed for each type of learning to occur.

So there are two bases for the classification of learning outcomes: (1) the performance manifested is entirely different for each type of learning; and (2) the conditions required are different for each type. Some of the essential internal conditions required for the various types of learning are now presented.

Internal Conditions. For an intellectual skill to be learned, it is necessary that certain previously learned prerequisites be recalled. For example, before a person can learn to classify objectives as belonging to appropriate domains of outcomes, the person must be able to recognize that two outcomes are different (e.g., that being able to *state* a rule is different from being able to *use* the rule).

For an attitude to be learned, the learner needs to be able to recall a respected model exhibiting the attitude (e.g., a famous athlete eating a breakfast cereal). Cognitive strategy learning is based on prior learning of intellectual skills, and information learning is facilitated if the learner can recall previous learning that is related to the new (e.g., recalling the names of major phyla of animal categories before learning species in each phylum).

External Conditions. Just as the internal conditions are different for each type of learning, so are the external conditions. For a concept to be learned, a person must have opportunities to practice distinguishing correctly between examples and

---

*Editor's note: *Conditions of learning* should not be confused with *instructional conditions* as defined in Chapter 1. Internal conditions of learning are in fact instructional conditions, but external conditions of learning are instructional methods (see next few sentences in text).

nonexamples. For motor-skill learning, it is important that the learner be able to practice the skill and receive immediate information on the correctness of the performance.

For cognitive strategies to be learned, there must be opportunities over a period of time to practice originating new solutions to problems. An essential external condition for learning verbal information is to have the information presented in a context that is meaningful to the learner. For an attitude to be learned, a model respected by the learner must be provided; direct or vicarious experience is thus one mechanism for attitude formation or change. Under some conditions, persuasive communications or conditioning techniques may be employed.

The preceding discussion presented only some of the essential conditions required for different varieties of learning to occur. Table 4.2 presents other conditions as well.

TABLE 4.2
Learning Conditions for Cognitive Strategies,
Verbal Information, Attitudes, and Motor Skills[a]

Type of Learning	Internal Conditions	External Conditions
Cognitive strategy	Recall of relevant rules and concepts	Successive presentation (usually over an extended time) of novel problem situations with class of solution unspecified
		Demonstration of solution by student
Verbal information	Recall of larger meaningful context	Present new information in larger context
Attitude	Recall of information and intellectual skills relevant to the targeted personal actions	Establishment or recall of respect for "source" (usually a person)
		Reward for personal action either by direct experience or vicariously by observation of respected person
Motor skill	Recall of component motor chains	Establishment or recall of executive subroutine (rules)
		Practice of total skill

[a]Source: From PRINCIPLES OF INSTRUCTIONAL DESIGN, 2nd edition, by Robert M. Gagné and Leslie Briggs. Copyright © 1974, 1979 by Holt, Rinehart and Winston. Reprinted by permission of Holt, Rinehart and Winston, CBS College Publishing.

TABLE 4.3
Subcategories of Intellectual Skills

Type of Intellectual Skill	Performance
Higher-order rule	Generate new rule for solving a problem
Rule	Demonstrate application of a rule
Defined concept	Classify objects, events, or states using verbal descriptions or definitions
Concrete concept	Identify instances of the concept by pointing to examples
Discrimination	Discriminate between stimuli that differ along one or more physical dimensions

Subcategories of Intellectual Skills

Some of the five categories of learning have subcategories of outcomes; most important are the subcategories in the intellectual-skills domain. These subcategories and the performance resulting when each type is acquired are shown in Table 4.3.

As mentioned previously, Gagné has shown that the essential internal condition that must be met for learning an intellectual skill is that necessary prerequisites must have already been learned. One important external condition is stimulating the learner to recall those essential prior learnings. In order for a person to demonstrate the use of a *higher-order rule* (i.e., by generating a new rule), the person must have learned various prerequisite *rules*. Because a rule is a relationship between two or more concepts, those *concepts* are prerequisite to learning the rule of which they are a part. Similarly, defined concepts often have as referents *concrete concepts* (e.g., the concept "chair" can be learned as a definition or as an object that can be physically identified). Before a concept can be learned, one must be able to make *discriminations* between critical attributes. For example, the learner must be able to indicate if a chair and a bench are different from one another before learning those two concepts. In addition, the most basic forms of learning include associations and chains. These types of learning are not described at all in this chapter; the reader should refer to Gagné (1970, 1977). Figure 4.1 illustrates the distinguishing feature of any type of intellectual skill—the necessity for acquisition of prerequisite skills.

At this point, the reader has been introduced to the system Gagné developed for classifying the various learning types according to their respective outcomes and the conditions required for learning to occur. The distinction between internal and external conditions was also explained, and the essential conditions for the respective types of learning were presented. The next section discusses some of the ways that this learning-theory background can be used in selecting objectives and sequencing instruction.

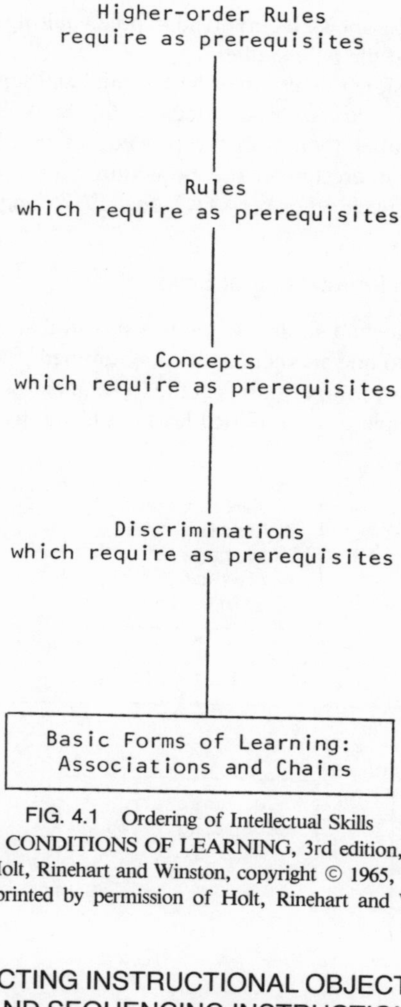

Higher-order Rules
require as prerequisites

Rules
which require as prerequisites

Concepts
which require as prerequisites

Discriminations
which require as prerequisites

Basic Forms of Learning:
Associations and Chains

FIG. 4.1   Ordering of Intellectual Skills

[a]Source: From THE CONDITIONS OF LEARNING, 3rd edition, by Robert M. Gagné. Copyright © 1977 by Holt, Rinehart and Winston, copyright © 1965, 1970 by Holt, Rinehart and Winston, Inc. Reprinted by permission of Holt, Rinehart and Winston, CBS College Publishing.

SELECTING INSTRUCTIONAL OBJECTIVES AND SEQUENCING INSTRUCTION

Prerequisites

An important consideration in sequencing instruction is to ensure that the learner has mastered the necessary prerequisites. There are two types. *Essential prerequisites* are those subordinate skills that must have been previously learned to enable the learner to reach the objective. Also these prerequisites become an integral part of what is subsequently learned. *Supporting prerequisites* are those that are useful to facilitate learning but are not absolutely essential for the learning to occur. The learning of these can make learning the objective easier or faster. An example of a supporting prerequisite is the positive attitude that a successful pole vaulter has about him- or herself, for the skills involved in pole vaulting are not dependent on the particular attitude of the pole vaulter.

The instructional designer determines the essential and supporting prerequisites by conducting a *learning-task analysis*. Because this book is concerned with prescriptive instruction rather than with the procedures used to derive those prescriptions, the reader interested in the procedures for conducting a learning-task analysis should consult other books (Gagné, 1977; Gagné & Briggs, 1979).

Learning Hierarchies for Intellectual Skills

In the domain of intellectual skills, Gagné has shown that essential prerequisites and their relationship to one another can be diagrammed in the form of a *learning hierarchy*, in which the terminal skill is at the top and below it are all the essential prerequisites. An example of a simplified learning hierarchy is shown in Fig. 4.2.

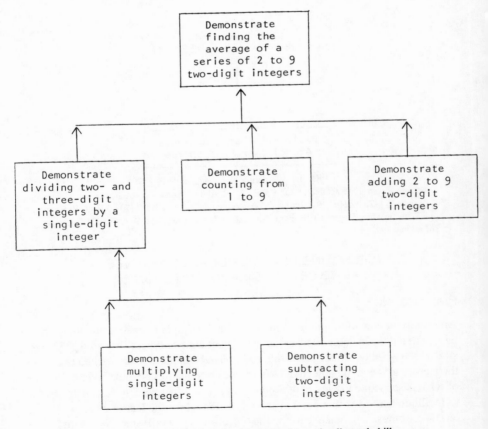

FIG. 4.2   A partial learning hierarchy for an intellectual skill.

In Fig. 4.2, the terminal objective is "demonstrate finding the average of a series of two to nine two-digit integers." The prerequisites of being able to add, count, and divide are listed below the terminal objective. The competency, "dividing two- and three-digit integers by a single-digit integer," has the prerequisites "subtracting two-digit integers" and "multiplying single-digit integers." Subtraction is itself composed of many subskills that could be further specified (see Gagné & Briggs, 1979).

Two points about learning hierarchies should be emphasized:

1. Constructing a learning hierarchy is pertinent *only in the intellectual-skills domain*.

2. A learning hierarchy shows the intellectual skills that must be learned; it *does not show the order in which those skills may be performed* once they have been learned (e.g., the sequence for *learning* the prerequisites for being able to do long division is learning addition, subtraction, and then division; the sequence for *performing* those operations when dividing is performing division, then multiplication, then subtraction.*

Selecting Objectives for Intellectual-Skill Outcomes

One of the most important contributions of Gagné to a prescriptive model of instruction is the specification of *what* to teach in order to achieve a desired outcome. The various skills identified as prerequisites must be selected as enabling objectives (and hence as part of the content) for the course, unit, or lesson, unless the learners have already mastered those prerequisite skills. The essential prerequisites also help prevent the designer from including nonessential objectives for a given instructional sequence.

Sequencing Instruction

Another important contribution of Gagné to a prescriptive model of instruction is that in addition to indicating what should be taught, a learning hierarchy provides a guide for planning the sequence in which the objectives should be achieved. Even though the analysis that results in constructing a learning hierarchy proceeds from the top down, instruction is sequenced from the bottom up.

In a fully developed hierarchy, at any given level, there may be two or more competencies that are prerequisites to a single skill at the next higher level. The sequence for learning such a cluster of prerequisites (and thus the sequence for teaching them) may not be critical so long as all of the prerequisites are mastered before moving to the skill at the higher level. For example, prerequisites for learn-

---

*Editor's note: This is similar to Gropper's distinction between *learning contingencies* and *performance contingencies* (see Chapter 5, p. 157).

ing the rule for writing an instructional objective using the Gagné and Briggs system (Gagné & Briggs, 1979, Chapter 7) are the following concepts: situation, learned capability, object, action, and tools or constraints. The order in which each of these concepts is learned is not critical, but all have to be learned in order to write an objective embodying the concepts.

Another point is that sometimes prerequisites may be taught at the same time For example, concepts may be presented as examples and nonexamples of one another (e.g., latitude and longitude, north and south, up and down, subject and predicate).

Although a learning hierarchy can serve as a guide to what must be learned, this does not mean that a particular instructional sequence must include instruction for each competency in the hierarchy. The reason is that some learners may already have learned a competency and do not, therefore, require instruction before moving on to a more complicated skill that has not yet been mastered. Thus, learning hierarchies provide a basis for determining what a learner has already achieved and for diagnosing what specific competencies have not been mastered—deficiencies that must be overcome before proceeding to subsequent learning.

Entry Level

Another use of a learning hierarchy is to designate a level at the lower part of the hierarchy as the *entry level* for given learners. This means that all the competencies below that level have to have been mastered before the learner can begin a particular instructional sequence that teaches the competencies above the entry level. For example, the learning hierarchy for solving algebraic equations with two unknowns would show, low in the hierarchy, that the student must have mastered basic math facts and operations. Such competencies would be considered as entry-level behaviors for instruction in algebra.

Although the designer may use some professional judgment in determining initially where the entry level should be, testing must be conducted to verify whether or not the designated entry level is correct. If it is not, the designer may have to raise or lower the entry-level requirements.

Sequencing Instruction in Other Domains

When the learning involves predominately intellectual-skill outcomes, the designer is usually advised to base the instructional sequencing on the prerequisites for those intellectual skills (Gagné & Briggs, 1979). Even though essential prerequisites can form the basis for many instructional sequences, supporting prerequisites must be considered, too. For example, an attitudinal learning outcome that a person will choose to ride a bicycle rather than drive a car to run short errands in the neighborhood has as a supporting prerequisite that the person knows how to ride a bicycle.

For learning a *motor skill*, it is sometimes advised to teach first the rule that governs the sequence that is followed in performing part skills that make up the total skill. Then these part skills are often best taught separately before they are practiced together. A coach may instruct a beginner in how to shot put by having the person learn such part skills as how and where to stand, how to step, how to grip the shot, where to hold it in relationship to the head, and how to follow through after putting the shot. When each of the part skills has been mastered, the person can practice them together in order to learn the timing and rhythm necessary for the smooth execution of the total skill.

For learning *verbal information*, the essential prerequisite is that the person have a way for relating previously learned information to the new. The sequence for learning verbal information is not critical, though. One may present historical facts in a chronological order or present them organized around such topics as transportation, government, and economics. The important point is that the learner be able to integrate the facts into a framework that has meaning for him or her. It does not matter whether that framework is a time line or a topic outline.

Cognitive strategies probably have as prerequisites various intellectual skills. Therefore, the sequence for instruction leading to a cognitive strategy outcome should include any of the skills that have not been previously acquired. In addition, there may be information about problem solutions that would have a bearing on the particular cognitive strategy—information that must be acquired before the cognitive strategy can be learned (Gagné & Briggs, 1979).

Table 4.4 summarizes the relationships among the five domains of objectives and their respective essential and supporting prerequisites that can serve as guides to the designer for making some decisions for sequencing instruction. The reader is advised to consult Gagné and Briggs (1979, Chapter 8) for a complete discussion of instructional sequencing.

In addition to offering guidelines for selecting objectives and prescribing sequences for learning the objectives, Gagné and Briggs offer useful information for prescribing the details of instruction through the application of instructional events, that are discussed in the following section.

INSTRUCTIONAL EVENTS

Understanding how *instructional events* function in different learning situations and for different types of learning provides direction to the designer in making appropriate instructional prescriptions.

Definition

What are instructional events? These are classes of events that occur in a learning situation. Each event functions to provide the external conditions of learning described previously. Therefore, one designs instruction in part by ensuring that the events used in instruction are planned to satisfy the necessary conditions of learning. Table 4.5 lists the events in the order in which they usually occur.

TABLE 4.4
Essential and Supportive Prerequisites for
Five Kinds of Learning Outcomes[a]

Type of Learning Outcome	Essential Prerequisites	Supportive Prerequisites
Intellectual skill	Simpler component intellectual skills (rules, concepts, discriminations)	Attitudes Cognitive strategies Verbal information
Verbal information	Meaningfully organized sets of information	Language skills Cognitive strategies Attitudes
Cognitive strategies	Specific intellectual skills (?)	Intellectual skills Verbal information Attitudes
Attitudes	Intellectual skills (sometimes) Verbal information (sometimes)	Other attitudes Verbal information
Motor skills	Part skills (sometimes) Procedural rules (sometimes)	Attitudes

[a]Source: From Gagné. R. M., Analysis of objectives, in L. J. Briggs, (Ed.), INSTRUCTIONAL DESIGN, Englewood Cliffs, N.J.: Educational Technology Publications, 1977, p. 141. Reproduced by permission of the copyright owner, Educational Technology Publications.

TABLE 4.5
Instructional Events

1. Gaining attention

2. Informing the learner of the objective

3. Stimulating recall of prerequisite learnings

4. Presenting the stimulus material

5. Providing learning guidance

6. Eliciting the performance

7. Providing feedback about performance correctness

8. Assessing the performance

9. Enhancing retention and transfer

Brief descriptions of each instructional event, including examples of appropriate prescriptions for applying each event, are given next.

Gaining Attention. An initial task in any instruction is to gain the learner's attention so that other instructional events can function properly. For example, in designing instructional motion pictures on inherently dull subjects, May (1965) suggested that two versions of the films might be produced. The first version would be designed to gain the viewer's attention, using many embellishments and rapidly changing stimuli, whereas the second version would have few special effects and would develop at a slower rate to enable the viewer to process and learn the information presented.

Informing the Learner of the Objective. The purpose of communicating the objective to the learner is to enable the person to answer the question: "How will I know when I have learned?" (Gagné & Briggs, 1979). Too often students are given an imprecise description of the content to the covered; for example, consider a biology teacher who introduces a unit on genetics by saying, "One thing you will learn about is homozygous and heterozygous genotypes." Such a statement does not communicate what the learning outcome will be. Will the students be able to state definitions of the concepts heterozygous and homozygous genotypes, or will the learners be able to classify genotypes as homozygous or heterozygous and name the kind of resulting phenotype?

Stimulating Recall of Prerequisite Learnings. As explained earlier in the discussion of conditions of learning, essential capabilities must be available for recall before new learning can occur. Sometimes, this event can be accomplished by the instructor's simply reminding the individual of previous learning: "Remember that you learned the difference between the numerator and denominator in a fraction. Now we can learn how to find common denominators." At other times, a formal review may be required: "Class, before we learn how to look up words in a dictionary, let's review how to alphabetize words that have the same first two or three letters."

Presenting the Stimulus Material. The range of stimulus materials is as varied, of course, as the range of instructional objectives. Stimulus material may be in the form of statements of verbal information ("Here are the essential provisions of Public Law 94–142, The Education for All Handicapped Children Act of 1975."); examples of concepts ("This is a monocotyledon plant; this is a dicotyledon."); or demonstrations of motor skills ("Watch this demonstration of how to high dive."). The actual form of the stimulus material will also be determined by the subject matter* and such factors as the characteristics of the learners and the media used. Selection and utilization of media are discussed later in the chapter.

---

*Editor's note: This matter is discussed in considerably more detail in most other chapters in this unit.

Providing Learning Guidance.   The function of learning guidance is to help the learner acquire the particular capabilities specified in the objectives. For example, in teaching a concept, the learning guidance would ensure that the learner understood the critical attributes of the concept; in teaching a procedure to follow for diagnosing trouble in a piece of malfunctioning equipment, the learning guidance might be in the form of a checklist to teach the steps to follow and the sequence in which they are performed.

Some learners require more guidance than others,* a principle utilized in programmed instruction which has extensive branches.

Eliciting the Performance.   In order to determine if a learner is in fact acquiring a particular internal capability, it is important to have the learner perform an overt action. The instructor may ask a question or give directions to elicit a response: "Class, is this an example of a simile or a metaphor?" or "Here are some problems to solve."

It is important that the response called for is the same as that required in the objective so that the learner is getting practice that is relevant to the desired learning outcome. If the terminal objective specifies that the learner will be able to classify statements as similes or metaphors, it would be inappropriate to ask the individual how to spell the words *simile* and *metaphor*.

Providing Feedback about Performance Correctness.   Providing feedback is a crucial instructional event. To be most effective, feedback should be informative. Rather than writing on a composition "needs improvement," the experienced English teacher explains the kinds of improvements that are required: "These sentences are not parallel," "These sections are redundant," or "The pronouns and their antecedents do not agree."

Assessing the Performance.   The purpose of this event is to determine if the learner obtained the objective and can consistently perform what was intended. A variety of test items may be employed and used over a period of time. Of course, the assessment should be congruent with the objective.

Enhancing Retention and Transfer.   Instructional designers cannot assume that learners will be able to transfer learning from one situation to another; such retention and transfer should be included as part of the instruction. For intellectual skills, providing spaced reviews helps. For verbal information, providing linkages between information learned at different times is recommended.

Suggestions have just been given for enhancing retention and transfer for intellectual skills and information. Table 4.6 lists recommendations that Gagné and Briggs (1979) give for this instructional event in other domains of learning. Table 4.6 also describes ways to provide all of the instructional events in each domain of learning.

---

*Editor's note: This is similar to Gropper's concern for *degree of attention,* discussed in Chapter 2.

Now that each instructional event has been described, the next section looks at some of the events according to the amount of variation there is in the function they perform.

Differential Effects

Some events function in essentially the same way regardless of the type of learning. Examples of such events include "gaining attention," "informing the learner of the objective," "eliciting performance," and "providing feedback." For these events, though, the details of application depend on the characteristics of the learners. First-year medical students would probably not have to have motivating events built into instruction, whereas first-grade children learning to read would most likely need some external motivation. Also, the way that objectives are communicated may vary considerably depending on the task and the age of the learners. But the function of providing an expectation would be served in any case.

Other events function entirely differently depending on the type of learning. The two events for which this *differential effect* is most important and crucial are the events "stimulating recall of prerequisite learnings" and "providing learning guidance." It is with these events that the designer pays special attention to the particular conditions of learning in order to determine instructional prescriptions.

The nature of the essential prerequisites for stimulating recall of prerequisite learnings is different for each type of outcome because the internal conditions are different. For example, before a rule can be learned, it is necessary that concepts incorporated in the rule be learned. However, before information can be learned, it is necessary that a meaningful framework be established for relating the new information to that previously acquired.

Similarly, the function of learning guidance will be different for each type of learning because the external conditions are different. Thus, the instructional prescription is often determined by the kind of learning guidance that is required. For example, an objective in a history course may involve learning about the events leading to World War II. The designer might plan for the information to be presented in an expository mode through well-organized lectures and readings. Consider, though, another objective in the same course involving the interpretation, from an economic perspective, of the events leading up to World War II. This later objective, a problem-solving task, might be best taught through use of simulation exercises to enable the students to learn the relationship between economic and political events.

Providing the events of instruction involves making prescriptions for various media, which is discussed in the following section.

INSTRUCTIONAL MEDIA

Briggs (1970) defined *instructional media* broadly as all means by which stimuli are presented to provide the events of instruction. In this sense, media include the full range of audiovisual materials, print, and the voices of the teacher and learners.

TABLE 4.6
Instructional Events and the Conditions of Learning
They Imply for Five Types of Learned Capabilities[a]

| | | | Type of Capability | | |
Instructional Event	Intellectual Skill	Cognitive Strategy	Information	Attitude	Motor Skill
1. Gaining attention			Introduce stimulus change; variations in sensory mode		
2. Informing learner of objective	Provide description and example of the performance to be expected	Clarify the general nature of the solution expected	Indicate the kind of verbal question to be answered	Provide example of the kind of action choice aimed for	Provide a demonstration of the performance to be expected
3. Stimulating recall of prerequisites	Stimulate recall of subordinate concepts and rules	Stimulate recall of task strategies and associated intellectual skills	Stimulate recall of context of organized information	Stimulate recall of relevant information, skills, and human model identification	Stimulate recall of executive subroutine and part skills
4. Presenting the stimulus material	Present examples of concept or rule	Present novel problems	Present information in propositional form	Present human model, demonstrating choice of personal action	Provide external stimuli for performance, including tools or implements
5. Providing learning guidance	Provide verbal cues to proper combining sequence	Provide prompts and hints to novel solution	Provide verbal links to a larger meaningful context	Provide for observation of model's choice of action, and of of reinforcement received by model	Provide practice with feedback of performance achievement

6. Eliciting the performance	Ask learner to apply rule or concept to new examples	Ask for problem solution	Ask for information in paraphrase, or in learner's own words	Ask learner to indicate choices of action in real or simulated situations	Ask for execution of the performance
7. Providing feedback	Confirm correctness of rule or concept application	Confirm originality of problem solution	Confirm correctness of statement of information	Provide direct or vicarious reinforcement of action choice	Provide feedback on degree of accuracy and timing of performance
8. Assessing performance	Learner demonstrates application of concept or rule	Learner originates a novel solution	Learner restates information in paraphrased form	Learner makes desired choice of personal action in real or simulated situation	Learner executes performance of total skills
9. Enhancing retention and transfer	Provide spaced reviews including a variety of examples	Provide occasions for a variety of novel problem solutions	Provide verbal links to additional complexes of information	Provide additional varied situations for selected choice of action	Learner continues skill practice

[a]Source: From PRINCIPLES OF INSTRUCTIONAL DESIGN, 2nd edition, by Robert M. Gagné and Leslie Briggs. Copyright © 1974, 1979 by Holt, Rinehart and Winston. Reprinted by permission of Holt, Rinehart and Winston, CBS College Publishing.

Instructional Events and Media

Moreover, Briggs recommended that media be selected after the requirements for providing the instructional events for a given instructional sequence had been determined. Using the events of instruction as a guide for selecting media often results in more than one medium being used, due to the different functions and stimuli requirements for each event.

A short course on cardiopulmonary resuscitation (CPR) illustrates how a multimedia approach provides the events of instruction:

1. A printed, programmed manual teaches information, concepts, and rules. (Presenting stimulus materials, eliciting the performance, and providing feedback)
2. Sound motion pictures and slide/tapes demonstrate the various techniques that must be learned to perform CPR properly. (Presenting stimulus materials)
3. A printed checklist teaches the sequence of steps to follow in doing CPR. (Providing learning guidance)
4. Life-sized manikins enable learners to practice performing CPR in a realistic way. (Eliciting the performance)
5. Electronic devices in the manikins monitor the rate of hand thrusts on the chest. (Providing feedback)
6. An instructor shares personal experiences in performing CPR (gaining attention), relates these experiences to the classroom and programmed learning activities (enhancing retention and transfer), diagnoses problems learners have and suggests ways to solve them (providing learning guidance), checks learner performance (providing feedback), reviews materials (enhancing retention and transfer), and tests the learners over all of the course objectives (assessing the performance).

Learner Characteristics and Media

In addition to considering each instructional event in selecting and using media, the designer must also be concerned with such learner characteristics as age, experience, and capability for learning from various media.

As one guide for matching media prescriptions with learner and task variables, Briggs (1970) suggested using Dale's Cone of Experience. Dale (1969) organized the full range of media in a cone in which the most concrete medium (direct, purposeful experience) is at the lowest level on the scale incorporated in the cone and the most abstract (verbal symbols) are at the highest level. Briggs (Gagné & Briggs, 1979) offers the following design heuristic: "Go as low on the scale as you need in order to insure learning for your group, but go as high as you can for the most efficient learning" (p. 181).

Of course, there are many other considerations for selecting and using media, such as cost, practicality, availability, and time for development. All of these factors are described fully in other books, and detailed procedures to follow for selecting media are given (Briggs, 1970, 1972, 1977; Briggs & Wager, 1981; Gagné & Briggs, 1979).

CONCLUSION

This chapter has discussed aspects of the work of Gagné and Briggs that may be considered as a prescriptive model of instruction. The salient points can be summarized as follows:

1. Different sets of conditions are required for various types of learning to occur. Instructional objectives can be classified according to the type of learning involved.
2. In selecting instructional objectives to be learned in the domain of intellectual skills, learning hierarchies indicate which competencies must be acquired.
3. Learning hierarchies also provide guidance in ways to sequence instruction so that competencies which are prerequisite to other competencies are taught in their proper order.
4. The events of instruction provide the external conditions of learning that are required to activate the support the internal processes of learning.
5. Instructional prescriptions are made to ensure that each instructional event functions to achieve the desired learning outcomes.
6. A variety of instructional media can be used as the means for applying the respective instructional events.

Briggs has integrated the concepts discussed in this chapter and several others not mentioned here (Briggs, 1970, 1972; Briggs & Wager, 1981) and has presented them in the form of a complete procedure for the design of prescriptive instruction. Often referred to as *instructional systems design*, the procedure is appropriate whether instruction is presented by conventional teaching methods or by self-instructional modules. The procedure is applicable for course development, for units within a course, or for individual lessons.

GLOSSARY

Note: Terms are listed in the order discussed in the text. For more complete definitions, the reader should consult Briggs (1977).

Varieties of Learning

Varieties of learning are the several different and distinctive types of outcomes that result when various capabilities have been attained. There are five classes of learning outcomes: intellectual skills, attitudes, information, cognitive strategies, and motor skills. There are subcategories of intellectual skills.

Learned Capability

A learned capability is a particular competence that a person has acquired. Because it is an internal state, which is not observable, one can infer from a person's performance, which is observable, whether a particular capability has been learned.

Learning Outcome

A learning outcome is the observable performance that indicates that a particular capability has been acquired. Learning outcomes are often stated in the form of performance objectives.

Conditions of Learning

The conditions of learning are those internal states and external events that together are required for learning to occur. Different types of learning require different sets of conditions.

Internal Conditions

Internal conditions are those states within the learner that are involved in learning. Examples of internal conditions are motivational states and mechanisms involved in processing, storing, and retrieving information.

External Conditions

External conditions are those events outside the learner that activate and support the internal processes of learning. The appropriate provision of the external events is the framework for planning instruction.

Essential Prerequisite

An essential prerequisite is one that must be mastered before subsequent learning can occur. This kind of prerequisite is also incorporated into the new learning. For example, learning of concrete concepts requires discriminating the essential features of examples of objects belonging to a class, called concepts.

Supporting Prerequisite

A supporting prerequisite is prior learning that assists in achieving an objective but is not an integral part of the new learning. Supporting prerequisites for intellectual-skill learning may involve information or attitudes.

Learning-Task Analysis

Learning-task analysis is the process of (1) classifying learning outcomes according to types of learning; and (2) determining, for a given outcome, the essential and supporting prerequisites that are involved.

Learning Hierarchy

A learning hierarchy results when a learning-task analysis is conducted for an objective in the intellectual-skills domain. Starting with a terminal objective, the essential prerequisites are specified until the designer is assured that the entry-level skills have been identified. The hierarchy serves as a basis for sequencing instruction.

Instructional Events

Instructional events provide the external conditions that are necessary for learning to occur. Some events function in the same way regardless of the type of learning, whereas other events function differently depending on the type of learning.

Differential Effect

Differential effect refers to the way that some instructional events function differently depending on the type of learning involved. The instructional events "stimulating recall of prerequisites" and "providing learning guidance" function most differently depending on the type of learning.

Instructional Media

Instructional media are all the materials and means for presenting stimuli required for providing the events of instruction for given learning tasks and learners. For example, spoken words may be presented by recordings or live by the teacher's or student's voice. Written words and symbols may be presented by a variety of projected or electronic means or by print. Similarly, still or motion pictorial stimuli may be presented by a variety of means.

Instructional Systems Design

Instructional systems design is the total set of procedures that are followed in planning, developing, implementing, and evaluating instruction. The procedures are derived from knowledge of human learning relevant for instruction and from the results of empirical data obtained during tryouts of preplanned instruction.

REFERENCES

Briggs, L. J. *Handbook of procedures for the design of instruction.* Pittsburgh: American Institutes for Research, 1970.

Briggs, L. J. *Student's guide to handbook of procedures for the design of instruction.* Pittsburgh: American Institutes for Research, 1972.

Briggs, L. J. (Ed.). *Instructional design: Principles and applications.* Englewood Cliffs, N.J.: Educational Technology Publications, 1977.

Briggs, L. J., & Wager, W. W. *Handbook of procedures for the design of instruction* (2nd ed.). Englewood Cliffs, N.J.: Educational Technology Publications, 1981.

Dale, E. A. *Audiovisual methods in teaching* (3rd ed.). New York: Holt, Rinehart & Winston, 1969.

Gagné, R. M. *The conditions of learning* (2nd ed.). New York: Holt, Rinehart & Winston, 1970.

Gagné, R. M. *Essentials of learning for instruction.*, New York: Holt, Rinehart & Winston, 1974.

Gagné, R. M. *The conditions of learning* (3rd ed.). New York: Holt, Rinehart & Winston, 1977.

Gagné, R. M., & Briggs, L. J. *Principles of instructional design* (2nd ed.). New York: Holt, Rinehart & Winston, 1979.

May, M. A. *Enhancements and simplifications of motivational and stimulus variables in audiovisual instructional materials* (Interim report, USOE Contract OE–5–16–006). Washington, D.C.: U.S. Department of Health, Education and Welfare, 1965.

5 A Behavioral Approach to Instructional Prescription

George L. Gropper
Digital Equipment Corporation[1]

George L. Gropper

George L. Gropper received an A.B. in Social Relations from Harvard College in 1948, an M.A. in Psychology from the University of California at Berkeley in 1953, and a Ph.D. in Psychology from the University of Pittsburgh in 1956. He is currently serving as a Principal Educational Specialist with the Educational Services Development and Publishing division of the Digital Equipment Corporation. There he serves as a consultant to technical writers who prepare technical manuals and to course developers who prepare courses on computer usage. Course delivery modes include: lectures, printed materials, CAI, and video disc presentations. In his role as consultant he provides advice and training on all major instructional design tasks. He also contributes to programs concerned with broader educational issues such as evaluation and quality assurance. He has been serving in these varied capacities for four years.

Previously, Dr. Gropper served for two years in a faculty development role at the University of Pennsylvania and for one year as a visiting professor in the Department of Educational Research at the Florida State University. Prior to that, he had been engaged for fifteen years in research and development activities at the American Institutes for Research. In those years he conducted research on the role of visuals in instruction, applied programming techniques to educational television, and formulated an instructional design model. He also prepared numerous instructional programs that were aimed at varied target audiences, covered varied subject matters, and were presented via various media.

His major publications, which document much of this R&D effort, include: Managing problem behavior in the classroom (Appleton Century Crofts, 1970); and (from Educational Technology Publications) the following three volumes—Criteria for the selection and use of visuals in instruction (1971); Instructional strategies (1974); and Diagnosis and revision in the development of instructional materials (1975). All these works were based on a behavioral approach to learning and instruction and, generally, to behavior change.

CONTENTS

Introduction   106
  Learning Concepts   106
    S-R Association   107
    Stimulus Control   107
    Discrimination   107
    Generalization   108
    Association   108
    Chains   109
  Instructional Concepts   109
    Cue   110
    Incrementing   110
    Shaping   110
    Fading   111
  Instructional Models   111
Conditions   112
  Skill Analysis   112
  Performance Analysis   114
  Conditions Affecting The Ease Of Skill Acquisition   115
    Similarity/Dissimilarity   115
    Number Of Stimulus/Response Properties   119
    Number Of Stimulus And/Or Responses   120
    Existing Associations   122
    Summary   122

Conditions Affecting Recall And Transfer   123
    Conditions Affecting Recall   123
    Conditions Affecting Transfer   123
    Individual Differences Among Students   123
Treatments   124
    Treatment Goals   125
        Performance In A Criterion Mode   125
        Performance Of All Constituent Skills   125
        Performance Under All Conditions   126
        Meeting Post-Instructional Requirements   126
        Summary   126
    Treatment Tools   126
    Cues   128
        Strength Of Association With Responses   128
        Degree Of Similarity With Responses   128
        Cue Interval   130
        Number Of Cue Attributes   130
        Summary   131
    Unit Of Behavior   131
        Amount Of Behavior Practiced   132
        Integrity Of Behavior Practiced   133
        Standards Of Performance   133
        Summary   133
    Stimulus And Response Mode   134
        Response Mode   134
        Stimulus Mode   135
    Varied Practice Examples   137
        Practice Content   138
        Frequency Of Practice   141
        Summary   141
    Treatment Organization   141
        Individual Practice Task   142
        Transitions Between Tasks   142
        Cumulative Series Of Practice Tasks   143
        Summary   143
Matching Treatments And Conditions   144
    Treatment Priorities   145
        Routine Treatments   146
        Shaping Progressions   146
        Specialized Treatments   147
    Matching Objectives And Treatments   148
        Recalling Facts   148
        Defining Concepts   150
        Giving Explanations   151
        Following Procedural Rules   152
Multiple Objectives   155
    Relationships Among Objectives   156

Vertical Relationships   156
Horizontal Relationships   156
No Relationships   157
Role Of Task Description   157
Performance Versus Learning   157
Contingencies   157
Sequencing Decicions   158
Summary   159

FOREWORD

Many of the roots of the discipline of instruction are in behavioral learning theory. From 1954, when B. F. Skinner published *The Science of Learning and the Art of Teaching,* until the early 1970s, a behavioristic orientation dominated instructional research and theory construction. Gropper's work represents an integration of the vast majority of the knowledge about instruction that has arisen out of the behavioristic tradition, and he has extended that knowledge base in important areas. The result is a number of different models of instruction on the micro level and one model on the macro level. One of the most outstanding features of Gropper's work is that his instructional models are among the most detailed and complete models described in the instructional-design literature.

On the micro level (for "single objectives") a different model is prescribed for each of five types of objectives. The types of objectives include: recalling facts, defining and illustrating concepts, giving and applying explanations, following rules, and solving problems. The model prescribed for *each* type of objective is responsive to the mix of skills (discriminations, generalizations, associations, and chains) that is characteristic of that type. It is also responsive to potential learning problems posed by an objective's specific stimulus-response characteristics.

Each model has three parts: (1) *basic* method components (called "routine treatments"), which are always present for an objective; (2) *standard enrichment* components (called "shaping progressions"), which are routinely added in when the objective is expected to be difficult for learners; and (3) *specialized enrichment* components (called "specialized treatments"), which are also added in when the objective poses particular types of learning problems. Naturally, practice and feedback (i.e., reinforcement) are the most important of the basic method components for all five models.

On the macro level (for "multiple objectives"), Gropper uses *learning* prerequisite relationshps and input-output *performance* relationships as the basis for both the *selection* of practice content and the *sequencing* of the content.

C. M. R.

---

[1]The views expressed in this chapter do not necessarily reflect those of the Digital Equipment Corporation.

A Behavioral Approach to Instructional Prescription

INTRODUCTION

Behavioral approaches to instructional design can trace their lineage to World War II when psychologists engaged in military training began identifying the outcomes of training in *performance* terms. From these early efforts instructional design inherited a commitment to "task description" and the techniques needed to identify tasks performed on the job. From film- and TV-mediated training conducted then and in subsequent decades instructional design inherited a commitment to "active practice" as an important condition for learning those tasks as well as school-related tasks. With the subsequent appearance of programmed instruction, active practice assumed an even more central and assured role in instruction. The operant tradition, which inspired programmed instruction and its active practice requirement, also identified "reinforcement" as a necessary condition for learning (Skinner, 1953). Both active practice and reinforcement continue to be key ingredients in behavioral and, it might be pointed out, other approaches to instruction.

The 1960s mark the beginning of detailed and systematic "behavioral analyses" of subject-matter objectives.* The prescription of treatments for teaching them also became more analytic and systematic (Gilbert, 1962; Mechner, 1967). Shortly thereafter, comprehensive instructional models and theories that were conceptually related to the behavioral tradition appeared (Gagné, 1970).** The behavioral instructional theory that is described in the major sections of this chapter in turn followed these pioneer efforts (Gropper, 1973, 1974, 1975).

This introductory section reviews key concepts in behavioral approaches to learning and instruction. The instructional theory described later in the chapter elaborates and builds on these concepts.

Learning Concepts

Learning theory describes the lawful ways in which changes in behavior occur. Its parameters identify: a unit of behavior to be analyzed; the conditions that produce changes in it; and the nature and permanence of the changes in it that can result.

---

*Editor's note: Probably the most important of these was Gagné's hierarchical analysis of intellectual skills (see Chapter 4).

**Editor's note: See also Chapter 4.

S–R Association

In a behavioral/reinforcement orientation, the unit of analysis is a stimulus–response (S–R) association. Depending on the purpose of the analysis, such S–R units can involve either microscopic or macroscopic amounts of behavior.

In driving situations, a red traffic light acts as a "stimulus." The "response" associated with it might be: for a driver, putting a foot on the brake; for a pedestrian, staying on the curb; for the school patrol, telling other school children not to cross the street; or, for a repair person, concluding that the traffic light is in working order.

In reading, the word itself—for example, *receive*—acts as a stimulus. The appropriate response is to read the word. In arithmetic, a column of numbers accompanied by a plus sign acts as a stimulus. The appropriate response to it is to add the numbers.

These examples illustrate the kinds of stimulus–response associations on which a behavioral analysis of any educational or training objective focuses.

Stimulus Control

When, upon repeated presentation of a stimulus, an appropriate response to it is made, the response is said to be "under the *control* of that stimulus." Predictably, the same response or a functional equivalent will be made on any subsequent presentation of it. Before learning occurs, such stimulus control does not exist. A column of numbers does not lead students to do correct addition; a red light does not lead to pumping the brake; or the word receive does not lead to a correct reading response. Following learning, these events do occur. On being confronted with a stimulus that is an appropriate occasion for a response, the now-competent performer consistently makes that response to it.

Appropriate occasions for a response may consist of such diverse *stimuli* as objects, words, symbols, or events, and so on. Verbal, symbolic, or motor behavior may constitute the appropriate *responses* to them. The consequences (reinforcement) that follow the responses may consist of physical, verbal, or symbolic stimuli.

Whatever the nature of the stimulus, the response, or the reinforcement, establishing stable stimulus control depends on the same two learning conditions: *practice* of an appropriate response in the presence of a stimulus that is to control it and delivery of *reinforcement* following its practice.

There are, in addition, preconditions to the establishment of stimulus control. Four types of skills must be mastered, including: discrimination, generalization, association, and chaining.

Discrimination

One of the preconditions for the establishment of stimulus control is a need to learn *discriminations*. The competent performer has to be able to discriminate between one stimulus and another. He or she has to be able to *tell them apart*. For example, to make an appropriate response to a red traffic light (and to green and amber lights as well), depends on a driver's being able to distinguish between these colors (stimuli). The reader who is color blind is more apt to appreciate the relevance of this particular discrimination as a precondition for the establishment of stimulus control.

The need to discriminate among stimuli is omnipresent. Classifying a particular object as either a solid, liquid, or a gas requires an ability to distinguish between instances of each. Cringing appropriately or beaming with approval appropriately when notes are sung requires an ability to distinguish between notes sung on or off pitch. Thus, recognizing a particular stimulus as an appropriate occasion for a particular response depends on an ability to discriminate or distinguish between it and other, often highly similar, stimuli.

Learning to discriminate among stimuli is facilitated by differential reinforcement. Reinforcement for one type of response to stimulus A and for another type of response to stimulus B facilitates the discrimination between the two types of stimuli. A red light is recognized as an appropriate context for stopping behavior, green for motion; the letter b is recognized as an appropriate context for "buh" sounds, the letter d for "duh" sounds. In each case successful performance reinforces the appropriate response.

Generalization

In the process of being reinforced for responding in a particular way to a particular stimulus, students also come to respond *in the same way* to other stimuli that are similar to or functionally equivalent to the original. Different shades of red elicit appropriate braking behavior. A new column of figures accompanied by a plus sign is also added. This phenomenon is called *generalization.*.

Whenever there is a *class* of stimuli, each of whose members requires the *same* response, generalization becomes a second precondition for effective stimulus control. All members of the class of stimuli must control that same response. For example, objects made of wood, iron, copper, or tin all belong to a class called *solids*. They must *all* be recognized as solids.

Any stimulus belonging to a *class* (e.g., all *liquids, prime numbers, fugues,* etc.) has to be recognized as being similar to all other stimuli belonging to the same class. They *all* have to be seen as appropriate occasions for the same response. For example, any instance of a prime number has to be recognized as a prime number. Successful performance could not occur unless a performer were able to *recognize* all instances of a class as being similar and therefore functional equivalents of one another.

Association

The ability to recognize a stimulus as being different from, or as being similar to, other stimuli does not exhaust the preconditions for performance mastery. In addition, particular responses have to come to be *associated* with the stimuli that must control them. It is not enough for a child learning to read to be able to discriminate between the letters b and d. The child also has to associate the letter b with the "buh" sound and the letter d with the "duh" sound. Thus, a third precondition for the establishment of stimulus control involves the "association" of a response with a stimulus that is the appropriate occasion for its being made.

In driving, red comes to be associated with braking/stopping behavior, green with putting an auto in motion. In arithmetic, plus signs are associated with adding behavior, minus signs with subtracting behavior. Successful performance of these activites could not occur unless a performer were able to *associate* a particular stimulus (or a class of stimuli) with a particular response.

Chains

Three skills are necessary for proficient performance. In the case of driving, drivers have to be able to *discriminate* between red and green. They have to be able *generalize* across various shades of each. And, they also have to be able to *associate* red with nonmotion and green with motion. Similarly, the performance of adding and substracting, of spelling, or of reading depends on the mastery of all three types of skills. Each S–R *unit* in these performances includes all three. And, in fact, any type of *performance* is similarly made up of S–R units that include all three skills.

Although S–R is the unit of analysis, most behavior involves multiple such units. They are all linked or "chained" together in a particular sequence. A green light becomes the occasion for a driver to remove his or her foot from the brake; the release of the brake becomes the occasion for the driver to put a foot on the gas pedal; subsequent driving conditions become the occasion for steering to the right or the left; and so on. Solving a complete addition problem, analyzing a poem for the dominant type of imagery used, or writing a chapter on instructional design involve similar, long chains of linked S–R units.

Before learning occurs, a stimulus in an individual S–R pairing does not predictably lead to an appropriate response. As learning progresses, the probability of the correct response being made to it increases. Finally, stable stimulus control is achieved. The probability of the correct response being made in the presence of that stimulus is now extremely high. Active practice of the correct response in the presence of that stimulus—followed by reinforcement—are the conditions necessary to make its occurrence so highly probable.

Stimulus-control requirements apply to all constituent S–R units in a chain. Thus, for a total performance to be learned, all as yet unlearned S–R units in the chain must be practiced. Successful performance of any activity could not occur unless a performer had learned all S–R units in it *and* had integrated them into a complete *chain*.*

Instructional Concepts

Instruction is not concerned with how behavior change in general *occurs*. Rather, its concerns are with techniques for bringing about specific changes in behavior. Experimental work conducted in operant laboratories provides a heuristic model for *engineering* these changes.

---

*Editor's note: Landa discusses a similar idea in Chapter 6, (pp. 197–202).

To describe the operant path for engineering stimulus control, it is necessary to distinguish between two types of stimuli: a criterion stimulus and a cue.

Criterion Stimulus

A red light, letters on a printed page, a column of figures, or a physical object are the appropriate occasions for stopping an automobile, reading, doing addition, or classifying an object as a solid. They are all examples of *criterion stimuli*. Criterion stimuli are the stimuli that must gain control over these responses by the time learning has been completed. Before learning has occurred, the stimuli do not possess such control. The goal of instruction is to impart it to them.

Cue

Instructional engineering consists of: (1) finding other, noncriterion stimuli, called *cues*, that already possess control over responses that have to be learned; (2) using these cues to elicit practice of those responses *in the presence of* the relevant criterion stimuli; and (3) ultimately transferring control (over those responses) from the cues to the criterion stimuli.

Oral instructions to an apprentice driver to stop at red lights act as a cue. In response, the driver practices stopping at red lights (the criterion stimulus). Eventually, with no one to remind the driver—to cue him or her—the driver stops at red lights on his or her own. Red lights now *control* "stopping" behavior. Control has been transferred from the cue, oral instructions to stop, to the criterion stimulus, a red light.

Because of their capacity to elicit the practice of appropriate responses, model demonstrations, pictures, words, symbols, and so on, can all serve as cues. Stimulus control is transferred from any of these types of cues to the criterion stimulus. At that point, even in the absence of a cue, the criterion stimulus is capable of eliciting a desired response. The criterion stimulus has achieved stimulus control.

Incrementing

Learning all the S–R units in complex behaviors may require an "incremental" or step-by-step approach. Each S–R unit may have to be learned by itself or in groups of two or more, and then be added on to and integrated with other previously learned S–R units in a chain.* For example, in instruction on driving, apprentice drivers might practice shifting alone, steering alone, starting the engine alone, and so on. Ultimately, these separate skills would have to be practiced togehter in order to be integrated into the total performance of driving a car.

Shaping

The mastery of complex criterion behaviors may also require progress through a *series of approximations*. Even with cues available to them students may be unable to make the fine-motor adjustments required in penmanship or to read words or sentences smoothly. To begin with, they may be capable of only a gross approxi-

---

*Editor's note: This is similar to Landa's step-by-step *snowball approach* (see Chapter 6, pp. 197–198).

mation to such criterion standards. What an instructional strategy must calculate is the sequence of practice events that can advance the approximation until finally students are able to perform at a criterion level.

The process of taking students from a partial, incomplete, or gangling performance to one that meets criterion standards is called *shaping*. Through a series of approximations to criterion standards, students are gradually nudged towards those more exacting standards.

Fading

Ultimately, students must be capable of performing correctly even when no cues are present. Still, early in the incrementing or shaping processes, cues must be provided. The cues must be strong enough (provide enough guidance) to elicit correct responses. To prepare students for those future occasions when cues will no longer be available, cues must be made gradually weaker. For example, a partial demonstration of a lab procedure provides weaker cuing than a complete demonstration of it. Fading is the process whereby students are *gradually weaned from the help* that cues provide.

To get students to criterion-level performance successfully requires the incremental and gradual shaping of behavior and the decremental and gradual elimination of cues. As cues are being faded, they are still capable of eliciting correct responses. This is so because parallel with their gradual weakening is the gradual strengthening of the responses that are being practiced. It no longer requires strong cues to elicit them. And, eventually, no cues are required.

Instructional Models

General principles of instruction, although more useful than general principles of learning, are still not apt to be of much help to practitioners. They must teach driving or reading or quantitative skills or concepts in physics. They need more specific guidance for teaching these skills than is provided by *general* principles. They need *concrete prescriptions* that they can apply directly to their highly specific goals: teaching the addition of two-digit numbers, or how to devise remedies for stagflation, or how to punctuate sentences, and so on.

Practitioners have to be able to identify the distinctive requirements of their specific goals. And, they have to be able to develop specific treatments* that are capable of fulfilling those requirements.

The remainder of this chapter condenses and updates a previously published behaviorally oriented instructional theory (Gropper, 1973, 1974, 1975). It begins with an enumeration of subject-matter characteristics (i.e., conditions) that a practitioner would look for in analyzing goals. It follows with an enumeration of instructional treatments that a practitioner has available for accommodating these

---

*Editor's note: These are *methods* as defined in Chapter 1.

subject-matter characteristics. It concludes with more explicit prescriptions for *matching* specific treatments and specific subject-matter requirements.

Fig. 5.1 summarizes all the key prescriptive ingredients discussed in the next several sections of this chapter. Column 4 identifies the types of *treatments* available for teaching any of the types of *objectives* that are listed in Column 3. Column 2 identifies the *skills* and the *performance conditions* that define learning requirements for any of these types of objectives.[2] Finally, Column 1 identifies the *subject-matter properties* that determine how easy or how difficult it is likely to be to learn these skills.

Columns 1, 2, and 3 add up to *conditions* that require attention. Column 4 identifies way to provide the kind and amount of attention (*treatments*) that can match these requirements. The text that follows discusses: Conditions, Treatments, and Matching Treatments and Conditions—in that order.

CONDITIONS

Instructional treatments must be responsive to highly specific subject-matter requirements. It is through a task analysis that *skill requirements* are identified for each objective. The taxonomy used for this purpose includes the four behaviorally defined *component skills*: discrimination, generalization, association, and chaining.

An objective is also analyzed for its *stimulus and response characteristics*, because it is these characteristics that determine how easily the component skills can be learned. Thus, a task analysis results in the identification of an objective's specific skill requirements and of the specific conditions that have the potential for making it difficult to learn these skills.

Postinstructional *performance requirements* are also analyzed. The taxonomy used for this purpose includes: *recall* of learned skills and their *transfer* to new, previously unencountered situations.

Skill Analysis

The behaviorally defined component skills are assumed to underlie *all* types of objectives (however one chooses to describe or classify them). They underlie those identified by many theorists and practitioners as: recalling facts, defining concepts and principles, following procedural rules to solve a problem, or inventing new rules to solve it. Competent performance of any type of objective requires mastery

---

[2]The taxonomy adopted in the model under discussion focuses on these skills and these conditions of performance—*not* on types of objectives. However, because of their greater familiarity to most readers, types of objectives are identified in this chapter. Although the subsequent discussion refers frequently to types of objectives used in taxonomies of other theorists, the taxonomy that is central to the model under discussion concentrates on component skills (discrimination, generalization, association, and chaining) and conditions of performance (recall and transfer). It is the distinctive mix of skills and performance conditions that characterizes an objective on which treatment selection for it depends.

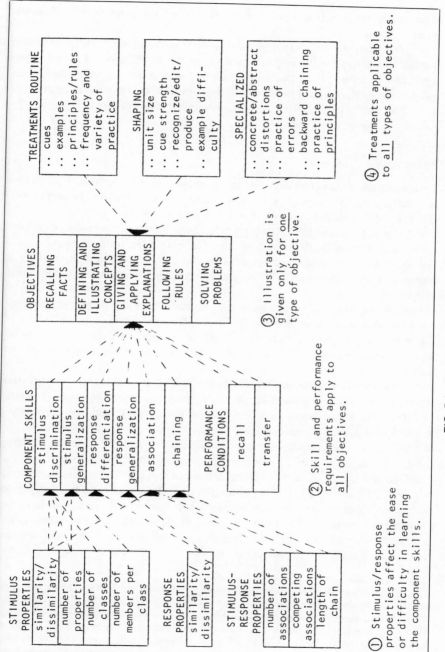

FIG. 5.1 Summary of strategy elements.

of *its* specific combination of component discriminations, generalizations, associations, and chains.

All objectives, whether of the same type or of different types, differ from one another with respect to the content, number, mode, or difficulty of their component skills. A major, early task in a behavioral approach to instructional design involves the *analysis* of any objective for its specific, distinctive *mix of component skills*. The results form the basis for prescribing a distinctive mix of strategies for teaching that objective.

Performance Analysis

Two additional parameters are used in an analysis of an objective. They define postinstructional conditions under which that objective will have to be performed. One is a *recall requirement*, the other a *transfer requirement*.

A recall requirement affects only what has been previously *encountered* during instruction. A stimulus that was used during instruction is, following the completion of instruction, again presented as an appropriate occasion for making a response. The response that had been previously made to it during instruction must now be made again.

Upon being required to respond to the presentation of any previously encountered stimulus (e.g., a word made into a plural, a tree classified as deciduous or coniferous, or a calculus problem solved), the competent performer is able to repeat the performance. The skills that are involved in the performance are recalled.

A postinstructional *transfer requirement* identifies previously *nonencountered* situations. It specifies that there are previously nonencountered instances of a class of stimuli that must also possess stimulus control. Even though these instances have not been previously encountered during instruction, they must still be capable of eliciting the same responses that the previously encountered instances are able (on a recall basis) to elicit. Upon being confronted with a new stimulus (e.g., a word not previously made into a plural, a tree not previously classified as deciduous or coniferous, or a calculus problem not previously solved), the competent performer is able to make the same response to it that he or she had made to those instances that were previously encountered. Thus, in addition to recalling skills applicable to already-encountered situations, students must be capable of transferring the same skills to new, relevant situations.[3]

---

[3]A task analysis finding that there is a *generalization* requirement indicates that there is a *class* of stimuli to be identified. During instruction, instances of the class may or may not all be encountered. When all the instances of a class *are* encountered (e.g., I, you, he, she, and it—all the instances of the class of singular pronouns that require a singular verb—have been used during instruction), subsequent performance depends only on recall. When they are not all encountered (e.g., only a sample of plural nouns that require plural verbs has been used during instruction), subsequent performance depends on *transfer*. A response that was previously made only to encountered instances must be transferred to new

Conditions Affecting the Ease of Skill Acquisition

Strategy formulation builds on an identification of the *level of difficulty* students can be expected to experience in learning new skills. For that assessment, the properties of the specific stimuli and of the specific responses that enter into the required skills are examined. It is these *stimulus and response properties* that determine how easy or how difficult it will be for students to learn those skills.

Figure 5.2 summarizes the stimulus and response properties that affect the ease with which the four behavioral component skills can be acquired, retained, and transferred.

Similarity/Dissimilarity

The similarity or dissimilarity of *stimuli* is assessed in order to determine how difficult it will be for students to identify it correctly. The following principles describe how these attributes can affect both discriminations and generalizations* (the basis for correct identifications). *Stimulus similarity* can have the following effects:

- The greater the similarity among stimuli that belong to *different* classes, the easier it will be to discriminate among them.

- The greater the similarity among stimuli that belong to the *same* class, the easier it will be to generalize from one instance to another.

Stimulus dissimilarity has the opposite effect on discriminations and generalizations.

- The greater the dissimilarity among stimuli that belong to *different* classes, the easier it will be to discriminate among them.

- The greater the dissimilarity among stimuli that belong to the *same* class, the more difficult it will be to generalize from one instance to another.

Effects on Discriminations.   To primary-grade students learning to read, the letters *b* and *d* or the letters *m* and *w* often appear similar. When this is the case, the students are likely to have difficulty *discriminating* between the members of either pair. Likewise, high-school students studying machines might *mistakenly* classify a pair of ice tongs and a nutcracker, which are highly similar in appearance, as belonging to the same *class* of levers. They will have failed to discriminate between instances of levers that belong to two different classes.[4]

---

instances. Thus, a task analysis revealing a generalization requirement indicates that there is a class of stimuli all of whose members require the same response. A task analysis revealing a transfer requirement indicates that not all members of that class will be encountered during instruction. This is likely to be the case whenever classes of stimuli are large.

*Editor's note: As defined in Chapter 1, these are descriptive principles of instruction.

[4]In ice tongs the effort force is applied between the load and the fulcrum. In the nutcracker, the load is in the middle—between the effort force and the fulcrum. These two levers belong to different classes.

	DISCRIMINATIONS	GENERALIZATIONS
STIMULUS PROPERTIES	Similarity of stimuli to be discriminated. Number of stimulus properties on the basis of which stimuli are discriminated from one another. Number of classes of stimuli to be discriminated from one another.	Dissimilarity of stimuli within a given class--all requiring generalization. Number of stimulus properties on which generalization is based. The number of stimulus members belonging to a class.
RESPONSE PROPERTIES	Similarity of responses that have to be differentiated from one another. The number of response properties forming the basis for response differentiation.	Dissimilarity among responses requiring response generalization. The number of response properties forming the basis for response generalization.
	ASSOCIATIONS	CHAINS
STIMULUS-RESPONSE PROPERTIES	Similarity of stimuli or responses in multiple stimulus-response pairings. The number of stimulus-response pairings. The strength of an existing stimulus - response association and the requirement that a new response be associated with the original stimulus.	The length of a chain (the number of stimulus-response pairings in the chain). Any of the other conditions listed in this table that are applicable to any individual stimulus-response pairing or unit in the chain.

FIG. 5.2   Conditions affecting the ease of learning component skills.

In general, the greater the *similarity* among stimuli, the more likely are they to be confused. This applies to unique stimuli that do not belong to a class (e.g., the letters *b* and *d*, people like Tom, Dick, and Harry, etc.) as well as to stimuli that do belong to a class (e.g., machines, trees, genres, etc.). Instead of responding to these stimuli differently (e.g., pronouncing them differently or classifying them differently), students are apt—incorrectly—to respond to them in the same way (e.g. to pronounce them in the same or to classify them in the same way). Stimulus *similarity* can make for such discrimination failures; and, for that reason, stimuli that make up an objective are examined for its presence. Based on the degree of similarity between stimuli, its potential effects on discriminations are assessed.

Effects on Generalizations. Problems in generalizing from one instance of a class to another can arise when the stimulus instances belonging to that class are highly *dissimilar*. Generalizing across instances (of any class) that are characterized by surface, irrelevant dissimilarities *is* likely to pose difficulties. Subvarieties of a class are then not likely to be easily recognized.

Consider the following three instances of a *third-class* lever: a shovel, a pair of ice tongs, and an arm—all seemingly different. Yet, with respect to the critical attributes of third-class levers (relative positions of effort force, fulcrum, and load), they are alike. In each case, the effort force is applied between the load and the fulcrum—the definition of a third-class lever. The potentially distracting surface dissimilarities can make the identification of this *essential* similarity difficult. One or more of these instances of a third-class lever might easily be mistaken for other types of levers.

In general, the more *dissimilar* the subvarieties of the same stimulus class, the more likely are they to be treated as instances of other classes. A failure in stimulus generalization will have occurred. Stimulus *dissimilarity* can make for such generalization failures; for that reason, objectives are examined for stimulus dissimilarity, and its potential effects are assessed.

Effects on Responses. The similarity or dissimilarity of *responses* also poses potential learning problems. Response *differentiation*, the ability to distinguish one response from another, can be affected. Response *generalization*, the ability to identify a similarity among responses, can also be affected. Response similarity and dissimilarity can have the following effects:

- The greater the *similarity* among responses, the more difficult it will be to differentiate among them.

- The greater the *dissimilarity* among (functionally equivalent) responses, the more difficult it will be to generalize from one instance to another.

Due to response similarity, responses requiring *differentiation* may be confused with one another and, incorrectly, may be used interchangeably. On the other hand, due to response dissimilarity, responses requiring generalization may not be used interchangeably (as they should be).

The ability of novice singers to sing on pitch can be affected by marginal and therefore barely detectable differences in the *act* of producing notes that are on or off pitch. Primary-grade students struggling to produce hand-written script that meets teacher specifications can have difficulty detecting differences between their production and the "correct" way of going about it. Similar difficulties can be experienced in learning to speak in foreign language, to act in plays, or to hit a backhand in tennis. The greater the overlap or *similarity* between correct and incorrect (or between different) responses, the more difficult will response differentiation be.

Response differentiation becomes more difficult the narrower the gap between right and wrong or between alternative ways to do something. In contrast, response generalization is more likely to be affected by *apparent*, wide gaps between what are alternative, functionally equivalent ways to do the same thing. For example, students who have to learn to multiply two numbers—starting with the right-hand-most digit of the multiplier—may have difficulty identifying the acceptability and equivalence of starting with the left-hand-most digit. Thus, although there may be alternative, equally valid ways to perform the same function, an apparent but irrelevant dissimilarity may make it difficult to identify that equivalence.

For these varied reasons, responses that make up an objective are examined for similarity and dissimilarity, and the potential effects of each are assessed.

Effects on Associations. The similarity or dissimilarity of either stimulus or response can also pose obstacles to the learning of *associations*. This is particularly likely to be the case when there are multiple associations to be learned.

> • The greater the *similarity* among either stimuli or responses in multiple S-R associations, the more difficult it will be to learn the associations.

In learning to read Chinese, for example, students have to associate either a Chinese word or an English-language equivalent with a Chinese ideograph. There are thousands of such ideographs, many of them differing from one another by what, to Westerners, appears to be a stroke or two. Difficulty in discriminating among highly similar ideographs can make it hard to learn the associations between them and the words they represent.

Summary. Stimulus discrimination and generalization are part of the simplest and most routine behaviors, as well as of the most complex and atypical behaviors. Putting a shoe on the correct foot depends on them. Diagnosing a skin condition depends on them. At any point in long division (a chain), estimating how many places in a dividend a particular divisor will go depends on them. Identifying a novelist's attitude to his or her characters depends on them. The more nearly similar the stimuli in such behaviors are, the more difficult these key discriminations can be. Conversely, the more dissimilar the stimuli within a given class, the more difficult the required generalizations can be.

Stimulus or response similarity and dissimilarity are potential obstacles to the learning of discriminations, generalizations, and associations. And, because all three skills make up each unit of a chained performance, these attributes can also affect the learning of a chain. Therefore, an analysis of an objective will include a search for the presence of stimulus and response similarity or dissimilarity at any point in a chain that has to be learned.

Number of Stimulus/Response Properties

Stimuli or responses are rarely unidimensional. For example, the quality of a diamond is judged on the basis of multiple properties: color, freedom from flaws, size, number of facets, and so on. Discriminating among diamonds of unequal quality depends on an ability to recognize all these properties. Generalizing across diamonds of equal quality also depends on an ability to recognize all these properties. Similarly, all criterion stimuli are usually characterized by multiple properties, and competent performance depends on being able to apprehend them all.

Effects on Component Skills.   The number of properties that define a stimulus or a response can affect the ease or difficulty of discriminating between that stimulus and other stimuli or between that response and other responses. Also, the number of properties that define a *class of stimuli* or a *class of responses* can affect the ease or difficulty in identifying similarities among stimuli or among responses within those classes (generalizing).

It is not possible to postulate a uniformly linear relationship between the number of stimulus or response properties and difficulty levels. For example, a traffic light can be identified by two properties, color and position on a pole—a clear boon to the color blind. In this case, a property in addition to color makes a correct response possible. But, there is reason to expect that increases in the number of relevant properties that *define* the essential nature of a stimulus can increase learning difficulty.

The number of properties that stimuli or responses possess can have the following effects:

- Stimulus discrimination and generalization are likely to be adversely affected the larger the number of *stimulus properties* that must be attended to.

- Response differentiation and generalization are likely to be adversely affected the larger the number of *response properties* that must be attended to.

In elementary physics, students who have to classify instances of levers need to be able to discriminate among instances belonging to three different classes and to generalize across multiple and varied instances within each class. Were the discrimination or the generalization based just on where the fulcrum is located or just on where the load is located or just on where the effort force is applied, students would be less likely to have difficulty classifying instances than they typically do. It is all three properties, relative to one another, that determine to which class of levers any instance (a shovel, a wheelbarrow, a pair of tongs, or an arm) belongs. In classifying any of these levers, students must attend to all three.

It is not possible to identify the *number* of properties that forms the cutoff point dividing what is or is not likely to make the learning of skills difficult. Because a uniformly linear relationship between "number of properties" and "level of difficulty" cannot be described with certainty, just how serious the problems posed by "multiple properties" are likely to be may require a case-by-case, empirical assessment during the analysis of an objective.

Number of Stimuli and/or Responses

The sheer number of stimuli and responses entering into a performance can affect the ease with which all four skill elements can be learned.

Effects on Component Skills.   The *number* of stimuli or responses can have the following effects:

- The larger the number of *classes of stimuli* to be discriminated, the more difficult it will be to discriminate among instances belonging to those classes.

Consider the varieties of moods, voices, or tenses of verbs on which good usage depends. At issue here is not the ability to *produce* a verb in the correct mood, voice, or tense. Rather, it is the ability to *select* a correct verb for a particular *context*. It is the ability to identify contexts correctly on which their respective use depends, because it is based on context that decisions have to be made as to which mood, which tense, or which voice to use.

Consider the following tense options in English language usage.

PAST	PRESENT	FUTURE
He *saw* his doctor this morning.	I *see* what you meant by that statement.	I *will see* my doctor.
He *has already seen* his doctor.	At this moment he *is seeing* his doctor.	I *see* my doctor tomorrow.
He *had seen* his doctor before being advised to do so.	He *does see* your point.	Harry *is to see* his doctor tomorrow.
He *was to see* his doctor on Tuesday.		Dick *will have seen* his doctor by tomorrow.
He *did see* his doctor daily.		

The problem in correct English-language usage is *not* learning how to produce these differing verb forms. Rather, it is to learn *when* to use each of the three present-tense options, *when* to use each of the four future-tense options, and *when* to use each of the five past-tense options. Speakers or writers have to discriminate among meaningful contexts calling for each of the subvarieties within each of the three tenses. In addition, each subvariety constitutes a *class* of similar contexts.

Thus, English-language usage requires discriminations among a large number of classes of meaningful contexts and generalization across instances within each class.

By way of contrast, in Chinese-language usage there is only one past, one present, and one future. Thus, correct Chinese-language usage requires discriminating among meaningful contexts calling only for past, present, or future. Only three classes of contexts need to be discriminated as compared to 12 in English-language usage. Thus, the English language, with its larger number of classes of stimuli to be discriminated (meaningful contexts to be distinguished), is clearly the more difficult language to learn—at least with respect to verb inflection.

> • The larger the *number of instances* within a class (requiring generalization), the more difficult it will be to generalize from one instance to another (with qualifications).

Per se the *number of instances* within a class does not invariably make generalization more difficult (consider the large number of one dollar bills). In interaction with *dissimilarity*, it is highly likely to. For example, chairs come in so many shapes, sizes, colors, and materials that young children learning the concept *chair* may have difficulty identifying the essential similarity that all instances of it share. The more subvarieties there are within a class, the more difficult generalization can be.

> • The larger the number of discrete stimulus–response *associations* to be learned, the more difficult it will be to learn them.

In chemistry, students typically have to *associate* an atomic symbol, number, and weight with each chemical element. Today, with 103 known elements, students are likely to have greater difficulty learning these associations than they would have had at an earlier time, when considerably fewer elements were known. Similarly, learning a foreign language requires learning a large number of associations. The larger the vocabulary (associations between words in two different languages), the more difficult the learning problem. Here, numbers alone work a detrimental effect.

> • The larger the *number of stimulus–response units* linked in a chain, the more difficult it will be to learn the entire chain.

The more extended the performance—that is, the more steps or S–R units that make it up—the more difficult it is to learn. For example, an automobile mechanic learning to assemble or disassemble an engine is likely to experience less difficulty with a diesel engine and its fewer parts than with a conventional internal-combustion engine. In the latter case, because there are more parts to be assembled or disassembled, there are more steps—more S–R units—to be learned and chained in sequence. The longer any chain is, the more difficult it is to learn.

In summary, numbers of stimuli or responses (number of classes, number of instances within a class, number of stimulus–response associations, or number of S–R units) can affect the learning of the component skills. Thus, numbers constitute an important condition to be explored when objectives are analyzed.

Existing Associations

Learning associations has to occur in the face of other associations that have been learned in the past.

Effects on Component Skills. Existing associations between old responses and old stimuli can *interfere* with the learning of new responses to those same stimuli. For example, an American driving an automobile in England is required to reverse the use of lanes. The left-hand lane, which the driver has previously learned to avoid, is now the lane he or she must seek out and use. Or, if the locations of letters on a typewriter keyboard were rearranged, a typist would have to seek out these new locations. Such old associations can be expected to offer competition to the new ones. Existing associations can have the following effect:

> ● The stronger the *association* between
> a stimulus and a response, the more
> difficult it will be to associate a
> new response with that *old* stimulus.

The competing nature of existing associations can be most vividly seen in many types of remedial training. The learning of new motor behaviors is particularly vulnerable to the competition posed by existing habits. The tennis player or the golfer wishing to change strokes can testify to the difficulty of trying something new. Language usage can be similarly affected. Consider the difficulty teachers have in urging students to give up "with him and I" in favor of "with him and me." The older (or stronger) the existing association, the greater the competition it can be expected to offer.

Summary

In summary, there are objects, words, people, symbols, and events that constitute appropriate stimulus occasions for varied verbal, symbolic, or motor responses. Determining what is an appropriate occasion depends on stimulus discrimination and generalization. The ability to make an appropriate response on that occasion depends on response differentiation, response generalization, stimulus–response association, and chaining. Whether any of these skills will be learned easily or with difficulty depends on *properties* that stimuli, responses, and stimulus–response pairings (populating these skills) possess. Thus, analyses of objectives and their constituent skills also include a search for the presence of these properties and an assessment of their potential effects.

Conditions Affecting Recall and Transfer

What conditions affect the *recall* of skills already learned and their *transfer* to new situations?

Conditions Affecting Recall

With the passage of time, newly acquired skills are variably subject to being forgotten. The likelihood of their being forgotten is a function of: *how often* they were originally practiced and reinforced; the *length* of the interval between the conclusion of instruction and the occasion when they must be exhibited again; the *frequency* with which they are practiced in that interval; and the *amount* of competing, new learning that occurs during that interval.

Typically, instructional design is much more concerned with problems of initial learning than it is with recall. In training environments, this neglect is likely to be of little consequence. Trainees almost always have frequent on-the-job opportunities to rehearse and thereby maintain newly acquired skills. It is school learning—unapplied—that is most vulnerable to being forgotten. Lack of use over time is the major source of such recall failures.

Conditions Affecting Transfer

Generalization and transfer impose a common requirement on students. Students must be able to identify *similarities* among different stimuli that belong to the same class. The conditions likely to affect transfer overlap those affecting generalization. They include stimulus dissimilarity, the number of stimulus properties, and the number of instances belonging to a class. In addition, they also include the strength of (ability to recall) the generalization to which it is related.

Individual Differences Among Students

Learner characteristics can also determine how easy or difficult it will be to learn specific objectives. A behavioral, reinforcement orientation is not a particularly rich source for identifying what those characteristics might be. It is an orientation that is allied to an experimental tradition that is more concerned with uniformities than with individual differences. Thus, it is not surprising that there are no distinctive or proprietary principles about aptitudes or readiness that can be quickly labeled "behavioral."

It is possible to speculate about the role played by individual differences in student *capacity* to learn the "behavioral" component skills: discriminations, generalizations, associations, and chains (Gropper, 1974). Evidence of stable differences among students in the ease or difficulty with which they learn these skills would be a useful finding. It would permit the prescription of proven treatments to accommodate the overlay of problems that individual differences contribute. The possibility of using the same types of treatments to meet joint *subject-matter* and *individual-difference* requirements would make for a parsimonious approach to the prescription of treatments.

A contrasting approach to the accommodation of individual differences has also been described (Gropper, 1976). It calls for the *reduction of individual differences* rather than for their differential accommodation. It calls for training students to be self-reliant learners.* It calls for training them to search for information in texts, lectures, demonstrations, and so on, that is relevant to course objectives. More importantly, it calls for training them to search for information relevant to the component skills that underlie them.

Students could be given statements of objectives and a description of their component skills. These advance organizers would provide the necessary guidance to initiate student search for information relevant to those skills. For example, an objective might read: "Define and contrast *kinetic* and *potential* energy and give examples of each." Instructions about relevant skills to consider might read: "Look for information that will help you to *distinguish* between kinetic and potential energy and to identify the *similarities* among the varied examples of each of these concepts." In effect, students would be encouraged to act as behaviorally oriented task analysts.

Given sufficient encouragement, guidance, and practice in searching for information relevant to underlying skills, students could ultimately become self-reliant. They could become adept at searching for similar types of information even in the absence of explicit instructions to do so—a useful ability given how much learning does or can go on outside of school and training settings.

It is hypothesized that enhanced skill in "learning to learn" would reduce individual differences. If it is given a behavioral orientation, this skill could effectively complement instructional treatments that also reflect that orientation.

For a summary of all of the conditions discussed in this section of this chapter, refer back to columns 1 and 2 of Fig. 5.1.

TREATMENTS

Practice is central to all treatments devised to assure mastery. Two major types of progressions or series of practice tasks are available for devising appropriate treatments. One, a *preparatory* progression, is applicable to instruction for an *individual* objective. The other, a *contingent* progression, is applicable to instruction for *multiple* objectives.** Strategy formulation focuses on both types of progressions as a means of building competence in a gradual and orderly way.

---

*Editor's note: This is somewhat similar to Landa's advocacy of the teaching of *learning algorithms* (Chapter 6, p. 178) and *general algo-heuristic procedures* (chapter 6, p. 203).

**Editor's note: These correspond exactly to micro and macro strategies, respectively (see Chapter 1).

This section of the chapter enumerates the varied treatment options available for creating *preparatory* progressions that are suitable for an *individual* objective. The discussion that follows describes what treatments must accomplish (i.e., their goals), what tools are available for accomplishing them, and what organizing principles govern the use of those tools.

Treatment Goals

The progression of practice tasks that is devised for an individual objective must prepare students to meet four performance criteria. At the conclusion of instruction students must be able to:

- perform in a *criterion* mode;

- exhibit those skills under *conditions* that typically affect them; and

- exhibit all of an objective's *constituent skills*;

- meet *post-instructional* requirements.

Performance in a Criterion Mode

The criterion mode of an objective is defined in terms of both stimulus and response. The *stimulus mode* of prose to be interpreted is *verbal*. For a biological cell to be classified it is concrete and *visual*. For a mathematical function to be differentiated it is quantitative and *symbolic*. Competent performance requires an ability to respond to stimuli that are encountered in these very criterion modes.

If an objective calls for a *response mode* that is verbal (e.g., describing a novel) or that is quantitative (e.g., differentiating a power function) or that is motor (e.g assembling an electric motor), competent performance requires an ability to respond in these criterion modes. Similarly, if an objective calls for students to "*produce*" an answer, being able only to "*select*" one from options will not do. In this case, criterion performance requires a "*production*" response mode.*

Upon being confronted with a stimulus presented in a criterion mode, students have to be able to respond to it in a criterion mode.

Performance of All Constituent Skills

The number, the mix, and the relative importance of each of the four component skills vary from one type of objective to another. In the "recall of facts," *associating* one set of information with another plays a predominant role. In "rule following," *chaining* plays a predominant role. In problem solving, *chaining, discriminations,* and *generalizations* (at decision points) all play a predominant role.

However, much of the "predominant" skills may characterize a particular kind of objective, all four skills generally enter into its performance. Students have to be able to exhibit *all* the constituent skills—predominant and secondary ones alike (see columns 2 and 3 of Fig. 5.1).

---

*Editor's note: Merrill's Component Display Theory (Chapter 9) incorporates this idea.

Performance Under All Conditions

Competent performance requires an ability to exhibit component skills even under conditions that make it difficult to do so. It requires an ability to make classifications (of trees, machines, novels, etc.) even if *similarity* among instances to be classified makes the necessary discriminations difficult or even if *dissimilarity* among instances makes the necessary generalizations difficult. It requires an ability to recall facts even though the *number* of stimulus-response pairs is large. It requires an ability to follow algorithms even though the *number* of steps chained together is large.

Students have to be able to exhibit all of an objective's constituent skills— under any set of conditions that may apply to those skills.

Meeting Post-Instructional Requirements

Competent performance requires an ability to exhibit newly acquired skills immediately following instruction. It may also require them to be able to exhibit those skills at some more distant time. Students have to be able to meet both of these types of *recall* requirements.

Competent performance also requires an ability at some future time to respond to new situations—those not previously encountered during instruction. Students have to be able to meet such a *transfer* requirement.

Summary

In summary, there are four treatment goals. Students must be prepared: to perform all the component skills of an objective; to perform them in a criterion mode; to perform them under any condition that might prevail; and to meet post-instructional requirements for them.

Treatment Tools

The following treatment tools are available for use in designing practice tasks as a means of promoting treatment goals (see Fig. 5.3).

- the *degree of cuing* that is provided for a practice task;
- the *size of the unit of behavior* that is practiced in a practice task;
- the *mode* of stimulus and response that is required in a practice task;
- the *variety* that is built into a practice task;
- the *content* that is built into a practice task; and
- the *frequency* with which a task is practiced.

Typically, each of these tools is *not* used alone. Most often the tools are used in varied combinations. The use of two or more of them allows for adjustments in the demands put on students—both up and down—at any particular stage in a practice progression.

TREATMENT TOOL	PARAMETERS		
CUE STRENGTH	Degree of association between a cue and a response to be elicited.	Degree of similarity between a cue (as a model) and a response to be elicited.	Number of cue attributes that possess control over a response.
SIZE OF UNIT OF BEHAVIOR	Amount of the criterion behavior to be practiced.	Integrity of the criterion behavior to be practiced.	Length of the interval between cue presentation and response practice. Standards for the behavior to be practiced.
MODE OF STIMULUS AND RESPONSE	Concreteness vs. abstractness of stimulus or response.	Familiarity vs. the technical nature of a stimulus.	Mode of responding: (recognizing vs. editing vs. producing a response).
VARIED EXAMPLES	Variety of examples provided.	Difficulty level of examples based on: .. familiarity of examples .. similarity of example to other examples .. saliency of defining characteristics	
PRACTICE CONTENT	Exaggeration of stimulus or response examples.	Paired practice of errors and a correct performance.	Sequence of practice (reverse order of steps). Practice of non-criterion behaviors (principles about procedures)
FREQUENCY OF PRACTICE	Frequency of repetition of practice tasks.		

FIG. 5.3   Treatment tools and parameters that allow for variations in their use.

Cues

Cues provide the "help" and guidance that students need. Lectures, demonstrations, job aids, definitions, gimmicks, a single word or symbol, and so on, can all serve as cues. In that capacity they identify: how to *define* a concept or what its appropriate instances are; what the *algorithm* is for a procedural activity; what the *facts* are that need to be remembered; or what *techniques* are useful in solving problems. Thus, cues are a principal means for providing guidance to any type of performance.

Cues lend themselves readily to the shaping of behavior. Early in the learning process, when students are most in need of help, *strong* cues an be used. As mastery gradually increases and, therefore, as learner needs for cues diminish, cue strength can be *gradually diminished*. Cues are finally *eliminated* at that point when students are judged capable of responding to a criterion stimulus alone. Cues can play these differential roles because it is feasible to vary the degree of help they provide.

The *strength* of a cue (and, therefore, the degree of help it provides) may be defined in terms of and, therefore, varied on the basis of the following parameters: the *strength of association* between the cue and the response to be elicited; the *degree of similarity* between the cue (serving as a model) and the response it serves to elicit; the *size of the interval* between presentation of the cue and the occasion set for response practice; and the *number of controlling attributes* that the cue possesses (see row 1 of Fig. 5.3). These parameters enter into a consideration of cues that might be used at different stages in a progression of practice tasks. They make it possible to select cues that provide varying, appropriate amounts of help. Each of these is discussed below.

Strength of Association With Responses

The strength of association between a cue and a response is a function of students' learning histories. The frequency of past experience with words, objects, or symbols determines how dependably they can be relied on to function as cues. For example, school populations are likely to have had different histories in their use of the words "stop" and "desist." The word "stop," likely to have been used more often, can serve more dependably as a cue for calling a halt to an activity. Highly familiar cues, like the word "stop," are used early in a series of practice tasks. They are used to make sure that the responses that students must practice will in fact be elicited. Once students begin practicing those responses and the association between the responses and the criterion stimulus begins to develop, weaker cues can be relied on to perform the same function.

In the early stages of practice maximum help is provided through the use of highly familiar examples (e.g., animals or objects) or through the use of other highly familiar visual, symbolic, or verbal cues (e.g., colors or diagrams). These cues are selected because they are *strongly associated* with the responses that need to be

EXAMPLES	EARLY PRACTICE	INTERMEDIATE PRACTICE	FINAL PRACTICE
1.	Finger nails and typewriter keys are color coded (matched) to cue the touch method of typing.	Color intensity is gradually faded or some of the colors are eliminated.	No colors are available as cues.
2.	Pictures of animals, objects, etc. are used to elicit reading of their names.	Repeated practice of the same word with occasional omission of a picture.	No pictures are provided during reading practice.

Examples of strength of association with responses.

practiced and, therefore, can be relied on to elicit those responses. The number of practice stages that are made to intervene between early practice offering maximum cuing and final criterion practice offering no cuing at all, is a function of anticipated learning problems and the amount of help judged to be necessary for dealing with them.

Degree of Similarity with Responses

A model demonstration of a procedural performance (e.g., adjusting a carburetor, balancing a chemical equation, etc.) can also serve as a cue. It is used to elicit student repetition of the performance he has observed and others like it.

It is possible to vary the degree of guidance a model demonstration provides. At one extreme, a model demonstration, identical in content and mode to a criterion behavior, offers maximum cuing strength. No demonstration represents the other extreme. For points between these extremes, the degree of cuing strength can be manipulated by varying the *degree of similarity* between a model and the behavior to be practiced.

A model demonstration can be presented realistically; or it can be presented in words (*telling* rather than *showing* students "how to"). The former is assumed to offer greater guidance because of its greater similarity to the behavior that must be practiced. The more nearly similar a model demonstration is to the behavior to be practiced, the greater its capacity to act as an effective cue (model).

It is also possible to vary the degree of similarity among *examples* of a concept as a means of providing varying degrees of guidance for learning that concept. The more nearly similar a model example and other examples are, the greater its capacity to facilitate generalization from one instance of a concept to another. The cuing strength an example provides (i.e., its capacity to guide student classification of other examples) depends on how similar it is to the other examples.

EXAMPLES	EARLY PRACTICE	INTERMEDIATE PRACTICE	FINAL PRACTICE
1.	For penmanship, model script is provided. Students trace over it.	Model script is still provided. Students copy it. They do not trace over it.	Students write with no cues available.
2.	French is spoken on tape. Students imitate it.	Students speak in French—reading from a printed text.	Students speak in ordinary conversation.
3.	Examples of types of levers and rules for their classification are provided. Students practice classifying other examples.	Only rules for classification are provided. Students classify old and new examples.	No aids are provided. Students classify old and new examples.

Examples of degree of similarity with responses.

Cue Interval

It is also possible to manipulate the strength of a cue by varying the length of the *interval* between cue presentation and the start of student practice. Typically, it is not the interval per se that is varied (although administrative considerations may dictate that too). Rather, it is the *length of a presentation* (a lecture, a reading passage, or a demonstration) that is varied. It is presentation length that dictates the length of the interval. The longer the presentation, of necessity, the longer practice must be delayed. For example, reading one page of text (provided as a cue) will cause less of a delay than reading 20 pages of text. Forgetting resulting from prolonged delays can be expected to diminish the strength of cues (lectures, demonstrations, etc.) and, hence, their capacity to function as they are meant to.

Number of Cue Attributes

The *number of attributes* that a cue possesses can also determine its strength and usefulness for eliciting responses. The more cue attributes there are that control the responses that must be practiced, the more likely is a cue (with those attributes) to be effective in eliciting them.

A cue may have one or more attributes that possess stimulus control over a response. For example, on a geography map both "lines" and "color" can demarcate boundaries and assist (cue) students to identify neighbors, relative sizes of countries, and so on. Maps that do not use color must rely on lines alone to elicit these identifications. They are likely to function less well in eliciting the identifications than the maps with two controlling attributes.

EXAMPLES	EARLY PRACTICE	INTERMEDIATE PRACTICE	FINAL PRACTICE
1.	Video demonstration of soldering plus audio instructions are provided as cues.	Only audio instructions on soldering are provided as cues.	Students solder with no cues available.
2.	Rules for and examples of the use of "that" and and "which" in restrictive and non-restrictive clauses are provided.	Only rules for correct usage are provided during writing of "that" and "which" clauses.	Students write restrictive and non-restrictive clauses without any guidance.

Examples of number of cue attributes.

In early practice activities that require strong cues it may be necessary to use cues with multiple attributes. In the final stage of practice, when students are expected to be able to practice correct responses in the presence of the criterion stimulus alone, all cues are withdrawn. In between, cues with gradually fewer (controlling) attributes may be used.

Summary

Cues vary in their capacity to elicit responses. This may be due to: the *strength of the association* between a cue and a response to be elicited (the familiarity of the cue); the *similarity* between a cue (as a model) and a response; the *length of the interval* between cue presentation and response practice; and the *number of cue attributes* that possess stimulus control over a response to be practiced (see row 1 of Fig. 5.3).

Cues are typically used in combination with other treatment tools. The use of cues makes it possible to reduce the number of practice stages required by these other means. Cues help to bring students up to criterion standards as quickly and as efficiently as possible. They contribute to this outcome by supplying a needed degree of guidance. The amount of guidance provided is geared to the type of practice a practice task demands and is thus geared to a practice task's position in a progression of similar practice tasks.

Unit of Behavior

The "size" of the unit of behavior that is practiced may be defined in terms of such parameters as: *how much* of the criterion behavior students are required to practice; the degree of *integrity* of the criterion behavior that is maintained; and the *standards* that students have to meet when they practice a criterion behavior or some portion of it (see row 2 of Fig. 5.3). Each of these is discussed below.

EXAMPLES	EARLY PRACTICE	INTERMEDIATE PRACTICE	FINAL PRACTICE
1.	Estimating how many places in a dividend a divisor will go.	Doing each intermediate division step by itself: multiplying, subtracting, etc.	Doing an entire long division problem.
2.	Punctuating sentences.	Writing sentences or paragraphs.	Writing short essays.

Examples of amount of behavior practiced.

Amount of Behavior Practiced

An individual practice task can call on students to practice varying *amounts* of a criterion behavior. Students may be required to practice the entire criterion behavior, only one of its component skills, or a portion of it lying anywhere in between these extremes. A *progression* of practice tasks can start with small units, continue with "n" units of intermediate size, and end with the largest unit, the entire criterion behavior.

The *size* and *complexity* of a criterion behavior determine how necessary it may be to break it up into small units. They also determine how many units will be necessary and how large each unit should be (they need not all be of equal size). The more difficult procedural decisions are or the more procedural steps there are, the greater the need to break up a criterion behavior into small units. The degree and extent of *expected learner difficulty* are the relevant parameters.

EXAMPLES	EARLY PRACTICE	INTERMEDIATE PRACTICE	FINAL PRACTICE
1.	Students practice driving in a deserted parking lot on a Sunday morning.	Students practice driving on city streets very early on weekday mornings —with limited amounts of traffic present.	Students practice driving during rush hour traffic.
2.	Students practice tennis strokes using a light-weight racket or a loosely strung racket (or a smaller racket for children).	Students practice with a medium weight racket or a moderately tight one or a medium sized one.	Students practice with tennis rackets of criterion dimensions: weight, size, and tightness of strings.

Examples of integrity of behavior practiced.

Integrity of Behavior Practiced

It is possible to dispense with the *integrity* or fidelity of a criterion behavior in order to make practice easier. Attributes of the criterion behavior can be eliminated or modified. Students are then required to cope only with the simplified remainder.*

In early practice stages, attributes of a criterion behavior can thus be either removed or diminished, gradually re-introduced as practice progresses, and included in their entirety during criterion practice.

Standards of Performance

Early in instruction, standards of performance, either quantitative or qualitative, can be varied to accommodate learner needs. Lesser standards are accepted at the beginning of practice, criterion standards at the end, and varying, intermediate levels in between.

Summary

These varied kinds of adjustments in "unit size," either in the *amount* practiced, or in the *integrity* of the criterion behavior, or in the *standards* set for practice tasks, carry students from low to high levels of competence gradually (see row 2 of Fig. 5.3) The level of performance required at any stage in a preparatory practice progression is selected so as to match estimated student readiness at that stage.

EXAMPLES	EARLY PRACTICE	INTERMEDIATE PRACTICE	FINAL PRACTICE
1.	Ragged penmanship is accepted.	Increasingly closer approximations to criterion penmanship standards are required.	Criterion penmanship standards are required.
2.	A moderate number of typing errors per fixed unit of time is accepted.	Gradually fewer errors per the same unit of time are required.	A criterion number of typing errors for that unit of time is required.
3.	Diagnosing computer faults in two hours is considered acceptable.	Gradually smaller durations for diagnosis completion are required.	Diagnosis must be completed in thirty minutes (the criterion).

Examples of standards of performance.

---

*Editor's note: This bears some similarity to the Elaboration Theory (Chapter 10), except that this discussion relates to the *micro* level.

Stimulus and Response Mode

As performance in a *criterion* mode is a key goal of instruction, practice in that mode is a necessary ingredient of a preparatory progression. But, it is sometimes useful to schedule prior practice in other, easier modes. A stimulus mode or a response mode can be deliberately selected for its capacity to make early practice tasks easy and later ones progressively more difficult.

Response Mode

A criterion *response mode* typically requires the *production* of some behavior or its output. Students may be required: to divide and get a quotient; to formulate a reserach hypothesis; to play from a musical score; or to discuss the role of fiscal

EXAMPLES	RECOGNITION PRACTICE	EDITING PRACTICE	PRODUCTION PRACTICE
1.	14 +37 ———	24 +48 ——— 62	34 +39 ———
	which is the correct answer? ——a. 41 ——b. 51	The above total is incorrect. Correct it.	Add these numbers.
2.	Which of the follwoing is an example of extinction? ——a. Not acknow-ledging an answer a child has blurted out. ——b. Telling a child not to blurt out an answer.	"Ignoring a child's persistent begging is an example of punishment." Is this a correct statement? Correct it if it is not.	"Withholding a reprimand when a child has a tantrum." Classify the above example of a classroom management tech-nique.
3.	Which of these letters comes at the beginning of the word "boy"? ——b ——d	Look at the animal in this picture. Look at the word under it. ("bog") Is that correct? If not, tell me what it should be.	Read the following words. boy dog dot bet bad

Examples of response mode.

and monetary policy in controlling the economy. A less difficult task can be posed for students by altering this requirement. Students may be required simply to *edit* a response that is provided, or even less difficult, to *recognize* and select a correct response from among options. And, when judged to be necessary, a complete "recognize-edit-produce" (REP) progression may be scheduled (see row 3 of Fig. 5.3).

As is the case for progressions using any of the other treatment tools, the full "recognize-edit-produce" (REP) sequence is used *only* in those situations judged to require it. Elsewhere, because of the *efficiency* it confers, requiring a "production" practice mode from the very beginning is to be preferred.

Recognition practice can be used for purposes other than that of simply making practice tasks easier. It lends itself to *types* of practice that are particularly suited to common learning problems. The *pairing of two stimuli* or (two responses) in a recognition task lends itself to the practice of discriminations and generalizations. Example #3 illustrates the use of a recognition task that can help grade school students to discriminate between the similar appearing letters "b" and "d". A presentation of *paired* instances of different types of levers, triangles, leaves, or poetry, may be used to facilitate the identification of differences between them.* Or, *pairs* may be used to facilitate the identification of similarities among instances of stimuli belonging to the same class. Such *recognition practice* can facilitate the identification of attributes that mark instances as belonging to the same class and that distinguish instances belonging to different classes.

Stimulus Mode

The mode of a simulus or of both stimulus and response can also be varied to create a preparatory progression. It is possible to precede an abstract and potentially difficult mode (the criterion mode) with more concrete and, hence, easier modes (see row 3 of Fig. 5.3). Three types of concrete presentations can be sequenced *before* an abstract version to make the teaching of concepts and principles easier: the use of verbally described, *concrete examples;* the use of concrete, *visual examples;* and the practice of *concrete procedures.*

Learning to define and illustrate concepts is apt to be difficult if definitions are offered in abstract, technical language. One way to prepare students for this more abstract type of presentation is to precede it with one that employs *everyday language* or *concrete, verbal examples.*

Familiar examples and everyday language are used to elicit the practice of responses that the criterion stimuli (more abstract and unfamiliar language) cannot yet elicit. Through practice with the concrete and familiar, students learn concepts and explanations more easily. Afterward the technical or more abstract language is associated with them.

---

*Editor's note: This is the same as Merrill's "matched nonexamples" (Chapter 9, p. 325) and Markle's "close-up nonexamples" (Markle & Tiemann, 1969).

EXAMPLES	EARLY PRACTICE	FINAL PRACTICE
1.	Verbal examples depict teachers ignoring student fighting or blurting out of answers when not called on (attention seeking behaviors).	Technical definition of "extinction" is provided: (the withholding of both reinforcement and punishing for attention seeking behavior.)
2.	Homely, verbal examples depict "pushes" and "pulls" being applied to objects such as wagons, blocks of ice, etc. The movement that results is also depicted.	The concepts "force" and "motion" are defined and their relationships described.

Examples of verbal stimulus mode.

A *visual mode* can create a similar kind of experience. Non-verbal stimuli, responses, or both—generally already familiar to students—can be used to teach concepts, principles, or procedures. Following a concrete experience students are then better able to respond to a technical or abstract treatment—*verbal* or *symbolic*.

These examples illustrate how students can be helped to respond in an abstract, verbal way (as in the second example) or in an abstract, symbolic way (as in the first example). Properties of visual objects or events that already control

EXAMPLES	EARLY PRACTICE	FINAL PRACTICE
1.	A number line is used to demonstrate the addition of positive and negative numbers.	Problems in adding positive and negative numbers are presented and solved symbolically.
2.	In an animated film, air is shown passing by the upper and lower parts of an airplane wing at different rates. The resulting lift is also represented. Students verbally describe the relationships among these concrete events.	A more abstract verbal account of Bernouilli's Principle is provided. Students practice stating and illustrating the principle—using technical terms.

Examples of visual stimulus mode.

behaviors are used to elicit practice of those behaviors. Concepts, principles, or procedures can be learned through the practice of these concrete behaviors. Technical language is subsequently associated with the concepts, principles, or procedures, which, by that time, are already understood.

Students sometimes have to learn principles *about* procedural activities: principles about doing research, doing instructional design, or doing therapy. To make it easier for students to learn principles (*about* procedures), prior practice of the procedures themselves can provide a concrete introduction to them.*

EXAMPLES	EARLY PRACTICE	FINAL PRACTICE
1.	Students practice doing a task description. They also use the results as a basis for performing other course development tasks (e.g., stating objectives).	Students practice stating or applying principles about the role of task description in course development.
2.	Students practice withholding attention (positive or negative) following the occurrence of attention-seeking behavior. They also practice observing the change in frequency of such behavior.	Students practice stating or interpreting behavioral principles (re: "extinction") as applied to the management of classroom problem behaviors.

Examples of procedures before principles.

The observation of relationships between actions and outcomes or between events serves as a concrete introduction to *issues* about them. This kind of experience can be effective in facilitating learner ability—in more abstract ways—to state, interpret, or apply principles governing those relationships.

Practice in a concrete mode—use of concrete, verbal examples, use of visual examples, or practice of concrete procedures—is not meant to replace practice in an abstract, criterion mode (see row 3 of Fig. 5.3). Practice in these other modes is used to make it easier for students subsequently to engage in practice in the more difficult, criterion mode.

Varied Practice Examples

The use of varied practice examples (of concepts or of problem tasks) is indispensable for promoting *generalization* and *transfer*. It is a principal means for

---

*Editor's note: This contradicts Mayer's (1976) finding that meaningful knowledge should precede rote (calculational) knowledge. Nevertheless, Gropper's prescription here is intuitively appealing. Clearly, further research is needed in this area.

preparing students to identify any instance of: a second class level, a scalene triangle, baroque music, a prime number, research design violations, and so on. Exposure to varied *practice* examples facilitates the correct identification (e.g., classification) of *new* instances of a class of objects, ideas, symbols, or situations.

The *sequence* in which practice examples are presented may be used to create a progression of practice tasks. Practice examples judged to be easy can be scheduled early, highly difficult ones late, and gradually more difficult ones in between.

What makes practice examples "easy"? Some instances of objects, events, ideas, or symbols are more easily identified as belonging to a particular class than others. Three attributes of instances can contribute to this effect: *familiarity, similarity* to other instances, and *saliency* of their defining characteristics. Some instances are already known and *highly familiar* and, therefore, easily recognizable. Also, some instances within a class are *highly similar* to one another and therefore are readily recognizable as examples of that class. Other instances belonging to different classes are dissimilar and therefore easily distinguishable from them. Finally, the defining characteristics of some instances are *highly visible or salient,* making those instances easily recognizable. Or, their other non-defining characteristics may be less visible, making them less likely to be mistaken for instances of other classes. Practice examples judged to be "easy" or "difficult" based on such considerations can be used to create a progression of practice tasks that range from easy to difficult (see row 4 of Fig. 5.3).

Since *practice examples,* whether easy or difficult, frequently constitute "criterion stimuli" to which students will have to respond, they are prime candidates for use in practice designed for most educational and training objectives.

Practice Content

The principal content of most practice tasks is an intact criterion behavior or some portion of it. It is, after all, the very practice of the criterion behavior itself that increases the likelihood of its successful mastery. But, as we have seen earlier, practice tasks can also depart from this ideal. *Cues* can be added to them.

EXAMPLES	INITIAL PRACTICE	INTERMEDIATE PRACTICE	FINAL PRACTICE
1.	Students form plurals for regular nouns (dog, boy, cat, etc.)	Students form plurals for nouns ending in "s" and "s" sounds (lens, loss, horse, etc.)	Students form plurals for irregular nouns (man, sheep, series, etc.)
2.	Students design experiments involving only one variable.	Students design experiments involving two variables.	Students design experiments involving multiple, interacting variables.

Examples of varied practice examples.

Or, their *mode* requirements can be altered. Or, only *parts* of them can be practiced. Still other departures are possible. Also available are such treatment tools as: *distortions* or exaggerations of stimulus or response; practice of *errors;* altered (non-criterion) performance *sequences;* and the practice of behaviors totally *different from the criterion behavior* (see row 5 of Fig. 5.3) Each of these departures can have a specific, constructive role to play, and each is described below.

Distortions. For some objectives a key component skill may require the making of fine-grained distinctions among stimuli or among responses. Initial *exaggeration* of stimuli to be discriminated or responses to be differentiated can be a useful strategy in preparing students for such fine-grained distinctions.

A music student is often required to detect the difference between notes performed on pitch or minutely off pitch. Musical notes that are markedly off pitch can be used to pose an easy, initial discrimination. Subsequent practice tasks can present notes that are less and less off pitch. Gradually notes are made to approximate the criterion, a note recognized to be just a hair-off pitch. By starting with *exaggerated practice examples* that students can easily identify, progressions of this type gradually prepare students to identify examples that are minutely different from other examples—a more difficult discrimination.

Whenever there are fine-grained and difficult response differentiations to be learned, it is strategic to consider the use of exaggerated response examples (e.g., a tennis stroke that is very much exaggerated).

Errors. Practice opportunities are usually designed to prevent the *practice of errors*. Nevertheless, there are situations for which it makes sense to promote the practice of errors. These include: behaviors that are known to be error prone; remediation for behaviors that are currently being performed incorrectly; and behaviors that routinely require a performer to monitor and correct his or her own performance.

Practice of errors can help students to *discriminate* between the right and wrong way to do something. Being able to make this discrimination can help them to avoid learning an error, to discontinue an already learned error, or, on the basis of self-generated feedback, to make corrective adjustments when an error occurs.

The *paired* practice of both the right and wrong way to do something can be used in a variety of situations. Speakers of nonstandard English may be required to practice successive use of a correct and an incorrect grammatical form. For example, they may be required to say in succession "he be there" and "he is there" or "the three boy" and "the three boys." Such practice can help them to hear the difference between a correct and incorrect version and to identify which version is correct.

Criterion behaviors that involve motor skills (e.g., playing the violin, wielding a scalpel, playing golf, etc.) and that are naturally subject to slight variations in execution can also profit from the practice of "right" and "wrong." Being able to discriminate between the feel of a correct and incorrect motor response resulting from such practice can provide useful feedback. It permits the competent performer to monitor and adjust his or her ongoing performance. It is useful both during and after completion of instruction.

Altered Sequences. For some types of learning problems, practice of the criterion behavior itself is retained but the *sequence* in which its elements are practiced can be altered. Procedural tasks made up of a long chain of steps can be practiced in a reverse order. Prescription of such *backward chaining* is usually based on a reinforcement rationale (Gilbert, 1962).

Procedural or problem-solving activities (such as differentiating power functions, assembling a motor, designing instruction, etc.) are potential candidates for backward chaining. They all share a common requirement: the need to chain a series of steps in a correct sequence.

A "modeling" rationale has also been offered to account for the value of backward chaining (Gropper, 1974). One of the volumes being summarized in this chapter employs a backward "modeling" approach (Gropper, 1973). Students first learn to try out and revise instructional materials (the last major task in the instructional-design process). They are given model outputs for prior design tasks—from task description through materials development. They then practice doing tryout and revision. By the time they work their way back in the chain and are required to perform such tasks as "strategy formulation," or "sequencing," or "task analysis," they have had an opportunity to inspect several *model products* for each of these tasks. They can base their own subsequent performance of those tasks on the models they have observed.

Noncriterion Behaviors. The "content" subvarieties discussed thus far have required the practice of criterion behaviors albeit in an altered version (exaggerations, errors, and altered sequences). Preparatory progressions can also require the practice of *noncriterion* behaviors. These other-than-criterion behaviors are selected for their assumed capacity to facilitate the practice and performance of the criterion behaviors. For example, *principles* may be taught as a means of facilitating the learning and subsequent performance of procedures—the criterion behavior. Often these principles concern how equipment operates and not the procedures that must be mastered. For example, military trainees who are to maintain electronic equipment are taught principles of electronics. Computer trainees who are to write software programs are taught facts and principles about how computer systems work—the internals of the systems. Underlying this instructional strategy is the assumption that the learning of these principles about something other than the procedures to be learned will facilitate the learning of those procedures.

This is an unsettled area. Judgments about what is "required" and what is "nice to know" are difficult to make. For those developers for whom "efficiency" of instruction is not critical, "nice to know" may be an acceptable option. For those for whom it is critical, the burden is on them to demonstrate that there is a connection between the principles they teach and a criterion behavior that must be mastered.

The types of practice content are summarized in row 5 of Fig. 5.3.

Frequency of Practice

A major treatment tool for creating a progression of tasks is *repetition*. It is important for acquisition and retention alike. For difficult problem areas it is possible to require the repeated practice of the same task (the same stimulus example and the same response to it) before moving on to a new task (with a new stimulus example and either the same or a different response to it).

Repetition leads to gradual increases in response strength. Students are more able to undertake each new repetition—even as they are being weaned of assistance. They are also more able to undertake different kinds of tasks. Frequency, along with variety, is a major tool in facilitating the acquisition, retention, and transfer of behaviors.

Summary

In summary, the list of treatment tools just concluded is quite long (see Fig. 5.3). It includes variations in: cue strength, behavior unit size, stimulus and response modes, practice example variety, content of practice, and frequency of practice. Some of these tools are staples in all types of instruction. Others are infrequently used. For any given objective a developer is likely to select only a few of them at a time. However, all are available on an as-needed basis for creating *graduated*, preparatory progressions. All are available for fashioning the kinds and amounts of attention suitable for anticipating student difficulties in meeting subject-matter requirements.

Treatment Organization

An ideal instructional sequence accomplishes its goals with the minimum amount of practice and in the minimum amount of time possible. Strategy formulation must take into account the practicalities of devising appropriate and sufficient practice opportunities while at the same time deviating as little as possible from this ideal.

The most direct route to instructional efficiency is to have students practice a criterion behavior in its *entirety*—straightaway and without help. Unfortunately, there are not many criterion behaviors for which students are able to do this. Indeed, that constitutes the raison d'etre for instruction.

Instruction must *prepare* students to be able to perform a criterion behavior (in its entirety) when required to do so. How much prior preparation and what kinds of prior practice are necessary are functions of the *learning problems* that characterize a particular criterion behavior (see the previous section on conditions). The planning of instruction revolves around: (1) an identification of those problems; (2) an assessment of their severity; and (3) a selection of the kinds and amount of practice necessary to cope with them.[*]

---

[*]Editor's note: This is an overview of an instructional-development model, as distinct from an instructional theory: Rather than indicating *what* the instruction should be like, it indicated *how* to go about making it, regardless of what it should be like.

The design of enabling learning experiences for an individual objective revolves around decisions about the use of three principal organizational components:

- the individual practice task;
- transitions between practice tasks; and
- a cumulative series of practice tasks.

Successful and efficient instruction for any criterion behavior is achieved through the systematic design and use of all three components.

Individual Practice Task

The fundamental unit in a total instructional sequence (for a given objective) is the individual practice task. In scope and complexity it can range from the practice of a total criterion behavior—a total chain—to the practice of only one component skill in that chain.

The practice task has virtually no (technical) limits obstructing its design. As is indicated in Fig. 5.3, the individual practice task can vary in: the *content* of what is practiced; the *mode* of practice; the *amount* of the criterion behavior included; and, not least, the kind and amount of *help* (cuing) provided.

A desideratum in practice task design is the prevention of learner practice of errors. The *unplanned* practice of errors can result in an increase in the strength of an incorrect behavior or of a behavior that can compete with the learning of the desired, correct behavior or in a need for remedial instruction. The help or guidance (cuing) that is provided for practice tasks is meant to prevent these possibilities. The other attributes of practice tasks—content, mode, and amount—are similarly manipulated with this end in mind.

Successful learner completion of an individual practice task contributes to an overall learning experience. The individual practice task provides an opportunity for a criterion response to be practiced in the presence of a criterion stimulus. Learner ability to recall that response—when presented with that criterion stimulus —is incrementally strengthened. The probability of that response being made in its presence on a succeeding task increases.

Successful learner completion of the individual practice task also contributes incrementally to learner ability to *transfer* a response to varied instances of a criterion stimulus. New instances of the criterion stimulus (e.g., a previously non-encountered tree or machine or classroom problem behavior to be classified) become increasingly more capable of eliciting the same response. Thus, appropriately designed individual practice tasks, which students negotiate successfully, contribute incrementally to an ability to recall and to transfer criterion skills.

Transitions Between Tasks

Because the individual practice task is typically embedded in a series of other practice tasks, the nature of the *transitions* between it and those other practice tasks can affect its difficulty level. Thus, the design of transitions between tasks is very important.

Ultimately, students have to be able to practice a criterion behavior—a practice task of maximum difficulty. A prior succession consisting solely of *easy* tasks is unlikely to provide suitable preparation for it. Only if students practice *progressively more difficult* tasks can they be expected to be ready for practice tasks of criterion difficulty levels. The character of successive practice tasks has to be deliberately varied (i.e., made progressively more difficult) so that they provide that kind of necessary preparation.

The design of transitions concentrates on student progress from relatively easy to relatively difficult practice tasks. For example, early tasks can involve only a small portion of a criterion behavior, later tasks virtually all of it. Early tasks can use easy examples, later tasks more difficult ones. Early tasks provide maximum help, later tasks minimal or no help. Early tasks can stress the concrete, later tasks the abstract. Or, early tasks can require recognizing a correct answer, later tasks producing one. It is the progression from easy to more difficult—in any of these ways—that prepares students to handle the ultimate difficulty level. At the end, students are capable of exhibiting the criterion behavior in its entirety, in a proper mode, and without help.

Transitions afford the principal means by which students can be brought—in stages—to approximate the end goal: performance of the criterion behavior.

Cumulative Series of Practice Tasks

Effective instruction for an individual objective requires the successful design of individual practice tasks, of transitions between tasks, and of a total series of tasks. The design of a total, cumulative series of practice tasks for an individual objective takes into consideration such additional parameters as: the *frequency* of practice (including the total number of practice tasks as well as the number of repetitions of the same task) and the nature and amount of *variety* that is built into practice tasks.

Control over the frequency of practice is a principal means for assuring *recall*. Control over the variety of practice is a principal means for assuring *transfer*. Together they assure student ability to meet these two postinstructional requirements.

It is the very last stage of a progression of practice tasks that a criterion behavior—in the proper mode, without help, requiring all its constituent skills, and with new examples—is practiced. All the easements that were used to prepare the learner are now abandoned.

Summary

In summary, the individual practice task, transitions between tasks, and a cumulative series of tasks constitute principal treatment components. It is the systematic and analytic design of all three on which the attainment of treatment goals depends.

MATCHING TREATMENTS AND CONDITIONS

Each objective has its own idiosyncratic skill and performance requirements. But, for all its uniqueness, an objective shares with other objectives requirements that are susceptible to a *common* treatment. Consider any objective calling for the "recall of facts." It requires the association of one set of information with another. It might require an association between the names of states and their capitals, or chemical elements and their atomic weights. These types of objectives share a common learning requirement: multiple associations. Strategies appropriate for teaching a large number of associations (e.g., repeated practice) is likely to be appropriate for teaching *any* objective with such a requirement.

Taxonomies for classifying objectives vary from instructional theory to instructional theory. Five categories often used to classify the objectives taught in school and training settings include: recalling *facts*, defining and illustrating *concepts*, giving and applying *explanations*, following *rules*, and solving *problems*. The predominant learning requirements of an objective belonging to any one of these categories typically differ from those of objectives belonging to the others. But, most importantly, an objective is likely to share *common skill requirements* with other objectives belonging to the same category. This availability of common strategies for *objectives of the same general type** can to some extent simplify the design process.

A *common*, routine *strategy* can be devised to satisfy the common mix of skill requirements that any objective shares with other objectives in the same category. For the surplus, idiosyncratic requirements that *each* objective will inevitably have (based on its specific stimulus and response properties), strategies can be devised in a less time-consuming, ad hoc way.

In behavioral instructional theories each objective is *dissected* and its component skills identified. This is done for every S–R unit in an entire chain. Treatments are made responsive to the specific skills that are discovered. Thus, even though any two objectives of the same general type may share common requirements, they are likely to *differ* from one another in the number, difficulty, content, and mode of these component skills. They are also likely to differ in the number of these skills that will depend on recall or on transfer for correct (postinstructional) performance. For example, one "rule-following" objective may consist of many steps that depend on recall and only a few that depend on transfer. For another "rule-following" objective the reverse may be true. It is to these differences that prescribed, behavioral treatments provide an *idiosyncratic* response. Thus, treatment prescription combines both a "common" and an "idiosyncratic" response to the requirements of any objective.

---

*Editor's note: Notice the similarity to Gagné's work: prescribing methods on the basis of types of objectives.

Treatment Priorities

Treatments that are selected to accommodate any type of learning requirement can be assigned to three priority groupings: treatments to be considered routinely (and first) for all types of objectives; treatments to be considered next if "easier," graduated practice is judged to be necessary; and specialized treatments to be considered when specialized learning requirements dictate them. Fig. 5.4 summarizes these groupings in the order in which it is recommended that they be considered.

These priorities are assigned on the basis of the relative *efficiencies* that these types of treatments can afford. They have little to do with instructional effectiveness. Treatments in columns 2 and 3 of Fig. 5.4 are likely to be as *effective* as those in column 1 and are, therefore, interchangeable with them. But, by definition, they require the addition of other types of practice prior to (intact) criterion practice. Therefore, the principal disadvantage of the treatments in columns 2 and 3 is that they may make instruction long and less efficient. For that reason it is desirable that they be used only when routine treatments alone cannot meet learning requirements.

Routine Treatments	Shaping Progressions	Specialized Treatments
.. cues (telling "what" and "how") .. examples or demonstrations .. rules re: performance provided . . .	.. unit size reductions .. strength of cues varied .. recognize-edit-produce sequence of tasks .. difficulty of examples varied . . .	.. concrete/abstract progressions .. distortions of stimulus or response .. practice of errors .. backward chaining .. practice stating principles . . .
Associated Practice .. practice of an intact criterion behavior	Associated Practice .. practice of easier versions of the criterion behavior followed by practice of the criterion behavior	Associated Practice .. practice of something other than the criterion behavior followed by practice of the criterion behavior

FIG. 5.4   Treatment priorities.

Routine Treatments

It is maximally efficient to have students practice *intact* criterion behaviors at the very outset if such is possible. Students may be required to do long division in its entirety, design a research study, or do close reading of a novel. To be able to carry out such tasks, students require some form of help. The routine treatments to be considered for helping students to perform such intact criterion behaviors include:

- telling students what to do and how to do it;*
- providing varied examples of an implemented performance;** and
- providing rules governing the performance.

After exposure to these treatments, students are required to practice performing an intact criterion behavior. *Frequency* of such practice assures recall; *varied practice* assures transfer.

If students were expected to define, distinguish between, and illustrate "monetary" and "fiscal" policy (definitions), instructional materials designed to help them to practice this behavior would: provide a definition of these terms; provide varied examples of them; and (optionally) provide some principles governing this task. Or, if students were expected to issue commands to make use of a computer system's utilities (rule following), instruction would: identify the commands and the utilities they call up; illustrate how to call up the utilities; and provide some general rules relevant to the use of the system.

Guided by this three-part *routine* treatment, students practice an intact criterion behavior as frequently as is necessary to acquire and recall it and with as many varied instances as is necessary to assure transfer to new instances (that will be encountered later). There is no *added*, prior practice devoted to isolated portions of the criterion behavior nor is there any subsequent practice devoted to the integration of separate portions into a whole. Thus, the practice of an entire, intact criterion behavior by itself makes for maximum instructional efficiency. For that reason, when practicable, it is a first choice in strategy selection.

Shaping Progressions

There will always be objectives whose requirements exceed what routine treatments can accommodate. Objectives that involve many steps, that require multiple or complex interim decisions, or that pose transfer problems are all likely candidates for treatments that go beyond the routine, Such objectives may require a progression of practice tasks that gradually shapes approximations to an intact criterion behavior. Available for and particularly suited for this purpose is the use of *varieties* in the following treatment tools:

---

*Editor's note: This is similar to Landa's *algorithms* (Chapter 6), Scandura's *rules* (Chapter 7), and Merrill's *generalities* (Chapter 9).

**Editor's note: These are similar to Landa's *demonstrations* (Chapter 6) and Merrill's *examples* (Chapter 9).

- cue strength;
- the size of the unit of practice;
- the mode of practice; and
- example difficulty.

The use of each of these treatment tools, either alone or in combination, requires the practice of a noncriterion behavior prior to, and in addition to, the practice of a criterion behavior. It is this nonroutine, prior practice that is used to accommodate the requirements of a "difficult" objective. Its purpose is to prepare students for eventual practice of the criterion behavior.

All four treatment tools are capable of dealing with expected student difficulty in learning component skills for any type of objective. For example, for rule-following objectives that involve many steps chained together (e.g., computing a correlation, dissassembling an airplane engine, or operating controls in a television studio), an entire procedural performance can be *broken up* into its constituent parts—with one or more of the parts practiced by itself. Detailed *job aids* (cues) can provide guidance to student practice of one or more procedural steps. *Recognition practice* can help students to distinguish between correct and incorrect versions of such components of a procedural performance as: steps, the sequence in which they are performed, or decisions about interim or final outcomes. Also, examples of problems, for which the procedures produce a solution, can be sequenced in *increasing order of difficulty*. Or, finally, two or more of these tools can be used in combination.

All four tools are similarly suitable for creating a progression of practice tasks to deal with potential learning obstacles posed by other types of objectives—for example, recalling facts, defining and illustrating concepts, giving explanations, and solving problems.

In the interest of preserving instructional *efficiency*, it is important to keep departures from routine treatments to a minimum. It is efficient to: break up a criterion behavior into *as few* units as possible; to use cues at the *minimum strength* needed to assure correct practice (and to abandon them as early as possible); to resort to recognition and editing practice *only* when production practice alone cannot succeed; and to expose students to *difficult* practice examples as quickly as possible.

The use of a shaping progression is a strategic response to the conditions that make it difficult to acquire, retain, or transfer constituent skills (see the previous section on conditions). When *difficult conditions* obtain, shaping progressions can be considered the "routine" treatment of choice.

Specialized Treatments

Other even more specialized treatments are available for dealing with likely learning difficulties. These treatments include (see Fig. 5.4 earlier):

- concrete/abstract progressions;
- distortions of stimulus or response;

- practice of errors;
- backward chaining; and
- practice stating principles.

The problem areas for which these specialized treatments are suitable are varied. When remedial instruction is judged to be necessary for dealing with competing associations, the successive practice of the new and the old, or of the right way and the wrong way, can be helpful. For long procedural chains, backward chaining can be helpful. For fine-grained stimulus discrimination or response differentiation, distortion of stimulus or response can be helpful. For objectives containing new technical or abstract terms, concrete/abstract progressions can be helpful. These more highly specialized and less frequently used treatments are worthy of consideration when specialized needs arise and when either routine treatments or shaping progressions are judged unlikely to provide sufficient help for them. They are given the lowest priority because they are likely to be more (technically) difficult to develop and less efficient to implement. However, specialized treatments are likely to be no less *effective* in meeting learning requirements than routine or shaping treatments.

Matching Objectives and Treatments

The ingredients that enter into the decisions for selecting instructional strategies were summarized earlier in Fig. 5.1. They include: characteristics of stimulus and response; component skills and conditions of performance; types of objectives; and types of treatments. All are considered in strategy formulation.

The relationships among all these strategy ingredients can be illustrated for each of the specific types of objectives that are identified in Fig. 5.1.*

Recalling Facts

Learning Requirements.   The design of routine treatments for *all* objectives that require the recall of facts must accord with the following distinctive set of learning *requirements:*

- multiple S–R *associations* must be learned; and
- facts (the multiple S–R associations) must be recalled at *delayed intervals* following completion of instruction.

It is this particular mix of requirements that distinguishes "recalling facts" from other types of objectives.

---

*Editor's note: Each of the following sections describes a different *instructional model,* which is prescribed on the basis of type of objective. Each model in turn has variations represented by the nonroutine treatments, which are prescribed on the basis of subject-matter characteristics. The complete set of models plus the basis for prescribing them (the types of objectives) comprise an *instructional theory.*

Routine Treatments.   The routine treatments appropriate to the distinctive skill and performance requirements involved in the recall of facts include:

- *telling* students what the facts are; and
- requiring students to *practice* and review either stating or applying the facts (or both).

An instructional sequence implementing these types of treatments might identify: the names of English kings and the dates associated with them; computer commands and the functions associated with them; or English words and the French-language equivalents associated with them. For their part, students would be required to practice stating or applying these facts (preferably the latter).

Stimulus–Response Characteristics.   Whether *shaping progressions* or *specialized treatments* need to be invoked for the recall of facts depends on the specific stimulus/response attributes that characterize a particular objective. The *characteristics* most likely to make recalling facts difficult and (potentially) to require treatments that go beyond the routine include:

- the *number* of S—R associations to be learned;
- *competition* from existing associations; or
- *similarity* of stimulus or response in multiple associations.

Nonroutine Treatments.   Several nonroutine treatments are suitable for coping with these potential learning obstacles.

For *large numbers of associations* (e.g., historical events and their dates, names of chemical elements and their atomic weights, pairs of numbers and their products, two treatment types (beyond extra practice or review) recommend themselves. *Cues* that call greater attention to (highlight) the associations can be used. For example, listings or tables that isolate pairings and make them more salient can more readily control learner attention—directing it to the associations to be learned. Or, the practice of associations in *applied or meaningful contexts* (e.g., using atomic weights in computations) can create opportunities for additional criterion stimuli to acquire control over the responses to be made. It is likely to be easier for a correct association to be formed if more than one stimulus or if more than one attribute of a stimulus is capable of gaining control over required responses.

For *competing associations* (e.g., one English-language–foreign-language association has already been learned and another has to be learned; or incorrect noun–verb agreement has already been learned and correct agreement has to be learned; etc.), three treatment types suggest themselves: recognition practice, practice of errors, and extra cuing. *Recognition practice* (pairing the old and the new as options and requiring students to *select* the desired alternative) allows students to practice discriminating between the options. The successive practice of correct and incorrect (*practicing errors* in a production mode) is capable of performing a similar function. Additionally, extra *cues* (e.g., verbal instructions) can be used to call attention to the old and new or to the correct and incorrect and to what it is that distinguishes them.

For stimulus or response *similarity* (e.g., multiple alphanumeric acronyms, only marginally different from one another, have to be associated with names of computer commands or with file specifications; or Chinese ideographs and the words they signify have to be associated, etc.), the following treatment types suggest themselves: *Tables* can be created with the information that needs to be discriminated (similar stimuli) located in physically adjacent areas—thus calling attention to the relevant differences. Or, attention can be drawn to specific differences in stimuli that only appear similar through explicit, verbal *instructions*.

Any specific objective calling for the "recall of facts," even though it shares common requirements with other objectives of the same type, has its own *specific requirements* that only a task analysis can reveal. It is to meet these idiosyncratic requirements that the varied, nonroutine treatments, at whatever priority level, are used.*

Defining Concepts

Objectives often call for students to state a definition of a concept, to identify a relevant instance of it, or to supply their own instances, or to do all of the preceding. For example, students may be required to define "phoneme," "romanticism," or "buoyant force" and either identify or produce an instance of these concepts.

Learning Requirements.   The design of routine treatments for *all* such objectives must accord with the following set of distinctive learning *requirements:*

- instances of a concept have to be *discriminated* from noninstances (i.e., from instances of other concepts);
- all encountered instances of the concept have to be identified as such *(generalization);*
- a definition of the concept has to be learned (a verbal *chain*);
- these skills have to be recalled at *delayed intervals* following instruction; and
- these skills have to be *transferred* to instances (of that concept) that are *not* encountered during instruction.

Routine Treatments.   The routine treatments appropriate to this distinctive mix of requirements include:

- providing a definition of the concept;
- providing *examples* and *nonexamples* of the concept;
- (optional) providing a list of defining attributes or *principles* governing the inclusion and noninclusion of instances; and

---

*Editor's note: This model has some notable similarities with the Gagné–Briggs model for *verbal-information* objectives.

- *practice* requiring students to state the definition of the concept and either to identify or produce instances of it.

An instructional sequence for the concept "fiscal policy" might provide: a definition of it, examples of it, contrasting examples of "monetary policy," and some guidelines or principles for distinguishing between the two concepts.

Stimulus–Response Characteristics.   The need for treatments that go beyond the routine depends on how many and which of the following subject-matter *characteristics* apply to a particular objective.

- a high degree of *similarity* between instances of a concept and noninstances of it;
- a high degree of *dissimilarity* among instances of the same concept;
- a *large number* of stimulus properties forming the basis for discrimination or for generalization;
- a *large number* of classes (concepts) to be discriminated; and
- a large class (concept) *size* (it contains many instances).

Nonroutine Treatments.   Nonroutine treatments suitable for facilitating the learning of stimulus discrimination and generalization, and transfer as well, include: the use of special *cues* such as diagrams or information maps that distinguish between instance and noninstance or that call attention to properties that instances possess; *recognition* practice that pairs instances and noninstances of different concepts, or the subvarieties of instances of the same concept; presenting examples in a sequence of *graduated difficulty;* presenting *widely differing* examples and the gradual narrowing of differences among them; and the learning of *principles* governing the grounds for class inclusion and noninclusion. For example, students can be shown instances and noninstances of a phoneme and be required to select the correct option; or instances can be ordered by level of difficulty with practice starting with easy instances, and so on.

The mix of skill and performance requirements for "definition of concepts" differs markedly from that for "recall of facts." There are other types of objectives whose mix of requirements is less markedly different.

Giving Explanations

Objectives often call for students to provide explanations for particular phenomena. In addition, they may call for students to identify instances of the phenomena to which the explanations are relevant. Or, they may call for students to supply their own instances. Students may be required: to explain how reinforcement, punishment, and extinction affect the acquisition of behavior and its maintenance; to identify which of these three types of consequences are at play for given instances of behavior change or nonchange; or to supply their own instances.

"Defining concepts" and "giving explanations" have similar outcomes and learning requirements. But, whereas the former deals in a single concept (sometimes to be discriminated from other related concepts), the latter generally deals in the *relationships* among two or more concepts. Explanations thus have to do with "principles" that describe these relationships. They describe the logical, temporal, or causal relationships that exist among concepts. It is these relationships that "explain" phenomena.

The discussion of treatments for "defining concepts" is applicable to "giving explanations." The latter phrase may be substituted for the former in that discussion. The same skill and performance *requirements* apply. The recommended *routine* and *nonroutine* treatments are also applicable. And, objectives involving explanations can be examined for the same kinds of stimulus/response properties.

Although the learning requirements for these two types of objectives are similar, those for "giving explanations" can quite naturally be expected to pose the greater problem. *Additional treatments* can be recommended for dealing with the learning problems that may arise. *Specialized cues* can be designed to assist students to chain verbal statements that correctly relate multiple concepts. For example, *flow charts* can be used to represent abstract relationships in concrete, visual terms. Other *concrete/abstract progressions* can be helpful in making complex relationships more readily understandable. For example, a *demonstration* of the apparent reduction in the weight of a submerged object (attached to a hanging scale) may be more helpful in explaining Archimedes' principle than a solely verbal discussion of it. Or, *practice in using* reinforcement and extinction techniques in an actual classroom and observing the changes in behavior that they bring about may be helpful in making *principles* of "contingency management" more readily understandable to student teachers.

Following Procedural Rules

Objectives often call for students to perform tasks according to well-defined rules or algorithms. Students may be required to: multiply two numbers, bisect an angle, balance a chemical equation, operate a movie projector, capitalize proper nouns, play from a piano score, and so on.

Learning Requirements. The design of treatments for all such procedural objectives must accord with the following distinctive *requirements:*

- tasks to be performed by one set of procedures have to be *discriminated* from tasks that are performed by other sets of procedures;
- subvarieties of tasks, all of which are to be performed by the same set of procedures, have to be identified as being similar *(generalization);*
- discriminations and generalizations for the *outcomes* of one interim step have to be mastered so that the appropriate next interim step can be adopted;
- a series of steps (S–R associations) must be *chained* into a complete performance;
- discriminations and generalizations for acceptable/unacceptable final outcomes have to be mastered; and
- postinstructional *recall* and *transfer* requirements have to be met.

Although all these requirements apply to any "rule-following" objective, the relative importance of the individual requirements may vary from one "rule-following" objective to another.

Routine Treatments. The routine treatments appropriate to this general but distinctive mix of "rule-following" requirements include:

- identifying the *steps* to be followed;
- *demonstrating* or illustrating their implementation;
- providing *rules* to be observed in performing the steps;
- repeated learner *practice* of the steps; and
- repeated learner practice with *varied examples* of the tasks requiring these procedural steps.

Thus, an instructional sequence (using routine treatments) for teaching the threading of a film projector might: list the steps to be followed; demonstrate their implementation; and provide some rules about threading the film. For their part students would be required to practice threading a projector.

Stimulus–Response Characteristics. The need for treatments beyond the routine for a rule-following objective depends on *which* skill or performance requirements are relatively more important. It also depends on which particular requirements are difficult and which are not. This in turn depends on which and how many of the following stimulus or response *characteristics* apply to a particular objective:

- tasks requiring alternative algorithms are similar and therefore difficult to discriminate;
- interim and/or final outcomes are similar and therefore difficult to discriminate;
- subvarieties of tasks or of outcomes are dissimilar, making generalization and transfer difficult;
- the number of properties of stimuli (tasks or outcomes), the number of classes of stimuli, or the number of members per class is large, making discriminations and/or generalizations difficult;
- responses to be differentiated are similar and therefore difficult to tell apart;
- responses requiring generalization are (apparently) dissimilar, making identification of their essential similarity difficult; and
- chains are long.

Nonroutine Treatments. Nonroutine treatments that can be used to deal with these complications (when they apply) include: the use of job aids or checklists (*cues*) to overcome difficulties traceable to the length of a chain; the listing of *criteria* to facilitate discriminations or generalizations about tasks, interim outcomes, or final outcomes; the *breaking up* of a long or difficult chain into smaller units and requiring the practice of individual units; the use of a *recognize–edit–produce*

(REP) progression for discrimination and generalization problems or for chaining problems; *backward chaining* for long chains; the practice of errors for error-prone activities; or *exaggerated differences* for response differentiation or generalization problems.

In the interest of efficiency, only one or two of these shaping and specialized treatments are likely to be selected as a complement to the routine treatments that are adopted for a rule-following objective.

Solving Problems

Objectives can also call upon students to perform tasks according to rules that are relatively unstructured or according to rules that they themselves must invent. Students may be required: to write a computer program for dealing with an application problem; to design an experiment; to diagnose equipment malfunctions; to analyze and interpret music or literature; to develop an instructional model, and so on. Clearly, for such activities there are no *complete* sets of fixed rules that can be put to work.*

Because of the absence of fixed algorithms for carrying out necessary steps, "solving problems" is a more complex version of "rule following." *Task identification* (determining what the problem is) will clearly be more difficult. Identifying $4 + 3 = ?, 4 - 3 = ?, 4 \times 3 = ?,$ or $4 \div 3 = ?$ as a request to add, subtract, multiply, or divide is not apt to pose much difficulty for students. In contrast, being required to create remedies for degenerative diseases brought on by aging, to propose strategies for teaching children to read, or to recommend solutions for inflation do pose more complex problems. The nature of the task (the problem) to be performed must first be identified. In addition, procedures must be selected for coping with that task or new ones must be invented.

Even though "solving problems" is more complex than "rule following," the treatments applicable to the latter are also applicable to the former. Their focus can shift to the specific leaning requirements that typify "problem solving" (for example, task identification). Both the routine and nonroutine treatments recommended for "rule following" can be adapted to deal with the mix of skill and performance requirements that characterize "solving problems." That mix would focus on those particular requirements that characterize "problem solving" and that distinguish it from "rule following."

Summary

Some *version* of the same routine treatments is applicable to any type of objective. Whether an objective calls for recalling facts, defining and illustrating concepts, giving and applying explanations, following procedural rules, or solving prob-

---

*Editor's note: This is somewhat similar to Landa's distinction between *heuristics* and *algorithms* (see Chapter 6).

lems, three basic treatment types apply: *telling* students what to do and how to do it; providing *examples* of that performance; and providing some guiding *principles*. Practice always follows.

Because types of objectives differ in their requirements, the particular version (of the routine treatments) that is implemented will reflect those differences. However, the version selected for any specific objective will be applicable to any other objective of the same general type. A "common" *routine treatment* can be given first consideration when analyzing the needs of an objective of that type.

In selecting *nonroutine treatments,* special consideration is given to those particular skill requirements that predominate and therefore typify a given objective. Further, both stimulus and response properties need to be examined in order to determine whether (and which) nonroutine treatments will be necessary for it.

A *selection* from the mix of nonroutine treatments appropriate to a type of objective and responsive to the special problems that tend to characterize all objectives of that type makes for a less cumbersome and less inefficient design process. However, each objective has its own idiosyncratic requirements that have to be met. Strategy formulation therefore revolves around the selection of both "common" and "idiosyncratic" treatments (at whatever priority level) to meet both the "common" and "idiosyncratic" requirements of a given objective.

MULTIPLE OBJECTIVES

A behavioral orientation has a good deal to say about how practice tasks for an *individual* objective should be sequenced. When judged to be necessary, practice tasks are sequenced as a "preparatory progression" so that approximations to a criterion behavior can be shaped. The rationale and the techniques for accomplishing this derive from the operant tradition. The nonroutine treatments described earlier build and elaborate on techniques used in that tradition.

The routine and nonroutine treatments described earlier are limited to the specification of the what, when, and how of practice for an individual objective. A behavioral orientation has no comparable, distinctive, or proprietary prescriptions for the order in which *multiple* objectives should be practiced relative to one another.* Rational, but atheoretic, considerations, must fill this void.

The *order* in which multiple objectives are practiced may have facilitative, neutral, or potentially interfering effects on student ability to learn them. For that reason it is important to make analytic and systematic decisions about that order. To make sure that the effects produced are facilitative, a progression of practice tasks, comparable in intent if not in execution to that for an individual objective, needs to be designed. If learning objective A can facilitate the learning of objective B, these two objectives should be learned in that order. What are the conditions (the charac-

---

*Editor's note: This is referring to *macro strategies* as defined in Chapter 1.

teristics of objectives) on which decisions about such a *contingent* progression can be based?

Relationships Among Objectives

The relationships among multiple objectives (described in the following paragraphs) bear on decisions that are made about the order in which they should be taught. These relationships are revealed not through behavioral analysis but through the conduct of a *task description*. Behavioral analysis reveals the *component skills* that make up an individual objective. Task description reveals three principle *performance relationships* that two or more objectives can have to one another: vertical, horizontal, or no relationship.

Vertical Relationships

A task description identifies hierarchies of objectives. It identifies the objectives that are prerequisites for other objectives. Performance of objective *A* is contingent on an *ability* to perform subordinate (prerequisites) objective *B*.* For example, the student who cannot multiply (a subordinate objective *B*), cannot be expected to do division (a superordinate objective *A*). It is such superordinate–subordinate *ability contingencies* that task description reveals and, when graphically represented, are shown as *vertical* relationships.

Some behaviors are clearly prerequisites for others. Primary-grade students cannot be expected to do long division without being able to add, subtract, and multiply. Nor can they read for meaning without being able to decode letters. Adults cannot disassemble a motor without being able to use the tools needed to do that task. It is the job of a task description to identify such contingent "performance" relationships.

Horizontal Relationships

A *horizontal* performance relationship identifies a coordinate status among objectives. It identifies which of two objectives is performed *temporally* prior to the other. The output of a temporally prior objective becomes the input or starting point for that other objective. For example, in long division, a single digit in the quotient multiplied times the divisor produces a product (an output). It is this product that becomes the subtrahend of the next "subtraction" step. In performances of this kind, one objective cannot *begin* until another has been completed. Unlike the vertical relationship, this type represents a temporal, not an "ability," contingency. Task descriptions showing such temporal contingencies are typically displayed— in graphic representations (e.g., flow charts)—horizontally.

---

*Editor's note: This is identical to Gagné's *learning prerequisites*.

No Relationship

Finally, an objective may bear neither a prerequisite nor a coordinate relationship to any other objective. It is the job of task description to reveal the absence of any relationship among objectives as much as it is its job to reveal vertical and horizontal ones.

Role of Task Description

A major purpose in performing a task description is to obtain a comprehensive, hierarchical portrait of superordinate and subordinate behaviors. The resulting hierarchy is inspected and judgments are made about that point in the hierarchy below which all subordinate behaviors are assumed to be in the repertoire of a target audience and above which all superordinate behaviors are not in that repertoire. It is these superordinate behaviors that need to be taught.* The hierarchy is also used as a basis for deciding the order in which separate behaviors, some of them prerequisites for others, will be taught.**

Task description also reveals that some behaviors do not bear such a hierarchical relationship to one another. Some must be completed before others can begin. The relationship is a temporal one. The output of one becomes the input to the other. Repair cannot begin until diagnosis has been completed. Similarly, the statistical significance of the difference between means cannot be assessed until the difference has been computed. Or, the editing of prose cannot begin until a draft has been written. It is also the job of a task description to identify this second type of contingent relationship.

A major purpose or a horizontal representation of these temporal performance relationships is to identify coordinate relationships comprehensively. They too enter into sequencing decisions (as explained later).

Performance versus Learning Contingencies

The vertical and horizontal relationships describe "performance" contingencies. In the one case, an expert cannot perform Y unless he or she is also *able* to perform X. In the other, the expert cannot perform Y unless he or she has *completed* performing X. A *learning contingency*, the order in which a learner must practice X and Y, need not inevitably parallel these performance contingencies. For example, even though X, in performance, must be completed before Y, under some circum-

---

*Editor's note: This is a *selection strategy* as defined in Chapter 1, and it is identical to the Gagné-Briggs selection strategy (Chapter 4, p. 89).

**Editor's note: This is a *sequencing strategy* as defined in Chapter 1, and it is also identical to the Gagné-Briggs sequencing strategy (Chapter 4, p. 89).

stances it may be effective to schedule the learning of Y first. Or, even though being able to perform X depends on an ability to perform Y, there may be occasions when learning the two *together* may be effective.

There is good reason to expect that most vertical performance contingencies will require a particular learning order. If the ability to perform Y is contingent on the ability to perform X, it is reasonable to expect that in most learning situations X should be learned first. At the least, they should be learned together. This is an instance of a learning contingency's paralleling a vertical performance contingency.

A horizontal performance contingency does not require a particular learning order. Even though one is temporally contingent on the other—in performance—a reverse learning order may be facilitative. It may be facilitative to learn repair before diagnosis, play before bidding in bridge, editing before writing, or interpreting research results before designing research. The two explanatory accounts for the merits of *backward chaining* that were cited earlier (i.e., feedback and modeling) are pertinent to an explanation of the potentially facilitative effect of this counter-to-performance ordering of the learning of multiple objectives.

Sequencing Decisions

Two types of contingent *performance* relationships have been identified. In one, a given objective is a prerequisite for another. In the second, a given objective bears a coordinate input–output relationship to another objective. Two additional relationships are relevant to sequencing decisions.

Objectives can bear *no relationships* to one another. For example, the concepts "balanced force" and "unbalanced force" may be analyzed for two subordinate concepts: "strength of a force" and "direction of a force." These latter subordinate concepts bear no relationship to one another. It is possible to understand one without the other. (The order in which they are learned would seem to make little difference.)

A final relationship can be identified, that of *shared elements*. Two or more objectives may share the same subordinate objective. For example, the component skills (discriminations, generalizations, associations, and chains) are subordinate skills for all five types of objectives—recalling facts, defining concepts, giving explanations, following rules, and solving problems. Because all five share the component skills as prerequisites, efficiency is served if instructional-design students learn about these "skills" first.

Sequence prescriptions for multiple objectives may be summarized as follows:

- If X is a prerequisite for Y, X should be taught first. However, it may be possible to schedule them together.
- When subordinate objectives are shared by more than one superordinate objective, all the *shared elements* should be scheduled first (in the interest of efficiency).
- *Coordinate* objectives that bear an input–output relationship to one another in performance can be scheduled in either order.

- Objectives that bear *no relationship* to one another may be scheduled in any order.

Performance relationships among objectives are identified by the use of task-description techniques. The prescriptions for the order in which they should be learned are not "behaviorally" derived. They could easily be prescriptions arrived at by adherents of any other orientation. They are based on rational but atheoretic considerations.

SUMMARY

At the heart of a *behavioral* instructional model is a requirement that students practice a designated response in the presence of the criterion stimulus that must control it. Because students must be able to identify which stimulus constitutes the appropriate occasion for that response, they must be given an opportunity to practice discriminating between what is and what is not the relevant criterion stimulus and to practice generalizing to other appropriate instances of it. They must also be given the opportunity to practice associating the criterion stimulus and the criterion response. Finally, to learn a *total* performance, they must also be given the opportunity to practice chaining the total series of stimulus–response associations that make up that performance.

The four constituent skills (discrimination, generalization, association, and chaining) are building blocks for *all* types of objectives that are taught in both school and training settings. One frequently used taxonomy categorizes these objectives as: recalling facts, giving and illustrating definitions, giving and applying explanations, following rules, and solving problems. These varied types of objectives differ from one another in the distinctive mix of skill elements that characterize them. But, all objectives falling *within* any one of these categories are made up of the same general mix of skill elements. Each specific objective within that category is also characterized by an idiosyncratic surplus. Instruction must address both these common and idiosyncratic requirements.

Instruction must anticipate how easy or how difficult it will be to learn the constituent skills and to meet the performance requirements (recall and transfer) of a particular objective. Difficulty in learning that objective can be expected to be largely a function of *its* specific *stimulus and response characteristics*. The characteristics potentially applicable to an objective include: similarity/dissimilarity; number of stimulus and response properties; number of classes and number of members per class; number of associations; competing S–R associations; and the length of a chain. It is how many and which of these characteristics that apply to the particular objective that determine its idiosyncratic requirements and how difficult it will be for students to learn it.

In a behavioral approach to the design of instruction, each objective is analyzed for the presence or absence of these *stimulus and response characteristics*. The results indicate whether there will be obstacles to learning the component skills of that objective. The *performance requirements* of recall and transfer for that objective are also analyzed. Thus, in a behavioral approach it is not enough merely to categorize an objective as "recalling facts" or "giving definitions" or "following rules," and so on. It is also necessary to identify its constituent skills and its stimulus–response properties that can determine how difficult it will be to learn those skills. *Treatments* are selected based on their suitability for teaching these skills and for dealing with these stimulus–response properties that will make learning them difficult.

Treatments must accord an individual objective both the types and amounts of attention it requires. They can do so by delivering routine, shaping, or specialized attention. For any type of individual objective it is strategic, first of all, to consider providing *routine* attention. Telling students what to do and how to do it, illustrating that performance, and, as needed, providing principles governing the performance together deliver that kind of attention.

When learning obstacles are anticipated, *shaping* routines can bring students up to criterion levels of performance gradually. Relying on a series of graduated approximations to the criterion behavior represents an adaptive way of dealing with those obstacles. Shaping routines can rely on one or more of the following techniques: breaking a performance up into parts and requiring students to practice the performance part by part; providing cues that offer varying degrees of help—with students practicing first with the aid of strong cues and then with gradually weaker ones; scheduling practice in alternative, noncriterion modes with students first practicing in easier modes and only at the end in a criterion mode; providing examples varying in difficulty and requiring students to practice first with easy examples and then with progressively more difficult ones.

For specialized learning problems, *specialized* types of attention can be considered. For remedial training it might be the paired practice of the right and wrong way to do something; for performance involving long chains it might be backward chaining; for difficult discriminations it might be recognition practice or practice with distorted stimuli; or for difficult transfer problems it might be the practice of principles.

In the interest of efficiency, reliance on the routine is given first priority. The nonroutine, because it increases the duration of instruction, is invoked only for adequate cause.

Integral to all these treatment types is practice and feedback to assure acquisition, repetition to assure retention, and varied practice to assure transfer to new situations.

These *behavioral* considerations apply to teaching of an individual objective. For the teaching of multiple objectives, it is necessary to turn to rational, atheoretic considerations. Here, it is task-description results that reveal relevant "performance" relationships among multiple objectives.

Some objectives are "prerequisites" for others. Students cannot be expected to perform one without being able to perform the other. Prerequisite objectives must be taught before, or, minimally, at the same time as, the objectives that are dependent on them. By way of contrast, some objectives share a *coordinate* status with other objectives. They must be completed before the others can begin. Thus, although in performance they occur temporally before the others, in instruction either may occur first. Still other objectives bear no relationship to one another. They, too, may be learned in either order.

Practice is central to behaviorally derived prescriptions. It is central to prescriptions for teaching both a single objective and multiple objectives. To make the learning of either effective and efficient, practice tasks are sequenced as enabling progressions.

REFERENCES

Gagné, R. M. *The conditions of learning* (2nd ed.). New York: Holt, Rinehart, & Winston, 1970.

Gilbert, T. F. Mathetics: The technology of education. *Journal of Mathetics,* 1962,7–73.

Gropper, G. L. *A technology for developing instructional materials.* Pittsburgh: American Institutes for Research, 1973.

Gropper, G. L. *Instructional strategies.* Englewood Cliffs, N.J.: Educational Technology Publications, 1974.

Gropper, G. L. *Diagnosis and revision in the development of instructional materials.* Englewood Cliffs, N.J.: Educational Technology Publications, 1975.

Mechner, F. Behavioral analysis and instructional sequencing. In P.C. Lange (Ed.), *Programmed Instruction.* Chicago: NSSE, 1967.

Skinner, B. F. *Science and human behavior.* New York: Macmillan, 1953.

Skinner, B. F. Science of learning and the art of teaching. *Harvard Educational Review*, 1954, *24*, 86–97.

6 The Algo-Heuristic Theory Of Instruction

Lev N. Landa
The Institute for Advanced Algo-Heuristic Studies, New York

Lev N. Landa

Lev N. Landa was a resident of the USSR until 1976. He received a doctoral degree in psychology from the Institute of General and Educational psychology, Moscow, a postdoctoral degree in educational psychology from the University of Leningrad, and a life-long title of Professor granted to him by the Ministry of Higher Education of the USSR. From 1963 to 1976 he was Professor and Director of a department at the Institute of General and Educational Psychology in Moscow. Concurrently, beginning in 1972, he was a Professor at the Institute of Advanced Training of University and Pedagogical College Teachers at the USSR Academy of Pedagogical Sciences, Moscow. From 1976–1979 he was Visiting Professor at universities in Europe and the USA. Presently he is Director of The Institute for Advanced Algo-Heuristic Studies, New York, and President of the New York based

Landamatic Systems Corporation. More than one-third of his more than 100 published books and articles have been translated into 15 languages.

Dr. Landa has developed the algorithmico-heuristic (algo-heuristic) theory and method of performance, learning and instruction that has been labeled "Landamatics" in the USA. This theory deals with componential and systemic analysis of knowledge and cognitive operations involved in the acquisition and application of knowledge and the formation of cognitive and psycho-motor skills and abilities.

Algo-heuristically-based courses have been developed for many disciplines. Landamatics is being applied in academia, industry, business, government, and the military and, wherever used, has permitted a significant increase in the efficiency of performance, learning, and instruction.

CONTENTS

What Is The Algo-Heuristic Theory Of Instruction About?   166
  Basic concepts   166
  Relationships Between Learning, Performance, And Instruction   170
Building And Testing Models Of Unobservable Cognitive Processes   172
    Breaking Down Complex Cognitive Processes Into More
    Elementary Operations   172
  Systems Of Operations And Their Models   176
  Verification   177
Algo-Heuristic Prescriptions As A Means Of Increasing
    The Efficiency Of Instruction   178
Some Shortcomings Of Conventional Instruction   180
Students Are Not Taught Processes   180
Students are Taught Uncertain, Vague Prescriptions   182
Additional Definitions   186
Some Methods Of The Management And Development Of
    Algo-Heuristic Processes   190
  1. Process-Oriented Vs. Prescription-Oriented Instruction   190
  2. Teaching Processes Through Prescriptions Vs.
    Demonstrations   191
  3. Teaching Ready-Made Algo-Heuristic Procedures Vs.
    Getting Students To Discover Them On Their Own   194
  4. Teaching Algo-Heuristic Procedures As A Whole Vs.
    Teaching Them In A Step-By-Step Manner   195
  5. Teaching General Vs. Particular Algo-Heuristic Procedures   203
An Integrated Model Of Instruction   204
Concluding Remarks And Summary   207

FOREWORD

In contrast to Chapter 4 and Chapter 5, which describe instructional theories deriving primarily from a behavioral orientation, this chapter describes an instructional theory from a cognitive orientation. Although the cognitively oriented instructional models of Bruner and Ausubel predate it, Landa's algo-heuristic theory of instruction (increasingly referred as to "Landamatics") is the oldest of the cognitively oriented instructional theories and models described in this book.

In spite of its cognitive orientation, Landa's theory is highly compatible with behaviorally oriented theories. The latter focus more on observable procedures (i.e., overt behaviors), whereas Landa's focuses more on unobservable procedures (i.e., cognitive processes). Nevertheless, the essential similarities among procedures, whether or not they are observable, require essentially similar methods of instruction. In fact, Landa prescribes his methods for "motor operations," just as Gropper does the reverse (e.g., in his prescriptions for teaching problem-solving skills). In addition, great similarities exist between Landa's theory and each of the two cognitively oriented theories that follow in Chapter 7 and Chapter 8.

Landa's theory tends to emphasize the macro strategies of selection and sequencing of the instructional content. With respect to *selection*, the most important feature of this theory calls for breaking down complex, unobservable cognitive operations that can be unambiguously (or less ambiguously) communicated to learners. It is the resulting "elementary" cognitive operations that are then selected as the instructional content. With respect to sequencing, perhaps the most important feature of Landa's theory is what he calls the *snowball method* for teaching a chain of cognitive operations (which make up the complete cognitive process). This method entails the following sequence: (1) the first elementary operation in the chain is taught and practiced alone; (2) then the second elementary operation is taught alone, practiced alone and then is practiced together with the first; (3) then the third is taught alone, practiced alone and then practiced together with the first two: and so on, until all elementary operations have been taught separately but practiced together.

One of the most interesting features of Landa's theory is his treatment of the expository-discovery controversy.[1] Landa indicates that these are not two different approaches for achieving the same goals—rather they are approaches for achieving different goals. Landa provides prescriptions as to which approach should be used when.

---

[1] See also the Foreword to Chapter 8, p. 249.

This analysis represents an important contribution to the discipline by resolving a major source of conflict among instructional theorists and thereby bringing us closer to a truly integrative, common knowledge base in instructional design.

Another point of interest is Landa's identification of two kinds of "general algorithms" (which represent generic skills similar to Gagnés *cognitive strategies* and Scandura's *higher-order rules*). One kind comprises those algorithms that help a student to *discover* other algorithms (see Chapter 8 for more about discovery). The other kind comprises those that are "more general" and hence serve to teach more efficiently the content and skills that need to be taught (see Chapter 7 for more about such "higher-order rules").

Like the two theories that have been described so far. Landa's theory describes several major kinds of "objectives" that require different methods of instruction. However, Landa does not really describe more than one model. As with other theorists, Landa acknowledges that there are important areas in which more research, model building, and theory construction are needed.

C. M. R.

The Algo-Heuristic Theory of Instruction

WHAT IS THE ALGO-HEURISTIC THEORY OF INSTRUCTION ABOUT?[2]

Basic Concepts

As is well known, instruction may have different objectives: to equip students with knowledge about certain phenomena, to develop the skills to handle these phenomena, and to form students' abilities, motives, and even personality traits (like persistence, industriousness, self-discipline, self-regulation and control, and some others).

The instructional process may pursue multiple objectives but it may be directed, at certain stages, at attaining some limited ones, such as providing students with knowledge about certain phenomena or developing their particular skills. The *outcomes* of instructional activities are specific psychological phenomena (knowledge, skills, abilities, etc.) that interact with each other in a certain manner in the process of their formation and that are interconnected after having been formed.

---

[2]This chapter represents a brief discussion of some aspects of the algo-heuristic theory of performance, learning, and instruction that the author began to develop in 1952 while a resident of the USSR.

For example, one can develop in a student a knowledge about some chemical processes, but this knowledge does not automatically generate a skill to deal with these processes. *Skills* draw upon certain knowledge, having the latter as their prerequisites, but the knowledge does not amount to the skills.* Each skill is an ability *to apply* knowledge and manifests itself in special *actions* on knowledge and/or its objects. Knowledge is a necessary but not sufficient condition for the development of a skill. To develop a skill, one has to teach a different psychological thing, specifically *operations* on objects, on their images, and on concepts, in addition to teaching images and concepts themselves. These specific instructional objectives require specific instructional methods.

Kinds of Knowledge

We have mentioned knowledge and operations as two psychological phenomena with which the algo-heuristic approach to instruction deals. Without trying to give definitions of these two concepts (which is difficult because they are basic categorical concepts), let us give an idea of them by examples. Take an object—for example, an isosceles triangle. While cognizing it, we reflect it in our mind. This reflection is knowledge. The knowledge emerges in three forms. When we watch the triangle we have a *perceptive image* of it. When we close our eyes we have a *mental image* of it in our heads.

But a person who may have a mental image of an isosceles triangle and may be able to draw it on paper may not be aware of its characteristic features and may not be able to answer the question, "What is an isosceles triangle?" by describing its characteristic features. This means that he or she has an image of it but does not have its concept. A *concept* is a form of knowledge that represents an object as a set of its characteristic features (that is, the object can be described by a person through these characteristic features).

A person, however, may know not only characteristic features of an object but also its relationships with other objects, its constituent elements, their relationships, and so on. This knowledge presents itself in the form of *propositions* about the object. Definitions, axioms, postulates, theorems, laws, and rules are all examples of propositions.

All concepts may express themselves in the form of propositions, but concepts and propositions are different things. For example, one may have a correct concept of an object but may not be able to give a correct definition of it. To list characteristic features of an object and to construct a correct defintion of this object are different abilities displaying different psychological forms of knowledge. Thus, we can give the following classification of the major forms of knowledge:

---

*Editor's note: This distinction between knowledge and skills is similar to Gagnés, distinction between *verbal information* and *intellectual skills* (see Chapter 4) and to Merrill's distinction between the *remember level* and the *use level* (see Chapter 9).

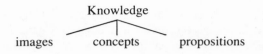

Kinds of Operations

In contrast to knowledge, *operations* are *transformations* (or changes) of either real material objects or their mental reflections (images, concepts, propositions). For example, we can physically turn around a material isosceles triangle composed of matches; we can also physically change its shape, size, and other characteristics. Operations that transform material objects are called *motor* (or material) *operations.* But transformations we perform on real material objects can be performed on their mental images as well. We can turn around an image of an isosceles triangle in our minds in a way similar to that by which we turn around a real material triangle. We can also change the form of the image, its size, and so on. These transformations are real transformations, but of images of material objects rather than of objects themselves. They are called *cognitive* (or mental) *operations.*

We can transform (or change) not only images but concepts as well. For example, we can add, subtract, or replace the indicative features of an object that we hold in our minds in the form of a concept. This transforms (or changes) the *concept.* And, of course, we can transform definitions, theorems, laws, rules, and so on. This is transformation of *propositions.* But both motor and cognitive operations are real transformations that change their objects, their attributes, their elements, or their relationships.[3]

The classification of operations may be presented as follows:

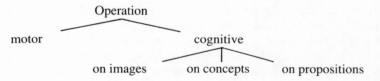

Kinds of Knowledge Revisited

Earlier we spoke about three forms of knowledge (images, concepts, and propositions), but we did not classify knowledge in terms of differences in their objects. Among all possible distinctions, of importance for us are the division of knowledge into knowledge about *objects* of different kinds (things, their attributes, their relationships, etc.) and knowledge about *operations* on objects (motor or cognitive). In this respect, knowledge can be classified like this:

---

[3]Transformation is understood here in a broad sense. In this sense a mental separation of an attribute of an object is also a transformational operation, because originally the attribute was reflected as an aspect (side) of the object but then was *torn out* of this initial connection and appeared as a separate cognitive object. The relationship between the object and its attribute was cognitively (in the mind) changed.

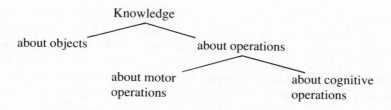

The significance of these distinctions becomes clear from a simple example. We may have knowledge about an automobile engine and its controls but we may not *know what to do* in order to start a car. Having a knowledge about an *object* does not automatically mean that we have a knowledge of *operations* to be performed on the object in order to achieve some goal.

On the other hand, we may *know what to do* in order to achieve a certain goal or to perform some activity but we may *not be able* to perform the operations. For example, we may know what to do in order to swim (i.e., know all the operations to be performed to swim), but still not be able to swim.

There may also be the opposite situation. A person may have a mastery of motor and/or cognitive operations (may successfully execute them while solving certain problems or performing some activities), but be *unaware* of what he or she is doing when performing the activity. He or she has a mastery of operations but not a knowledge of them. A simple example is an athlete or musician who may perfectly perform without being aware of the movements, or at least most of the movements, that are executed while performing; he or she is also unable to give an account of them. This situation often occurs on the mental level. An expert in an area may find a solution to a difficult problem through performance of many operations but may not be able to explain how he or she arrived at the solution: He or she is unaware of the operations performed while looking for a solution.

Processes

From the preceding discussion, we know what knowledge is and what an operation is. Human beings' activities, however, rarely consist of performing a single operation. Usually, it is a set or a system of operations organized in some structure. A functioning system of operations (whether motor or cognitive) is called a *process*. Designation of operations by words constitute a *description* of a process. Another important concept is that of a *prescription*. When we tell a person what he or she should do in order to accomplish some task or to solve some problem, we give him or her a set of *directions:* Do this, then do this, and so on. Such a system of directions is a *prescription*.

Very often, when the directions of which a prescription consists are general enough and may be used for solving different specific problems, a prescription is called a *method*. The degree of generality of methods may be different.

In the following discussion, we use the terms *process* and *precription* in the sense we have just defined. The term *method* is used for designation of both general *systems of operations* (processes) and general *systems of instructions* (prescriptions) in accordance with the two meanings in which the word *method* is used in everyday life and science. Indeed, when one says that "Mr. N. *solved* a problem by a simple method," a system of *operations* is meant. On the other hand, when one says that "Mr. N. *formulated* a method for solving problems of a certain type," it is clear that a system of *statements* (instructions, directions) is meant. Thus in many cases the context unambiguously suggests the meaning in which the word *method* is used.

The question may arise as to why we need the term *method* at all if we have the unambiguous terms *process* and *prescription*. The term *method* conveys the idea of generality of a process or a prescription. There are systems of operations and their corresponding prescriptions that provide for a solution to individual and specific problems only. Such systems of operations (processes) and systems of instructions (prescriptions) are not methods. Thus the term *method* is a needed one. The sense in which we use it here is clear from the context or it is specified.

What has been said with regard to the term *method* refers also to the term *procedure*, with the exception that *procedure* does not generally imply a *general* procedure. A procedure may be both general and individual. But, as in the case of *method*, it may designate a process ("Mr. N. *used* an effective procedure to solve the problem") or a prescription ("Mr. N. *formulated* a procedure for solving the problem"). From time to time we use the term *procedure*, for stylistic purposes, as a substitute for *process* and/or *prescription*, and its meaning is also clear from the context or it is specified.

Relationships Between Learning, Performance, and Instruction

Just as knowledge is a necessary but not sufficient condition for developing a skill, so a particular skill is a necessary but not sufficient condition for developing an *ability* in the conventional sense of the word. To develop an ability (which is always a generalized psychological phenomenon), one has to generalize a skill by transforming a particular skill into a more general one. This is a special instructional task that requires special methods on the part of the teacher and particular activities on the part of a student.

The same is true with regard to the development of *personality traits*. Any personality trait (for example, industriousness) generally rests upon certain knowledge, skills, and abilities; but these do not amount to that personality trait. A person may have skills to do many things and even highly developed abilities, but may not like to work—may not be industrious. Additional psychological phenomena (like specific positive motives, a need to be involved in activities, and some others) should be developed in a person in order to transform skills and abilities into personality traits. This requires other specific methods that are different from those required for developing skills and abilities.

The algorithmico-heuristic (algo-heuristic, for brevity) *theory of learning and performance* deals primarily with understanding and describing specific processes—operations and their systems—that turn knowledge into skills and abilities, underlie the latter and the performances that realize them, and allow a person not just to know something but to apply this knowledge to solving problems and performing certain activities (motor and/or cognitive). The algo-heuristic *theory of instruction* deals with the problem of how to use the information about these operations in order to purposefully and effectively develop them in the course of instruction. Another subject of the algo-heuristic theory of learning and performance—less developed at the moment—deals with systems of operations that turn skills and abilities into personality traits.

We mentioned earlier that the *operations* underlying the transition from knowledge to skills and abilities and from the latter to personality traits is a subject of the algo-heuristic theory of learning and performance. But operations underlie not only the transition from knowledge to skills and abilities but also the acquisition of knowledge itself. The composition and structure of these operations and the methods of their detection and description are also subjects of the algo-heuristic theory of learning and performance, and the *effective formation of these operations* in the course of instruction represents the major focus of the algo-heuristic theory of *instruction*.

The application of knowledge to the solution of problems and to effective performance in general requires specific operations both on the objects of knowledge and on knowledge itself. This fact raises the question about what these operations are like: What is their nature, composition, and structure? Only on the basis of information about operations that underlie skills and abilities can we develop them in students consciously, purposefully, efficiently, and in a systematic way.

The first question here is how to get the necessary information about these operations. The discussion of this question is beyond the topic of this chapter. We only note that the answer will be different depending on the nature of the operations in question, including, first and foremost, whether the operations are motor or cognitive. Two characteristic features of motor operations are that they are *observable* and that in many cases their performers are aware of them and can give an account of them. So the necessary information about motor operations involved in a performance can be obtained from external observations and, to a great extent, from accounts of their performers.

Cognitive operations—which are involved in many practical activities (along with motor operations) as well as in all "pure" cognitive activities—are *unobservable,* and their performers are often unaware or only partially aware of them. Therefore, in many cases they are not able to give an account of them, or they can give only a very incomplete account. Asked how he or she came to a solution of a difficult problem, a performer (especially a master performer, because his or her operations are automatized) often responds: "A solution came by itself," "I saw it immediately," "My intuition suggested it to me," and the like.

As in the case of motor operations, in order to teach cognitive operations purposefully, systematically, and effectively, one has to know their composition and structure.* This is the subject of the next section of this chapter.

BUILDING AND TESTING MODELS OF
UNOBSERVABLE COGNITIVE PROCESSES

Breaking Down Complex Cognitive Processes in Relatively Elementary Operations*

Most instructional theories proceed from a certain model of the psychological processes to be formed by the methods offered by the theory. One of the characteristic features of the algo-heuristic theory of instruction is the requirement to analyze operations, especially cognitive ones, to such a degree of *elementariness* that we know how to construct them in the course of instruction. We have called this approach *constructive* (Landa, 1976).

This requirement is not met in many instructional theories, where the psychological processes to be formed are often described in very general and ambiguous terms like: A learner (or problem solver) should be able to "analyze the situation," "identify relevant factors," "establish relationships between them," "draw conclusions," and the like. This level of description is too general and indefinite and does not suggest the ways of producing these processes. If a teacher tells a student: "Analyze the situation" or "Identify relevant factors," the student may ask: "How do I do this?" In order to answer this question and be able to produce these skills or abilities in a student, it is necessary for a teacher to know the more *elementary operations* that comprise each of these general activities.

Reducing complex psychological phenomena to their more simple constituent elements has been a thrust of a number of theories and approaches during the last

---

*Editor's note: Like Gagné–Briggs and Gropper, Landa is hereby placing a large emphasis on the analysis of what is to be taught and on using the results of that analysis to prescribe methods of instruction. So far, Landa's *taxonomy of objectives* might be characterized as the following hierarchy:

personality traits
↑
abilities
↑
skills
↑
knowledge

**Editor's note: This corresponds roughly to a task-analysis process, although it differs in important ways from other task-analysis procedures.

15 years (Bloom, 1956; Gagné, 1968, 1977;* Mager, 1962; P. Merrill, 1977; Scandura, 1974**). It should be mentioned, however, that the emphasis in these theories and approaches was on two things: (1) breaking down complex tasks into more elementary ones when a task could be viewed as the performance of a pretty elementary *motor operation* like, according to Gagné (1965), "putting a radar set into operation [p. 31]"; and (2) on breaking down complex and ambiguous instructional objectives like "understanding" or "appreciating" of some material by a student into observable and unambiguously assessible terminal behaviors that again represented *motor operations* (cf. Mager, 1962).

It is important not to underestimate the theoretical and practical significance of these theories and approaches. However, the thrust of the algo-heuristic theory of instruction from its very inception about 25 years ago (Landa, 1955) was not just breaking down complex tasks into more elementary ones or ambiguous objectives into observable and unambiguously assessible behaviors (or motor operations), but breaking down *complex, unobservable, cognitive* processes into more *elementary* but *also unobservable cognitive operations* that could be *unambiguously* executed by learners in the course of learning and performance and *reliably produced* by teachers in the course of instruction. Our approach is closer in its ideology to what later appeared under the label "information-processing theories" (cf. Newell & Simon, 1972; Reitman, 1965; Simon, 1969) and "structural learning theory" (Sdandura, 1973, 1977**), although none of the mentioned theories completely coincides with the algo-heuristic theory, either in the scope and nature of problems covered or in the approaches to their treatment and resolution.[4]

Elementariness of Operations****

As has been mentioned, the algo-heuristic theory requires breaking down complex unobservable cognitive processes into more elementary cognitive operations, but the concept of *elementariness is relative*. An operation elementary for one person may not be elementary for another, and vice versa. Algo-heuristic theory offers some criteria of, and a method of identification for, whether or not a given operation is elementary for a given student.[5] One of the criteria is the ability of a learner (or a performer in general) to execute uniformly, in a standard, regular way, an action or a series of actions (motor and/or cognitive) under one and the same conditions.

---

*Editor's note: See also Chapter 4.

**Editor's note: See also Chapter 7.

**Editor's note: See also Chapter 7.

****Editor's note: This is identical to Scandura's notion of *atomic components*, (Chapter 7, p. 230).

[4]For a deep and comprehensive analysis of different approaches to and theories of learning and instruction see, for example, Snelbecker, 1974.

[5]For more detail on the relativity of the concept of elementary operation and on the methods for identification of elementariness, see Landa, 1974.

It may seem strange that *a series* of actions may be viewed as *one* elementary operation. But if a learner is always able, for example, to correctly find a subject in a sentence using a single procedure, then the whole procedure (consisting of a number of operations) may be viewed as one elementary operation for the learner.* In other words, *a block* of operations constituting an entity may be viewed as an elementary operation. But the size of the block that can be viewed as elementary is different for different people. Although finding a subject in a sentence (which is always a set of operations) is viewed as an elementary operation for a student who performs it as a single act (i.e., the constituent operations have formed themselves in a block), it is viewed as a nonelementary operation for a student who does not know how to find a subject, or for a student who sometimes succeeds in finding it and sometimes does not, or for a student who does it differently in different cases (which shows a lack of uniformity), or for a student who does it slowly (which shows that the operations have not yet formed themselves into a single block). Similar objective criteria, the average time of performance included, may be used in other instances for defining whether or not an action or a set of actions may be viewed as an elementary operation for a given student.

The possibility of viewing a set of operations as one elementary operation also agrees with our everyday instructional practice, when, for example, a teacher— who knows for sure that a student can always find a subject in a sentence easily, unmistakenly, and instantaneously—refers to this activity as one elementary operation. The teacher knows that it is enough to say to the student, "Find a subject" *without* any specifications as to how to do this, and the subject will be found.

The latter suggests another criterion of elementariness of operations that proceeds from the notion of an elementary direction and its relativity. If a learner, or a performer in general, understands the direction to perform an activity unambiguously and performs it with the characteristics mentioned previously, then this direction is elementary for the student, and an action or a system of actions constituting this activity may be viewed as elementary for this student. This can be put in another way. The direction is elementary for a given student when it is *unambiguously understood* by him or her and always brings about an action or a set of actions that are *performed without error*, in a *uniform* standard way, or as a single act having the characteristics mentioned earlier.

In certain cases, it is impossible or not advisable, from an instructional point of view, *to break processes* into such elementary components where each of them represents an elementary operation in a defined sense. For many problems it is also impossible or unadvisable *to formulate directions* that would completely and unambiguously determine the operations to be performed in order to solve any given problem in a guaranteed way. This is the case, for example, when elementary

---

*Editor's note: This is similar to the Merrill–Reigeluth distinction between the micro level and the macro level (see Chapter 1) and to Gropper's distinction between single objectives and multiple objectives (see Chapter 5). The micro level and single objectives are both on the level of elementary operations.

operations and directions are *not known* in the field at a given moment of time, or when it is impossible to indicate the directions whose carrying out will lead to a solution because the general procedure of solving these problems *does not exist*. It may be also the case when the amount of directions addressed to elementary operations is so *huge* (as in chess playing or solving some mathematical problems) that carrying out of all the detailed directions becomes practically inexpedient or even impossible. ʻʻhat is why the directions that are possible or advisable to formulate would contain this or that degree of uncertainty or indeterminacy.

Algorithmic and Heuristic Processes

A process consisting of a series of relatively *elementary opeations* that are performed in some *regular, uniform way* under defined conditions to solve all problems of a certain class is an *algorithmic process*. A prescription determining these operations is an *algorithmic prescription*, or an *algorithm*.

A process consisting of a series of *nonelementary operations* (which a performer does not know beforehand how to perform) or of elementary operations that are *not performed in a regular or uniform way* under the same conditions is a *heuristic process*. A prescription determining these operations is a *heuristic prescription*.

Examples of an algorithmic process include systems of operations that people perform: (1) while making a telephone call from a pay telephone (they first lift the receiver, then drop a coin, etc.); and (2) while starting a car. Many processes of an algorithmic nature (without being named algorithmic) have been known for centuries, such as practical activities carried out by means of motor operations. People had to devise algorithmic processes because without them it was difficult to effectively perform many tasks. In many cases corresponding prescriptions (algorithmic in nature) were also formulated, but formulation of such prescriptions was not generally a very difficult problem because motor operations were observable and their performers were aware of them.

Quite different was the situation with algorithms of cognitive activity because, as was mentioned earlier, cognitive operations are unobservable and people are often unaware of them. Here algorithms were devised and used mainly in mathematics (for example, the algorithm for division of one number by another one). This explains why, up until after World War II, algorithmic processes and algorithms were viewed as specific mathematical phenomena, and the concept of algorithms was considered mathematical.

Examples of heuristic processes may be these: (1) operations of choosing an attribute of a geometrical figure among existing or known attribuets while solving a problem of proof; normally it is not known which of all the attributes is to be used in each particular case and no unambiguous directions that guarantee the solution to the problem can be given; (2) operations of searching for a tool capable of solving some technical problem when no available tools (or those coming to mind) can solve the problem; normally, when the solution and the process of its searching are not known, it is impossible to give a precise and determinate direction as to where and how to look for a tool that would be a solution. In these cases, no direction can guarantee finding a solution.

Because the degree of indeterminacy or uncertainty in different directions may be different, we have divided heuristic directions into semialgorithmic, semiheuristic, and heuristic (in the true sense of the word), according to the nature and degree of their uncertainty and indeterminacy.[6] However, for purposes of this chapter, we do not make such fine distinctions, but rather refer to all three types of directions as heuristic.

Systems of Operations, and Their Models

As soon as we have detected the operations underlying certain performances, skills, and abilities, it is necessary to identify the system, or structure, of the operations detected and then visualize the functioning of the *whole system* as a mechanism of a specific kind that consists of certain components that interact with each other in a certain way. Because cognitive operations—which are components of psychological mechanisms—are not observable, most mechanisms visualized will be, of necessity, hypothetical mechanisms. The description of a hypothetical mechanism may be called its *descriptive model*. Depending on whether the mechanism under consideration consists of algorithmic or heuristic operations, a descriptive model will be algorithmic or heuristic. Because the functioning of any mechanism—whether psychological or not—represents a process, we may speak of hypothetical algorithmic and heuristic processes as models that we build in the course of psychological cognition.

The significance of the algo-heuristic theory of learning and performance consists in the discovery that it is possible to analyze complex cognitive processes (by special methods of componential analysis) into relatively elementary operations in practically all subject areas. In the algo-heuristic theory of instruction this manifests itself in the generalization of the requirement to break down as far as possible complex, unobservable, cognitive activities—and not just observable practical activities—into relatively elementary operations, even in cases when cognitive processes seem further unbreakable (as in processes of identification, figuring out, ability to see relations between objects or their parts, attributes, etc.). Moreover, the algo-heuristic theory includes methods of *analyzing complex cognitive processes* into elementary components (i.e., methods of uncovering algorithmic and heuristic processes),* methods of *formulating algorithmic and heuristic prescriptions*, and methods of managing performance and *improving*

---

[6]The notion of heuristic processes and directions in the broader sense of the word is equivalent to that of nonalgorithmic processes and directions. For more details, see Landa, 1976, Chapters 5 and 6.

*Editor's note: This is a *development procedure*, not to be confused as a part of Landa's instructional theory, but it is essential to the application of that theory to the design of instruction.

learning and instruction on the basis of discovered algorithms and heuristics. All these problems are outside the subject of mathematics as a science and are not naturally even raised in it.

The algo-heuristic theory's requirement to break down complex cognitive processes into relatively elementary operations and to find and teach algorithms is *not absolute*. When it is impossible to find algorithms or it is not advisable to teach them, the algo-heuristic theory requires one to try to find effective heuristic processes (procedures) and to formulate heuristic prescriptions (methods) that will be the least uncertain and ambiguous possible. This allows one to improve both the *management* of performing heuristic processes and to increase the efficiency of *learning* them in the course of instruction.[7]

Earlier we called a description of an hypothetical algorithmic process a *descriptive algorithmic model* and similarly a description of an hypothetical heuristic process a *descriptive heuristic model*. When a prescription is built on the basis of a descriptive model, then it is natural to call an algorithmic prescription (i.e., an algorithm) a *prescriptive algorithmic model* and a heuristic prescription a *prescriptive heuristic model*.

Verification

After a model has been built, a problem arises as to whether our hypothetical notion of unobservable algorithmic or heuristic processes underlying certain performances, skills, and abilities are adequate and complete or whether they are not. This requires their verification.

There are several ways of verification: (1) confronting subjects with problems, (i.e., giving them specified inputs) and *observing their performance* (outputs) from the point of view of whether the performance corresponds to the expected one, where the latter is derived from the hypothetical model; (2) *computer simulation* of subjects' hypothetical processes; (3) *error analysis* where real errors are matched with those that are predicted to occur under certain circumstances, and some others. We dwell here upon the first of these methods of verification— namely, the utilization of prescriptions in a specially organized experimental instruction.

The idea underlying this method of verification is simple. Suppose we have built an hypothesis about what is going on in the head of an expert performer that allows him or her to perform at an expert level. On the basis of our hypothetical knowledge of the operations he or she should perform, we can compose a prescription (algorithmic or heuristic) as to what one should do in order to perform at an expert level. Now we can consider subjects who are poor performers: They may not be able to

---

[7]An example of how this can be done in teaching geometrical reasoning and problem solving can be found in Landa, 1976.

solve "relating" problems, or may solve them erroneously, inefficiently, and so on. We provide the subjects with a prescription that reflects our hypothesis about correct operations and develop these operations in our subjects. If, after they have mastered these operations, they start to perform as experts do, then our model (hypothesis) is very likely correct. If their performance does not improve or improves insufficiently, then our hypothesis (model) was incorrect or incomplete and we have to improve it. Thus we verify our hypothetical model through instruction, where we try to form in the subjects the processes that, according to our hypothesis, underlie expert performance. Hence, the algo-heuristic theory offers methods for improving the hypothetical models as well as for designing the instruction.

ALGO-HEURISTIC PRESCRIPTIONS AS A MEANS OF INCREASING THE EFFICIENCY OF INSTRUCTION

It is important to distinguish between three types of prescriptions: (1) prescriptions for *performers*, which indicate to them what they should do in order to be able to perform on a mastery level (these are called *performance* algorithms or heuristics);* (2) prescriptions for *learners*, which indicate to them what they should do in order to learn how to perform on a mastery level (these are called *learning* algorithms or heuristics);** and (3) prescriptions for *teachers*, which indicate to them what they should do in order to develop in performers and/or learners algo-heuristic processes (these are called *teaching* algorithms or heuristics.)[8]****

In order to be able to solve problems effectively and perform on a mastery level, the learner must acquire and master the cognitive operations underlying mastery. Instructionally, this can be done in a variety of ways.

A student may be put in a number of problem situations in which he or she will have to *discover by trial and error* the necessary operations and their systems. This may turn out to be very time-consuming, and there is no guarantee that any student will discover the required operations. However, an advantage is that the teacher does not have to know the operations underlying mastery performance and learning and does not have to know how to directly handle them.

Another approach is for a student to *discover by examples.***** Any master performer, a teacher included, may demonstrate by examples what he or she does

---

*Editor's note: These represent the content for instruction.

**Editor's note: These are similar to Grooper's concern for *learning to learn* (Chapter 5, p. 124).

***Editor's note: These are methods of instruction.

****Editor's note: Collins and Stevens have developed a similar approach in considerable detail (see Chapter 8).

[8]Teaching algorithms or heuristics can also be called *instructional* algorithms or heuristics. For more detail about the difference between performance and learning algorithms on the one hand, and teaching, or instructional, algorithms on the other hand, see Landa, 1974.

in each particular situation and may even explain why he or she does so in each of the situations. The teacher, however, does not describe the general method that he or she actually (and often unconsciously) uses while handling different particular situations. The general algorithmic or heuristic procedures remain hidden for students to discover.

There are other varieties of instructional methods in which the teacher does not directly manage students' cognitive processes and may even not know anything about their make-up and structure. In such cases the teacher deals with a student as with a kind of black box. He or she manages the student's input (providing him or her with problem situations, examples, explanations about the content to be learned, and the like) and output (reacting to the student's actions, solutions, and other responses by providing a certain kind of feedback). How the inputs are converted into outputs may not be known to a teacher, and he or she does not directly control (in a cybernetic sense) intermediary cognitive processes inside the psychological black box.

The principal difference between the instructional methods just described and a method based on a more or less *complete knowledge* of the unobservable cognitive processes underlying performances, skills, and abilities—the mediating connections between inputs and outputs—is that here a teacher handles not just inputs and outputs but also understands and purposefully, in a more direct way, *influences the internal processes* taking place inbetween.

The greater potential of such instruction in terms of reliability, effectiveness, and efficiency is evident. It does not mean that students should never be put in situations in which they have to discover methods of cognitive activity independently, either through trial and error or through examples or through other kinds of indirect guidance. (For more about achievements in discovery learning, see Shulman & Keislar, 1966.) It is just to say that *methods of discovery of algo-heuristic processes* (metamethods) should also be *explicitly taught* in order to make discovery learning manageable and more reliable and efficient.[9]* If we assume that rather elementary

---

[9]Some examples of the practical realization of this approach and direct, explicit teaching of general metamethods leading to students' discovery of general operations and methods can be found in Landa, 1974, and Landa, 1976.

*Editor's note: Cognitively oriented instructional theorists have seemingly conflicted with respect to advocacy of explicit methods (e.g., Ausubel) versus discovery methods (e.g., Bruner). I believe that this apparent conflict is attributable to differing goals of instruction rather than to differing methods for attaining the same goals. Advocates of discovery methods have the learning of methods of discovery as one of their major goals (see, for example, the Collins–Stevens model in Chapter 8), whereas advocates of explicit methods have the learning of a specific subject-matter content as their only goals. Landa makes an important contribution to discovery instruction in his advocacy of using *explicit* methods to teach methods of *discovery*, rather than falling into the "chicken and egg" dilemma of expecting students to discover how to discover. Once again we see the importance of prescribing methods on the basis of different kinds of goals, or objectives. Gagné would probably classify discovery as a *cognitive strategy* (see Chapter 4) and Gropper would put it in the category of *learning to learn* (see Chapter 5).

skills—like reading, writing, and counting—should be taught to students rather than be discovered on their own, then why should not much more complex and creative skills like discovering algorithmic and heuristic methods also be explicitly taught?

Incidentally, it is not quite correct to believe that only simple skills have an algorithmic nature and that all complex skills are heuristic. Algorithmic skills may be extremely complex in terms of the number of underlying operations and their structures. On the other hand, many complex skills that seem heuristic today may be of an algorithmic nature: We just might not yet have discovered the algorithms underlying the processes that appear to be heuristic.

Thus, the algo-heuristic theory of instruction is one in which unobservable and often unconscious cognitive processes in a psychological black box are made the subject of a specially designed analysis directed at: *isolating* them, *breaking them down* into relatively elementary components, explicitly *describing* their composition and structure, *creating prescriptions* on the basis of descriptions, and directly *managing and developing* processes through the management and development of their known elementary components and their structures.

Before we move on to consideration of some possible ways, rules, and methods of such a management and development—the core of the algo-heuristic theory of instruction—let us discuss some of the most frequent shortcomings in conventional instruction and some ways of overcoming them with algo-heuristically based instruction.

SOME SHORTCOMINGS
OF CONVENTIONAL INSTRUCTION

With regard to teaching students cognitive processes rather than just knowledge, the following shortcomings are observed fairly often:

1. Students are *not taught processes* (operations) at all because teachers themselves are not aware of them.
2. Students are *taught the wrong make-up* and/or system of operations (procedures).
3. Students are *taught an incomplete repertoire* and/or system of operations (procedures).
4. Students are *taught particular rather than more general operations* and their systems.
5. Students are *taught uncertain, vague, or ambiguous prescriptions*, which leave unclear what specifically should be cognitively done in order to be able to solve problems.

Students Are Not Taught Processes

Let us start with an example of the first shortcoming. It is known that there are languages in which articles exist (for example, English) and languages in which articles do not exist (for example, Russian). One of the most difficult problems in teaching article-having languages to speakers of article-lacking languages is determining *factors that should be taken into account* by a learner in order to make a decision as to which article to use in each particular case: indefinite, definite, or no article. The second problem here is *what operations should be performed* on a linguistic situation and on the factors relevant to make a correct decision, such as, for instance, meanings to be conveyed.

In most textbooks *factors* are described very uncertainly and ambiguously. Operations on situations or factors are in most cases either not indicated at all, or they are incorrect or incomplete. Let us cite some explanations from a widely used grammar of English for Russians (Barkhudarov & Steling, 1973):

> A definite article is individualizing. Association of a noun with a definite article designates a single object, which differs from other ones and which is particular or specific. . . . An indefinite article is classifying. Association with an indefinite article answers the questions: "What kind of object is this one?", "How can it be named?", "What kind of objects can be attributed to it?", "How can it be classified [p. 50]?"

Suppose now that a student of English as a foreign language goes home, pulls out a book from a briefcase, and wants to say to his or her mother: "I have just bought _____ very interesting book." *A* book or *the* book? Following the conditions for using a definite article ("it designates a single object, which differs from other ones, etc."), one should say "the book", because the book bought was single and different from other ones. On the other hand, following the conditions for using the indefinite article, one should say "a book," because it answers the question "What kind of object is this one?" How do you solve this problem? What operations should be performed to this end? This problem was not even raised by the authors.

This situation is typical of most textbooks on English grammar designated for learners of English as a foreign language. There is, however, a grammar (Kachalova, 1964) in which the author managed to find unambiguous factors and to indicate unambiguous operations that allow one to solve the problem (to be more precise, a subset of all problems involved in defining the proper article) successfully. Here is a translation of an excerpt from Kachalova's (1964) book:

1. If before a (countable) noun in Russian (in singular) one can put *some, one, any, each*, then with a corresponding noun in English one should use a classifying article (i.e., an indefinite article).
2. If . . . one can put *this* or *that*, then with a corresponding noun in English one should use an individualizing article (i.e., a definite one).
3. If before a Russian noun one can put a possessive pronoun, then with a corresponding English noun one should use a corresponding English pronoun.
4. If none of the above-mentioned Russian words can be put before a Russian noun, then an English classifying article (i.e., indefinite) should be used [p. 25].

It is clear that our previous example falls into category 1: "I have just bought *one* (or *some*) interesting book," from which follows that an indefinite article should be used: "I have bought *an* interesting book."

The rules given by the author can be converted into an economical algorithm like this:

Algorithm

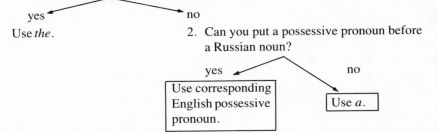

1. Can you put *this* or *that* before a countable noun in Russian?

yes ← → no

Use *the*.   2. Can you put a possessive pronoun before a Russian noun?

yes ← → no

Use corresponding English possessive pronoun.   Use *a*.

We do not maintain that this algorithm is perfect or complete even with regard to countable nouns in the singular because we do not know whether the rules given by Kachalova are correct and complete. This example demonstrates, however, how explanations that do not provide one with a method for solving pertinent problems —or at least do not allow one to solve problems unambiguously—can be stated in the form of a method, on the basis of which even an unambiguous algorithm—or quasi-algorithmic procedure—can be formulated.[10] The instructional value of such an approach is evident.

When problems are heuristic in nature, it is impossible to remove uncertainty from instructions completely (i.e., it is impossible to convert a heuristic process into an algorithmic one and a heuristic prescription into an algorithmic one). What is important in such cases is to *decrease the degree of uncertainty* and ambiguity as much as possible in order to make heuristic prescriptions *more concrete and specific* and, thus, to increase their instructional value.

Students Are Taught Uncertain, Vague Prescriptions

We now skip over a number of the shortcomings indicated previously and dwell upon the last of them. One of the problems with instruction when algorithms are not known and heuristic prescriptions are used is to try either to *turn a heuristic prescription into an algorithmic one* (when it is possible and advisable) or to

---

[10]See Landa (1955, 1974) and Bung (1973) on quasi-algorithmic procedures or quasi-algorithms.

specify its constituent instructions by breaking them down into more elementary ones to such a degree that learners would know more specifically what they should cognitively do in order to be able to solve certain problems and effectively perform the required activities. It is a problem of lending heuristic prescriptions greater managing power so as to raise the efficiency and reliability of the instructional process.

How vague, ambiguous, and unmanaging many heuristic prescriptions are may be illustrated by these examples. The following prescription as to what should be cognitively done in order to solve legal problems or answer the questions raised in a case appears in a book for high-school students that has as one of its objectives teaching students legal thinking (Fisk & Mietus, 1977): "To answer the question raised in a problem or case, first read it carefully. Be sure you understand the question. Then analyze the situation, determine the rule of law involved, and reach a decision [p. XI]."

" . . . Read it carefully." How do you do this? It is good if a student knows how to read carefully. What if, however, he or she does not? Careful reading differs from uncareful reading by the performance of certain specific operations on the text. Which operations? What should be cognitively done in order to make reading careful? If a student does not know this, the advice given will be of no use for him or her. "Read carefully" is similar to advice like "Be wise," "Be thoughtful," and so on.

" . . . Be sure you understand the question." How can you be sure? How do you control one's understanding in order to be sure?

" . . . Then analyze the situation." How? What should be done in order to analyze it?

" . . . Determine the rule of law involved." How?
" . . . Reach a decision." How?
Another example has been taken from a book on legal drafting (Dickerson, 1965), in which the author tried to break down the process of drafting into steps and to teach the process of drafting step by step:

Step 1: Preparing a first draft.
. . .

Step 2: Revision

The draftsman revises his work as many times as necessary to produce the desired result . . . It is no disgrace to revise a draft a dozen times . . . A good draftsman may make as many as fifteen to twenty revisions to iron out an extremely difficult provision. The important thing to remember is that, ideally, he should keep on revising until he feels that the draft is 99 percent right, unless, of course, the economics of the situation make some compromise necessary [pp. 44–45].

In order to reveal the instructional value of this description, which automatically transfers itself into a prescription, we have flowcharted it. This is what we got:

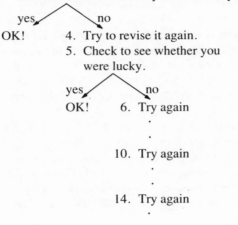

How to improve a draft

1. Check to see whether the draft is satisfactory.

OK!   2. Try to revise it.
       3. Check to see whether you were lucky.

OK!   4. Try to revise it again.
          5. Check to see whether you
             were lucky.

          OK!   6. Try again

                 .
                 .

                 10. Try again

                 .
                 .

                 14. Try again

                 .
                 .

                 20. Try again
                 21. Check to see whether
                     the draft is 99% right.

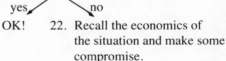

                 OK!   22. Recall the economics of
                             the situation and make some
                             compromise.

The only operations indicated by the author are "check whether the draft is satisfactory," "try to revise the draft," "make some compromise." The question that arises here is the same: "How?" How do you check? How do you try? How do you make a compromise? For a person who does not know how to do all this, the prescription says nothing; it is not able to manage his or her cognitive operations and therefore is of no use for him or her.

By the way, it is widely believed that an algorithm is the same thing as a flow chart and to algorithmize a process means to flowchart it. From this example it is clear that this is not true. Every algorithm may be presented in a flow chart form (although there exist other forms of presentation), but *not every flow chart is an algorithm*. Flow charts may be such vague, uncertain, and ambiguous prescriptions that they do not determine the process of performance to any substantial degree (as in the example cited). Only that flow chart is an algorithm whose instructions are *completely comprehensible* for a person and *clearly determine what should be done* in order to solve any problem belonging to a certain class. That is why the major problem in finding algorithms for solving problems is not flowcharting but breaking the uncertain, vague, and ambiguous operations down to such relatively *elementary* ones (i.e., elementary for a given person) that a person knows how to perform them, can perform them, and can reliably solve the problem.

We do not know which elementary operations are involved in the process of the revision of a draft, but this can be found out as a result of the special algo-heuristic analysis. But let us give an idea as to how an uncertain instruction such as "analyze the situation" may be *made more specific* so as to begin to direct and determine the process of analysis. Very often, all situations, whether they are legal, medical (diseases),grammatical, and so on, may be divided into groups or *classes*. Each class may be described through a set of *attributes*. "To analyze a situation" means to isolate in a situation those attributes and their structurally organized sets that allow you to relate a situation to a certain class. But this can be done only on the basis of a knowledge as to what sets of attributes and what type of their structure constitute a certain class. This can be expressed in propositions of the type: If a situation has attributes (*a* & *b*) or *d*, then it belongs to class *M*; if it has attributes *a* & *b* & not-*d*, then it belongs to class *P*; if it has attributes *a* & not-*b* & c, then it belongs to class *S*, and so on.

As soon as all this has been discovered, a *precise prescription* as to what should be done in order to analyze a situation and attribute it to a certain class can be formulated. Let us take a concrete, although general, example. Let us suppose that in some area of some broader field of knowledge, there are three important (from the viewpoint of certain purposes) situations that may belong to three classes *M*, *P*, *S*. These classes are defined by the following attributes:

$$a(x) \mathbin{\&} b(x) \longrightarrow x \in M.$$
$$a(x) \mathbin{\&} \bar{b}(x) \longrightarrow x \in P.$$
$$\bar{a}(x) \longrightarrow x \in S.$$

where $a(x)$ means that situation x has an attribute a, $\bar{a}(x)$ means that situation x does not have an attribute a, $\rightarrow$ means "if . . . , then", and sign ϵ means "belongs to class . . . ."

For example, the first proposition reads: If situation x has an attribute a and an attribute b, then the situation x belongs to class M.

Now, instead of giving some uncertain, unmanaging direction like "analyze the situation," a prescription can be given as to what precisely should be done in order to analyze the situation.[11]

---

[11]The prescription "How to improve a draft" was not an algorithm. But if the operations had been elementary, the prescription would have been an algorithm. The function of such an algorithm is to *trans-*

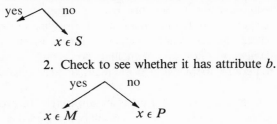

1. Check to see whether the situation has an attribute *a*.

yes / no

$x \in S$

2. Check to see whether it has attribute *b*.

yes / no

$x \in M$ $x \in P$

There may be cases when a person knows precisely what are the criteria of all the attributes and how to unambiguously identify them. In this case this prescription will be algorithmic. If the person, however, does not know this precisely or if there is some uncertainty as to how to qualify each (or at least some) of the attributes, then this prescription will be heuristic. What we want to underline, however, is that even if this prescription is heuristic and contains this or that degree of uncertainty, it is *much more specific and managing* than the original extremely uncertain and unmanaging instruction "analyze the situation." A concrete example of how a very uncertain and unmanaging heuristic prescription may be converted into a set of much less uncertain and more manageable (although also heuristic) prescriptions may be found in Landa (1976).

ADDITIONAL DEFINITIONS

Before we move to the description of some principles and rules of instruction in algo-heuristic processes, let us dwell upon some concepts of a theory of instruction that we plan to use:

1. An instructional process is a system of influences exercised by a teacher[12] and directed at a student in order to transform the student's present state of psychological processes and behaviors to a *desired* state. This desired state emerges as an *objective* of an instructional process (or any fragment thereof) or its *desired outcome*.

---

form one initial situation (object, etc.) into some other situation. Algorithms performing this function have been called *transformation algorithms*. The problem being discussed now is of another type: It is not necessary to transform the situation, it is necessary to determine (identify) the class to which the situation belongs. We call algorithms that solve this type of problem *identification algorithms*. An example of such an algorithm follows this discussion. For a discussion of relationships between transformation and identification algorithms, see Landa, 1974.

[12]For convenience, the term *teacher* is used here to designate any teaching agent, whether it is a live teacher or "mechanical teacher" (a textbook, audiovisual instructional means, a mechanical teaching machine, an electronic computer, etc.).

2. Instructional processes are effected through the *teacher's actions** or *instructional operations** directed at eliciting certain performance and learning actions in a student and thus bringing about performance and learning processes.

3. A *system* of learning operations directed at attaining a specified objective is often called an *instructional method,*** each constituent being a *method component.*[13]

4. Each instructional process is not only directed at attaining specified objectives, but is also effected under certain *conditions*. Conditions are numerous and diversified. They include different types of external conditions, psychological characteristics of students (e.g., the content and level of knowledge they have, the characteristic features of their skills, abilities, motives, character traits, etc.), the teachers' knowledge, skills, abilities, and character traits, and some others.

5. *Teaching* may be viewed as the solving of a series of instructional problems. Each *instructional problem* is a situation in which a teacher has to determine and perform the actions that should be executed in order to attain a specified objective (desired outcome) under given conditions.

6. The connections between objectives, conditions, and instructional actions may be described in the form of specific *instructional propositions,* which may be instructional rules, value judgments, definitional statements, and some others.[14]

There exist three types of *instructional rules:* descriptive, prescriptive, and permissive.

6.1. *Descriptive rules* are statements about *what occurs* (i.e., which instructional outcomes emerge) when certain instructional actions are effected under certain instructional conditions.*** The logical structure of descriptive instructional rules is this:

"*If* one applies instructional actions A to a student under conditions α, *then* outcome α occurs,"

where A, a *and* α may be composite phenomena consisting of a number of components.

What follows as a consequence of the given conditions (i.e., after the *then*) may be of deterministic or probabilistic nature, which means that they may follow necessarily or with some degree of probability. In the area of instruction the consequences

---

*Editor's note: These are what were defined as *instructional methods* in Chapter 1.

**Editor's note: This is what has been referred to as an *instructional model* so far in this book.

***Editor's note: In Chapter 1 these were referred to as *descriptive principles of instruction.*

[13]Not infrequently the term *strategy* is used in the same sense as *method*. However, more often a *strategy* implies *method* in its second sense—that is, method as a more or less general system of directions (a prescription) rather than a system of operations (a process). This is the case when one speaks of "working out a strategy," "applying a strategy," and the like.

[14]On instructional rules see, in particular, Markle (1978) and Stolurow (1065a, and 1965b).

are in most cases probabilistic, with a higher or lower degree of probability. It is relatively rare that it is possible to achieve desired results with 100% probability—that is, to formulate completely deterministic rules. Normally, the rules called deterministic are in fact "close to deterministic."

6.2 *Prescriptive rules* are statements about *what should be done* in order to attain some specified objectives under some given conditions.* The logical structure of prescriptive rules is this:

"*In order* to attain the outcome (objective α under the conditions a, use action A."

Prescriptive rules can be stated also in the "if . . . , then" form:

"*If* you have an objective α and there are conditions a, *then* use the action A."

In the precise sense of the word, descriptive instructional rules (i.e., the rules of the first type discussed earlier) are not rules but *instructional laws* or *regularities;* rules are only propositions of the second type (i.e., prescriptive) because only they indicate instructional actions to be performed in order to achieve specified goals under certain conditions. Unfortunately, the term *rule* is very often used in the scientific literature indiscriminately, designating propositions that are not rules because they do not indicate what should be done in order to achieve a certain goal.

6.3 Closely related to prescriptive rules are *permissive rules* (the third type of rules). Changing the command "*use* the action A" in the latter rule for the permission "*may use* the action A" creates a permissive rule:**

"If there are conditions a and you have the objective α, then you may use the action A."

"May" means that the action A will lead to the desired outcome, but it is not the only action that is capable of leading to the outcome. "May" states that A is a sufficient condition for achieving the objective α, whereas "use" (which means "you *have to* use") means that it is not only a sufficient but also a necessary condition,* or at least the *best one*** that is recommended by the author of the rule.

7. Besides instructional laws (regularities) and rules that establish connections between conditions, instructional actions, and outcomes, there exist other types of instructional propositions that are statements about desirable general characteristics of the instructional process and its individual components and aspects. We call

---

*Editor's note: In Chapter 1 these were referred to as *prescriptive principles of instruction.*

**Editor's note: This is another kind of *prescriptive principle of instruction* as defined in Chapter 1.

***Editor's note: This is similar to the Collins-Stevens notions of necessary and sufficient factors (see Chapter 8).

****Editor's note: This is very common and very important in instructional theory: prescribing the *best* of the available methods for achieving the desired outcomes under the given conditions.

such propositions, which are based on certain accepted value systems, *accepted general "must" statements* (or, for brevity, just *instructional "must" statements*). Some examples are: "One should teach students not only knowledge, but the ability to think as well." and "The instruction should be meaningful" (whatever is implied by meaningful).

Instructional "must" statements are *value judgments* rather than rules because they state what we *desire* from the instructional process—what we want it to be——rather than what we should do in order to achieve the established goals. "Must" statements may be different in different societies, cultures, social and political systems, educational schools, and philosophies. As propositions of a higher level, they determine to a great degree the concrete instructional objectives set in education, the conditions to be created, and the instructional rules or actions to be performed in order to attain specific objectives.

8. There exist other types of instructional propositions that describe *properties* of instructional processes and their components (for example, properties of objectives, instructional actions, interactions between a teacher and a student, etc.). These propositions are neither "must" statements nor rules. We call them, without further specification here, *empirical propositions,* because, being theoretical in nature, they are established empirically.*

9. If an individual instructional rule prescribes what should be instructionally done in order to attain a single instructional objective, a set of instructional rules should be used in order to attain a set of instructional objectives that may be different in nature and content. A structured set of all types of instructional propositions— which includes definitions, "must" statements, empirical propositions, rules, and some others—constitutes an *instructional theory*.

Strictly speaking, for a set of propositions to be a theory, it is not necessary for it to be comprehensive and to encompass all the phenomena in a given area. For example, the concept of chemical theory does not imply that all chemical substances and processes are described by the theory: They may be pertinent to a specific substance and specific processes, being a theory of these substances and processes. The same is true of instructional theory. The latter *may* be comprehensive, comprising all the "instructional objects"; but it may instead be pertinent to certain types of objectives. For example, it could be a theory of knowledge formation, or a theory of developing practical skills, and so on. The algo-heuristic theory of instruction is a theory of shaping different performances, abilities, behaviors, and character traits on the basis of a knowledge of their underlying operations through the explicit, systematic, and purposeful formation of these operations and their systems.

---

*Editor's note: These were referred to as *instructional concepts* in Chapter 1.

SOME METHODS OF THE MANAGEMENT
AND DEVELOPMENT OF
ALGO-HEURISTIC PROCESSES

1. Process-Oriented versus
Prescription-Oriented Instruction

Must Statement 1

In instructing *students* it is more important to develop algo-heuristic *processes* in them rather than to get them to learn algo-heuristic *prescriptions.**

Substantiation. Knowledge of a prescription as to what to do in order to solve problems of a certain class is only one of the means to learn operations, enabling the process of solution. Any *process* of solving problems is an information-transforming process that expresses itself in the transformation of images, concepts, and/or propositions. Knowledge of a *prescription* as to what should be done in order to solve problems does not transform anything in itself. But this knowledge of operations to be performed can actuate the operations, put them to work, and thus touch off an information-processing *process*.

Must Statement 2

In instructing *teachers* (including future teachers) and all those who have to guide other people in their activities, it is equally important to teach them both algo-heuristic *processes* and algo-heuristic *prescriptions*.

Substantiation. Teachers and all those who guide other people's activities have to be able not only to solve problems on their own, but to *instruct* others how to do this. In order to effectively instruct other people in methods of solving problems, one has to know constituent operations and be able to communicate them to other people in the form of *prescriptions*.

Instructional Rule 1

If one teaches *students* and has an objective to develop in them only an ability to solve problems, then one has to develop primarily algo-heuristic *processes*, using prescriptions only when necessary as a means of developing the processes (see empirical proposition 1 later).

Instructional Rule 2

If one teaches *teachers* or those who have to guide other people's activities and has an objective to develop in them both the ability to solve problems and to teach other people to do so, then one has to develop in them both algo-heuristic *processes* and a knowledge of corresponding *prescriptions*.

---

*Editor's note: Recall that a *prescription* is a set of directions that can be learned as "knowledge" (equivalent to Gagné's *verbal information* and to Merrill's *remember level*, whereas a *process* is a set of operations that exist as "skills" (equivalent to Gagné's *intellectual skills* and Merrill's *use* level).

These two instructional rules can be presented in the form of the following decision-making algorithm:

Algorithm

1. Do you have to teach students or teachers or those who will guide other people's activities?

| students | teachers or guiders of others |

2. Do you want to develop in them only an ability to solve problems?

2. Do you want to develop in them only the ability to solve problems or also the ability to teach others to do so?

| yes | no | only one ability | both abilities |

Develop in them primarily algo-heuristic *processes*, using prescriptions only as a means of developing processes.

Develop in them both algo-heuristic *processes* and knowledge of corresponding *prescriptions*.

2. Teaching Processes through Prescriptions versus Demonstrations

Empirical Proposition 1

Two explicit and direct ways of actuating existent and forming new algo-heuristic operations and their systems (processes) are: *prescriptions* and *demonstrations* of operations. (For mastering the operations and their subsequent perfecting, *practice* is also necessary.)*

Empirical Proposition 2

Motor operations, which are always observable, can be taught by *prescriptions* and/or *demonstrations*; cognitive (unobservable) operations can be actuated and formed by *prescriptions only*, with the exception of when cognitive operations have motor prototypes that may be demonstrated on material objects or their materialized models.[15]

---

*Editor's note: This is similar to the Component Display Theory's call for *generalities*, *examples*, and *practice* for instruction on the "use" level (see Chapter 9).

[15]Remember our example of the cognitive operation of turning around an image of an isosceles triangle. This cognitive operation has its prototype in the motor operation of turning around a real material triangle, and this prototype operation can be demonstrated to a student.

Empirical Proposition 3

Depending on their individual psychological characteristics, some students learn easier and faster from *demonstration* of operations and their systems (processes) when demonstration is possible, others from *prescriptions*, and still others from a *combination* of both of them. There also exist students who learn equally well from demonstrations and prescriptions.

Must Statement[16]

If a student learns poorly from prescriptions and effectively from demonstrations, it is (or may be) important to develop in him or her an *ability to work with prescriptions* and to learn from them, even if it is more difficult for the student.

Instructional Rule 1

If: (1) it is possible to teach certain operations both by prescriptions and demonstrations; and (2) a student learns more easily through demonstrations; and (3) the teacher does not have the objective to develop in the student the ability to learn better through prescriptions, then *demonstrations should be used* as a major method.

Instructional Rule 2

If: (1) it is possible to actuate and form certain operations both by prescriptions and by demonstrations; and (2) a student learns more easily through prescriptions; and (3) the teacher does not have the objective to develop in the student the ability to learn better through demonstration, then the teacher should *use prescriptions* as a major method.

Instead of listing all the rules separately, let us throw them together into a single algorithm, each branch of which represents a specific rule (see Fig. 6.1.) This algorithm proceeds from the assumption that first, we know the individual psychological characteristics of each student and, second, we can effect individualized instruction and thus adapt to these characteristics. If either or both of these conditions are not met, the following rules apply:

Rule 1

If you do not know the individual psychological characteristics of a student, but can effect individualized instruction, then *try both means* (prescriptions and demonstrations) by turns and find out which of them is *easier* for the student. Having identified the individual characteristics of the student, turn to the preceding algorithm and use it.

---

[16]Earlier we indicated some factors that determine the content of "must" statements. Among the factors may also be empirical phenomena and their corresponding empirical propositions. This is the case now.

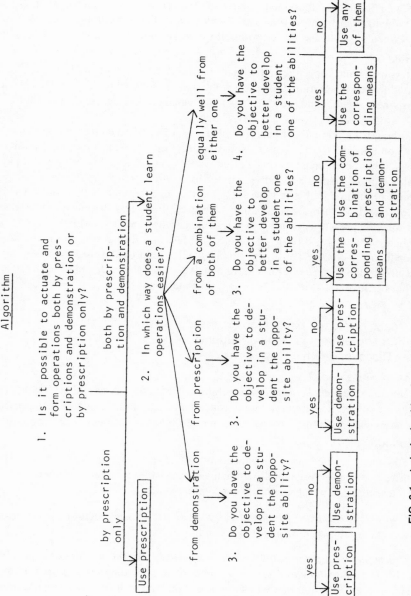

FIG. 6.1 A single algorithm for deciding on prescriptions or demonstrations to teach processes.

Rule 2

If you know the individual characteristics of a student, but cannot effect individualized instruction, then use a *combination* of prescriptions and demonstrations when possible and prescriptions alone when demonstrations are impossible.

Rule 3

If you neither know the individual characteristics of students nor can effect individualized instruction, then use a *combination* of prescriptions and demonstrations when possible and prescriptions alone when demonstration is impossible.

Although individualized adaptive instruction has more educational potentials than nonindividualized and nonadaptive instruction, from an economical point of view the increment in educational effectiveness may be less than the price of psychological diagnostics and individualized instruction. (How to measure them is a special problem.) If this is the case, then the instructional method indicated in Rules 2 and 3 ("use a combination of prescriptions and demonstrations when possible and prescriptions alone when demonstrations are impossible") should be applied. What has just been said is easy to state in a formal rule form. It is also evident how to construct an algorithm that would comprise the preceding algorithm and all the rules just cited. This algorithm will be of a higher order than the one stated earlier because it will include it as one of its outcomes.

3. Teaching Ready-Made Algo-Heuristic Procedures versus Getting Students to Discover Them on their Own

Must Statement 1

Teaching students *how to discover* algo-heuristic procedures and getting them to discover any particular procedure is educationally far more valuable than providing them with ready-made procedures and just teaching them how to use them.*

Empirical Proposition 1

Students learning via an independent (and even guided) discovery of algo-heuristic procedures is generally a much *more difficult and time-consuming* process than learning and mastering ready-made procedures.

Consequence 1 from Empirical Proposition 1. An instruction using solely a discovery strategy is practically impossible .

Consequence 2 from Empirical Proposition 1. In the instructional process, teaching students *how to discover* algo-heuristic procedures and getting them to discover them in particular cases should be combined in other cases with providing the students with *ready-made procedures* that they have to learn, master, and

---

*Editor's note: This is similar to Gropper's concern for *learning to learn* (Chapter 5, p. 124) and with Collins-Stevens' concern for *learning how to derive a general rule or theory* (Chapter 8, p. 258).

apply in order to develop quickly and efficiently certain performance and learning skills and abilities.

It is perhaps impossible to indicate the optimal proportion of time for teaching students to discover algo-heuristic procedures versus providing them with ready-made ones. We can state only the following very unspecific (heuristic) method, which contains many uncertainties and draws upon a number of the teacher's subjective estimates:

1. Conduct a special lesson devoted to teaching students *how to discover* algorithms (a method of conducting such a lesson and one of its possible applications is given following step 3 here).

2. On the next occasion, when it comes to getting students to learn some algo-heuristic procedure, make an estimate, on the basis of your experience, as to *how long it would take* for students to discover this procedure under your guidance.

3. Check whether the required time is *available* in your course plan.

yes	no
Get students to discover the procedure on their own under your guidance.	4. Check to see whether the discovery of this particular procedure is, from your standpoint, of great educational value for students.

	yes	no
	5. Check to see if you can make time for it at the expense of something less educationally valuable.	Provide students with the ready-made procedure.

yes	no
Get students to discover the procedure on their own under your guidance.	Provide students with the ready-made procedure.

4. Teaching Algo-Heuristic Procedures as a Whole versus Teaching Them in a Step-By-Step Manner

Empirical Proposition 1

If the algo-heuristic procedure is too long, it is ineffective or even impossible to teach it *integrally* and a *step-by-step* (operation-by-operation) approach should be used.

Empirical Proposition 2

The concept of "too long" is *relative* and depends on the students' individual psychological characteristics: Some can effectively handle and learn one operation at a time, others several. The length is different for different students.

Empirical Proposition 3

The size of the step is determined by which operation is elementary for a given student and by how many elementary operations he or she can handle and learn at a time.[17]

Empirical Proposition 4

Criteria of elementarity may be only experimental (for discussion of these criteria see Landa, 1974).

We do not describe here *methods of determining* which operation is elementary for a student and which is not.* The interested reader is referred to the description of this method in Landa (1974). Nor do we describe here the method for defining the *length of a chain* of operations that a student can comfortably handle and learn at a time. The experimental method for solving the latter problem is essentially the same as the method for defining the elementarity of a single operation for a student. Only the object of experimentation will be different: chains of operations of varying sizes rather than individual operations of different sizes.

Rule 1

In order to effectively teach students algo-heuristic processes, *break down* each process into operations *elementary* for a given student using the methods just referred to.

Rule 2

In order to effectively teach algo-heuristic processes, define the *length of chains* of operations that a student can comfortably handle and learn at a time, using methods similar to the ones referred to previously. The length of the chain will determine the *size of the step* optimal for a given student. In order to determine which method of instruction to use—integral or step-by-step—one can apply the following simple algorithm.

---

[17]As was mentioned earlier (see Landa, 1974), "elementarity of an operation" is a relative notion: An operation elementary for one student may not be elementary for another one, in which case it should be broken down into components that are elementary for a given student.

*Editor's note: These methods are development procedures, not part of an instructional theory. However, they are essential for effectively implementing the instructional theory.

Algorithm

1. Check to see whether the procedure to be taught is longer than the optimal size of a chain for a given student.

| yes | | no |

| Use the step-by-step approach. | | Use the integral approach. |

The integral approach presupposes that a teacher has a possibility to conduct individualized and adaptive instruction, in the course of which he or she can diagnose the level of elementarity of operations and the optimal length of the chain of operations for each student. As such conditions are not available in mass education, the *step-by-step approach should be used* as a pretty safe and sufficiently reliable approach. The level of elementarity of particular operations is determined on the basis of the teacher's experience: Each teacher knows approximately which operations are elementary for the students of the given age and grade and which ones are not. This knowledge is, of course, of empirical statistical nature and may not be true with regard to each particular student, but "on the average" one can proceed from this knowledge as a starting point, making corrections when possible in the course of instruction itself. Instruction that is based on estimations rooted in the teacher's experience is always less effective than instruction based on a preliminary *psychological diagnosis*. But when it is impossible to conduct a psychological diagnosis of each particular student and then use its results for individualized adaptive instruction, then there is no alternative to orientation on the "average student."

Method 1: The Step-by-Step Approach

The following is a description of the step-by-step approach:

1. *Present* an algorithmic or nonalgorithmic procedure to students and *demonstrate* to them how, by means of the procedure, one can easily solve problems that are to be learned how to solve.

2. Develop the *first operation* in students. (The method of developing individual operations* in students is described later; it includes practicing each operation and bringing it to mastery.)

3. Present problems to the students that require application of the first operation, and have the students *practice* the operation until they master it.

4. Develop the *second operation* in the students.[18]

---

*Editor's note: Landa is referring here to micro methods as defined in Chapter 1.

[18]In the cases of branched algo-heuristic procedures, there may be two second operations, each starting a separate branch. There may be several methods of working with branches, discussion of which is a special topic. It is important to develop systems of operations that correspond to each branch.

5. Present problems to the students that require application of *both operations* and have the students *practice* these operations until they master their system.

6. Develop the *third operation* in the students.

7. Present problems that would require application of *all three operations*.

8. Continue to proceed in the same way until all operations in the process are mastered.

This method is called the *snowball method* and the principle underlying it is called the *snowball principle of developing multioperation procedures*.

Whether prescriptions are used just as a means of learning algo-heuristic operations and their systems or also as a special subject of learning, the snowball method allows students to learn them without the special task of memorization. With this method, a student has to keep in mind, at any given moment of learning, only one instruction from a set of instructions of which a prescription usually consists. He or she moves to the next instruction only after mastering the previous one and does not need to even remember it. Each learned operation will be actuated automatically or nearly automatically by the givens of the problem and/or by other operations. The magnitude of the "snowball" are enlarged gradually by joining new operations to it. Thus, using this method, it is possible to develop a very large and complex system of operations (complex algo-heuristic processes) without the student's having to memorize long prescriptions.

Example

Let us consider an example of a step-by-step snowball method of shaping an algo-heuristic procedure when it consists of only two operations. There are three English verbs—"to suggest," "to offer," and "to propose"—all of whose meanings are conveyed in Russian by a single verb *predlozhit'*:

Russian	English
1. I want to *predlozhit'* you an interesting book.	1. I want to *offer* you an interesting book.
2. I want to *predlozhit'* you to take a bus.	2. I want to *suggest* to you that we take a bus.
3. I want to *predlozhit'* a resolution.	3. I want to *propose* a resolution[19]

The problem for a Russian learner of English is to know which English word to use instead of *predlozhit'* in one case or another. The problem for a teacher of English is how to teach Russian students so they are able to make the correct choice. English-speaking persons make these decisions unconsciously, without being aware of the cognitive operations they perform (i.e., nobody is able to give

---

[19]It is not a characteristic feature of relationships between Russian and English that one Russian word is conveyed by a number of English words. In other cases, the situation is opposite. For example, a single English word "snow" is conveyed in the Eskimo language by some 20 words.

an account of what he or she is doing in his or her head when attempting to convey the meaning contained in the Russian *predlozhit'*): Most reply, "I just know," "I feel," "I make the decision intuitively," and the like.

As our experience and experiments showed, Russian students have difficulties and make mistakes for years and even dozens of years. This is because they are not taught the operations that English-speaking persons unconsciously perform and that allow them to solve the problem correctly. What cannot be taught in conventional instruction for years can be—and was—taught within 15 to 20 minutes as soon as the operations underlying the decisions made by native English-speaking people have been identified, described explicitly, and expressed in the form of an algorithm indicating what a nonnative speaker of English should cognitively do in order to be able to solve this problem as native English speakers do. The reader can easily verify this by conducting a similar and simple instructional experiment.

Such an algorithm was composed by I. Pavlova, graduate of the Moscow Institute for Teaching Foreign Languages, who collaborated with us on applying the algorithmic approach to teaching foreign languages. This is the algorithm in somewhat modified form:

Algorithm
for choosing among "to suggest," "to offer," and "to propose" something

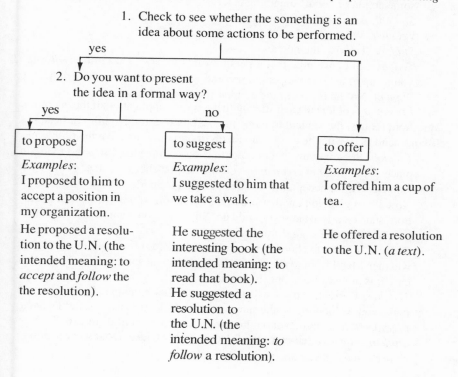

1. Check to see whether the something is an idea about some actions to be performed.

| yes | no |

2. Do you want to present the idea in a formal way?

| yes | no |

to propose   **to suggest**   **to offer**

Examples:
I proposed to him to accept a position in my organization.

He proposed a resolution to the U.N. (the intended meaning: to *accept* and *follow* the the resolution).

Examples:
I suggested to him that we take a walk.

He suggested the interesting book (the intended meaning: to read that book).
He suggested a resolution to the U.N. (the intended meaning: *to follow* a resolution).

Examples:
I offered him a cup of tea.

He offered a resolution to the U.N. (*a text*).

The following is an application of the snowball method to teaching this algorithm:

1. *Present the procedure* to the students and demonstrate to them how, by means of the procedure, one can easily perform as required.

> *Teacher*: (the teacher explains the problem to students in the way it was just explained and shows how the problem of choice can be easily solved by using the algorithm)

2a. *Develop the first operation* in students.

> *Teacher*: In order to know which English word to choose in place of *predlozhit'* in one case or another, you have to perform all the operations indicated in the prescription (i.e., algorithm). Let us start by learning and mastering the first one. What should you do first in order to determine which English verb to use?
>
> *Student*: I have to check to see whether the "something" I want to present is an idea about some action to be performed or not.
>
> *Teacher*: Correct.

2b. *Check* whether each student understands the meaning of the instruction and its corresponding operation.

> *Teacher*: Suppose one person wants to say to another person: "I want to *predlozhit'* you to go to the movies." Is the person presenting an idea about some action or about something else?
>
> *Student*: An idea about an action.
>
> *Teacher*: What action?
>
> *Student*: To go to the movies.
>
> *Teacher*: Suppose now that a person wants to say: "I want to *predlozhit'* you a cup of tea." Is the person presenting an idea about some action?
>
> *Student*: No, he is presenting an idea about some object.

3. *Present a problem* to each student that requires application of the operation in question; request the student to name the operation or to give him- or herself a self-command as to what he or she should do first in order to solve the problem.

> *Teacher*: So you know that in order to choose which English word to use in place of the Russian *predlozhit'* you should first check whether or not what is presented for acceptance or consideration is an idea about some *action*. Now I will give you another problem, but before you perform your operation, state clearly what you should do. Suppose, you want to say: "I want to *predlozhit'* you a suggestion."
>
> *Student*: In order to choose a proper English word, I first have to ask myself whether what I want to *predlozhit'* is an idea about some action. No, in this case it is not an idea about some action.
>
> *Teacher*: Correct. Now I will give you another example, but before you make your response give the same command silently to yourself: "I want to *predlozhit'* a resolution about how to react to our enemy's threats."
>
> *Student 1*: (gives a self-command) No, it is not an idea about some action to be performed. It is a document—a resolution.

Student 2: (after having given a self-command) I do not agree. I want to *predlozhit'* how to react and I do this by means of a resolution. It is an idea about some action to be performed and expressed as a resolution.

Teacher: Both of you are right. The first of you may mean that you want to *predlozhit'* a *document* in which the actions are described; the second may mean that you want to *predlozhit'* the *actions* described in the document. According to the algorithm, each of you will have to use different English verbs for conveying your meaning. What are these verbs?

Student 1: (states them.)

Teacher: What should you do if you want to *predlozhit'* something that is not an idea about some action to be performed?

Student 1: I have to draw a conclusion that I have to use "to offer" in place of *predlozhit'*.

Teacher: And what should you do when what you want to *predlozhit'* is an idea about some action?

Student 1: I have to check whether I want to present the idea in a formal or informal way.

Teacher: Correct. Now we will work on the second operation . . .

In the same way in which the teacher developed the first operation in students, he or she now begins to work on the second operation. After the students have enough practice on the second operation and master it, the teacher gives them some problems that require application of both operations. After some practicing in using both operations, a block of operations is formed and students are able to successfully solve all the problems covered by the algorithm and hence can easily choose English verbs correctly. The process of solution before final automatization of operations looks like this:

Teacher: "I want to *predlozhit'* you an interesting idea." Which English word should you choose?

Student: Is the idea an action that I present to you? No, it isn't. Then "offer": "I want to offer you an interesting idea."

Teacher: "I want to *predlozhit'* you a book."

Student: What do you mean: to read a book or a book as an object?

Teacher: To read a book.

Student: So you want to *predlozhit'* me an action. Do you want to do this formally?

Teacher: No.

Student: Then "suggest" : "I want to suggest you a book."

Teacher: And if I want to *predlozhit'* you a book as a gift?

Student: Then it is not an idea about some action, and "offer" should be used: "I want to *offer* you a book."

After some period of training, students will not give themselves any self-commands and will perform checking operations immediately and simultaneously. It will lead to an instant *automatized reaction* with a proper English verb to any communication task that arises. The final psychological mechanism will be the same as is characteristic of native speakers. In some time the students may completely forget the directions and the process will become "unconscious." This will be the stage when students may even not be able to give any account of their processes and will choose proper words intuitively, intuition being nothing other than instantaneously and unconsciously solving problems on the basis of performance operations without being aware of them.

We have just given an example of the snowball method of forming *algorithmic* processes. An example of application of this method to forming *heuristic* processes can be found in Landa (1976).

Method 2: Developing Individual Operations*

Now that we have considered a method of teaching whole procedures by the step-by-step approach, let us cite (without examples) a method[20] for developing *individual operations* constituting a procedure:

1. Check whether the student *understands the meaning* of the direction in a prescription and its corresponding operations (the meaning of the concepts used in the direction, the role and the function of the operation, etc.).**

yes	no

2. Present to the student a *problem* that requires application of the operation in question.
3. Request the student to *name* the operation or to give him- or herself a *self-command* as to what he or she should do in order to solve the problem, before he or she *executes the operation.*
4. Present the *next problem* and request that the student give the self-command internally.

2. *Explain* what the student does not understand.

3. *Test* the correctness of his or her understanding by asking questions or presenting problems, the solution of which will provide some *practice* in applying the new knowledge, and at the same time, will serve as a test for the student's understanding and for his or her ability to apply the new knowledge. If the student

---

*Editor's note: This is on the micro level, as defined in Chapter 1.

[20]Although we are describing this method in a flow-chart form, we do not call it an algorithm because some of its constituent directives are not algorithmic. As was mentioned, each algorithm may be described in flow-chart form, but not all flow charts are algorithms.

**Editor's note: This is similar to Gagné's third *instructional event*—stimulating recall of prerequisite learnings (see Chapter 4, p. 93).

5. Keep having the student *practice* the operation. Do this by presenting different problems to solve until he or she starts to solve all of them without mistakes and with a speed that you consider to indicate *mastery* of the operation.[21]*

did not pass the test, provide him or her with *additional explanation or or practice,* depending on the reasons for his or her difficulties and/or mistakes. If he or she passed the test, then ⎯

5. Teaching General versus Particular Algo-Heuristic Procedures

Empirical Proposition 1

There exist *different degrees of generality* of problems, operations, their systems (processes or procedures), and their corresponding prescriptions.**

Must Statement 1

From educational and developmental points of view, it is important to teach students processes (procedures) that are *as general as possible* so that a learner who has mastered a procedure will be able to successfully solve most diverse problems within a certain area, as well as be able to see the commonality in situations and problems belonging to different areas and to transfer methods of solution from one area to another.

Empirical Proposition 2

According to the algo-heuristic theory of instruction, the just-mentioned general systems of operations (general procedures) and their corresponding general prescriptions (general methods of thinking or activity) underlie *general abilities* whose development is one of the most important tasks of instruction and education.

Empirical Proposition 3

There exist procedures and methods that are *so general* that they do not depend on the content of the subject matter or on the specific nature of the problems to be solved.*** This enables one and the same method to be applied to different subjects and leads to the successful solution of problems within them. These most general methods, which are often called "cognitive strategies" (cf. Gagné, 1977; Reigeluth, 1980; Rigney, 1978), underlie most general cognitive abilities and are, to a great degree, content independent.

---

[21]In order not to make the description of the method too cumbersome, we have not included in it such evident teaching operations as reactions to incorrect answers or decisions, providing students with feedback, and a number of others. These are routine operations that have to be performed in the framework of different instructional methods.

*Editor's note: This is the major part of Gropper's micro strategy (see Chapter 5).

**Editor's note: This is similar to Scandura's notion of higher-order rules (see Chapter 7).

***Editor's note: These are the same as Gagné's *cognitive strategies* (see Chapter 4).

Must Statement 2

Educationally it is much more important to teach students *how to derive most general methods* of solving problems from logical structures of subject matters than to provide students with these general methods in a ready-made form.[22]

Empirical Proposition 4

Learning a general method of deriving general methods (i.e., a higher-order method) will provide students with a general ability to *derive algorithms* when necessary. As a result, they will be able not only to learn and apply algorithms derived by someone else but also to derive them on their own.

Empirical Proposition 5

As soon as students have learned a general method of deriving general methods, it may be impractical to have them derive each particular algorithm on their own (this may be too time-consuming). As in the case described previously, it is impossible to establish a precise proportion of time between teaching students general methods of deriving general methods and providing them with ready-made general methods of solving problems. Having in mind the task of teaching students general methods of deriving general methods, each teacher will easily find a right proportion, based on the specific conditions of his or her instructional work in each particular case.

AN INTEGRATED MODEL
OF INSTRUCTION

We mentioned earlier that we would demonstrate the method of teaching students how to discover algorithms. Let us now demonstrate this by an example of a particular case of a *guided discovery*—namely the discovery of a very general algorithm for identification of phenomena. A part of the discovery process is deriving identification algorithms from the logical structure(s) of indicative features of phenomena to be identified by means of the algorithm.

The method that is described is directed at solving several instructional problems and achieving several instructional objectives: providing students with knowledge of the nature of general methods for solving problems, getting them to discover (through the teacher's utilization of the snowball principle) necessary operations, getting them to learn and master these operations and their systems (i.e., to develop in them some general cognitive abilities), and some others. The method demonstrated is a synthesis in the sense that it combines in a single instructional model particular instructional procedures that achieve the particular instructional objectives described earlier.

---

[22]On the relationships between logical and linguistic connectives in language, see, in particular, Beilin (1975).

Instead of describing the method as a set of directions and then giving an example of its application, we indicate at each step of the description the method component, referring the reader to an example of practical implementation of this method component set forth in the so-called "Logic Lesson" in Landa (1974). Evidently, this method is just one of the possible methods for solving the instructional problems of the type for which it was designed. As in any instructional situation, there exist many, or at least several, methods for achieving the same instructional objectives.* Our experience, however, showed that the method we developed and applied proved to be effective and easily led to achieving the goals set.

We have conducted the instruction described here in the framework of teaching 11- to 12-year-old students one of the topics of Russian grammar (although such instruction can be conducted in the framework of any other subject matter, in no connection with any specific subject matter at all, and with children of different ages). Although we conducted this piece of instruction in conjunction with teaching some grammatical knowledge and skills, the overall objective of the instruction was more general: to get the students to understand the nature and role of general methods of thinking (solving problems) and to get them to learn a general method of discovering such general methods of thinking, master them, and be able to effectively apply them.

Step 1

Objective

To get students to *realize the importance* of the ability to distinguish different and yet similar grammatical phenomena in order to correctly solve grammatical problems—that is, to write grammatically.

Conditions

The instruction is conducted in a classroom setting with students of approximately equal educational background; there is no possibility to individualize the instructional process and to make it adaptive to individual psychological differences of individual students.[23]

Instructional Operations (Method Components)

1. Explaining the *importance* of correct identification of grammatical phenomena in order to write grammatically.

2. Demonstrating, by examples, how the inability to identify phenomena will lead to mistakes in writing.

---

*Editor's note: This is similar to Gropper's thesis in Chapter 2. However, the question becomes "Are all of these alternative methods equally effective?" If not, only the most effective should be included.

[23]Because these conditions are the same throughout the whole piece of instruction described here, we omit indication of these conditions in each subsequent "step" to avoid unnecessary repetitions.

(For the example of implementation of this step, see paragraph 1 in Landa, 1974, p. 352.)

Step 2

Objectives[24]

1. To get students to realize: (1) that the correct identification of a grammatical phenomenon is a particular case of the ability to identify phenomena in general; and (2) that the ability to identify phenomena depends on the knowledge of their indicative features.

2. To get students to learn scientific terminology for factors on which the identification process depends.

Instructional Operations

1. Explaining that procedures for identification of grammatical phenomena do not in principle differ from procedures for identification of other phenomena.

2. Confronting students with a *familiar everyday situation* when they have to identify (recognize) an object in order to solve their problem.

3. Asking questions intended to lead students to a realization of the *factors* on which the ability to identify depends.*

4. Acquainting students with *scientific terms* designating these factors.

(For the example of implementation of this step, see paragraphs 2 to 7 in Landa, 1974, p. 352.)

Step 3

Objectives

1. To urge students to *single out the features* of the object (in the example referenced, the features of Ivan Ivanovich) that will allow them to recognize it.

2. To develop in students the notions of a *good* and a *bad* indicative feature.

3. To bring students to the concept of *sufficient* and *insufficient* indicative features.**

4. To bring them to awareness of the *cognitive operations* that should be used in order to establish whether an indicative feature (or a given set of indicative features) is a sufficient condition for drawing an inference, whether the object belongs to a certain class or does not belong.

---

[24]An objective may be complex or composite (i.e., consist of a number of subobjectives). This is an example of such an objective.

*Editor's note: This is similar to the Collins-Stevens approach (see Chapter 8).

**Editor's note: Again, note the similarity with Collins' and Stevens' *sufficient and insufficient factors* (see Chapter 8, pp. 252–3).

Instructional Operations

1. Asking students which indicative features of the object (in the example referenced, that of Ivan Ivanovich) they can indicate in order to be able to recognize it.

2. Asking students whether the features indicated by them are unambiguously recognizable.

3. Asking the students whether the features named by them are sufficient for recognizing the object.

4. Assessing their answers and making such comments on them as would lead to the formation in the students of the notions and concepts that should be developed in them according to the stated objectives.

(For the example of implementation of this step, see paragraph 7 (the last sentence) on p. 352 through paragraph 1 on p. 355 in Landa, 1974).

The whole model can be described in a similar manner. For the example of implementation, see the remaining part of the "Logic Lesson" in Landa (1974, pp. 355–380).

CONCLUDING REMARKS AND SUMMARY

As was mentioned earlier, algorithms have been known in mathematics as a mathematical notion for many centuries. Heuristics were used as a means for directing problem-solving processes also for centuries. However, until recently there did not exist a single *psycho-pedagogical algo-heuristic* theory that would be aimed at the development of cognitive processes and behavior in the course of instruction and that would organically synthesize the algorithmic and heuristic approaches. The development of such a theory has allowed us to bring up and resolve a number of problems that have not been previously raised or solved by using some coherent systematic approach.

The psycho-pedagogical algo-heuristic theory (sometimes referred to for brevity as Landamatics—a term suggested by Dr. A. Berkowitz—professor of CUNY) can be described as a theory and technique for:*

1. *Uncovering* conscious and unconscious processes underlying abilities of expert learners and performers to perform on mastery level.

2. Explicitly *describing* the uncovered processes in the form of hypothetical descriptive models.

3. *Testing* out the correctness and completeness of the descriptive models by designing prescriptions on the basis of descriptions (i.e., prescriptive algorithmic

---

*Editor's note: The following 11 steps comprise an instructional *development* model (or procedure), not an instructional model.

and nonalgorithmic models), the latter being used for producing, in a formative pedagogical experiment, psychological processes whose models are to be tested.

4. *Improving* the models, if necessary.

5. *Optimizing* the models when there exist criteria of optimization.[25]

6. *Designing* final algorithmic or nonalgorithmic ideal procedures enabling nonexperts to perform on a mastery level (learners' performance algorithms or heuristics).*

7. *Identifying* the *learning procedures* leading to the development in learners of performance algorithms or heuristics (i.e., identifying learners' learning algorithms or heuristics).**

8. *Designing* algo-heuristic *teaching procedures* capable of effective development of algo-heuristic performance and learning procedures in students.**

9. *Designing* algo-heuristically based *training courses and materials* (textbooks, manual workbooks, systems of exercises, etc.).***

10. Creating, if necessary, computer-based or other *media-based programs* on the basis of algo-heuristic training programs.

11. Designing methods for *evaluating* the efficiency of Landamatic methods of learning and instruction as compared with other methods.

The algo-heuristic theory and methods of performance, learning, and instruction began to develop in the USSR and East-European countries after the appearance of the first publications in Russian starting in 1955 to 1959 (cf. Landa, 1955; Landa & Belopol'skaya, 1959). Among further publications are, in particular, Belopol'skaya (1963), Clauss (1965a, 1965b), Günter (1965), Kelbert (1963), Klix, Neumann, Seeber, & Sydow (1963), Korelyakov (1974), Maliř (1967), Menschel (1969), Pesočin (1970), Pohl (1964), Šolomij (1969, 1973), Volynskaya (1974), Weiser (1969), Yudina (1973), and many others.

After translations from Russian into West-European languages starting in 1962, the algo-heuristic approach to learning and instruction became known in West-European countries, the United States, and Japan. The research on this theory and methods began to develop there (cf. Bung, 1968; Bussman, 1970; Carplay, 1976; Coscarelli, 1978; Edwards, 1967; Gentilhomme, 1964; Gerlach, Reiser, & Brecke, 1977; Horabin & Lewis, 1977; Kopstein, 1974; Lánský; 1969, 1970; Lewis, 1967; Scandura, Durnin, Ehrenpreis, & Luger, 1971; Schmid, Portnoy, & Burns, 1976; Tulodziecki, 1972; Vermersch, 1971; Zierer, 1971, 1972; Zock, 1980; and others).

---

[25]Not any improved model is an optimal model; it may be better than a previous model but not an optimal one.

    *Editor's note: This is a selection strategy.

    **Editor's note: This is also a selection strategy.

    ***Editor's note: The instructional theory (set of models) provides the details for doing this.

REFERENCES

Barkhudarov, L., & Steling, D. Grammatika anglijskogo jazyka (English grammar). Moscow: Vysšaja škola, 1973.

Beilin, H. Studies in the cognitive basis of language development. New York/San Francisco/London: Academic Press, 1975.

Belopol'skaya, A. R. Opyt primenenija obučajščich algoritmov (An experiment in application of instructional algorithms). Vestinik vysšey školy, 1963, 6.

Bloom, B. S. (Ed.). Taxonomy of Educational Objectives: The Classification of Educational Goals. Handbook 1. Cognitive Domain. New York: McKay, 1956.

Bung, K. A model for the construction and use of adaptive algorithmic language programmes. In K. Bung (Ed.), Programmed learning and the language laboratory, 1. London: Longmac, 1968.

Bung, K. Towards a theory of programmed language instruction. The Hague/Paris: Mouton, 1973.

Bussmann, H. Die Anwendung der Algorithmentheorie L. N. LANDA's auf eine anschauliche Problemlösungsaufgabe aus der pädagogischen Psychologie. Dissertation. Die Philosophische Fakultät der Rheinisch-Westfälischen Technischen Hochschule Aachen, 1970.

Carplay, J. A. M. Foreign language teaching and meaningful learning. A Soviet Russian point of view. ITL Review of applied linguistics, University of Leuven, 1976, 161–187.

Clauss, G. Zur Anwendung der Informationstheorie auf lernpsychologische Probleme. Pädagogik, 1965, 1. (a)

Clauss, G. Zur Handlungsanalyse durch Algorithmen und ihre Anwendung im Unterricht. Pädagogik, 1965, 4. (b)

Coscarelli, W. Algorithmization in instruction. Educational Technology, 1978, 2.

Dickerson, R. The fundamentals of legal drafting. Boston/Toronto: Little, Brown, 1965.

Edwards, K. Algorithms and the teaching of grammer. Audio-Visual Language Journal, 1967, 1.

Fisk, M., & Mietus, N. Applied business law. Cincinnati: South-Western Publishing, 1977.

Gagné, R. The analysis of instructional objectives for the design of instruction. In R. Glaser (Ed.), Teaching machines and programmed learning, II. Washington, D.C.: NEA, 1965.

Gagné, R. Learning hierarchies. Educational Psychologist, 1968, 6, 1–9.

Gentilhomme, I. Optimisation des algorithmes d'enseignement. La Pédagogie Cybernetique, 1964, 4.

Gerlach, V., Reiser, R., & Brecke, F. Algorithms in education. Educational Technology, 1977, 10.

Günter, K. Algorithmen als Mittel zur realisierung der Russischunterrichts. Fremdsprachenunterricht, 1965, 11.

Horabin, I., & Lewis, B. Fifteen years of ordinary language algorithms. Improving Human Performance, Quarterly, 1977, 2–3.

Kachalova, K. Grammatika anglijskogo jazyka (The grammer of English). Moscow: Vnestorgizdat, 1964.

Kelbert, H. Über die Anwendung der Algorithmen von Liapunov in der Berufspädagogik. In: Mathematische und Physikalisch-Technische Probleme der Kybernetik. Berlin: DDR, 1963.

Klix, F., Neumann, J., Seeber, A., & Sydow, H. Die algorithmische Beschreibung des Lösung-sprinzips einer Denkaufforderung. Zeitschrift der Psychologie, 1963, 1–2.

Kopstein, F. What is algorithmization of instruction? Educational Technology, 1977, 10.

Korelyakov, Ju. Formirovanije u učaščichsja obščich metodov rassuždenija pri rešeniji zadač na objasnenije (Development of general methods of thinking in students in the process of solving problems of explanation). Dissertation abstract (avtoreferat), Moscow, 1974.

Landa, L. K psichologii formirovanija metodov rassuždenija (na materiale resenija geometriceskich zadač na dokazatelstv (On formation of methods of reasoning in students (on material of students' solution to geometrical problems by proof). Dissertation abstract (avtoreferat). Moscow, 1955.

Landa, L. Algorithmization in learning and instruction. Englewood Cliffs, N.J.: Educational Technology Publications, 1974. (Russian edition, 1966; German edition, 1969.)

Landa, L. *Instructional regulation and control: Cybernetics, algorithmization, and heuristics in education.* Englewood Cliffs, N.J.: Educational Technology Publications, 1976.

Landa, L. & Belopol'skaya. A. Formirovanije u ucascichsja obscich schem umstvennych dejstvij kak uslovije effektivnogo obučenija metodam umstvennoi raboty (Formation in students of general strategies of cognitive actions as a condition of effective teaching the methods of cognitive activities). In: *The proceedings of the first convention of Psychological Society of the USSR,* Moscow, 1959.

Lánský, M. Learning algorithms as a teaching aid. In *RECALL: Review of educational cybernetics and applied linguistics.* London: Longmac, 1969.

Lánský, M. VERBAL: An algorithm which determines the optimal distribution of explanations in a teaching program. In *RECALL: Review of educational cybernetics and applied linguistics.* London: Longmac, 1970.

Lewis, B. *Three essays in ordinary language algorithms.* London: London University Institute Monograph, 1967.

Mager, R. *Preparing instructional objectives.* Palo Alto: Fearon Publishers, 1962.

Maliř, F. Der russische Imperative. *Fremdsprachenunterricht.* 1967, 1–2.

Markle, S. *Designs for instructional designers.* Champaign, Ill: Stipes Publishing, 1978.

Menschel, H. Algotiymizacija i poetapnoje formirovanije umstvennych dejstvij kak sredstovo razvitija myšlenija na urokach fiziki (Algorithmization and stage-by-stage formation of mental actions as a means of thought development on physics lessons). Dissertation abstract (avtoreferat). Moscow, 1969.

Merrill, P. F. Task analysis—An information processing approach. *NSPI Journal,* 1976, *15*(2), 7–11.

Merrill, P. F. Algorithmic organization in teaching and learning: Literature and Research in the U.S.A., *Improving Human Performance Quarterly,* 1977, *6,* 2–3.

Merrill, P. F. Representations for algorithms. *NSPI Journal,* 1980, *19,* 8.

Mitchell, M. C. Jr., The practicality of algorithms in instructional development. *Journal of Instructional Development,* 1980, *4,* 1.

Newell, A., & Simon, H. A. *Human problem solving.* Englewood Cliffs, N.J.: Prentice-Hall, 1972.

Pesočin, A. *Formirovanije algorithmičeskich processov kak sredstvo obučenija ponimaniju inostrannogo teksta (The formation of algorithmic processes as a means of instruction in the comprehension of a foreign language text).* Dissertation abstract (avtoreferat), Moscow, 1970.

Pohl, L. Die methodische Behandlung des Participe Passé. *Wissenschaftliche Zeitschrift der Friedrich-Schiller-Univerität Jena.* Gesellschafts-und sprachwissenschaftliche Reihe, 1964, 2.

Reigeluth, C. M. *Meaningfulness and instruction: Relating what is being learned to what a student knows* (Working Paper No. 1). Syracuse, N.Y.: Instructional Design, Development, & Evaluation Program, School of Education, Syracuse University, 1980.

Reitman, W. *Cognition and thought. An information processing approach.* New York: Wiley, 1965.

Rigney, J. W. Learning strategies: A theoretical perspective. In H. F. O'Neil, Jr. (Ed.), *Learning Strategies.* New York: Academic Press, 1978.

Scandura, J. The role of higher-order rules in problem solving. *Journal of Experimental Psychology,* 1974, *120,* 984–991.

Scandura, J. *Problem solving: A structural process approach with instructional implications.* New York/San Francisco/London: Academic Press, 1977.

Scandura, J. *Structural learning I. Theory and research.* New York/London/Paris: Gordon and Breach, 1973.

Scandura, J. M., Durnin, J. H., Ehrenpreis, W., & Luger, G. *An algorithmic approach to mathematics: Concrete behavioral foundations.* New York: Harper & Row, 1971.

Schmid, R., Portnoy, R., & Burns, K. Using algorithms to assess comprehension of classroom text materials. *Journal of educational research,* 1976, *69,* 309–312.

Shulman, L., & Keislar E. (Eds.). *Learning by discovery: A critical appraisal.* Chicago: Rand McNally, 1966.

Simon, H. A. *The science of the artificial.* Cambridge, Mass: MIT Press, 1969.

Snelbecker, G. *Learning theory, instructional theory and psychoeducational design.* New York: McGraw-Hill, 1974.

Solomij, K. O različii mezdu algoritmičeskimi i nealgoritmičeskimi programmami (On the difference between heuristic and non-heuristic programs) *Voprosy psikhologii,* 1969, 2.

Solomij, K. Ob odnom iz formal'nych metodov sozdanija optimal'nych algoritmov raspoznavanija (On one of the formal methods for design of optimal identification algorithms). In L. Landa (Ed.), Problemy algoritmizacii i programmirovanija obučenija. Vol. 2 (Problems of algorithmization and programming of instruction, Vol. 2). Moscow: Pedagogica, 1973.

Stolurow, L. A model and cybernetic system for research on the teaching–learning process. *Programmed learning,* 1965, 10. (a)

Stolurow, L. Model of the master teacher or master the teacher model. In J. D. Krumboltz (Ed.), *Learning and educational process.* Chicago: Rand McNally, 1965. (b)

Tulodziecki, G. *Beiträge der Algorithmenforschung zu einer Unterrichtswissenschaft. Athenäum, Padagogischer Verlag Schwann et al., 1972.*

Vermersch, P. *Les algorithmes en psychologie et en pedagogie. Definition et intérêts. Le travail humain,* 1971, 1.

Volynskaya, Ž. *Issledovanije vozmožnosti i čelesoobraznosti programmirovannogo obučenija elementarnoj teorii muzyki (A research into possibility and advisability of programmed instruction of the theory of music).* Dissertation abstract (avtoreferat), Moscow, 1974.

Weiser, G. *Formirovanije metodov rassuždenija učaščichsja v processe rešenija fizičeskich zadač (Formation of methods of reasoning in students in the process of solving physics problems).* Dissertation abstract (avtoreferat), Moscow, 1969.

Yudina, O. *Diagnostica psichologočeskich pričin ošibok učaščichsja pri algoritmičeskom i nealgoritmičeskom obučenii (Diagnostics of psychological causes of students' errors in algorithmic and non-algorithmic instruction).* In L. Landa (Ed.). Problemy algoritmizacii i programmirivanija obučeniya (Problems of algorithmization and programming of instruction, Vol. 2). Moscow: Pedagogica, 1973.

Zierer, E. Die algorithmische Methode bei Übersetzen in die Zielsprache. In K. G. Schwestal (Ed.) *Grammatik, kybernetik, kommunikation.* Bonn: Dümmlers, 1971.

Zierer, E. Using algorithmic procedures in foreign language learning. In *RECALL: Review of educational cybernetics and applied linguistics.* London: Longmac, 1972.

Zock, M. *Du "savoir" au "savoir-faire": Strategies en production verbale. Doctoral dissertation, Paris, 1980.*

7 Instructional Strategies Based on the Structural Learning Theory

Joseph M. Scandura
University of Pennsylvania

Joseph M. Scandura

Joseph M. Scandura, Ph.D., is the author of over 135 publications, including 7 books. In addition to articles in mathematical, experimental, and educational psychology in artificial intelligence and educational research and other research journals, his major works include *Structural Learning I: Theory and Research* and *Research and Structural Learning II: Issues and Approaches.* Gordon & Breach Science Publishers, 1973 and 1976; *Problem Solving: A Structural / Process Approach with Instructional Implications,* Academic Press, 1977; *Structural / Process Theories of Complex Human Behavior,* Sijthoff, 1978; and *Structural Learning and Concrete Operations: An approach to Piagetian Theory,* Praeger, Special Studies (Div. Holt, Reinhart & Winston), 1980.

In addition to his research, he has organized an ongoing series of interdisciplinary conferences and an international society on structural learning, including a NATO Advanced Study Institute, "Structural / Process

Theories of Complex Human Behavior." He is currently director of Interdisciplinary Studies in Structural Learning, Instructional Systems and Computer-Based Instruction at the University of Pennsylvania and president, Scandura Training Systems, a company specializing in the development of advanced instructional systems for use on microcomputers. In 1955, he won the National AAU freestyle wrestling championship and was named the tournament's outstanding wrestler. He also coached championship wrestling teams at Syracuse University while pursuing doctoral studies.

Dr. Scandura received his B.A. and M.A. degrees from the University of Michigan and his Ph.D. degree from Syracuse University in 1962. He also has taught at the State University of New York, Buffalo; Syracuse University, and Florida State University, and has been a post-doctoral research fellow or scholar in residence in experimental, mathematical, and educational psychology and artificial intelligence at Indiana University, University of Michigan, E.T.S., Stanford University, and M.I.T., respectively. He completed a one-year U.S.O.E. senior post-doctoral fellowship at the Institute for Mathematical Studies in the Behavioral Sciences at Stanford University during 1968–69 and won Fullbright Awards to West Germany in 1975 and 1976. He has recently been notified of his prospective presidential appointment to the National Council on Educational Research.

CONTENTS

A Prototypic Instructional Strategy Based On The
    Structural Learning Theory   217
Essentials Of Instructional Theory   224
Overview Of The Structural Learning Theory   227
    What Must Be Learned   227
        Problem Domain   227
        Rules   229
        Higher-Order Rules   231
    The Process Of Structural Analysis   232
    The Learner   237
    Assessing Individual Knowledge   240
    Instructional Systems   240

FOREWORD

This chapter describes another cognitively oriented instructional model. As is true of most of the early pioneers in the discipline of instruction (e.g., Bruner, Ausubel, Skinner, Gagné, Landa), Scandura's work has been a combination of learning theory, instructional theory, and instructional-development procedures. Because our purpose is to focus on his instructional-theory ideas, it is important for the reader to understand that Scandura's Structural Learning Theory is considerably more extensive than what is presented in this chapter.

Scandura's instructional theory is similar to Landa's in many ways. It is cognitively oriented. It is comprised exclusively of selection and sequencing strategies (in Landa's the major emphasis was the same). Selection is made on the basis of *rules,* which serve a similar function to Landa's *algorithms.* The rules are broken down into *atomic components,* similar to Landa's *elementary operations.* And Scandura's instructional theory prescribes replacing as many rules as possible with *higher-order rules,* which can be used to generate those rules whenever needed. In his chapter Landa uses *general algorithms* to convey a similar idea. (This results in reducing the amount of content that needs to be taught, while at the same time increasing transfer.) However, there are also important differences. With respect to sequencing, in contrast to Landa's *snowball method,* Scandura prescribes teaching the *simplest path* through a rule first and then proceeding to teach progressively more complex paths until the entire rule has been mastered.

Although his strategies can be (and have been) used for group instruction, Scandura believes that the advantages of his theory become most apparent in individualized instruction. A major part of his selection strategy is to do a thorough analysis as to which paths of which rules each student has and has not mastered and then to teach each student only those paths of those rules that the student has not already learned. It remains to be seen as to whether this is, or will be, a cost-effective approach to instruction. Computer implementations, such as a series being developed by Scandura and his associates, may provide the key to answering this question.

In contrast with other theories elaborated in this book, Scandura's instructional theory tends to place more emphasis on such philosophical concerns as generality, parsimony, and cohesiveness. Relatively less emphasis is placed (1) on describing what we referred to as micro strategies in Chapter 1 (such as Gagné's nine *events of instruction,* Gropper's *preparatory progressions* for individual objectives, and Landa's *methods for developing individual operations*); and (2) on describing different models of instruction for different kinds of objectives. In Scandura's opinion, his instructional theory "has a rigorous base that makes it particularly useful in designing individualized instruction, especially in a computer environment."

Scandura has undeniably made important contributions to instructional theory. To name two, the selection of higher-order rules and the simple-to-complex sequencing of instruction on a rule on the basis of the complexity of its paths are both very important contributions to a common knowledge base—a comprehensive set of models of instruction.

C.M.R.

Instructional Strategies Based on the Structural Learning Theory

On the occasion of various professional/social events, I have frequently been asked to "explain the essentials of my Structural Learning Theory." Often the unstated implication is that this should be accomplished in no more than 5 minutes and preferably in a short verbal paragraph. It is easy to satisfy such constraints, of course, by presenting vacuous truisms at a high level of abstraction. But, so doing would serve little useful purpose; indeed, it would do a distinct disservice to the listener who goes away with a few chosen "key" words to be misued in future social situations.

Along with the other contributors to this book, I have been asked to write a chapter briefly describing the Structural Learning Theory, with specific emphasis on its prescriptive implications for instruction. I try to do this. In so doing, however, I feel compelled first to mention several caveats:

1. Instructional theory MUST be prescriptive. Any theory that does not provide some means of controlling or influencing learning would by definition not be an instructional theory. Although descriptive (explanatory) theories are desirable in many scientific fields, this is not the case in instruction, or indeed in any "science of the artificial," where theory derives its value from its ability to achieve predetermined ends.*

2. Proper understanding of the Structional Learning Theory in its philosophical and methodological, as well as theoretical and pragmatic, aspects requires extended, serious study. Indeed, the Structural Learning Theory is not really a theory at all. The Structional Learning Theory refers collectively to certain distinctive research methodologies, along with a broad, comprehensive CLASS of con-

---

*Editor's note: See Chapter 1, pp. 21–23, for further discussion of this topic.

tent and population-specific structural learning theories, a large number of which currently exist. As argued elsewhere, this class of theories and methodologies is a necessary consequence of certain very basic assumptions that most scientists would agree are crucial to instructional theory (e.g., Scandura, 1971a, 1973, 1977b, 1978b, 1980).

3. Most current "instructional theories" consist largely of taxonomies and techniques. Most of these taxonomies and techniques are designed to meet immediate practical ends and, therefore, tend to be highly discrete and peculiarly related to particular needs. In most cases, they only minimally satisfy the requirements of good theory: completeness, cohesiveness, parsimony, precision, and operationality. As a consequence, and when looked at from a deeper theoretical perspective, many of the pragmatic or taxonomic distinctions made are more apparent than real.

In line with my assigned task, what I would *like* to do is to show in detail: (1) how existing taxonomies and techniques, along with others that have been used in instructional design, may be derived from the Structural Learning Theory; and (2) why pragmatically proven techniques are good and how those of questionable value might be improved. Important as these tasks might be, I must settle for more modest goals. With a few major exceptions (e.g., Scandura, 1973, 1977b), my previous writings in this area are fairly widely scattered.

In the following pages, I begin by "epitomizing" the Structural Learning Theory in its prescriptive aspects. Specifically, using a very simple task as a prototype, I show how the theory lends itself to prescribing instruction for *individual students*.* Incidentally, it is noted why the analytic approach, which characterizes structural learning theories, avoids certain complications inherent in more taxonomic and/or pragmatic techniques.

Subsequent sections deal more generally with the essentials of what I consider to be a scientifically and (practicably) viable approach to instructional theory, along with a summary of some of the theoretical and empirical progress we have made using this approach.

A PROTOTYPIC INSTRUCTIONAL STRATEGY BASED ON THE STRUCTURAL LEARNING THEORY

Instructional implications of the Structural Learning Theory are perhaps most easily seen by illustration. In this section, we consider column subtraction problems as a simple prototype.

In order to utilize structural learning principles in designing instruction, the ESSENTIAL first step is to identify: (1) the educational goals—what the learner is

---

*Editor's note: Such individualization, of course, may not be cost effective in many instructional settings. In this case, Scandura recommends the use of what he calls "approximation" methods (e.g., Lowerre & Scandura, 1973). For a comparison, note how Landa deals with this problem (see Chapter 6, p. 194).

to be able to do after instruction* and (2) prototypic cognitive processes—how the learner is to perform tasks associated with educational goals.** By educational goals I am not referring to "behavioral objectives," at least not just in the highly restricted traditional sense (Scandura, 1971a). Thus, for example, educational goals may vary at one extreme from something as specific as "saying cat when shown a cat" to something as broad as "being able to devise an operational theory to explain any given set of behavioral phenomena." Clearly, no one could reasonably be expected to achieve the latter goal with perfection; but, from the present perspective, that is not essential. What IS essential is that we can distinguish between those things that a learner might do that are relevant and those that are not.

Prototypic cognitive processes refer essentially to what the learner must (according to the teacher) master in order to perform as desired.

In the Structional Learning Theory, what must be learned is one or more *rules*.*** Rules are theoretical constructs that may be used to represent all kinds of human knowledge. Each rule consists of a *domain,* or set of encoded inputs to which it applies, a *range* or set of undecoded outputs that it is expected to generate, and a restricted type of *procedure,* which applies to elements in the domain.

For example, consider a rule for adding "ed" to verbs. In this case, the domain of the rule is the set of all verbs to which "ed" can be added. The range of the rule consists of the resultant verbs (i.e., the verbs with "ed" added, properly spelled). The procedure of the rule may be described as follows:

1. If the last letter (of the verb) is a "c," then add a "k" and then "ed."
2. Otherwise, if the last three letters are of the form consonant—vowel—consonant, then double the final consonant and add "ed."
3. Otherwise, if the verb ends in "e," then drop the final "e" and add "ed."
4. Otherwise, if the last letter is "y" preceded by a consonant, then change "y" to "i" and added "ed."
5. Otherwise, just add "ed."

The Structural Learning Theory provides a general method of analysis, called Structural Analysis,**** by which the rules to be learned can be derived from suitably operationalized educational goals. Although there are many details still to be completely objectified, the method is relationship systematic and has been applied successfully in analyzing a wide variety of content. (More details are given in the following section on structural analysis.)

---

*Editor's note: In spite of an apparent similarity with the previous theories, goals are not used as a basis for prescribing methods in Scandura's theory. Rather, they serve as a starting point for further analysis.

**Editor's note: Note the similarity with Landa's cognitively oriented theory (see Chapter 6).

***Editor's note: Although there are important differences, this notion is similar to Landa's *algorithms* (see Chapter 6).

****Editor's note: This is a development procedure, not a part of an instructional model or theory. However, it is essential for the implementation of the instructional theory.

The first step in structural analysis involves *selecting a representative sample of problems* associated with the educational goal in question. Representative problems may be defined as problems that the "teacher" feels best represent how a knowledgeable person should solve the problems. In the case of simple subtraction, this might include problems like:

$$\begin{array}{c} 9 \\ \underline{-5} \end{array} \qquad \begin{array}{c} 879 \\ \underline{-325} \end{array} \qquad \begin{array}{c} 432 \\ \underline{-129} \end{array} \qquad \text{and} \quad \begin{array}{c} 402 \\ \underline{-124} \end{array}$$

The second step in structural analysis involves *identifying rules* for solving each of the selected problems. Identifying such rules involves several identifiable substeps:

1. Assumptions must be made regarding the minimal encoding and decoding *capabilities of the students* in the target population.* In the case of second graders, for example, the teacher/analyst would normally assume that all students are able to distinguish "the minus sign," the individual digits 0, 1, . . . 9, the columns, and the rows, and that all are able to write the individual digits in desired locatioins. The present illustration builds on this assumption. Consequently, the remainder of the analysis is inadequate JUST to the extent that these assumptions are in error for students in any given target population.

2. The analyst must decide the *scope of each representative prototype problem.* This scope effectively defines the domain of the rule associated with the prototype.** The problem

$$\begin{array}{c} 432 \\ \underline{-124} \end{array}$$

for example, might be held prototypic of the entire class of column subtraction problems—namely, those formed by varying the individual digits (0, 1, . . . , 9) and/or the number of columns. Indeed, in the present case, each of the selected representative problems is prototypic of this same domain. Consequently, in the present case, it is reasonable to assume that there is only one domain, the domain of column subtraction problems.

3. Next, the analyst must *identify the steps* (operations and decisions) involved in solving each of the representative problems.*** These operations and decisions must be sufficiently simple that using them refers only to abilities that are assumed available to ALL students in the target population (i.e., encoding/decoding capabilities).**** The operations must also be *atomic* in the sense that, for each student

---

*Editor's note: In the Gagné-Briggs theory, these were referred to as *entry-level behaviors* (see Chapter 4).

**Editor's note: This is similar to Gropper's notion of *stimulus properties* (see Chapter 5, p. 116).

***Editor's note: This is similar to Landa's *performance algorithms* (see Chapter 6, p. 178).

****Editor's note: This is similar to Landa's notion of *elementariness of operations* (Chapter 6, p. 173) and to Gagné's *entry-level behaviors* (Chapter 4, p. 90).

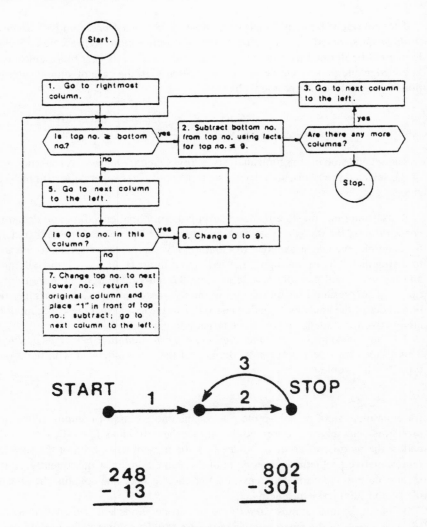

FIG. 7.1   Subtraction rule (algorithm) and sample subtraction problems.

in the target population, the ability to correctly use an operation once is indicative of uniform success, and conversely for failure.

The flow diagram in Fig. 7.1 depicts the procedural portion of a rule based on borrowing, more commonly known as the "borrowing algorithm." In this rule, it is implicitly assumed that each operation acts only on digits, rows, and columns—hence, the previously referred-to need to assume certain minimal encoding/decoding abilities. In addition, the decisions of this rule (e.g., Is top number greater than bottom number?) constitute additional assumptions concerning minimal cognitive ability. Only to the extent that these assumptions are met will this subtraction rule, according to the Structural Learning Theory, provide a useful and operationally precise basis for designing efficient and effective instructional strategies.

More could be said about the actual processes by which such rules are constructed but this area is still largely virgin territory, and going more deeply into it here would detract from our main concern with instructional strategies. The essential thing to emphasize is that use of the Structural Learning Theory for purposes of designing instruction necessarily begins with a *rule-based analysis of the subject matter* (broadly conceived) in question. Notice, in particular, that I have said nothing about a taxonomy of subject-matter content; according to a structural learning perspective, ALL content must be analyzed. Some types, of course, such as our subtraction example, are easier to analyze than others. Indeed, if one were to propose a taxonomy of content types, such a taxonomy might most usefully derive from the extent and nature of the analyses necessary. In the theoretical part of this chapter, for example, I sketch what is involved in analyzing more complex content (e.g., geometry construction problems), which involves a wide variety of rules and higher-order rules representing interrelationships among them.

Once an analysis has been completed, designing an effective instructional strategy follows directly and precisely from the theory. Specifically, once an analysis has been completed, one knows: (1) what the student *is to be able to do* once he or she has achieved the educational objective (e.g., solve arbitrary column subtraction problems); and (2) what the student *must learn* in order to be able to do that (i.e., the borrowing rule).*

Given this information, the first thing one must do in designing an effective instructional strategy is to *determine what each student already knows*—specifically, that part of what the student knows that is directly relevant to what one wants the student to learn. The process by which this is accomplished is described in the section entitled *Assessing Individual Knowledge* in the context of describing the theory more generally and thus is not considered here. It is sufficient for present purposes to observe that solving particular subtraction problems involves following one and only one *path* through the subtraction rule.** In effect, there is a unique class of problems associated with each path through the rule.

For example, one path through the subtraction rule (procedure) described in Fig. 7.1 may be described as:

1. Go to the rightmost column.

2. If the top number is greater than or equal to the bottom number, subtract the bottom number from the top number using facts for the top number less than or equal ($\leq$) 9.

---

*Editor's note: These prescriptions are limited to *selection* strategies—that is, the structural analysis reveals what rules should be selected as instructional content.

**Editor's note: For a more thorough (yet concise) discussion of *paths* and *path analysis,* see Scandura (1971b, 1973, 1973b) and P. Merrill (1978).

3. Go to the next column to the left and repeat step 2. This is adequate for solving all, but only, those column subtraction problems in which the top number in each column is greater than or equal to the bottom number. (Incidentally, notice that there is a finite number of paths associated with any given rule).

Given the previously described assumption concerning atomicity (of basic operations and decisions), success or failure on any one problem associated with such a class provides complete information as to the availability to the student of the particular path in question. For example, the problem

$$
\begin{array}{r}
879 \\
-325 \\
\hline
\end{array}
$$

is solved by following the path defined by operation 1 (go to rightmost column), then 2 (subtract bottom number from top number), then 3 (go to next column to left), and back to 2, before stopping.

By testing on a small, finite set of problems, it is possible to identify precisely and unambiguously which parts of the subtraction rule any given individual knows and which parts that student does not know. Such testing, in effect, defines the student's entering level. In this regard, more can be said about such things as testing in situations in which more than one rule is involved and about increasing efficiency via sequential testing (e.g., Scandura, 1971a, 1973, 1977b), but this is not necessary for present purposes.

Prescribing the content of instruction, then, follows directly from what the student knows. All one needs to do is to identify the missing portions of the desired (subtraction) rule and to present them to the student. The theory is neutral on whether this information should be presented, say, in an expository or a discovery manner. Thus, for example, deciding on the appropriate method of presentation depends on secondary objectives that the teacher may (or may not) have in mind (e.g., to help students learn how to detect regularities). The important part, insofar as being able to perform subtraction is concerned, is simply to be able to perform according to the rule.

As an illustration, suppose a student's knowledge may be represented by the flow diagram in Fig. 7.1, minus only the loop involving operation 6 (change 0 to 9). In this case, the instructor would need only to make sure that the student knows, at the appropriate points, how to test whether the top number in a column is zero, how to change zero to 9, and how to proceed to the next column (operation 5). When the student knows less, of course, one would start with the simpler prototypes (partial rules representing what the student knows) and gradually "elaborate," or add increasing detail, until the student has mastered the entire rule.*

In the structural learning theory, then, diagnosis and instructional prescription begin with structural analysis, in which rules are broken down into atomic compo-

---

*Editor's note: This is a *sequencing* strategy—a prescription as to how to order the content that has been selected for instruction.

nents (i.e., steps that are so simple that each student in the target population may be assumed able to perform each step either perfectly or not at all). Given the results of such analysis, one can identify which parts of to-be-taught rules individuals already know. Success on any path of a rule implies success on all atomic components. Conversely, failure on a path implies that at least one component has not been mastered. By comparing mastered and unmastered paths, it is possible to pinpoint exactly which atomic components must be taught in order for the student to perform as desired. Elaboration, in effect, consists of presenting needed components in an order (typically more than one order will do) that results in complete mastery of increasing numbers of previously failed paths. Readers of this book, hopefully, will notice that my use of the term *elaborate* was intended to make clear connections between this process and that proposed by Reigeluth and Merrill under the label *Elaboration Theory*.

The close relationship between instructional strategy and basic underlying theory has a number of other important advantages, not the least of which is the integration of what sometimes appear to be different concepts. In more taxonomic and/or pragmatic theories, for example, a distinction is frequently made between *Macro* and *Micro* instructional strategies. Macro strategies, as the name implies, refer to global aspects of instruction—for example, how to combine or sequence atomic[1] (component) rules as discussed previously in order to teach some overall rule like subtraction. Micro strategies, then, refer to more detailed or elemental aspects of instruction—like how to sequence instances (e.g., examples or problems) so as to optimize the learning of component (atomic) rules.*

When viewed from the current theoretical perspective, this distinction is totally arbitrary and depends solely on the preferred level of analysis. The point is that individual atomic rules are themselves simply rules. They too may be "broken down" into still more basic components. Operation 2 "Subtract bottom number from top number using facts for top number ≤ 9," for example, may, and with many student populations should, be represented in more detail in terms of the individual "facts" involved. In this case, the instructional strategies for teaching operation (rule) 2 would be identical to those used with other rules—namely, start with the known paths and "elaborate."

What the distinction between macro and micro strategies does is to allow one the option of NOT engaging in a more rigorous analysis of atomic components.

---

[1]Given *fixed* assumptions concerning encoding and decoding capabilities, there is always some minimal level of atomicity. Further refinement of atomic components in such cases requires more detailed characterization of such capabilities. For further discussion of this and related issues, see the following sections and Scandura (1973, 1977b).

*Editor's note: See Chapter 1 for more detail about macro and micro strategies. See also Gropper's distinction between *preparatory progressions* (for single objectives) and *contingent progressions* (for multiple objectives: see Chapter 5, p. 155), and Landa's distinction between *methods for developing individual operations* and his other kinds of methods (see Chapter 6, p. 202). These concepts are indeed relative, but that enhances rather than diminishes their usefulness.

Instead, one can use such pragmatic and/or empirically validated "rules of thumb" as "teach instances that vary maximally over the domain of the rule." With respect to subtraction, for example, we have the basic facts at one extreme and problems that involve mixed nonborrowing, borrowing, and borrowing across zero at the other. Having conducted what are some of the earliest studies dealing with related problems on rule learning (e.g., Scandura 1967b, 1968, 1969), I am happy to endorse such "rules of thumb." They are, however, just that: rules of thumb. More rigorous and thereby efficient treatment requires prior analysis of the sort proposed earlier. In this case, rather than just presenting subtraction problems of different degrees of difficulty, instruction would consist of presenting exactly those components that diagnosis showed to be lacking, and presenting them in an order consistent with the natural hierarchical ordering of paths.

In concluding this section, it must be emphasized that the preceding illustration of prescriptive aspects of the Structural Learning Theory constitutes only a simple prototype. It "epitomizes" the prescriptive theory in this sense. The theory itself provides a far more generalized basis for instructional prescription—which in principle may be used with any subject matter (or educational goal) that might be of interest.

In the hope that they may be suggestive of even more fertile fields of application, the theoretical foundations of the Structural Learning Theory as they pertain to instruction are summarized in the following sections.

ESSENTIALS OF
INSTRUCTIONAL THEORY

Any viable theory of teaching must include, first of all, some way of specifying what must be learned—that is, some way to represent knowledge. In addition, a fully adequate theory of teaching must allow for the growth of knowledge over time as learners interact dynamically with a changing teaching environment.

During the past two decades considerable progress relevant to various aspects of the above has been made in such fields as artificial intelligence (e.g., Bobrow & Collins, 1975; Minsky & Papert, 1972), individual differences measurement (e.g., Cronbach & Snow, 1977; Glaser, 1963; Hively, Patterson, & Page, 1968), and cognitive psychology (e.g., Anderson, 1976; Kintsch, 1974), as well as in instructional psychology per se (e.g., Gagné, 1962; Glaser & Resnick, 1972; M. D. Merrill & Boutwell, 1973; P. F. Merrill, 1978; Rothkopf, 1972; Tennyson & Rohen, 1977).

There have also been important developments in dealing with the instructional process as a whole (e.g., Landa, 1976; Pask, 1976) and with relationships to general systems theory (especially Pask, 1976). Specifically, significant progress has been made in understanding the interrelationships among content, cognition, and individual differences and in the way they interact over time as a result of instruction.

Global considerations, of course, necessarily play some role, even in the most prescribed research, as does actual human behavior in global systems-oriented theories. Nonetheless, the extent to which "top-down" considerations have influenced the former and the extent to which "hard data" have influenced theorizing about instructional systems have generally been quite limited. Somewhat orthogonal to the just described dichotomy has been the widely sensed gap between theory and practice (see Scandura, Frase, Gagné, Groen, & Stolurow, 1978).* Typically, theories associated with the various academic disciplines have been perceived as having at best peripheral relevance to instruction. On the other hand, pragmatically generated teaching techniques and/or design principles have been largely devoid of theory.

To date, the only theory that appears to have seriously probed the "unexplored land" between these alternative views and concerns is the Structural Learning Theory (e.g., Scandura, 1971a, 1973, 1977b).** This theory and a rather large body of supportive empirical research have been well documented in the literature, most recently and comprehensively in my books on Structural Learning and Problem Solving (Scandura, 1973, 1977b). I do not attempt to even survey this literature here.[2] Rather, I emphasize essential historical, global, and methodological considerations, with special attention to relationships to the instructional process.

Historically, development of the Structural Learning Theory was motivated by instructional considerations. Specifically, the goal of my very first piece of serious research (Scandura, 1962, 1964) was to help clarify the roles of expository and discovery modes of problem-solving instruction. I found that it is essentially impossible to obtain reliable results no matter how precisely one attempts to specify instructional treatments. More critical than *how* information was imparted was *when* that information was given in relationship to what learners knew at the time.***

---

*Editor's note: The "theory" referred to here is mostly *learning* theory. Instructional theory by its very nature is closely related to practice. See Chapter 1 for further discussion of this difference.

**Editor's note: Because it is the purpose of instructional theory to bridge the "gap between (learning) theory and practice" (see Chapter 1, p. 5), all of the theories and models described in this book do the same. The differences reside primarily in the emphasis on basic theory versus instructional application.

***Editor's note: Hence, Scandura's emphasis on the macro strategies of *selection* and *sequencing* to the exclusion of micro concerns, such as the Gagné—Briggs *nine events of instruction* (Chapter 4), Gropper's *preparatory progressions* (Chapter 5), and Landa's *method for developing individual operations* (Chapter 6).

[2]Early beginnings followed by a large body of related research on rule learning appeared in print as early as 1962 (Scandura, 1962, 1964, 1969, 1970). The earliest systematic presentation of the theory (Scandura, 1971a), although somewhat outdated, still provides perhaps the best introduction, although Scandura (1977c) also provides a useful survey. Volume 1 of Structural Learning (Scandura, 1973) provides a relatively formal treatment, but the more recent book on problem solving (Scandura, 1977b) provides perhaps the clearest version along with important refinements, extensions, and applications to education. *Instructive Commentaries on Problem Solving* are included in Scandura and Brainerd (1978) and the *Journal of Structural Learning* (volume 6, no. 4).

If information was presented too early, pupils were not only unable to use the information but also they gradually learned not to attend when presented with subsequent information.

Nonetheless, although certain analytical tools were used (e.g., the use of algorithms to represent what was to be learned), a major problem with this research was the inability to operationalize individual knowledge. Specifically, it was difficult to tie the phenomena being studied in with the S–R and concept-learning studies, or with the computer simulation studies of the day. Given what seemed to me to be an inadequate S–R language and unnecessarily cumbersome computer programs, I turned my attention in the early and mid-1960s towards the development of a simple but suitably general scientific language for theorizing about such phenomena.

Others during that period, most notably Gagné (1962), also were concerned with clarifying relationships between simple S–R and more complex kinds of learning. Rather than attempting to represent rule, problem solving, and other complex forms of learning as complications of S–R learning, however, it seemed to me both more parsimonious and more useful to take the rule as basic and to explain simpler types of learning as special cases (e.g., Scandura, 1967a, 1970b). This type of formulation appeared to be considerably more precise, thereby making it possible to avoid certain problems that arise, for example, in attempting to represent rules or principles in terms of concepts or associations (see Scandura, 1967a, especially p. 339; 1970b, pp. 517–521).

In the Set-Function Language developed as a result of this work, the emphasis was on *sets* of observable input–output (stimulus–response) pairs and on rule (function) constructs needed to explain how outputs were to be generated from the inputs. Specifically, rules were characterized as triples, each rule having: (1) a *domain*, or set of conditions to be satisfied by inputs; (2) a *range*, or set of anticipatory conditions characteristic of the outputs the knower expects the rule to produce; and (3) an *operation* or procedure (algorithm) that, when applied to inputs in the domain, generates a unique output (e.g., Scandura, 1970b).*

During the 1960s my students and I used rules, so defined, in the analysis and empirical study of a wide variety of rule-based phenomena, ranging from simple to complex. (Many of these studies are summarized in Scandura, 1969, 1976.) This characterization was subsequently adopted in research by a number of influential educational psychologists (e.g., M. D. Merrill & Boutwell, 1973; P. F. Merrill, 1978; Schmid & Gerlach, 1977 personal communication) and apparently is now widely accepted.[3]

---

*Editor's note: The *domain* and *range* are similar to Gropper's *class of stimuli* and *class of responses*, respectively, and *operation* is similar to Landa's *algorithm*.

[3]Since its early development, this characterization has undergone a number of important refinements. For example, although rules are similar to "productions," as originally conceived by the logician Post (see Minsky, 1967) and later utilized for psychological purposes by Newell and Simon (1972) and other members of the Carnegie school, they are *not* identical. Specifically, the operations/ procedures in rules, although restricted as to form, are *more general* than those in productions. Also,

OVERVIEW OF THE
STRUCTURAL LEARNING THEORY

The Structural Learning Theory is a natural extension of this early work and provides a unifying theoretical framework within which to view the teaching–learning process. As noted previously, the theory is not really a (specific) theory at all, but rather it defines a *class* of theories much as is the case, for example, with Stimulus Sampling Theory of S–R behaviorism (e.g., Estes, 1959).

The Structural Learning Theory, however, is not simply a scientific language. As we see, very definite assumptions are made about how and why people behave as they do. Furthermore, numerous specific realizations of the theory have been detailed and empirically tested to good effect (e.g., Scandura, 1977b; Scandura & Scandura, 1978).

As shown in Fig. 7.2, the theory is concerned with: (1) the specification of *what must be learned* (to perform as desired on the given educational goals); (2) the characterization of cognitive essentials of *individual learners*; and (3) the ongoing and goal-directed *interactional process* between teacher and learner.

What Must Be Learned

Problem Domain

In the theory, *content* is effectively characterized in terms of the tasks, or problem situations, that the teacher wants the learner to master (or to deal with effectively), and is referred to as a *problem domain*.[4] The prototypic processes that collectively make it possible to solve problems in a problem domain are referred to as rules of competence. (Rules of competence are defined as indicated earlier.) Collectively, the set of competence rules is called a *competence account* of the problem domain and constitutes what the learner must learn in order to master the *content*.[5]

It is important here not to confuse problem domain with sets of *behavioral objectives*. Although the latter may constitute a problem domain, the converse is not necessarily true. As observed in an earlier exposition (Scandura, 1971c) the behavioral objectives approach has a major disadvantage:

> Because the (solution) rules (for each objective) are discrete, they cannot account for behaviors which go beyond the given corpus (i.e., for tasks not associated with one of the given behavioral objectives). . . . For example, suppose a set of behavioral

---

productions *do not distinguish* ranges apart from what one gets when an operation is applied. Both differences, although seemingly technical, are crucial in converting the rule construct into an operational scientific theory that is sufficiently broad to encompass the instructional process.

[4]In structural learning theories, problems are formally characterized (represented) in tems of finite sets of elements, relations, and operations defined on the elements, and higher-order relations and operations. (Unlike standard mathematical systems, the relations and operations need not be defined on the same domains and ranges.)

[5]Note: What is referred to here as *content* corresponds to what others sometimes call educational goals.

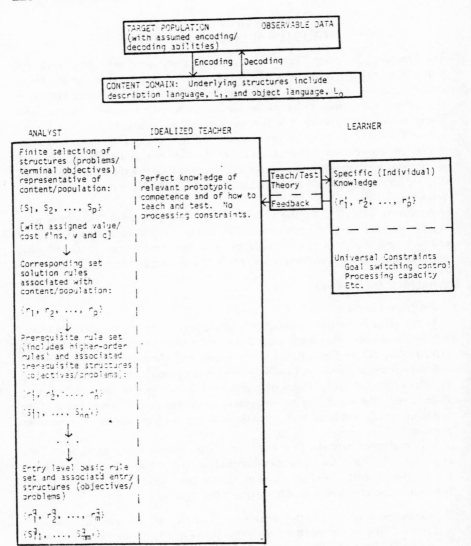

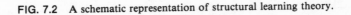

FIG. 7.2 A schematic representation of structural learning theory.

objectives in arithmetic) only involved rules for adding, subtracting, multiplying, and dividing. In this case, the subject would be unable to even generate the addition fact corresponding to a given subtraction fact, although one might reasonably expect this type of behavior from a person . . . well versed in arithmetic. One might counter, of course, that it would be a simple matter to add a new rule to the original list. (Such a rule might map $5 - 3 = 2$ into $2 + 3 = 5$, for example.) In effect, when

confronted with the criticism that their objectives do not constitute a . . . viable curriculum (curriculum constructors) would simply say we can add more objectives. . . . This sort of argument . . . misses the point entirely. Not only would such an approach be *ad hoc*—which really says nothing in itself except to convey some ill-defined dissatisfaction—but it would be completely infeasible where one is striving for completeness. To see this, it is sufficient to note that a new rule would have to be introduced for every conceivable interrelationship, and that the number of such interrelationships is indefinitely large. One could easily envision a number of rules so large that no human being could possibly learn all of them. . . . The sum total of all mathematical knowledge, for example, is so vast that no one has or could possibly acquire all of it. As vast as this knowledge is, however, a really good mathematician is capable of generating any amount of new mathematics which does not appear in print anywhere. That is he can *create*. Much of the new mathematics might be utterly trivial, of course, but the very fact that it exists at all strongly suggests that any (behavioral objectives) characterization would almost certainly miss much that is important [pp. 28–29].

In the theory, then, the term problem domain is used in a broad sense, and, in principle, may encompass anything from arithmetic to language or moral behavior. Orthogonally, problem domains may be narrow in scope (e.g., two-digit subtraction problems) or comprehensive (e.g., an elementary-school mathematics curriculum).

Rules

A central problem in all scientifically viable cognitive theories is that of how to represent competence, and the Structural Learning Theory is no exception (Scandura, 1971a, 1973). A variety of constructs have been proposed for this purpose; these range from relational networks (e.g., Quillian, 1968) and frames (e.g., Minsky, 1975), which tend to emphasize static considerations, to productions (e.g., Newell & Simon, 1972) and procedures (e.g., Minsky & Papert, 1972), which emphasize cognitive operations.

Rules (e.g., Scandura, 1970b) fall in the latter category.[6] More specifically, it is assumed in the Structural Learning Theory that the competence underlying any

---

[6]In general, inferences drawn about cognitive processes from observable behavior necessarily involve both encoding/decoding and internal processes—in a combination that cannot be determined via observation alone. Specifically, a theorist may equally well absorb most of the explanation into the encoding/decoding (of static structures) or into internal cognitive operations. (See Anderson [1976] for a good discussion of the issues involved.)

Hence, technically speaking, rules in the Structural Learning Theory do not operate on observable inputs but rather on (static) cognitive representations (structures) of such inputs. Similarly, rules do not generate observable outputs but rather internal structures representing such outputs. (These distinctions between observables and representations of these observables are schematized at the top of Fig. 7.2.)

To avoid the ambiguity mentioned earlier, the Structural Learning Theory does not attempt to explain encoding and decoding processes; rather it requires that all of the targeted students (and the teacher) agree on what are the minimally effective operating inputs and outputs (i.e., what are the

given problem domain can be represented in terms of finite sets of rules (e.g., Scandura, 1971c), each of which may be represented in terms of elementary or atomic components (e.g., Scandura, 1970b, 1976). Each rule can be broken down into *atomic components* (i.e., steps that are so simple that each individual in the target population may be assumed to be able to perform each step either perfectly or not at all).* In line with our previous discussion, it is worth emphasizing that what are atomic units relative to one population may not be atomic units with respect to another (e.g., less-sophisticated) population.

Because success on any path of a rule depends on success on all atomic components, each path through the rule also acts in atomic fashion. Furthermore, there is only a *finite number of behaviorally distinct paths*: We do not distinguish paths according to the number of repetitions of loops, because the same cognitive operations and decisions are required regardless of how many times a given loop is traversed in carrying out a given "cognitive computation."

Collectively, the paths of the subtraction rule impose a partition on the domain of column subtraction problems: That is, they define a set of distinct, exhaustive, and homogeneous *equivalence classes*** of subtraction problems such that each problem in a given equivalence class can be solved via exactly one of the paths.

One path through the aforementioned subtraction algorithm of Fig. 7.1 is represented schematically at the bottom of Fig. 7.1, along with two-column subtraction problems to which that path applies (the first node designates START). Operation (arrow) 1 says to go to the rightmost column. The second node, then, asks whether the top number is greater than the bottom number. Because the answer is "yes,"

---

encoded and to-be-decoded structures representing the inputs and outputs). In this regard, it is important to emphasize two things:

1. Assuming the uniform availability of certain minimal encoding and decoding capabilities is not a practical or even an in-principle limitation. Not only have psychologists long made such assumptions implicitly, but it is always possible to reduce the amount assumed sufficiently so that the capabilities of students in the target population are not exceeded. In effect, assumed encoding and/or decoding processes can always be detailed in terms of (internal) rules, together with simpler forms of encoding or decoding. Given a problem like

$$\begin{array}{r} 45 \\ +34 \\ \hline \end{array}$$

for example, it is normally assumed that all students will encode the digits in the standard way. Although such an assumption might be quite realistic with most second graders, this is not necessariy the case with children who cannot yet read or write. In the latter case, for example, the assumed decoding capabilities could be reduced, by absorbing into the rules the processes by which simple line segments, curves, and corners are combined to form the digits. (Correspondingly, notice that one could analyze the writing process in this way.)

2. By assuming minimal encoding/decoding capabilities in this way, it is possible to make unambiguous inferences concerning cognitive processes; the rules (and certain cognitive universals mentioned later) contain all that is important insofar as explaining, predicting, and controlling behavior on the given problem domain concerned.

*Editor's note: This is identical to Landa's notion of elementariness of operations (p. 173).

**Editor's note: This is related to Markle and Tiemann's (1969) notion of *minimum rational set*, which is a set of examples comprised of one example from each *equivalence class*.

Operation 2 is applied (i.e., the bottom number is subtracted from the top number). Next (node 3), we ask if there are any more columns. If there are, we proceed to the next column (operation 3) and repeat. Otherwise we STOP.

Theoretically, the problems associated with any given problem domain can be solved in any number of ways (e.g., via any number of rule sets). In practice, however, only a *small number of alternative rule sets* are normally compatible with how a teacher wants the students to go about solving them. It would make a big difference, for example, whether the teacher simply wants the students to be able to perform successfully on a given class of tasks (e.g., subtraction problems) or whether he or she also wants the students to do so with "understanding" (e.g., to be able to relate the process to concrete reality; for example, German children are taught the equal additions method of subtraction, whereas American children are taught borrowing). The underlying rules of competence necessarily reflect these preferences. (Note: In the unrestricted Structural Learning Theory (i.e., not limited to instruction), rules of competence are more generally viewed as prototypic of some subject population—for example, prototypic of how concrete operational children are assumed to solve conservation tasks (Scandura & Scandura, 1978.)

Whereas teacher expectations place constraints on the *form* of what is to be learned, the entering capabilities of the student population determine the *level of detail* with which competence rules must be specified. Thus, for example, whereas reading may be assumed to be an elementary or atomic operation for most college students, this certainly is not true of third graders. In general, underlying rules must be represented in sufficient detail that all of the specified components make direct contact with assumed minimal capabilities of (all) students in the target population. Specifically, these components must be either uniformly available or atomic in the sense that they are so (relatively) simple that the students in question cannot master part of such a component without mastering it all. (Basic mathematical considerations guarantee some such level of representation—Scandura, 1970a, 1976; Suppes, 1969.)

Higher-Order Rules

In solving problems (i.e., in generating outputs associated with given inputs), it is not necessary that this be accomplished directly by applying rules individually. Rather, in the Structural Learning Theory, solutions may be generated indirectly because rules are allowed to operate in *higher-order* fashion on other rules[7] to generate new rules. The new rules, in turn, may generate the solutions.

The term *higher-order rule*, as it is used here, should not be confused with other common uses of the term, especially with a rule that is associated with higher levels in learning hierarchies (cf. Ehrenpreis & Scandura, 1974; Gagné, 1970; Scandura, 1970b). Whereas the latter (e.g., Gagné, 1970) involve combinations of lower-order rules, our higher-order rules include, for example, the processes by

---

[7]More accurately, higher-order rules operate on data structures that contain rules. See preceding footnote. Also see Scandura, 1977c.

which lower-order rules, associated with any number of different hierarchies, are *combined* to form correspondingly more complex rules (i.e., higher-order rules in Gagné's terminology).

This is not to say that the only thing higher-order rules are good for is to combine lower-order rules in learning hierarchies. A wide variety of behavioral phenomena can be accounted for in this way: learning (rule derivation/"invention"), breaking problems into subproblems (including constructing hierarchies of subproblems), assigning meanings, motivation, or rule selection, problem definition, storage and/or retrieval from memory, automatization, and so on (see Scandura, 1973, 1977b, 1978a). The basic differences in each case reside in the general types of higher-order rules required. "Invention," for example, may involve higher-order *analogy rules*, which construct new rules having the same form as given ones, as well as higher-order *composition rules*, which serve to integrate component rules into more comprehensive wholes.

The explicit introduction of higher-order rules has a number of important general advantages:

1. Higher-order rules represent interrelationships in a way that appears to allow for "creative potential" (i.e., unanticipated outcome). In addition, the introduction of higher-order rules, as well as lower-order ones, often makes it possible to account for relatively complex domains in an unusually efficient manner (e.g., Scandura & Durnin, 1977).

2. As indicated later in the section on *The Learner*, higher-order rules (along with lower-order rules) appear to provide a general and viable means for representing individual knowledge (i.e., actual human behavior potential). Moreover, their introduction for this purpose is highly consistent with what is known (or at least what may safely be assumed) about how humans function as information processors.

3. As we see in discussing individual-differences measurement, higher-order rules, just as rules in general, are fully operational. It is possible by testing to determine which parts of which higher-order rules have and have not been acquired by individual learners at any given stage of learning.

4. Finally, the introduction of higher-order rules appears to facilitate the relatively difficult task of specifying the competence underlying complex problem domains. The quasisystematic form of analysis that has been used or this purpose is called *structural analysis*.

The Process of Structural Analysis*

Detailed structural analyses have been undertaken of several rather comprehensive problem domains, including geometry construction problems (Scandura, Durnin,

---

*Editor's note: This is an instructional-development procedure and should not be confused with an instructional model or theory. However, because of the predominant role of selection strategies in Scandura's instructional model, this procedure is included in some detail here to shed further light (albeit indirect light) on the nature of Scandura's selection strategies.

& Wulfeck, 1974), an entire mathematics curriculum for elementary-school teachers (Scandura, Durnin, Ehrenpreis, & Luger, 1971), algebraic proofs (Scandura & Durnin, 1977), arithmetical skills (Scandura, 1972), and, most recently, the domain of Piagetian conservation problems (Scandura & Scandura, 1978). Empirical evaluations strongly supportive of the analyses involving geometry construction problems (Scandura, Wulfeck, Durnin, & Ehrenpreis, 1977), the mathematics curriculum (Ehrenpreis & Scandura, 1974), arithmetical skills (Scandura, 1972), and conservation (Scandura & Scandura, 1978) have been completed.

The point to emphasize here, perhaps, is that the constraints imposed on (the representation of) competence in structural learning theories go beyond those normally associated with a scientific language. As we see, these constraints play an important role in satisfying the needs of instructional theory. Also, unlike most cognitive theorizing, considerable attention has been given to the crucially important problem of *how to identify* the rules of competence underlying given problem domains. In the case of instruction, for example, it is one thing for a teacher to be able to give examples of the kinds of problems he or she wants the students to solve; it is quite something else to be able to identify precisely what it is that the students need to learn in order to solve them. Clearly, being able to represent needed competence involves much more than simply being able to solve problems by oneself.

In general, structural analysis involves: (1) specification of the *problem domain*, including both the individual problems and the extent of the domain; and (2) specification of the *rules* needed to solve the problems. In the case of relatively simple domains, for example the domain of subtraction problems, both the problems and the underlying solution rules can be specified relatively easily (see Fig. 7.1). In addition to mastery of the content, the major prerequisites for reliable analysis in simple cases such as this one would appear to be: (1) some facility in constructing flow diagrams and (2) representing them at a level of detail (i.e., in terms of atomic components) that is appropriate for the students in question.[8]

The situation with more complex domains is far less obvious. For one thing, it is not always easy to identify the effectively operating problems, or the extent of the given *problem domain*. Both factors had to be dealt with in our recent analysis of the Piagetian stage of concrete operations (Scandura & Scandura, 1978), but, as yet, little has been done by way of devising reliable, systematic, and efficient means for achieving such specification. The constraints on structural analysis, as presently practiced, reside primarily: (1) in the required form of representation

---

[8]In recent work, we have discovered what appears to be a close relationship between devising prototypic solution rules and "top-down" programming, a general method often used in computer programming to construct what are called *structured programs*. (See Haskell [1978] for a highly readable introduction.) Use of this method to supplement existing forms of structural analysis appears to have considerable promise and could lead to the development of reliable, systematic, and efficient methods of analysis. Research in this direction is currently under way.

(e.g., of problems as a type of structure[9]); and (2) in the need for, if not an analytic description of, the domain, and then the existence of some oracle (e.g., teacher) who given an arbitrary problem can determine whether or not it belongs to the domain.

Considerably more work has been done to identify the *rules of competence* underlying complex domains. Specifically, in addition to rules of competence per se, progress has been made towards the development of systematic and relatively efficient methods of structural analysis (designed to identify rules of competence).

Unlike simple domains, complex domains are not easily reduced to single rules of competence: Some domains may not be so reduced in principle or in practice. This difficulty is circumvented to some extent in structural analysis by adopting a modular approach.

In schematic form, structural analysis begins with some given domain of problems and involves the following steps:

1. Select a representative sample of *problems*.
2. Identify a *solution rule* for solving each of the sampled tasks. (These solution rules are designed to reflect the way in which successful subjects in a given target population might solve the sampled problems; the initial set of solution rules is denoted *R*.)
3. Identify *higher-order rules* that reflect parallels among the initial solution rules and that operate on lower-order rules.
4. *Eliminate* lower-order rules made unnecessary by the higher-order rules.
5. *Test and refine* the resulting rule set on new problems from the problem domain.
6. *Extend* the rule set when necessary so that it accounts for both familiar and novel problems in the domain.

Collectively, the higher- and lower-order rules of step 3 constitute a more basic set of rules from which the initial solution rules, among others, may be derived.

Steps 1 and 2

Consider, for example, step 1—two sample problems from the domain of geometry construction problems—and step 2—their corresponding solution rules.

Sample Problem 1:   Using only a straight edge and compass, construct a point *X* at a given distance *d* from two given points *A* and *B*:

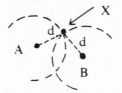

Solution Rule 1:   [Set (the radius of) the compass to distance d, put the point of the compass on point A, and draw a circular arc (i.e., the "locus" of points at distance d from point A)]; [place the compass on point B and draw another circular arc]; [label the point(s) of intersection of the two circles X].

Sample Problem 2:   Given a point A, a line l and a distance d, construct a circle with radius d that goes through point A and is tangent to line l.

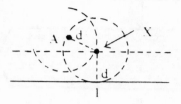

Solution Rule 2:   [Construct a circle with center at A and radius d]; [construct a locus of points at distance d from line l (i.e., parallel line at distance d from line l)]; [construct a circle with center X (the intersection of the circle and the parallel line) and radius d].[10]

Step 3

Notice that the two solution rules have the same general structure [set off by brackets]. Although the component rules of these solution rules differ substantially, each solution rule involves two independent "locus" constructions, with the X of the two loci playing a critical role. In the first problem, X is the solution. In the second problem, it is the center of the desired goal circle.

In general, each type of structural parallel can be realized concretely in the form of higher-order rules. (The above type of parallel is only one of several basic kinds that may be shared by two or more rules.) In the present illustration, for example, both solution rules can be derived by applying the higher-order "two-locus" rule of Fig. 7.3 to the respective component rules. This higher-order two-locus rule operates on simple locus rules (e.g., for constructing circular arcs and parallel lines) and generates solution rules (i.e., combinations of the simpler locus rules). It is important to emphasize that the two-locus higher-order rule can be used to derive solution rules for a wide (potentially infinite) range of problems, not just for the two sampled problems.

(Incidentally, notice also that the higher-order rule is only represented schematically. For example, the notion of a "locus condition" in the first decision would almost certainly not be atomic (i.e., sufficiently elementary) with respect to most populations of learners. For this purpose, "locus condition" must be detailed in terms of the more basic conditions shown in Fig. 7.4—such as the "picture"

---

[10]Each step in Solution Rule 2 can be detailed in terms of the more molecular operations of setting a compass, using a fixed compass to construct a circular arc, and using a straight edge to construct a line segment.

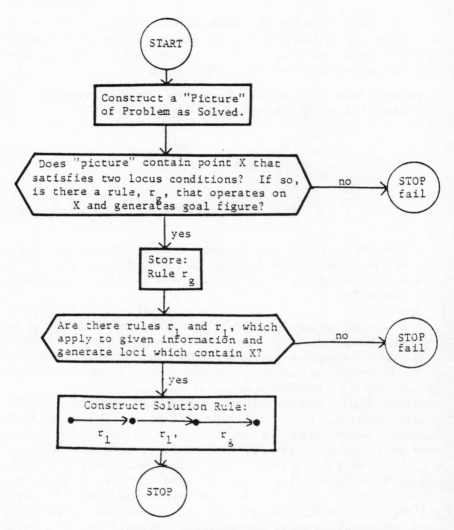

FIG. 7.3   High-level description of higher-order two-loci rule.

contains a point X that is a given distance from two given points or lines or is equidistant from two pairs of given points or lines.)

Step 4

Given the higher-order two-locus rule and the lower-order component rules, the solution rules themselves may be eliminated as redundant because they can be derived from the former rules acting collectively.

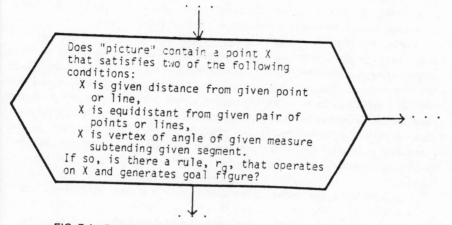

FIG. 7.4   Partial specification of First Decision of higher-order two-loci rule.

Illustrating steps 5 and 6 of structural analysis would require more space than is available, but the general intent is clear. For details of the analysis, see Scandura et al. (1974).

It is important to notice that structural analysis may be applied iteratively (i.e., repeatedly). Given an initial set of solution rules, one need not stop by deriving a more basic rule set (e.g., a set including both higher- and lower-order rules). The derived rule set, in turn, can be subjected to precisely the same type of analysis with the result being a rule set that is still more basic. In general, structural analysis may be reapplied as many times as desired, each time yielding a rule set that is more basic in two senses: (1) individual rules are simpler; and (2) the new rule set as a whole has greater generating power (i.e., it provides a basis for solving a greater variety of tasks; see Scandura, 1973, 1977b).

The Learner*

Prototypic competence is not the same as rules of knowledge that characterize individual behavior potential. It is assumed in the Structural Learning Theory that what an individual does and can learn depends directly and inextricably on what he or she already knows. More particularly, as shown in Fig. 7.2 earlier, it is assumed that human cognition may be adequately characterized in terms of: (1) *universal characteristics* of the human information processor; and (2) *individual knowledge*. As we see, the latter is operationally defined in terms of rules (of both higher- and

---

*Editor's note: This section describes aspects of a *learning* theory rather than of an *instructional* theory. However, it provides an important rationale for the instructional theory. See Chapter 1, p. 23, for a discussion of the distinction between the two.

lower-order) relative to prototypic competence (prototypic competence being associated with given problem domains and learner populations).

Clearly, instruction is concerned primarily with individual knowledge. From an instructional point of view, universal characteristics are best thought of as those aspects of human cognitive functioning that are inherent to humans generally; they need not, and indeed in some cases cannot, be taught. But higher-order rules do not provide a sufficient basis for explaining individual behavior. A complete theory must include (control) mechanisms that explain how and why various rules are used in particular situations. In this regard, the Structural Learning Theory postulates a simple *goal-switching control mechanism* that makes minimal assumptions about the processor, assumptions that appear to be generalizable to all people.

Given a problem, the human information processor is assumed to first check to see if a solution is directly available. If not, the processor is assumed to search through (the ranges of) his or her available rules to see which, if any, might solve the problem. A rule is a potential solution rule if its range "matches" the problem goal and its domain includes the given problem. If a unique rule is found, then the rule is applied and the output is tested to see if it solves the problem. If there are no potential *solution rules*, then the search takes place at a still deeper level. In this case, control directs the search for *higher-order rules* that generate potential solution rules.

If such a higher-order rule is found, then it is applied; the newly generated rule is added to the set of available rules and the search reverts to the next lower level. The augmented rule set is then checked as before; only this time the newly derived (potential) solution rule is available. In general, whenever there are no rules (or more than one rule) that apply at a given level of search, control moves to a still *deeper level*. Conversely, whenever a match is achieved (so that a rule is applied), control reverts to the preceding level.

This simple "goal-switching" mechanism[11] is hypothesized to be common to all humans and to govern all cognition, irrespective of the specific knowledge involved. Consider, for example, the problem of rule derivation, of how individuals

---

[11]In earlier formulations (e.g., Scandura, 1971a, 1973, 1977b), emphasis was given to switching between higher- and lower-level goals and, correspondingly, the control mechanism was referred to as the *goal-switching mechanism*. The preceding description is behaviorally equivalent to these earlier formulations. However, although it is beyond the scope of this chapter to discuss the reasons, recent theoretical advances and computer implementations of the mechanism convince me that the formulation just sketched is preferable. Among other things, it makes it possible to program the control mechanism in a way that is completely independent of content (i.e., specific rules of competence). The latter can be removed, replaced, and/or modified without requiring any change in control. Strictly speaking, implementation of the goal-switching mechanism, as originally conceived, is not possible. In this case, it is necessary either to restrict oneself to incomplete approximations (e.g., Wulfeck & Scandura, 1977) or to introduce minor but nonetheless ad hoc assumptions concerning specific sets of competence rules.

derive new solution rules for solving new problems they have never seen before. According to the Structural Learning Theory, rule derivation takes place as a result of applying higher-order rules to other rules. Various higher-order rules may serve to *combine* component rules, to *generate* analogous rules, to *generalize* given rules, and so on. The more general term *derivation rule* refers to the potential solution rules that may result.

To make things concrete, suppose a child knows rules for converting yards into feet (multiply by 3) and for converting feet into inches (multiply by 12) and that the child is asked, "How many inches are there in 2 yards?" Clearly, this problem can be solved by combining the two available rules, the rule for converting yards into feet and the rule for converting feet into inches. But how does the child know how to combine the given rules? Knowing component rules is surely not logically equivalent to knowing when and how to use them.

A basic assumption in the Structural Learning Theory is that new rules are derived by application of certain rules to other rules. In the present case, a child might be expected to succeed if he or she knows a higher-order rule that operates on pairs of rules of the form $A \rightarrow B,\ B \rightarrow C$ (i.e., like but not limited to those previously described), and combines them to form a composite rule of the form $A \rightarrow B \rightarrow C$, in which the components are performed in sequence.

Although knowing both requisite *higher-order rules* and requisite *lower-order rules* is a necessary condition for solving problems, this is *not* sufficient. In order to effectively use available rules to derive solution rules and to solve problems, some type of *control mechanism* is needed to determine when each rule is to be used and how.

I must caution that this simple control mechanism is an idealization and applies only in situations in which processing capacity is not a factor, and specifically in which all of the requisite higher- and lower-order rules are learned perfectly and are active in "working" memory (see Scandura, 1971a, 1973, 1977b). Perhaps surprisingly, however, this limitation has not proved to be as critical as one might expect. Empirical support has been strong, although not deterministic, even under "real-world" conditions. Ehrenpreis and Scandura (1974), for example, found that higher-order (as well as lower-order) rules underlying a college course for teachers could be identified in a systematic manner and that instruction on such rules had a highly positive effect on prespecified kinds of "far transfer." Furthermore, the degree of transfer was directly related to the degree to which the test conditions deviated from the ideal (Scandura, 1977b).

When used in conjunction with appropriate kinds of higher- (and lower-) order rules, the goal-switching control mechanism provides an adequate basis for explaining, predicting, and controlling a wide variety of behaviors; these include: solving analogy problems, generalizing given rules, motivation (rule selection), problem definition (subgoal formation), automatization, and rule retrieval. For details and related empirical support, the interested reader is referred to Scandura (1973, 1977b).

Assessing Individual Knowledge

In contrast to universal cognitive constraints, *specific knowledge* is assumed to vary over individuals. The theory shows how prototypic competence (i.e., competence prototypic of given populations) may be used to operationally define the knowledge available to actual individual members of such populations. More generally, the theory tells how, through a finite testing procedure, one can identify which parts of to-be-taught rules *individual* subjects know—even when any (finite) number of higher- and lower-order rules may be involved. The *rules* in a very real sense serve as *rulers* of *measurement* and provide a sufficient basis for the operational definition of human knowledge (see Scandura, 1977b).

The fact that each *path* is associated with a unique subclass of column subtraction problems makes it possible to pinpoint through a finite testing procedure exactly what it is that each subject knows relative to the initial rule. It is sufficient for this purpose to test each subject on one randomly selected item from each *equivalence class*. Success on each item, according to our atomicity assumptions, implies potential success on all other items from the same equivalence class, and conversely for failure.

It would appear that any viable theory of instruction must take into account underlying competence. Not only do rules of competence (associated with populations of subjects) provide a basis for measuring individual knowledge and for providing remedial instruction, but they also provide an explicit basis for selecting appropriate test items.

Equally important, the structural approach to assessing behavior potential makes it possible to identify precisely not only what individuals can and cannot do, but also what the learner does and does not know relative to the particular rules involved. A simple basis for instructional decision making follows directly: Assume the paths the learner already knows and gradually "build in" those that he or she does not.

Instructional Systems

It is not easy to reduce complex and sometimes subtle interrelationships to linear form (as in writing). I have, nonetheless, tried in the preceding sections to stress some of the more crucial interrelationships that exist among content, cognition, and individual differences in the context of instruction.

In each area we have seen that the choice of representation (i.e., the theoretical constructs, the way they are characterized, and their mode of operationalization) is crucial. Specifically, the rule construct was defined as it was (i.e., as a triple consisting of a domain, a range, and a restricted type of procedure) to meet certain very critical requirements that appear essential in any viable theory of instruction that deals with individual behavior in specific situations.

Thus, for example, the aforementioned method of operationalizing individual knowledge (i.e., for assessing individual behavior potential) depends crucially on both the restrictions placed on the procedures (operations) of rules and on the previously described assumptions concerning encoding and decoding. The procedures in question are *restricted* to those that can be represented concretely as structured programs (e.g., Alogic & Arbib, 1978; Haskell, 1978).[12]

This restriction on rule procedures (i.e., the procedures of rules) is made possible by the cognitive separation between specific knowledge and control, which in turn is made feasible by strongly supporting data, which suggests the universality of goal-switching control. This separation of specific knowledge and control has the effect of extracting goal-switching from unrestricted procedures.

To summarize, restricting the procedures of rules, together with the encoding/decoding assumptions referred to previously, greatly simplifies the representation of competence without reducing generality. These constraints "force" competence into a form that both is unambiguous (relative to encoding/decoding assumptions) and has considerable heuristic power insofar as operationalizing individual knowledge is concerned.

Other features of the rule representation are equally crucial. For example, attaching ranges (to rules) that are *independent* of the domains and the procedures plays a crucial role in goal-switching control. Given the assumption that people may be characterized as goal-directed information processors, it stands to reason that rule use depends on what the knower *expects* rules to do and not just on how and where they can do it. What a person expects a rule to do is not necessarily the same as what the rule actually will do. In tightening a joint, for example, a plumber might expect (hope?) to stop a leak; instead, he or she might cause the pipe to break (and get drenched?).

---

[12]Unrestricted procedures, for example, allow for the generation of new (sub) procedures and their subsequent use in executing such procedures. In effect, goal switching in unrestricted procedures, rather than being distinguished from specific competence, is *intertwined* with it. This confounding leads to unnecessarily complex procedures, and moreover, procedures that seem to have little heuristic power in so far as individual-differences measurement is concerned.

At the other extreme, the operations of simple productions (e.g., Post in Minsky, 1967) are *too restrictive*. Productions disallow the possibility of internal decisions, for example, and effectively act as atomic rules. The domains and operations, consequently, may not act independently of one another—something that seems at variance with everyday observation. It is quite possible, for example, for a person (e.g., a child) to be able to identify any given column-addition problem without necessarily knowing how to find its sum.

Although the *necessary richness* might be obtained by introducing (sets of) production systems (e.g., Newell & Simon, 1972) to represent competence, doing so would destroy much of the heuristic value gained by representing competence in terms of rules. Independent justification for this observation can be gleaned from the fact that, although Siegler and Klahr (e.g., Klahr, 1978), for example, have used production systems in much of their work, the (finite) decision trees they used for diagnostic purposes are, in fact, rules. When represented in terms of production systems, the underlying processes appear to lose their heuristic power almost entirely. In effect, although there are any number of scientific languages that are sufficiently rich to characterize competence/knowledge, formal equivalence is not the same as psychological equivalence, even less so when the needs of instruction are taken into account.

Goal-switching control, in turn, not only has found strong and direct empirical support in its own right, but it also provides a pragmatically useful basis for *identifying what must be learned* in instructional situations. Thus, the separation of specific knowledge/competence from control greatly *simplifies* the task of dealing with high-level interrelationships that are frequently involved in complex domains. Specifically, taking the control mechanism as given not only makes it possible to represent competence in a modular fashion (in terms of independent rules) but also makes it easier to identify this competence.

In the latter regard, I have been concerned in my theoretical work only in part with specifying constraints on the representation of competence (i.e., what must be learned). I have been equally concerned with the problem of *how* to identify the competence underlying given problem domains. Clearly, knowing the way in which such competence is to be represented (i.e., the type of representation) is not the same as being able to construct such representations in the first place. As a result of carrying out an increasing number and diversity of structural analyses and related research, I believe that it may be possible to construct structural-learning—based competence theories in a relatively efficient, systematic, and objective manner.[13] This is especially so in the case of competence theories that are intended to be used for instructional purposes.

Our understanding of how to analyze content has increased dramatically over the past several years; and the future looks even more promising. To see this, one has only to mention the important contributions made by traditional task analysis in this direction (e.g., Gagné, 1962, 1970) and to point out that this method of analysis is a special case of structural analysis.[14] The main advantages of the latter are that it is more precise and that it enables one to analyze more complex domains, where higher-order relationships play an important role.

In many ways, the problem of how to *devise* specific competence theories is more basic than any of the others. Prior structural analysis of a given body of content is the essential prerequisite for realizing particular structural learning theories. Given an analyzed (and evaluated) problem domain, the rest of the theory follows directly: the assessment of individual knowledge, the specification of what

---

[13]I am not implying the possibility of automatic theory construction (i.e., of theories based on sets of rules), however. I very much doubt that we will ever have a completely general or complete method of analysis. (Related questions of possibility and impossibility have been considered in the theory of computation—e.g., Rogers, 1967; but such questions are hard to prove in the context of human behavior because they require making explicit assumptions that one might not be willing to make about (real) people. To my knowledge, the possibility of systematic construction of structural learning theories remains an open question.)

[14]Although going into the matter here would detract from present concerns, it would be easy to show that other common and pragmatically based methods of analysis, used in instructional planning, are also special cases. The *elaboration* theory proposed by Reigeluth and Merrill provides a case in point. It corresponds directly to starting with the paths a learner knows and progressively adding more elaborate ones.

individual learners will do and/or learn in particular problem situations, and detailed plans for sequencing the instruction. It is worth emphasizing in this regard that the assessment method proposed, the assumed universals used to (partially) characterize human cognition and instructional methods refer to the entire *class* of structural learning theories (i.e., to the Structural Learning Theory) and not just to particular realizations.

ACKNOWLEDGMENTS

Portions of this chapter have been abstracted and adapted from Theoretical Foundations of Instruction: A Systems Alternative to Cognitive Psychology, *Journal of Structural Learning*, 1980, *6*, 347–394. Preparation of this chapter was supported in part by a grant from the Spencer Foundation, and in part by Scandura Training Systems, Inc.

REFERENCES

Alogic, S., & Arbib, M. A. *The design of well-structured and correct programs.* New York: Springer-Verlag, 1978.

Anderson, J. R. *Language, memory and thought.* Hillsdale, N.J.: Lawrence Erlbaum Associates, 1976.

Bobrow, D. G., & Collins, A. (Eds.). *Representation and understanding: Studies in cognitive science.* New York: Academic Press, 1975.

Cronbach, L. J., & Snow, R. E. *Aptitudes and instructional methods: A handbook for research on interactions.* New York: Irvington, 1977.

Durnin, J. H., & Scandura, J. M. An algorithmic approach to assessing behavior potential: Comparison with items forms and hierarchical analysis. *Journal of Educational Psychology*, 1973, *65*, 262–292. (Also in J. M. Scandura, *Problem solving.* New York: Academic Press, 1977.)

Ehrenpreis, W., & Scandura, J. M. Algorithmic approach to curriculum construction: A field test. *Journal of Educational Psychology*, 1974, *66*, 491–498.

Estes, W. K. Component and pattern models with Markovian interpretations. In R. Bush & W. K. Estes (Eds.), *Studies in mathematical learning theory.* Stanford: University Press, 1959.

Gagné, R. M. The acquisition of knowledge. *Psychological Review*, 1962, *59*, 355–365.

Gagné, R. M. *The conditions of learning* (2nd ed.). New York: Holt, Rinehart & Winston, 1970.

Glaser, R. Instructional technology and the measurement of learning outcomes: Some questions. *American Psychologist*, 1963, *18*, 519–521.

Glaser, R., & Resnick, L. B. Instructional Psychology. *Annual Review of Psychology*, 1972, *23*, 207–276.

Haskell, R. E. *Fortran programming using structured flowcharts.* Chicago: Science Research Associates, 1978.

Hively, W., II, Patterson, H. L., & Page, S. A "universe defined" system of arithmetic achievement tests. *Journal of Educational Measurement*, 1968, *5*, 275–290.

Kintsch, W. *The representation of meaning in memory.* New York: Wiley, 1974.

Klahr, D. Information processing models of cognitive development. In J. M. Scandura & C. J. Brainerd (Eds.), *Structural/process models of complex human behavior.* Leyden, Netherlands: Sijthoff & Noordhoff International Publishers, 1978.

Landa, L. N. *Instructional regulation and control.* Englewood Cliffs, N.J.: Educational Technology Publications, 1976.

Lowerre, G., & Scandura, J. M. Development and evaluations of individualized materials for critical thinking based on logical inference. *Reading Research Quarterly*, 1973, *IX*, 185–205.

Merrill, M. D., & Boutwell, R. C. Instructional development: Methodology and research. In F. N. Kerliger (Ed.), *Review of research in education*. Itasca, Ill.: F. E. Peacock, 1973.

Merrill, P. F. *Algorithmic organization in teaching and learning: The literature and research in the U.S.A.* Manuscript, 1978.

Minsky, M. L. *Computation: Finite and infinite machines.* Englewood Cliffs, N.J.: Prentice-Hall, 1967.

Minsky, M. L. A framework of representing knowledge. In P. Winston (Ed.), *The psychology of computer vision*. New York: McGraw-Hill, 1975.

Minsky, M., & Papert, S. *Research at the laboratory in vision, language, and other problems of intelligence* (Artificial Intelligence Progress Report Memo 252). Cambridge, Mass.: Massachusetts Institute of Technology, Artificial Intelligence Laboratory, 1972.

Newell, A., & Simon, H. A. *Human problem solving.* Englewood Cliffs, N.J.: Prentice-Hall, 1972.

Pascual-Leone, J. A mathematical model for the transition rule in Piaget's developmental stages. *Acta Psychologica*, 1970, *63*, 301-345.

Pask, G. *Conservation theory.* Amsterdam: Elsevier, 1976.

Quillian, M. R. Semantic memory. In M. Minsky (Ed.), *Semantic information processing*. Cambridge, Mass.: MIT Press, 1968.

Resnick, L. B., & Glaser, R. Problem solving and intelligence. In L. B. Resnick (Ed.), *The nature of intelligence*. Hillsdale, N.J.: Lawrence Erlbaum Associates, 1976.

Rogers, H. J. *Theory of recursive functions and effective computability.* New York: McGraw-Hill, 1967.

Rothkopf, E. Z. Structural text features and the control of processes in learning from written materials. In J. B. Carroll & R. O. Feedle (Eds.), *Language comprehension and the acquisition of kowledge*. Washington, D.C.: Winston & Sons, 1972.

Rumelhart, D. E., & Lindsay, P. H., & Norman, D. A. A process model for long-term memory. In E. Tulving & W. Donaldson (Eds.), *Organization of memory*. New York: Academic Press, 1972.

Scandura, A. M., & Scandura, J. M. *Structural learning and concrete operations: An approach to Piagetian Conservation.* New York: Praeger Spec. Studies, 1980.

Scandura, J. M. *The teaching-learning process: an exploratory investigation of expository and discovery modes of problem solving instruction.* Unpublished dissertation, Syracuse University, 1962.

Scandura, J. M. An analysis of expository and discovery modes of problem solving instruction. *Journal of Experimental Education*, 1964, *33*, 149—159.

Scandura, J. M. The basic unit in meaningful learning—association or principle? *The School Review*, 1967, *75*, 329–341. (a)

Scandura, J. M. (Ed.). *Research in mathematics education.* Washington, D.C.: NCTM, 1967. (b)

Scandura, J. M. New directions for theory and research on rule learning: I. A Set-Function Language. *Acta Psychologica*, 1968, *28*, 301–321.

Scandura, J. M. New directions for theory and research on rule learning: II. Empirical research. *Acta Psychologica*, 1969, *29*, 101–133.

Scandura, J. M. A research basis for mathematics education. *High School Journal*, 1970, *53*, 264—280. (a) (*Also in Educational Studies in mathematics*, 1971, *3*, 229—243; and *Journal of Structural Learning*, 1970, *2*, 1—18.)

Scandura, J. M. The role of rules in behavior: Toward an operational definition of what (rule) is learned. *Psychological Review*, 1970, *77*, 516–533. (b)

Scandura, J. M. Deterministic theorizing in structural learning: Three levels of empiricism. *Journal of Structural Learning*, 1971, *3*, 21–53. (a)

Scandura, J. M. *Mathematics: Concrete behavioral foundations.* New York: Harper & Row, 1971. (b)

Scandura, J. M. A theory of mathematical knowledge: Can rules account for creative behavior: *Journal of Research in Mathematics Education*, 1971, *2*, 183–196. (c)

Scandura, J. M. Plan for the development of conceptually based mathematics curriculum for disadvantaged children. Part II: Applications. *Instructional Science*, 1972, *2*, 363–387.

Scandura, J. M. *Structural learning I: Theory and research.* London/New York: Gordon & Breach Science Publishers, 1973.

Scandura, J. M. The role of higher-order rules in problem solving. *Journal of Experimental Psychology*, 1974, *120*, 984–989. (Also in J. M. Scandura, *Problem solving: A structural/process approach with instructional implications.* New York: Academic Press, 1977.) (a)

Scandura, J. M. The structure of memory: Fixed or flexible? *Catalog of Selected Documents in Psychology*, 1974, Spring, 37–78. (Abridged version in F. Klix (Ed.), *Organismische Informationsverarbeitung*, Bericht uber ein Symposium, September 11–14, 1973. Berlin: Akademic-Verlag, 1974.) (b)

Scandura, J. M. (Ed.) with contributions by Arbib, M., Corcoran, J., Domotor, Z., Greeno, J., Lovell, K., Newell, A., Rosenbloom, P., Scandura, J., Shaw, R., Simon, H., Suppes, P., Wittrock, M., & Witz, K. *Structural learning II: Issues and approaches.* London/New York: Gordon and Breach Science Publishers, 1976.

Scandura, J. M. A deterministic theory of teaching and learning. In H. Spada & W. F. Kempf (Eds.), *Structural models of thinking and learning.* Bern: Huber, 1977. (a)

Scandura, J. M. *Problem solving: A structural/process approach with instructional implications.* New York: Academic Press, 1977. (b)

Scandura, J. M. Structural approach to instructional problems. *American Psychologist*, 1977, *32*, 33–53. (c)

Scandura, J. M. Discussion of selected issues in structural learning. In J. M. Scandura & C. J. Brainerd (Eds.), *Structural/process models of complex human behavior.* Leyden, Netherlands: Sijthoff, 1978. (a)

Scandura, J. M. Human problem solving: A synthesis of content, cognition, and individual differences. *Journal of Structural Learning*, 1978, *6*. (b)

Scandura, J. M. Theoretical foundations of instruction: A systems alternative to cognitive psychology. *Journal of Structural Learning*, 1980, *6*, 247–394. (Also in Scandura, J. M. & Scandura, A. B. *Structured learning and concrete operations: An approach to Piagetian Conservation.* Praeger Spec. Studies, 1980.

Scandura, J. M. & Brainerd, C. J. (Eds.) *Structural/process models of complex human behavior.* Leyder, Netherlands: Sijthoff, 1978.

Scandura, J. M., & Durnin, J. H. Structural (algorithmic) analysis of algebraic proofs. In J. M. Scandura, *Problem solving.* New York: Academic Press, 1977.

Scandura, J. M., & Durnin J. H. Assessing behavior potential: Adequacy of basic theoretical assumptions. *Journal of Structural Learning*, 1978, *6*, 3–47.

Scandura, J. M., Durnin, J. H., Ehrenpreis, W., & Luger, G. *An algorithmic approach to mathematics: Concrete behavioral foundations.* New York: Harper & Row, 1971.

Scandura, J. M., Durnin, J. H., & Wulfeck, W. H., II. Higher-order rule characterization of heuristics for compass and straight-edge constructions in geometry. *Artificial Intelligence*, 1974, *5*, 149–183. (Also in J. M. Scandura, *Problem solving.* New York: Academic Press, 1977.)

Scandura, J. M. (Chair), Frase, L., Gagné, R. M., Groen, Storulow, L., and others. Current status and future directions of educational psychology as a discipline (A detailed report based on 2½ years work). *Educational Psychologist*, 1978, *13*, 9–22.

Scandura, J. M., Woodward, E., & Lee, F. Rule generality and consistency in mathematics learning. *American Educational Research Journal*, 1967, *4*, 303–319.

Scandura, J. M., Wulfeck, W. H., Durnin, J. H., & Ehrenpreis, W. Diagnosis and instruction of higher-order rules for solving geometry construction problems. In J. M. Scandura, *Problem solving.* New York: Academic Press, 1977.

Schmid, R. F., Portnoy, R. C., & Burns, K. Using algorithms to assess comprehension of classroom text materials. *Journal of Educational Research*, 1976, *69*, 309–312.

Summary and discussion of issues in studying developmental change by R. Siegler. *Journal of Structural Learning*, 1978, 6, in press.

Suppes, P. Stimulus–response theory of finite automata. *Journal of Mathematical Psychology*, 1969, 6, 327–355.

Tennyson, R. D., & Rothen, W. Pretask and on-task adaptive design strategies for selecting number of instances in concept acquisition. *Journal of Educational Psychology*, 1977, 69, 586-592.

Voohries, D., & Scandura, J. M. Determination of memory load in information processing. In J.M. Scandura, *Problem solving*. New York: Academic Press, 1977.

Wulfeck, W. H. Comments on Siegler's contribution. *Journal of Structural Learning*, 1978, 6, in press.

Wulfeck, W.H., & Scandura, J. M. Theory of adaptive instruction with application to sequencing in teaching problem solving. In J. M. Scandura, *Problem solving*. New York: Academic Press, 1977.

8 A Cognitive Theory of Inquiry Teaching

Allan Collins
Albert L. Stevens
Bolt Beranek and Newman, Inc.

Allan Collins

Allan Collins is a Principal Scientist at Bolt Beranek and Newman Inc., a research firm in Cambridge, Massachusetts. He is a specialist in the fields of cognitive science and human semantic processing and also in the use of computers in education. He is one of the founders and served as the first chairman of the Cognitive Science Society, and he is widely known for his work with Dr. M. R. Quillian on semantic memory. He was also one of the original editors of the journal, *Cognitive Science*.

Dr. Collins received his doctorate in Psychology at the Human Performance Center of the University of Michigan. His work there was in human information processing with Dr. P. M. Fitts, and then in language and memory with Drs. E. Martin and A. W. Melton. Before that, he received a Master's degree in Communication Sciences where he acquired a background in artificial intelligence, mathematical logic, and linguistics.

From 1970 to 1973 Dr. Collins directed a project with the late Dr. Jaime Carbonell on the SCHOLAR CAI system, where knowledge was structured like human memory so that it could be used in a variety of ways.

From 1975 to 1979 Dr. Collins directed a project to develop an intelligent CAI system (the WHY system) that used a Socratic (or case) method for tutoring causal knowledge and reasoning. In conjunction with this project he developed a formal theory of Socratic tutoring in computational form, derived from analyses of a variety of inquiry teaching dialogues.

CONTENTS

Introduction   250
    Terminology Used In The Theory   251
    Independent And Dependent Variables In Different Domains   253
    Data Analyzed   255
The Theory   257
    Goals Of Teachers   257
    Strategies For Inquiry Teaching   259
        1. Selecting Positive And Negative Exemplars   260
        2. Varying Cases Systematically   262
        3. Selecting Counterexamples   263
        4. Generating Hypothetical Cases   264
        5. Forming Hypotheses   265
        6. Evaluating Hypotheses   267
        7. Considering Alternative Predictions   268
        8. Entrapping Students   269
        9. Tracing Consequences To A Contradiction   271
        10. Questioning Authority   273
    Dialogue Control Structure   274
Conclusion   276

FOREWORD

The Collins-Stevens instructional theory is the most recently developed of those described in this unit. In spite of this, their approach to theory construction is the closest I have encountered to a pure *inductive* approach to theory construction. The authors have obtained transcripts of performances of a number of teachers and have analyzed those transcripts for: (1) the strategies that the teachers used; and (2) the goals and conditions for which they used each of those strategies. In spite of such an inductive approach, the theory has been developed within a distinctly *cognitive* metatheory (witness the title of the chapter). However, there are two major "camps" within the cognitive orientation: an expository approach such as that of Ausubel and a discovery approach such as that of Bruner. The Collins-Stevens instructional theory is definitely in the *discovery* tradition. Similar to Scandura's, the Collins-Stevens theory is intended mostly for individualized instruction but is often applied in classes.

The main features of this instructional theory are: (1) a set of goals that teachers have; (2) a set of strategies for achieving those goals; and (3) a mechanism (or "control structure") for deciding which goal to pursue when. The *control structure* specifies what are in essence selection and sequencing strategies. It calls for selecting and sequencing content on the basis of the particular "misconceptions" that a student has at a given time, which requires: (1) constant assessment of each student's knowledge; and (2) individualized prescriptions based on that assessment. (This is remarkably similar to Scandura's approach to rule selection and sequencing.)

With respect to *goals*, Collins and Stevens distinguish between teaching students to *apply* a specific *rule* or *theory* (similar to Gagné's *rules,* Gropper's *explanations,* Scandura's *rules,* and Landa's *particular algo-heuristic procedures*), and teaching them how to *derive a rule or theory* (similar to Gagné's *cognitive strategies* Scandura's *higher-order rules,* and Landa's *how to discover algo-heuristic procedures*). Nevertheless, *unlike* Gagné and Landa (but like Scandura), the authors do not clearly delineate a separate set of strategies for each of these two kinds of goals. With respect to *strategies,* many bear a marked similarity to Gropper's shaping and cuing strategies, whereas others represent methods particular to learning how to discover. It is interesting that this cognitively oriented theory bears as many similarities (if not more) to Gropper's theory as to Landa's or Scandura's (see Editor's notes in the text).

Several of the more important limitations (i.e., boundaries) to this theory are: (1) it is not appropriate for all kinds of content (it is primarily appropriate for principles—"causal" relationships—as well as for discovery skills), and it is generally not appropriate for facts or concepts); (2) it is not self-sufficient, in that in most cases some other form of instruction such as written materials must be used to provide the background knowledge (of facts and concepts) that is necessary for the discovery process to be able to occur (see the various examples throughout the chapter); and (3) for learning specific rules or theories the discovery process is probably less efficient than an expository approach (see, for example, the section *Teaching Ready-Made Algo-*

Heuristic Procedures), and it may be less effective as well, to the extent that it becomes necessary to correct many errors and misconceptions that perhaps could have been avoided through appropriately designed expository instruction.

Nevertheless, there is increasing recognition that cognitive strategies (or higher-order rules) such as "how to discover" are among the most important types of content for public education. Hence, these should be explicitly taught. And many of the Collins-Stevens strategies, although on one level represent a discovery approach to teaching specific rules, on another level represent components on an expository approach to teaching such cognitive strategies. And for these higher-level goals, the Collins—Stevens theory identifies useful strategies that the other instructional theories overlook.

C. M. R.

A Cognitive Theory of Inquiry Teaching

INTRODUCTION

We have been studying transcripts of a variety of interactive teachers. The teachers we have studied all use some form of the case, inquiry, discovery, or Socratic method (Anderson & Faust, 1974; Davis, 1966; Sigel & Saunders, 1979). The topics they are teaching range over different domains: mathematics, geography, moral education, law, medicine, and computer science. But we think it is possible to abstract common elements of their teaching strategies, and to show how these can be extended to different domains. In this way we think it is possible to identify the most effective techniques that each of these teachers has discovered, so that they can be made available to anyone who wants to apply these techniques in their own teaching (Collins, 1978).

In a related paper (Collins & Stevens, 1982), we have attempted to specify a formal theory to describe the goals and strategies of the teachers we have been analyzing. In this chapter we instead want to pick the most striking *techniques* they are using, and show how these can be applied across widely disparate domains.

The theory of instruction we are developing in these two papers is at base a *descriptive theory* in the terms of Reigeluth (Chapter 1, this volume). We are trying to describe expert performance, in the current tradition of cognitive science (e.g., Chase & Simon, 1973; Larkin, 1979; Simon & Simon, 1979). By focusing on experts, the descriptive theory becomes a *prescriptive theory* as well. That is to say, a descriptive theory of expert performance is in fact a prescriptive theory for the nonexpert performer.

Our theory of inquiry teaching is *domain independent*. That is not to say that this is the only useful kind of analysis of expert teaching. There is much to be gained from careful examination of the kinds of misconceptions students have in different domains (e.g., Brown & Burton, 1978; Stevens, Collins, & Goldin, 1979) and of the specific methods suited to teaching a particular domain (e.g., VanLehn & Brown, 1980). But at the same time, task analysis can be used to abstract the significant generalizations about teaching that cut across domains. Comparison across diverse domains makes it possible to see what teachers are doing in a more general way, and forces insights into teaching that might not otherwise be noticed.

Our theory of inquiry teaching is cast in a framework similar to that used by Newell and Simon (1972) to describe human problem solving. It contains three parts:

1. The goals and subgoals of teachers.
2. The strategies used to realize different goals and subgoals.
3. The control structure for selecting and pursuing different goals and subgoals.

Teachers typically pursue several *goals* simultaneously. Each goal has associated with it a set of strategies for selecting cases, asking questions, and giving comments.* In pursuing goals simultaneously, teachers maintain an *agenda* that allows them to allocate their time among the various goals efficiently (Collins, Warnock, & Passafiume, 1975; Stevens & Collins, 1977). The theory therefore encompasses goals, strategies, and control structure.

Terminology Used in the Theory

Many of the teaching strategies we describe serve to communicate the teacher's understanding of the causal structure** of a domain to a student. Thus we need a way to notate a causal structure. One way of representing causal dependencies is in

---

*Editor's note: Notice the similarity with the previous chapters that have emphasized prescribing methods on the basis of the type of objective.

**Editor's note: In Chapter 1 this *causal structure* was labeled as *principles* or *theories*. This instructional theory is probably not useful for teaching all types of content (e.g., facts).

terms of an *and/or graph* (Stevens & Collins, 1980). Fig. 8.1 shows such a graph for the causal dependencies derived by a student in a dialogue on growing grain in different places (Collins, Warnock, Aiello, & Miller, 1975). Each place that was discussed functioned as a *case* in the terminology of the theory. In the figure, rice growing is the *dependent variable* and is treated as a function having two possible *values*: Either you can grow rice or you cannot. In other sections of the dialogue, wheat growing and corn growing were discussed as alternative dependent variables. Unlike grain growing, which the student treated as a threshold function, many dependent variables are treated as continuous functions (e.g., a place is colder or warmer), where there is a continuous range of values.

During the course of the dialogue, the student identified four principal *factors* affecting rice growing: fresh water, a flat area, fertile soil, and warm temperature. These were configured as shown in the the diagram. These factors (or *independent variables*) are linked to rice growing through *chains* with various *intermediate steps*. In fact, any step in a chain can be considered as a factor.

Given a set of factors and a dependent variable, a *rule* is any function that relates values of one or more factors to values of the dependent variable. A rule can be more or less complete depending on how well it takes into account all the relevant factors and the entire range of values of the dependent variable. For example, a rule about rice growing might assert that growing rice depends on heavy rainfall and fertile soil. Such a rule is obviously incomplete with respect to the minitheory shown in Fig. 8.1. A *theory* specifies the causal structure interrelating different rules. In complex domains like rice growing and medicine, no theory is ever complete.

Given the dependencies in the diagram, it is apparent that a factor like heavy rainfall is neither *necessary* nor *sufficient* for rice growing. It is not necessary

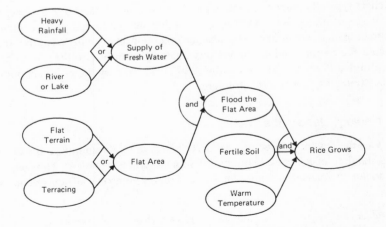

FIG. 8.1   A student's analysis of the causal factors affecting rice growing.

because obtaining a supply of fresh water (which *is* a necessary factor) can also be satisfied by irrigation from a river or lake. It is not sufficient* because other factors, such as a warm temperature, are required. When prior steps are connected into a step by an "or," any of the prior steps is sufficient and none is necessary. For example, either heavy rainfall or a river or a lake is a sufficient source for fresh water, but neither heavy rainfall nor a river nor a lake are necessary. In contrast, when prior steps are connected into a step by an "and," all of the prior nodes are necessary and none is sufficient.** For example, fresh water is necessary to flood a flat area, but it is not sufficient. Any variable not included as a factor in the diagram is effectively treated as *irrelevant* to the theory.

Independent and Dependent Variables in Different Domains

Table 8.1 illustrates how the terminology applies to teaching strategies in different domains. We believe that these teaching techniques can be applied to virtually any domain. In Table 8.1 we are not trying to list all possible independent and dependent variables, nor are we ruling out other possible assignments; these are merely meant to indicate the most common assignments that teachers make.

Let us briefly explain these examples:

1. In arithmetic, a student solves problems in order to learn how to handle different operations, numbers, variables, and so on. Because of the procedural emphasis in arithmetic, it is the domain that fits our terminology least well.

2. In art history, the teacher attempts to teach students how different techniques, uses of texture or color, structural interrelationships, and so on, create certain effects on the viewer.

3. In law, historical cases are used to teach students how different variables (historical precedents, laws, aspects of the particular case, etc.) affect legal outcomes.

4. In medicine, the goal is to teach students how to diagnose different diseases, given patterns of symptoms, their course of development, and the patient's history and appearance.

5. In geography, most variables are treated both as independent and dependent variables on different occasions. For example, average temperature is a dependent variable with respect to the first-order factors, latitude and altitude, and general second-order factors, distance from the sea, wind and sea currents, tree and cloud cover, and so on. But, in turn, temperature is a factor affecting dependent variables such as population density, products, land types, and so on.

---

*Editor's note: This is similar to Landa's notion of *sufficient and insufficient indicative features* (see Chapter 6, p. 206).

**Editor's note: The "and—or" distinction here is similar to Landa's distinction between *prescriptive rules* and *permissive rules* (see Chapter 6, p. 188).

TABLE 8.1

Elements that Function as Cases, Independent Variables,
and Dependent Variables in Different Disciplines

Discipline	Cases	Independent Variables	Dependent Variable
Arithmetic	Problems	Numbers, operators, variable assignments	Answers
Art history	Pictures, sculptures	Techniques, relation of parts	Effects on viewer
Law	Legal cases	Laws, past rulings, facts of case	Court decisions
Medicine	Medical cases	Symptoms, history, course of symptoms	Diseases
Geography	Places	e.g., latitude, altitude, currents	e.g., climate
Moral education	Situations, events	Actions, rules of Behavior	Fairness
Botany	Particular plants	Shapes, leaf and branch structure	Type of plant

6. In moral education, teachers try to teach rules of moral behavior by considering different situations with respect to the actions and motives of the participants.

7. In botany, one learns what configurations of the shape, branches, leaves, and so on, go with what plant names.

Whether a variable is treated as a dependent or independent variable depends on what the teacher is trying to teach. It does not depend on the direction of causality. What functions as a dependent variable is merely what one tries to make predictions about in the real world.

Data Analyzed

The dialogues we have analyzed range over a variety of subject-matter domains and take place in a variety of situations. Some are with individual students and some with groups of students. The students range in age from preschoolers to adults. In some cases the teacher has a well worked-out plan as to where the dialogue will go; in others, the teacher does not. We can illustrate the variety by describing briefly each of the dialogues we have analyzed, which we have listed in Table 8.2.

1. In arithmetic Professor Richard Anderson of the University of Illinois systematically varied different variables in problems of the form $7 \times 4 + 3 \times 4 = ?$ until the student discovered the shortcut to solving them based on the distributive law (i.e., $(7 + 3) \times 4$).

2. In geography Anderson compared different places to get the student to see that average winter temperature depends on distance from the ocean as well as latitude.

3. In moral education Anderson compared the American revolutionaries to draft resistors to force the student to consider what factors make rebellion right or wrong.

4. In one dialogue Professor Max Beberman of the University of Illinois had junior-high students figure out the pattern underlying the wrong answers in an arithmetic test ($5 + 7 = 57$, $1/2$ of $8 = 3$), where the answers were derived by manipulating the symbols (i.e., numerals) rather than number concepts. His goal was to teach the difference between numbers and their symbols.

5. In the other Beberman dialogue he got students to abstract the rules for addition of real numbers. He gave them problems to work on graph paper by drawing lines to the right for positive numbers and lines to the left for negative numbers.

6. In two dialogues on grain growing, Collins (the first author) questioned adults about whether different places grow rice, wheat, and corn in order to extract the factors that determine which grains are grown.

7. In two dialogues on population density, Collins asked why different places have more or fewer people to determine what factors affect population density.

TABLE 8.2
Teachers, Students, Domains, and Topics
in the Analyzed Transcripts

Teacher	Student	Domain	Topic
Anderson, R. C.	Junior-high girl	Arithmetic	Distributive law
Anderson, R. C.	Hypothetical student	Geography	Factors affecting temperature
Anderson, R. C.	Hypothetical student	Moral education	Morality of American revolutionaries
Beberman, M.	Junior-high students	Arithmetic	Numbers versus numerals
Beberman, M.	Junior-high students	Arithmetic	Addition of real numbers
Collins, A.	Adults	Geography	Grain growing
Collins, A.	Adults	Geography	Population density
Mentor	Hypothetical student	Medicine	Diagnosis of disease
Miller, A.	Adults	Law	Fairness of sentences
Schank, R.	Graduate students	Computer science	Types of plans
Socrates (Plato)	Slave boy	Arithmetic	Area of squares
Stevens & Collins	Adults	Geography	Causes of rainfall
Warman, E.	Preschoolers	Moral education	Who can play with blocks
Warman, E.	Preschoolers	Moral education	Character's morality in Peter Pan

8. Mentor is a computer system developed by Feurzeig, Munter, Swets, & Breen (1964). In its medical dialogues the student tries to identify a particular disease by asking the system about symptoms and test results. In turn, the system interrogates the student about his or her hypotheses.

9. In a television series Professor Arthur Miller of Harvard Law School conducted a dialogue with his audience on whether or not there should be mandatory sentencing, by considering what would be fair sentences for various hypothetical crimes.

10. In his computer-science class Professor Roger Schank of Yale asked students first to define a plan, then to form a taxonomy of different types of plans, and finally to analyze a real plan in terms of the taxonomy.

11. In the Meno dialogue, Socrates (Plato, 1924) uses systematic questioning to get a slave boy to figure out that the area of a square can be doubled by multiplying each side by $\sqrt{2}$.

12. In the Stevens and Collins (1977) dialogues, several adults were questioned about the factors leading to heavy rainfall or little rainfall in different places.

13. In a dialogue with a class of preschoolers, Eloise Warman tried to get the students to solve the problem that arose because the boys were always playing with the blocks, thus preventing the girls from playing with them.

14. In another dialogue, Warman questioned the children about the morality of different characters after the children had seen a film of Peter Pan.

We show excerpts from many of these dialogues as we discuss the various strategies that inquiry teachers use to get their students to solve different problems.

THE THEORY

Our theory of inquiry teaching has three parts: (1) the goals of teachers; (2) the strategies teachers use; and (3) the control structure governing their teaching. Each of these is discussed here.

Goals of Teachers

There are two top-level goals that teachers in inquiry dialogues pursue: (1) teaching students *particular rules* or theories; and (2) teaching students how to *derive rules* or theories.* There are several subgoals associated with each of these top-level goals. The top-level goals and subgoals that we have identified are shown in Table 8.3.

---

*Editor's note: These are similar to Gagné's *rules* and *cognitive strategies*, respectively, and to Scandura's *rules* and *higher-order rules*, respectively (see Chapter 7), and to Landa's *teaching students particular algo-heuristic procedures* and *teaching students how to discover algo-heuristic procedures* (see Chapter 6).

TABLE 8.3
Goals and Subgoals of Teachers

1. Teach a general rule or theory (e.g., Beberman, Anderson, Collins).
   a. Debug incorrent hypotheses (e.g., Beberman on numbers and numerals, Socrates, Stevens & Collins, Feurzeig et al., Anderson on moral education and geography).
   b. Teach how to make predictions in novel cases (e.g., Beberman, Anderson in arithmetic, Warman, Collins, Feurzeig et al.).

2. Teach how to derive a general rule or theory (e.g., Schank, Warman).
   a. Teach what questions to ask (e.g., Schank, Warman).
   b. Teach what is the nature of a theory (e.g., Schank, Beberman, Stevens & Collins).
   c. Teach how to test a rule or theory (e.g., Anderson in geography, Schank).
   d. Teach students to verbalize and defend rules or theories (e.g., Warman, Miller, Schank).

The most frequent goal is for the student to derive a *specific rule* or theory that the teacher has in mind. For example, in arithmetic Beberman tried to get students to derive the rule for addition of real numbers, and Anderson the distributive law. In geography Anderson tried to get the student to understand how distance from the ocean affected temperature, and Stevens and Collins tried to get students to build a first-order theory of the factors affecting rainfall.

Along with trying to teach a particular rule or theory, teachers often try to elicit and *debug incorrect rules* or theories. The teachers want the student to confront incorrect hypotheses during learning, so that they will not fall into the same traps later. This kind of goal is evident in Beberman's dialogue in which he tries to teach the difference between numbers and numerals, in Socrates' dialogues in which he traces the consequences of his student's hypothesis down to a contradiction, and in Anderson's dialogues on geography and moral education in which he entraps students into revealing their misconceptions.

Another goal that frequently pairs with teaching a given rule or theory is teaching students how to make *novel predictions* based on the rule or theory.* Simply knowing the structure of a theory is not enough; one must be able to operate on that structure to deal with new problems. For example, in mathematics Anderson gives harder and harder problems for the student to predict the answer.** In geography Collins and Stevens start with cases that exemplify first-order factors and gradually move to more difficult cases to predict. Feurzeig et al. are trying to get students to diagnose novel cases. This goal emphasizes the ability to use the theory one has learned.

The other top-level goal of inquiry teachers is to teach students *how to derive* a new rule or theory. For example, Schank tried to get his students to formulate a new theory of planning, and Warman tried to get her preschoolers to devise a new rule for allocating blocks. Many of the dialogues had a similar aim.

---

*Editor's note: This goal is definitely on an application level of learning (e.g., Gagné's intellectual skills and Gropper's *giving and applying explanations*).

**Editor's note: This is identical to Gropper's *shaping treatments* (except that Gropper's treatments specify detailed ways in which practice examples are (or can be made) easier or harder.

One related ability is knowing *what questions to ask* in order to derive a new rule or theory on your own. For example, Warman teaches her preschoolers to evaluate any rule by how fair it is. Schank tries to get students to construct a theory by asking taxonomic kinds of questions. Feurzeig et al. emphasize considering different diagnoses before reaching a conclusion.

A goal that underlies many of the dialogues is to teach students what *form* a rule or theory should take. In Schank's case, the structure of a theory is a set of primitive elements as in chemistry. In one of Beberman's dialogues he taught students the form of arithmetic rules, where variables replace numbers in order to be general. Stevens' and Collins' (1977) notion of a theory of rainfall was a hierarchically organized, process theory. The principal method for achieving their goal seems to be to construct rules or theories of the idealized type.

Occasionally in the dialogues the teachers pursue a goal of teaching students how to *evaluate* a rule or theory that has been constructed. For example, in teaching about what affects temperature Anderson tried to get the student to learn how to control one factor while testing for another. After his students had specified a set of primitive plan types, Schank tried to get them to test out their theory by applying it to a real-world plan (i.e., becoming president). The strategies teachers use are specific to the kind of evaluation methods being taught.

Finally, it was a clear goal of both Warman and Schank to get their students to *verbalize and defend* their rules or theories. For example, it is clear why Warman's children were always interrupting to give their ideas: She was constantly encouraging and rewarding them for joining in. Similarly, Schank tried to get each student in the class to either offer his or her ideas, adopt one of the other's ideas, criticize one of the other's ideas, and so on. Both Warman and Schank stressed the questioning of authority in their dialogues as a means to push students to formulate their own ideas.

These are the top-level goals we have been able to identify so far. They are summarized in Table 8.3 earlier. In pursuing these goals, teachers adopt supporting goals of identifying particular omissions or misconceptions and debugging them (Stevens & Collins, 1977). Thus these top-level goals spawn supporting goals that drive the dialogue more locally. This is discussed more fully in the section on control structure.

Strategies for Inquiry Teaching*

We have decided to focus on 10 of the most important strategies that inquiry teachers use. The 10 strategies are listed in Table 8.4 together with the teachers

---

*Editor's note: It may be helpful to keep in mind that there is a difference between inquiry and discovery approaches to instruction. *Inquiry* approaches start with a question, and the remainder of the instruction attempts to bring the student to an understanding of the answer to that question, by means of either an expository approach or a discovery approach. On the other hand, *discovery* approaches do not present a rule (or generality) to the student until after the student discovers it. The student may be led to discover something without having first formulated a question related to such

TABLE 8.4
Different Instructional Techniques
and their Practitioners

---

 1. Selecting positive and negative exemplars (Anderson, Miller, Stevens & Collins)
 2. Varying cases systematically (Anderson, Stevens & Collins)
 3. Selecting counterexamples (Collins, Anderson)
 4. Generating hypothetical cases (Warman, Miller)
 5. Forming hypotheses (Warman, Schank, Anderson, Beberman)
 6. Testing hypotheses (Anderson, Schank)
 7. Considering alternative predictions (Feurzeig et al., Warman)
 8. Entrapping students (Anderson, Collins, Feurzeig et al.)
 9. Tracing consequences to a contradiction (Socrates, Anderson)
10. Questioning authority (Schank, Warman)

---

who used them. Our plan is to show excerpts of the teachers illustrating each of these techniques, and then show how the technique can be extended to two other domains.

The domains we use to illustrate the techniques are mathematics, geography, moral education, medicine, and law. These domains cover radically different kinds of education: Mathematics exemplifies a highly precise, procedural domain; moral education and law exemplify domains in which loosely structured belief systems are paramount (Abelson, 1979), and geography and medicine exemplify domains in which open-ended, causal knowledge systems are paramount (Collins, Warnock, Aiello, & Miller, 1975).

Selecting Positive and Negative Exemplars

Teachers often choose positive or negative paradigm cases in order to highlight the relevant factors. *Paradigm cases* are cases in which the relevant factors are all consistent with a particular value of the dependent variable. This strategy was most evident in the geographical dialogues of Stevens and Collins (1977), but it is also apparent in Anderson's arithmetic dialogue, and Miller's law dialogues.

We can illustrate this strategy for geography in terms of selecting paradigm cases for rainfall. In the beginning of their teaching, Stevens and Collins chose positive exemplars such as the Amazon, Oregon, and Ireland where all the relevant factors had values that lead to heavy rainfall. They also chose negative exemplars* like southern California, northern Africa, and northern Chile where all the relevant factors have values that lead to little rainfall. Only later would they take up

---

discovery, in which case it would not be an inquiry approach to discovery. Although Collins and Stevens are clearly interested in a model of inquiry instruction, it appears that some of the teachers whose instruction was analyzed may not have been using an inquiry approach, and that care should be exercised by a teacher or instructional designer to use the strategies described in this section in such a way as to implement an inquiry rather than a noninquiry approach to discovery.

*Editor's note: These are similar to Gropper's *practice of errors* (Chapter 5, p. 139) and Merrill's *matched nonexamples* (Chapter 9, p. 325).

cases like the eastern United States or China where the factors affecting rainfall have a more complicated pattern.*

The method that Anderson used to select cases to illustrate the distributive law in arithmetic was based on the strategy of selecting positive exemplars. For example, the first problem he presented was $7 \times 5 + 3 \times 5 = ?$ He wanted the student to see that because the 5 entered the equation twice, the problem could be easily solved by adding 7 and 3 and multiplying by 5. There are a number of aspects of this particular problem (and the subsequent problems he gave) that make it a paradigm case: (1) because 7 and 3 add up to 10, the 5 appears as the only significant digit in the answer; (2) the 5 appears in the same position in both parts of the equation; (3) the 5 is distinct from the other digits in the equation. All these serve to highlight the digit the student must factor out.**

In his work on discovery learning, Davis (1966) advocated a similar strategy for selecting cases. In getting students to discover how to solve quadratic equations by graphing them, he gave problems of the form: $X^2 - 5X + 6 = 0$, where the roots are 3 and 2, or $X^2 - 12X + 35 = 0$, where the roots are 5 and 7. The fact that both roots had the same sign was essential to getting the students to make the correct discovery; only when there are roots of the same sign is it readily apparent that the X coefficient is the sum of the two roots.

This same attempt to pick paradigm cases is apparent in Miller's law dialogues. In considering what should be a mandatory sentence for a crime, he considers worst cases, in which all the relevant factors (e.g., tough guy, repeat offender, no dependents) would lead a judge to give a heavy sentence, and best cases, in which all the relevant factors (e.g., mother with dependents, first offender) would lead to a light sentence. This exactly parallels the Stevens and Collins strategy in geography.

There are also two other strategies for picking positive and negative exemplars that we have named *near hits* and *near misses* after Winston (1973). *Near misses* are cases in which all the necessary factors but one hold.*** For example, Florida is a near miss for rice growing, because rice could be grow there except for the poor soil. Near misses highlight a particular factor that is necessary. *Near hits* are their counterparts for sufficient factors: cases that would not have a particular value on the dependent variable, except for the occurrence of a particular sufficient factor.**** For example, it is possible to grow rice in Egypt despite little rainfall, because of irrigation from the Nile. Near misses and near hits are important strategies for highlighting particular necessary or sufficient factors.

---

*Editor's note: This is reminiscent of Gropper's *shaping routines* wherein more difficult examples are only presented after easier examples are presented.

**Editor's note: These are identical to what Gropper refers to as *cues* (see Chapter 5, p. 128).

***Editor's note: This is identical to Merrill's notion of a *matched nonexample* (see Chapter 9, p. 325) and Markle and Tiemann's (1969) notion of a *close-in nonexamplar.*

****Editor's note: This is similar to Merrill's notion of *divergent examples* (see Chapter 9, p. 325), Markle and Tiemann's (1969) notion of *divergenc exemplars,* and Gropper's notion of *varied practice examples* (see Chapter 5, p. 137).

2. Varying Cases Systematically

Teachers often choose cases in systematic sequences to emphasize particular factors that they want the student to notice. This is most evident in the dialogue in which Anderson got a junior-high-school girl to derive the distributive law in arithmetic. He started out giving her problems to work, like $7 \times 5 + 3 \times 5$ and $7 \times 12 + 3 \times 12$, in which the only factor that changed was the multiplier, which shows up in the answer (50 or 120) as the significant digits. He then gave problems in which he varied the addends systematically—$70 \times 8 + 30 \times 8$ and $6 \times 4 + 4 \times 4$—but preserved the fact that the multiplier formed the significant digits. Then he relaxed that constraint to examples like $11 \times 6 + 9 \times 6$, $110 \times 4 + 90 \times 4$, and finally $4 \times 3 + 8 \times 3$, so that the student would formulate the distributive law in its most general form. Anderson was systematically varying one factor after another in the problems he gave the student, so that the student could see how each factor in turn affected the answer.*

We can illustrate this technique in geography by showing how teachers can systematically choose cases to vary the different factors affecting average temperature. First, the teacher might systematically vary latitude while holding other variables constant (e.g., the Amazon jungle, the Pampas, Antarctica), then vary altitude while holding other variables constant (e.g., the Amazon jungle, the city of Quito, the top of Kilimanjaro), then other factors such as distance from the ocean, sea and wind currents, cloud and tree cover, and so on. The separation of individual factors in this way is precisely what Anderson was doing in arithmetic.

In moral education it is possible to consider what punishment is appropriate by considering cases in which the punishable behavior is systematically varied in different respects. For example, the teacher could systematically vary the malice of the intention, the severity of the act, and the damage of the consequences one at a time while holding each of the other factors constant.

In Collins and Stevens (1982) we point out four different ways this kind of systematic variation can occur. The cases already cited involve differentiation; in *differentiation* a set of nonfocused factors is held constant, while the teacher shows how variation of one factor affects the dependent variable. Its inverse, *generalization*, occurs when the teacher holds the focused factor and the dependent variable constant, while varying the nonfocused factors.** The two other strategies highlight the *range of variability* of either the focused factor or the dependent variable: In one strategy the teacher holds the focused factor constant while showing how widely the value of the *dependent variable* may vary (because of variation in nonfocused factors); in the other strategy the teacher holds the dependent variable constant and shows how widely the value of the *focused factor* may vary.*** These four strategies allow teachers to stress various interactions between different factors and the dependent variable.

---

*Editor's note: Again notice the similarity with Gropper's various *shaping routines*, especially his *varied practice examples* (see Chapter 5).

**Editor's note: These two correspond to Gropper's *discrimination* and *generalization*.

***Editor's note: These two are similar to Gropper's *varied practice examples* (see Chapter 5).

3. Selecting Counterexamples

. A third method of choosing cases that teachers use in the dialogues we have analyzed is selecting counterexamples. We can illustrate two different kinds of counterexamples in the following short dialgue on growing rice from Collins (1977):

AC: Where in North America do you think rice might be grown?
S: Louisiana.
AC: Why there?
S: Places where there is a lot of water. I think rice requires the ability to selectively flood fields.
AC: OK. Do you think there's a lot of rice in, say, Washington and Oregon? (Counterexample for an insufficient factor)
S: Aha, I don't think so.
AC: Why?
S: There's a lot of water up there too, but there's two reasons. First the climate isn't conducive, and second, I don't think the land is flat enough. You've got to have flat land so you can flood a lot of it, unless you terrace it.
AC: What about Japan? (Counterexample for an unnecessary factor)
S: Yeah, well they have this elaborate technology I suppose for terracing land so they can flood it selectively even though it's tilted overall.

The first counterexample (for an insufficient factor) was chosen because the student gave rainfall as a sufficient cause of rice growing. So a place was chosen that had a lot of rainfall, but no rice. When the student mentioned mountains as a reason why no rice is grown in Oregon, Japan was chosen as a counterexample (for an unnecessary factor), because it is mountainous but produces rice.* As can be seen in the dialogue, counterexamples like these force the student to pay attention to different factors affecting the dependent variable.

One can see this same strategy for choosing a counterexample applied to moral education in the following excerpt from Anderson (in Collins, 1977):

RA: If you'd been alive during the American Revolution, which side would you have been on?
S: The American side.
RA: Why?
S: They were fighting for their rights.
RA: You admire people who fight for their rights. Is that true?
S: Yes.
RA: How about the young men who broke into the draft office and burned the records? Do you admire them? (Counterexample for insufficient factors)
S: No, what they did was wrong.

What Anderson did was to pick a counterexample for an insufficient factor. He knew the student does not admire everyone who fights for his or her rights, so there

---

*Editor's note: This is a form of feedback on the practice (see, for example, Gagné's seventh instructional event in Chapter 4)—a form in which the student is led to discover his or her own error.

must be other factors involved. This line of questioning forces the student to think about some of the different factors that determine the morality of an action.

We can illustrate the use of counterexamples in mathematics with an example from analytic geometry. Suppose a student hypothesizes on the basis of the graph for $x^2 + y^2 = 1$ (which yields a circle of radius 1) that the term on the right of the equation is the radius of the circle. Then the teacher might ask the student to plot the graph of $x^2 + y^2 = 4$. The student will find that this yields a circle of radius 2 rather than radius 4, and may infer that the radius is the square root of the term on the right. Learning to construct counterexamples is particularly useful in mathematics, where many proofs and intuitions rest upon this skill.

Two kinds of counterexamples were seen in the first excerpt from geography: a counterexample for insufficient factors, and one for unnecessary factors. There can also be counterexamples for irrelevant factors and incorrect values of factors (Collins & Stevens, 1982).

4. Generating Hypothetical Cases

In the dialogues of Eloise Warman on moral education and Arthur Miller on fairness of sentencing, these teachers often generate hypothetical cases to challenge their students' reasoning. Warman's use of the strategy was most apparent in a class discussion about a problem that arose because the boys (B) in the class were always playing with the blocks, thus preventing the girls (G) from playing with them. Two examples of Warman's use of the strategy occur in the following excerpt:

B: How about no girls play with anything and boys play with everything.
EW: OK. Let's take a vote. Boys, how about if you don't play with any toys here in school? Would you like that? (Hypothetical case)
B: No
G: Yea.
EW: OK. David said something. What did you say?
B: I would stay home.
EW: He would stay home. OK. How about if we had boys could play with everything but blocks? (Hypothetical case)
B: No. Rats.

What Warman does systematically is to illustrate the unfairness of the current or a proposed situation by reversing the roles as to who gets the advantage.* Thus in the first hypothetical case she reverses the boy's proposed rule by substituting boys for girls. In the second hypothetical case she reverses the current situation in which girls do not get to play with the blocks. She reverses the polarity of some factor in the situation to force the students to see what factors will make things fairer.

A somewhat different version of this strategy is used by Miller in his television show Miller's Court. In a show on sentencing, for example, he carried on a dialogue along the following lines with one man (M):

---

*Editor's note: Again, this is a form of *feedback by discovery*.

AM: You believe that there should be mandatory sentences? What do you think should be the sentence for armed robbery?

M: 10 years.

AM: So if a hardened criminal robs a bank of $1000, he should get 10 years in prison with no possibility of parole? (Hypothetical case)

M: Yes that seems fair.

AM: What if a poor young woman with children, who needs money to feed her kids, holds up a grocery store with an unloaded gun. Should she get 10 years too? (Hypothetical case)

What Miller does is entrap the man into a confirmation of a harsh rule of sentencing with one hypothetical case. His second case faces the man with the opposite extreme (as did Warman's) in which the man's rule is satisfied (armed robbery), but in which other factors override the man's evaluation of the fairness of the rule. Both Miller and Warman use hypothetical-case construction to force their respondents to take into account other factors in forming a general rule of behavior.

We can illustrate how this technique can be extended to geography with an example. Suppose a student thinks rice is grown in Louisiana because it rains a lot there. The teacher might ask "Suppose it didn't rain a lot in Louisiana; could they still grow rice?" In fact, irrigation could be used to grow rice. In the Collins and Stevens (1982) paper, we outline four different kinds of hypothetical cases the teacher can construct; these parallel the four kinds of counterexamples.

5. Forming Hypotheses

The most prevalent strategy that teachers use is to get students to formulate *general rules* relating different factors to values of the dependent variable. We can illustrate these attempts in all three domains by excerpts from Beberman, Anderson, and Warman.

In one dialogue Beberman was trying to get students to formulate a general rule for addition of real numbers. To this end he gave students a procedure to work through on graph paper to add a set of real numbers, by going right for positive numbers and going left for negative numbers. After a while students found a shortcut for doing this: They would add together the positive numbers, then the negative numbers, and take the difference. Beberman subsequently tried to get them to formulate this shortcut procedure into a few general rules for adding real numbers, which can be seen in the following dialogue excerpt:

MB: I want to state a rule here which would tell somebody how to add negative numbers if they didn't know how to do it before. Christine?

S: The absolute value—well—*a* plus *b* equals uh—negative—

MB: Yes, what do we do when we try to do a problem like that? Christine is on the right track. What do you actually do? Go ahead, Christine.

S: You add the numbers of arithmetic 5 and 7, and then you—

MB: I add the numbers of arithmetic 5 and 7; but how do I get the numbers of arithmetic when I'm talking with pronumerals like this?

We can illustrate the attempt to get students to formulate rules in geography with an excerpt from Anderson (in Collins, 1977) on the factors affecting average temperature. In an earlier part of the dialogue the student had been forced to the realization that there were places in the northern hemisphere that were warmer on the average than places to the south of them. The following excerpt shows Anderson's (in Collins, 1977) emphasis on hypothesis formation:

S: Some other factor besides north–south distance must also affect temperature.
RA: Yes! Right! What could this factor be?
S: I don't have any idea.
RA: Why don't you look at your map of North America. Do you see any differences between Montana and Newfoundland?
S: Montana is in the center of the country. Newfoundland is on the ocean.
RA: What do you mean by "in the center of the country"?
S: It's a long way from the ocean.
RA: Do you suppose that distance from the ocean affects temperature?
S: I'm not sure. It would just be a guess.
RA: True! The name for such a guess is a hypothesis. Supposing the hypothesis were correct, what exactly would you predict?
S: The further a place is from the ocean, the lower the temperature will be in the winter.

In her dialogue on who could play with blocks Warman never explicitly asked the children to formulate a new rule, but she stated the problem and encouraged them strongly whenever anyone offered a new rule for allocating the blocks. This can be seen in the following two short excerpts; in the first Warman rejects a proposed rule because it is the same as the current rule, and in the second she accepts the rule as the solution to the problem:

G: I've got a good idea. Everybody play with blocks.
EW: What do you think about that?
B: Rats.
EW: Isn't that the rule we have right now? That everyone can play with blocks. But what's the problem?

————

B: I've got one idea.
EW: Oh, Greg's got a good idea. (Reward rule formulation.)
B: The girls can play with the big blocks only on 2 days.
EW: Hey, listen we come to school 4 days a week. If the girls play with the big blocks on 2 days that gives the boys 2 other days to play with blocks. Does that sound fair? (Restate rule. Ask for rule evaluation.)
G: Yea! Yea!

There are a variety of strategies for *prodding* students to formulate hypotheses about what factors are involved and how they affect the dependent variable.*

————————

*Editor's note: This is similar to Gropper's notion of *cuing* (see Chapter 5).

These are enumerated in Collins and Stevens (1982) as strategies for identifying different elements in a rule or theory.

6. Evaluating Hypotheses

Sometimes teachers follow up the hypothesis-formation stage by trying to get students to systematically test out their hypotheses. This strategy is seen most clearly in the Anderson and the Schank dialogues. Anderson tries to get the student to test his hypothesis by comparing temperature in different places in the real world. Schank tries to get his students to test out their notions about what are the basic elements in planning by applying their taxonomy to a real-world problem, such as running for president. We now show how testing hpypotheses can be applied to the three previous examples of hypothesis formation.

We start with the Anderson example, in which the student's hypothesis was that distance from the ocean affects average temperature. The dialogue continued as follows:

RA: How could you test your hypothesis?
S: By comparing temperatures of places different distances from the ocean.
RA: Very good. Let's do that. Suppose we take St. Louis, Missouri. Which would be best to compare, Atlanta, Georgia, or Washington, D.C.?
S: I'm not sure.
RA: Why don't you look at your map? Maybe that will help you decide.
S: I would pick Washington.
RA: Why?
S: Because it's at the same latitude as St. Louis.
RA: Why is that important?
S: Well, if Atlanta were warmer, I wouldn't know whether it was because it was nearer the ocean or further south.

What Anderson is doing here is teaching the student how to hold other variables constant when testing out a hypothesis. This is also one of the strategies used by teachers in the systematic variation of cases described earlier.

After Beberman got the students to formulate several rules for the addition of real numbers, he could have had students test their rules by generating widely different examples to see if the rules as formulated could handle them. For example, one rule the class formulated was "If both a and b are negative, add the absolute value of a and the absolute value of b and give the sum a negative sign." There were such rules to handle different cases. To test out the rules he could get students to generate different pairs of numbers to see if the rules produce the same answers as the line-drawing procedure. In this case it is particularly important to make sure the rules work for special cases, such as when a or b equals zero.

In the Warman excerpt in which Greg formulates a rule that boys get to play with the blocks on 2 days and girls on 2 days, Warman explicitly asks students to evaluate the rule for fairness. This in fact led later to one amendment, that the girls get to go first because they have been deprived previously. Warman could have gone further in evaluating Greg's rule by asking the students to consider its fairness for all the people involved: boys, girls, teachers, particular children, and so on. If they had done this, they might have amended the rule further to let the child (or children) who was playing with the blocks invite one member of the opposite sex to play, because one of the boys had expressed a desire to play with one of the girls. They could have tested the rule even farther in this situation by trying it out for a day on which the boys got the blocks half the time and the girls half the time, to see whether the new rule worked.

There are different aspects to hypothesis evaluation, such as controlling variables or testing out special cases, that are important for students to learn. These can be brought out by getting students to systematically evaluate their hypotheses.

7. Considering Alternative Predictions

Hypothesis formation is concerned with identifying *different factors* and how they relate to values of the dependent variable. Thus Anderson was trying to get students to consider different factors that affect temperature and to specify a rule relating to factors to temperature. Sometimes, teachers, particularly in the Feurzeig et al. and Warman dialogues, try to get the students to consider different alternative values for the dependent variable.*

We can see the teacher trying to get the student to consider alternative predictions in the following dialogue on medical diagnosis (Feurzeig et al., 1964):

> T: We've considered one possibility (i.e., pulmonary infarction). Do you have another diagnosis in mind?
> S: No.
> T: In that case I'd like to talk about viral pneumonia. The tachycardia, high WBC, elevated respiratory rate, shaking chills, bloody sputum, and severe pleural pain all lend weight to that diagnosis—right?

What the teacher is doing here is trying to get the student to consider how the values of the known factors fit with different possible values of the dependent variable. This forces the student to weigh different alternatives in making any predictions or judgments. This same strategy was applied by Collins in his dialogues on the factors affecting grain growing when he asked students to consider whether wheat or rice or corn could be grown in the same place.

An excerpt from Warman illustrates the same strategy applied to moral education. The excerpt is from a dialogue discussing the morality of the different characters in Peter Pan, which the children had just seen:

> EW: Are the Indians good in Peter Pan?
> S: Good.

---

*Editor's note: Considering that the real content here is *how to derive a general rule or theory* (goal 2 in Table 8.3), this—like many of the other strategies here—is just a form of *practice*, in which the student is required to practice one of the parts of the algo-heuristic procedures for deriving a general rule or theory.

EW: Why are the Indians good?

S: No. It's the Chief, because he catched all of the boys.

EW: So the Chief catches all the boys; so is the Chief good?

S: Nope. He's bad.

EW: He's bad? Is he always bad? Or is he good sometimes, or what do you think? That's a tough question. Is the Indian Chief always bad, or is he sometimes bad? What would you say?

Here Warman tries to get the children to consider different points on the morality continuum, in relation to where the actions of the Indian Chief fall on that continuum. Sometimes dependent variables have a discrete set of values as in medicine, and sometimes they are continuous variables, as in moral education, but in either case it is possible to get students to consider different possible values.

This strategy can be illustrated in mathematics with an example from geometry. Suppose the teacher wants the student to figure out what the regular polygon is with the most number of sides that can cover a plane surface. The student might have decided that four must be the answer, because you can cover a surface with triangles and squares but not with pentagons. The teacher might press the student to consider six, eight, and twelve as possible answers. Part of a mathematician's skill depends on being able to systematically generate other plausible solutions and to prove they cannot hold.

Encouraging students to consider other values of the dependent variable forces them into the more powerful methods of differential diagnosis or comparative hypothesis testing as opposed to the more natural tendency to consider only one alternative at a time.* This is particularly important to prevent people from jumping to a conclusion without considering the best alternative.

8. Entrapping Students

The teachers we have analzyed often use entrapment strategies to get the students to reveal their underlying misconceptions. This is most apparent in the dialogues of Anderson, Collins, and Feurzeig et al. We can illustrate the use of entrapment in the different domains by excerpts from three of the dialogues.

Anderson frequently uses a kind of entrapment strategy in which he takes the student's reasons and turns them into a general rule.** One example of this occurred in the excerpt in which he formulated the general rule "You admire people who fight for their rights," and then suggested a counterexample. This strategy can be seen later in the same dialogue, when the student defended the American revolutionaries:

S: They were in the right. They didn't have any voice in the government. There was taxation without representation.

---

*Editor's note: This supports the contention in the preceding Editor's note.

**Editor's note: This kind of entrapment seems to be mostly *feedback* on practice, where the *student's reasons* is the student's response on the practice.

RA: So you would say that people do have a right to disobey laws if they don't have a voice in the government? (Formulate a general rule for an insufficient factor.)

Anderson's formulation of general rules can be applied not only to reasons based on insufficient factors, as in these two examples, but also to unnecessary factors, irrelevant factors, and incorrect values of factors (Collins & Stevens, 1981).

Another somewhat different kind of entrapment can be seen in the following dialogue excerpt from Collins (1977):

AC: Is it very hot along the coast here? (points to Peruvian coast near the equator) (Entrapment into a prediction based on insufficient factors)
S: I don't remember.
AC: It turns out there's a very cold current coming up along the coast; and it bumps against Peru, and tends to make the coastal area cooler, although it's near the equator.

Here the teacher tries to entrap the student into a wrong prediction based on the equatorial latitude, which is an insufficient factor overridden in this case by an ocean current. Anderson (in Collins, 1977) also uses this kind of entrapment in his geographical dialogue when he asks "Which is likely to have the coldest winter days, Newfoundland or Montana?" The student is likely to guess Newfoundland because it is further north.* Entrapment into incorrect predictions can also occur in different forms (Collins & Stevens, 1981).

Another kind of entrapment occurs in the medical dialogues of Feurzeig et al. (1964). This can be seen in the excerpt in which the teacher suggests that several symptoms lend weight to a diagnosis of viral pneumonia. In fact, all the symptoms mentioned either have incorrect values or are irrelevant to a diagnosis of viral pneumonia.** Here the entrapment takes the form of a suggestion that particular factors lead to a given value of the dependent variable.

We can illustrate how entrapment might be used in mathematics by considering Socrates' dialogue with the slave boy in the Meno dialogue (Plato, 1924), in which Socrates tried to get the boy to figure out the area of a square:

Soc: So the space is twice two feet?
Boy: Yes.
Soc: Then how many are twice two feet? Count and tell me.
Boy: Four, Socrates.
Soc: Well could there be another such space, twice as big; but of the same shape, with all the lines equal like this one?
Boy: Yes.
Soc: How many feet will there be in that, then?

*Editor's note: This second kind of entrapment seems to be a combination of practice item divergence (i.e., Gropper's *varied practice examples*) and feedback on that practice.
**Editor's note: This third kind of entrapment seems to be primarily practice item divergence.

Boy: Eight.

Soc: Very well, now try to tell me how long will be each line of that one. The line of this one is two feet; how long would the line of the double one be?

Boy: The line would be double, Socrates, that is clear.

Here the boy is entrapped into a wrong hypothesis, that double the area is produced by a side double in length, in a manner similar to the previous geographical example.* The entrapment would have been even stronger if Socrates had suggested, "Would the line of the double square be twice as long?" This is entrapment into an incorrect prediction, but other forms of entrapment are equally applicable with respect to mathematical rules or factors.

Entrapment is used to force the student to face difficulties that may arise later in other circumstances. By getting the student to reveal and correct misconceptions during learning, the teacher assures that the student has a deeper understanding of the subject matter.**

9. Tracing Consequences to a Contradiction

One of the ways teachers try to get students to correct their misconceptions is to trace the consequences of the misconceptions to some conclusion that the students will agree cannot be correct.*** This kind of approach is most evident in Socrates' Meno dialogue and Anderson's moral-education dialogue.

We can illustrate Socrates' use of this technique by picking up just after the slave boy had predicted that to double the area of a square, you must double the length of the side (the line segments are shown in Fig. 8.2) (Plato, 1924):

Soc: Then this line (ac) is double this (ab), if we add as much (bc) to it on this side.

Boy: Of course.

Soc: Then if we put four like this (ac), you say we shall get this eight-foot space.

Boy: Yes.

Soc: Then let us draw these four equal lines (ac, cd, de, ea). Is that the space which you say will be eight feet?

Boy: Of course.

Soc: Can't you see in it these four spaces here (A, B, C, D), each of them equal to the one we began with, the four-foot space?

Boy: Yes.

Soc: Well how big is this new one? Is it not four times the old one?

---

*Editor's note: This is reminiscent of Gropper's *practice of errors* (see Chapter 5).

**Editor's note: An interesting question here is whether the instruction might not be more effective and efficient if, through an expository or "explicit" approach (such as Gropper's), those misconceptions were avoided (i.e., dispelled before they developed) and hence did not have to be "unlearned" later on through such entrapment techniques. Of course, this question becomes moot when the goal of the instruction is to "teach how to derive a rule or theory" rather than just to "teach a specific rule or theory." (See Landa's algorithm in Chapter 5, p. 195, for an excellent basis for deciding whether a discovery or expository approach is preferable.)

***Editor's note: This is a form of feedback on practice.

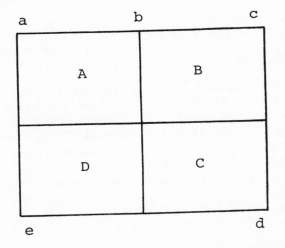

FIG. 8.2   Diagram referred to by Socrates in the Meno dialogue.

Boy: Surely it is!
Soc: Is four times the old one, double?
Boy: Why no, upon my word!
Soc: How big then?
Boy: Four times as big!
Soc: Then, my boy, from a double line we get a space four times as big, not double.
Boy: That's true.

What Socrates did was to follow the chain of consequences until the slave boy recognized the contradiction.

Anderson applied this same strategy in his dialogue comparing the Vietnam draft resistors to the American revolutionaries. In the segment shown there is a series of four questions in which he traces out several different consequences of the student's previous statements until the student finally finds a distinction that differentiates the two cases for him:

S: I don't think Viet Nam is such a good thing, but you just can't have individuals deciding which laws they are going to obey.
RA: So, you would say the American revolutionaries should have followed the law.
S: Yes, I guess so.
RA: If they had obediently followed all the laws we might not have had the American Revolution. Is that right?
S: Yes.
RA: They should have obeyed the laws even if they believed they were unjust. Is that right?
S: I'm not sure. I suppose I have to say yes.
RA: In other words what the American revolutionaries did was wrong. That's true isn't it?

S: No, damn it. They were in the right. They were fighting for their liberty. They didn't have any voice in the government. There was taxation without representation.

We can illustrate how this same technique can be extended to geography with an example from one of Stevens' and Collins' dialogues on the causes of rainfall in the Amazon. When asked from where the moisture evaporated that caused the heavy rainfall in the Amazon jungle, the student incorrectly answered the Amazon River. The implications of this could be traced with a series of questions such as: (1) Does most of the water in the river evaporate or flow into the ocean? (2) If most of the water flows into the ocean, won't the process soon dry up? The student will quickly be forced by this line of reasoning to see that most evaporation must occur from the ocean rather than from the river.

Tracing consequences in this way forces students to actively debug their own theories. This may prevent students from making similar mistakes in the future, and it teaches them to evaluate a theory by testing out its consequences.

10. Questioning Authority

A striking aspect of both the Schank and Warman dialogues is the effort these teachers make to get the students not to look to the teacher or the book for the correct answers, but rather to construct their own theories. This is a particularly important strategy to Schank's and Warman's goals of teaching students how to develop their own rules or theories.

We can illustrate how Schank and Warman apply the strategy with short excerpts from their class sessions. The segment from Schank shows him trying to get students to form a taxonomy of basic types of plans. He complains when he recognizes that the students are just repeating what they read in the book:

RS: Give me some categories of plans.
S2: Bargain object. (laughter)
RS: Give me a better one than that. Anyway it's not a category, that's a plan.
S1: Plans to obtain objects. (Schank writes it down)
S4: Is there a reason why we want that category?
RS: No, I'm just looking for gross categories.
S2: Plans to establish social control over something.
RS: The two of you are agreeing that everything from the book is gospel. It's all right. Give me something new—I wrote those—invent something.

Warman comes to the same problem in her dialogue when she is trying to get her preschoolers to develop a new rule to decide who is allowed to play with the toy blocks in the classroom. The current rule is that anybody can play with anything, but the boys are dominating the use of the blocks, thus keeping the girls from them. The following excerpt shows her argument against deciding by authority:

EW: Do you think that it should be all right for only one person should get to make all the choices (sic) for who gets to play with blocks. Or do you think it should be something we all decide on?

G: I think it should be the teacher's.

EW: But why just the teacher's? It doesn't seem to work. We had an idea. We've been trying.

The questioning of authority is an important strategy for getting students to think like scientists, to get them to try out theory construction on their own, and to get them to question those things that may appear to be givens.

Dialogue Control Structure

The control structure that the teacher uses to allocate time between different goals and subgoals may be the most crucial aspect for effective teaching.* An earlier attempt at a theory of the control structure was developed in Stevens and Collins (1977), based on tutors' comments about what they thought a student knew after each answer and about why they asked each question. The four basic parts of the control-structure theory are: (1) a set of strategies for *selecting* cases with respect to the top-level goals; (2) a student model; (3) an agenda; and (4) a set of *priority rules* for adding goals and subgoals to the agenda.

Given a set of top-level goals, the teacher selects cases that optimize the ability of the student to master those goals. There appear to be several overall strategies that the teachers apply in selecting cases:

1. *Selecting cases that illustrate more important factors before less important factors.* For example, in teaching about rainfall, Stevens and Collins move from cases like the Amazon and Ireland that exemplify a first-order theory to cases like eastern America or Patagonia where the factors are more complex.**

2. *Select cases to move from concrete to abstract factors.* Teachers tend to select cases that emphasize concrete factors initially, in order to make contact with the student's experience, and then move to cases that emphasize more abstract factors.***

3. *Select more important or more frequent cases before less important or less frequent cases.* Other things being equal, a geography teacher will select cases like the United States, Europe, and China, which are more important. A medical professor will select the most frequent diseases and the ones that are most important to diagnose.

---

*Editor's note: To a large extent the authors are talking here about the importaqnce of a *selection* strategy. A *sequencing* strategy is also involved to some extent (see following discussion).

**Editor's note: This is a bit unclear because importance and complexity are two different things. With respect to complexity, this prescription is similar to Gropper's *shaping routines* and Sandura's *elaboration on the simplest path*. With respect to importance, it is similar to the Elaboration Theory of Instruction (see Chapter 10), except that the latter is a macro-level strategy.

***Editor's note: This is similar to Gropper's *concrete and abstract stimulus/response modes* (see Chapter 5, pp. 135–137).

When a case is selected, the teacher begins questioning students about the values of the dependent and independent variables, and the rules interrelating them. The answers reveal what the student does and does not know with respect to the teacher's theory (Stevens & Collins, 1977).* As the teacher gains information about the student's understanding, factors in the teacher's theory are tagged as known, in error, not known, and so on. This is the basic student model.

The teacher's model of the student also includes a priori expectations of how likely any student is to know a given piece of information in the theory (Collins, Warnock, & Passafiume, 1975). As a particular student reveals what he or she knows, his or her level of sophistication with respect to the teacher's theory can be gauged. From this, an estimate can be made as to the likelihood that the student will know any given factor in the theory. This enables the teacher to focus on adding information near the edge of what the student knows a priori. The details of how this operates are given in Collins, Warnock, and Passafiume (1975).

As specific bugs (i.e., errors and omissions) in the student's theory or reasoning processes are identified, they create subgoals to diagnose the underlying causes of the bug and to correct them. Often the questions reveal multiple bugs. In such cases the teacher can only pursue one bug at a time. Thus there has to be an *agenda*, which orders the subgoals according to which will be pursued first, second, third, and so on.**

In adding subgoals to the agenda, there must be a set of priority rules. The priorities we found in the earlier work (Stevens & Collins, 1977) were:

1. Errors before omissions.
2. Prior steps before later steps.***
3. Shorter fixes before longer fixes.
4. More important factors before less important factors.

Errors take priority over omissions because they have more devastating consequences. Prior steps take priority because the teacher wants to take things up in a rational order, to the degree the order is not determined by the student's responses. Shorter fixes, like telling the student the right answer, take priority because they are easier to complete. More important factors take priority because of the order implied by the overall goals.

When more than one bug has been diagnosed, the teacher holds all but the one pursued on the agenda, in order of their priority. When the teacher has fixed one

---

*Editor's note: This serves the same function as Scandura's procedures for assessing individual knowledge (Chapter 7, p. 240). It has the same limitation of only being applicable in individualized instruction contexts.

**Editor's note: This is clearly a sequencing strategy.

***Editor's note: This is similar to Gropper's *forward chaining*. As Gropper argues, this may be the least important criterion.

bug, he or she takes up the next highest priority bug, and attempts to fix that. Sometimes when trying to fix one bug, the teacher diagnoses another bug. If the new bug is of a higher priority, the teacher sometimes *interrupts* the goal he or she is pursuing to fix the higher priority bug. Thus in the dialogues, there is a pattern of diagnosing bugs at different times and holding them there until there is time to correct them.

CONCLUSION

These techniques of inquiry teaching are designed to teach students to construct rules and theories by dealing with specific cases,* and to apply these rules and theories to new cases. In this process the student is learning two kinds of things: (1) specific theories about the knowledge domain; and (2) a variety of reasoning skills (see Table 8.3). In some sense the inquiry method models for the student the process of being a scientist.

The kinds of reasoning skills we think the student learns from this process are: forming hypotheses, testing hypotheses, making predictions, selecting optimal cases to test a theory, generating counterexamples and hypothetical cases, distinguishing between necessary and sufficient conditions, considering alternative hypotheses, knowing the forms that rules and theories can take, knowing what questions to ask, and so on (see Table 8.4). In short, all the reasoning skills that scientists need arise in this model of teaching.

Furthermore the technique is exceptionally motivating for students.** They become involved in the process of creating new theories or recreating theories that have been developed over centuries. It can be an exhilarating experience for the students.

In summary, by turning learning into problem solving, by carefully selecting cases that optimize the abilities the teacher is trying to teach, by making students grapple with counterexamples and entrapments, teachers challenge the students more than by any other teaching method. The students come out of the experience able to attack novel problems by applying these strategies themselves.

ACKNOWLEDGMENTS

This research was sponsored by the Personnel and Training Research Programs, Psychological Sciences Division. Office of Naval Research under Contract Number N00014-79-C-0338. Contract Authority Identification Number NR154-428.

---

*Editor's note: This is what Landa refers to as *discovery by examples* (see Chapter 6, p. 178).
**Editor's note: See Chapter 11 for a description of some of the reasons why.

We thank Dean Russell Zwoyer of the School of Education at the University of Illinois, Champaign–Urbana, for sending us transcripts of Professor Max Beberman, Dr. Irving Sigel of the Educational Testing Service for sending us a tape and transcript of Eloise Warman, Dr. Richard C. Anderson for sending us various tapes, transcripts, and other materials illustrating Socratic tutoring, and Natalie Dehn for recording Professor Roger Schank during one of his classes at Yale.

REFERENCES

Abelson, R. P. Differences between belief and knowledge systems. *Cognitive Science*, 1979, *3*, 370–385.

Anderson, R. C., & Faust, G. W. *Educational psychology: The science of instruction and learning.* New York: Dodd, Mead, 1974.

Brown, J. S., & Burton, R. R. Diagnostic models for procedural bugs in basic mathematical skills. *Cognitive Science*, 1978, *2*, 155–192.

Chase, W. G., & Simon, H. A. The mind's eye in chess. In W. G. Chase (Ed.), *Visual information processing*. New York: Academic Press, 1973.

Collins, A. Processes in acquiring knowledge. In R. C. Anderson, R. J. Spiro, & W. E. Montague (Eds.), *Schooling and the acquisition of knowledge*. Hillsdale, N.J.: Lawrence Erlbaum Associates, 1977.

Collins, A. *Explicating the tacit knowledge in teaching and learning.* Paper presented at American Educational Research Association, Toronto, 1978.

Collins, A., & Stevens, A. L. Goals and strategies of effective teachers. In R. Glaser (Ed.), *Advances in instructional psychology* (Vol. 2). Hillsdale, N.J.: Lawrence Erlbaum Associates, 1982.

Collins, A., Warnock, E. H., Aiello, N., & Miller, M. L. Reasoning from incomplete knowledge. In D. Bobrow & A. Collins (Eds.), *Representation and understanding: Studies in cognitive science*. New York: Academic Press, 1975.

Collins, A., Warnock, E. H., & Passafiume, J. J. Analysis and synthesis of tutorial dialogues. In G. H. Bower (Ed.), *The psychology of learning and motivation* (Vol. 9). New York: Academic Press, 1975.

Davis, R. B. Discovery in the teaching of mathematics. In L. S. Shulman & E. R. Keisler (Eds.), *Learning by discovery: A critical appraisal*. Chicago: Rand McNally, 1966.

Feurzeig, W., Munter, P., Swets, J., & Breen, M. Computer-aided teaching in medical diagnosis. *Journal of Medical Education*, 1964, *39*, 746–755.

Larkin, J. Information processing models and science instruction. In J. Lochhead & J. Clement (Eds.), *Cognitive process instruction*. Philadelphia: The Franklin Institute Press, 1979.

Miller, A. Sentencing. Shown on *Miller's Court, WCVB, Boston on October 12, 1979.*

Newell A., & Simon, H. A. *Human problem solving.* Englewood Cliffs, N.J.: Prentice-Hall, 1972.

Plato. *Laches, Protagoras, Meno, and Euthydemus.* (W. R. M. Lamb, trans.) Cambridge, Mass.: Harvard University Press, 1924.

Sigel, I. E., & Saunders, R. An inquiry into inquiry: Question-asking as an instructional model. In L. Katz (Ed.), *Current topics in early childhood education*. Norwood, N.J.: Ablex, 1979.

Simon, D. P., & Simon, H. A. A tale of two protocols. In J. Lochhead & J. Clement (Eds.), *Cognitive process instruction*. Philadelphia: The Franklin Institute Press, 1979.

Stevens, A. L., & Collins, A. The goal structure of a Socratic tutor. *Proceedings of Association for Computing Machinery National Conference*, Seattle, Washington, 1977.

Stevens, A. L., & Collins, A. Multiple conceptual models of a complex system. In R. Snow, P. Federico, & W. Montague (Eds.), *Aptitude, learning, and instruction: Cognitive process analysis*. Hillsdale, N.J.: Lawrence Erlbaum Associates, 1980.

Stevens, A. L., Collins, A., & Goldin, S. Misconceptions in students' understanding. *International Journal of Man-Machine Studies*, 1979, *11*, 145–156.

VanLehn, K., & Brown, J. S. Planning nets: A representation for formalizing analogies and semantic models of procedural skills. In R. Snow, P. Federico, & W. Montague (Eds.), *Aptitude, learning and instruction: Cognitive process analysis*. Hillsdale, N.J.: Lawrence Erlbaum Associates, 1980.

Winston, P. Learning to identify toy block structures. In R. L. Solso (Ed.), *Contemporary issues in cognitive psychology: The Loyola Symposium*. Washington, D.C.: Winston, 1973.

9

Component Display Theory

M. David Merrill
University of Southern California

M. David Merrill

M. David Merrill, Professor of Educational Psychology and Technology at the University of Southern California, is an internationally recognized instructional research scientist. His work includes major theoretical positions on instructional strategies (as represented by Component Display Theory described in the chapter) and Content Structure (as represented by Elaboration Theory as described in the chapter by Charles M. Reigeluth). He has authored or coauthored 9 books related to instructional design and has authored or coauthored 10 chapters in edited books. He and his associates have completed more than 100 research studies on instructional processes, many of which have appeared in educational research journals.

Dr. Merrill received the Ph.D. degree in 1964 from the University of Illinois. He has served on the faculty of George Peabody College for Teachers (1964–66), Brigham Young University (1966–67; 1968–79), Stanford University (1967–68) and the University of Southern California (1979–present). At BYU Dr. Merrill founded and directed the Division of Instructional Research,

Development and Evaluation (now called The David O. McKay Institute). He also founded and chaired the Department of Instructional Science.

Dr. Merrill is a popular lecturer who has delivered more than 40 presentations at professional meetings and has conducted or participated in more than 50 seminars and workshops throughout the United States, Europe, and Indonesia.

As a consultant, Dr. Merrill has contributed to many military and industrial development efforts. He was a founder and director of Courseware Inc., an instructional research and development company, and served as Vice President for Research from 1974 until 1979.

As a researcher Dr. Merrill has directed projects totalling over $.5 million. He was codirector of the TICCIT project (over $5 million of NSF money). He directed the team that prepared the courseware design for the TICCIT system. (TICCIT is a computer based instructional system currently being marketed by Hazeltine Corp. Its unique design includes built-in instructional strategies featuring learner control.)

CONTENTS

Introduction   283
   Context   283
   Background   284
The Performance–Content Matrix   285
   Performance Categories   287
   Content Categories   287
   Performance-Content Classification   288
   Specifying Objectives   289
   Specifying Test Items   291
   A Subject-Matter Taxonomy   296
   A Performance Taxonomy   300
Presentation Forms   305
   Primary Presentation Forms   305
   Secondary Presentation Forms   307
   Process Displays   310
   Procedure Displays   310
Performance-PPF Consistency   311
Content-PPF Consistency   313
   Generalities   313
   Instances   315
   Instance Practice   317
   Generality Practice   319
Adequacy Rules   320
   Secondary Presentation Forms   320
   Interdisplay Relationships   325
Learner Control   327
Student Conscious Cognitive Processing   328
Training Materials For Component Display Theory   330
Research Support For Component Display Theory   330
   The Primary Presentation Forms   331
   Sequence Of Primary Presentation Forms 331
   Secondary Presentation Forms   331
   Interdisplay Relationships   331
   Learner Control   332
   Process Displays   332

FOREWORD

Like the Gagné—Briggs instructional theory, Merrill's component display theory (CDT) integrates knowledge about learning and instruction from all three major theoretical perspectives: behavioral, cognitive, and humanistic. However, by comparison CDT is considerably *narrower*: It only deals with the cognitive domain (Bloom, 1956); and within the cognitive domain it only deals with the micro level (e.g., with aspects of instruction that relate to teaching a single idea, such as a single concept or principle). Also, it does not yet systematically integrate knowledge about the motivational design of instruction (see Chapter 11). In exchange for its present narrowness, CDT provides a level of *detail* that is sorely lacking in the Gagné—Briggs theory. Its greater detail makes it more useful—that is, more reliable in the production of effective instruction—within its limited domain; and attempts are currently under way to expand that domain (see Chapters 10 and 11).

Like the previous models and theories of instruction, CDT is a language on one level and a set of prescriptions on another level. As a *language*, it is a set of concepts that describe the conditions, methods, and outcomes of instruction. This language is perhaps more complete and comprehensive within its domain than that of other models and theories. Hence, it provides a useful medium for analyzing and understanding those aspects of other theories and models that deal with the same domain. As a set of *prescriptions*, CDT attempts to indicate what set of method components (i.e., what model) is most likely to optimize achievement of the desired outcomes under the specified conditions. Merrill has made no explicit attempt to integrate systematically the work of others in the field; rather his approach has been one of internalizing such work as it is reported, and (often unconsciously) modifying it and integrating it with his ever-evolving conception of CDT, by which time there is a tendency to lose sight of the intellectual antecedents of those ideas. Hence, much of the work that CDT builds on and integrates is not explicitly referenced, even though Merrill acknowledges that it should be. In point of fact, CDT has built its models from strategy components developed by such researchers and theorists as Bruner, Evans—Glaser—Homme, Rothkopf, Skinner, Kulhavy, Gropper, Markle, Klausmeier, Landa, and many more.

One of the outstanding features of CDT (aside from its highly integrative nature) is its basis for prescribing which model to use when. Like most of the previous theories, its models are prescribed on the basis of goals, or objectives. But unlike other theories, CDT classifies objectives on two dimensions: (1) type of *content* (facts, concepts, principles, and procedures); and (2) desired level of *performance* with that content (remember, use, and find). Hence, an objective can call for remembering a concept (e.g., memorizing the definition), using a concept (e.g., classifying new examples of it), or finding a concept (e.g., discovering a way of categorizing phenomena). Merrill's system is, in fact, quite compatible with Gagné's. Merrill's three levels of performance correspond to Gagné's three cognitive domains: verbal information, intellectual skills, and cognitive strategies; and within the intellectual-skills domain, Gagné distinguishes between what are in effect content types, including concepts and rules. However, Gagné did not explicitly extend the content distinctions to either the verbal-information domain (which I find very useful), or the cognitive-strategies domain (which may not be the most useful kind of distinction to make here). It should be noted that Merrill has not yet explicitly developed a model or models for the "find" level (i.e., the cognitive-strategies domain).

Another important feature of CDT's basis for prescription is the notion of *level of richness*. Each of the models (that are prescribed on the basis of content/performance classification) can exist at a variety of levels of richness (i.e., levels of support provided by the instruction). For a relatively difficult objective in relation to student ability and experience, a relatively rich version of the appropriate model would be used, whereas for an easy objective a lean version would be prescribed.

Finally, a very significant feature of CDT is what Merrill refers to as *learner control*. CDT prescribes formating instruction in such a way as to make it easy for learners to pick and choose the strategy components that best fit their momentary state aptitudes and their more permanent trait aptitudes. In this way, the instruction not only makes learning as easy as possible by making it completely "individualized" to each student's needs, but it also teaches the student *learning strategies* that will be of great value in less structured learning environments.

Although much work remains to be done to develop CDT to its full potential (especially in the areas of motivational-strategy components and cognitive strategies), it is indicative of the highly integrative, multiperspectived approach to model building and theory construction that is sorely needed at this point in the evolution of instructional design. In addition, its extensive base of empirical support—both formal research and real-world field testing—assure that the practicing designer can already benefit greatly from its prescriptions.

C. M. R.

Component Display Theory

INTRODUCTION

How do you know that a given presentation will enable a student to acquire a particular knowledge or skill? Most descriptions of instruction identify three primary components: objectives, learning activities, and tests. Objectives state what is to be learned; learning activities are events in which the student must participate in order to acquire the objectives; and tests are events that assess the degree to which the student acquired the objectives. Component Display Theory (CDT) is a set of prescriptive relationships that can be used to guide the design and development of learning activities. The degree to which these relationships are incorporated into the learning activities has been found to correlate with the degree to which the learning activities promote acquisition of the objectives.

CDT defines several categories of objectives using a two-dimensional classification system with performance level as one dimension and content type as the other dimension. CDT also defines a set of primary and secondary presentation forms. The theory postulates that for each type of objective there is a unique combination of primary and secondary presentation forms that will most effectively promote acquisition of that type of objective. The relationships specified by the theory state that performance on a particular type of objective will be a function of the degree to which: the presentation forms used in the learning activities correspond to the prescribed combination; the presentation forms include certain enhancing characteristics; and the presentation forms are sequenced and interrelated in specified ways.

This chapter presents CDT in a way that we hope will be useful to teachers, instructional designers, and others interested in improving the instructional process. We also attempt to present a little of the underlying rationale and a summary of some of the empirical support for the theory.

Context

Reigeluth and Merrill (1978) identified three major categories of instructional variables: organizational strategies, delivery strategies, and management strategies.* Organizational strategies are those decisions involved in the design of learning activities, including the types of displays to be presented to the student, the sequence of these displays, the topics to be included, the sequence and structure of these topics, the type of practice, the nature of feedback, and other decisions regarding the nature of the presentation. *Organizational strategies* can be subdivided into two subcategories: *micro* strategies and *macro* strategies. Micro strategies are concerned with the individual displays—including their characteristics, interrelationships, and sequence—that are to be presented to the student.

---

*Editor's note: See also Chapter 1.

Micro strategies might also be characterized as presentation strategies because they are concerned with the details of each individual presentation to the student. Macro strategies are concerned with the selection, sequence, and organization (structure) of the subject-matter topics that are to be presented.

Delivery strategies are those decisions affecting the way the information will be carried to the student. Delivery strategies affect the selection of the instructional media that will be used to present the learning activities.

Management strategies are those decisions affecting the way the individual student will be helped to interact with the learning activities. Management strategies involve motivational techniques, individualization schemes, scheduling, resource allocation, and other implementation activities.

In its present form Component Display Theory is concerned almost exclusively with micro strategies. CDT is independent of the macro strategy, the delivery system, or the management system used to implement the instruction. In other words, a given micro strategy, as specified by CDT, can be used with a wide variety of subject matters and content organizational schemes, with virtually any delivery system, and with a wide variety of different techniques for managing the instruction.

This theory's being limited to micro strategies does not detract from its importance as an instructional-design tool. It has been found that all else being equal, a given subject matter can be carried by a wide variety of media-delivery systems. It has been found that student can learn in a considerable range of different management structures. However, it has also been shown that changes in micro strategies result in considerable differences in student achievment regardless of the delivery-system or management-system context in which these changes occur. When attempts are made to improve a particular instructional system, the greatest gains in performance occur when changes are made in the macro strategies used, and the second greatest gains result from changes in the micro strategies (this is the area in which CDT is applicable). Changes in delivery or management system often result in significant differences in cost, efficiency, and administrative convenience, even though there are not parallel changes in effectiveness.

Background

Robert Gagné (1965, 1970, 1977) postulated that different types of learner outcomes required different conditions of learning.* CDT evolved from attempts on the part of the author to clarify the Gagné theory for his students. Early publications on the ideas, which have led to CDT, reflect this orientation (See Merrill, 1971; Merrill & Boutwell, 1973). CDT is founded on the same assumption as Gagné's work—namely that there are different categories of outcomes and that each of these categories requires a different procedure for assessing achievement

---

*Editor's note: See also Chapter 4.

and a different procedure for promoting the capability represented by the category. However, a one-dimensional classification system such as that originally proposed by Gagné's (1965) seemed too limiting; hence a two-dimensional classification system was proposed (Merrill & Boutwell, 1973; Merrill & Wood, 1974) with *performance* (Gagné's only dimension) forming one dimenion and type of *content* forming the other.

Gagné attempted to describe the conditions necessary for the acquisition of each outcome category in terms of traditional learning-psychology variables. It seemed desirable to cast these conditions in terms more readily understood by teachers, authors, and instructional designers. In an attempt to formulate a more presentation-oriented prescription, it was postulated that instructional materials could be characterized in terms of discrete displays and that very few different types of displays could account for a wide variety of different presentations. Thus four primary presentation forms were described together with secondary presentations that are elaborations of these primary presentations. The resulting formulation (Merrill & Boutwell, 1973; Merrill, Reigeluth, & Faust, 1979; Merrill, Richards, Schmidt, & Wood, 1977; Merrill & Wood, 1974) resembles the RULEG language suggested by Evans, Homme, and Glaser (1962). Whereas Evans, Homme, and Glaser limited their formulation to programmed instruction, CDT postulated that these primary presentations characterized all cognitive instruction.

CDT, like Gagné's work, assumes that learned capabilities can be categorized into a limited number of categories; it assumes that the most useful classification system has two dimensions: performance and content type; it assumes that for each performance–content category there is a combination of primary and secondary presentation forms that will result in more effective, efficient, and appealing acquisition than will any other combination of displays. This chapter describes the performance–content classification scheme, the different types of primary and secondary presentation forms, and the prescriptive relationships between outcome capability and presentation displays that have been found to most adequately promote each type of outcome.

CDT draws on the work of many other investigators, especially those involved in programmed instruction, instructional-systems design, and task analysis. Merrill, Kowallis, and Wilson (1981) attempted to describe the interrelationships between this theory and other significant theoretical developments in educational psychology during the past two decades.

THE PERFORMANCE-CONTENT MATRIX

The Gagné assumption that different outcomes require different conditions of acquisition further assumes that appropriate outcome categories can be identified, specified, and measured reliably and validly. The outcome categories for CDT are specified by the two-dimensional performance–content matrix illustrated in Fig. 9.1. This classification scheme is an extension of the categories originally pro-

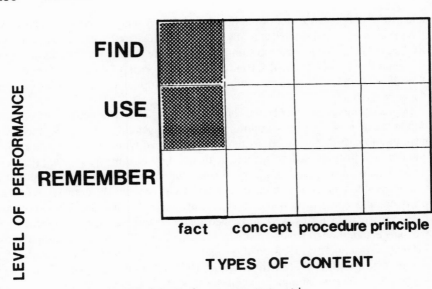

FIG. 9.1   Performance-content matrix.

posed by Gagné (1965; see also Merrill, 1971). The modifications in Gagné's scheme were made to facilitate outcome classification by designers, teachers, and others interested in applied instructional design. It was also found that the content distinctions made by the performance–content matrix resulted in important differences in conditions for promoting acquisition, which were often overlooked by previous classification schemes.

In this section on the performance–content matrix we first define and illustrate each major cell of the classification matrix. The next two parts of this section describe considerations that are necessary for adequately specifying and classifying objectives and text items using the performance–content matrix. Finally, in the last two parts of this section we briefly describe a subject-matter taxonomy that, in part, explains the choice of content categories. We also briefly describe a performance taxonomy that, in part, explains the choice of performance categories. These presentations are necessarily brief and therefore oversimplified and incomplete. These sections can be skipped by the reader interested primarily in the empirically based propositions of the theory rather than in the possible justifications for the category system used.

The heart of CDT is the performance–content classification system illustrated in Fig. 9.1. Three performance levels are indicated: remember, use, and find. Four content dimensions are indicated: fact, concept, procedure, and principle. These categories are defined and illustrated in the following paragraphs.

Performance Categories

Remember is that performance that requires the student to search memory in order to reproduce or recognize some item of information that was previously stored. *Use* is that performance that requires the student to apply some abstraction to a specific case. *Find* is that performance that requires the student to derive or invent a new abstraction.*

For example, consider the following test items:

1. The symbol for a resistor is _____?
2. What would happen in the circuit shown below if the load resistance were shorted? (circuit diagram shown)
3. Invent a simple circuit that will gradually slow a direct current motor until it stops.

The first item is at the remember level, the second is at the use level, and the third is at the find level.

Content Categories

Facts are arbitrarily associated pieces of information such as a proper name, a date or an event, the name of a place or the symbols used to name particular objects or events. The following test items involve facts:

1. The symbol for a resistor is _____.
2. Name the principal part of the eye.
3. Who is the president of the United States?
4. What is the value of *G*, the gravity constant?

Concepts are groups of objects, events, or symbols that all share some common characteristics and that are identified by the same name. Most of the words in any language identify concepts. The following test items involve concepts:

1. What characteristics distinguish Impressionist paintings from Renaissance paintings?
2. Which of the following photographs show cumulus clouds?
3. Does the analysis of the data given below require the use of a one- or two-tail statistical test?

Procedures are an ordered sequence of steps necessary to accomplish some goal, solve a particular class of problem, or produce some product. The following test items involve procedures:

---

*Editor's note: These categories correspond to Gagné's *verbal information, intellectual skill,* and *cognitive strategy,* respectively (see chapter 4).

1. What are the steps required to find the current in a DC circuit?
2. Use a hand-held calculator to find the mean and standard deviation of the following set of numbers.
3. Solve the following linear equations.

Principles are explanations or predictions of why things happen in the world. Principles are those cause-and-effect or correlational relationships that are used to interpret events or circumstances. The following test items involve principles:

1. In the following circuit explain what will happen to the intensity of the light by explaining the electron flow in the circuit.
2. Given the following case study, explain the subject's antisocial behavior in terms of reinforcement theory.
3. As concisely as possible explain the first law of motion.*

Performance-Content Classification

According to CDT, all objectives or test items can be classified into one or more cells of the performance–content matrix. The following examples illustrate this two-dimensional classification:
Remember–fact:

1. On a topographic map what is the symbol for a church?
2. What is the value of pi?

Facts have no general or abstract representation, so there is no Use–fact or Find–fact level in the matrix.
Remember–concept:

1. What are the characteristics of a conifer?
2. Define positive reinforcement.

Use–concept:

1. Is the mountain pictured in this photograph an example of a folded mountain?
2. Read the following short story. Identify that paragraph that best represents the climax of the story.

Find–concept:

1. Sort the rocks on this table into several different piles. Indicate the characteristics by which one of your classmates could sort them into the same piles.
2. Figure out a way to group students in a classroom that assures a range of ability, a range of sex, and a mix of ethnic background in each group.

*Editor's note: These last three categories are somewhat similar to Gagné's *concept* (defined and concrete), *rule*, and *higher-order rule*, respectively.

Remember—procedure:

1. What are the steps in balancing a checkbook?
2. Describe the steps in making a black-and-white print in the darkroom.

Use—procedure:

1. Demonstrate how to clean a clarinet.
2. Make a whip or tongue graft in a fruit tree.

Find—procedure:

1. Write a computer program that will index and retrieve recipes.
2. Devise a technique for randomly assigning students to experimental treatments as they enter the laboratory.

Remember—principle:

1. Explain each of the three projection techniques for making maps of the earth's surface.
2. What happens when water evaporates? Explain in terms of molecule movement and heat.

Use—principle:

1. Read the following case study of an ecological system. In this system the rodents are increasing in number. Predict some possible hypotheses based on your knowledge of life cycles and the interdependence of species in this ecological system.
2. Below are pictures of two ocean vessels. One is floating very high in the water and the other is floating very low. Explain at least three different reasons that could account for this difference.

Find—principle:

1. Set up an experiment to assess the effect of tabacco smoke on plant growth. Report your findings.
2. Set up a demonstration that will allow you to illustrate how water gets into a well.

Specifying Objectives*

There have been many prescriptions for writing objectives for instruction. Most have been modeled on Mager's (1962) classic work and have included at least

---

*Editor's note: Unless objectives are to be included in the instruction, this section is not a part of an instructional model or theory. In most cases, this will be a step in an instructional-development procedure. I am allowing it to be included in this chapter primarily for the benefit of those who believe in including objectives in the instruction.

three components for an adequately stated objective: conditions, behavior, and criterion. The IDI (Instructional Development Institute) version added a specification of audience and the mnemonic specification of *A B C D* for the components: audience, behavior, conditions, and degree (criterion). Gagné and Briggs (1979) made another modification by suggesting that the statement should include a classification of the type of learning involved: affective, psychomotor, intellectual skills, verbal information, or cognitive strategies. The purpose of this classification was to facilitate the specification of the necessary conditions for learning.

As already indicated in a previous section of this chapter, CDT is founded on the same assumption that underlies the Gagné and Briggs prescriptions (i.e., that there are different kinds of objectives and that each type of objective requires a unique set of conditions to promote optimal acquisition of the capabilities specified by the objective). In our view, the identification of categories as part of the specification of an objective is not merely another component of form but adds the dimension of *substance* to the specification. In other words, specifying the category makes it possible to indicate particular conditions, particular behavior, and particular criteria that are acceptable for a given outcome category. The addition of this dimension also changes the nature of the task of specifying objectives from one of invention to one of selection. If the taxonomy (category system) for outcomes is complete, then it can be claimed that there is only a limited set of possible objectives, and that objectives of a single type differ only in the topics that are included but do not differ significantly in either form or substance. Hence, the task for the designer is not to invent an objective but rather to select that objective that corresponds to the intended performance–content level. This addition greatly simplifies the process of specifying objectives.

Fig. 9.2 summarizes the substantive conditions, behavior, and criteria that characterize each of the categories of the performance–content matrix. The categories are listed along the left-hand column. Reading across a given row, the entries in each column indicate the conditions, behavior, and criteria that are necessary to specify an objective for that performance–content category. Each component is divided into two columns, one indicating that part of the compoent that is fixed or necessary for the objective to characterize the specified category and the other indicating those aspects of the component that can vary and still not affect the classification of the objective. For example, for the remember–fact category, the fixed condition (column 3) is to present the symbol, object, or event that is to be named (*A*) and, if a set of such facts has been learned, to present the elements in random order. These two conditions are necessary for an objective to be included in the remember–fact category. However, the way that the object, event, or symbol is represented to the student can vary considerably—for example, it could be a drawing, a picture, a diagram, a model, or the actual object. The form of representation does not change the classification of the objective.

Fig. 9.2 is formated so that reading across provides a rather complete statement of a given objective. Thus, reading across the remember–fact row, an objective would be stated as follows:

Given a drawing (column 1) of an eye (*A*) with the parts numbered in random order (column 2) the student will be able to recall the name of each part (B) (column 3), by writing the name opposite the number corresponding to that part (column 4) with no errors and no delay (column 5) as shown by one point for each part named correctly and one point subtracted from the score for each 10 seconds over 1 minute required to complete the exercise (column 6).

Note that the author of this objective was required to fill in the topic *A* and to select the specific mechanisms for presenting the item and for scoring the item but that the rest of the objective was specified by the table.

Specifying Test Items

Like objectives, there have been many prescriptions provided for writing correctly formated test items. Also like the prescriptions that have been provided for objectives, most of these prescriptions concentrate on the correct format for these test items rather than on the *substance* of the test items. It is not expedient for us to repeat these prescriptions in this chapter; rather we concentrate our discussion on those aspects of test items that affect the degree to which they measure the specified objectives.

An objective, when adequately specified, defines a class of acceptable test items, each of which should provide some degree of measurement for the performance–content combination represented by the objective. Hence, not only does Fig. 9.2 provide guide for specifying objectives, but it also provides a guide for the formulation of test items designed to measure those objectives. Many of the prescriptions for test items divide test items into various forms of tests, including true-false, multiple-choice, matching, short answer, essay, and other types of items. These item formats are independent of the performance–content levels specified by CDT. A particular category of the performance–content matrix can be assessed to some extent by any form of test item. Conversely, a given form of test item can be used to assess almost any performance level.

Input–Output Conditions. In order to test, it is necessary to provide information and material that will be used by the student to demonstrate competence. We refer to this information and material as *input* for the item. The response of the student or the product resulting from this response is the second part, or *output*, of a test item. It is this information that will be evaluated to assess the student's capability. The condition column of Fig. 9.2 specifies the type of input required for each type of test item and the behavior columns specify the type of output required. Other input–output formats may occur to the reader, and some of these are acceptable for assessing a given performance–content combination. However, formats recommended by Fig. 9.2 are those most appropriate for each category.

Timing Conditions. On every test students are allowed a certain amount of time to respond to the items. The fixed criterion column on Fig. 9.2 specifies these

	Given: of/for: CONDITIONS		the student will be able to: by: BEHAVIOR		with: as shown by: CRITERION	
	VARIABLE	FIXED	FIXED	VARIABLE	FIXED	VARIABLE
USE CONCEPT	DRAWINGS PICTURES DESCRIPTIONS DIAGRAMS	NEW EXAMPLES	CLASSIFY	WRITING SELECTING POINTING SORTING ETC.	SOME ERRORS SHORT DELAY	
USE PROCEDURE	WORD MATERIALS EQUIPMENT DEVICE	NAME NEW TASK	DEMONSTRATE	MANIPULATING CALCULATING MEASURING REMOVING	SOME ERRORS TIMED or UNTIMED	CHECK LIST
USE PRINCIPLE	WORD DESCRIPTIONS DRAWINGS FIGURES	NAME NEW PROBLEM	EXPLAIN or PREDICT	PREDICTING CALCULATING DRAWING GRAPHING ETC.	SOME ERRORS UNTIMED	
FIND CONCEPT	DRAWINGS PICTURES DESCRIPTIONS DIAGRAMS OBJECTS	REFERENTS From unspecified categories	INVENT CATEGORIES	.SORTING AND OBSERVING ATTRIBUTES .SPECIFYING ATTRIBUTES	UNTIMED .HIGH CORRELATION when others use concept	
FIND PROCEDURE	DESCRIPTION DEMONSTRATION ILLUSTRATION SPECIFICATION	DESIRED PRODUCT or EVENT	DERIVE STEPS	EXPERIMENT ANALYSIS TRIAL + ERROR	UNTIMED Demonstration of utility	
FIND PRINCIPLE	DESCRIPTION ILLUSTRATION OBSERVATION	EVENT	DISCOVER RELATIONSHIP	EXPERIMENT ANALYSIS OBSERVATION DEMONSTRATION	UNTIMED .Appropriate Research Design or Scholarship	

Given: of/for: the student will be able to: by: with: as shown by:

	CONDITIONS		BEHAVIOR		CRITERION	
	VARIABLE	FIXED	FIXED	VARIABLE	FIXED	VARIABLE
REMEMBER FACT	DRAWINGS PICTURES DIAGRAMS OBJECTS	<u>A</u> in any order	RECALL <u>B</u>	WRITING DRAWING POINTING CIRCLING ETC.	NO ERRORS NO DELAY	1 point for each correct symbol within 10 sec.
REMEMBER CONCEPT	WORD SYMBOL	<u>NAME</u>	STATE DEFINITION	WRITING SELECTING CIRCLING CHECKING ETC.	FEW ERRORS SHORT DELAY	1 error for each characteristic
REMEMBER PROCEDURE	WORD SYMBOL DIRECTIONS	<u>NAME</u>	STATE STEPS	DRAWING FLOW CHARTING LISTING ORDERING ETC.	FEW ERRORS SHORT DELAY	1 error each step
REMEMBER PRINCIPLE	WORD SYMBOL	<u>NAME</u>	STATE RELATIONSHIP	WRITING DRAWING FORMULA GRAPH ETC.	FEW ERRORS SHORT DELAY	1 error each relationship

NOTES:
1. Variable condition refers to representation of stimulus materials given to the student.
2. Variable behavior refers to type of performance used by the student to show capability.
3. Variable criterion refers to how a particular type of item will be scored.

FIG. 9.2 Specification of objectives.

293

timing conditions for each performance–content category. For the remember–fact or the recall of specific instances of a concept or the recall of a fixed procedure, there should be *no delay* in response. For the remember–definition, procedure, or principle level where the student is required to paraphrase or to recognize a paraphrased statement, it is necessary to allow a *short delay,* because searching memory for a paraphrased response does require some processing time. For the use–concept level, the student should also be allowed a *short delay* to allow time to study the instance and classify it. For the use–procedure and use–principle level, the performance should be *untimed* unless a timed response is required by the specific nature of the procedure. The find level requires considerable thinking and study and therefore should be tested by power (*untimed*) tests.

Prescoring Feedback.   It is valuable for feedback (knowledge of correct responses) to be provided after the test is complete (meaning after the student's performance has been scored), but any feedback that appears before the student has finished the test could have either a positive or negative influence on the student's performance. It is desirable, therefore, to delay all feedback on the testing situation until after the test has been scored.

Prompts.   Prompts consist of any information that enables the student to determine the correct response by other than the desired level of performance. There are several kinds of potential prompts in the testing situation. *Deliberate* hints, attention focusing, or other information is sometimes added to the content to facilitate acquisition of the information. All such prompting should be eliminated during the testing phase of the instruction. There are *inadvertent* prompts that sometimes are included through inappropriate format, information provided by other items on the test, and other sources of help not intended by the instructor. These sources of extraneous information should also be avoided. Finally, *feedback* provides a source of prompting for subsequent items. As already indicated, feedback should be delayed until after the test has been scored.

Most tests do not consist of isolated test items, but are arranged to include a set of test items often measuring the acquisition of a number of different instructional components. There are certain characteristics related to the *interrelationships* between these several test items that should also be considered in order to assure adequate tests.

Number of Items.   Criterion-referenced tests, those intended to measure specific objectives, should be considered as a series of subtests in which the items pertaining to a single objective are considered together and separate from those items pertaining to a second objective (see Popham, 1975). Therefore, the question "How many items?" is a question about the number of items required to adequately test a *single* objective rather than a question about how many items should be included in the entire test designed to measure a number of different objectives.

Most achievement tests err in having too few items for a single objective, therefore making measurement of the objective somewhat unreliable.

Test items for remember–facts should have one item for each fact to be learned. Test items for remember–definitions, statements of procedures, and statements of principles should require one item if the statement is to be remembered verbatim but may require two or more items if a paraphrased statement is to be recognized or recalled. Use–level items require a sample of new examples, tasks, or problems. The number of instances in this sample depends on the complexity of the phenomenon, the variance that occurs within the class of events included, and the difficulty of the classification demonstration, or explanation. It is not possible to make adequate inference about yet-to-be-encountered situations from a single test item; reliable assessment requires demonstration of competence in a variety of specific situations. Often, one of the greatest mistakes in testing is that, because of time constraints, the more complex the situation, the fewer the items that are included for assessment. However, for reliable measurement the reverse should be the case. At the find level, the question of how many items is not as meaningful because the situation usually dictates that the students need as much information as may be required to find the solution.

Divergence and Difficulty.   Whenever a test requires more than one item having the same input–output form and assessing the same objective, these items should vary from each other in such a way as to represent the variation present in the population of possible items related to this objective. If all of the items are very similar, then the increased reliability that would otherwise result from multiple item testing of the same objective will not be gained from the repeated measurement. A similar argument can be made for item difficulty. Whenever a test requires more than one item for the same objective, these items should represent a range of difficulty from easy to hard. Presenting all easy or all hard items results in a potential distortion of the student's performance capability.

Criterion.   A fixed standard criterion such as 80% or 90% does not apply to all performance–content levels. The criterion should vary according to the category. The fixed criterion column in Fig. 9.2 indicates some general criterion guidlelines for each level. The figure indicates that for remember–fact there should be no errors. Either a student knows a fact or he or she does not. It makes little sense to know four of the five notes represented by the lines on the treble cleff, for example. Hence facts should be all or none, 100% correct. A similar argument holds for verbatim recall. Whenever the objective is to remember something verbatim, the criterion should be 100% correct. However, when a student is asked to paraphrase, we introduce a chance for misinterpretation even when the student remembers the definition, procedure, or principle being assessed. It may be that what is unknown is one of the words used in the paraphrase rather than the desired information itself.

Because of this possibility, we should allow for some margin of error. The figure specifies this as "few errors" and would be implemented by a criterion of something like 90%. At the use level, the margin for ambiguity increases considerably. Even experts may make mistakes in some situations. The criterion should allow for this margin of error. Perhaps an 80% criterion is more appropriate. It is sometimes desirable to have a *split criterion* at the use level, at which the student is expected to get 95% or 100% of the easy items correct but is given considerably more room for error on the more difficult items—for example, 60% or 75%. At the find level, the number of errors seems like an inappropriate criterion because the student is discovering or inventing new information. Fig. 9.2 suggests that a better criterion is some demonstrating that the new knowledge works. For concepts, the definition is adequate if associates can use the new category to classify yet new instances. The procedure works if it produces the desired product or outcome. The principle is appropriate if it explains the phenomenon or allows one to make predictions about similar situations.

A Subject-Matter Taxonomy*

The categories of fact, concept, procedure, and principle were not arbitrarily chosen, but are based on some assumptions about the nature of subject matter (see Reigeluth, Merrill, & Bunderson, 1978). It is assumed that subject matter is organization that is imposed upon the world by humans. The world, it is proposed, consists of numerous objects and events that are without organization until humans group them together into classes that share common characteristics. These groupings are called *concepts*. Hence, the first step in the development of subject matter is the invention or definition of a concept class. Objects or events can be grouped in innumerable ways; thus the mere definition of concepts still does not comprise subject matter. It is only when a relationship between two or more concepts is discovered that a subject matter begins to emerge.

Fig. 9.3 illustrates this creation of subject matter. In Fig. 9.3 the language of set-function theory (see, for example, Scandura, 1968) has been adopted to describe the components of subject matter. The objects and events that exist in the world are called referents. They are referents in the sense that they are potential instances of concepts. A circle has been used to indicate that a group of such referents are grouped together because they share common characteristics or attributes. The relationship between concepts is depicted as involving a set of domain concepts— that is, those classes of events or objects that will be acted upon; operational concepts—that is, the operation or change that will be imposed upon the instances of

---

*Editor's note: This section and the next provide rationales for the performance–content matrix. Many readers may view these two sections as advanced topics because they are not necessary for an understanding of the instructional theory itself, in which case it would be appropriate to skip to the section *Presentation Forms*.

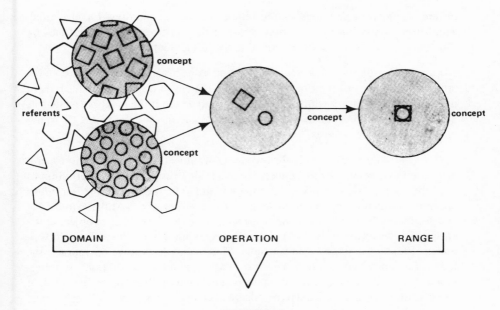

DOMAIN   OPERATION   RANGE

CONSTRUCT

REFERENT (INSTANCE). A referent (or Instance) is an object, event, or symbol which exists, or could exist, in our real or imagined environment.

CONCEPT. A concept is a set of common characteristics (attributes) referenced by a particular name or label, that can be applied to a set of referents (instances of that concept).

OPERATION. An operation is a function set or a set of operators which specifies a particular mapping between a domain and a range.

DOMAIN. A domain is a set of referents upon which the operation acts or to which it is applied.

RANGE. A range is a set of referents which results from the application of an operation to a domain.

CONSTRUCT. A construct is a structure consisting of a domain, an operation, and a range.

FIG. 9.3   The composition of a content construct.

the domain concept; and range concepts—that is, the result of the operation or action. This domain–operation–range relationship is called a *subject-matter construct*. By analogy, if concepts are the atoms, subject-matter constructs are the molecules of subject matter.

One of the ways to characterize subject matter is as an attempt to identify those types of operations that relate one set of concepts to another set of concepts. As indicated in Gagné and Merrill (1976) and Merrill (1973), a number of possible relationships between domain and range concepts have been explored. The criterion for selecting a classification system was suggested by Gagné (1965)—that is, different kinds of operations should require different conditions for promoting acquisition. Based on this criterion, some of the most pervasive operations are illustrated in Fig. 9.4 and are described in the following paragraphs.

Identity Operations. For an identity operation the instances of the range concept are set in a one-to-one relationship with the instances of the range. In this type of operation, it is arbitrary which is the domain and which is the range, inasmuch as the operation is bidirectional. The operation is represented by the words "is equivalent to," or "is the same as."

Descriptive Operations. In the formation of subject matter, descriptive operations are those relationships between concepts that result from the definition of concept classes. Two operations have been found to be useful; the first is a *subset operation,* which is equivalent to saying "*x* is a subset of *y*." At the extreme, of course, this is the same as saying "*x* is an instance of *y*," or "*x* is an object in the class *y*." However, subsets also include classes within classes, thus creating taxonomies of relationships between concepts. The second descriptive operation is the logical function of *intersection*. This is the basic operation of definitions. A definition is an identification of attribute concepts such that an object that shares each of those attributes is thus defined as a concept class by itself. Hence, the range labels the concept class, and the domain indicates the attributes or characteristics of that class. The use of descriptive operations enables us to have concepts that are used to define other concepts. Eventually this leads to tautological statements. At the same time, however, this use of descriptive operations makes concepts a very pervasive and powerful element with which to build subject matter.

Productive Operations. A productive operation is distinguished from a descriptive operation in that a descriptive operation is an invention, is arbitrary, is imposed upon the world. A productive operation, on the other hand, results in some change that can be empirically observed, or has the potential of being observed. Thus, descriptive operations can never be described as true or false, whereas productive operations can be assigned a truth value depending on their correspondence with experience. Two productive operations have been identified. The first is an *ordering operation,* which is represented by "do this first and then do this," or "place this here, and then place this here." Order in this context also suggests spatial ordering as well as temporal ordering. For ordering operations, the instances of the domain concepts are the things to be ordered. The product or event that results from the ordering is the range concept. A *causal relationship* is the second productive operation. The word causal is used in the broadest sense to include correlational relationships. In this case, the instances of the domain concepts are combined or separated to produce some new concept or new event.

The choice of content dimensions for the performance–content matrix was derived from this analysis of subject matter. In the early versions of the performance–content matrix (see Merrill & Boutwell, 1973; Merrill & Wood, 1974,

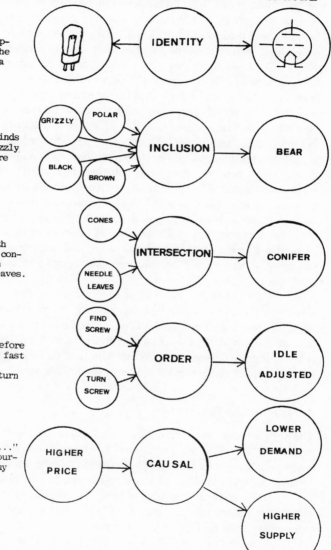

CONSTRUCT

FACT
Operation = "is represented by..." The symbol represents a vacuum tube.

SUBSET
Operation = "are kinds of..." Polar, grizzly black, and brown are kinds of bear.

CONCEPT
Operation = "if both are present..." A conifer is a tree with cones and needle leaves.

STEP
Operation = "do 1 before 2 ..." To adjust a fast idle 1) locate the idle screw, and 2) turn clockwise.

PRINCIPLE
Operation = "causes..." A rise in price encourages consumers to buy less and producers to make more.

FIG. 9.4   Examples of five types of constructs.

1975), these operations—identity, descriptive, and productive—were used for the content side of the matrix. However, CDT is designed to facilitate instructional design, and not just to be an academic theory to promote research. Instructional designers, teachers, and others who were using the theory found these terms cumbersome and difficult to use. Thus, everyday terms were substituted for these dimensions, and subsequently we had facts, concepts, and rules (Merrill & Wood, 1974). The word *rule*, however, takes on many meanings. At one point in the development of CDI *rule* meant a subject-matter construct, while at the same time it meant a causal relationship. In actual practice, designers began to use the word *rule*, for ordering relationships, and for procedural types of tasks. To avoid this confusion, the word *rule* was abandoned, and the productive category was divided into procedures and principles corresponding to the ordering relationship and the causal relationship. We did not separate the subset and intersection descriptive relationships, however, but merely substituted the word *concept*. One of the arguments for this is that in the definition of a concept it is usually necessary to define the superordinate class as well as the intersecting classes in order to adequately state a definition. It would be possible, of course, and perhaps desirable, to include subset and intersection as dimensions on the content matrix. The reader should recognize that the technical terms *identity, subset, intersection, ordering,* and *causal* are more accurate than the vernacular terms *fact, concept, procedure,* and *principle*.

Finally, it should be observed that any subject-matter taxonomy is somewhat arbitrary. The excuse for any given category system is its usefulness in relationships of a procedural or causal nature. As explained later in this chapter, the CDT also attempts to identify those prescriptive relationships. The categories thus identified do require unique strategies for testing and for acquisition. Thus, there seems to be useful verification of the subject-matter taxonomy.

A Performance Taxonomy*

The categories on the performance dimension of the performance–content matrix previously described are not arbitrarily chosen but are derived on the basis of assumptions about the nature of human memory and learning processes. The following explanation, although based on current ideas related to cognitive processing, is not a complete learning theory. Its purpose is to identify some of the assumptions about learning that seem to be valid and that underlie the choice of categories for the performance dimension.

A basic assumption of CDT is that there is more than one kind of learning and perhaps more than one kind of memory structure. These are hypothetical con-

---

*Editor's note: This section, like the previous one, provides a rationale for a part of the performance–content matrix. Because it is not necessary for an understanding of CDT, you may wish to view it as an advanced topic and skip to the section *Presentation Forms*.

structs, and do not necessarily imply any anatomical separation. At least functionally there are differences in the way memory seems to occur.

Gagné and White (1978) cite four kinds of memory structures. These are propositions, images, episodes, and intellectual skills. The authors indicate that the performance outcome for propositions is knowledge stating, whereas the performance outcome for intellectual skills is rule application. Two of these memory structures, propositions and intellectual skills, seem to have particular relevance for the performance dimension of the performance–content matrix. We would prefer to call the propositional memory structure *associative memory,* and the intellectual-skills memory structure *algorithmic memory.*

Figure 9.5 is an outline of some of the functions of these two types of memories. Episodic and image memory are also shown. Although these types of memories play an important role in learning and instruction, they have not been considered in this discussion of performance levels. The various characteristics of each of these

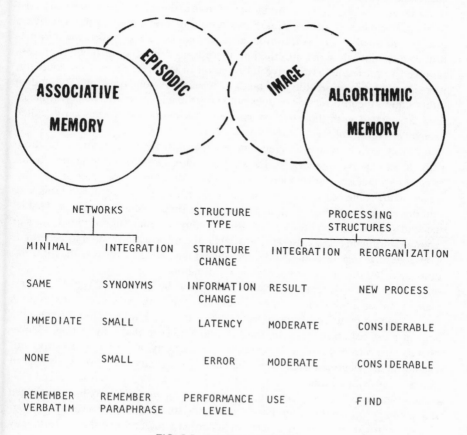

	NETWORKS		STRUCTURE TYPE	PROCESSING STRUCTURES	
MINIMAL	INTEGRATION	STRUCTURE CHANGE	INTEGRATION	REORGANIZATION
SAME	SYNONYMS	INFORMATION CHANGE	RESULT	NEW PROCESS
IMMEDIATE	SMALL	LATENCY	MODERATE	CONSIDERABLE
NONE	SMALL	ERROR	MODERATE	CONSIDERABLE
REMEMBER VERBATIM	REMEMBER PARAPHRASE	PERFORMANCE LEVEL	USE	FIND

FIG. 9.5   Memory structures.

memory systems are indicated in the center of the figure. The first characteristic is structural type; the second is structural change; the third is information change; the fourth is the latency associated with retrieval; the fifth is the error level associated with retrieval; and the sixth is the performance level related to that particular kind of memory. These performance levels correspond to the categories on the performance–content matrix.

Associative Memory. In our view, associative memory is composed of a hierarchical network structure. Students can assess this associative memory in two ways: first, by a literal storage and retrieval. Used as literal storage, items are retrieved from memory in almost the identical form in which they are stored. When a student puts an item of information into associative memory, and then retrieves it in the same form in which it is stored, there is minimal structural change. As a result, there is also minimal search required. Retrieval requires the student to access the network structure at a node identical with, or close to, the information to be retrieved. Consequently, if a student remembers the information, and can find it in his or her memory structure, retrieval should be immediate, with virtually no delay or minimal delay. As a consequence, the student either knows the information or does not know the information; there is no derivative or thought process involved in retrieving associative information in identical form. Consequently, there should be no error. Retrieval tends to be an all-or-none function. The student either knows the information or does not know the information. The performance level associated with the literal storing and retrieving of information is called *remember–verbatim*.

It is also possible to use the subordinate, superordinate, and coordinate relationships in associative memory for the storage and retrieval of information. In this mode a new piece of information is placed in the structure subordinate to, or coordinate with, some other information. Using the associative memory in this way requires some types of integration as the student encodes the information. That is, the student must search the structure for a synonym from a superordinate class or from a coordinate class with which to relate the information that is to be stored. Consequently, in a decoding mode, the student may not only retrieve the information itself, but may retrieve coordinate information or superordinate–subordinate information that is related to the item stored. When the student is asked to retrieve a paraphrase, or a synonym for the information stored, the search time required is more than that required for the literal retrieval of stored information, because the student must search the tree structure to find the associated information. Consequently, the retrieval time is increased by the necessity of searching the structure. Furthermore, when the student is searching for synonyms, there is always an increased possibility that errors will occur. The student may not have had an adequate structure in the first place and, in integrating the material, may have integrated it in an inappropriate location. Furthermore, the student may not be able to recognize the equivalence of a given term in his or her structure, and the retrieval may result in a term that is not equivalent or is judged not to be equivalent by whomever is judging the performance. Because of this probability of error, it is still possible that a student may have correctly encoded the information into the structure, and that the retrieval might not be anticipated by the performance judge. Consequently, there is a possibility of error even when the student has more or less adequately encoded the information. The performance level associated with the integration of ideas into associative memory is called *remember–paraphrase*.

In the performance categories that were identified in the performance–content matrix, no distinction was made between verbatim and paraphrased information. However, there is a performance distinction, and the subsequent presentation rules associated with these two categories are different. In some versions of the performance–content matrix we have made this distinction (Ellis & Wulfeck, 1978; Merrill et al., 1977), and this draws to a large extent on the work of prose learning theorists, such as Rothkopf and Frase.

Algorithmic Memory. The other type of memory that is assumed is algorithmic memory. This is a more dynamic memory in which the information is modified as it is integrated into the structure. Fig. 9.5 identifies the structural type as processing strategies or schema. Students encoding information into this memory do not encode it in the literal form in which it is given, but attempt to transform and integrate it into the existing processing structures. There are two possible ways that information can be integrated into algorithmic memory. The first is an *integration* in which a schema is called forward by the student to accommodate the new information. Once a possible schema is identified, the student attempts to instantiate the variables of that schema. When the information is decoded or retrieved, the student provides a result of this integration, rather than merely retrieving the information itself. Because this is active processing, retrieval from this memory usually (depending on the amount of practice) requires considerably more processing time than is required to retrieve a synonym type of associative memory. Therefore, the response requires some moderate amount of time. It is also likely that there is considerable room for error. Even though the student may have created an appropriate processing structure, he or she may still not be able to correctly recognize a new instance, or correctly apply a procedure to a new situation, even though the student may have an appropriate structure. This kind of processing is called *use level*. Use means to use a general rule to process specific information. In this case, he student uses a schema to process new input and make decisions about that input.

Perhaps an explanation in terms of the learning of a concept may be helpful in understanding the aforementioned ideas related to algorithmic memory and the integrative use of such memory. When a student is presented a definition, this definition is compared with existing schemata within the student's memory to determine if an appropriate structure already exists. If not, it is assumed that a student may modify an existing schema to create a new schema. The new schema is a framework in which placeholders are established for the various categories identified by the definition. The next step in active processing is for the student to instantiate those placeholders. This can be done in one of two ways; the student may query his or her existing memory, either associative or algorithmic, to see if there are items that could instantiate this particular schema. Often students do not go to this effort, but merely leave the variables open. When an example is presented to the student, and is identified as an example, the student then compares the attributes of that example with the variables. If they fit, the student then would store or remember information about those attributes in each of the variable slots. When a second example is presented, the student would compare the attribute values of the former example with the attribute values of this new example. If the second example is very similar to the first example, then the student may dismiss it and not store details in the variable slots. If, however, the new example is very different from the existing example, the student would then store this new example in the variable slots as a second possibility to broaden his or her generalization capability. Later when a student is asked to classify yet a new example, he or she would compare this new example with the values already stored in the variable slots. If they compare favorably, the example would be classified as belonging. If one or more of the attributes do not compare favorably, the example would be classified as not belonging. Granted, this is an oversimplified explanation of the workings of algorithmic memory, but perhaps it is sufficient to give some idea about the assumptions underlying the *use* category. A similar argument could be made for the storing of procedures or principles, both of which have many of the same characteristics as the classification storage just described.

The second way for the student to use algorithmic memory is *reorganization*. Reorganization means that new schemata are created internally rather than being established by external stimuli, as in the case just described. The student would use an inductive process by examining a set of phenomena and creating a new schema to account for similarities, differences, or changes that may be observed in the phenomena being presented. Consequently, the information change is not a result of establishing a schema and using it, but is a creation of a new shema, which can then be shifted and used, as can a presented schema. The process involved in modifying existing structure often requires a great deal of thought effort on the part of the student. Consequently, the latency involved in establishing new schemata can be very long. Sometimes even an exceedingly long latency is not sufficient for the student to adequately create the reorganization necessary to come up with a new schema. Creating a new schema is also frought with potential error; many false starts and wrong paths can be chosen by the student. Consequently it is difficult to judge the adequacy of a student's efforts until the result is known and a new process has been tested on real-world applications of that process. This type of processing is called *find level*, which means that the student is finding a new generality or is finding a higher-level process.

There is no pretense on the part of the author that the preceding explanation is an adequate representation of a learning theory. Our purpose here is merely to indicate that the categories on the performance level do have some base in processing differences that may occur in the human learner. The purpose of this explanation is to indicate that the categories suggested for the performance levels are not arbitrary. They are based on some assumptions about how human beings encode and decode information using various types of memory structures. Even though our explanation may not be very precise, we believe that it is consistent with some of the current thought concerning cognitive processing.

PRESENTATION FORMS

Primary Presentation Forms

Generalities and Instances

We have previously described two descriptive components of CDT: a category system for subject matter and a set of categories for student performance. The third component of CDT is a presentation taxonomy.* It is postulated that all cognitive subject matter can be represented on two dimensions. The first dimension is the specificity of subject matter. All cognitive subject matter can be represented at either a *general* level or a *particular* level. It was previously suggested that the basic component of subject matter is the concept, defined as a set of objects or events. This set of objects is described by a definition. A definition is a general statement that refers to all of the objects or events in a given class. In a parallel way, a statement of a procedure is a list of the steps involved. These steps are general in that they can be applied in a wide variety of specific situations. In a parallel way, a statement of a principle represents the general law that applies to the many specific situations to which that general law is applicable. These general statements of definition, procedure, and principle are called *generalities*.

Whereas a concept, procedure, and principle can be described by a generality, they may also be identified by the specific case. For a concept, a specific object or event that is defined by the concept class can be used to identify the concept. Also a specific execution of the procedure or a specific phenomenon described by the principle constitutes the specific case. These specific cases are called *instances*. Therefore, a given conceptual subject matter can take the form of either a generality or an instance.

Facts are distinguished by having no generality. A fact is always a specific case. In Fig. 9.1 illustrating the performance–content matrix, no use or find level for facts is indicated because these levels were defined in terms of the application of a general case to a specific case.

---

*Editor's note: This is a description of methods of instruction, which are then prescribed on the basis of content type and performance level (the condition variables and desired-outcome variables).

	TELL OR EXPOSITORY (E)	QUESTION OR INQUISITORY (I)
GENERALITY (G)	RULE or GENERALITY EG TG RU	G-PRACTICE IG G-TEST QG RU
INSTANCE (eg)	EXAMPLE Eeg Teg EG	eg-PRACTICE Ieg eg-TEST Qeg EG

FIG. 9.6   Primary presentation forms.

Expository and Inquisitory Presentations

The other dimension of presentation deals with the responsive expectation for the student. A generality or an instance can be presented in an expository way, which entails merely telling, illustration, or showing the student, or it can be presented in an inquisitory fashion, in which the student is expected to respond by completing the statement or applying a given generality to a specific case. In previous papers (Ellis & Wulfeck, 1978; Merrill et al., 1977), the words *tell* and *question* were used as a more vernacular description of this dimension. Fig. 9.6 illustrates these two dimensions for a given concept. The entries in the cells also indicate the various terms that have been used to describe each of these four cells. These four display types are referred to as the *primary presentation forms*. It is argued that all cognitive subject matter can be presented using a series of primary presentation forms and that any existing presentation can be segmented into these primary presentation-form components.

By substituting symbols, a number of familiar instructional strategies can be described by merely writing a formula for the strategy. For example, *EG1, EG2, EG3, . . .* would represent an expository presentation consisting of one generality after another. A presentation that consisted of *EG1, Eeg1, EG2, Eeg2, . . .* would represent an expository presentation in which generalities were followed by illustrations. A presentation that consisted of *Eeg1, Eeg2, Eeg3* followed by an *IG*

PRIMARY PRESENTATION FORM

TYPE OF ELABORATION	EG	Eeg	Ieg	IG
CONTEXT (c)	EG$'$c	Eeg$'$c	Ieg$'$c	IG$'$c
PREREQUISITE (p)	EG$'$p	Eeg$'$p		
MNEMONIC (mn)	EG$'$mn	Eeg$'$mn		
MATHEMAGENIC HELP (h)	EG$'$h	Eeg$'$h	Ieg$'$h	IG$'$h
REPRESENTATION (r)	EG$'$r	Eeg$'$r	Ieg$'$r	IG$'$r
FEEDBACK (ca) correct ans. (h) help (u) use			FB$'$ca FB$'$h FB$'$u	FB$'$ca FB$'$h FB$'$u

FIG. 9.7 Secondary presentations.

would represent some type of discovery strategy in which a series of instances were presented and the student was expected to respond by finding the generality.*

Secondary Presentation Forms

To be complete, it is necessary to designate another form of presentation called secondary presentation forms (see Fig. 9.7). For the most part, secondary presentations are elaborations of the primary presentations, The prime (′) has been used

---

*Editor's note: It is important to note that this taxonomy of methods is not an instructional model or theory in itself; rather it is a language (a set of concepts) that can be used to describe *any* method of instruction (expository, discovery, inquiry, etc.).

to designate a secondary presentation (EG'). Primary presentation forms are the major vehicle of the instruction. Secondary presentation forms are those methods that are used to facilitate the students' processing of the information or to provide items of interest, such as contextual background.

EG Elaborations.   Following the presentation of a generality, the instructor may find it desirable to present additional information, information that is designed to facilitate learning but that is secondary to the primary purpose of the presentation. If this information consists of definitions of the concept components comprising the generality, it is designated as *prerequisite elaboration (EG'p)*.* If the elaboration consists of contextual or historical background (who discovered the principle, where did it come about, or why is it important), it is called *contextual elaboration (EG'c)*. If the elaboration consists of mnemonic information or other memory aids to assist the student in remembering the generality, it is called *mnemonic elaboration (EG'mn)*.** If the elaboration consists of attention-focus-ing devices such as arrows, color, or boldface type, which are designed to help the student identify critical attributes and to see how the generality applies to a specific instance, it is called *mathemagenic elaboration*.[1] The vernacular term for mathe-magenic elaboration is *help*; consequently, the symbol that we have used for mathemagenic information is *h (EG'h)*. If the generality is represented in some other form, such as a diagram, a chart, a formula, or even in other words, it is called *representational elaboration* or *alternate representation (EG'r)*.***

In summary, elaborations of a generality are designated as secondary presentation forms. Other types of elaboration of a generality could be identified, but the ones indicated have been found to have the most relevance for instructional design.

Eeg Elaborations.   In a like manner all of the just-mentioned secondary pre-sentation forms can also be associated with expository instances. In an expository instance, mathemagenic elaboration would be information added to the content for the purpose of focusing the student's attention or facilitating the student's ability to relate the instance to the generality. Numerous devices can be used for this type of elaboration (including color, numbering, arrows, exploded drawings, graphics of various types) for the express purpose of facilitating the student's acquisition of the information. Mathemagenic elaboration is usually called *help (Eeg'h)*.

It is also possible to elaborate an expository instance by providing *context*, adding information of interest, or adding asides. Often, a given instance consists

---

*Editor's note: This is very similar to Gagné's instructional event number 3: "Stimulate recall of prerequisite learnings" (see Chapter 4, p. 93).

**Editor's note: This draws on the work of many people who have done work on mnemonics.

[1]*Mathemagenic* is a word that was coined by Earnst Rothkopf to refer to those behaviors on the part of students that were thought to promote learning. The word was borrowed to refer to information that is supplied to facilitate the student's learning.

***Editor's note: This draws on the work of many people who have done work in this area, including Bruner (enactive, iconic, and symbolic representations) and Dwyer.

of a story or a vignette that has far more detail than is necessary to the generality being taught. This secondary information is a form of elaboration that may increase interest or may make the example more meaningful to the student. An example of such contextual information would be the story in a story problem in which the focus is teaching a mathematical principle; the story merely provides a vehicle and hence is of secondary importance. It is sometimes desirable to have an historical elaboration of instances. If an instance happens to be a famous scientific experiment, the instruction might present the context of that experiment: Who was involved? or How did it come about ($Eeg'c$)?

It is sometimes desirable to present the same instance using more than one form of representation. If the format of the problem is modified, it may facilitate the student's understanding or ability to solve the problem. This alternate presentation of an instance is called *representational elaboration (Eeg'r)*.

Ieg Elaborations. Inquisitory instances also have secondary presentations. The most important is *feedback*, or knowledge of results. When a student is asked to respond to a question and is then provided information about the nature of the response or the correct answer to the question, this is a form of secondary presentation. Elaborative feedback may vary from the presentation of the correct answer or merely the words "you're right" or "you're wrong" to a complete reworking of the problem with the student.* This reworked instance is very similar to an expository presentation of the instance. Because of its importance, feedback is represented symbolically by the letters FB' where the subscripts indicate the extent of the feedback. A correct answer is indicated by $FB'ca$ whereas a reworked problem is indicated by $FB'h$, where the h indicates help or mathemagenic information.

An inquisitory instance may also be associated with *preresponse mathemagenic elaboration*. As in the case of an expository instance, this would be information presented to the student for the express purpose of facilitating his or her answering of the question. This type of help is a form of prompting ($Ieg'h$). An inquisitory instance may also have *contextual elaboration*. Here again, the story problem is a good example when the story is merely a vehicle to provide context in which to couch the question to which the student is expected to respond ($Ieg'c$). It is also possible to have secondary contextual elaboration of classical problems when some historical facts associated with the items are presented to the student ($Ieg'c$). Finally, inquisitory instances may also be *represented* in more than one way to provide an opportunity for a student to see a problem in several formats ($Ieg'r$).

IG Elaborations. Inquisitory generalities may also have secondary presentations. As with inquisitory instances, the most important secondary elaborations are feedback ($FB'ca$, $FB'h$, and $FB'u$). Correct-answer feedback consists of providing the student with the correct statement of the generality and is the most frequently used secondary presentation for inquisitory generalities. Alternate representations

---

*Editor's note: This draws on the work of many people who have developed prescriptions for feedback, especially Kulhavy.

(*IG′r*) often consist of graphic or pictorial presentations of relationships. Helped generalities (*IG′h*) usually demonstrate the application of the generality to a specific example. These secondary presentations (*IG′r* and *IG′h*) are useful for assessing a student's ability to recognize the same relationship ina paraphrased or different form than that used in the presentation. Contextual elaboration (*IG′x*) for inquisitory generalities, like that for expository generalities, consists of historical information, prerequisite information, and information about the importance of the relationship. Such information is sometimes requested from the student.

By using symbols to represent an instructional strategy, consider the following: *EG, EG′c, EG′p* . . . would indicate the presentation of a generality followed by some contextual elaboration followed by some prerequisite elboration in which the component concepts were defined or illustrated for the student. A presentation that consisted of *EG, EG′p, Eeg, Eeg′c, Ieg, FB′h* would indicate a presentation in which generality was presented, some prerequisite information involved in the generality was defined, an example was presented that involved contextual information such as a story problem, the student was asked a practice question, and the student was given feedback regarding that practice question. The illustration is sufficient to indicate to the reader how symbolism can be used to describe existing instruction or to prescribe an instructional presentation.

The symbolism that has been adopted is similar to that suggested by Evans et al. (1962) in an article titled "The RULEG System . . . ." The original conceptualization was to describe various forms of programmed instruction. Although primary presentation forms were not originally derived from the RULEG idea, the description of the type of information involved in each of the primary presentation forms is similar to that suggested by the authors of RULEG. The notion has been considerably expanded and applied to a much broader context, rather than being limited to programmed instruction.

Process Displays

Process displays are a third type of presentation form that is different from either primary or secondary presentation forms. A process display consists of instructions or directions presented to the student suggesting how he or she should consciously process the information that is presented. Such directions might be things like "Close you eyes and try to say the generality in your own words." or "Think back over the past several days and try to find an object stored in your memory that illustrates the generality." or "Try to form a picture of the generality in an odd or unusual way so as to remember it more accurately." Any type of information directing the student how to think about or how to process the information being presented would be labeled as a process display.

Procedural Displays

Procedural displays are a fourth type of presentation form. Procedural displays are directions to the student indicating how to operate the equipment being used to present the material. Directions like "Turn the page now." or "Turn on the audio recorder." are examples of procedural displays.

PERFORMANCE-PPF CONSISTENCY*

Categorizing a given area into concepts is useful only if each category enters into propositions that can be empirically verified. in this chapter three taxonomies have been presented: a performance taxonomy, a subject-matter taxonomy, and a presentation taxonomy. The remainder of this chapter presents the propositional relationships that comprise CDT. Each of the propositions in the following sections either has been, or could be, verified by experimental investigation.

Consistent with the orientation of other chapters in this volume, CDT can be conceptualized as several different models of instruction corresponding to the performance levels of the performance-content matrix. Figure 9.8 and Fig. 9.10 are organized so that the rows in each figure correspond to one of these models. This section describes the combination of primary presentation forms that comprises the skeleton of each model. The next section provides additional detail about each of those models by describing the characteristics that each primary presentation form should have, depending on the type of content involved. These are in essence variations on the basic models shown in Fig. 9.8. The following section further fleshes out each model by describing secondary presentation elaborations. It also elaborates the use and find models by describing important relationships between primary and secondary presentation forms.

The first set of propositions is concerned with the consistency between the performance classification and the primary presentation forms used to present this information. The consistency hypothesis is based on Gagné's (1965) assumption that there are different kinds of instructional outcomes and that each of these different kinds of outcomes requires a different set of conditions to promote its acquisition.

The performance–PPF consistency propositions are summarized in Fig. 9.8. The vertical dimension indicates the three performance categories with subcategories indicated for the remember level. The horizontal dimension indicates the presentation, practice, performance phases of instruction. Performance refers to postinstruction testing rather than real-world performance. In many cases postinstruction testing and real-world performance are very similar or identical. In other cases, because of expense, danger, or inaccessibility, the testing may involve representations of real-world objects or events.

The cells of the matrix indicate the prescribed combination of primary presentation forms for each performance level. In the next section, the consistency between

---

*Editor's note: This section begins the heart of the instructional theory: the prescriptions for different methods based on different conditions or desired outcomes. Although Merrill has opted not to describe a complete model from beginning to end for each cell of the content–performance matrix, the prescriptions will enable you to do so.

	PRESENTATION	PRACTICE	PERFORMANCE
FIND		legs.N, IG.N	legs.N, IG.N
USE	EG, Eegs	legs.N	legs.N
REMEMBER GENERALITY PARAPHRASE	EG, Eeg	IG.P	IG.P
REMEMBER GENERALITY VERBATIM	EG	IG	IG
REMEMBER INSTANCE PARAPHRASE	Eeg	legs.r	legs.r
REMEMBER INSTANCE VERBATIM	Eeg	leg	leg

NOTES: Eegs = 2 or more examples
         N = New examples or generality (previously unencountered)
        .P = Paraphrase
        .r = alternate representation

FIG. 9.8 Performance-PPF consistency.

the presentation forms and the types of content are described. In this section, combinations of presentation forms that constitute an adequate strategy for each of the
performance levels is presented.

Because the conditions vary sufficiently to warrant such distinctions, Fig. 9.8
indicates several subdivisions of the remember category in the performance
dimension. In the previous description of the performance–content matrix, performance levels were divided into remember, use, and find. In the presentation of the
performance taxonomy, an additional distinction between verbatim and paraphrase was introduced. Having described primary presentation forms, it is meaningful to introduce one additional distinction: that between remembering a generality and remembering an instance. The conditions necessary to promote each of
these types of remembering are different; therefore, the consistency rules are
different.

Distinctions between variations on the primary presentation forms are also indicated. Some of these variations include the relationship of one primary presentation form to another. In the presentation column, *eg* suggests the presentation of a

single instance, whereas *egs* represents the presentation of a set of instances. In the practice column, *IG* means that the generality is requested from the student in the same form as in the presentation. The *IG.p* means that a paraphrase version of the generality is requested or presented to the student for his or her response. The *IG.n* indicates that a new generality (one not previously used in the presentation) is requested from the student. Distinctions are also indicated for three variations of inquisitory instances. *Ieg* means that the incomplete instance in practice is identical to the instance used in the presentation. *Iegs.r* means that a set of two or more instances are presented and that they are represented in some form different from that used in the presentation. *Iegs.n* indicates that a set of two or more instances, not used in the presentation, are presented to the student for response. A strategy for a given performance level is determined by reading horizontally across the chart for the row associated with that type of performance.* For example, at the use level, the presentation should consist of an expository generality (*EG*) and a set of instances (*Eegs*). Practice should consist of a set of new inquisitory instances (*Iegs.n*). Performance should consist of another new set of instances (*Iegs.n*).

The performance column has the same entries as the practice column. This indicates several things. First, practice items and test items should be similar; however, the specific items should be a new set for use and find. Other distinctions between tests and practice are made as part of the adequacy propositions described later.

CONTENT-PPF CONSISTENCY

Having prescribed which primary presentation forms are appropriate for each level of performance, we now indicate that one of the reasons for distinguishing various types of *content* is that the characteristics of the presentation forms should differ from one content type to another. That is, the specification of a generality for a concept is different from the specification of a generality for a procedure or a principle. Hence, the following prescriptions qualify the nature of each of the models shown in Fig. 9.8. Fig. 9.9 summarizes the principal characteristics of generalities, instances, instance practice, and generality practice for each of the four types of content specified in the performance–content matrix. The following paragraphs briefly elaborate these various conditions.

Generalities

As previously indicated, there is no generality for a fact.

---

*Editor's note: In other words, each row represents a different model of instruction. Additional specifications for each model are provided by the content–PPF consistency prescriptions and the adequacy rules described later.

TYPE OF CONTENT	EG GENERALITY	Eeg INSTANCE	Ieg INSTANCE PRACTICE	IG GENERALITY PRACTICE
FACT		SYMBOL-SYMBOL SYMBOL-OBJECT SYMBOL-EVENT A B	SYMBOL- ? OBJECT- ? EVENT- ? A ?	
CONCEPT	DEFINITION: .name .superordinate class .attributes .relationships	EXAMPLE: .name .object, event symbol .attributes present .representation	CLASSIFY: .new object event, or symbol .attributes present .representation ? (name)	STATE DEFINITION: .name .paraphrase or verbatim ?(definition)
PROCEDURE	PROCESS: .goal .name .steps .order .decisions .branches	DEMONSTRATION: .goal .name .materials .sequential execution .representation	DEMONSTRATE: .goal .new materials .response representation ?(execution)	STATE STEPS: .goal .paraphrase or verbatim .response representatio ?(steps, decisions, branches, sequence)
PRINCIPLE	PROPOSITION: .name .component concepts .causal relationships	EXPLANATION: .name .event, situation, or problem .representation	EXPLAIN: .name .new problem .response representation ?(solution, prediction)	STATE RELATIONSHIP: .name .paraphrase or verbatim .response representatio ?(proposition

FIG. 9.9 Content-PFF consistency.

The generality for a *concept* is labeled by the term *definition*. A definition consists of the name of the concept, a superordinate class, a list of the intersecting attributes that define the concept, and the nature of the relationship between those attributes. For example, the definition of a conifer might be as follows: "A conifer is a tree that has needle-like leaves and seed-bearing cones." An analysis of this definition shows that to define conifer, a superordinate class of objects, of which conifer is one subclass, should be identified first. That superordinate class is the concept tree. It can be argued that it is impossible to define any concept without first identifying some superordinate class of which the concept is a member. The ultimate superordinate class may be the concept "thing." If all else fails, a concept can be defined as "a thing that . . . " followed by the definition of the attributes. For the definition of conifer, the attributes are needle-like leaves and seed-bearing cones. The nature of the relationship between these attributes is specified by the term *and*, meaning that it is an intersection relationship. If a tree has both needle-like leaves and seed-bearing cones, then it is a conifer. If a tree has needle-like leaves but no seed-bearing cones, it is not a conifer.

The generality for a *procedure* is different from a definition. The general term that labels a procedural generality is *process*. Another label might be the term *algorithm*. Whereas the definition of a concept is characterized by an intersection operation, the generality for a procedure is characterized by an ordering relationship. The generality consists of the goal or outcome to be produced by the process, the name of the procedure, some identification of each of the steps involved, some device to indicate the order in which those steps occur, a distinction between process steps and decision steps, and some indication of alternatives that might result from a particular decision in the procedure.

A generality for a *principle* is different from either a definition or a process. The word *proposition* is used to indicate a generality for a principle. A proposition would include the name of the principle, some identification of the component concepts that comprise the principle, and some statement of the causal relationship. One of the forms that principles often take, especially in the sciences, is the form of mathematics. For example, Ohm's law might be stated as $I = E \div R$. This is a highly abstract representation of the principle relating current, voltage, and resistance. Each of the symbols I, E, and R stand for a particular concept: I is the current, measured in amps; E is the voltage, measured in volts; and R is the resistance, measured in ohms. The formula indicates the proportional relationship (causal) between voltage and resistance.

Instances

Just as generalities are different for each of the various kinds of content, so also the instances for each kind of content are different from one another. In the case of a *fact*, there is no generality, but facts are instances. The form of these instances, as indicated in Fig. 9.9, is a one-to-one relationship between a symbol and another symbol, between an symbol and an object, between a symbol and an event. An instance of a fact indicates that A is equivalent to B, the same as B, or stands for B. For example, a zigzag symbol is a circuit-diagram representation of a resistor. A dot on the first line of the treble cleft is known by the letter E. These symbol–object or symbol–symbol relationships are specific instances of a given fact. The relationship between the two parts or the particular note and the particular wavelength is one of equivalence. It is an arbitrary association that cannot be represented by a generality. Historical facts fall under the same category. The date associated with a given event is essentially an accidental and hence arbitrary association. Proper names are also arbitrary associations of a particular label (name) with a particular object (the person).

An instance of a concept is labeled by the term *example*. It may be well to distinguish between the use of the term *example* and the use of the term *instance*. In this sytem the term *instance* is the specific case of a concept, procedure, or principle, whereas the term *example* is limited to instances of a concept. The instance of a concept is a specific object, event, or symbol that is a member of the class under consideration. This instance should consist of the concept name, the particular object, event, or symbol that is being presented, or some representation of the object, event, or symbol being presented.

It is not always possible in instruction to present the actual object, event, or symbol, but it is usually possible through some form of medium to represent these objects, events, or symbols. Whenever the actual object, event, or symbol is not involved, one must be concerned with the question of fidelity. Fidelity means the degree of correspondence between the actual object, event, or symbol and its representation. The representation of the example should usually include all of those defining characteristics that make the object or event a member of a particular class. For example, if a mammal is defined as a fur-bearing animal that suckles its young, then it may not be sufficient to indicate that a cat is a mammal. The word *cat* is a label for animals that have particular characteristics. If the learner knows those characteristics and has seen or understands how a cat suckles its young and has felt that a cat has fur on its body, then it may be an adequate example.

The nature of this problem can be illustrated if we indicate that a platypus is an example of a mammal. Can you, the reader, represent to yourself the way that a platypus suckles its young? If you do not know how a platypus suckles its young, then you have not had represented to you the critical characteristic of suckling that characterizes it as a mammal. Therefore, it becomes a fact that you must take on faith. You're merely being told that a platypus is a mammal; this does not illustrate to you the characteristic of mammalness—namely, the characteristic of suckling its young. Many seeming examples of concepts should properly be labeled pseudo-examples because they suffer from the "platypus problem"—that is, they do not have the critical attributes present in the representation of the concept that is presented to the student.

An instance of a procedure is different from an instance of a concept. The term *demonstration* has been used to characterize an instance of a procedure. A demonstration should consist of an indication of the outcome desired, the name of the procedure being demonstrated, the materials and other pieces of equipment that will be manipulated, and some actual execution of the procedure using those materials (or if the procedure cannot be actually done in the instructional situation, then a representation of that procedure). If the procedure is represented through some form of medium, it is critical that this representation contain all of the process steps as specified by the generality, all of the decision steps, and a demonstration of some or all of the alternatives that result from making those decisions.

The instance of a principle is labeled as an *explanation*. In this case some event occurs and the explanation is some description of what is actually happening as a result of this event's occurrence. This explanation should include the name of the principle that is being explained. It should include the problem situation, including the conditions and constraints that define the problem. It should contain some description of what happens during a time sequence as the components interact, and it should include some description of the causal relationships involved. Of course, these descriptions need not (and often should not) be verbal. As with concepts and procedures it may be difficult to bring the actual event into the instructional situation. The principle may also require some form of representation. The fidelity of that representation must be such that all of the component concepts are represented and all of the causal events can be observed or at least inferred from the situation that is presented.

The importance of representation in the presentation of instances deserves some further comment. There are some who would argue that the higher the fidelity of the representation (that is, the more real-world-like that a representation is), the better. This may not always be the case, however (see, for example, Bruner's (1966) discussion of enactive, iconic, and symbolic representations). Much of the real-world representation may consist of a contextual secondary presentation that may divert the student's attention from those critical characteristics that define the instance of a concept class, that represent the steps of the procedure, or that constitute the components of the causal relationship. It may be that early in the instruction a lower fidelity representation may be more instructionally effective than a very high fidelity representation. It is important, however, that the distinction be maintained between those critical aspects of the representation that are necessary to make the instance an illustration of the generality and those secondary aspects of the representation that provide context for the instance.

Instance Practice

Generalities and instances consist of expository presentations. Evans et al. (1962) suggested that inquisitory presentations were merely incomplete expository presentations in which the student was expected to complete the item. Perhaps their definition characterizes the nature of practice instances for the various categories of outcome.

Instance practice for a *fact* consists of presenting one side or the other of the associated pair. If the fact is a symbol–symbol pair, one symbol is presented and the student is asked to recognize or reproduce the other symbol. If it is a symbol–object pair, the object is presented and the student is asked to reproduce or recognize the symbol. Unlike the other types of practice, instance practice for a fact is always a verbatim type of memory in which the student is asked to literally reproduce or recognize what was presented.

Instance practice for a *concept* is labeled *classify* because this verb best characterizes the type of performance required by the student. An instance for instance practice of a concept would consist of an object, event, or symbol that has not been previously presented to the student during the instruction. The student is asked to complete the example by supplying the name or by otherwise indicating the class to which the instance belongs. There are various ways this can be done, but essentially it is a matter of supplying or matching the name with the object. It is critical, as with the presentation of an example, that the practice instance also have all of the relevant attributes present. It must not suffer from the "platypus problem."

Instance practice for *procedures* consists of the student's demonstrating the procedure. The input here would consist of presenting the goal, the name, the materials, and equipment that may be required, and asking the student to manipulate these materials and symbols by using the steps of the procedure. There are two parts to the response when a student is demonstrating. One is the correct execution of the steps and the second is the product from carrying out the procedure. As with previous explanations, it may be necessary that the student carry out the procedure in a symbolic way or in some form of representation, rather than actually manipulate the materials or the objects involved. However, when such representations are used, it is critical that the student be required to demonstrate all of the steps, decisions, and branches involved. It is also necessary that the representation used is of sufficient fidelity that all the critical steps are required. Simulations are a type of representation for the execution of complex procedures when the actual execution may be dangerous, difficult, or impossible to manage.

The instance practice for a *principle* entails the presentation of a problem situation to the student. The name of the principle may or may not be given, and the student is asked to explain what happens. This explanation may take the form of a prediction about the outcome, or it may take the form of a solution to the problem. Representation again plays an important role. If it is impossible to have the actual objects and events present, then they must be represented. The representation must be sufficient so that all of the critical aspects of the cause-and-effect relationship are represented for the student.

The least ambiguous incomplete examples of instance practice, have been described. It is possible to manipulate other things and create other item forms. In some circumstances these alternate item forms may have validity and be important ways to facilitate the student's acquisition of the capability being taught. For instance, in the case of a concept, the student may be given the name and be told to find some objects or events. This is the "example from home problem." It may be a valid way to have the student practice the concept. However, there is a danger that the degree of divergence that the student exercises may be less than what should be exercised. Divergence is discussed under the adequacy section later.

It is possible in a demonstration to have the student watch the execution of the procedure and recognize whether the procedure is being executed correctly or not, rather than having the student actually execute the procedure. This may be a way to partially assess the student's capability without having the student actually perform the procedure.* Such a recognition form has obvious limitations. The purpose of this paragraph is not to itemize the alternative practice items that could be used but rather to acknowledge that various other possibilities exist and to indicate that these alternatives may still be consistent with CDT.

Generality Practice

Generality practice can be used for either a memory level or a complex problem-solving level depending on the context in which the student is asked to come up with a generality. The information in Fig. 9.9 describes generality practice in a remember–generality mode. The differences that would be found at a find level are noted as the various categories are described.

Because there are no generalities for facts, there is obviously no generality practice.

For a *concept* the words *state definition* characterize the behavior when a student is asked to respond to the definition of a concept. A typical item form would present the name and ask the student to produce or recognize the definition. It is possible for the student to recognize the definition verbatim, exactly as it was stated, or to paraphrase the definition by recasting it in his or her own words. There are various item forms that could be used. For example, the definition could be presented and the student could be asked to come up with the name.

At a *find* level the student would not be given the name of the definition but would be asked to identify those attributes that the instances in a given class, either created by the teacher or created by the student, share. In this case, a student is inventing or finding the definition that might be present. Even though the student is still asked to find the definition, the idea of verbatim and paraphrase no longer make sense, because in this situation the student will always be casting the definition in his or her own words.

At the *procedure* level, generality practice for rememberng the generality is a matter of having the student state the steps in the process or draw a flow chart representing the procedure. Here the student would be presented the goal and

---

*Editor's note: This is similar to Gropper's recognize-edit-produce distinction for response modes (Chapter 5, p. 135).

would then be asked to indicate all of the steps, decision steps, and alternative branches that might be part of the procedure. Again the recall may be verbatim or paraphrased—that is, the student may recall exactly what was presented, or may recast it in his or her own words or representation. One further consideration must be the representation form of the response; the student could be asked to draw flow charts, make a list, or draw a picture. There are many types of response formats, and this should be specified to the student.

At the find level, the nature of the question changes somewhat in that the student is presented an outcome, either a product or a result, and is asked to derive a procedure that would enable him or her to come to that outcome. In this case the outcome would substitute for the name of the procedure; the rest would be similar in that the student would have to state the steps required and represent them in some form. However the paraphrase–verbatim distinction becomes meaningless in that the student would be stating the procedure in his or her own words. In a find situation the student might also be asked not only to state the procedure, but also to go on and demonstrate its use. This, of course, would shift back to the instance-practice type of situation.

At the *principle* level, generality practice for remembering the proposition requires the student to state the relationship. The student would typically be given the name of the principle involved, and be asked to state the proposition. The student may be asked to state in verbatim or paraphrased, and there may be various ways in which he or she could represent the response. The common ways are to have it stated as a mathematical relationship, as a verbal expression, or in a graph format.

As with the find level of concepts and procedures, if a student is asked to discover a new principle or relationship, the nature of the statement may be in the form of some conclusion; but rather than being given the name and being asked to state the principle, the student would be given a problem and would be asked to find some solution to that problem or some explanation of that phenomenon that tends to work. There is a wide variety of research and scholarly methodology that may come to play in the find-a-principle situation.

ADEQUACY RULES

Secondary Presentation Forms

In the section on presentation forms, a number of secondary presentation forms were introduced. The first set of adequacy rules prescribes the inclusion of secondary presentation forms to augment the primary presentation forms needed for consistency. Even when a presentation is consistent, as prescribed by Fig. 9.8, there are still additional strategy considerations that will result in improved performance. Fig. 9.10 is an extention of Fig. 9.8. The primary presentation forms head

	EG GENERALITY	Eeg INSTANCES	INSTANCE Ieg PRACTICE	GENERALITY Ig PRACTICE
FIND				FB'u
USE	EG'h EG'p, EG'r	Eeg'h, Eeg'r	Ieg'r, FB'h	
REMEMBER GENERALITY PARAPHRASE	EG'mn	Eeg'h		FB'ca.h
REMEMBER GENERALITY VERBATIM	EG'mn			FB'ca
REMEMBER INSTANCE PARAPHRASE		Eeg'r	Ieg'r, FB'ca.h	
REMEMBER INSTANCE VERBATIM			FB'ca	

ca = correct answer
u = use level

NOTES: See Fig. 9.8
h = help or attention
    focusing information
p = prerequisite
r = alternate representation
mn = mnemonic

FIG. 9.10 Secondary presentation from adequacy.

the columns. The cell entries indicate secondary presentations that should be added to the primary presentations.

Feedback

The first adequacy rule that should be observed from Fig. 9.10 is feedback. Feedback should always accompany practice at every performance level. Feedback is recommended for both correct and incorrect responses. Note that this feedback varies in form from one level to another. At the remember—verbatim level, correct answer (*ca*) feedback is most appropriate. The feedback, in essence, provides a second presentation of the verbatim response that the student was to have made. At the remember—paraphrase level, for both instances and generalities, not only correct answer, but some degree of attention focusing feedback is prescribed. This helping information should indicate to the student how the alternative representation of the example, or how the alternative statement of the generality, corresponds to the original.

At the use level, helped feedback is recommended. This feedback is recommended for both correct and incorrect responses. In the use situation, feedback should indicate to the student why the instance is an example of the concept class being presented, how the execution of the procedure implements all of the steps, how the explanation of the phenomena in a particular situation relates to the generality. The feedback should tie the response or the execution to the original generality.

Feedback at the find level takes a different form. As indicated by $FB'u$, feedback here should be generated by the student as follows: In a concept situation, the definition invented by the student should be presented to another student to see if this other student can use the definition to classify instances. If he or she can, this is feedback as to the adequacy of the concept that was invented. At the procedure level, the procedure should be executed in a new situation to see if it produces the desired result. If it does, then this information provides feedback to the student on the adequacy of the new procedure. At the principle level, a prediction should be made for a new situation. If the prediction is verified, then this information provides feedback to the student as to the adequacy of the new principle. Essentially the student drops down to the use level and uses the new generality with a new set of instances. If it works, then this information provides feedback as to the adequacy of the new generality.

Although feedback is recommended for all practice, a qualification needs to be noted. When students know that, by touching a button, turning a page, or answering a question, they will receive immediate confirmation of their actions, there is sometimes a tendency to engage in self-deception—that is, the student will assume that he or she knows how to work the problem and turns to the feedback before the work or answer is carefully checked. This leads to less adequate learning on the part of the student and consequently to a decrement in test performance. The solution to this problem is to introduce procedures that delay the feedback until the student has checked the adequacy of the response. Various management or incentive systems could be employed to promote more careful performance prior to providing feedback (see Sassenrath, 1975; Surber & Anderson, 1975).

Elaboration

At each of the performance levels, certain types of elaboration are indicated to be added to the generality. At the remember level mnemonic elaboration is recommended. The student should be presented some mnemonic device to facilitate his or her ability to recall the generality. At the use level, helping information is recommended. Helping elaboration includes attention-focusing devises that focus the student's attention on critical aspects of the generality and how they relate to an instance. This type of elaboration could take the form of exploded drawings, arrows, color, or diagrams. Prerequisite elaboration is also recommended at the use level. Prerequisite elaboration includes information about prerequisite concepts and facts that are required to understand the definition, the procedure, or the principle that is being presented. This form of elaboration includes definitions or an instance of these prerequisite component concepts. A third type of generality elaboration is to present the generality using some alternate form of representation. If the generality was presented as a verbal statement, perhaps a diagram indicating the relationship may be desirable. If the generality was presented as a formula, perhaps a verbal statement would be an appropriate alternative representation. The amount of elaboration required depends to some extent on the complexity of the generality being presented. In a given instructional presentation, the use of all of these forms of elaboration may be unnecessary. As the generality gets more complex, it is more likely that the student will acquire the capacity being taught if all of these forms of elaboration are included.

The second column in Fig. 9.10 indicates the secondary presentation forms that should be added to instances. Helping information should accompany instances presented at the use level, and also at the remember–generality–paraphrase level. At the use level it is suggested that each of the instances be accompanied by attention-focusing information that indicates why this particular instance is an illustration of the generality. This information should also focus the student's attention on the critical aspects of that instance. The form of this elaboration would vary depending on the nature of the content. In a concept, it should focus the student's attention on the relevant attributes in the instance that define the instance as a member of a particular concept class. In a procedure, it should focus the student's attention on critical decisions, branches, and the ordering of the steps. In a principle, it should focus the student's attention on instances of the critical concepts and how they are combined to produce the change that is described by the principle. Secondary helping information should accompany the instance used in a remember–generality mode. In this case, there is only a single instance. The secondary presentation should help the student see why the example is an instance of the generality. In this case, the purpose is to help the student remember the generality, and the instance should be a commonly encountered instance that would facilitate the student's ability to remember the generality.

A cautionary note must accompany the recommendation to include helping information. Some students become help dependent in that this attention-focusing information guides the mental processing necessary for the student to learn. Too much help means the student may never have to internalize this mental processing and hence will learn less, resulting in a performance decrement. To avoid over-dependence on help, it should be gradually eliminated while the directions encourage the student to perform this attention-focusing procesing for him or herself. This caution is similar to the fading recommendations from programmed instruction (see Markle, 1969).*

An additional type of secondary presentation associated with examples deals with representation. In this case the medium representation of that instance would change. This is important for the use level because the student needs to see the variety with which the instances can be represented. A particular instance presented in more than one representation form may facilitate the student's ability to recognize new instances using alternative forms of representation. It is not necessary that every instance be represented alternatively, but some of the instances should be represented in more than one way. This is also important for the remember–instance–paraphrase level. Paraphrase at this level means that the student should be able to remember the instance even if it is represented in some other form. Therefore, it is important that the students see more than one representation form.

The third column in Fig. 9.10 indicates the secondary presentations that should be added to instance practice items. We have already discussed the feedback additions. In addition it is suggested at the use level that practice instances be presented using alternative representation forms. Representation is a form of variety that the student will encounter in real-world situations. Failure to experience some of this variation in practice will likely decrease the student's ability to generalize to new representations and hence decrement the performance. This alternative representation is the meaning of paraphrase for the remember–instance–paraphrase level. Alternative representation may not be something one would want to do with every single item. However, some items should be represented in more than one way.

For the remember-paraphrase and use levels one might be inclined to include helping information. This would constitute a form of prompting. Such helping information has not been included for practice. Prompting on the practice may give the student a false sense of security resulting in a decrement in performance rather than facilitating performance. However, if complex content is being taught, it may be that for the early practice items some prompting is desirable. This prompting would then be eliminated so that the student would have an opportunity to respond to unprompted items. As a rule of thumb, it is suggested that helping information should always accompany the expository presentation of the examples at the use level, whereas this type of prompting should not accompany the practice items in a use–level presentation. There are variations on this particular rule as to the amount of secondary helping presentations that might be desirable.

The fourth column in Fig. 9.10 prescribes secondary presentations to accompany inquisitory generalities. As previously indicated, at the remember level the

---

*Editor's note: See also Chapter 5.

secondary presentation that should be used is feedback that indicates to the student a correct response. As previously described, at the find level feedback consists of the student's ability to demonstrate the generality.

Interdisplay Relationships

In the previous section, it was suggested that the addition of certain secondary presentation forms increases the probability of an increment in the student's performance. This section deals with the relationships *between* primary presentation forms. These rules apply to the use and find levels of the performance–content matrix. At both of these levels, the consistency rules call for a set of examples to be presented and a set of practice items to be included as part of a consistent presentation. Interrelationships are those ways in which one display in this set is affected by another display in the set.

Isolation. Primary and secondary presentation forms have been identified for the purpose of analyzing and describing instructional presentations. In a given presentation, the clear identification of these various presentation forms is often not made explicit to the student. That that is the generality and that that is elaboration of the generality may seem obvious to the instructor, who is familiar with the subject matter. However, it is often not obvious to the students. It is typical of much instruction to include examples with generalities in such a way that it may be difficult for students unacquainted with the subject matter to separate the main ideas from the illustrative material. This situation is called *instructional hide-and-seek,* because the student must look for the key ideas that are embedded in the more elaborate textual presentation. The isolation rule indicates that the primary presentation forms should be clearly *separated* and *identified* for the student by means of some type of graphic or auditory convention.

Divergence. The divergence rule indicates that the instances for a particular generality should be divergent. This means that the critical characteristic of these instances should be as different as possible. This set of instances represents a sample from all of the possible instances that could be included in the concept class being taught, the set of procedures being taught, or the set of phenomena to which the principle applies. The divergence rule suggests that this sampling needs to be somewhat representative. It is often impractical to attempt to systematically represent each of the irrelevant characteristics by means of an example (see Markle & Tieman, 1970). The divergence rule is a compromise that approximates a more systematic sampling procedure. If the divergence rule is applied, then it is probable that the sample of instances presented to the student will be representative of the population of instances that may be encountered in the real world.

Matching. There has been considerable discussion in the educational-psychology literature concerning the role of nonexamples. Frequently this literature suggests that nonexamples should not be included in instructional materials. However, the matching rule suggests that during the expository presentation, examples should be matched with nonexamples. Matched means that the nonexample should be selected in such a way that it enhances the student's ability to discriminate between characteristics that are relevant and those that are not relevant.

The matching rule takes different forms for the different types of content. For a concept, matching exists when all of the irrelevant characteristics of the example and the matched nonexample are as similar as possible. The critical characteristics, of course, would differ. A matched nonexample might be thought of as a potentially confusing instance to which the student might overgeneralize were it not for this discrimination training.

For a procedure, a matched nonexample would demonstrate potentially incorrect ways to execute the procedure in this situation. The student should be shown the correct way and then be shown typical or frequently occurring errors. The consequence of those errors should be pointed out. There is some controversy as to whether or not the presentation of such wrong procedures will confuse the student. In a matched correct and incorrect execution of a procedure it is therefore critical that the correct steps be clearly identified so the student can easily discriminate the correct execution from the incorrect execution.

For a principle, a matched nonexample would take the form of a frequent but incorrect explanation. Here is a place where previous myths or incorrect interpretations can be contrasted with the correct, or more recent, explanations of the phenomena being explained or predicted. The consequence of such incorrect predictions should be pointed out to the student. The incorrect explanations that should be included are those that may be potentially confusing, that may be in the common folklore, that may have been taught in the past, or for which there is some probability for the student to otherwise be confused.

A cautionary note must also be attached to the preceding recommendations for matched nonexamples. Like feedback and attention-focusing help, matching directs mental processing, which facilitates comparing and contrasting instances. If all examples are matched to nonexamples, the student may not learn to internalize this compare-and-contrast operation. Therefore it is important that external matching be eliminated as the instruction progresses and that the student be directed to perform the compare-and-contrast operation with instances previously stored in memory.

Difficulty.   It has been found that for almost any concept, procedure, or principle some of the instances are more easily classified, executed, or explained than others. If a student is presented all typical examples, there is a tendency to undergeneralize, and thus to fail to adequately perform when difficult instances are presented. On the other hand, if only difficult examples are used, a student may have a tendency to overgeneralize. Overgeneralization occurs when the student includes examples in the concept class that do not belong, attempts to apply the procedure to situations in which it is inappropriate, or attempts to explain situations to which the explanation does not apply. The most effective presentation is one that includes a sample of instances representing a range of difficulty. Some easy instances should be included to which it is expected that most of the students would respond correctly, as well as some very difficult instances, to which it is expected that many of the students would be unable to respond appropriately. By giving the student experience with a wide range of difficulty levels, the probability of transfer to new situations is increased. There is some overlap between the difficulty rule and the divergence rule in that presenting a divergent set of examples often includes examples of a wide range of difficulty.

Sampling in inquisitory presentations.   The same rules of divergence, matching, and difficulty can also be applied to inquisitory presentations. However, there are some exceptions that should be noted. The sample set of practice instances should include a divergent set, as with the expository instances. Sample instances should also include a range of difficulty. For adequate practice it is important that the student have an opportunity to respond to instances representing the entire range of the potential population. The sampling rules have been purposely simplified to facilitate their use in instruction design. More systematic sampling procedures could be used, but for most instructional situations, it is adequate to make a conscious effort to informally include a range of difficulty and a range of divergence rather than to systematically sample all the potential instances.

In the inquisitory mode, it is important that the matching rule *not* be included. A matched example–nonexample pair for which the student is asked to classify which is the example and which is not, or is asked to recognize which is the correct execution of a procedure and which is not, provides an unintentional prompt for the student, thereby making the execution of the procedure, the classification, or the explanation easier than it would be were the matched relationship not present. It is desirable in most cases to present instances in the practice mode in *random order* so as to avoid the potential presentation of matched examples and non-examples.

LEARNER CONTROL

CDT is *not* a set of propositions for adapting instruction to individual learners. Rather it is a set of propositions for designing instruction for groups of learners, within which there may be a range of individual differences. If all of the CDT prescriptions are implemented for a given lesson, the resulting instructional materials are very rich in facilitating techniques. It is unlikely that a single student will need all of the material provided, but it is equally probable that in a group of students each of the components included will be used by at least some of the students. If every student is required to use every prescribed component, the materials will be considerably less efficient than is necessary.

CDT assumes that some degree of learner control will be available to the student. Learner control subsumes a range of variables. Learner control of *content* includes curriculum selection, lesson or objective selection, and segment or module selection. Learner control of *strategy* includes display selection (number and type of primary and secondary presentation forms) and selection of conscious cognitive processing. CDT assumes some form of learner control over display selection including PPF sequence, the number of examples and practice items, and the amount of elaboration needed (see Merrill, 1980, in press).

Learner control of displays is not a characteristic that must be deliberately designed into instructional materials. All instructional materials allow some degree of learner control. Lectures, films, videotapes, and other paced presentations severely limit the amount of control available to the student. Textbooks, workbooks, self-administered tape–slide presentations, and other self-paced instructional materials allow considerable learner control depending on the degree of isolation employed.

Implementing a full range of CDT prescriptions is most appropriate for *self-paced* instructional materials. For paced presentations, the prescriptions are still valid, but compromises in the number of displays and the amount of elaboration must be made in order to pace the materials for some middle point of the intended audience.

Research on learner control (see later section *Learner Control*) shows that merely providing the opportunity for student choice and a rich array of displays from which to choose are not sufficient. Bright students seem to benefit most, whereas less able students need more direction in using the materials available to them. It would seem that having designed the materials to implement CDT prescriptions may not be enough. An adaptive *instructional management system* that assists the student to use those displays from the available array would seem to be a necessary addition for many students. It is also possible that students can be *taught* to use learner control more effectively. The research to date has been insufficient to determine the feasibility or best approach for such training.

CDT seems to ignore individual differences, but this is not quite the case. CDT assumes that individual differences will affect primarily the number of displays and the amount of elaboration (secondary presentations and interdisplay relationships) that may be necessary for a given student to learn. On the other hand, CDT also assumes that all students, regardless of aptitude or ability, will require at least the primary presentation forms appropriate to a given performance–content category in order to learn. Students obviously vary in their ability to use previously learned information to compensate for information or elaboration that may be missing (according to CDT) from the presentation. Our current work on conscious cognitive processing is an attempt to expand CDT to include this consideration.

STUDENT CONSCIOUS COGNITIVE PROCESSING

This section looks into the future rather than a part of CDT that currently exists. It is hypothesized that, in addition to a particular set of primary presentation forms, associated secondary presentations, and appropriate interdisplay relationships, there is also an associated *conscious cognitive process* that would facilitate the student's acquisition of the behavior specified by a given performance–content category. What is a conscious cognitive process? It is generally acknowledged that students are not passive when they are interacting with instructional materials. For example, when a student is presented a generality in order to teach a concept, there are a number of options as to what the student can do with that information. The student could read it, paraphrase it, look through memory to find an example of the thing being defined, remember it by applying some mneumonic system, or remember it by creating a unique mnemonic representation. All of these activities represent alternative conscious cognitive processing activities that the student could apply to the display that is presented.

Rigney (1978) suggested a classification of instructional materials in which system control and student control constitute one dimension, and embedded and detached constitute the other. Using this scheme, learning strategies activated by CDT are embedded and system controlled. The various primary and secondary presentation forms and the relationships between them have been selected in a way that promotes certain kinds of processing on the part of the student by virtue of the information that is available. However, the presentation of appropriate information interrelated in certain ways may not be sufficient. Although this embedded structure may increase the probability that a student will engage in appropriate processing, there is still a considerable range of less appropriate activities that the student may use. This is especially true for presentations that may be inadequate according to the prescriptions of CDT. It is possible that when a presentation is inadequate, the student, with appropriate direction, could provide compensating cognitive activity. That is, the student could search his or her memory for the information that was not supplied, or could provide elaboration for material that is not related in a way that is appropriate for acquisition. In effect, the student is redesigning the instruction by means of conscious processing. It is hypothesized that not only are there particular combinations of primary presentations, secondary presentations, and interrelationships that are appropriate for each content–performance class, but that there are also appropriate processing strategies associated with these displays. If a student engaged in this conscious processing, the probability of acquiring of the material is higher than if he or she engaged in some other type of processing.

The use of processing displays has considerable implications for instructional design. If processing that is appropriate for a given piece of information within the context of a given performance–content outcome can be identified, then it may be possible to enhance the learning that takes place from existing instructional materials merely by adding process display overlays. Existing materials could be overprinted with directions on how the student should process the information. If these processing displays enable the student to compensate for some lack in the instructional design of the existing materials, then this technique provides an inexpensive resynthesis process that would enhance the learning that could take place from existing materials. According to Rigney's classification, such processing directions are *detached* rather than embedded learning-strategy activators. This explicit direction of processing appropriate for a given display in the context of a given outcome class may be an interim step leading to learner control of appropriate learning strategies.

TRAINING MATERIALS FOR CDT

The brevity of this chapter makes it necessary to present primarily generalities with few examples and no practice. Submitted to evaluation using the CDT, this chapter would rate poorly as instructional material. Some training materials related to CDT is available to the interested reader. For the use–concept cell of the performance–content matrix, *Teaching Concepts: An Instructional Design Guide* (Merrill & Tennyson, 1977) provides a more instructional presentation. The *Instructional Strategy Diagnostic Profile: Training Manual* (Merrill et al., 1977) and the Navy adaptation of this material, *Interim Training Manual for the Instructional Quality Inventory* (Ellis & Wulfeck, 1978) present CDT as a tool for evaluating existing instructional materials. Courseware, Inc. has produced training materials to teach an earlier version of CDT, called the *Author Training Course* (1977),[2] which consists of five training manuals: (1) *Classifying Instructional Objectives;* (2) *Developing Specifications for Fact Instruction;* (3) *Developing Specifications for Concept Instruction;* (4) *Developing Specifications for Procedure Instruction;* (5) *Developing Specifications for Rule Instruction*. This course has been described in O'Neal, Faust, and O'Neal (1979).

RESEARCH SUPPORT FOR CDT[3]

There is not room in this chapter in this particular volume for a detailed presentation of the research evidence for CDT. Some of the early evidence was summarized by Merrill, Olsen, and Coldeway (1976). In this section the findings for some of that research, which has been done by the author and his associates over the part decade, are cited. More than 50 experimental studies concerned with aspects of CDT have been conducted by the author and his associates. To conserve space and because many of these studies have been published only as working papers, we have not referenced them here. The following paragraphs summarize the principal findings.

---

[2]The Author Training Course is available from Courseware, Inc., 10075 Carroll Canyon Road, San Diego, California, 92131, (714) 578-1700.

[3]A list of research studies pertaining to CDT is available from the author. Copies of individual research reports are also available for interested readers. Contact M. David Merrill, Professor of Educational Psychology and Techology, WPH 801, University of Southern California, Los Angeles, California, 90007, (213) 743-6263.

The Primary Presentation Forms

Considerable work has been done on the consistency relationships between various performance categories and the primary presentation forms recommended. The conclusion of this research is that the consistency rules do indeed hold. At the use level it has been found that whenever all three primary presentation forms are present, the performance is more adequate than if only two of the primary forms are present. It has also been demonstrated that if the primary presentation forms appropriate for one performance category are used in an attempt to teach another performance category, then there is a decrement in performance.

Sequence of Primary Presentation Forms

CDT does not recommend a particular sequence of primary presentation forms. To some extent, a generality, example, practice sequence is implied. Several research studies tend to support this particular proposition. However, the support at the use level is not completely consistent. The studies show that students who receive generalities prior to instances usually do better than students who receive instances prior to generalities. It has also been demonstrated that students who receive practice do much better than students who do not receive practice. It has not been consistently shown that practice should always occur at the end. It is possible for practice to occur immediately after the generality, or after the example. In some cases, the practice can occur first, and then be followed by generalities and examples.

Secondary Presentation Forms

There is considerable evidence to support the recommendations for secondary presentation forms. Students who receive mnemonics tend to do much better than students who do not receive mnuemonic support. Students who receive help (mathemagenic information), either for generalities or for instances, do better than students who do not receive such help. There is limited support for the notion that alternative representation forms are important. However, this is an area in which we need to do more research; the evidence is not as firm as it should be.

Interdisplay Relationships

Studies investigating isolation of presentation forms have demonstrated that learning is more efficient and often more effective for the isolated treatments.

A number of studies have shown that matching, divergence, and difficulty are important variables, especially in the teaching of concepts. Appropriate manipulation of these variables always results in an increment in classification behavior. The evidence for the type of matching suggested for principle and procedure using in somewhat sketchy and represents another area in which additional research is needed. There is considerable evidence, however, that divergence and a range of difficulty are important to teach adequate transfer in the procedure and principle using areas (as well as concept using).

Learner Control

Studies investigating learner control have shown that students are able to determine how many instances or practice items they need to optimize test performance. Learner control of presentation forms does not result in performance differences when compared to performance of students in fixed-order treatments. Learner control of generality help results in superior test performance, but learner control of example and practice help results in a performance decrement. Students at the college level with minimal directions do not make good use of learner-control options. Amount of training in the use of learner control to optimize performance has not been adequately investigated.

Process Displays

The research has just begun to scratch the surface in the area of process displays. A couple of studies indicate that giving processing directions to students considerably enhances their performance.

REFERENCES

Bloom, B. S. (Ed.) *Taxonomy of educational objectives: Cognitive domain.* New York: David McKay, 1956.

Bruner, J. S. *Toward a theory of instruction.* New York: Horton, 1966.

Courseware, Inc. *Author training course.* San Diego: Courseware, Inc., 1977.

Ellis, J. A., & Wulfeck, W. H., II *Interim training manual for the instructional quality inventory* (NPROC TN 78–5). San Diego: Navy Personnel Research and Development Center, 1978.

Evans, J. L., Homme, L. E., & Glaser, R. The RULEG system for the construction of programmed verbal learning sequences. *Journal of Educational Research,* 1962, *55,* 513–518.

Gagné, R. M. *The conditions of learning.* New York: Holt, Rinehart & Winston, 1965.

Gagné, R. M. *The conditions of learning* (2nd ed.). New York: Holt, Rinehart & Winston, 1970.

Gagné, R. M. *The conditions of learning* (3rd. ed.). New York: Holt, Rinehart & Winston, 1977.

Gagné, R. M., & Briggs, L. J. *Principles of instructional design* (2nd ed.). New York: Holt, Rinehart & Winston, 1979.

Gagné, R. M., & Merrill, M. D. The content analysis of subject matter; a dialogue between Robert Gagné and M. D. Merrill. *Instructional Science,* 1976, *5,* 1–28.

Gagné, R. M., & White, R. T. Memory structures and learning outcomes. *Review of Educational Research,* 1978, *50,*, 625–646.

Mager, R. F. *Preparing instructional objectives.* Belmont, Calif.: Fearon, 1962.

Markle, S. M. *Good frames and bad* (2nd ed.). New York: Wiley, 1969.

Markle, S. M., & Tiemann, P. W. *Really understanding concepts: Or in frumious pursuit of the jabberwock* (3rd ed.). Champaign, Ill.: Stipes Publishing, 1970.

Merrill, M. D. Necessary psychological conditions for defining instructional outcomes. In M. D. Merrill (Ed.), *Instructional design: Readings.* Englewood Cliffs, N.J. Prentice-Hall, 1971.

Merrill, M. D. Content and instructional analysis for cognitive transfer tasks. *AV Communication Review*, 1973, *21*, 109–126.

Merrill, M. D. Learner control in computer based learning. *Computers and Education*, 1980, *4*, 77–95.

Merrill, M. D. Learner control. In C. R. Dills, (Ed.), *Instructional development: The State of the art*, in press.

Merrill, M. D., & Boutwell, R. C. Instructional development: Methodology and research. In F. N. Kerlinger (Ed.), *Review of research in education* (Vol. #1). Itasca, N.Y.: Peacock, 1973.

Merrill, M. D., Kowallis, T., & Wilson, B. G. Instructional design in transition. In F. H. Farley & N. J. Gordon (Eds.), *Psychology and education: The state of the union*. Berkeley: McCutchan, 1981.

Merrill, M. D., Olsen, J. B., & Coldeway, N. S. *Research support for the instructional strategy diagnostic profile* (Report No. 3). San Diego: Courseware, Inc., 1976.

Merrill, M. D., Reigeluth, C. M., & Faust, G. W. The instructional quality profile: Curriculum evaluation and design tool. In H. F. O'Neal, Jr. (Ed.), *Procedures for instructional systems development*. New York: Academic Press, 1979.

Merrill, M. D., Richards, R. E., Schmidt, R. V., & Wood, N. D. *The instructional strategy diagnostic profile: Training manual*. San Diego: Courseware, Inc., 1977.

Merrill, M. D., & Tennyson, R. D. *Teaching concepts: An instructional design guide*. Englewood Cliffs, N.J.: Educational Techology Publications, 1977.

Merrill, M. D., & Wood, N. D. Instructional strategies: A preliminary taxonomy. *Mathematics Education Report* (ERIC for Science, Mathematics, and Environmental Education). Ohio State University, 1974.

Merrill, M. D., & Wood, N. D. An instructional strategy taxonomy: Theory and applications. *Journal for Research in Mathematics Education*, 1975, *6*, 195–201.

O'Neal, H. L., Faust, G. W., & O'Neal, A. F. An author training course. In H. L. O'Neal, Jr. (Ed.), *Procedures for instructional systems development*. New York: Academic Press, 1979.

Popham, W. J. *Educational evaluation*. Englewood Cliffs, N.J.: Prentice-Hall, 1975.

Reigeluth, C. M., & Merrill, M. D. A knowledge base for improving our methods of instruction. *Educational Psychologist*, 1978, *13*, 57–70.

Reigeluth, C. M., Merrill, M. D., & Bunderson, C. V. The structure of subject matter content and its instructional design implications. *Instructional Science*, 1978, *7*, 107–126.

Rigney, J. W. Learning strategies: A theoretical perspective. In H. F. O'Neal, Jr. (Ed.), *Learning strategies*. New York: Academic Press, 1978.

Sassenrath, J. M. Theory and results of feedback and retention. *Journal of Educational Psychology*, 1975, *67*, 894–899.

Scandura, J. M. New directions for theory and research on rule learning: I. A set-function language. *Acta Psychologica*, 1968, *28*, 301–302.

Surber, J. R., & Anderson, R. C. Delay–retention effect in natural classroom sittings. *Journal of Educational Psychology*, 1975, *67*, 170–173.

10

The Elaboration Theory of Instruction

Charles M. Reigeluth
Faith S. Stein
Syracuse University

Charles M. Reigeluth

Charles M. Reigeluth received an A.B. in Economics from Harvard University in 1969 and a Ph.D. in Instructional Psychology from Brigham Young University in 1977. He taught science at the high school level for three years before his graduate studies, and after a one-year post-doctorate at Brigham Young, he joined the faculty of the Instructional Design, Development and Evaluation program at Syracuse University in 1978.

Dr. Reigeluth's major professional interest lies in improving public education. Based on the conviction that an educational system should place greater emphasis on well designed resources as the source of knowledge, he has devoted his efforts to contributing to the development of a comprehensive knowledge base to guide the development of such resources, with particular emphasis on computer-based resources. His first major integrative effort was the Elaboration Theory of Instruction, whose initial development was funded by the Navy Personnel R and D Center; and work still continues on the development of the Elaboration Theory. His next major integrative effort was a project to synthesize into a single procedure the state of the art in task analysis methodologies, which play an important role in planning the details of what to teach and the order in which to teach it. This project, funded by the Army's Training and Doctrine Command, resulted in the Extended Task Analysis Procedure (ETAP). Reigeluth's third effort to help integrate existing knowledge into a common knowledge base was this book, which took over two years to prepare. His most recent integrative effort was a project that has enabled him to integrate and extend all of his previous efforts. This project, funded by the Army's Training and Doctrine Command, resulted in the Extended Development Procedure (EDeP). EDeP includes a synthesis of what appears to be the best methods for such diverse forms of instruction as tutoring, lecture, discussion, group activities, individualized resources, and projects, plus a set of criteria for deciding which of these should be used when.

CONTENTS

Introduction   338
   Context: Scope And Limitations Of The Elaboration
     Theory   338
   History: Origins And Precursors   338
   Organization Of This Chapter   340
An Analogy   340
   Use Of The Elaboration Approach   341
Strategy Components   342
   1. An Elaborative Sequence   342
   2. A Learning-Prerequisite Sequence   356
   3. Summarizer   358
   4. Synthesizer   358
   5. Analogy   360
   6. Cognitive-Strategy Activator   361
   7. Learner Control   362
   Micro Strategies   363
   Summary Of Strategy Components   363
The Elaboration Model   364
   1. Present An Epitome   364
   2. Present Level-1 Elaborations   365
   3. Present Level-2 Elaborations   366
   4. Present Additional Levels Of Elaboration   366
   Other Comments   366
   Summary Of The Elaboration Model   367
Variations Of The Model   368
   The Three "Organizations"   368
   Other Kinds Of Variations   369
   Summary Of Variations   370
Using The Elaboration Theory   370
Support For Validity   372
   Research Support   372
   Learning-Theory Support   373
   Support From Educational Practice   378
Conclusion   379

FOREWORD

The purpose of the Reigeluth–Merrill elaboration theory of instruction is to extend the Component Display Theory (CDT) to the macro level (i.e., to such concerns as selection, sequencing synthesizing, and systematic review of related ideas). In other words, its purpose is to integrate as much as possible of our current knowledge about learning and instruction on the macro level. Like CDT, it only deals with the cognitive domain; but unlike CDT, it already includes many motivational-strategy components, and work is currently underway to integrate more of Keller's work with the elaboration theory.

The elaboration theory's prescriptions are based both on an analysis of the structure of knowledge and on an understanding of cognitive processes and learning theories. As with other theories, goals form the basis for prescribing models. The most important aspect of all three models is a specific kind of simple-to-complex sequence, which is an extension of Ausubel's *subsumptive sequencing*, Bruner's *spiral curriculum*, and Norman's *web learning*. This sequencing pattern helps to build stable cognitive structures, provides a meaningful context for all instructional content, and provides meaningful application-level learning from the very first "lesson." Gagné's learning-prerequisite sequences are then introduced only as they become necessary within each lesson, and systematic integration and review are provided at the end of each lesson and unit. Also, each lesson is adjusted in certain ways to make it appropriate for the ability level of the students in relation to the complexity or difficulty of the content.

Like CDT, the Elaboration Theory organizes instruction in such a way as to facilitate learner control; but on the macro level this means control over selection and sequencing of ideas as well as control over frequency and timing of such strategy components as synthesizers and reviews. Simple-to-complex sequencing allows the learner to make an informed decision as to what ideas interest him or her the most and hence warrant "zooming in" for more detail about those ideas. The use of analogies is another important feature of the elaboration theory.

Although much work remains to be done to develop the Elaboration Theory to its full potential, it (like CDT) is indicative of the integrative, multiperspectived approach to model building and theory construction that is sorely needed at this point in the evolution of the discipline. Particularly useful right now would be some extensive research and field tests.

C. M. R.

The Elaboration Theory
of Instruction

INTRODUCTION

Context: Scope and Limitations of the Elaboration Theory

The field of instructional science is concerned with understanding and improving methods of instruction so as to make them more effective, more efficient, and more appealing. In Chapter 1 of this book, a distinction is made between the micro level (which deals only with methods for teaching a single idea, such as the use of examples of that idea) and the macro level (which deals only with methods that relate to several ideas, such as sequencing those ideas). The Elaboration Theory is exclusively on the *macro* level—it prescribes methods that deal with many related ideas, such as how to sequence them. (The preceding chapter in this book presents a compatible theory that deals only with the micro level.) Chapter 1 also describes three major kinds of instructional methods: organizational, delivery, and management. The Elaboration Theory makes no attempt to deal with either delivery or management strategies, although these are important variables that need to be integrated into any instructional model or theory if it is to be sufficiently comprehensive to be optimally useful to instructional developers and planners.

The Elaboration Theory thus deals only with organizational strategies at the macro level. The macro level is made up mainly of four problem areas. We have referred to these as the *four S's*: selection, sequencing, synthesizing, and summarizing of subject-matter content. The Elaboration Theory attempts to prescribe optimal methods in all four of these areas.

The Elaboration Theory of instruction prescribes that the instruction start with a special kind of overview that teaches a few general, simple, and fundamental (but not abstract) ideas. The remainder of the instruction presents progressively more detailed ideas, which elaborate on earlier ones. The theory also prescribes the use of prerequisite sequences within parts of the simple-to-complex sequence, and it prescribes the systematic use of review and synthesis, among other things (see section on "Strategy Components" later).

History: Origins and Precursors

During the past 10 or 15 years, considerable new knowledge has been generated about isolated aspects of macro strategies. Robert Gagné (1968, 1977) identified an important kind of relationship in subject matter: the *learning prerequisite* (see Chapter 4, this volume). The concept of a learning prerequisite involves the fact that some knowledge must be acquired before other knowledge can be acquired. One must understand the concept "volume" before one can understand the principle that describes the relationship between volume, pressure, and temperature. A complete set of learning prerequisites for a given idea comprises what is called a *learning hierarchy* (see Chapter 4). This has given rise to the hierarchical approach to task analysis. Various theorists have more complex methodologies for conducting more precise and thorough hierarchical task analyses (see, for example, the review by Bergan, 1980), but such complexity and precision is of questionable utility to instructional developers.

However, the learning prerequisite is only one important kind of relationship to guide instructional design. Another important one is represented by the information-processing approach to task analysis. This *procedural* type of relationship describes the order in which tasks must be performed, as opposed to the order in which they must be learned. One can *learn* how to do the last step in a procedure first, but one cannot *do* the last step first in a performance of that complete procedure. Gropper (1974), Landa (1974), P. Merrill (1971), Resnick (1973), and Scandura (1973) were among the first to emphasize the importance of this kind of relationship for instructional design on the macro level. For an excellent review of task-analysis methodologies, see Resnick (1976).

David Ausubel (1963, 1968) pioneered some important knowledge about kinds of *instructional sequences* that help instructional content to be more meaningful for a learner and that thereby help the instruction to result in better learning and retention. He advocated initiating instruction with general-level knowledge that "subsumes" the content that is to follow; the remainder of the instruction is then a process of *successive differentiation*—the gradual introduction of more detailed and specific knowledge about the general-level ideas. This is similar to (although much more highly developed than) Bruner's (1960) notion of a *spiral curriculum*. Recent developments under the rubric of *schema theory* (Anderson, Spiro, & Montague, 1977; Collins & Quillian, 1970; Lindsay & Norman, 1977; Rumelhart & Ortony, 1977) have reinforced and supported the general-to-detailed sequencing advocated by Ausubel. In fact, Norman's (1973) notion of *web learning* is similar to the spiral curriculum and successive differentiation patterns of sequencing instruction.

These isolated advances in our knowledge about methods of instruction on the macro level (i.e., hierarchical, information-processing, and cognitive-elaboration approaches to sequencing) have often appeared to compete with and even (in a superficial sense) occasionally contradict each other. But they each accurately and truthfully describe different aspects of the structure of knowledge, the process of learning, and/or the process of instruction. Therefore, the purpose in developing the Elaboration Theory was to create a comprehensive set of macro-level models that would integrate all of this recent knowledge in a way that would greatly improve our ability to design good instruction. In the process of doing this, it was sometimes necessary to attempt to fill in gaps that became apparent in our knowledge about instruction at the macro level.

Organization of This Chapter

The Elaboratory Theory is comprised of: (1) three *models* of instruction; and (2) a *system for prescribing* those models on the basis of the goals for a whole course of instruction.* Like all models of instruction, each of these three models is made up of *strategy components*. It is important to understand that the Elaboration Theory is by no means static; rather, it continues to develop and improve as research reveals weak strategy components that should be eliminated from the models and new strategy components that should be integrated into the models.

The following are the major sections of this chapter:

1. An *analogy* that helps to give a general idea of what the Elaboration Theory is.
2. A description of each individual *strategy component*.
3. A description of the *general model* (i.e., the common features of the three models that comprise the Elaboration Theory).
4. A description of the ways in which the *three models* differ from each other and the system for *prescribing* when each model should be used.
5. A summary of some *procedures for using* the elaboration model in the development or evaluation of instruction.
6. Some support for the *validity* of the Elaboration Theory.

AN ANALOGY

A good introduction to the nature of the Elaboration Theory of instruction is an analogy with a zoom lens. Studying a subject matter "through" the elaboration model is similar in many respects to studying a picture through a zoom lens on a movie camera. A person starts with a wide-angle view, which allows him or her to see the major parts of the picture and the major relationships among those parts (e.g., the composition or balance of the picture), but without any detail.

The person then zooms in on a part of the picture. Assume that, instead of being continuous, the zoom operates in steps or discrete levels. Zooming in one level on a given part of the picture allows the person to see more about each of the major subparts. After having studied those subparts and their interrelationships, the person could then zoom back out to the wide-angle view to review the other parts of the whole picture and to review the context of this part within the whole picture.

The person continues this pattern of zooming in one level (or one additional level) to see the major subparts of a part and zooming back out for context and

---

*Editor's note: This pattern should be quite familiar by now!

review. The person could be forced to complete all of one level before proceeding to the next level. Or the person could be forced to go to the full depth of detail (to zoom in as far as the camera will go) on one part before proceeding to another part of the picture. Or the person could be allowed to choose to follow his or her own interests in viewing the picture, in which case the person can make an informed decision (on the basis of information from the wide-angle view) as to what part of the picture would interest him or her the most. The only restriction is that the person may not view any part of the picture unless he or she has already viewed it from the next higher (wider-angled) level.

In a similar way, the Elaboratory Theory of instruction starts the instruction with a special kind of *overview* of the simplest and most fundamental ideas within the subject matter; it adds a certain amount of *complexity* or *detail* to one part or apsect of the overview; it *reviews* the overview and shows the *relationships* between the most recent ideas and the ideas presented earlier; and it continues this pattern of elaboration followed by summary and synthesis until the desired level of complexity has been reached on all desired parts or aspects of the subject matter. It also allows for informed learner control over the selection and sequencing of content.

Of course, it must be remembered that the zoom-lens analogy is just an analogy and therefore that it has nonanalogous aspects. One such dissimilarity is that all the detail of the picture is actually present (although usually not noticed) in the wide-angle view, whereas the complexity is not there at all in the overview.

Now, some people, ask, "Don't you have to go through a lot of learning prerequisites (Gagné, 1968) to teach the overview?" The answer is a definite "No." In fact, like Bruner's (1960) *spiral curriculum*, few unmastered learning prerequisites (if any) exist at the level of the overview. As learners work to deeper levels of complexity, increasingly complex prerequisites exist, but many of them will already have been taught as parts of previous lessons. Hence, if prerequisites are held back until the lesson for which they are immediately necessary, there will be only a few prerequisites for a lesson at any level of complexity, and the learners will want to learn those prerequisites because they will see their importance for learning at the level of complexity that now interests them.

Use of the Elaboration Approach

The simple-to-complex sequence prescribed by the Elaboration Theory helps to ensure that the learner is always aware of the context and importance of the different ideas that are being taught. It allows the learner to learn at the level of complexity that is most appropriate and meaningful to him or her at any given state in the development of one's knowledge. And the learner never has to struggle through a series of learning prerequisites that are on too deep a level of complexity to be interesting or meaningful at the initial stages of instruction.

Unfortunately, a zoom-lens approach has not been widely used in instruction, in spite of its fundamental simplicity and intuitive rationale. Many textbooks begin with the "lens" zoomed in to the level of complexity deemed appropriate for the intended student population; and they proceed—with the "lens" locked on that level of complexity—to pan across the entire subject matter. This has unfortunate consequences for synthesis, retention, and motivation. Using a hierarchical approach, many instructional developers have used a sequence that in some ways resembles beginning with the lens zoomed all the way in and proceeding in a highly fragmented manner to pan across a small part and zoom out a bit on that part; pan across another small part and zoom out a bit, and so on, until the whole scene has been covered and, to some limited degree, has been integrated by the very end of the instruction. This has also had unfortunate consequences for synthesis, retention, and motivation. And some educators have intuitively groped for an elaboration-type approach with no guidelines on how to do it. This has resulted in a good deal less effectiveness than is possible for maximizing synthesis, retention, and motivation.

The major reason for the lack of utilization of an elaboration approach in instruction is probably that the hierarchical approach has been well-articulated and is a natural outgrowth of a strong behavioral orientation in educational psychology, which was very much in vogue until recently. This in effect put "blinders" on most of the few people who have been working on instructional-design strategies and methodology.

The Elaboration Theory does not reject the hierarchical approach; in point of fact, an idea cannot be learned before its true learning prerequisites have been learned. Rather the Elaboration Theory integrates hierarchical sequencing within the overall structure of an elaborative sequence. As an approach that attempts to integrate the best strategies of a wide variety of researchers and theoretical perspectives, the Elaboration Theory prescribes the use of a number of major strategy components, including learning prerequisite sequencing, at various points during the instruction.

STRATEGY COMPONENTS

The Elaboration Theory presently utilizes seven major strategy components: (1) a special type of simple-to-complex sequence (for the main structure of the course); (2) learning-prerequisite sequences (within individual lessons of the course); (3) summarizers; (4) synthesizers; (5) analogies; (6) cognitive-strategy activators; and (7) a learner-control format. These components are described briefly here.

1. An Elaborative Sequence

An elaborative sequence is a special kind of *simple-to-complex sequence.*But there are many different ways to form a simple-to-complex sequence for a single course, and naturally some of them are better than others. For example, one could start a history course by summarizing the major events in history, then proceed to provide a little more detail about each of those events and to add a few of the next most important events, and so on, until the desired level of detail is reached for that course. The use of such things as overviews (Hartley & Davies, 1976), advance organizers (Ausubel, 1968), web learning (Norman, 1973), and the spiral curriculum (Bruner, 1960) are all attempts to use a simple-to-complex sequence to some degree. The Elaboration Theory proposes that an *elaborative sequence* (of which there are three kinds) is the best for reasons that are outlined here, but further research is needed to adequately test this hypothesis.

An *elaborative sequence* is a simple-to-complex sequence in which: (1) the general ideas *epitomize* rather than summarize the ideas that follow; and (2) the epitomizing is done on the basis of a *single type of content.*

Epitomizing versus Summarizing

Epitomizing differs from summarizing in two important ways. It entails: (1) presenting a very *small number* of the ideas that are to be taught in the course; and (2) presenting them at a concrete, meaningful, *application level.* On the other hand, summarizing usually entails presenting a considerably larger number of the ideas but at a more superficial, abstract, memorization level. For example, a summary of an introductory course in economics might present a label for, or even a statement of, each of the most important principles of economics, whereas an *epitome* of that course would teach the one or two most fundamental and simple principles (such as the law of supply and demand) at the application level. The application level is what Merrill refers to in Chapter 9 as the *use a generality* level, and in this case it means that the student would be able to use each of those principles to predict or explain novel cases. To epitomize is not to lightly preview all of the important course content; rather it is to teach (on an application level, complete with examples and practice that enable the learner to relate it to previous knowledge and experience) a *few fundamental and representative ideas* that convey the essence of the entire content. Those ideas are chosen such that all the remaining course content provides more detail or more complex knowledge about them.

Single Type of Content

With respect to a single type of content, the process of epitomizing is done with just one of three types of content: concepts, procedures, or principles. A *concept* is a set of objects, events, or symbols that have certain characteristics in common. Knowing a concept entails being able to identify, recognize, classify, or describe what something is. For example, "sonnet" is a concept. A *procedure* is a set of actions that are intended to achieve an end. It is often referred to as a skill, a technique, or a method. Knowing a procedure entails knowing how to do something. For example, "the steps for critically analyzing a sonnet" are a procedure. A *principle* is a change relationship; it indicates the relationship between a change in one thing and a change in something else. It may also be called a hypothesis, a proposition, a rule, or a law, depending on the amount of evidence for its truthfulness. Usually, it describes causes or effects, either by identifying what will happen as a result of a given change (the effect) or why something happens (the cause). For example, "including an introduction in a written composition will result in a more effective communication" is a principle.*

One of these three types of content—concept, procedure, or principle—is chosen as the most important type for achieving the general goals of the course. Henceforth the elaboration sequence is characterized as having a *conceptual organization*, a *procedural organization*, or a *theoretical organization*, in which the respective type of content (which is called the *organizing content*) is epitomized at the beginning of the course and is gradually elaborated on throughout the remainder of the course, in such a way that most lessons not only elaborate on a previous lesson but also epitomize several later lessons. The other two types of content and rote facts (which are all called the *supporting content*) also appear throughout the length of the course, but they are only introduced when they are highly relevant to the particular organizing content ideas that are being presented at each point in the course sequence.

In essence the process of epitomizing entails: (1) selecting one type of content as the organizing content (concepts, principles, or procedures); (2) listing all of the organizing content that is to be taught in the course; (3) selecting a few organizing content ideas that are the most basic, simple, and/or fundamental; and (4) presenting those ideas at the application level rather than the more superficial and abstract memorization level. Detailed procedures have been developed to guide instructional developers, and they are summarized later in this chapter.

General versus Simple versus Abstract

Because the terms *general, simple,* and *abstract* are often confused, we discuss them here. These terms are parts of three different continua: (1) general to detailed; (2) simple-to-complex; and (3) abstract to concrete (Reigeluth, 1979a). These three continua are illustrated in Fig. 10.1. The first two are very similar to each other, but the third is very different.

The *general-to-detailed* continuum refers primarily to a continuum formed by subdividing ideas (either concepts or procedures) or by lumping ideas (subordinate concepts or subprocedures) together. *General* has breadth and inclusiveness (i.e., lots of things lumped together), whereas *detailed* is usually narrow (subdivisions). In Fig. 10.1(a), "polar bear" is a more detailed concept than "animal"; it requires finer discriminations (polar bears are more similar to other kinds of bears than animals are to nonanimals) and has fewer examples (there are fewer polar bears than there are animals). Since general concepts entail fewer and grosser discriminations, they are also simpler than detailed concepts.

---

*Editor's note: See Chapter 1, p. 14, for more about principles.

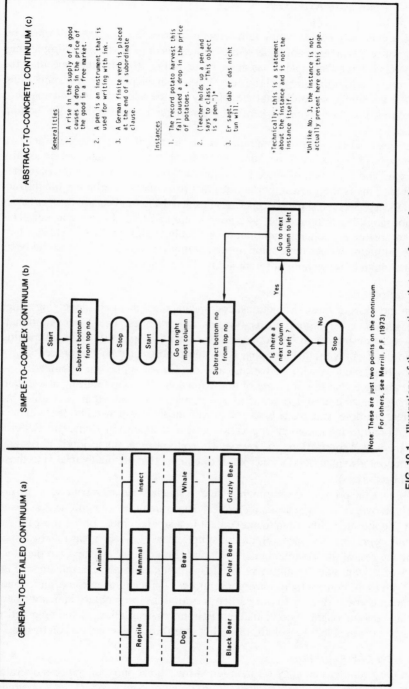

FIG. 10.1 Illustrations of three continua that are often confused.

345

The *simple-to-complex* continuum refers primarily to a continuum formed by adding or removing parts of ideas (either principles or procedures). "Simple" has few parts, whereas "complex" has many parts. In Fig. 10.1(b), the procedure for subtracting multidigit numbers is more complex than the procedure for subtracting single-digit numbers. Additional complexity can be added by introducing sub-procedures for "borrowing" when the top number is smaller than the bottom number.

The *abstract-to-concrete* continuum refers to tangibility, and there are two major types of tangibility. First, *generalities* are abstract, and instances are usually concrete: The definition of a tree is not tangible, but a specific tree (an object) is tangible. This is the most important abstract-to-concrete continuum for instructional theory. Second, some concepts are considered abstract because their instances are not tangible. "Intelligence" is a good example of an abstract concept. This second abstract-to-concrete continuum is largely irrelevant for our present purposes, although it does have some important implications as to what would be an optimal model for teaching different kinds of concepts.

The Epitome

On the basis of these distinctions, epitomizing always entails identifying either very *general* or very *simple* ideas, but *not abstract* ones. The concept "animal" is no more abstract than the concept "polar bear," the procedure for subtracting whole numbers without borrowing is no more abstract than the procedure for subtracting fractions with borrowing, and the law of supply and demand is no more abstract than the principle of utility maximization. Epitomizing also entails teaching the epitomized content at the application level—that is, with some concrete examples and practice, as well as with an abstract generality. (See Chapter 9 for more information about application-level instruction.) In essence the elaboration theory's "special kind of overview" epitomizes a single kind of content (although it also includes the other kinds of content that are highly related to those epitomized ideas).

Because the process of epitomizing yields a special kind of overview, we do not call it an overview—we call it an *epitome*. The content for an epitome is selected by: (1) epitomizing the organizing content to a small number of the most fundamental, representative, general, and/or simple ideas (i.e., the ideas that best subsume the rest of the organizing content); and (2) including whatever of the other types of content that are highly relevant (including learning prerequisities). Fig. 10.2 shows the content for a conceptual epitome, a procedural epitome, and a theoretical epitome. Contrary to our earlier prescriptions, preliminary indications are that an epitome ought to contain about 10 hours of instruction, including practice exercises (Pratt, 1982; Reigeluth, 1982), but more research is needed on this issue.

Levels of Elaboration

In the zoom-lens analogy we mentioned that the zooming-in process operates in steps or levels. Each level provides more detail or complexity about something in the preceding level. Hence, the *first level* of elaboration elaborates on the

Content for a Conceptual Epitome for an Introductory Course in Statistics
1. Organizing content (concepts)
   Kinds of measures
      a. Elevation (or central tendency)
      b. Spread
      c. Proportion
      d. Relationship
   Kinds of methods
      a. Description
      b. Estimation
      c. Hypothesis testing
2. Supporting content
   (Learning prerequisites for the aforementioned concepts)
Practically all concepts in statistics can be viewed as elaboration
on these concepts, through development of parts or kinds conceptual
structures.

Content for a Theoretical Epitome for an Introductory Course in Economics

1. Organizing content (principles)
   The law of supply and demand
      a. An increase in price causes an increase in the quantity
         supplied and a decrease in the quantity demanded.
      b. A decrease in price causes a decrease in the quantity
         supplied and an increase in the quantity demanded.
2. Supporting content
   The concepts of
      a. Price
      b. Quantity supplied
      c. Quantity demanded
      d. Increase
      e. Decrease
Practically all principles of economics can be viewed as elaborations
on the law of supply and demand, including those that relate to mon-
opoly, regulation, price fixing, and planned economies.

Content for a Procedural Epitome for an Introductory Course in Literature

1. Organizing content (procedures)
   There are four major steps in the multidimensional analysis
   and interpretation of creative literature.
      a. Identifying elements of the dramatic framework--
         character and plot.
      b. Combining the elements into composites appropriate
         for analysis of their literal meaning--analysis of
         character in terms of plot.
      c. Figuratively interpreting the elements--symbolism
         through character, mood, tone.
      d. Making a judgement of worth--personal relevance,
         universality.

FIG. 10.2   (continued)

(This procedure is simplified by introducing only <u>two</u> elements for the analyses in a and b, <u>three</u> in c, and <u>two</u> in d. It is further simplified by introducing only those procedures and concepts necessary for the analysis and interpretation of a <u>short poem</u>. Complexity is later added by increasing the number of elements used in each stage of analysis or interpretation and by introducing procedures and concepts needed for analyzing and interpreting more complicated types of creative literature.)

2. Supporting content
        Concepts necessary for performing the procedure in 1.
            a. Character
            b. Plot
            c. Symbolism
            d. Mood
            e. Tone
            f. Universality
Practically all procedures for analyzing and interpreting creative literature can be viewed as elaborations on these four steps.

FIG. 10.2   The instructional content for a conceptual epitome, a procedural epitome, and a theoretical epitome.

organizing content presented in the epitome; the *second level* elaborates on the organizing content presented in the first level, and so on. A lesson on the first level is in effect an epitome of all those lessons on the second level that elaborate on it. Figure 10.3 shows a partial example of a level-1 lesson by showing some organizing content that elaborates on the conceptual epitome in Fig. 10.2, some organizing content that elaborates on the procedure epitome in Fig. 10.2, and some organizing content that elaborates on the theoretical epitome in Fig. 10.2. The most important supporting content is also listed.

To give a clearer idea of what each of the three types of elaborative sequences—conceptual, procedural, and theoretical—is like, it is necessary to understand a little about the structure of knowledge. A *knowledge structure* is something that shows relationships among pieces of knowledge (i.e., among facts, concepts, principles, and procedures). The elaboration theory proposes that there are four major types of relationships that are important for purposes of instruction: conceptual relationships, procedural relationships, theoretical relationships, and learning-prerequisite relationships (Reigeluth, Merrill, & Bunderson, 1978; Reigeluth, Merrill, Wilson, & Spiller, 1980). The first three kinds of relationships are described next, and learning-prerequisite relationships are described later under strategy component 2, *A Learning Prerequisite Sequence.*

A *conceptual structure* shows superordinate/coordinate/subordinate relationships among ideas. There are three important types of conceptual structures: *parts* conceptual structures, which show concepts that are components of a given concept; *kinds* conceptual structures, which show concepts that are varieties or types of a given concept; and *matrices* or tables, which are combinations of two or more conceptual structures. Figs. 10.4, 10.5, and 10.6 show examples of each kind of conceptual structure.

Content for an Elaboration on the Conceptual Epitome

1. Organizing content (concepts)
   Kinds of measures

a.1 Mean	a.2 Median	a.3 Mode
b.1 Variance	b.2 Standard deviation	
c.1 Percent	c.2 Decimal	c.3 Fraction
d.1 r_s	d.2 r_{pb}	d.3 r_ϕ

2. Supporting content
   (Learning prerequisites for the aforementioned concepts)
   Additional elaborations would define kinds of methods for each
   kind of measure (e.g., methods of hypothesis testing for spread).

Content for an Elaboration on the Theoretical Epitome

1. Organizing content (principles)
   a. Effects of changes in supply schedules on equilibrium price.
   b. Effects of changes in demand schedules on equilibrium price.
   c. The principle of why changes occur in supply schedules or
      demand schedules.
2. Supporting content
   a. The concepts of supply, supply schedule, and supply curve.
   b. The concepts of demand, demand schedule, and demand curve.
   c. The concept of changes in supply schedules or demand
      schedules.
   d. The concept of equilibrium price.
   Beyond this point, elaborations would split into those that
   elaborate on the supply side (i.e., production and costs) and
   those that elaborate on the demand side (i.e., consumption and
   utility).

Content for an Elaboration on the Procedural Epitome

1. Organizing content* (procedures)
   a. Procedures for identifying the remaining elements of the
      dramatic framework: setting, perspective, and language
   b. Procedures for combining elements into appropriate compo-
      sites for analysis of literal meaning:
         -Character, plot, and setting
         -Perspective, character, and plot
         -Language
2. Supporting content:
   a. Concepts: setting, perspective, language, imagery
   b. Procedure: the analysis of patterns of imagery
   *This organizing content elaborates only on steps a and b (which
   must be elaborated simultaneously because of their interrelatedness). The elaboration involves the addition of elements that
   must be identified (stage a) and analyzed in combination
   (stage b).

FIG. 10.3 The instructional content for level-1 elaborations on the conceptual,
theoretical, and procedural epitome in FIG. 10.2.

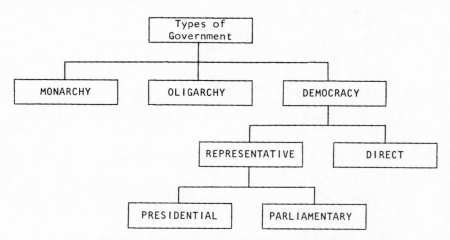

FIG. 10.4   An example of a kinds conceptual structure.

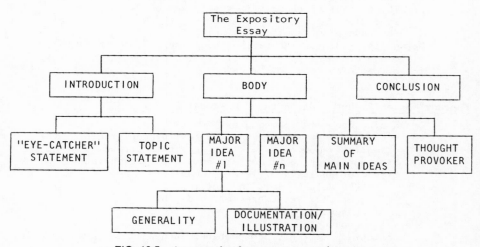

FIG. 10.5   An example of a parts conceptual structure.

A *procedural structure* shows relationships among steps of a procedure. There are two important kinds of procedural relationships: *procedural-order* relationships, which specify the order(s) for performing the steps of a procedure; and *procedural-decision* relationships, which describe the factors necessary for deciding which alternative procedure or subprocedure to use in a given situation. Figure 10.7 and Fig. 10.8 show examples of each kind of procedural structure.

A *theoretical structure,* or theoretical model, shows change relationships among events. There are two major kinds of theoretical structures. The most common kind of theoretical structure is one that describes *natural* phenomena—that is, it is a branching chain of interrelated *descriptive* principles. The other important

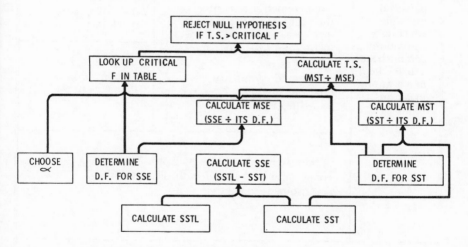

	REPTILES	MAMMALS	BIRDS	FISH	INSECTS
HERBIVORES	TURTLES ...	COWS ...	CHICKADEES ...	MINNOWS ...	ANTS ...
CARNIVORES	SNAKES ...	LIONS ...	VULTURES ...	SHARKS ...	LADY BUGS ...
OMNIVORES	LEOPARD LIZARDS ...	DOGS ...	ROBINS ...	CARP ...	BLACK STINK BUGS ...

FIG. 10.6   A portion of a matrix structure (or table) combining two kinds conceptual structures.

KEY: In this matrix, each box is a kind of both its row heading and its column heading.

FIG. 10.7   An example of a procedural-order structure.

KEY: The arrow between two boxes on different levels means that the lower box must be performed before the higher box can be performed.

kind describes phenomena that optimize (or sometimes merely influence) some desired outcome—that is, it is a branching chain of interrelated *prescriptive* principles. Usually it will merely identify the desired outcome(s) (e.g., as a heading), and then prescribe the "causes" in a way that shows how they should all be interrelated. Theoretical structures can be arranged on a continuum from purely descriptive to purely prescriptive, in which case a purely prescriptive theoretical structure (or model) is very similar to a procedural-order structure. Figure 10.9 and Fig. 10.10 show examples of each.

EB FLOW CHART FOR MATCHED PAIRS

SELECTION CRITERIA

For two independent samples see page 302.	Parametric tests on means. These tests are equivalent to each other. They apply also to medians if both distributions are assumed symmetric.	Have M_1, M_2, S_1, S_2, r_{12} already been computed? No	Better-known method
			Quicker method
			Yes
		p. 251	

Relatively powerful methods which can be used to demonstrate a difference in elevation in various limited senses	Nonparametric tests of the null hypothesis that difference scores are distributed symmetrically around zero. (Remember symmetry does not imply normality.) pp. 274, 349, 251	Powerful, fairly quick test
		Very quick test with lower power than any above
	A nonparametric test on medians. This test applies also to means if both distributions are assumed symmetric.	
p. 296		

A method with power comparable to EB10 which can demonstrate a range of complete dominance

p. 296

FIG. 10.8   (continued)

More About Epitomizing

Considering these three major kinds of knowledge structures, we can now elaborate a bit on the nature of the three types of elaborative sequences and how each differs from a summarizing approach to simple-to-complex sequencing.

Procedural content can be sequenced in any of five major ways: (1) forward chaining, which occurs at a single level of complexity and entails teaching all the

METHODS

EB7*★★★	***t* TEST FOR MATCHED PAIRS** Compute $D = X_1 - X_2$ for each person. $t = \dfrac{M_D}{S_D/\sqrt{N}}$ **df** $= N - 1$ M_D, S_D are the mean and standard deviation of D's <div align="right">p. 344</div>
EB7a★	**SANDLER *A*, MODIFIED** Compute $D = X_1 - X_2$ for each person. $A' = \dfrac{(\Sigma D)^2}{\Sigma D^2}$ <div align="right">p. 345</div>
EB7b★★★	***t* TEST FOR MATCHED DATA USING INTERMEDIATE STATISTICS** $t = \dfrac{M_1 - M_2}{\sqrt{\dfrac{S_1^2 + S_2^2 - 2r_{12}S_1 S_2}{N}}}$ **df** $= N - 1$ <div align="right">p. 347</div>
EB8★★	**WILCOXON SIGNED-RANKS TEST FOR MATCHED PAIRS** For each person compute $D = X_1 - X_2$. Then use Method **EA4** (p. 286) to test the null hypothesis $\mu_D = 0$. <div align="right">p. 348</div>
EB9★★	**SIGN TEST FOR MATCHED PAIRS** Count the number of matched pairs for which $X_1 > X_2$, and the number for which $X_1 < X_2$. Redefine N as the sum of these two numbers, thus ignoring pairs for which $X_1 = X_2$. Enter the two numbers counted into Method **PA1** (p. 436) or Method **PA2** (p. 437). <div align="right">p. 349</div>
EB10★★	**SIGN TEST FOR PERCENTILE SCORES** Divide the scale at some point P; no score in either group should exactly equal P. Count the number of pairs for which $X_1 < P$ and $X_2 > P$. Count the number of pairs for which $X_1 > P$ and $X_2 < P$. Redefine N as the sum of these two numbers. Enter the two numbers into Method **PA1** (p. 436) or **PA2** (p. 437). <div align="right">p. 350</div>
EB11★	**SIGN TEST FOR EACH POINT ON AN OD CURVE** See Method Outline <div align="right">p. 351</div>

FIG. 10.8 An example of a procedural-decision structure.

steps in the order in which they are performed; (2) backward chaining, which also occurs at a single level of complexity but entails teaching all the steps in the opposite of the order in which they are performed; (3) a hierarchical sequence, which entails teaching all possible substeps (parts) of a step before integrating them, then doing the same for another step, and so on, until all parts have finally been taught and integrated; (4) a general-to-detailed sequence based on summarizing, which

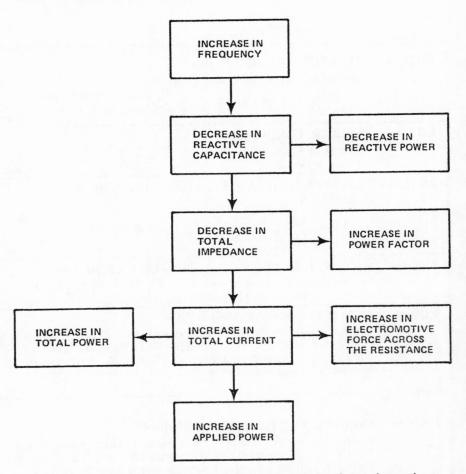

Key: The arrow between two boxes means that the change in one box causes the change in the other box to occur.

FIG. 10.9   An example of a descriptive theoretical structure.

entails something like presenting a general-level flow chart or list of all steps (or clusters of steps) at the very beginning of the instruction, followed by elaborating them down to the application level; and (5) a simple-to-complex sequence based on epitomizing, which entails presenting the shortest path (or shortest procedure) at the application level at the very beginning of the instruction, following by elaborating it out to the desired breadth and complexity of alternative paths (or procedures), each additional path usually being progressively more complex. These last two methods respectively entail: (1) abstract breadth followed by elaborating down to the application level; and (2) narrow application followed by elaborating out to the required breadth and complexity of paths (or procedures).

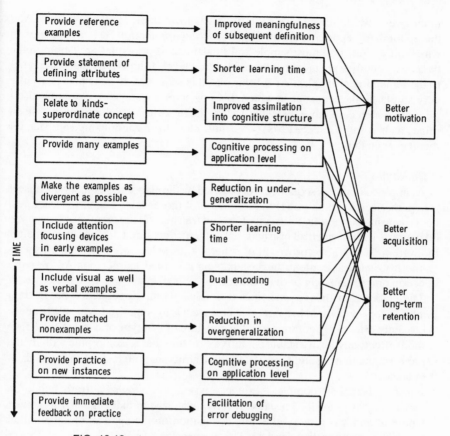

FIG. 10.10   An example of a prescriptive-theoretical structure.

KEY: Each arrow means "causes."
NOTE: In the extreme, the prescriptive-theoretical structure is practically identical to a procedural-order structure, in that the middle and right-hand columns of boxes drop out (or more precisely, are incorporated into a statement of the goals and conditions that provide the basis for prescribing it).

In the case of *concepts*, the summarizing approach is also one of *abstract breadth*: It is a sequence in which all of the important concepts are listed in the overview, followed by elaborating each down to the application level. And the epitomizing approach is also one of *narrow application*: It is a sequence in which only a few (the most general and inclusive) concepts are taught in the overview, but they are taught at the application level, followed by elaborating out to the remaining concepts (which are configured as being "down" on a conceptual structure because they are more detailed and less inclusive).

Finally, in the case of *principles,* the summarizing approach is also one of *abstract breadth*: It is a sequence in which all of the important principles are listed in the overview, followed by elaborating each down to the application level. And the epitomizing approach is still one of *narrow application*: It is a sequence in which only a few (the most simple and fundamental) principles are taught in the overview, but they are taught at the application level, followed by elaborating out to the remaining principles. As it turns out, this sequence of principles is usually very similar to the sequence in which those principles were discovered in a discipline, in which case those texts that follow the historical development of a discipline (such as some science texts) come quite close to an epitomizing approach for theoretical content.

Rationale

A simple-to-complex sequence is prescribed by the elaboration theory because it is hypothesized to result in: (1) the formation of more stable cognitive structures, hence causing better long-term retention and transfer; (2) the creation of meaningful contexts within which all instructional content is acquired, hence causing better motivation,* and (3) the provision of general knowledge about the major aspects of the instructional content, hence enabling informed learner control over the selection and sequencing of that content.

The elaboration theory prescribes a simple-to-complex sequence based on a *single kind of relationship* in the content because it is hypothesized to enable learners: (1) to more effectively comprehend the structure of that type of content and hence to more effectively form a stable cognitive structure that is isomorphic with it; and (2) to form the most useful type of cognitive structure with respect to the goals of the course.

Finally, a (simple-to-complex) sequence based on *epitomizing* (rather than on summarizing) is prescribed because it is hypothesized to make the learning more meaningful and less rote by effecting acquisition on the application level rather than on the memorization level.** This is expected to result in easier and more enjoyable learning and better retention.

Perhaps the best instructional model will be one that uses some combination of summarizing and epitomizing. Some support for these prescriptions is provided in the last section of this chapter, but there is clearly a great need for research in this area.

2. A Learning-Prerequisite Sequence

A learning-prerequisite sequence (Gagné, 1968) is based on a *learning structure,* or learning hierarchy. (The term *learning hierarchy* has come to mean many different things to different people. For instance, may consider parts conceptual

---

*Editor's note: This is similar to Keller's concern for *relevance* (Chapter 11). Also, for a discussion of the effects of a simple-to-complex sequence on a student's *expectancy for success,* see Chapter 11.

**Editor's note: This also relates to Keller's concern for *relevance* (Chapter 11, pp. 406–415).

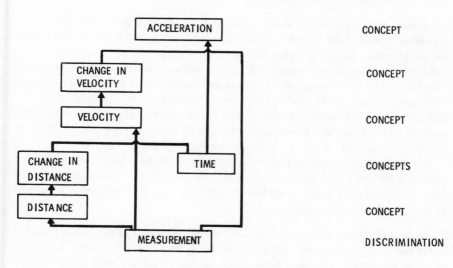

Key: The arrow between two boxes on different levels means that the lower box must be
learned before the higher box can be learned.

FIG. 10.11   An example of a learning structure.

structures to be learning hierarchies. Hence, we prefer to use the less ambiguous
term, learning structure.) A learning structure is a structure that shows what facts
or ideas *must* be learned before a given idea can be learned (see Fig. 10.11 for an
example). Hence, it shows the *learning prerequisites* for an idea. For example,
one cannot learn what a quadratic equation is until he or she has learned what its
defining characteristics (e.g., in this case "second power" and "unknown variable") are. Similarly, one cannot learn the principle that "force equals mass times
acceleration" until he or she has learned the individual concepts of mass, acceleration, and force. It is also necessary to understand the relationships represented by
"times" and "equals." Before the learner has mastered these ideas, he or she is
incapable of understanding the principle "force = mass x acceleration." However,
the learner is capable of substituting values and calculating results (a rote
procedure).

Learning prerequisites can be considered *critical components* of an idea. The
critical components of principles are: (1) concepts; and (2) change relationships.
The critical components of concepts are: (1) defining attributes; and (2) their
interrelationships (e.g., conjunctive and disjunctive). And the critical components
of procedures are, in the case of regular steps (i.e., the steps represented by rectan-
gles in a flow chart): (1) a more detailed description of the actions involved in the
step (i.e., the verbs that describe the step's actions in greater detail); and (2) concepts that relate to those actions (e.g., objects of or tools for the actions), or, in the
case of decision steps (i.e., the steps represented by diamonds in a flow chart):

(1) a more detailed description of the factors that influence the decision; (2) concepts that relate to those factors; and (3) rules for considering the factors in making the decision (see Reigeluth & Merrill, 1981, for details).

Learning-prerequisite structures are often confused with the other three types of structures. The best means of differentiating learning structures from the other three types is to consider that learning prerequisites must be acquired before the learner is *able to learn* the subsequent idea. On the other hand, the ideas in conceptual, procedural, and theoretical structures can be learned in any order (although we believe that some orders are better than others.

A *learning-prerequisite sequence* is the presentation of content ideas in an order such that an idea is not presented until after all of its learning prerequisites have been presented (that is, all of its learning prerequisites that the students had not mastered before this lesson).

Relationship to the Other Kinds of Structures.   Learning prerequisites exist for every box in all three of the other kinds of structures (conceptual, procedural, and theoretical). Hence, you could picture, say, a kinds conceptual structure on a sheet of paper that is held horizontally in the air. Then, there would be a learning structure dangling down from each box in that conceptual structure. It is also common for a concept in a conceptual structure to also appear as part of a principle in a theoretical structure or as part of a step in a procedural structure.

3. Summarizer

In instruction it is important to systematically review what has been learned, so as to help prevent forgetting. A summarizer is a stretegy component that provides: (1) a *concise statement* of each idea and fact that has been taught; (2) a reference example (i.e., a typical, easy-to-remember example) for each idea; and (3) some diagnostic, self-test practice items for each idea. There are two kinds of summarizers in the elaboration theory. One is an *internal summarizer,* which comes at the end of each lesson and summarizes only the ideas and facts that are taught in that lesson. The other is a *within-set summarizer,* which summarizes all of the ideas and facts that have been taught so far in the "set of lessons" on which the learner is currently working. A set of lessons is any one lesson, plus the lesson on which it elaborates, plus all of the other lessons (coordinate lessons) that also elaborate on that lesson (see Fig. 10.12).

4. Synthesizer

In instruction it is important to periodically interrelate and integrate the individual ideas that have been taught, so as to: (1) provide students with that valuable kind of knowledge; (2) facilitate a deeper understanding of the individual ideas through comparison and contrast; (3) increase the meaningfulness and motivational effect of the new knowledge by showing how it fits within a larger picture (Ausubel,

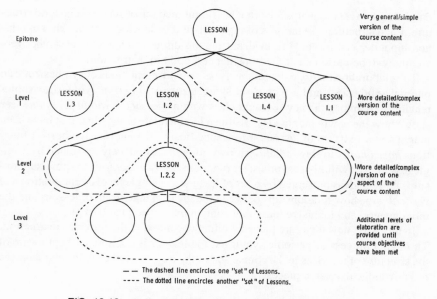

FIG. 10.12   A diagrammatic representation of a set of lessons.

1968; Keller, Chapter 11, this volume); and (4) increase retention (i.e., reduce forgetting) by creating additional links among the new knowledge and between the new knowledge and a learner's relevant prior knowledge (Ausubel, 1964; E. Gagné, 1978; Norman, Rumelhart, & the LNR Research group, 1975; Quillian, 1968).

In the elaboration theory, a *synthesizer* is a strategy component for relating and integrating ideas of a *single type* (e.g., for relating and integrating a set of concepts or a set of procedures or a set of principles). This is done by presenting: (1) a generality in the form of one (or more) of the kinds of knowledge structures (previously described) and, if necessary, explaining what it means; (2) a few integrated reference examples—ones that illustrate the relationships among the ideas; and (3) a few integrated, diagnostic, self-test practice items. A single type of relationship is advocated for each synthesizer so as to not confuse the learner as to what kind of relationship is being depicted by any given line in the diagram. Hence, kinds conceptual relationship should be presented in a different synthesizer (diagram) from parts conceptual relationships (unless a table or matrix structure is used to combine them in a clear way). And procedural and theoretical relationships should be presented apart from each other and from conceptual relationships, even though the same concept (e.g., velocity) may appear in all of those different synthesizers. Like the alternative conceptual relationships, descriptive and prescriptive theoretical relationships should be presented separately; but procedural order and procedural-decision relationships are often best combined into a single procedural structure. Each structure—regardless of type—should be labeled as to the kind of relationship it depicts. It should be evident from this discussion that several synthesizers are likely to be presented at the same general point in instruction.

The elaboration theory calls for the use of two different kinds of synthesizers: an internal synthesizer and a within-set synthesizer. An *internal synthesizer* shows relationships among the newly taught ideas within a lesson. A *within-set synthesizer* shows how the newly taught ideas within a lesson relate to the ideas that have been taught so far in its set of lessons. More specifically, the internal synthesizer functions *horizontally* to show relationships among ideas that were presented by a single lesson. The within-set synthesizer functions both *horizontally* to show relationships among ideas presented by a set of lessons at a single level of elaboration and *vertically* to show relationships between the ideas in that group of lessons and the more general and inclusive ideas that contain them (see Fig. 10.12).

In this way, new ideas are placed within the context of the previous instruction. Through a process of periodic synthesis, the learner is continually kept aware of the structure of the ideas in the course and of the relevance of each individual piece of knowledge to related pieces.

5. Analogy

An analogy is an important strategy component in instruction because it makes it easier to understand new ideas by relating them to familiar ideas (Dreistadt, 1969; Ortony, Reynolds, & Arter, 1978; Raven & Cole, 1978). An *analogy* describes similarities between some new ideas and some familiar ones that are outside of the content area of immediate interest. Fig. 10.13 shows examples of an analogy. An analogy is helpful whenever the to-be-acquired ideas are difficult to understand and lack direct meaningfulness for the learner. By relating this difficult and unfamiliar content to familiar knowledge in some other content area, the new content acquires meaning; it becomes familiar.* For example, a lesson or group of lessons on meter in poetry can be introduced by an analogy that compares metrical patterns in poems to rhythms in music.

As long as the instruction carefully identifies the limits of the relationship and the points at which the analogy breaks down, an analogy can be a strong and effective strategy component. The larger the number of similarities, the more effective an analogy will be. Also, the larger the number of ideas that can be made familiar through the analogic comparison, the more useful the analogy will be. Moreover, the greater the familiarity and meaningfulness of the analogy to the learner, the more useful it will be. However, if the number of differences between the new and analogic ideas is great, then the analogy may be more confusing than helpful.

---

*Editor's note: For a discussion of the motivational effects of analogies, see Chapter 11, pp. 403–404.

NEW IDEA   ANALOGIC IDEA

1. RESISTOR   VALVE
    BOTH REDUCE THE AMOUNT OF FLOW OF SOMETHING.

2. EXPERIMENTAL ERROR   STATIC
    RANDOM INTERFERENCE IS A CENTRAL PART OF BOTH.

3. HUMAN BRAIN   COMPUTER
    BOTH STORE, PROCESS, AND RETRIEVE INFORMATION.

4. TOUCHING KEYS   TOUCHING A HOT STOVE
    BOTH HAVE THE SAME QUICK MOVEMENT AND LIGHT TOUCH.

FIG. 10.13 Examples of analogic ideas that can be used to facilitate learning new ideas.

More than one analogy may be available for use at a given time. In such a case, it is often advisable to include more than one, especially if there are considerable individual differences among the learners. Then each learner may be encouraged to skip some of the analogies and to choose the particular analogy that is most useful for him or her. It is also important to note that if highly similar analogous ideas are not part of a learner's prior knowledge, it will still be worth teaching them if the amount of learner effort that they save is greater than the amount of effort that their instruction costs.

6. Cognitive-Strategy Activator

Instruction is more effective to the extent that it requires learners to consciously or unconsciously use relevant cognitive strategies (Bruner, 1966; Gagné, 1977; Rigney, 1978), because how a student processes the instructional inputs is a crucial link in the learning process. *Cognitive strategies,* sometimes called generic skills, include learning skills and thinking skills that can be used across a wide variety of content areas (hence the name "generic"), such as creating mental images and identifying analogies.

Cognitive strategies can and should be activated during instruction. Two means of accomplishing this have been described by Rigney (1978). First, the instruction can be designed in such a way as to force the learner to use a particular cognitive strategy, often without the learner's being aware that he or she is, in fact, using that strategy. These *embedded* strategy activators include the instructional use of pictures, diagrams, mnemonics, analogy, paraphrases, and other devices that force the learner to manipulate or interact with the content in certain specific ways.

The second form of activator is the *detached*-strategy activator, which directs the learner to employ a previously acquired cognitive strategy. Directions to "create a mental image of the process you just learned" or to "think of an analogy for this concept" serve two functions. First, they improve the learner's acquisition and retention of the new content. But just as importantly, the conscious use of cognitive strategies increases the learner's competence with them.

In addition, cognitive strategies can and usually should be taught along with the subject matter of interest. The inclusion of detached-strategy activators, along with some brief instruction on the use of those cognitive strategies (for those learners unfamiliar with them) takes very little instructional time and increases both the effectiveness of the instruction and the learner's capacity to manipulate and understand other similar kinds of learning tasks. Such use of detached activators serves to provide practice that, if interspersed with appropriately labeled examples (embedded activators) for the same cognitive strategies, should help the learner to learn *how* to use those cognitive strategies on his or her own. It should also help the learner to learn *when* to use each cognitive strategy by focusing the learner's attention on the types of cognitive strategies that are appropriate for particular learning tasks. This latter strength becomes an important issue to consider for the next strategy component, learner control.

7. Learner Control

According to Merrill (1979), the concept of learner control refers, in its widest sense, to the freedom the learner has to take command of the *selection* and *sequencing* of: (1) the *content* to be learned (content control); (2) the *rate* at which he or she will learn (pace control); (3) the particular *instructional-strategy components* he or she selects and the *order* in which they are used (display control); and (4) the particular *cognitive strategies* the learner employs when interacting with the instruction (conscious cognition control). Merrill (1979) has described the characteristics of each of these types of control, as well as the limitations that instruction places on each. The elaboration theory affords possibilities for learner control over the selection of content (1), instructional-strategy components (3), and cognitive strategies (4). (The second category, pace, is only controllable at the micro level.) Merrill hypothesizes a *metacognition* model inside each learner that orchestrates how the learner chooses to study and learn. In terms of this model, we hypothesize that instruction generally increases in effectiveness, efficiency, and appeal to the extent that it permits informed learner control by motivated learners (with a few minor exceptions).

Many opportunities can and usually should be made for the informed learner to select and sequence instructional content and strategies and to activate cognitive strategies in accordance with his or her own metacognition model. With respect to learner control over *content*, elaborative sequencing makes it possible for a learner to pick that aspect of the epitome—or of any other lesson—that interests him or her the most and to study it next. Only a simple-to-complex sequence can allow a learner to make an *informed* decision about the selection of content. The learner can then continue to select more detail in that area, or he or she can return to an earlier lesson and pick a different aspect of it for further elaboration. For more information about learner control over content, see Merrill (1980) and Reigeluth (1979b).

Aside from the selection and sequencing of content, learner control can also be provided for the selection and sequencing of strategy components. The learner could be given greater freedom to decide when and if he or she wants to view a summarizer or a synthesizer or an analogy. The learner could also be given the freedom to select the cognitive strategies that are most appropriate and useful for him or her at that particular point in the instruction.

One of the major ways for giving competent learners a large measure of control over strategy is formating. Clearly *separated* and *labeled* instructional components make it easier for the learner to select and sequence these components according ot his or her personal needs and interests, including the selective review and study of summarizers and synthesizers. Also, clearly separated and labeled cognitive-strategy activators (detached or embedded) increase the learner's fluency with these strategies and permit the learner to choose how he or she will manipulate and interact with the content. They also facilitate review and study of these strategy components.

Micro Strategies

One additional aspect of the Elaboration Theory, although it could hardly be called a strategy component, is that it calls for the use of Merrill's Component Display Theory (see Chapter 9) for designing the instruction on the individual ideas and facts comprising the instructional content (i.e., for designing the instruction on the micro level).

Summary of Strategy Components

In summary, the Elaboration Theory is comprised of seven major strategy components (plus some minor ones that have not been mentioned):

1. An elaborative sequence.
2. A learning-prerequisite sequence.
3. A summarizer.
4. A synthesizer.
5. An analogy.

6. A cognitive-strategy activator.
7. A learner-control format.

In addition, the Elaboration Theory prescribes the use of Merrill's Component Display Theory (see Chapter 9) for teaching each individual idea and fact.

It is hypothesized that instruction is more effective, more efficient, and more appealing to the extent that each of these seven strategy components is employed in the instruction. However, these strategy components could be combined in many different ways. The elaboration model of instruction specifies a particular way of combining them that is hypothesized to optimize learning. The next section of this chapter describes that particular way of combining these strategy components.

THE ELABORATION MODEL

We said earlier that the Elaboration Theory is comprised of *three models* of instruction and a *system for prescribing* these models in accordance with the goals or purpose of a course or curriculum. The seven strategy components just described are present in all three models, but some characteristics of those components vary from one model to another. The constancy of all seven components in all three models allows us to talk about a *general model* of instruction—a set of unvarying characteristics for all instruction designed according to the Elaboration Theory. This general model is described next. It provides a "blueprint" or description of what the instruction should be like, from beginning to end, for objectives in the cognitive domain.

1. Present an Epitome

The general elaboration model of instruction starts by presenting an epitome (a lesson that epitomizes a single type of content and includes whatever of the other types of content are highly relevant). The epitome might start with a *motivational-strategy component* such as the creation of an incongruity (see Chapter 11); but such strategy components have not yet been adequately integrated into the Elaboration Theory. Then it presents an *analogy,* if a good one can be found and is believed to be necessary or useful. Next, it presents the *organizing content ideas* in a "most fundamental, most representative, most general, and/or most simple first" sequence.[1] However, each of these ideas is directly preceded by all of its *learning prerequisites* that have not yet been mastered by all of the target learner population. Each of the organizing content ideas may also be directly followed by any of the other *supporting content ideas* that have been selected as highly relevant to it.

---

[1]In the case of procedural organizing content, a forward chaining sequence is recommended for presenting the organizing content ideas.

Alternatively, it may be best to group all of those supporting ideas for presentation after all of the organizing content ideas have been presented, especially if those supporting ideas are highly interrelated. All of the ideas in the epitome are presented according to *Component Display Theory* specifications (see Chapter 9). Finally, a *summarizer* and a *synthesizer* are presented. The synthesizer shows the part of the organizing structure whose ideas have been taught in the epitome. Also, *cognitive-strategy activators* (embedded and detached) are included whenever they are needed and appropriate, as are additional motivational-strategy components (see Chapter 11).

2. Present Level-1 Elaborations

Next, the general elaboration model makes all of the level-1 lessons available to the learner. There will usually be about four to eight level-1 lessons—lessons that elaborate directly on various aspects of the epitome's organizing content. Each level-1 lesson takes one (or sometimes two) aspects of the epitome's organizing content and presents slightly more detailed or more complex organizing content that elaborates on it. Each lesson has all the characteristics of the epitome lesson described earlier: motivational-strategy components, a new analogy or an extension of the earlier analogy if appropriate, the organizing content ideas directly preceded by their prerequisites and succeeded by their other supporting content, and an internal summarizer and internal synthesizer. Naturally, the Component Display Theory is still used to present each individual idea and fact, and cognitive-strategy activators and additional motivational-strategy components are used whenever needed and appropriate.

However, one additional component is added on to the end of each level-1 lesson: an *expanded epitome*. This expanded epitome begins with a within-set summarizer, which summarizes ideas among the already-taught lessons within that set of lessons. Then it relates the new organizing content (via a synthesizer) to the within-set organizing content that has already been taught. It does this via synthesizers and integrative generalities, examples, and practice, as prescribed by the Component Display Theory (see Chapter 9). This is equivalent to the zoom-out-for-context-and-review activity in the zoom-lens analogy.

Usually the level-1 lesson that elaborates on one aspect of the epitome should not include *all* of the more detailed or complex knowledge on that aspect. Rather, a level-1 elaboration should itself be an epitome of all the more detailed or complex knowledge on that aspect of the epitome, just as zooming in one level provides a slightly more detailed wide-angle view of one part of the whole picture. It is important to note that an aspect is not the same thing as an idea. It is possible that a level-1 elaboration may elaborate to some extent on all of the ideas in the epitome or perhaps even on a relationship among those ideas, or even on an exception to those ideas.

The depth to which a level-1 elaboration should elaborate on an aspect of the epitome is somewhat variable (i.e., the discrete levels on the zoom lens are variable, not always constant and equal in the amount of detail added). The most important factor for deciding on the depth of a given level-1 elaboration is the *student learning load*. It is important that the student learning load be neither too large nor too small, for either will impede the instruction's efficiency, effectiveness (especially for retention), and appeal. The number of ideas that represent the optimal student learning load will vary with such factors as student ability, the complexity of the subject-matter ideas, and student prefamiliarity with the ideas. We expect that the breadth of a level-1 elaboration will usually be fairly difficult to adjust. Hence, optimizing the student learning load in a given elaboration can often be done mainly by varying the depth of the elaboration. But we hypothesize that both ways are equally acceptable.

3. Present Level-2 Elaborations

The general elaboration model makes level-2 lessons available to the learner as soon as he or she has reached mastery on the level-1 lesson on which those level-2 lessons elaborate. Each level-2 lesson is of identical nature to the level-1 lessons except that it elaborates on an aspect of a *level-1* lesson's organizing content instead of elaborating on an aspect of the epitome's organizing content.

4. Present Additional Levels of Elaboration

The general elaboration model continues to make more detailed or complex levels of lessons available to the learner as soon as he or she has reached mastery of the lesson on which those lessons elaborate, until the desired level of detail or complexity (as represented by the objectives of the course) is reached. And each of those lessons is of similar nature to the other lessons, with the exception that it elaborates on an aspect of the previous level's organizing content instead of a higher level's organizing content.

Other Comments

According to the general elaboration model, elaborations that are on the *same level* are very different from each other with respect to the instructional content they contain (i.e., their ideas are very different from each other), but elaborations that are on *different levels* are very similar with respect to their instructional content (i.e., their ideas are very similar), because each level has basically the same content as the previous level, only presented in greater detail or complexity. This provides an important systematic review mechanism.

It should be noted that there are three ways in which systematic review takes place. First, each level of elaboration covers *similar content* to that in the previous level (only with some additional detail or complexity). Learning this more-detailed version of the same content stimulates or incorporates review of that earlier aspect of the course content. Second, the *internal summarizer* at the end of each elaboration reviews the content that was just presented in that elaboration by providing a concise generality for each idea. And third, the *expanded epitome* (including the external summarizer) at the end of each elaboration constantly reviews and integrates the major content that was presented in earlier elaborations.

Summary of the Elaboration Model

In summary, the elaboration model is as follows (see Fig. 10.14). First the *epitome* is presented to the student. Then the *level-1 lessons* are made available to elaborate on the various aspects of the organizing content in the epitome. An internal summarizer and synthesizer come in the last part of each lesson, and an *expanded epitome* is presented after each lesson. Also, as soon as a learner reaches mastery on a level-1 lesson, *level-2 lessons* are made available that elaborate on that level-1 lesson. Additional levels of lessons are made available in the same way—an elaboration followed by an expanded epitome—until the level of detail specified by the objectives is reached.

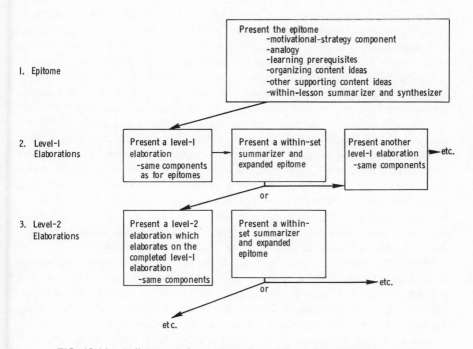

FIG. 10.14   A diagrammatic representation of the general elaboration model.

Each lesson, including the epitome, should contain: motivational-strategy components if needed, an analogy if appropriate, the organizing content ideas directly preceded by their prerequisite supporting content and succeeded by their other supporting content, and an internal summarizer and internal synthesizer. The component display theory is used to present each individual idea and fact, and cognitive-strategy activators and additional motivational-strategy components are used whenever needed and appropriate. In addition, each lesson except for the epitome should end with an expanded epitome, which begins with a within-set summarizer and proceeds to horizontally and vertically integrate the organizing content (and occasionally supporting content) via synthesizers, integrative generalities, examples, and practice.

VARIATIONS OF THE MODEL

The Three "Organizations"

As we said earlier, several different models of macro organization can be generated from the general model. In fact, the Elaboration Theory is comprised of: (1) three different models; and (2) a basis for prescribing when each model should be used. These three different models are the conceptually organized model, the procedurally organized model, and the theoretically organized model. Although all three models have the characteristics described previously, the nature of the epitome, the elaborations, and the synthesizers varies considerably according to whether the organization of the course is conceptual, procedural, or theoretical.

For example, a *conceptually organized* course, such as a course in basic biology might be, uses a conceptual (perhaps matrix) structure, in which the most general concepts are presented in the epitome (as, for example, the animal phyla). The epitome is quite different from the other two types of epitome, not just in that it centers around concepts, but also in that its organizing content is more general than the remaining organizing content (i.e., most of the remaining concepts are either parts or kinds of the epitome's concepts). Succeeding elaborations are different in that they provide more detailed and narrow subclassifications of the epitome's concepts, until the most detailed concepts specified by the objectives are mastered. Students learn to make progressively finer and more precise discriminations among narrower and more exclusive categories as levels of elaboration progress. The synthesizers also differ in that they utilize conceptual structures.

On the other hand, a course in applied statistics would probably use a *procedural organization,* in which the simplest and most generally applicable statistical procedure is taught first (at the application level) as the organizing content for the epitome. A procedural epitome is often identical to what information-processing analysts refer to as the "shortest path" through a procedure (or a set of alternative procedures). The remaining procedures are not parts or kinds of the epitome's procedure; rather they are more complex and often more narrowly focused procedures that are necessary for achieving basically the same ends under different and often more difficult conditions. The elaborations are different from the other two kinds of elaborations in that they teach progressively more detailed and complex condition-specific versions of or alternatives to the simple epitome procedure, until a large variety of procedures—each of which is used under fairly limited conditions—has been taught. The synthesizers mostly take the form of procedural structures, although some kinds and parts structures are often used.

Finally, an introductory course in economics would probably use a theoretical organization, in which the most fundamental principle of economics (the law of supply and demand) is taught first (at the application level) as the organizing content for the epitome. This principle is often identified by asking an experienced teacher or subject-matter expert, "If you could only teach one principle (or two), what would it be?" The elaborations are different from the other two kinds of elaborations in that they teach progressively more complex, narrow, and situation-specific versions of, or qualifications of, the fundamental epitome principle(s), until the desired level and breadth of explanation or prediction have been reached. The synthesizers mostly take the form of branching chains of cause-and-effect statements, which are usually represented diagrammatically (if they are qualitative statements) but are occasionally represented mathematically (if they are quantitative as well).

Moreover, the need to nest particular *types of supporting* structures within each elaboration requires further variations among the models. For example, conceptual supporting content requires a different kind of synthesizer than does procedural supporting content. Thus the nature of each type of structure, both organizing and supporting, represents a different variation of the general model.

It should be noted that any of the three organizations can be used for almost all subject areas. For example, although a conceptual organization is usually more consistent with the goals of a high school biology course, a theoretical organization would be quite reasonable (centered around such principles as survival of the fittest and genetic variability), and a procedural organization would also be possible (e.g., a course centered around how to make hybrids).

Other Kinds of Variations

In addition to these standard variations among the three models based on the type of organizing content selected, variations of the general model also derive from the nature of the "zooming in" from simple to complex. These variations could be viewed as the learner-controlled model, the system-controlled model, and the fixed model. The *learner-controlled* model was described as the general model. In the *system-controlled* model, the teacher or other delivery medium uses information about each learner to select and sequence the content and strategy components. Finally, the *fixed* model uses one set of content and strategy components (including sequence) for all students.

The Elaboration Theory hypothesizes that the learner-controlled model should usually be used whenever possible, as long as the learners are properly instructed in the effective use of learner control. The increased motivation that results when a learner is allowed to study in depth a particular aspect of the organizing content that is especially interesting to that individual will usually completely offset any decrease in learning efficiency that might result from this variation; and it is likely that increases in learning efficiency would be the rule rather than the exception, due mostly to increased motivation.

In addition, it should be noted that there are several types of *fixed models*. For example, following the epitome, the instruction could zoom in on all level-1 elaborations before proceeding with any level-2 elaborations, thus offering the learner the same level of detail and complexity across the breadth of the ideas covered in the epitome. Alternatively, the instruction might zoom in on only one level-1 elaboration, then proceed to a level-2 elaboration on only that content presented in the single level-1 elaboration, and then proceed to a level-3 elaboration on that same small set of ideas. This latter variation would provide learners with considerable depth on one part of the organizing content before giving them much breadth at all. Hence, the former variation of the fixed model will usually be preferable when the fixed model is necessary.

Summary of Variations

In summary, two important types of variations are possible within the elaboration model. The first concerns the type of *organization* selected for a particular course or curriculum. The second concerns the degree of *adaptability* of the sequencing to the individual learner and the degree of control given learners over the sequencing in the "zooming-in" process. Hence, the second type of variation also concerns the development and use of metacognition models with which the learner approaches learning tasks.

USING THE ELABORATION THEORY

We have developed a fairly detailed set of procedures for designing instruction according to the Elaboration Theory (see Reigeluth, Merrill, Wilson, & Spiller, 1978, for general procedures; see Reigeluth & Darwazeh, 1982, for the conceptual approach; see Reigeluth & Rodgers, 1980, for the procedural approach; and see Sari & Reigeluth, 1982, for the theoretical approach). Although the procedure varies in important ways depending on which of the three models is chosen, all three procedures are characterized by six general steps (see Fig. 10.15).

First, one must select an organization—either conceptual, procedural, or theoretical—on the basis of the goals or purpose of the instruction. Second, one must develop an organizing structure that depicts the organizing content (either concepts, procedures, or principles) in the most detailed/complex version that the

Step 1: Choose the type of organizing content

Conceptual
Procedural
Theoretical

Step 2: Develop organizing structure

2a. Conceptual Develop all useful parts and kinds conceptual structures, select the most important one(s), and combine into a matrix (if appropriate).

2b. Procedural Identify all useful steps and alternative paths to be learned, and combine them into procedural structures.

2c. Theoretical Identify all important principles to be learned, and combine them into theoretical structures.

Step 3: Allocate organizing content to levels of elaboration

Decide on the organizing content that should comprise the epitome and each level of elaboration.

3a. Conceptual Prune the organizing structure to the epitome content. Add back pruned content to form each level of elaboration.

3b. Procedural Find the shortest path to identify the epitome content. Add back progressively more complex paths to form each level of elaboration.

3c. Theoretical Use the most fundamental principle(s) as the epitome content. Use rank-order of fundamentalness and/or a parallel conceptual structure to identify principles for each level of elaboration.

Step 4: Allocate supporting content to levels of elaboration

Identify all supporting content that is highly relevant to the organizing content for each level. Then identify all unattained learning prerequisites for both organizing and supporting content.

Step 5: Allocate all content to individual lessons

Allocate all content on each level of elaboration to individual lessons, according to the aspect of the epitome, or of an elaboration, that it elaborates on.

Step 6: Sequence all content within each lesson

For each lesson list and sequence the following:

• motivational strategy components

• analogies

• each organizing content idea and its prerequisites

• each supporting content idea and its prerequisites

• within-lesson summarizer and synthesizer

• within-set summarizer and expanded epitome.

Micro Design

FIG. 10.15   The six step design procedure for designing instruction.

student needs to learn. This is a form of content analysis or task description. Third, the organizing structure is analyzed in a systematic manner to determine which aspect(s) of the organizing content will be presented in the epitome and which aspects will be presented in each level of elaboration. In this way the "skeleton" of the instruction is developed on the basis of epitomizing and elaborating on a single type of content.

The fourth major step is to embellish the "skeleton" by adding the other two types of content plus facts at the lowest appropriate levels of detail. Thus, the remaining kinds of subject-matter content are "nested" within different parts of the skeleton. Learning prerequisites are among the considerations that enter in at this point.

Having allocated all of the instructional content to the different levels of elaboration, it is now important to establish the scope and depth of each lesson that will comprise each level. The scope is usually predetermined by the organizing content ideas and their important supporting content. The depth is determined on the basis of achieving an optimal student learning load, as described earlier.

Sixth and finally, the internal structure of each lesson within each level is planned. The sequence of ideas and facts within a lesson is decided on the basis of several factors, the most important of which are learning-prerequisite relationships and contribution to an understanding of the whole organizing structure. Motivational-strategy components and analogies are planned, and the locations of internal synthesizers and summarizers are also determined. Finally, the content of each expanded epitome is specified.

This concludes the "macro" design process, at which point the "micro" design process begins: decisions as to how to organize the instruction on a single idea or fact.

We have spelled out these procedures for designing instruction in much greater detail elsewhere (Reigeluth & Darwazeh, 1982; Reigeluth et al., 1978; Reigeluth & Rodgers, 1980; Sari & Reigeluth, 1982).

SUPPORT FOR VALIDITY

The Elaboration Theory is very new and therefore lacks an extensive support base for its validity. Nevertheless, some support is to be found from three sources: formal research, learning theory, and educational practice.

Research Support

Although some research is currently in progress, only one study directly on the Elaboration Theory has been completed. However, because the Elaboration Theory integrates much work of other theorists and researchers, there is empirical support for aspects of the Elaboration Theory. It is beyond the scope of this chapter to conduct an extensive review of such research support. The following is a summary of the major lines of existing empirical support.

The research literature on advance organizers lends some support to the strategy of a general-to-detailed sequence (see Mayer, 1979, for a review and analysis of that literature). However, this research is mute on the question of epitomizing versus summarizing. The "path-analysis" literature for the information-processing approach to task analysis lends some support to epitomizing as opposed to summarizing. A procedural epitome is often the same as what information-processing analysts refer to as the "shortest path" through a procedure (see for example, P. Merrill, 1978).

With respect to the learning-prerequisite sequencing aspect of the Elaboration Theory, the research on hierarchical approaches to sequencing lends direct support to this aspect of the Elaboration Theory. See White (1973) and Resnick (1976) for excellent reviews of this research literature.

Although this piecemeal research does lend some support to the Elaboration Theory, it leaves many important questions unanswered. Of particular importance is research on the way in which all of the pieces have been integrated into the Elaboration Theory. This kind of research can only be done by including a treatment group that receives everything that the Elaboration Theory prescribes. The disadvantage is that such research requires extensive development of instructional materials, especially because it is likely that, for relatively short pieces of instruction, the human mind can compensate for most of the weaknesses in macro strategies. Full semester or year courses are likely to show some important differences, but they are very expensive to develop treatment materials for and to conduct. As of yet, federal agencies have been unwilling to support such expensive research. Until there is a change in this situation, research support for the Elaboration Theory will remain inadequate.

Learning-Theory Support

Theoretical support for the validity of the Elaboration Theory comes from several sources (see Merrill, Kelety, & Wilson, 1981, for a more extensive review). Two extremely important areas of cognitive psychology that provide the most support are: (1) theories about cognitive representational structures; and (2) related memory processes such as encoding, storage, and retrieval mechanisms. A discussion of these two areas of cognitive psychology is followed by a description of ways in which each supports specific aspects of the Elaboration Theory. Finally, several other sources of support are discussed.

Cognitive Structures

An early, primary focus of cognitive theory appears in the work of Ausubel (1963, 1964, 1968), who argued that new knowledge is acquired and acquirable to the extent that it can be meaningfully related to and subsumed within existing (i.e., previously learned) knowledge. Ausubel maintained that knowledge is organized within the learner's memory primarily in hierarchical fashion. More general, inclusive, and abstract content subsumes (or assimilates) newer, more specific, and concrete knowledge. The more firmly anchored and differentiated these subsuming structures are, the more useful they are as ideational anchorage. Additionally, Ausubel proposed that the various pieces of information integrated within a particular knowledge structure are highly interrelated, linked by some type of semantic similarity. Thus, previously acquired, more general and abstract knowledge can facilitate the acquisition of new subordinate content.

Ausubel described three necessary conditions for the meaningful learning of new content. The learner must possess a stable cognitive structure capable of subsuming the new content; the new content must be nonarbitrary (i.e., capable of being subsumed meaningfully in nonverbatim fashion); and the learner must have a cognitive "set" of previously acquired knowledge already in cognitive store to which the new content can be meaningfully related.

Ausubel's conceptualization of learning as assimilation (or, to use his earlier term subsumption) is echoed and extended in Mayer's (1977, 1979) theory of "assimilation to schema." A schema, according to Mayer, is any grouping of information that is organized in some meaningful fashion. Schemata facilitate the integration of the knowledge by serving an assimilative (or subsumptive) function; new knowledge is assimilated into a hierarchy of progressively more detailed, specific, and differentiated content within the learner's cognitive store. Thus, the basic learning process is the assimilation of new knowledge within hierarchically ordered schemata.

Mayer's theory posits that the nature of the learner's existing cognitive structure (i.e., the content and organization of knowledge in memory) is the major factor influencing the meaningful acquisition of new knowledge. In particular, both Ausubel and Mayer emphasize the importance of shaping the content and arrangement of antecedent learning conditions so as to facilitate the assimilation of new knowledge. The use of assimilative sequences of content that begin with very general and inclusive information can provide ideational anchorage for more specific and detailed information, thus providing the means for integrating new content within existing knowledge.

More explicit and detailed models of schema theory have been developed by Quillian (1968), Norman and Rumelhart (1975), and Anderson (Anderson, Spiro, & Anderson, 1978; Anderson, Spiro, & Montague, 1977). In these theories, schemata are perceived as organizational structures that serve both to interrelate separate pieces of information into a single conceptual unit and to channel new information to appropriate organizing structures on the basis of relatedness or semantic similarity. These schemata serve both to provide a representational scheme for the organization of knowledge and to offer a theoretical framework for accounting for the acquisition of new knowledge. According to Anderson et al. (1978), the schemata a learner already possesses are the primary determinants of what content the learner will be able to acquire.

Norman and Rumelhart (1975) view schemata as analogous to language structure. In their theory, information can be represented as a network of interrelated concepts and contexts that modify and are modified by incoming knowledge. Schemata permit the making of inferences by providing contextual information that allows, and defines the limits of, conclusions not directly contained within the related pieces of information constituting a schema.

Proponents of semantic networking theories (Norman & Rumelhart, 1975; Quillian, 1968) emphasize that schemata form multiple links with each other such that each piece of information is ultimately related to every other piece. Moreover, the relationships are diverse in nature; they are directional and substantial and determine the nature of what is acquired, stored, and retrieved. These relationships include subordinate, superordinate, and coordinate linkages; Collins and Quillian (1969, 1970) have demonstrated that retrieval is a function of the locatability of content within hierarchical structures.

Memory Structures

Research on the nature of encoding processes in memory has provided evidence for two kinds of memory: episodic and semantic. Semantic encoding processes are associated with deeper, more complex processes and more durable memory traces. Craik's work with semantic encoding processes (Craik & Lockhart, 1972; Craik & Tulving, 1975) indicates that information is encoded and stored in organizing structures similar to schemata. Both Estes' (1970) conceptualization of *control elements* (semantic categories that subsume appropriate pieces of information) and Kintsch's (1970) notion of *markers* (types of semantic topics that assimilate and store bits of related information) describe mechanisms and structures through which incoming information is analyzed, interpreted, and related to existing knowledge structures in memory. Similar notions of semantic organization have been proposed by other theorists. All assume that semantically encoded information is stored in a hierarchically interrelated manner with topical categories as focal units. Norman and Rumelhart's (1975) semantic networks represent one approach to the organization of knowledge in memory in terms of relationships among ideas. Because any one idea can be encoded in many different ways, depending on which of its semantic attributes are salient for any given structure, multiple relational linkages are created between that content and various existing knowledge structures, resulting in a broad network of interrelated knowledge.

Retrieval processes are generally characterized in terms of search mechanisms. Norman and Bobrow (1979) describe two separate stages of search operations. The first stage involves creating a description of the desired target information; the second involves the actual searching, including a recursive review of memory structures and ideas until the targeted information is identified. Anderson et al.

(1977) and Norman and Bobrow (1979) conceptualize such a search process in somewhat different forms; however, the common thread through these and other similar retrieval models involves the assumption that memory consists of highly organized knowledge structures through which searches proceed in hierarchical fashion, from the most general and inclusive to the progressively more detailed and specific knowledge, until the targeted content is located. Thus retrieval is facilitated or hindered to the extent that organizational structures in memory are available as guides for search operations.

Cognitive Psychology and Elaboration Theory

The assumptions and propositions of cognitive models of learning and of acquisition, storage, and retrieval processes previously described provide direct support for the Elaboration Theory. First, the subsumption, assimilation, and schema theories all imply the instructional use of a *general-to-detailed sequence* of content that begins with the most general and inclusive set of constructs available to provide ideational anchorage for the subsequent content. Progressively more detailed, specific, and complex ideas can then be acquired more easily as derivations or elaborations of the more general content. The use of a general-to-detailed sequence of content thus provides the learner with a progression of anchoring knowledge that subsumes, integrates, and organizes the more detailed or complex knowledge.

Second, cognitive learning theories argue the importance of *providing or activating* particular ideas in memory that are at an appropriate level of generality and inclusiveness for serving as ideational anchorage for new knowledge. Such ideas serve several important functions. They provide the *scaffolding* for later learning by their ability to incorporate, integrate, and assimilate more detailed information. They make explicit the *relevance* of later information. And they provide *form and structure* for the later content by identifying both kinds of relationships to be learned and the individual ideas involved in those relationships. In particular, the elaboration theory advocates the use of two principal kinds of relational strategies: (1) a general-to-detailed sequence; and (2) synthesizers (which provide progressive integration and reconciliation of content at each level of detail). Both of these strategies rely heavily on types of knowledge structures in terms of both a single, pervasive organization structure and appropriate supporting structures.

The use of the general-to-detailed sequence is supported by the assimilation and schema theories' assertions that the subsumptive function served by schemata in incorporating and integrating new knowledge at varying levels of generality and inclusiveness facilitates the creation of schemata for assimilating more detailed and specific content. As new knowledge is integrated within the developing hierarchical structure, learning is made more efficient and effective.

Synthesizers provide integration of content at regular points during the general-to-detailed progression of ideas and explicitly teach the interrelatedness of ideas. The resulting synthesis assists the learner in comprehending and utilizing the particular kinds of relationships that characterize a given content area. Equally, the use of a single type of organizing structure makes explicit the critical primary inter-relationships that constitute a particular idea. Both organizing and supporting structures provide functional encoding structures for the learner. At each level of elaboration, the expanded epitome assists the learner in integrating the various supporting structures within the primary organization structure.

Moreover, the principle of providing an organizational schema in the form of an epitome results in an encoding structure that requires less processing effort by the learner, because content in the epitome is selected for the learner in a manner compatible with what is already known about encoding mechanisms. Expanded epitomes further facilitate encoding operations through indicating the semantic linkages to be formed at each level of elaboration. The use of a general-to-detailed or simple-to-complex sequence and the periodic synthesis and reconciliation of content create an input structure reflective of our current understanding of the organization and operations of memory.

Additionally, retrieval, in the form of search processes through memory, is facilitated to the extent that information in memory is organized in hierarchically integrated—that is, searchable—form. Also, the greater the number of interrelationships accessible to search operations, the more unlikely it is that failure of a particular retrieval strategy will preclude location of target information. Instead, the learner has available multiple avenues of accessibility through activation of alternate relational paths.

Support for Additional Strategy Components

Another strategy component hypothesized to increase the relatability and stability of new knowledge is the analogy. Analogies function as lateral anchorage between familiar or previously acquired content and new knowledge. By identifying points of tangency between existing knowledge structures and new information and by helping learners to perceive the new in terms of the previously acquired, the analogy assists learners in integrating new, highly unfamiliar content meaningfully.

Ortony (1975, 1976; Ortony et al., 1978) asserts the importance of analogic structures (including metaphor and simile) as both communicative and instructive tools. He argues that such verbal devices assist literal language by permitting us to fill in the gaps created by a language's inability to communicate adequately the continuous nature of experience. Such structures communicate large chunks of experience that cannot be captured in literal terms. At their best, they transmit entire structures of meaning far beyond the capacity of denotative symbol systems. Ortony cites Paivio's (1979) work with imagery as evidence of the effectiveness of figurative devices as instructive tools.

Paul Merrill's work with information-processing models of task analysis underlies the development of strategy prescriptions for content defined as having procedural organization goals. When the subject matter to be acquired is algorithmic in nature, P. Merrill (1976, 1978) argues for the use of path analysis, which results in a sequence of component skills or operations similar to the Elaboration Theory's simple-to-complex epitomization approach.

Robert Gagné's contribution to the theoretical bases of the Elaboration Theory are more primal and pervasive. His concern for developing a theory of learning that accounts for the various different capabilities a learner may acquire led him to postulate his cumulative theory of intellectual-skills acquisition. Gagné (1977) argues that certain kinds of skills must be acquired before other kinds can be acquired. The learning-prerequisite sequences prescribed by the elaboration theory are based on this learning theory, and all the related research applies equally to validate this aspect of the Elaboration Theory.

Bruner's (1960, 1966) *spiral curriculum* is an approach to sequencing instruction that entails teaching ideas initially in a greatly simplified yet "intellectually honest" form, and periodically cycling back to teach those same ideas in progressively more complete and complex forms, like an ever-widening and rising spiral. Although the original intention of the spiral was for it to be applied to a whole curriculum, its intent and function are highly similar to the intent and function of the elaboration theory.

Norman's (1973) *web-learning* model provides similar parallels with Elaboration Theory. In his model, Norman advocates use of an initial broad conceptual outline of to-be-acquired content, followed by progressively more detailed and specific information. The outline serves the dual purposes of the epitome and single organization structure by teaching specific conceptual relationships as the means of facilitating creation and use of organizational schemata. Again, the hierarchical and integrative structure is the heart of the model.

It should be noted, however, that neither Ausubel's nor Bruner's nor Norman's model prescribes instructional strategies in sufficiently precise and detailed form. The Elaboration Theory has attempted to extend and articulate precisely the necessary strategy components for actual implementation of the cognitive (learning theory) principles discussed earlier. The elaboration theory is a highly precise specification of pedagogical requirements for teaching different kinds of content and for achieving different kinds of goals.

Support from Educational Practice

In addition to the previously cited empirical and theoretical support for the Elaboration Theory, there is some support for the elaboration theory from "the field." We have discovered that, for a theoretical organization, the sequence in which the principles in a field end up being taught is often remarkably similar to the sequence in which they were discovered in that field. Hence, textbooks and teachers who have used a chronological approach to teaching theoretically oriented content have often ended up using a sequence that is remarkably similar to that prescribed by the Elaboration Theory. In fact, such a historical approach has been very commonly used for theoretically oriented courses, ranging from physics to economics. The popularity of this approach seems to indicate that teachers feel it has good results. Finally, in several teachings of the most fundamental Elaboration Theory ideas to inservice teachers, we have received enthusiastic reception of the approach. Such intuitive appeal to experienced educators, although not experimental data, does nevertheless provide important support for the Elaboration Theory.

CONCLUSION

The Elaboration Theory and development procedures as described here have undergone very limited field testing and no systematic, integrated research. It is likely that aspects of the Elaboration Theory will be modified as research and field testing are performed. For example, it may turn out that having a complete expanded epitome (versus a more narrow one) after every single lesson is inefficient and unnecessary. It is also likely that a large, full-scale field test of the design procedures will reveal more effective and efficient steps for designing instruction according to the theory. In addition to the likelihood of modifications of existing aspects of the Elaboration Theory, there is a continuing need to integrate more of our expanding knowledge about instructional and learning processes.

The Elaboration Theory as developed to date is a tentative move in a much needed direction. It does not yet have the maturity and validation of the currently used approaches to instructional design on the macro level. But the need for such integrative alternatives should be clear. Hopefully, the Elaboration Theory will contribute towards meeting that need.

REFERENCES

Anderson, R. C., Spiro, R. J., & Anderson, M. C. Schemata as scaffolding for the representation of information in connected discourse. *American Educational Research Journal*, 1978, *15*, 433–440.

Anderson, R. C., Spiro, R. J., & Montague, W. E. *Schooling and the acquisition of knowledge*. Hillsdale, N.J.: Lawrence Erlbaum Associates, 1977.

Ausubel, D. P. *The psychology of meaningful verbal learning*. New York: Grune & Stratton, 1963.

Ausubel, D. P. Some psychological aspects of the structure of knowledge. In E. M. Elam (Ed.), *Education and the structure of knowledge*. Chicago: Rand McNally, 1964.

Ausubel, D. P. *Educational psychology; A cognitive view*. New York: Holt, Rinehart & Winston, 1968.

Bergan, J. R. The structural analysis of behavior: An alternative to the learning-hierarchy model. *Review of Educational Research*, 1980, *50*, 625–646.

Bruner, J. S. *The process of education*. New York: Vintage Books, 1960.

Bruner, J. S. *Toward a theory of instruction*. New York: W. W. Norton & Co., 1966.

Collins, A. M., & Quillian, M. R. Retrieval time from semantic memory. *Journal of Verbal Learning and Verbal Behavior*, 1969, *8*, 240–247.

Collins, A. M., & Quillian, M. R. Does category size affect categorization time? *Journal of Verbal Learning and Verbal Behavior*, 1970, *9*, 432–439.

Craik, F. I., & Lockhart, R. S. Levels of processing: A framework for memory research. *Journal of Verbal Learning and Verbal Behavior*, 1972, *11*, 671–684.

Craik, F. I. M., & Tulving, E. Depth of processing and the retention of words in episodic memory. *Journal of Experimental Psychology: General,* 1975, *104,* 268—294.

Dreistadt, R. The use of analogies and incubation in obtaining insight in creative problem solving. *Journal of Psychology,* 1969, *71,* 159–175.

Estes, W. K. *Learning theory and mental development.* New York: Academic Press, 1970.

Gagné, E. Long-term retention of information following learning from prose. *Review of Educational Research,* 1978, *48,* 629–655.

Gagné, R. M. Learning hierarchies. *Educational Psychologist,* 1968, *6*(1), 1—6.

Gagné, R. M. *The conditions of learning* (3rd ed.). New York: Holt, Rinehart & Winston, 1977.

Gropper, G. L. *Instructional strategies.* Englewood Cliffs, N.J.: Educational Technology Publications, 1974.

Hartley, J., & Davies, I. K. Preinstructional strategies: The role of pretests, behavioral objectives, overviews, and advance organizers. *Review of Educational Research,* 1976, *46,* 239–265.

Kintsch, W. *Learning, memory, and conceptual processes.* New York: Wiley, 1970.

Landa, L. *Algorithmization in learning and instruction.* Englewood Cliffs, N.J.: Educational Technology Publications, 1974.

Lindsay, P. H., & Norman, D. A. *Human information processing: An introduction to psychology.* New York: Academic Press, 1977.

Mayer, R. E. The sequencing of instruction and the concept of assimilation-to-schema. *Instructional Science,* 1977, *6,* 369–388.

Mayer, R. E. Twenty years of research on advance organizers: Assimilation theory is still the best predictor of results. *Instructional Science,* 1979, *8,* 133–167.

Merrill, M. D. *Learner-controlled instructional strategies: An empirical investigation.* Final report on NSF Grant No. SED 76–01650, February 16, 1979.

Merrill, M. D. Learner control in computer based learning. *Computers and Education,* 1980, *4,* 77—95.

Merrill, M. D. Reigeluth, C. M., & Faust, G. W. The instructional quality profile: A curriculum evaluation and design tool. In H. F. O'Neil, Jr. (Ed.), *Procedures for instructional systems development.* New York: Academic Press, 1979.

Merrill, M. D., Richards, R. E., Schmidt, R. V., & Wood, N. D. *The instructional strategy diagnostic profile training manual.* San Diego: Courseware, Inc., 1977.

Merrill, M. D., Kelety, J. C., & Wilson, B. G. Elaboration theory and cognitive psychology. *Instructional Science,* 1981, *10*(3), 217–235.

Merrill, P. F. *Task analysis—an information processing approach* (Technical Memo No 27). Tallahassee, Fl.: CAI Center, Florida State University, 1971. (Also in *NSPI Journal,* 1976, *15*(2), 7–11.)

Merrill, P. F. Hierarchical and information processing task analysis: A comparison. *Journal of Instructional Development,* 1978, *1*(2), 35–40.

Miller, G. A. The magical number seven, plus or minus two: Some limits on our capacity to process information. *Psychological Review,* 1956, *63,* 81–97.

Norman, D. A. Memory, knowledge, and answering of questions. In R. L. Solso (Ed.), *Contemporary issues in cognitive psychology: The Loyola symposium.* Washington, D.C.: Winston, 1973.

Norman, D. A., & Bobrow, D. G. Descriptions in intermediate stage memory retrieval. *Cognitive Psychology,* 1979, *11,* 107–123.

Norman, D. A., Rumelhart, D. E., & the LNR Research Group. *Explorations in cognition.* San Francisco: Freeman, 1975.

Ortony, A. Why metaphors are necessary and not just nice. *Educational Theory,* 1975, *25,* 45–54.

Ortony, A. On the nature and value of metaphor: A reply to my critics. *Educational Theory,* 1976, *26,* 395–398.

Ortony, A., Reynolds, R. E., & Arter, J. Metaphor: Theoretical and empirical research. *Psychological Bulletin,* 1978, *18,* 919–943.

Paivio, A. *Imagery and Verbal Processes.* Hillsdale, N.J.: Lawrence Erlbaum Associates, 1979.

Pratt, D. A cybernetic model for curriculum development. *Instructional Science,* 1982, *11*(1), 1—12.

Quillian, M. R. Semantic memory. In M. Minsky (Ed.), *Semantic information processing.* Cambridge, Mass.: MIT Press, 1968.

Raven, R. J., & Cole, R. Relationships between Piaget's operative comprehension and physiology modeling processes of community college students. *Science Education,* 1978, *62,* 481–489.

Reigeluth, C. M. In search of a better way to organize instruction: The elaboration theory. *Journal of Instructional Development,* 1979, *2*(3), 8–15. (a)

Reigeluth, C. M. TICCIT to the future: Advances in instructional theory for CAI. *Journal of Computer-Based Instruction,* 1979, *6*(2), 40–46. (b)

Reigeluth, C. M. *An investigation on the effects of alternative strategies for sequencing instruction on basic skills.* A final report submitted to the Navy Personnel R & D Center, San Diego, CA, 1982. Also presented at the annual meeting of the American Educational Research Assoc., New York, 1982.

Reigeluth, C. M., & Darwazeh, A. N. The elaboration theory's procedure for designing instruction: A conceptual approach. *Journal of Instructional Development,* 1982, *5*(3), 22—32.

Reigeluth, C. M., & Merrill, M. D. *The extended task analysis procedure (ETAP) user's manual.* Final report. Submitted to the US Army Training and Doctrine Command (TRADOC), Fort Monroe, Virginia, September 1980.

Reigeluth, C. M., Merrill, M.D., & Bunderson, C. V. The structure of subject-matter content and its instructional design implications. *Instructional science,* 1978, *7,* 107–126.

Reigeluth, C. M., Merrill, M.D., Wilson, B. G., & Spiller, R. T. *Final report on the structural strategy diagnostic profile project.* A final report submitted to the Navy Personnel Research and Development Center, San Diego, July 1978.

Reigeluth, C. M., Merrill, M.D., Wilson, B. G., & Spiller, R. T. The elaboration theory of instruction: A model for sequencing and synthesizing instruction. *Instructional Science,* 1980, *9,* 195–219.

Reigeluth, C. M., & Rodgers, C. A. The elaboration theory of instruction: Prescriptions for task analysis and design. *NSPI Journal,* 1980, *19*(1), 16—26.

Resnick, L. B. Issues in the study of learning hierarchies. In L. Resnick (Ed.), Hierarchies in children's learning: A symposium. *Instructional science,* 1973, *2,* 312–323.

Resnick, L. B. Task analysis in instructional design: Some cases from mathematics. In D. Klahr (Ed.), *Cognition and instruction.* Hillsdale, N.J.: Lawrence Erlbaum Associates, 1976.

Rigney, J. W. Learning strategies: A theoretical perspective. In H. F. O'Neil, Jr. (Ed.), *Learning strategies.* New York: Academic Press, 1978.

Rumelhart, D. E., & Ortony, A. The representation of knowledge in memory. In R. C. Anderson, R. J. Spiro, W. E. Montague (Eds.), *Schooling and the acquisition of knowledge.* Hillsdale, N.J.: Lawrence Erlbaum Associates, 1977.

Sari, I. F., & Reigeluth, C. M. Writing and evaluating textbooks: Contributions from instructional theory. In D. Jonassen (Ed.), *The technology of text: Principles for structuring, designing, and displaying text.* Englewood Cliffs, N.J.: Educational Technology Publications, 1982.

Scandura, J. M. *Structural learning* (Vol. 1). New York: Academic Press, 1973.

White, R. T. Research into learning hierarchies. *Review of Educational Research,* 1973, *43,* 361–375.

11 Motivational Design of Instruction

John M. Keller
Syracuse University

John. M. Keller

John M. Keller is an associate professor in Instructional Design, Development, and Evaluation at Syracuse University. Dr. Keller's work has centered on aspects of instructional systems design, with a special emphasis on problems of motivation and human performance in instructional settings. His research includes a number of published studies in specific areas of motivation including locus of control and learned helplessness. Currently, he is completing a handbook of motivational strategies for use by course designers and instructors. The handbook is based on the model described in the present book. It has been used in both the public schools and military training with positive results. Dr. Keller is a frequent consultant to schools, corporations, and the military.

Dr. Keller received his undergraduate degree in philosophy from the University of California at Riverside. After teaching in the secondary schools in San Diego county for a number of years, he began doctoral study at Indiana University. He was awarded the Ph.D. in instructional systems technology with a minor in organizational behavior in 1974. Upon graduating, he accepted an appointment at Syracuse University. In 1975 he received the Outstanding Young Researcher Award from the Association for Educational Communications and Technology. He was recently awarded a Research Fellowship by the University of Twente in The Netherlands. He will be in residence there for one semester to continue his writing, and to study with the faculty of the Instructional Science Department.

CONTENTS

Problems In The Study Of Motivation   387
  A Concern For Motivation   387
  A Need For Better Measures   388
Motivation And Learning   390
Motivational-Design Model   395
  Four Motivational Components   398
Interest   398
  The Concept Of Interest   398
  Interest: Conditions And Strategies   400
Relevance   406
  The Concept Of Relevance   406
  Relevance: Conditions And Strategies   407
    Personal-Motive Value Strategies   408
    Instrumental-Value Strategies   414
    Cultural-Value Strategies   414
    Summary   415
Expectancy   415
  The Concept Of Expectancy   415
    Expectations Of Others   416
    Expectations Of Oneself   416
  Expectancy: Conditions And Strategies   418
Outcomes   422
  The Concept Of Outcomes   422
  Outcomes: Conditions And Strategies   424
Conclusions   429

FOREWORD

John Keller's work represents an aspect of instructional design that has received relatively little attention: strategies for making the instruction more appealing. Of the theories and models described in this book, only the Gagné–Briggs theory and the Elaboration Theory explicitly include motivational-strategy components, and neither does so in a very pervasive or systematic manner.

Because it has received such little attention, work on motivational strategies for teaching cognitive objectives is at a considerably earlier stage of theory development than are other aspects of instructional design. Hence, the work described in this chapter does not yet represent a true instructional theory, or even a true model of instruction. Nevertheless, this chapter has been included: (1) because motivational strategies are so important; (2) because it is hoped that their inclusion here will encourage others to contribute to this area or to incorporate aspects of it in their own attempts to build integrative models of instruction; (3) because this chapter is highly integrative in that it draws on knowledge from many theoretical perspectives in its attempt to develop prescriptions for instructional design (which is a central theme of this book); and (4) because this chapter presents many useful prescriptions that can provide much guidance to instructional designers right now.

Keller has identified four major dimensions of motivation: (1) *interest,* which refers to whether the learner's curiosity is aroused and whether this arousal is sustained appropriately over time; (2) *relevance,* which refers to whether the learner perceives the instruction to satisfy personal needs or to help achieve personal goals; (3) *expectancy*, which refers to the learner's perceived likelihood of success and the extent to which he or she perceives success as being under his or her control; and (4) *satisfaction,* which refers to the learner's intrinsic motivations and his or her reactions to extrinsic rewards. Keller describes a smorgasboard of instructional strategies that can be used to improve each of these four dimensions of motivation and some bases for deciding when each of those straegies may and may not be appropriate to use.

In fact, each of Keller's four dimensions of motivation could be viewed as a potential "obstacle" to learning (see Chapter 2). In this case, Gropper's suggestion that "whether an obstacle is treated" is more important than "how it is treated" could become manifested in a model that specifies a menu of alternative strategies for treating each of the four potential obstacles.

This chapter represents a very significant, highly integrative contribution to an aspect of instructional design that is sorely in need of more attention.

C. M. R.

Motivational Design of Instruction

Ms. Thrush said, "Ok, that's it for the lesson. Now it's time for practice." She began handing out dittos. Each person received two. Several comments were directed to the teacher about these sheets.

"Are we gonna get more dittos?" No answer.

"How many of these do we have to do?" one boy asked.

"Twelve of them," she replied.

"BORING!" Carl said out loud.

"Ms. Thrush, how many of these do we have to do?" asked Millie from the other side of the room.

"A lot more than 12 if you keep asking me that," Ms. Thrush said, Don't forget, you've got a test on Friday."

This actual dialogue illustrates a teacher who is trying to solve several instructional-design problems at once. For example, she wants the students to respond actively, and to practice with concrete examples of the concepts she has been teaching. Both of these strategies are consistent with well-established instructional-design principles. However, she is also trying to solve a motivational problem, that of keeping the children's attention directed towards the task during the entire class period. Her approach is familiar, as we can easily remember how we or our children have suffered through endless reams of deskwork aimed at keeping us busy.

The children's comments clearly indicate that Ms. Thrush's motivational strategy is not successful. The children are variously bored, irritated, or apprehensive. This teacher's problem, which resulted despite her well-intentioned effort, simply illustrates an important problem in our knowledge of instructional design. As Chapters 4 to 10 indicate, our understanding of how to arouse and maintain student interest in learning lags far behind our knowledge of how to facilitate learning once the student has the desire to achieve.

This lack of attention to motivation is mirrored in the assumptions of various researchers, for motivation has played a curious role in instructional design and instructional theory. It is not explicitly included in some approaches to instruction (e.g., Carroll, 1963), it is subsumed under more general terms such as *aptitude* in others (e.g., Cronback & Snow, 1976; Walberg, 1971), it is equated with reinforcement or feedback in some (Skinner, 1968), and it is not regarded as essential to learning in still others (e.g., Ausubel, 1968). More commonly, however, motivation is explicitly labeled as an element in a given model (e.g., Bloom, 1976; Cooley & Lohnes, 1976; Gagné, 1977; Reigeluth & Merrill, 1979), but procedures for influencing motivation are never presented with the detail or precision of the procedures to facilitate concept acquisition.

Why, one might wonder, is there so much diversity, even in the definitions of where motivation belongs in a theory of instruction and learning? Some answers to this question are included in the following pages, but the primary purpose of this chapter is to offer the initial version of a systematic, theory-based approach to designing motivating instruction. For brevity, this approach is called *motivational design* and, in a later section, is distinguished from other elements of instructional design.

The accomplishment of this chapter's goal requires a number of steps. The first is to clarify some of the *problems* faced by the instructional researcher or designer who wants to study and influence motivation. The problems that have impeded progress in this area are by no means solved, but some progress has been made. The second step is to present a *theory** that illustrates the role of motivation in relation to other psychological and environmental factors in the learning situation. This theory provides the context for understanding the parameters of motivation in contrast to other influences on learning.

The third, and major, portion of the chapter is the presentation of a *model* for motivational design. This section begins with a general overview of the model and is followed by a detailed presentation of its four elements. The final section of the chapter highlights approaches to implementation, limitations of the model, and a number of areas in need of research and validation.

PROBLEMS IN THE STUDY OF MOTIVATION

There are many problems to be faced by the instructional designer who is interested in motivation. To discuss all of these issues would require a thorough historical review of the topic, and that is not the purpose of this chapter. However, there are two particular problems that warrant attention before proceeding. The first is attitudinal, whereas the second is technical and refers to both the theory and measurement of motivation.

A Concern for Motivation

The first problem in trying to develop and implement a systematic approach to motivational design lies in the traditional attitudes and definitions used by instruc-

---

*Editor's note: This is a *descriptive learning theory* as defined in Chapter 1, and to some extent it serves as a metatheory for the instructional-design model presented in this chapter.

tional technologists (not to mention their clients). For example, we often read that the goal of instructional technology is to design effective and efficient instruction. Unfortunately, these criteria make it easy to *exclude a specific concern for motivation,* or the appeal of instruction. The assumption all too often has been that if instruction is of good quality, motivation will take care of itself. Unfortunately, this assumption has been found to be only partly true. When we examine the meaning of "quality instruction," we discover that it generally refers to results in more or better learning per unit of time than other comparable methods of instruction.

Given this definition of quality, we can illustrate that it does not adequately account for motivation. It is true that one consequence of motivation is to contribute to better learning, and this is consistent with the previous definition of quality. But, another consequence of motivation is intensity of performance at a task. People tend to persist longer, or more intensely for a shorter period, at tasks when they are motivated than when they are not. However, in several cases it has been found that high-quality instructional programs resulted in superior learning when the students finished the entire course, but that large numbers of people dropped out or procrastinated excessively relative to the comparison groups. These results have been particularly noticeable in self-paced, independent-study courses (e.g., Alderman & Mahler, 1973; Johnston, 1975). Thus, we can have courses that are of demonstrably better quality with respect to the learning objectives, but less appealing than the comparison groups.

This distinction is important because it helps to identify motivation as an influence in instructional design that is not subsumed by the influences on efficiency and effectiveness that have traditionally been researched by instructional theorists. The growing concern for more research in this area was noted particularly by Cooley and Lohnes (1976), who indicated the need for improved measures of motivation that can be used in survey research. This could help in the understanding of the specific nature of motivation in relation to performance, and in relation to noncognitive variables such as quality of experience in school.

A Need for Better Measures

A second, more technical problem concerns the characteristics of motivation and efforts to measure it, particularly when contrasted with the concept of ability. In this chapter, a rather traditional distinction between motivation and ability is maintained. This is in contrast to the tendency established by Cronbach and Snow (1976) and Walberg (1971) to subsume all human characteristics under the term *ability*. In the present chapter, motivation refers, in a general way, to what a person *will* do, whereas ability refers to what a person *can* do. This usage is consistent with the preponderance of research and the associated technical definitions of the two terms in the literature.

In comparing the research on motivation and ability, there seems to be little doubt that people are much more stable, or consistent, in their *ability* to be successful at a given task once they are committed to it than they are in the *commitments* they make. The *variability* of personal choices, and the associated degree of effort exerted, are reflected in the variability shown in many of the measures of motivation. This issue of variability has been discussed by both Weiner (1974) and Mischel (1973), but from different perspectives. Weiner (1974) categorizes ability and effort respectively as stable and variable human characteristics that serve as two types of internally oriented attributions for the cause of given performance outcomes. Mischel (1973) discusses the issue more in terms of the difficulties of establishing a solid line of research and application in the area of motivation that would compare to the steadier progress in the study of ability and performance. In both cases, the characteristics of motivation as described by these two writers underscore the need to examine the concept of motivation and some of the theoretical issues that make it difficult to study.

It is *difficult to operationalize* the concept of motivation in as straightforward a manner as the concept of ability. Even though ability has been studied from many perspectives ranging from a general ability factor to a host of highly specific abilities, there are a number of different ways to measure ability. Furthermore, the measures of general ability tend to be consistently correlated with each other and with performance.

Motivation, by definition, refers to the magnitude and direction of behavior. In other words, it refers to the *choices* people make as to what experiences or goals they will approach or avoid, and the *degree of effort* they will exert in that respect. As such, motivation is influenced by myriad internal and external characteristics. People respond to their environment on the basis of inner reflexes, impulses, perceptions, and goals, and on the basis of perceived and actual opportunities and reinforcements in the external environment. Historically, various theories of motivation have tended to incorporate specific personal or environmental variables, but until recently almost none have tried to systematically incorporate both (Weiner, 1972).

Consequently, the term motivation is interpreted in many ways. The resulting difficulties in developing an adequate *theory* of motivation have been accompanied by corresponding difficulties in developing adequate *measures* of motivation, particularly academic motivation. Surrogate measures, such as family socioeconomic status, have been shown to have a substantial and consistent relationship to performance in school (Walberg, (1971), but direct measures of motivation tend not to be highly correlated with performance or with each other (Keller, Kelly, & Dodge, 1978). *Direct measures* are needed, because they will assist in the process of identifying specific motivational problems and the effects of instructional techniques on motivation. Surrogate measures only help to predict initial motivation with respect to the general importance of schol in one's development.

The need for more adequate measures of academic motivation has been identified by many researchers (e.g., Cooley & Lohnes, 1976), and this need is underscored in the present argument by the need for *better theory* upon which to base *better measures*. At the same time that these concerns are being expressed, there has been rapid growth recently in psychological research on a number of motivational concepts. In a recent review (Keller et al., 1978) of measures of several of the better known of these concepts in an academic context (e.g., locus of control, achievement motivation, curiosity), several questionnaire-type, self-report measures were found for each concept. However, the availability of these instruments does not help the instructor know which one to use under a given set of circumstances. And, it would not be feasible in most instructional situations, whether for research or practice, to use a battery of instruments to measure each of several motivational concepts. Hence, there still exists the need for a measure of general academic motivation. A few of these were found (Keller et al., 1978), and some had promise (especially Moen & Doyle, 1978), but none systematically measured specific aspects of motivation within the framework of a general theory of motivation and instruction. Such a measure is in prepration and has undergone preliminary testing (Keller & Keller, 1981).

MOTIVATION AND LEARNING

Of equal or greater importance than the two problems just discussed is the need for an adequate *theoretical basis* for understanding motivation in education. Such a theory provides the basis for a systematic approach to developing motivational-design strategies. In an earlier paper (Keller, 1979), a theory was presented that serves as the roots of the motivational-design approach described in this chapter. The following brief review highlights the key points of the theory together with a brief discussion of its characteristics and its relationship to the motivational-design model.

Motivation, as argued in the earlier paper (Keller, 1979), is the neglected "heart" of our understanding of how to design instruction. Historically, instructional science has benefited from the work of behavioral psychology and cognitive-learning psychology, but this has given us only partial knowledge of how people learn, and almost no knowledge of why they learn. Working from the perspective of behavioral psychology, early instructional scientists (e.g., Markle, 1969; Skinner, 1968) derived strategies for the organization of instruction to allow the effective use of feedback. This required active responding with minimal errors to provide a context for the contingent use of *feedback and reinforcement*. These approaches contributed to improvements in learning and, in a very qualified sense, to motivation. Given that a person is already interested in a subject and is actively responding, then the appropriate use of feedback will help maintain and sometimes increase that behavior.

Additional knowledge from cognitive psychology and information-processing research (e.g., Ausubel, 1968; Mayer, 1977) provided the basis for a better understanding of how to organize instruction to improve the acquisition and retention of knowledge and skills. Instructional scientists then developed strategies and prescriptions for the design of instructional materials (e.g., Gagné, 1977; Merrill, 1975; Reigeluth, 1979). These characteristics are also studied in relation to individual differences in ability and learning style (Cronbach & Snow, 1976).

Keller's (1979) theory of motivation, performance, and instructional influence illustrates how motivational theory can be integrated with these other two major influences in instructional science. On the one hand, this theory illustrates how to better understand what influences a person to approach or avoid a task. On the other hand, this theory illustrates how to approach the problem of making a task more interesting. This theory, building on the earlier work of Porter and Lawler (1968), clearly distinguishes between effort and performance as categories of behavior (see Fig. 11.1). *Performance* means actual accomplishment, whereas *effort* refers to whether the individual is engaged in actions aimed at accomplishing the task. Thus, effort is a direct indicator of motivation. We know that people are more or less motivated by the vigor or persistence of a behavior. In contrast, performance is a measure of learning and is only indirectly related to motivation; it is also influenced by ability and opportunity (learning design and management). Ironically, most studies of motivation in education use learning (as measured by grades or some other indicator of accomplishment) as the dependent variable.

A further distinction is made between performance and consequences. *Consequences* include both the intrinsic and extrinsic outcomes that accrue to an individual. These include emotional, or affective, responses, social rewards, and material objects. Consequences are related to motivation because they combine with cognitive evaluation (see Fig. 11.1) to influence changes in one's personal values or motives. These effects will, in turn, influence the degree of effort under similar circumstances in the future. This concern with the consequences of an immediate activity on future motivation for the activity has been discussed by Maehr (1976) as continuing motivation.

As illustrated in Fig. 11.1, this theory is in the tradition of field theory (Lewin, 1935), or social-learning theory (e.g., Hunt & Sullivan, 1974; Rotter, 1972), in which behavior is considered to be a function of the *person* and the *environment*:*

$$B = f(P \& E).$$

Keller's theory describes the influence of these two factors on three categories of responses: effort, performance, and consequences. This classification provides an effective means for integrating research. To illustrate, the preceding discussion of historical influences on instructional science can be quickly summarized in terms of this theory. For example, the study of reinforcement is an *E* variable that primarily influences consequences. There has been a great deal of research on this environmental factor, but relatively little on the *P* variable of cognitive evaluation. The

---

*Editor's note: In terms of the theoretical framework presented in Chapter 1, most person variables are instructional *conditions*, whereas most environment variables are instructional *methods*.

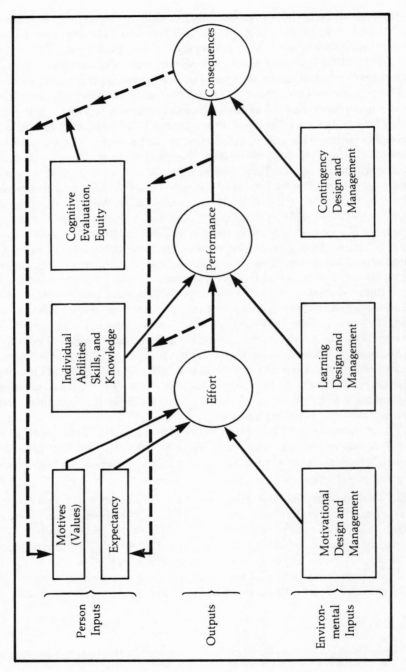

FIG. 11.1   A model of motivation, performance, and instructional influence.

work of Deci (1975), Condry (1977), and others suggests that there are important *P* factors that modify the effects of environmental contingencies.

Moving to the center of the model, there has been a great deal of research on *P* variables related to individual differences in performance, and there is a rapidly growing body of research and theory concerned with the optimal design of instruction (*E* variables) to maximize learning.

However, moving to the left, we come to the two primary areas of influence on motivation. There are many theories and lines of research on the individual characteristics of human motivation, *P* factors, but very little on ways to systematically influence motivation by means of instructional design, *E* factors.

Before elaborating further on this theory, particularly its motivational components and their relationship to the motivational-design model to be presented, it is worth considering what type of a theory this is. Keller's (1979) theory of motivation, performance, and school influence clearly is not in the tradition of micro theories* that have been in vogue for quite a number of years in psychology and education. In contrast, the purpose of this theory is to identify *major categories* of variables of individual behavior and of instructional design that are related to individual effort and performance. This theory incorporates the theories and paradigms that have received the major focus of attention in instructional science, and illustrates how motivational theory will interface with the earlier work. As such, the proposed theory is, in Kaplan's (1964) terms, a macro theory, or concatenated theory. It describes a network of relationships that provide a type of explanatory shell for the factors, or phenomena, that the theory attempts to explain.**

The present theory clearly attempts to be more analytic and inclusive than particular, and for several reasons. We technologists, in contrast to scientists, tend to be working with a rather larger base of knowledge and skills. We require syntheses of those areas of knowledge that are most likely to improve our decisions in practical problem solving. However, in contrast to the traditional linear view of science as discovering basic truths that then filter down to an applied level (of Hilgard & Bower, 1975), it is probably more likely that technology benefits selectively from science. Technology will benefit from useful syntheses of scientific knowledge if particular technologists *make the effort* to obtain the knowledge and write the syntheses (Kranzberg, 1968). In this same vein, these syntheses will be more meaningful and effective if they are presented in the context of an *organized structure* that facilitates their learning and retention. This is one of the purposes of the present theory. As a concatenated theory at the macro level, it serves as a "subsumer" in Ausubel's (1968) sense: It provides a structure in which to locate and remember many of the important concepts from the study of instruction and learning.

---

*Editor's note: *Micro theory* is not being used here in the same sense that it has been used in most of the other chapters of this book.

**Editor's note: It should be fairly clear to the reader that Keller's *macro* theory is what was referred to in Chapter 1 as a *metatheory* or *paradigm* or *theoretical framework*.

However, this organizational purpose would not be adequately served if the theory had no validity, and would be relatively trivial if "subsumption" were the only function of the theory. The present theory also provides *heuristic and predictive functions* and, following Snow's (1973) argument, both descriptive and prescriptive functions. At a descriptive level of explanation, the present theory leads to predictions about the relationships among motivation, learning, and performance. At a prescriptive level, it leads to predictions about how we can influence these human characteristics by manipulating various components of the instructional environment. Furthermore, the theory has, in our experience, proven to be rich in heuristic value; that is, testable working hypotheses are readily generated as we introduce more specifically defined variables and consider their impact on the theory.

The primary concern with this theory in the present context is to illustrate a systematic basis for a motivational-design model. As illustrated in Fig. 11.1, the primary "person" influences on effort are motives (values) and expectancies. Together, these factors represent a motivational theory generally known as *expectancy-value theory* (see Steers & Porter [1975] for a review). It assumes that motivation is a multiplicative function of values and expectancies; that is, a person will approach activities or goals that are perceived to be personally satisfying and for which the person has a positive expectancy for success.

Within the *value* category would fall the research in areas such as curiosity and arousal (Berlyne, 1965), personal needs (Maslow, 1954; McClelland, 1976; Murray, 1938; Rogers, 1969), and beliefs or attitudes (Feather, 1975; Rokeach, 1973). With the exception of curiosity, each of these areas of research is concerned with understanding how the internal structure of individual needs and beliefs is related to choices for action—that is, to the direction in which individuals will exert effort. Curiosity, as a line of research, stands apart in some respects. Berlyne (1965) defines curiosity in one sense as an individual-difference variable representing a personal motive or need. But, he also defines aspects of curioisity in terms of arousal, which is more of a physiological variable, and would be closer to a psychological explanation based in drive theory (Hull, 1943). Without entering into the controversies resulting from shifting to various modes of explanation (cognitive versus physiological), the position taken in the present approach is to treat curiosity and arousal as somewhat different from the other variables in the "value" category. This distinction will be quite apparent in the motivational-design model described later in this chapter.

The *expectancy* term in this theory of motivation also encompasses several lines of research. These include locus of control (Rotter, 1966, 1972), attribution theory (Weiner, 1974), self-efficacy (Bandura, 1977), learned helplessness (Seligman, 1975), and other influences on a generalized expectancy for success or failure (Jones, 1977; Perlmuter & Monty, 1977). A common element in all these approaches is the attempt to explain the formation and effect of personal expectancies for success or failure in relation to behavior and its consequences.

Although values (including curiosity) and expectancies are the foundation of the theory to explain individual motivational tendencies, the macro theory (see Fig. 11.1) also includes the effect of *reinforcement* on motivation. In this case it is represented as a joint influence of consequences and cognitive evaluation. Following a performance, a person will experience an emotional response, such as elation, pride, despair, or tranquility. The person may also receive an external reward such as applause, a smile, or cash. Deci (1975), Condry (1977), and others (e.g., Bates, 1979) have shown that the relationship between intrinsic and extrinsic reinforcement is not simple. There seem to be conditions under which an extrinsic reward will actually decrease intrinsic motivation. Thus, a concern for rewards and intrinsic motivation is represented by their influence on the *value* a person places on a given activity.

In summary, Keller's (1979) theory of motivation, performance, and instructional influence is a macro theory that incorporates cognitive and environmental variables in relation to effort, performance, and consequences. It also distinguishes between three types of influence of instructional design. The first is *motivational design*, the second is *learning design*, and the last is *reinforcement-contingency design*. The assumption is that any instructional event, whether it is a teacher in a classroom or a module on a microcomputer, will have these three influences; and the task of the instructional scientist is to understand and control them.

MOTIVATIONAL-DESIGN MODEL*

Turning now to the motivational-design model, it is presumed that there are four basic categories of motivational conditions that the instructional designer must understand and respond to in order to produce instruction that is interesting, meaningful, and appropriately challenging.** The four categories, which are derived from the preceding presentation, are interest, relevance, expectancy, and satisfaction (see Fig. 11.2). *Interest* refers to whether the learner's curiosity is aroused, and whether this arousal is sustained appropriately over time. *Relevance* refers to the learner's perception of personal need satisfaction in relation to the instruction, or whether a highly desired goal is perceived to be related to the instructional activity. *Expectancy* refers to the perceived likelihood of success, and the extent to which success is under learner control.

The final category, *satisfaction,* refers to the combination of extrinsic rewards and intrinsic motivation, and whether these are compatible with the learner's anticipations. For example, we would expect a student who finishes 10th in a class of

---

*Editor's note: It should be evident from Fig. 11.2 that this is an instructional-*development* model or procedure, not an instructional-design model (see Chapter 1, p. 24), but the central part of the model provides the basis for prescribing instructional-design models.

**Editor's note: These *motivational conditions* are condition variables as defined in Chapter 1.

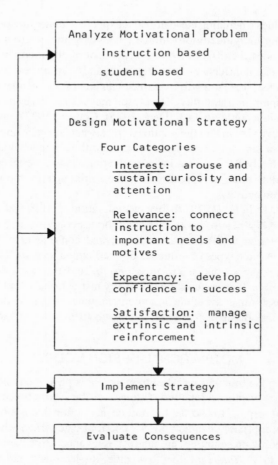

FIG. 11.2   A model for designing motivating instruction.

100 to feel good. But, if this student had a personal competitor whom he or she perceived to be inferior, and if the competitor came in seventh, then the student
would feel bad instead of good. Equity theory (Adams, 1965) provides another
approach to understanding the dynamics of social comparisons in relation to affective responses to outcomes.

This model serves three purposes. First, it provides a relatively parsimonious,
theoretically based model for *integrating* the numerous strategies for increasing
motivation. As indicated, this model is derived from the macro theory (Keller,
1979) that identifies the major categories of variables related to motivation.

Secondly, this model facilitates the effort to integrate motivation theory and motivational strategies with instructional-design theory.* Reigeluth and Merrill (1979 and Chapter 1 of this book), for example, have classified instructional variables into several sets of interrelated categories. One set of categories has three parts: conditions, methods, and outcomes. *Conditions* are variables that constrain or interact with methods, but that cannot ordinarily be directly manipulated by the instructional designer or educator. *Methods* are specific strategies for achieving different outcomes under different conditions. These are under the direct control of the instructional designer. *Outcomes* are the measurable influences of methods on the individual learner, a group of learners, or the learning institution. As illustrated in Fig. 11.3, these categories are further subdivided into three types of conditions and strategies and three levels of outcomes.

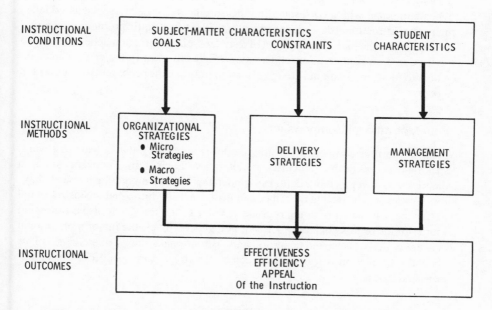

FIG. 11.3 A framework showing classes of instructional-method variables and the major condition variables that influence each. The classes of condition variables are *not* a complete list. Rather, they represent the conditions that are likely to have the strongest influence on each class of method variables. (This same figure was seen in Chapter 1.)

*Editor's note: The relationship between motivation theory and motivational strategies is similar to the relationship between learning theory and instructional strategies (see Chapter 1).

The identification of motivational conditions and strategies provides a convenient structure for presenting the present motivational model. Reigeluth and Merrill's distinction between conditions and methods corresponds roughly to Keller's distinction between two types of motivational problems: those located within the individual, and those located in the instruction. When there is a *severe* motivational problem in the individual, such as an extreme lack of confidence, then an intervention in the form of counseling or another type of behavior-modification strategy is needed. Normal instructional-design approaches would not solve this motivational problem. The assumption in the present model is that the students are within a normal range on the relevant motivational variables, and that an existing motivational problem is due to problems in the *instruction* rather than problems in the personality of the learner.

This leads us to the third major purpose of the present model. It allows a *problem-solving approach* to identifying the solving motivational problems. This model, when combined with a corresponding measurement approach, as discussed later, helps the instructional designer or educator to identify specific problems that might be depressing the motivational level of a student, classroom, or teacher. It can also be used in a preventative sense. The model helps to identify the critical areas on which to focus motivational-design efforts to improve the probability of success in a course.*

Four Motivational Components

Each of the four components of this model is a category that subsumes several specific concepts or micro theories of motivation. Each of these concepts or micro theories was developed in a context of understanding and predicting human behavior. As such, each concept describes a motivational condition that the instructional designer must match with appropriate parallel strategies. Each of the following four sections of this chapter describes, at a general level, the major motivational concept with its associated condition and instructional strategy or strategies. This general introduction is followed in each section by a more specific list of conditions and strategies.

INTEREST

The Concept of Interest

Practically every theory of learning includes some assumption about interest. A student has to at least be paying attention to a stimulus for learning to occur. As a motivational variable, interest encompasses several theories of *curiosity* and

---

*Editor's note: This shows great promise for providing a basis for prescribing different instructional models for the motivational design of instruction.

arousal. In education, one of the more widely used definitions of curiosity is that of Maw and Maw (1968). A curious person is one who:

1. reacts positively to new, strange, incongruous or mysterious elements in his environment by moving toward them or manipulating them;
2. exhibits a need or a desire to know more about himself and/or his environment;
3. scans his surroundings seeking new experiences;
4. persists in examining and exploring stimuli in order to know more about them [p. 2].

Given that these behaviors indicate curiosity, the challenge for the instructional designer is to know how to elicit them. Berlyne (1965) has been particularly interested in the properties of objects and conditions that *stimulate curiosity*. He found a number of such characteristics, which he called "collative" variables, including novelty, paradox, incongruity, and complexity. To include these characteristics in the design of instructional materials would enhance the likelihood of stimulating curiosity as defined in the first and third parts of the preceding definition of curiosity.

Another aspect of curiosity is reflected in the second and fourth parts of the definition. The inclusion of the collative variables in instruction will elicit curiosity, but it may be a rather passive, short-lived experience if the learners do not exercise their curiosity. Interest is more likely to be maintained if the students *engage in activities* that allow them to act on their curiosity by exploring and manipulating their environment. In many instructional settings, students are given very little encouragement or opportunity to explore, both in a physical and an intellectual sense.

Before looking at specific interent conditions and strategies, there are two distinctions and one caution that need to be made. These apply to curiosity in particular, and in some regards to motivation in general.

The first distinction is one that differentiates between two types of curiosity. Berlyne (1965) distinguishes between perceptual curiosity and epistemic curiosity. *Perceptual curiosity* is similar to attention; it refers more to a sensory-level reaction and selective attention in response to particular objects in the environment. Instructors and designers often capitalize on this type of curiosity by doing something startling at the beginning of or during a presentation. Of more interest to education, however, is *epistemic curiosity*. This refers to information seeking and problem-solving behavior that occurs as a result of the stimulation of curiosity. It is this type of curiosity that is evidenced when a child works at a jigsaw puzzle or a science problem.

A second distinction is made between state and trait curiosity. The term *trait* refers to the assumption that people have relatively stable proclivities with respect to such things as curiosity, need for achievement, anxiety, and so on. However, we see wide variations in behavior in different situations. Hence, *state* refers to the manifestation of a particular characteristic in a specific situation. Even though people have given proclivities, they may not be activated in a particular situation;

or due to the complex interrelationship of needs and desires, there may be motive conflicts in a given situation. A person who has a great deal of curiosity but dislikes responsibility may find that the exercise of curiosity in certain contexts leads to committee assignments. The person then may inhibit that tendency any time he or she anticipates its leading to unwanted responsibility. In this case, low *state* curiosity would inhibit *trait* curiosity.

In the classroom we often say that we want to foster creativity; we want students to do original thinking. Then we punish them for giving us "wrong" answers. Berlyne (1965) and others (e.g., Keller, 1978) have shown that people generally have to feel comfortable about the *consequences of taking risks* before they will exercise a great deal of curiosity. Therefore, in instructional design, we must be cognizant of whether we are designing educational situations that are consistent with the type of behavior we hope to observe.

A caution is in order that will apply throughout this model of motivation. The ancient Greek conception of balance and harmony, as exemplified in the "golden mean" of Aristotle, is very pertinent. Almost every motivational construct has an *optimal level* with respect to effective behavior. Stated in more modern terms, we are talking about the Yerkes and Dodson (1908) law, which suggests that the relationship between motivation and performance is, graphically, in the form of an inverted U. Too low a level of motivation results in less than optimal performance. On the other hand, excessive motivation also results in suboptimal performance due to anxiety and other sources of distortion and disorganization.

For example, achievement motivation has been shown to be at an optimal level with tasks of a *moderate level of risk*. Both low and high-risk challenges are related to a decrease in achievement motivation. Curiosity, and the closely associated concept of arousal, are presumed to follow the same law. In summary, it should never be assumed in the context of the model of motivational design that more of something is automatically to be preferred, as educators often do in the case of general intelligence. We are concerned with achieving a match between learners with a reasonable degree of curiosity, achievement motivation, and so on, and instruction that activates and fosters those characteristics.

Interest: Conditions and Strategies

In general, interest is a condition that exists when there is an *unexpected* or *inconsistent* event in the perceptual environment, or there is a *gap* between a given and desired state of knowledge. This two-part description is consistent with the previously defined distinction between perceptual and epistemic curiosity. It is especially useful for purposes of analysis and research, but only limitedly useful for design. In practice, some strategies are clearly identifiable as one or the other, such as slamming a book on the table, but many strategies have elements of *both*. It would be difficult, and seldom desirable, to develop a list of strategies that purported to be one or the other, especially because both types of curiosity are, within limits, desirable. *Perceptual curiosity* is certainly the easier of the two to arouse. There is a great deal of survival value for humans and other species in being sensitive and responsive to unexpected stimuli. However, most meaningful learning requires a *sustained* level of curiosity—or, as Aristotle would put it, wonderment— that is more challenging for the educator to sustain or nurture, and requires drawing on *epistemic curiosity*.

The following strategies begin with those that are simpler, operating more at the perceptual level, and progress to those that would contribute more to the development of epistemic curiosity. The last two are relatively complex and are represented by somewhat comprehensive models of teaching.

> *Strategy 1.*   To increase curiosity, use novel, incongruous, conflictual, and paradoxical events. Attention is aroused when there is an *abrupt change* in the status quo.

An unexpected stimulus, a puzzle, or *any device that creates perceptual or conceptual conflict* will increase attention and curiosity. People will seek information to explain or resolve the inconsistency. A lesson that begins with a question, statement, or other device that creates an *unusual perspective* in the mind of the learner will capture that learner's interest. A key element in this strategy is that it puts the learner into a problem-solving mode, even if the problem is nothing more than ascertaining the source and innocuousness of an unexpected stimulus (the slammed book).

The extent to which a student's curiosity can be held with this strategy depends on the *frequency* and *complexity* of its use. If students are bombarded with novel, incongruous, and conflictual stimuli, then the unusual can become commonplace and lose its effect, especially when there is insufficient time for the learner to actively respond to the situation in a problem-solving manner. This problem is probably best illustrated by the results of recent research on television. Children who watch large quantities of television, which provides such a continuous bombardment of stimuli, actually suffer impairments in learning and problem solving (Singer, Singer, & Zuckerman, 1980). The structure of a typical television show does not allow time for the rehearsal and transfer of information from short- to long-term memory, and it is a passive medium, one that encourages the undivided, passive attention of the viewer.

In summary, this strategy must be *applied judiciously*. Despite the preceding example of the consequences of excessive stimulation, the situation in school is more probably one of either understimulation or excessive complexity. That is, students are not likely to complain that they are being presented with too many novel and interestingly incongruous events. But, they are likely to develop confusions and misconceptions due to excessively complex and even unintended incongruities and paradoxes in the instructional material. In using this strategy, the students' curiosity must be aroused by perceiving a problem, but the students must also be given an opportunity to *resolve* the incongruity, or, in other words, to solve the problem.

> *Strategy 2.*   To increase curiosity, use anecdotes and other devices for injecting a *personal, emotional element* into otherwise purely intellectual or procedural material.

People are usually more interested in the concrete than the abstract, and in *real people and events* rather than humanity in general or hypothetical events. Consequently, the use of *personal language* and *concrete stories* about real people can help maintain curiosity and dispel boredom. Flesch (1948) created a simple formula to measure the human interest of prose material. His formula is based on the proportion of personal words and personal sentences in a passage. Research has demonstrated the validity of Flesch's formula, and underscores the assumptions underlying this strategy.

Dramatic evidence for this strategy appears in McConnell's (1978) article entitled "Confessions of a Textbook Writer." McConnel's introductory psychology text is one of the most widely used and has a very low end-of-year return rate. He attributes this success, in part, to the use of *personal anecdotes* throughout the text. He conducted extensive developmental testing while writing his text, a procedure seldom employed by textbook writers (which he acknowledges) and long prescribed by instructional-development models (which he does not acknowledge). His testing demonstrated the value of the personal stories about the famous psychologists in the text, and confirmed the admonition he received from a professor, Karl Dallenbach, who was one of his mentors and role models (McConnell, 1978): "If you want to capture the imaginations of young people, you have to tell them stories [p. 160]!" Although we often accept this uncritically when dealing with children, the work of McConnell and Flesch suggests that the strategy is true with both young people and adults.

> *Strategy 3.*   To arouse and maintain curiosity, give people the opportunity to learn more about things they *already know about* or believe in, but also give them moderate doses of the *unfamiliar* and unexpected.

On the one hand, this strategy seems contradictory, and on the other hand, it seems similar to the first strategy. It is true that people enjoy opportunities to learn more about things they already know and are interested in. That is why people subscribe to special-topic magazines, join clubs, do research, and attend political rallies of their own party persuasion rather than to learn about their opponents. Recognition of this by educators is reflected in the frequently heard admonition to present instruction at the student's level of ability and interest.

However, despite this commonplace observation, we often find a gap between instructional content and student interest, especially in areas other than reading where the teacher has some flexibility in selecting relevant stories. Even so, the strategy is valid and bears repeating in this context. One example of efforts to bridge the gap is provided by a teacher who uses *analogies* to help students find something familiar in material that might seem abstract and remote. For example, in teaching the structure of American government in seventh-grade social studies, this teacher asks the class how the three branches of government are like a two-story house with a basement. The students, in talking about the specific functions of the furnace in the basement, the return air ducts, the kitchen, living room, bedrooms, and so on, come up with the concepts of separate yet interdependent functions. In the teacher's experience, this has almost never failed to generate general interest in the class discussion, and increased interest in the functions of government. This particular analogy works well in New York, but might not in Arizona or southern California; however, the use of analogies is viable and is a good way to operationalize this strategy.*

The second part of this strategy is similar to the first strategy (using novel, incongruous, conflictual, and paradoxical events), but it is intended to focus more on unfamiliar, unexpected *content* or subject matter, as opposed to novelty in approach or example. Although there are individual differences in sensation-seeking tendencies among individuals (Zuckerman, 1971, 1978), people seem to enjoy moderate amounts of exposure to unusual or novel subjects. The inclusion of *unusual, or exotic, material* can help initiate or maintain curiosity in a group. However, even here a caution is in order. If a group is already highly curious about a particular subject, the inclusion of unexpected and divergent material can be irritating. For example, a group of doctors attending a briefing on the proper use of a recently licensed drug would want the essential information, and would want to get back to their practices as soon as possible. They would not appreciate extraneous material. In contrast, most designers are working with audiences that do not have as much inherent curiosity for the subject, and "human-interest" strategies will be helpful.

Strategy 4.   To increase curiosity, use analogies to make the strange *familiar* and the familiar *strange*.

An established design and teaching model that is very effective for stimulating and developing epistemic curiosity is synectics. *Synectics* was designed by Gordon (1961) specifically for the purpose of stimulating creativity in problem-solving situations, and creativity is highly correlated with curiosity (Vidler, 1977). Although originally used in industry to stimulate creativity within groups of people who work as problem solvers and product developers, it has now been developed into teaching models (Joyce & Weil, 1972; Weil, Joyce, & Kluwin, 1978) to stim-

---

*Editor's note: See Chapter 10, p. 360, for more about the use of analogies in instruction.

ulate imagination and creativity. As is often stated in readings on the topic, synectics can be used to help make the strange familiar and the familiar strange.

At the simplest level, synectics can be used to stimulate curiosity by: (1) presenting a *divergent situation* (an incongruous analogy); and (2) requesting *convergent thinking*. For example, a teacher who uses synectics in a high-school social studies class uses a series of metaphorical, or analogical, exercises to loosen up the class, and to lead into a level of understanding of the content that exceeds the level of simply memorizing facts, concepts, and examples. These examples and exercises, taken from a unit on World War II, begin with a warm-up exercise in which the teacher asks the students, "Which is deadlier, a gun or a rumor?" After a discussion of this analogy, the teacher tries to stretch the students minds a bit by asking, "Who has a better sense of humor, God or Hitler?" In this case, every student gave the "right" answer at first, then someone mentioned that he had no evidence as to whether God has a sense of humor, but he had seen a film in which Hitler did a brief "dance" when told of a Nazi military victory. The class was then given a brief written exercise on the topic of "How is a rattlesnake like a dictator?" and "How is a tornado like a blitzkrieg?" Additional exercises required the students to produce their own analogies. The benefits of this approach as used by this particular teacher were cognitive as well as motivational.* With respect to cognition, these exercises served an information-processing function in that they facilitated the integration of this new knowledge with what the students already knew.

The combined motivational and information-processing functions of synectics can be formalized by a process that might be called *metaphoric organizers*. It is similar to the concept of advance organizers (Ausubel, 1968), but with an important difference. The advance organizer model, as described in Ausubel's theory of meaningful learning, is concerned with a learner's cognitive structure—that is, a learner's knowledge of a particular subject matter and how well organized, clear, and stable it is. When this cognitive structure is defective, learning suffers. When the cognitive structure is effective, learning is enhanced, because new knowledge can be meaningfully integrated into, or subsumed by, the given cognitive structure.

However, in some cases, the material to be learned may be rather abstract and remote from the learner's experience—two factors that tend to reduce curiosity and learning. In these cases, metaphoric organizers can help the students relate the new, unfamiliar, abstract knowledge to something that is concrete and familiar. This is similar to Ausubel's use of comparative organizers to help relate new material to previously learned, related material. Common examples include comparisons between electronics and plumbing, mathematical equations and balance scales, and human cognition and computers (information processing). Weil, Joyce,

---

*Editor's note: For more on the cognitive benefits of analogies, see Chapter 10, p. 360.

and Kluwin (1978) offer many examples for the effective use of analogy in the context of synectics.

Strategy 5.   To increase curiosity, guide students into a process of question generation and *inquiry*.

A second design and teaching model that seems ideally suited to fostering epistemic curiosity is inquiry teaching.* This model, not to be confused with discovery learning, was developed (Suchman, 1966) to help students *learn how to learn* with respect to the process of inquiry. This model produces teaching situations that provide the students with a process that is similar to the process a scientist, or any disciplined inquirer (Cronback & Suppes, 1969), undertakes when investigating a problem. This is in contrast to traditional approaches to teaching science, in whic̓ɪ students are presented with laws and relationships during a lecture, then go to a laboratory to go through the motions of a series of "canned" experiments to verify what the lecturer has already told them.

It is noteworthy that the inquiry model begins with a *puzzling event,* something like an anamoly, a discrepancy between what is known and what will happen. This is followed by a learning process modeled after the *scientific method,* but it allows the students to investigate problems that are, in their eyes, original and capable of being solved at their level of understanding. The important factors in the present context are that this model both *stimulates* curiosity and provides the opportunity for students to *exercise* their curiosity. This model is well worth investigation by instructional designers (see Weil & Joyce, 1978).

In summary, one element of effective motivational design concerns the arousal and exercise of *curiosity* (or inteest) on the part of the learners. Because it is generally observed that students are understimulated far more often than they are overstimulated, instruction should benefit from efforts to incorporate the preceding strategies. The greatest danger is probably at the level of devising an extremely interesting opening, or "grabber," at the beginning of an instructional situation and not being able to follow through with an equally interesting program or presentation. That is why it is stressed in this section that the designer must be concerned with *arousing* and *sustaining* (or exercising) curiosity. To that end, the following principles (Keller, 1981) have been gleaned from the work on curiosity, and are offered for the assistance they might provide to the creative instructional designer:

With respect to curiosity, people tend to be:

1. Most interested in things they already know something about or believe in, but they also find the unfamiliar and unexpected to be intriguing in moderate doses.

---

*Editor's note: See Chapter 8 for an example of an inquiry approach to instructional theory.

2. More interested in real people and events than in humanity in general or abstract and hypothetical events.

3. Interested in anecdotes and other devices for injecting a personal, emotional element into otherwise purely intellectual or procedure material.

4. Interested in novel, incongruous, conflictual, and paradoxical events.

RELEVANCE

The Concept of Relevance

A second major motivational condition is that of relevance (see Fig. 11.2 earlier). Sustained motivation requirs the learner to perceive that *important personal needs* are being met by the learning situation. This general aspect of motivation has long been recognized as a progression of theorists have offered their explanations. One explanation is that of drive theory (Hull, 1943), in which motivation is defined primarily in terms of *physical deprivation*. Drives can range from primary physiological states such as hunger and thirst to secondary, acquired states such as fear and competitiveness.

In contrast, Murray (1938) explained motivation in terms of needs that act as "potentialities" of an organism to respond in particular ways under given conditions. Murray's explanation of the origin of a need is more *biological* than physical, and he identified a number of generalized needs. One of the best known of these is the *need for achievement,* which refers to a person's desire to do things rapidly and well, to overcome obstacles, to accomplish difficult tasks, and to attain high standards (Murray, 1938). Consequently, Murray viewed behavior as being goal directed: The organism will actively seek opportunities to change and grow in keeping with its need structures. This is in contrast to a more Hullian conception of a passive organism that responds to reduce stimulation—that is, taking a drink to reduce thirst, making friends to avoid loneliness, or achieving excellence to reduce job insecurity. However, there is still a similarity between the approaches represented by Hull and Murray. Both tend to see motivation as a difficult *tensional state* that persists until relief, or equilibrium, is obtained.

In keeping with Lewin (1935), Tolman (1949), and the general position taken in the present chapter, Murray assumed that behavior was a function of both *personal* and *environmental* characteristics. He is often recognized for his needs-press theory. A behavioral episode results from the press of the environment and the needs of the person. "Press" refers to obstacles, facilitation, and other characteristics of a situation that relate to the opportunity for need satisfaction.

Another major theorist in this context, McClelland, was influenced by the "why" of behavior (McClelland, Atkinson, Clark, & Lowell, 1953). Motives are learned and are represented by stimulus conditions that are associated with affective states. Furthermore, motives are aroused when there is a *discrepancy* between a present affective state and a desired or expected affective state. This theory includes the concept of equilibrium, as do the previous theories, but with a difference. In McClelland's affect arousal theory, equilibrium occurs when stimulation is at a point greater than zero. This is not, as it might seem, contradictory. It is analogous to a physiological state of equilibrium that requires a certain degree of stimulation for homeostasis. For example, understimulation, as in sensory deprivation, will cause hallucinations. In McClelland's theory, if a present level of stimulation is above or below that level, the organism will act to decrease or increase stimulation.

The three particular motives studied most thoroughly by McClelland and his associates are the needs for achievement, affiliation, and power. His definition of *achievement* is consistent with Murray's as previously described. *Affiliation* refers to the desire for close, personal relationships with other people. These would be regarded as two-way, meaningful relationships, and not as the desire to "do things" for other people. The latter is often an indication of the need for *power*, which is a desire to influence other people. The study of these particular motives has helped the understanding of motivation in relationship to performance in such diverse settings as entrepreneurship, managerial effectiveness, and education.

Although these are theories of the major theorists in this context, they are only a sampling. Also well known for their work in a context of identifying personal needs and values in relation to personal motivation are Maslow (1954), Rogers (1951), and Atkinson (Atkinson & Raynor, 1974).

Relevance: Conditions and Strategies

The general motivational condition related to relevance is that personal motivation will increase with increases in the perceived likelihood of a task to satisfy a *basic need, motive, or value*. This is the basic value term in the previously discussed expectancy-value approach to explaining motivation. With the exception of curiosity, which was included in the first of the four parts of this model (see Fig. 11.2), this category includes all of the approaches to describing particular values.

Consequently, this category encompasses a vast body of specific concepts, constructs, and attitudes. At the operational level, there is almost no limit to the number of specific desires that might impell a person to action. Without the guidance of theory, the instructional designer would be hard-pressed to determine what needs or values would characterize a particular audience, and what design strategies would be appropriate. Unfortunately, there is no single, and accepted, theory that is useful in this context. However, based on the theoretical approaches covered in the brief preceding review and on the results of research in the context of education, three specific categories of value will be used in the present model.

The three categories of value, each representing a subcondition under relevance, are personal-motive value, instrumental value, and cultural value. The first category, *personal-motive value,* suggests that increased value, or motivation, results when a given task or goal is perceived to offer satisfaction of a particular need or motive. Under personal-motive value are the lists of *needs* identified by researchers such as Murray (1938), Edwards (1970), Maslow (1954), and McClelland (1976). Among those that seem to be most pertinent to educational performance are three that are considered for illustrative purposes in this chapter. They are the needs for achievement, power, and affiliation. They have the advantage of a theoretical basis and a body of empirical study of their relationships to education (e.g., Atkinson & Raynor, 1974; McClelland et al., 1953).

The second category, *instrumental value,* refers to the increase in motivation to accomplish an immediate goal when it is perceived to be a required step for attaining a desired future goal. The effect of this future orientation and the perception of a series of contingent steps leading to a future goal has been described and studied most thoroughly by Raynor (1974).

Cultural value, the third category, is a well-known influence that parents, peers, organizations, and the culture at large have on motivation. Personal motivation increases when a desired goal is perceived to be consistent with the values of these reference groups. The values of these groups are not always consistent in a person's life, and *goal conflicts* can result, causing motivational problems. This is particularly noticeable with adolescents who develop peer-group allegiances that are incompatible with parental values.

Each of these motivational conditions suggests strategies for instructional design. Bear in mind that we are concentrating on strategies aimed at making instruction more motivating by being responsive to these three kinds of values. We are *not* presenting strategies designed to modify the motivational conditions in question, although that could be a consequence. For example, instruction that provides the opportunity for achievement need satisfaction could result in increases in the need for achievement in some learners. However, such results would be regarded as fortuitous in the present context. Following are several specific strategy suggestions in relation to each of the three relevance subcondition categories.

Personal-Motive Value Strategies

The following strategy descriptions are examples of the approach to take to connect motivational principles to instructional-design characteristics. They are not intended to encompass the vast amount of research that pertains to this general topic, but they do represent several of the major areas of study in an educational context.

> *Strategy 1.* To enhance achievement-striving behavior, provide opportunities to achieve *standards of excellence* under conditions of *moderate risk.*

A person's feeling of achievement is enhanced when the person believes success to be a *direct consequence* of his or her effort, when there is a moderate degree of *risk,* and when there is *feedback* attesting to his or her success. *Competition* can also be a factor in this process when the competition serves to inspire the participants to greater degrees of accomplishment. (There is another type of competition, as is described, that serves power needs rather than achievement needs.)

Specific approaches to operationalizing this strategy would include individual contracting with specified criteria for success, and non-zero sum-evaluation methods (described later). The principle of *individual contracting* can be utilized, as it traditionally is, in independent study; but it can also be embedded in a group activity. For example, deCharms (1976) described a learning activity called the Spelling Game. The instruction is designed so that each child in a classroom takes a pretest on the spelling list for the week. At the end of the week, the class is divided into two teams for a spelling bee. Each child has the choice of an easy, moderately hard, or hard word. An easy word is one that was spelled correctly by that particular child on the pretest. A moderately hard word is one spelled incorrectly on the pretest, but that the child has had several days to study. Finally, a hard word is one of comparable difficulty that the child has not seen before. Correct spelling of the word in the contest results in 1, 2, or 3 points, respectively.

This type of choice allows each child to establish his or her *own contract,* and to obtain immediate *feedback* regarding success. Furthermore, the social setting is such that the children are *encouraged* to do their best. There is nothing but social disapproval, another powerful form of feedback, for flamboyant, unrealistic attempts to answer difficult words, a condition that often prevails under normal contest situations. In addition, the achievement motive is stimulated in *all students*. Even poor spellers can earn 2 points by studying the words missed on the pretest. This type of structure can be used in other contexts to represent the general strategy description for achievement motivation, as can other approaches that stimulate moderate risk taking and the other characteristics listed in the strategy description.

A second example of design considerations in this context is the evaluation system in use. Alschuler (1973) points out that a *nonzero-sum scoring system* is best. Many types of competitive activities use a zero-sum scoring system. These systems require a penalty on one side for every gain on the other side. For example, grading on the curve, rank ordering, arm wrestling, chess, and standardized test taking are all zero-sum activities. In the spelling game *each child can be successful* independently of the overall outcome of the competition. Other examples include mastery learning, archery, performance contracting, and bowling. The nonzero-sum approach to evaluation allows each percon to *define standards of performance independently* of other persons, and competition is aimed at "passing the mark" established for the particular activity, rather than at simply "beating down" the rival.

In summary, there are entire books on the topic of increasing the level of achievement motivation in faculty and students (e.g., Alschuler, 1973; deCharms, 1976), and it is a challenging goal to bring about those changes. In contrast, the implications are clear for designing instruction to activate the achievement motive, given its presence in the learner. The challenge for the instructional designer is to implement *achievement-arousing strategies* concurrently with the other motivational requirements of the learners. The following strategies, which are presented more briefly, illustrate this problem.

> *Strategy 2.*   To make instruction responsive to the power motive, provide opportunities for *choice, responsibility,* and interpersonal *influence.*

The influence of *power* in learning environments is often negative. The negativity results from instructional-design approaches (including arbitrary requirements and teaching styles) that effect *controls* on the learners that are unnecessary or not clearly related to the learning objectives. Because power is the process of exerting influence, whether aggressive, persuasive, or unsolicited helping behavior, the teacher or designer who uses power inappropriately may initiate power struggles *instead of learning* in a given situation. This is illustrated in the excessive display of helping behavior of some teachers. One type of helping behavior is the Good Samaritan variety. It consists of a helping response when there is an obvious need for assistance. In contrast, the excessively helpful person is often high in need for power. A teacher who is too quick to show students how to do something, or to show them the "one right way to do it" will often generate negative reactions in the form of hostility or low effort. This teacher may not understand that the students are responding to the power influence, and do not like it because they want to "do it" for themselves.

It is important to realize that power and control are not equivalent. The power motive is revealed by a person's effort to gain a position of *influence* over other people. This influence could take the positive form of helping meet the dependency needs of a client or subordinate (McClelland & Burnham, 1976), or the more negative form of argument for argument's sake, classroom disruptions, or arbitrary "busywork" assignments. In both cases, the person enjoys the feeling of having influenced another person's life, but in the latter case the goal is influence for the sake of influence without an overriding goal of trying to establish control or resolve misunderstandings. In contrast, *control* is a type of power that is necessary to accomplish certain goals; it is a means rather than an end. A teacher needs classroom control in order for desirable learning to occur, and a person high on need for achievement likes to have personal control over the resources necessary to accomplish a goal. The teacher, who has to be prepared to use influence and to respond to student attempts to gain influence, will be more effective if he or she understands and enjoys the use of power.

The person high on need for *achievement* is often irritated by *power* struggles and tries to avoid them. This person sees control as a means of circumventing the "political" aspects of interacting with people to gain resources and personal advantages. Some Presidents of the United States experience this conflict, for example, Nixon and Carter, who had lofty achievement goals, but who tried to avoid the lengthy and demanding processes of building a base of influence with all of the key persons in Congress and other parts of the government (Winter, 1976). The desire for absolute control or, in a sense, absolute power, overshadowed the skill or desire for the process of competing for influence. In summary, when motive for power is strong, it means that the person derives pleasure from the process of wielding influence, whether or not achievement-type goals are obtained (McClelland & Burnham, 1976).

In instructional design, there are two problems with respect to power. One is to *avoid generating power conflicts* if possible, and the second is to *respond to students' power needs* when possible. The former is generally accomplished when rules are established and maintained consistently, providing that the rules are in the best interests of the students and that the students perceive this to be the case. Problems inevitably arise when a teacher, or the requirement in an instructional setting, is threatening and authoritarian and appears to serve only the personal power needs of the teacher.

However, even under the best of circumstances, some students will deliberately engage in power struggles with the teacher. This is one of the aspects of teaching that too few are prepared for before entering the classroom. Teachers generally have high, even idealized, expectations for the influence they hope to have on their students' lives. These teachers tend to be unprepared for students who fail to respond and who engage them in seemingly purposeless resistance. The resistance can be active, as with hostile, disruptive, and argumentative students, or passive, as with students who simply will not do the work.

These kinds of problems, coupled with other perhaps less dramatic signs of uncooperativeness, signal the need for more opportunities for students to satisfy their power needs. Sometimes this can be accomplished by *giving positions of authority* to students. We have all read stories about the social worker or teacher who converted a group of hostile opponents by identifying the leader, and winning the person over by giving the person a position of responsibility and enforcement. Similarly, elementary-school children experience a pleasant sense of personal power when they are selected for safety patrol, and get to leave class early. These leadership opportunities, when there is some *genuine authority* attached, give students experience with the exercise of personal influence.

In designing instruction to respond to the need for power in students, there are a number of strategies that may be employed. However, before describing them, a word of caution is in order. In a power context, the primary goal is *influence*. In an achievement context, the primary goal is *productivity*. Therefore, if the power motive is elicited without a corresponding requirement for goal accomplishment, these strategies may not have a beneficial educational consequence.

Power strategies are those that *provide the opportunity for influence or domination* over others, whether real or implied. Instructional strategies such as debating or the argumentative essay are traditionally acceptable strategies that elicit the power motive. These strategies require the utilization of knowledge and personal style for the purpose of "upstaging" an opponent, and not necessarily for the purpose of increasing truth or knowledge. Other power-motive strategies would include any types of *zero-sum games or simulations*. These, as indicated earlier, are games in which one person or team gains only at another's expense, as in chess and normative grading systems. This type of power motivation in curriculum design often has negative consequences, because students will use whatever means they can to achieve a favored position.

In summary, the power motive is difficult to address in instructional design. Students with a high need for power may become antagonistic if they have no opportunity to exercise power, and if they perceive the teacher to be exercising arbitrary and unwarranted power. The best solution seems to be for the teacher to have well-defined standards with consistently enforced rules, and to offer opportunities for students to assume responsibility. This responsibility could be in the form of administrative tasks in the classroom, or academic positions as in debates or argumentative essays.

> *Strategy 3.*   To satisfy the need for affiliation, establish *trust* and provide opportunities for *no-risk, cooperative interaction.*

The need for affiliation is expressed as a desire for close, friendly relationships with other people, and the desire to engage in cooperative, noncompetitive activities. As a motivational condition, the affiliation need is activated when *friendly cooperation* is the expected behavior in a group. This need is frustrated when students have to study in isolation from each other, when individual competitiveness is required, or when success is possible only at the risk of personal embarrassment or failure. Obviously, the need for affiliation seems to be in conflict with many of the typical requirements of school. Competing to achieve standards of excellence, or to gain positions of advantage are very much a part of the American classroom. Consequently, it would appear to be impossible to design instruction to simultaneously satisfy the needs for achievement, power, and affiliation; yet these are not mutually exclusive personality characteristics. A person can score high on any combination of these motives.

The point for instructional designers is that just as no one experience in life will satisfy all three motives, neither can they be satisfied *simultaneously* by a given instructional experience. Self-study may be a highly effective and efficient method for delivering some instruction, especially if it is appropriately challenging with frequent feedback. This would appeal to a person with a high need for achievement, but could become demotivating to persons with high needs for affiliation or power.

A solution to this dilemma is to *vary the instructional strategies* during a prolonged period of instruction. With respect to affiliation, this need for belongingness may be satisfied by several strategies. The first is to satisfy it as a prerequisite to more challenging risk-taking activities. Keller (1978) demonstrated how a lack of psychological security, which may be interpreted as a fear of personal rejection by others, can inhibit risk-taking behavior in a learning situation. Keller (1978) used a game in which the participants had to learn the rules by induction as they individually took turns trying to solve a concept-identification problem. Not until the participants learned the rules and overcame their fears of being embarrassed in front of the group did they relax and take the risks needed to find the solution. This is consistent with Maslow's (1954) hierarchy of human needs. It suggests that the need for affiliation must be satisfied *before* people will engage in the individual, competitive activities that lead to satisfaction of self-esteem needs.

The lesson for instructional designers is to include activities at the beginning of a learning situation that will *relax students' fears of social rejection.* In classroom situations, this often requires no more than taking a few minutes to establish personal contact with the group. In small groups, take a few minutes for introductions and personal comments. In large groups, as expert speakers well know, relate some human-interest information or anecdotes, and try to establish personal contact with one or two people in the group. In essence, one key motivational factor in relation to the need for affiliation is a negative one. That is, if people experience a *fear of rejection,* it may interfere with learning in a group setting. Therefore, the instructional designer has to *allay this fear* prior to engaging the students in the learning activity.

Two other design strategies are the inclusion of cooperative group activities, and shared-sum scoring systems. *Cooperative activities*, as opposed to competitive ones, allow people to enjoy social contact while trying to complete a task. An important part of the nondirective instructional-design model of Carl Rogers (1969) concerns the affiliative relationship of the teacher and learners. This relationship serves as a context within which individual, self-directed behavior can occur. The cooperative activity in this context may take the form of nonevaluative activities that allow the expression of warmth and responsiveness or the genuine acceptance of others as persons. Coffee breaks, "play" activities, and even group discussions of assigned material can serve this function, providing that the discussion leader is able to develop a sincere, positive atmosphere of acceptance in the groups. Another strategy is that of having students *work in groups* on an assignment. In teaching basic computing skills to children, it is helpful to have approximately three on a terminal. They tend to spontaneously work together in identifying mistakes, suggesting alternatives, and exploring options. The teacher in this setting has to ensure that the groups are compatible and that a single child does not dominate.

The final strategy described here is the shared-sum scoring strategy. Alschuler (1973) uses the example of team sports in which each member shares equally in the success or failure. This approach would also describe the instructional design and evaluation strategy in which students work as *team* and all get the same grade on their final product. This approach assumes that affiliative, cooperative behavior is required within the group in order for it to function effectively. The effect of this is seen in the comradery that is often developed among memebers of a team, or among the members of a class who move through a program together. However, there is a caution here, as every teacher knows. After assigning a group of students to work on a task, it is often confusing as to how the task can be subdivided into *distinct subtasks* for the individual students. In the absence of meaningful divisions of labor, it all too often happens that one person ends up doing "all" the work, and this becomes demotivating. It can also happen, as it does in team sports, that there is competition for favored positions or assignments.

The problem in this strategy is that, even though the evaluation system is shared sum, there is an interaction of affiliation and competition (or achievement) needs. Even though the team shares in the outcome, there is *individual assessment,* even if it is informal, of personal contributions to the success or failure. Therefore, in designing learning activities that require group activity and that employ shared-sum scoring, it would seem to be important to ensure *a clearly defined role for each person* to play and a sense that each role is *important.*

In summary, these are but three of the personal-motive value strategies that can be identified. At present, there is no comprehensive theory that succinctly categorizes all of the human motives that might influence the perceived relevance of instruction. The important principle for the instructional designer to retain is that motivation for learning is enhanced when the *perceived relevance* of the instruction is increased. The preceding discussion focused on strategies for increasing perceived relevance by making the instruction responsive to basic motivational needs in the students.

Instrumental-value Strategies

Another major category of influence in the perceived value of instruction, which is mentioned only briefly here, is perceived instrumentality. Raynor (1974) has demonstrated, as teachers have intuitively understood, that motivation is increased if a present goal or task is perceived to be an important or necessary prerequisite for the accomplishment of desired future goals. Correspondingly, design strategies that clarify the importance of a given segment of instruction should improve learner motivation. This can occur at the macro or micro level. At the broader level, teachers have traditionally used statistics and career education to illustrate how education leads to *greater earning power* and *career choice.* At the micro level, one function of learning *objectives,* although not generally identified as such, is to illustrate the importance of particular elements of instruction for goal accomplishment.

Cultural-Value Strategies

The final condition and strategy presented in this context is cultural value. Individual motivation to accomplish a given task is increased to the extent that the activity is positively valued by the individual's cultural reference groups. If the individual perceives that his or her family, friends, and society all think an activity is important, then the individual is more likely to think it is important. Problems erupt when, as sometimes happens in adolescence, there is a conflict between a child's family and peer group. At a broader level, there seems to be a growth in general cynicism about the value and quality of education in our culture, as evidenced by the publicized difficulties of Ph.D.'s and other graduates in getting jobs, and by highly critical news analyses, such as the recent report in *Time* magazine (e.g., Foote, 1980).

Instructional designers cannot necessarily be expected to introduce strategies that will solve psychological and social problems of this magnitude, but they can utilize strategies aimed at *improving the perceived cultural value* of instruction. Teachers try to use *positive role models,* by means of fiction and biography, in shaping student values. Similarly, in field testing his new, popular, introductory textbook in psychology, McConnell (1977) found that students were very interested in the *personal stories* about psychologists and other scientists. In one respect, these stories provided role models that attested to the cultural value of the subject matter. This suggests that when the motivational conditions are such that students are experiencing personal conflict or uncertainty about the value of a given course of instruction, the designer may increase perceived value by using culturally relevant *examples of accomplishment.* The insertion of anecdotes and personal examples into instruction could benefit this effort with adults as well as with children.

Summary

The concern for relevance is a major element in the motivational effect of instruction. It is not totally distinct from the earlier discussion of curiosity. As described in that section, curiosity is in one sense a motive that, when aroused by instruction, will make the instruction seem to be more relevant. Furthermore, some of the design strategies in that section deal directly with the problem of relevance, although from the standpoint of arousing and maintaining an appropriate level of stimulation. Together, the sections of this chapter dealing with curiosity and relevance combine into the *value* term of the expectancy-value theory of motivation (see Fig. 11.1).

The final two sections of this chapter are concerned with somewhat different motivational components. The first, *Expectancy,* refers directly to the other half of the expectancy-value theory. The final section, *Outcomes,* deals with the use of feedback and reinforcement, and other intrinsic and extrinsic consequences of behavior with respect to motivation.

EXPECTANCY

The Concept of Expectancy

The belief that a person's attitudes towards success or failure have a causal influence on actual events has a long history. The Greek myth of Pygmalian, the motivational workshops of Dale Carnegie, George Bernard Shaw's *My Fair Lady,* and Weiner Earhardt's EST are all based, at least in part, on this belief. Formal psychological studies based on this belief have taken several forms, but can be subdivided into two categories: expectations about *others* and expectations about *oneself*. The research on this topic is vast, so the remainder of this "concept" section contains brief introductions to some of the major theoretical approaches. These provide a sufficient basis for understanding the subsequent discussion of conditions and strategies.

Expectations of Others

One of the more widely known theories of expectancies concerns individual expectancies for the behavior of *others*. The theory was first defined as the self-fulfilling prophecy, which Merton (1968) describes as ". . . in the beginning, a false definition of the situation evoking a new behavior which makes the originally false conception come true [p. 423]."

Rosenthal and Jacobson (1968), who coined the term *Pygmalian Effect*, demonstrated this in an elementary-school classroom. Randomly selected children who were identified to the teacher as "intellectual bloomers" showed a 4-point gain in IQ over the control children in 1 year. Although the early work of Rosenthal and Jacobson was criticized on methodological grounds, subsequent research has supported the existence of a Pygmalian Effect (Jones, 1977; Strom, 1971).

A key factor in the self-fulfilling prophecy is the teacher's (or other professional's) belief that he or she can bring about the desired change. To tell a student, "You can do it if you try," is not an example of the self-fulfilling prophecy. To believe, "I know I can help this student despite the obstacles he or she presents." is an example. This was exactly the attitude of the fictional character of Professor Higgins in *My Fair Lady,* and of Anne Sullivan, the very real teacher of Helen Keller.

Expectations of Oneself

Turning to the more self-directed types of expectancies, there are several currently active concepts, including locus of control (Rotter, 1966), personal causation (Bandura, 1977; deCharms, 1976; White, 1959), and learned helplessness (Seligman, 1975). Each of these concepts explains an aspect of the effect of personal expectancies on one's own behavior.

The concept of *locus of control* (Lefcourt, 1976; Phares, 1976; Rotter, 1966) refers to a person's expectancy regarding the controlling influences on reinforcements. A person who tends to assume that good grades, friends, promotions, and other reinforcements are most likely to result from personal effort and initiative is an *internally* oriented person. In contrast, an *externally* oriented person tends to believe that irrespective of one's efforts, beneficial consequences are largely a matter of circumstances, either good luck or the favorable decision of a power-holding individual.

Weiner (1974) incorporated the concept of locus of control into the broader concept of *attribution theory*. He also broadened the concept from control over reinforcements to control over outcomes of behavior. His research suggests that attributions of successes or failures to relatively stable factors such as personal ability or task difficulty, in contrast to unstable factors such as effort and luck, are better predictors of performance than locus of control. Locus of control, which combines the *internal attributions* of ability and luck, and the *external attributions* of task difficulty and luck, is sometimes a better predictor of affect than performance (Keller, Goldman, & Sutterer, 1978; Weiner, 1979).

Another approach to the concept of personal expectancies is that of *personal causation,* or personal effectiveness. White (1959) introduced the concept of competence as an organism's capacity to interact effectively with its environment. A fuller development of this general idea is provided by Bandura (1977). Bandura's concept of *self-efficacy* refers to the personal conviction that one can execute the behavior required for successful performance. It does not refer to the relationship between performance and outcomes, which Bandura calls outcome expectations. These distinctions are virtually identical to those of Porter and Lawler (1968) who differentiate between the subjective expectancies that effort will lead to performance, and that performance will lead to reward. The same distinction is included in the theoretical bases of the present chapter (see Fig. 11.1).

Of more central interest to educators is deCharms' concept of personal causation (deCharms, 1968), which deCharms developed as the origin–pawn concept. *Origins* tend to be active authors of their own behavior, whereas *pawns* are more reactive and tend to let their goals and habits be dictated by others. However, deCharms has worked at a practical level to develop and validate programs for teachers and students to develop a higher degree of origin behavior (deCharms, 1976). Further reference to deCharms' work is included later in the discussion of strategies.

The final concept included in this section is *learned helplessness* (Seligman, 1975; Keller, 1975). Learned helplessness develops when a person wants to succeed, and when the person cannot avoid the situation in which success is expected but is in fact impossible. For example, a child in beginning algebra might be daydreaming, absent, or distracted by either a fear or amusement of the teacher during the time when some essential premises and operations are presented. Subsequently the child, who cannot avoid going to algebra every day and who would like to succeed, begins to fail. It is truly impossible for the child to be successful at this point without additional information that the child does not even realize is missing. Consequently, the child develops the deep-seated conviction that, "I can't do math." The child perceives no relationship between his or her effort and what happens as a consequence. Once established, this condition is extremely difficult to reverse. However, the studies that have been completed in an educational context (e.g., Chapin & Dyck, 1976; Dweck, 1975; Murphy, 1979) suggest that the condition can be reversed, particularly when it is interpreted and treated in a context of attribution theory (Abramson, Seligman, & Teasdale, 1978; Dweck & Goetz, 1977).

Expectancy: Conditions and Strategies

The general motivational condition related to expectancy is that personal motivation will tend to increase with increases in personal expectancy for success. Furthermore, personal expectancy for success is influenced by *past experience* with success or failure at the given task, *locus of control,* and *personal causation.* Before proceeding, one qualification is in order. When a task becomes extremely easy, it is not unqualifiedly true that personal motivation will increase. If tasks are very easy, hence an extremely high personal expectancy for success, a person may become bored or simply uninterested because the task represents no challenge. (Recall that persons high on need for chievement prefer tasks with a moderate level of difficulty.) In contrast, there are situations in which people enjoy tasks that are easy and relaxing. The point is that positive, as opposed to negative, expectancies for success are positively correlated with actual success, especially when the perceived control of success is internal rather than external.

Despite the rather large amount of research on expectancies, there has been rather little research on how to influence expectancies in an educational context. Most of the research on changing expectancies has been in a clinical-psychology context (e.g., Rudestam, 1980) or commercial self-help books and workshops (e.g., Lakein, 1973; Ringer, 1977). The major study conducted in schools was that of deCharms (1976); and his concern, like that of the clinical and commercial contexts, was how to develop a greater sense of personal causation in children who tended to be very low, or external, in this regard. DeCharms was concerned with what might be called a trait change—that is, a change in the students' generalized expectancies of personal effectiveness.

In contrast, as indicated earlier, the present chapter is concerned primarily with *state* changes: how to design instructional environments to stimulate students by responding to the motivational characteristics that may be expected to exist in a typical group. Students may be expected to be more interested in a class, and to perform better, if the class is designed in a way that stimulates their feelings of personal *competence* and *control.* The following list of strategies are not intended to solve the problems of either the extremely external or highly obsessive student. Such a student would need specialized help from a counselor, not an instructional scientist.

The following strategies encompass a number of instructional-design techniques, including some approaches from the previously mentioned work of deCharms (1976). Whenever possible, research supporting a strategy is mentioned, but in several instances the strategies, although based on sound arguments, need empirical investigation.

Strategy 1.   Increase expectancy for success by increasing *experience* with success.

This idea has a relatively long history of support in both theory and research. Rotter (1954) expressed the relationship in terms of generalized and specific expectancies, and provided a mathematical representation in a subsequent article (Rotter, 1972). Without our getting into mathematics we can understand that Rotter suggests that expectancy for success in a given situation is a combination of one's *generalized* expectancy for success and one's history of success in *similar situations*. In unfamiliar situations, a measure of generalized expectancy of success (such as that of Fibel & Hale, 1978)—not to be confused with locus of control, which refers to the perceived internal versus external control of reinforcements—is the best predictor of performance. If a person has a generally low expectancy for success or a specific history of failure in a given area, then a *series of meaningful successes* in that area will improve the person's expectancy for success (Feather, 1965; Feather & Saville, 1967).

There is a qualification that needs to be mentioned in connection with this strategy. The goal of such a strategy is to increase positive expectancies so students will be more successful under normal classroom conditions. Consequently, the success experiences used to build positive expectancies must be *similar* to those in the transfer situation. Success on a series of trivially easy tasks will not help a student who is confronted with tasks perceived to be moderately or extremely difficult.

This strategy is similar to the principle of error-free responding (Markle, 1969) in programmed instruction.* The strategy is based on a cognitive rather than behavioral assumption with respect to feedback. In this case it is assumed that feedback serves to verify the correctness of a response, but it is the *cognition of success* that increases the expectancy for success. This is different from the motivational influence of a reinforcement, which serves to maintain a response as long as the reinforcer is an incentive for the learner. In the present case, the focus is on increasing positive expectancies. Reinforcers are discussed in the last section of this chapter.

Strategy 2. Increase expectancy for success by using instructional-design strategies that indicate the *requirements* for success.

There are several instructional-design strategies—or, to be consistent with the present theoretical approach (see Fig. 11.1), learning-design strategies—whose effects on learning, have had considerable research, but not their effects on motivation. Two of these strategies are advance organizers and objectives. It has already been mentioned how *comparative organizers* can help generate a sense of relevance. In addition, both *comparative* and *expository* organizers (Ausubel, 1968) may serve to increase a student's expectancy for success.** By obtaining the superordinate relationships, or subsumptive structures, that facilitate the acquisition of unfamiliar material by overviewing its structure (expository

---

*Editor's note: See also Gropper's theory (Chapter 5).

**Editor's note: This applies to the elaboration theory's *epitome* as well (see Chapter 10).

organizers) or the integration of new but similar material (comparative organizers), the learner's motivation should increase due to increases in positive expectancies. Research is needed regarding these potential motivational effects.

Similarly, the presentation of *instructional objectives* to learners should increase the expectancy for success provided that there is consistency between the objectives and the evaluation of learning. A further assumption is that the stated objectives are the true objectives of the learning situations. All too often, relatively trivial aspects of a learning situation are stated in the objectives simply because the designers lacked the skill or imagination to describe the important goals in observable terms. Given these assumptions, well-stated objectives should have the dual motivational effect of reducing anxiety and increasing positive expectancies. Here again, research on the motivational properties of objectives is needed.

Strategy 3.   Increase expectancy for success by using techniques that offer *personal control* over success.

This strategy helps combine the concept of locus of control with expectancy for success. Strictly speaking, *locus of control* as developed by Rotter (1966) and others (e.g., Lefcourt, 1976; Phares, 1976) refers to the perceived internal versus external control over reinforcements. This implies something different from *expectancy for success* or failure, although the difference is not always clearly described. A person could have a positive expectancy for success at accomplishing a given task (e.g., "I will get that essay written by next Friday") and still have either an internal (e.g., "If I write it well, I'll get a good grade") or an external (e.g., "If the professor likes it I'll get a good grade") attitude towards reinforcement.

In essence, even though the two concepts are different, there is evidence that they are related. Internals tend to have a higher initial expectancy for success, especially with an unfamiliar task (Feather, 1965; Rotter, 1966). However, this difference tends to disappear with task experience.

The present strategy captures both concepts by suggesting that either personal control or predictable relationships (which is a form of control) over performance and reinforcement be established. An example of *personal control* would be individual contracting, assuming that the contract includes criteria for evaluation. An example of a *predictable relationship* would be mastery learning, again assuming that the mastery model is used properly with acceptable performance criteria specified.

Strategy 4.   Increase expectancy for success by using *attributional feedback* and other devices that help students *connect success* to personal effort and ability.

This strategy is particularly important when a student does not perceive a connection between his or her effort and its consequences, as in learned helplessness. This strategy is also one of the more difficult to implement, because it requires special attention from the designer and teacher.

Much of the nondirective approach of Rogers (1969) and the personal-causation approach of deCharms (1976) is concerned with helping students *develop internal attribution* for success and failure when such attributions are in fact appropriate. Both approaches emphasize the development of personal responsibilty and self-directedness. Rogers works in a context of human potential development and deCharms in a context of achievement motivation, and both authors have a number of specific suggestions for curriculum-design strategies. Those of deCharms (1976) are particularly helpful because concrete classroom activities are described. A similar approach to presenting Rogers' work in terms of concrete procedures is found in Weil et al. (1978).

A different and more direct approach to implementing this strategy requires the *direct intervention* of a teacher or tutor at an appropriate point. For example, a person who has developed a *learned-helplessness* attitude towards a particular subject simply does not perceive any causal link between behavior and its consequences. This person will tend to give an external attribution for success or failure. In math, this person will work on problems if they are easy, but will quit when the problems become challenging. This person often does not see the connection between ability and persistence as the key to success. In this situation, the designer must develop a sequence of problems (or other assignments depending on the context) that are *initially easy but become challenging.** After each success, the teacher gives *encouragement* to keep trying, and after success at the more difficult problems, the teacher gives verbal, *attributional feedback*. The student is told something like, "See, you succeeded because you kept trying. You are able to do that." Ordinarily it would take many such experiences to overcome a deep-seated helpless attitude. This approach has been demonstrated by Dweck (1975) in a mathematics context, and, with considerable revisions to fit the context, by Murphy (1978) in reading.

In summary, perceived expectancy of success is one of the two basic components of the basic expectancy-value theory of motivation. Jones (1977) has reviewed the research on expectancies, self-fulfilling prophecies, and the conditions related to the development of positive or negative expectancies. This research, incorporating both human and infrahuman subjects, supports the conclusion that *positive expectancies* lead to improved performance and success rates. A key factor in this principle is that the positive expectancies are not necessarily consistent with actual, or objective, predictions of success. Believing something can, apparently, help make it happen.

This principle, which is pushed to the unrealistic extreme in contexts such as "sales seminars" or by the "success merchants," is not advocated to the exclusion of the other motivational principles. *Excessive confidence* in success can lead to a narrowness of focus and an insensitivity to interpersonal feedback. Both of these consequences can interfere with the other motivational components of curiosity

---

*Editor's note: This easy-to-difficult sequence is an important part of Gropper's theory (Chapter 5) and Merrill's theory (Chapter 9).

and need satisfaction. However, it is seldom the case that students suffer from an excess of expectancy for success. Well-designed instruction should promote this perception.

OUTCOMES

The Concept of Outcomes

This category includes several specific factors that influence the satisfaction of goal accomplishment and the motivation to continue pursuing similar goals. It is assumed here, following the theory presented at the beginning of this chapter (see Fig. 11.1 for a representation); that both intrinsic and extrinsic outcomes follow a given performance. The *extrinsic outcomes* result from environmental controls and circumstances, and the *intrinsic outcomes* result from one's internal emotions and evaluations in response to the performance, the extrinsic consequences, and the relationship between them (Adams, 1965; Deci, 1975). The results of this cognitive evaluation feed back to motives and values, and thereby influence the motivation to continue to do the same kind of activity (see Fig. 11.1).

For example, a student, Deborah, may feel elated immediately after giving a speech in front of a class. She is elated because she remembered her entire speech and delivered it without fainting. A few minutes later her extrinsic "reward" from the teacher is being told that she was tense, barely audible, and obviously unrehearsed. Unless Deborah is an unusually stalwart person, or is driven by very powerful long-range goals, her intrinsic satisfaction has just been converted to embarrassment and, depending on her temperament, either shame or anger. The motive, or value, she attaches to this activity has been depressed and will survive only if there are other, overriding values for success in this activity. Furthermore, her subjective expectancy for success, with respect to the relationship between performance and consequences, has been reduced.

From a behavioral point of view, this example is a rather straightforward illustration of the interaction of internal and external consequences and evaluations of behavior. In a sense, it is simply an example of punishment, or a directly applied aversive consequence of behavior. However, in this case the relatively complex cognitive explanation might be preferable to a more parsimonious behavioral explanation. Recent research in intrinsic motivation versus extrinsic reinforcement suggests that there are a number of situations, similar to the preceding example, that are not explained satisfactorily by the more reductionistic behavioral theory (e.g., Bates, 1979; Condry, 1977; Deci & Porac, 1978). Space does not permit a thorough explication and review of the two positions, so the remainder of this section contains a brief overview. The next section, concerned with conditions and strategies, includes some of the principles that have been most heavily investigated and seem to have the most practical applicability.

Operant-conditioning theory assumes that behavior is controlled by its consequences. When a particular behavior is reinforced positively, it will increase in rate relate to a baseline, or nonreinforced, rate. Furthermore, if a variable-ratio reinforcement schedule is used, the behavior will persist for a relatively long time after reinforcement stops. However, once reinforcement terminates, the behavior will extinguish, which means that the rate of response will return to the baseline or slightly above it. Countless laboratory experiments confirm this observation (cf. Travers, 1977).

Despite the heavy support of conditioning principles, there are a growing number of observed situations that are not effectively explained by conditioning theory.* This is not surprising, as Kuhn (1970) has so aptly described, because the more rigorously we develop and apply a theory and its associated principles, the more we begin to notice the anomalies. For example, several studies have found conditions under which the removal of extrinsic reinforcement resulted in a decrease in response rate to *below the baseline* for the given activities (for reviews, see Bates, 1979; Condry, 1977; Deci, 1975). Typically these studies involve three phases. In Phase 1, subjects are observed working on fairly absorbing complex tasks such as solving puzzles, generating newspaper headlines, or creating artwork. An unobtrusive measure of time on task is obtained. In Phase 2, the subjects are given an extrinsic reinforcement such as praise or money for given units of performance. Then, in Phase 3, subjects are observed unobtrusively during a second period of "free play" with no extrinsic reward. During this second free-play period, the target behavior decreases significantly below the original baseline. Having controlled for fatigue and other sources of confounding, the researchers concluded that for some types of activity, *extrinsic reinforcement can decrease intrinsic motivation..*

This is not a new idea. Quite a number of researchers have commented on and studied the deleterious effects of extrinsic contingencies on intrinsic motivation and self-initiated, exploratory behavior (e.g., Festinger & Carlsmith, 1959; Harlow, 1953). However, a recent approach (Deci, 1975), especially in conjunction with the work of Condry (1977), is particularly appropriate for the overall approach of the present theory. Deci (1975) presented three propositions in support of cognitive evaluation theory. It is worth examining these because they form the basis of several strategies to be presented, and they form a linkage between this and earlier sections of the chapter.

The first two of Deci's propositions describe conditions that reduce intrinsic motivation. The first states that intrinsic motivation decreases as the perceived

---

*Editor's note: Contrary to the attitudes of some instructional scientists, the clear implication here is that we should not "throw out" such validated knowledge just because it cannot explain all phenomena. Different theoretical perspectives are like diffeent windows that allow one to look inside a mysterious house.

locus of causality shifts from internal to *external*. The second proposition states that there will be a decrease in intrinsic motivation if a person's feelings of *competence and self-determination* are *reduced*. The explanation for the relationship of external rewards to these two propositions lies in the third. It says that every reward, including feedback, has two elements, a controlling element and an informational element. If the controlling element is dominant, it will influence the perceived locus of causality. If the *informational element* is *dominant*, the influence will be a feeling of competence and self-determination. It is the controlling influence that is often responsible for the decrease in intrinsic motivation.

The research on intrinsic versus extrinsic motivation is still in somewhat of a formative state, and some of its findings are subject to criticism (Bates, 1979). Even so, there are several results that lead to prescriptions for strategies of instructional design and delivery. The following section contains several strategies concerned with the appropriate use of reinforcement for motivation and maintenance of intrinsic motivation.

Outcomes: Conditions and Strategies

The complexity of this section, caused in part by the number of sometimes conflicting propositions that must be accommodated, makes it difficult, if not impossible, to derive a single, guiding principle, except at a very abstract level. It is possible to state that to develop and maintain personal motivation for a given activity, *use reinforcement*, but do it in such a way that the controlling influences do not detract from the *intrinsic* satisfactions. This statement is intended to embrace standard reinforcement principles as modified by the research on intrinsic motivation.

The remainder of this section is concerned primarily with strategies based on the intrinsic-motivation research. The reason for this is practical, and not because of theory or personal biases of the author. Design principles based on reinforcement, or conditioning, theory have abounded in the literature of instructional technology for many years (Gagné, 1977;* Markle, 1969, 1977). Therefore, apart from some recent and not widely disseminated work of Tosti (1978), that work will not be repeated here.

Strategy 1.   To maintain intrinsic satisfaction with instruction, use *task-endogenous* rather than task-exogenous rewards.

Typically, one of the first questions asked in regard to intrinsic motivation is something like this: "If external rewards decrease intrinsic satisfaction, then how do you explain the effects of wages on job satisfaction?" The research on intrinsic motivation does not suggest that external rewards always imply external control with a reduction in intrinsic motivation. As previously indicated, a distinction is

---

*Editor's note: See also Chapter 4.

made between "controlling influence" and "external reward." Both Condry (1977) and Bates (1979) point out that an *endogenous reward* tends not to be perceived as having a controlling influence. An endogenous reward is one that customarily or naturally follows from a task. For example, a scientist participating in a "think tank" expects to be paid for his or her labor. However, the remuneration does not control the manner in which the scientist behaves. The scientist is free to speculate, task risks, and make personal decisions about how to spend his or her time.

In contrast, in some university departments, a university professor's annual salary increase is tied directly to the number and type of publications that he or she produces each year. This is an *exogenous-reward* situation. Research is not usually conducted on the basis of how many publishable articles it yields each year. It is generally approached with the idea that time is secondary to the requirements for valid inquiry aimed at finding the true consequences of given assumptions. Therefore, it is somewhat artificial to attach financial rewards to specific, arbitrary indictors of the rate of research that one reports. In this case, the exogenous reward might be expected to decrease intrinsic interest in research even though the quantity of research might increase for as long as the reinforcement system was operating, but the quality of research might decrease.

This seems to be a frequent finding despite the traditional assumption in behavior modification that clients, or students, would move from extrinsic to intrinsic reinforcers as a desirable behavior became established. In token-reinforcement systems, for example, desired behaviors, including both learning and classroom behavior, improve while the token system is in effect, but tend to extinguish rapidly when it is withdrawn (Kazdin, 1973; O'Leary & Drabman, 1971). Also, Levine and Fasnacht (1974) found that the use of tokenjs for rwards not intrinsic to the task led to decreases in self-initiated problem-solving behavior and less innovative solutions.

Of particular interest to designers and teachers in this regard is the work of Kruglanski, Riter, Amitai, Margolin, Shabtai, and Zaksh (1975) who report two studies using money-intrinsic and money-extrinsic tasks. These authors found that when monetary rewards (real or simulated) were normally associated with an activity such as coin tossing or a stock-market game, subjects gave higher ratings of continued interest when the rewards were paid than when not. Similarly, in money-extrinsic conditions such as athletic games and achievement activities such as a block-building game, subjects expressed greater continued interest when no monetary rewards were used.

The implication of this strategy is that extrinsic rewards should be *used selectively* and with consideration to the *nature of the task* to be reinforced. The remaining strategies in this section offer guidance as to the types and timing of various types of intrinsic and extrinsic reinforcers.

Strategy 2.   To maintain intrinsic satisfaction with instruction, use *unexpected, noncontingent* rewards rather than anticipated, salient, task-contingent rewards (except with dull tasks).

A number of studies have shown that extrinsic rewards are not as likely to decrease intrinsic interest if they are *unexpected* rather than expected (Greene & Lepper, 1974; Lepper & Greene, 1975; Lepper, Greene & Nisbett, 1973), and in some cases, if they are *noncontingent* rather than being tied to a specific performance criterion (see Bates, 1979, and Condry, 1977, for reviews). Similarly, Ross (1975) found that highly *salient* rewards, such as having the anticipated reward on a table in front of the subjects while they worked on a task, tended to decrease intrinsic interest.

There are, as one might expect, complexities and inconsistencies in this active area of research that require qualification of these simply stated principles, even though there seems to be a fair degree of support for them. For example, Calder and Staw (1975) found that rewards can increase interest in *dull tasks.* And, Kruglanski, Alon, and Lewis (1972) found that even unexpected rewards can decrease intrinsic motivation when the task is a type that is *often associated with reward.* Finally, there is a discrepancy between this strategy and the previous one, which included the observation that rewards inherent to the task content can increase intrinsic motivation (Kruglanski et al., 1975).

Despite these problems, it seems reasonable to conclude that designers and teachers should be particularly cautious about using expected, contingent, extrinsic rewards for tasks that do not typically have an inherent extrinsic reward. If there is a desire to use extrinsic rewards under these conditions, it would perhaps be better to use them in an unexpected and noncontingent manner.

> *Strategy 3.*   To maintain intrinsic satisfaction with instruction, use *verbal praise* and *informative feedback* rather than threats, surveillance, or external performance evaluation.

The preceding strategies have been primarily concerned with the conditions of reinforcement. In contrast, this strategy is more concerned with the types of *consequences* that will enhance or suppress intrinsic motivation. This also happens to be one of the more heavily researched areas of intrinsic motivation. Reviews of this research are provided by Bates (1979), Condry (1977), and Deci (1975). Again, as in the previous strategies, there tends to be a common theme despite the difficulties in interpreting and comparing the various studies. Intrinsic motivation tends to flourish to a far greater extent in a context of positive but *noncontrolling consequences* than when excessive evaluation and aversive forms of control are used.

For example, when working in a context that puts one before an audience frequently, as in the role of a teacher or professor, one can become as irritated with positive as with negative feedback. An educator must deal with many audiences including individual advisees, classes of students, principals or deans, consulting clients, and promotional review boards. The feedback from these various groups can sometimes serve to indicate that one's every move is being evaluated, and that can be irritating even when the results are positive. Similarly, the student's relationship to education, especially during the first 12 grade levels, is dominated by the evaluative role of the teacher. Indirectly, the instructional designer is part of this process, because the predominant modes of instructional design include *heavy doses of performance evaluation.* Consequently, it is not difficult to see at least part of the reason for the difficulty in maintaining the intrinsic interest of children in the school process.

A challenge for designers and teachers is to find ways of utilizing these strategies to maintain intrinsic motivation while meeting the sometimes rigid and competitive performance criteria that society and state education departments place on the schools. The two remaining strategies offer somewhat more specific advice in regard to operationalizing two aspects of these strategies.

> *Strategy 4.* To maintain quantity of performance, use *motivating feedback* following the response.

This traditional reinforcement principle, even with the modifications suggested in the preceding strategies due to intrinsic-motivation research, is still a powerful principle with a great deal of relevance. We are much more likely to repeat behaviors that have *pleasurable consequences* than those that do not. Additional discussion of this strategy, which becomes more interesting when contrasted with the following strategy, is included in the following Strategy 5 discussion.

> *Strategy 5.* To improve the quality of performance, provide *formative (corrective) feedback* when it will be immediately useful, usually just *before* the next opportunity to practice.

Tosti (1978) uses the terms *motivational* and *formative* to describe the traditional distinction between the two most frequently used types of feedback in learning and performance situations. The first, motivational, refers to positive reinforcement following a desired response. This could be praise for a student who finished an assignment or for a salesperson who sold a car, or it could be something tangible such as money or a grade. This type of feedback primarily affects the *quantity* of performance. It is the primary formulation of contingency management, and it signals that repetition of the same behavior is desirable.

The second type of feedback is formative; it is used to affect the *quality* of performance. In this sense, it signals a gap between the given versus a preferable performance, and it indicates the actions to take to close the gap. Consequently, formative feedback serves as a *correctant,* and it can produce rapid changes in behavior in contrast to the more tedious process of using shaping techniques with motivational feedback as a means of producing qualitative changes in behavior.

Typically these two types of feedback are used together, the first to encourage continued effort, and the second to encourage and assist improvements in quality. However, as observed by Tosti (1978), there are individual differences in style, and, as observed in subsequent research, differences in the effective use of the two types of feedback. When a student hands in a paper, some teachers will make a complementary comment such as, "I'm happy you finished. Your paper looks nice." Others would offer more corrective information such as, "You have missed some items. Here, let me show you your problem." Others, and this applies to supervisors in many contexts, not just teachers, mix the two types of feedback. This approach is easy to recognize because it always contains the word *but*, or a surrogate. For example, "I'm so pleased to see that you finished, but you do have a problem here." Or, "You did an excellent job of formulating these objectives for the math curriculum, but I would like for you to change the format." In both cases, the corrective feedback tends to *cancel the positive effect* of the motivational feedback.

How do we resolve this problem? Tosti suggests that the *timing* of feedback is critical. Motivational feedback should be given *immediately after* a performance, and should refer to those aspects of the performance criteria that were acceptable. In contrast, formative feedback should relate to those aspects of performance that are less than standard, and should be delivered *when it is immediately useful* (i.e., just before the next performance). In a telephone-sales organization, for example, the managers would listen to randomly selected calls and give the operators feedback on their performance at the end of each day. This use of feedback, following the traditional behavioral-modification pattern of immediate reinforcement, had little effect on the performance of the workers. When the corrective feedback was delayed until the beginning of the next day, performance improved dramatically.

Instructional designers and teachers would probably benefit from a similar application of this strategy. It is seldom the case that formative feedback is immediately useful just after a performance. An exception would be those situations in which a series of rehearsals or supervised practice exercises precede a final performance as in drama, athletics, and programmed instruction. More often, especially in academic subject areas, an assignment is given with, perhaps, some general advice or instruction on how to do the assignment, but no individual feedback on a student's *characteristic problems* with respect to successful performance. How many students who have trouble articulating the main idea in a prose passage receive personal guidance *just prior* to applying that skill? The appropriate use of formative feedback as suggested in this strategy statement underscores the need for a cumulative file for each student that is used for feedback purposes at the appropriate time. This would, of course, require extra work for teachers in the short run, which could probably be facilitated with a computer-management system, but if the performance improvements were substantial, there should be a long-range savings in teacher effort. Additional insights into teachers' uses of feedback is included in Brophy and Good (1970) and Cooper (1977).

In summary, the conclusions are far from being complete regarding intrinsic satisfaction and extrinsic reward. The precedinbg strategies reflect some of the recent research findings, and must now be operationalized and tested in terms of prescriptive design strategies. There seems to be little doubt that the emotional, attitudinal, and tangible consequences of a behavior will influence one's motivation to continue at that activity. However, the exact characteristics of these influences on each other and on continuing motivation require much additional study. From an instructional-design perspective, it is important to consider both the intrinsic and extrinsic consequences of our design strategies.

CONCLUSIONS

In summary, the present model uses the four categories of curiosity, relevance, expectancy, and outcomes to summarize research on human motivation, and to identify several strategies for generating motivation. Furthermore, these categories are derived from a macro theory of the relationships of individual and environmental characteristics on effort, performance, and outcomes (see Fig. 11.1).

There are a number of potential benefits of the present model for instructional science and instructional design, and there are some specific limitations. One of the benefits is that the model provides *four reasonably specific categories** of variables that help synthesize many of the lines of research concerned with motivation. This synthesis facilitates the development of applied-research projects because it helps identify several of the major sources of variance that operate simultaneously in a field setting. research on instructional design has to have external validity if it is to be of any use to designers. This means that major sources of variance have to be understood, not just controlled, in order to develop prescriptive strategies with descriptions of the conditions under which they will and will not work. Principles that require unrealistic controls simply are not useful. Newton's physical laws were a boon to theory, but their practical utility was limited, because they were unqualifiedly true only in a frictionless environment. Schools are, metaphorically speaking, anything but frictionless.

The present model appears to have heuristic value in that it incorporates specific categories of variables in a theoretical context that facilitates the development of research that has direct implications for motivational design. Several dissertations have been completed, and others are in progress (Keller, 1981) that were developed in the context of this model. Several of these studies are focusing on the development of prescriptive design strategies.

However, a limitation of the model, and of the state of the art in research in this area is the *lack of specific, prescriptive strategies*. The amount of research on motivation is vast, and the conditions that influence motivation are difficult to specify in concrete terms. A strategy that works today might not work tomorrow because it loses its novelty effect. Yet, it is shallow to assume that novelty has to always be present to stimulate and maintain motivation. The enduring characteris-

---

*Editor's note: These categories may correspond to Gropper's *obstacles* to meeting *learning requirements* (see Chapter 2). In this case, Gropper's suggestion that "whether an obstacle is treated" is more important than "how it is treated" could result in an instructional theory that specifies a menu of alternatives for treating each of Keller's four motivational requirements for appealing instruction.

tics of people and of instructional materials that contribute to sustained motivation are the ones that we want to capture. As we are able to do this in a systematic fashion, we will more frequently be able to make school appealing, even engrossing, as inspired teachers presently do.

REFERENCES

Abramson, L. Y., Seligman, M. E. P., & Teasdale, J. D. Learned helplessness in humans: Critique and reformulation. *Journal of Abnormal Psychology*, 1978, *87*, 49–74.

Adams, J. S. Inequity in social exchange. In L. Berkowitz (Ed.), *Advances in experimental social psychology* (Vol. 2). New York: Academic Press, 1965.

Alderman, D. L., & Mahler, W. A. *The evaluation of PLATO and TICCIT: Educational analysis of the community college components.* Princeton: Educational Testing Service, 1973.

Alschuler, A. S. *Developing achievement motivation in adolescents: Education for human growth.* Englewood Cliffs, N.J.: Educational Technology Publications, 1973.

Atkinson, J. W., & Raynor, J. O. (Eds.). *Motivation and achievement.* Washington, D.C.: V. H. Winston, 1974.

Ausubel, D. P. *Educational psychology: A cognitive view.* New York: Holt, Rinehart & Winston, 1968.

Bandura, A. Self efficacy: Toward a unifying theory of behavioral change. *Psychological Review,* 1977, *84*, 191–215.

Bates, J. A. Extrinsic reward and intrinsic motivation: A review with implications for the classroom. Review of *Educational research*, 1979, *49*, 557–576.

Berlyne, D. E. Motivational problems raised by exploratory and epistemic behavior. In S. Koch (Ed.), *Psychology: A study of a science* (Vol. 5). New York: McGraw-Hill, 1965.

Bloom, B. S. *Human characteristics and school learning.* New York: McGraw-Hill, 1976.

Brophy, J., & Good, T. Teacher's communication of differential expectations for children's classroom performance: Some behavioral data. *Journal of Educational Psychology*, 1970, *61*, 365–374.

Calder, B. J., & Staw, B. M. Self-perception of intrinsic and extrinsic motivation. *Journal of Personality and Social Psychology*, 1978, *31*, 599–605.

Carroll, J. B. A model of school learning. *Teachers College Record*, 1963, *64*, 723–733.

Chapin, M., & Dyck, G. Persistence in children's reading behavior as a function of N length and attribution retraining. *Journal of Abnormal Psychology*, 1976, 85, 511–515.

Condry, J. Enemies of exploration: Self-initiated versus other-initiated learning. *Journal of Personality and Social Psychology*, 1977, *35*, 459–477.

Cooley, W. W., & Lohnes, P.R. *Evaluation research in education.* New York: Halsted Press, 1976.

Cooper, H. M. Controlling personal rewards: Professional teachers' differential use of feedback and the effects of feedback on the students' motivation to perform. *Journal of Educational Psychology*, 1977, *69*, 419–427.

Cronbach, L. J., & Snow, R. E. *Aptitudes and instructional methods.* New York: Irvington, 1976.

Cronbach, L. J., & Suppes, P. (Eds.). *Research for tomorrow's schools: Disciplined inquiry for education.* New York: Macmillan, 1969.

deCharms, R. *Personal causation.* New York: Academic Press, 1968.

deCharms, R. *Enhancing motivation change in the classroom.* New York: Irvington, 1976.

Deci, E. L. *Intrinsic motivation.* New York: Plenum Press, 1975.

Deci, E. L., & Porac, J. Cognitive evaluation theory and the study of human motivation. In M. R. Lepper & D. Greene (Eds.), *The hidden costs of reward.* Hillsdale, N.J.: Lawrence Erlbaum Associates, 1978.

Dweck, C. S. The role of expectations and attributions in the alleviation of learned helplessness. *Journal of Personality and Social Psychology*, 1975, *31*, 647–695.

Dweck, C. S., & Goetz, T. E. Attributions and learned helplessness. In J. H. Harvey, W. Ickes, & R. F. Kidd (Eds.), *New directions in attribution research* (Vol. 2). Hillsdale, N.J.: Lawrence Erlbaum Associates, 1977.

Edwards, A. L. *The measurement of personality traits by scales and inventories.* New York: Holt, Rinehart & Winston, 1970.

Feather, N. T. The relationship of expectation of success to need achievement and test anxiety. *Journal of Personality and Social Psychology,* 1965, *1,* 118–126.

Feather, N. T. *Values in education and society.* New York: The Free Press, 1975.

Feather, N. T., & Saville, M.R. Effects of amount of prior success and failure on expectations of success and subsequent task performance. *Journal of Personality and Social Psychology,* 1967, *5,* 226–232.

Festinger, L., & Carlsmith, J. M. Cognitive consequences of forced compliance. *Journal of Abnormal and Social Psychology,* 1959, *58,* 203–210.

Fibel, B., & Hale, W.D. The generalized expectancy for success scale—a new measure. *Journal of Consulting and Clinical Psychology,* 1948, *46,* 924–931.

Flesch, R. A new readibility yardstick. *Journal of Applied Psychology,* 1948, *32,* 221–233.

Foote, T. (Ed.). Help! Teacher can't teach. *Time,* June 16, 1980, *115*(24), 54–63.

Gagné, R. M. *The conditions of learning* (3rd ed.). New York: Holt, Rinehart & Winston, 1977.

Gordon, W. J. *Synetics.* New York: Harper & Row, 1961.

Greene, D., & Leeper, M. R. Effects of extrinsic rewards on children's subsequent intrinsic interest. *Child Development,* 1974, *45,* 1141–1145.

Harlow, H. F. Motivation as a factor in the acquisition of new responses. In M. R. Jones (Ed.), *Nebraska symposium on motivation.* Lincoln: University of Nebraska Press, 1953.

Hilgard, E. R., & Bower, G.H. *Theories of learning* (rth ed.). Englewood Cliffs, N.J.: Prentice-Hall, 1975.

Hiroto, D. S., & Seligman, M. E. P. Generality of learned helplessness in man. *Journal of Personality and Social Psychology,* 1975, *31,* 311–327.

Hull, C. L. *Principles of behavior.* New York: Appleton-Century-Crofts, 1943.

Hunt, D. E., & Sullivan, E. V. *Between psychology and education.* Hinsdale, Ill.: Dryden, 1974.

Johnston, J. E. (Ed.). *Behavior research and technology in higher education.* Springfield, Ill. Charles C Thomas, 1975.

Jones, R. A. *Self-fulfilling prophecies: Social psychological and physiological effects of expectancies.* New York: Halsted Press, 1977.

Joyce, B., & Weil, M. *Models of teaching.* Englewood Cliffs, N.J.: Prentice-Hall, 1972.

Kaplan, A. *The conduct of inquiry.* San Francisco: Chaldler, 1964.

Kazdin, A. E. Role of instructions and reinforcements in behavior changes in token reinforcement programs. *Journal of Educational Psychology,* 1973, *64,* 63–71.

Keller, J. M. *Effects of instructions and reinforcement contingencies in the development of learned helplessness.* Unpublished doctoral dissertation, Indiana University, 1975.

Keller, J. M. Motivational needs game. *National Society for Performance and Instruction Journal,* 1978, *17*(6), 3–4, 21.

Keller, J. M. Motivation and instructional design: A theoretical perspectives. *Journal of Instructional Development,* 1979, *2*(4), 26–34.

Keller, J. M. *Motivational design research group annual report* (occasional paper). Syracuse: Syracuse University, Instructional Design, Development and Evaluation Program, 1981.

Keller, J. M., Goldman, J. A., & Sutterer J. R. Locus of control in relation to academic attitudes and performance in a personalized system of instruction course. *Journal of Educational Psychology,* 1978, *79,* 414–421.

Keller, J. M., & Keller, B.H. *Development of parallel self-report and teacher report measures of student motivation for specific school subjects* (occasional paper). Syracuse: Syracuse University, Instructional Design, Development and evaluation Program, 1981.

Keller, J. M., Kelly, E. A., & Dodge, B. *Motivation in school: A practitioner's guide to concepts and measures*. Syracuse: Syracuse University ERIC Clearinghouse for Information Resources, 1978.

Kranzberg, M. The disunity of science-technology. *American Scientist*, 1968, *56*, 21–34.

Kruglanski, A. W., Alon, I., & Lewis, T. Retrospective misattribution and task enjoyment. *Journal of Experimental Social Psychology*, 1972, *8*, 493–501.

Kruglanski, A. W., Riter, A., Amitai, A., Margolin, B., Shabtai, L., & Zaksh, D. Can money enhance intrinsic motivation?: A test of the content-consequence hypothesis. *Journal of Personality and Social Psychology*, 1975, *31*, 744–750.

Kuhn, T. S. *The structure of scientific revolutions* (2nd ed.) Chicago: University of Chicago Press, 1970.

Lakein, A. *How to get control of your time and life*. New York: New American Library, 1973.

Lefcourt, H. M. *Locus of control: Current trends in theory and research*. Hillsdale, N.J.: Lawrence Erlbaum Associates, 1976.

Lepper, M. R. & Greene, D. Turning play into work: Effects of adult surveillance and extrinsic rewards on children's intrinsic motivation. *Journal of Personality and Social Psychology*, 1975, *31*, 479-486.

Lepper, M. R., Greene, D., & Nisbett, R. E. Undermining children's intrinsic interest with extrinsic rewards: A test of the overjustification hypothesis. *Journal of Personality and Social Psychology*, 1973, *28*, 129–137.

Levine, F. M., & Fasnacht, G. Token rewards may lend to token learning. *American Psychologist*, 1974, *29*, 816–820.

Lewin, K. *A dynamic theory of personality*. New York: McGraw-Hill, 1935.

Maehr, M.L. Continuing motivation: An analysis of a seldom considered educational outcome. *Review of Educational Research*, 1976, *46*, 443–462.

Markle, S. M. *Good frames and bad: A grammer of frame writing* (2nd ed.). New York: Wiley, 1969.

Markle, S. M. Teaching conceptual networks. *Journal of Instructional Development*, 1977, *1*, 13–17.

Maslow, A. H. *Motivation and personality*. New York: Harper & Row, 1954.

Maw, W. H., & Maw, E. W. Self appraisal of curiosity. *Journal of Educational Research*, 1968, *61*, 462–466.

Mayer, R. E. *Thinking and problem solving: An introduction to human cognition and learning*. Glenview, Ill.: Scott, Foresman, 1977.

McClelland, D. C. *The achieving society*. New York: Irvington Publishers, 1976.

McClelland, D. C., Atkinson, J. W., Clark, R. W., & Lowell, E. L. *The achievement motive*. New York: Appleton-Century-Crofts, 1953.

McClelland, D. C., & Burnham, D. H. Power is the great motivator. *Harvard Business Review*, 1976, *52*(2), 100–110.

McConnell, J. V. *Understanding human behavior* (2nd ed.). New York: Holt, Rinehart & Winston, 1977.

McConnell, J. V. Confessions of a textbook writer. *American Psychologist*, 1978, *33*, 159–169.

Merrill, M.D. Learner control: Beyond aptitude-treatment interactions. *AV Communications Review*, 1975, *23*, 217–226.

Merton, R. K. The self-fulfilling prophecy. In R. K. Merton (Ed.), *Social theory and social structure*. New York: The Free Press, 1968.

Mischel, W. Toward a cognitive social learning reconceptualization of personality. *Psychological Review*, 1973, *80*, 252–283.

Moen, R., & Doyle, K. D., Jr. Measures of academic motivation: A conceptual review. *Research in Higher Education*, 1978, *8*, 1–23.

Murphy, F. *Alleviation of learned helplessness in high school remedial readers*. Unpublished doctoral dissertation, Syracuse University, 1979.

Murray, H. A. *Explorations in personality*. New York: Oxford University Press, 1938.

O'Leary, K. D., & Drabman, R. Token reinforcement program in the classroom: A review. *Psychological Bulletin*, 1971, *75*, 379–398.

Perlmuter, L. C., & Monty, R. A. The importance of perceived control: Fact or fantasy? *American Scientist*, 1977, *65*, 759–765.

Phares, E. J. *Locus of control in personality*. Morristown, N.J.: General Learning Press, 1976.

Porter, L. W., & Lawler, E. E. *Managerial attitudes and performance*. Homewood, Ill.: Richard D. Irwin, 1968.

Raynor, J. O. Relationships between achievement-related motives, future orientation, and academic performance. In J. W. Atkinson & J. O. Raynor (Eds.), *Motivation and achievement*. Washington, D. C.: V. H. Winston, 1974.

Reigeluth, C. M. In search of a better way to organize instruction: The elaboration theory. *Journal of Instructional Development*, 1979, *2*(3), 8–14.

Reigeluth, C. M., & Merrill, M.D. Classes of instructional variables. *Educational Technology*, 1979, March, 5–24.

Ringer, R. J. *Looking out for #1*. New York: Fawcett Crest, 1977.

Rogers, C. R. *Client centered therapy*. Boston: Houghton Mifflin, 1951.

Rogers, C. R. *Freedom to learn*. Columbus, Ohio: Charles E Merrill, 1969.

Rokeach, M. *The nature of human values*. New York: The Free Press, 1973.

Rosenthal, R., & Jacobson, L. *Pygmalion in the classroom*. New York: Holt, Rinehart & Winston, 1968.

Ross, M. Salience of reward and intrinsic motivation. *Journal of Personality and Social Psychology*, 1975, *33*, 245–254.

Rotter, J. B. *Social learning theory and clinical psychology*. New York: Prentice-Hall, 1954.

Rotter, J. B. Generalized expectancies for internal versus external control of reinforcement. *Psychological Monographs*, 1966, *80* (Whole No. 609).

Rotter, J. B. An introduction to social learning theory. In J. B. Rotter, J. E. Chance, & E. J. Phares (Eds.), *Applications of a social learning theory of personality*. New York: Holt, Rinehart & Winston, 1972.

Rudestam, K. E. *Methods of self-change*. Monterey, Calif.: Brooks/Cole, 1980.

Seligman, M.E. *Helplessness*. San Francisco: Freeman, 1975.

Singer, D. G., Singer, J., & Zuckerman, M. *Teaching television*. Dial Press, 1980.

Skinner, B. F. *The technology of teaching*. New York: Appleton-Century-Crofts, 1968.

Snow, R. E. Theory construction for research on teaching. In R. M. W. Travers (Eds.), *Second handbook of research on teaching*. Chicago: Rand McNally, 1973.

Steers, R. M., & Porter, L. W. *Motivation and work behavior*. New York: McGraw-Hill, 1975.

Strom, R. D. (Ed.). *Teachers and the learning process*. Englewood Cliffs, N.J.: Prentice-Hall, 1971.

Suchman, J. R. A model for the analysis of inquiry. In H. J. Klausmeier & C. W. Harris (Eds.), *Analysis of concept learning*. New York: Academic Press, 1966.

Tolman, E. C. *Purposive behavior in animals and men*. Berkeley: University of California Press, 1949.

Tosti, D. T. Formative feedback. *NSPI Journal*, October, 1978, 19–21.

Travers, R. M. W. *Essentials of learning* (4th ed.) New York: Macmillan, 1977.

Vidler, D. R. Curiosity. In S. Ball (Ed.), *Motivation in education*. New York: Academic Press, 1977.

Walberg, H. J. Models for optimizing and individualizing learning. *Interchange*, 1971, *2*, 15–27.

Weil, M., & Joyce, B. *Information processing models of teaching*. Englewood Cliffs, N.J.: Prentice-Hall Inc., 1978.

Weil, M., Joyce, B., & Kluwin, B. *Personal models of teaching*. Englewood Cliffs, N.J.: Prentice-Hall, 1978.

Weiner, B. *Theories of motivation: From mechanism to cognitioin.* Chicago: Rank McNally, 1972.

Weiner, B. (Ed.) *Achievement motivation and attribution theory.* Morristown, N.J.: General Learning Press, 1974.

Weiner, B. A theory of motivation for some classroom experiences. *Journal of Educational Psychology,* 1979, *71,* 3–25.

White, R. W. Motivation reconsidered: The concept of competence. *Psychological Review,* 1959, *66,* 297–323.

Winter, D. F. What makes the candidates run. *Psychology Today,* July, 1976, 47–49, 92.

Yerkes, R. M., & Dodson, J. D. The relation of stimulus to rapidity of habit formation. *Journal of Comparative Neurological Psychology,* 1908, *18,* 459–482.

Zuckerman, M. Dimensions of sensation seeking. *Journal of Consulting and Clinical Psychology,* 1971, *36,* 45–52.

Zuckerman, M. The search for high sensation. *Psychology Today,* February, 1978, 38–46, 96–97.

Unit III
COMMENTARY

This Unit provides commentary on instructional theory in general and on each of the particular theories presented in Unit II. Chapter 12's major contribution is some insightful *perspectives* on instructional theory: its producers and users, its history and some of its contemporary issues, its individual theories as represented in this book, and implications for its future. Of particular interest are discussions of: (1) the need for systematic synthesis of facts about instruction; (2) the role of personal values and prejudices in the constitution of instructional theory; (3) the relationship of instructional psychology to instructional theory; (4) skepticism as to whether comprehensive theories of instruction can in fact exist at all; (5) the need for systematic procedures for utilizing scientific knowledge to solve practical problems; (6) the tendency to select and restrict oneself to a single theory or theoretical orientation; (7) whether in fact any of the preceding chapters represents a true (comprehensive and valid) instructional theory; (8) the need for support for both the production and the utilization of better knowledge about instruction; and (9) the influence that the growing use of micro computers in education is likely to have on instructional theory. Discussion of these topics is complemented by an insightful commentary, comparison, and contrast of the individual theories described in earlier chapters of this book.

12

Is Instructional Theory Alive and Well?

Glenn E. Snelbecker
Temple University

Glenn E. Snelbecker

Education: B.S. in Business Education, Elizabethtown College, 1957. M.S. in Guidance and Counseling, Bucknell University, 1958. Ph.D. in Educational Psychology and Measurement (Major), with Minors in Child Development and Family Relationships and in Guidance and Counseling, Cornell University, 1961. He completed a post-doctoral training program in clinical and counseling psychology at the Brockton, Mass., Veterans Administration Hospital in 1961–1962. He also completed additional post-doctoral training programs in neuropsychology, electronic research equipment, and program evaluation.

Professional Experience: Dr. Snelbecker's current primary employment is at Temple University, where he is a Professor of Educational Psychology. Part time activities include work as an author, consultant, and evaluator; areas include microcomputers and other forms of technology, clinical psychology applications in business (e.g., stress management and productivity, improving communications, etc.), and the applications of instructional psychology in the design of education / training programs and general communications systems.

Scholarship: Dr. Snelbecker's work in instructional psychology spans more than two decades. This work includes empirical studies, historical analyses, critiques of theories, and systematic examination of ways in which scientific information is generated as well as ways in which it is used in practical contexts.

CONTENTS

Actual And Potential Audiences   440
   Knowledge Producers   440
   Knowledge Users   441
Historical And Contemporary Perspectives   442
   An Atheoretical Emphasis   443
   Emergence Of Instructional Theory?   444
     Influence Of The ASCD   445
     Influence Of Curriculum-Development Projects   447
   Relevance Of "Instructional Psychology"   447
   Some Issues Concerning Use Of Instructional Theory   449
Observations About The Total Group Of Theories   452
Observations About Individual Theories   456
   Aronson-Briggs-Gagné   457
   Gropper And Behavior Modification   459
   Three Cognitive Approaches   460
     Collins And Stevens   461
     Scandura   462
     Landa   463
   Summary Comments On The Three Cognitive Approaches   464
   Complementary Components Of A General Theory   465
     Merrill   465
     Reigeluth And Stein   466
     Keller   467
   Summary Comments On Complementary Components
     Of A General Theory   468
Conclusions: Status Of Instructional Theory And Implications
   For Users   468

FOREWORD

The major purpose of this chapter is to consider the present and probable future status of instructional theory. This is done by examining the theories that are presented in this book as state-of-the-art examples, keeping in mind both historical and contemporary perspectives, and by identifying ways in which different intended audiences are likely to perceive and to be influenced by these theories.

I selected the title of this chapter to convey some general attitudes and specific questions that, in my judgment, need to be raised if we are to gain a full understanding of the present status of instructional theory and to have a sound basis for projecting its probable future status. When we inquire if some thing or some person is alive and well, our question reveals a number of attitudes and concerns. There is an acknowledgment that some particular entity exists. There is at least implied (in most cases) some favorable support for this entity, including the hope that it *will* continue not only to exist but also to thrive. There are some assumed reasons for being. There is recognition that no person nor thing exists in a vacuum and that one's existence depends on at least a partly supportive environment. That the question is raised suggests that a negative answer is as plausible as a positive answer—that the thing or person *may not be* alive and well. In turn, this suggests that there may exist either hostile forces or potentially threatening inadequate supporting conditions. Moreover, as one considers each of these preceding concerns and implied questions, it becomes apparent that different people may have substantially different views about each concern and implied question.

C. M. R.

Is Instructional Theory
Alive and Well?

Is instructional theory alive and well? This chapter includes the following sections to provide answers and ideas relevant to this general question: *Actual and Potential Audiences; Historical and Contemporary Perspectives; Observations about the Total Group of Theories; Observations about Individual Theories; Conclusions: Status of Instructional Theory, and Implications for Users.*

ACTUAL AND POTENTIAL AUDIENCES

Who might be interested in instructional theory? Who might "care enough" about instructional theory to inquire about its current and probable future status? There are different groups that can be identified. But though they may *seem* to have similar characteristics because they are interested in instructional theory, in fact they have quite divergent reasons for asking what appear to be identical questions.

At least two major groups can be identified, with at least two subgroups within each major group. Described simply in terms of their reasons for inquiring about the status of instructional theory, they can be identified primarily as *knowledge producers* or primarily as *knowledge users*. (By including the word "primarily" here, it is implied that everyone is concerned with knowledge production and with knowledge use but that, in certain instances, personal and professional responsibilities dictate certain emphases.) Thus, one group that inquires about the status of instructional theory does so because of professional interests in the processes by which research is conducted and theory is constructed. Hereafter this is referred to as the "knowledge-producer" group. Another group is mainly interested in practical implications of research findings and theory. Hereafter the group is referred to as the "knowledge-user" group.

Knowledge Producers

The knowledge-producer group typically tends to view research findings, principles and theories as end results. There is a major concern with describing and explaining the phenomena related to the process of instruction. At least for many, there is little or no real concern with practical implications, other than that the object of study may include events occurring in "real-world" situations as well as in controlled laboratory contexts. The major objective is to obtain and to understand empirical findings relevant to the object of study.

Two subgroups can be identified within the knowledge-producer group. One subgroup is almost totally engrossed in the process of gathering facts, with minimal emphasis on interpretations beyond the research questions that have been posed. For this subgroup, it is sufficient to be aware of only those previous and current studies, principles, and theories that are clearly relevant to the particular object of study. These efforts optimally can culminate in a journal report of the results, followed by a series of related studies. Another subgroup displays a strong commitment to the gathering of facts but advocates the conviction that true science depends as much as the *systematic syntheses* of information (including but not limited to empirical facts) as it depends on the processes of gathering empirical facts. Whereas the first subgroup tends to judge statements mainly in terms of methodological and analytical aspects, the second subgroup is more apt to judge statements in terms of their *heuristic value*—especially as such statements draw on prior empirical facts and theoretical ideas to produce newer and more encompassing understandings about the total objects of study.

Both of these knowledge-producer subgroups might inquire about the current and probable future status of instructional theory. Both of these subgroups could display this interest in instructional theory without being concerned about the practical value of resultant ideas, per se. Both would be especially interested in the extent to which any specific theories or approaches have, somehow, advanced understanding of the processes of instruction. The first subgroup would particularly note the extent to which a specific theory or approach has been fostering sound research methodologies and appropriate analytic procedures to gather more facts about instruction. The second subgroup would particularly watch for ways in which a specific theory or approach has aided in compressing available empirical facts and ideas into compact principles and synthesizing explanatory systems.

Now that certain attributes have been delineated, hereafter I refer to these two knowledge-producer subgroups as researchers and theorists, respectively. This is done with the understanding that the differences are relative rather than absolute. The major purpose of making the distinction is to call attention to diffeent concerns and attitudes within the knowledge-producer group.

Knowledge Users

The knowledge-user group perennially is searching for information that it can use in practical situations. Although other sources of ideas exist and are utilized, there is more than a little pressure to encourage education and training practitioners to consider ways in which instructional research and theory might guide practitioners and might influence materials, methods, and procedures. For the knowledge-user group, it is as though the very raison d'être of instructional theory is practical application. For the knowledge-user group, it is not sufficient that instructional theory lead "merely" to journal publication—no matter how highly regarded the journal may be—nor to theory construction as an end itself—no matter how great the theoretical contribution might seem. For this group, the only "true" test of value for instructional theory lies in the extent, if any, to which it improves instruction and student learning.

Two subgroups can be identified within the knowledge-user group. The first subgroup consists of persons who work in teams while making decisions about the design of instruction, the administrative arrangements in a school, the development or the implementation of new curricula, and similar matters. I refer to this as the designer subgroup because, as far as instructional theory is concerned, this subgroup is mainly interested in ideas that can aid them in designing new or better instruction. The second subgroup consists of individuals who customarily work alone and whose activities are, at least to some extent, limited by the administrative and physical arrangements that have been set for them. Teachers constitute a convenient example of this subgroup, particularly when a teacher works alone in a classroom. However, because other educators also display similar responsibilities and concerns, I refer to this as the practitioner subgroup.

Both of these knowledge-user subgroups are interested in instructional theory primarily—perhaps, solely—because of the practical implications that may be derived. Their inquiries about the current or probable future status of instructional theory stem from the anticipated practical payoff. Their practical responsibilities keep them sufficiently busy that they have little time to even think about writing journal articles—especially those involving empirical data. Theory is almost totally judged in terms of its actual practical value or its perceived practical value.

However, the two knowledge-user subgroups often disagree as to how useful a particular research finding, principle, or theory may be. The designers can consider implementing some idea even if it takes some planning time or modification in the institution's physical or administrative arrangements. The practitioners may have some degree of "academic freedom" in carrying out their responsibilities, but they routinely encounter constraints within which they can make decisions and can implement some appealing idea. What may be useful for designers may simply not be feasible for practitioners. Conversely, what may seem inconsequential to designers may be taken as an important and helpful idea by practitioners. Thus, what is considered useful will reflect the two subgroups' respective responsibilities and working conditions as well as the nature of the idea under consideration.

Who might inquire about the status of instructional theory? Four subgroups have been identified. Even though additional subgroups could be described, these four should illustrate the various concerns and expectations that may be involved when someone inquires about the status of instructional theory. Thus, keep these four subgroups in mind as we explore the present and probable future status of instructional theory. Prepublication drafts of this book's chapters were reviewed critically by graduate students in several classes on learning theory and by advanced graduate students in a seminar on psychoeducational design. Because these students are representative of the four subgroups just described, their views have been considered in the preparation of the present chapter.

HISTORICAL AND CONTEMPORARY PERSPECTIVES

The descriptions of individual instructional theories and the various comments about instructional theory that have been provided in the previous chapters in this book obviously do not exist in a vacuum. Instead, these efforts are sometimes more easily understood if we take into account that they reflect contributions and controversies of earlier work in psychology and education. They can also be best understood if we take into account contemporary ventures to gain and to use scientific information in other practical contexts. Thus, it is very important that we draw on historical and contemporary perspectives as we consider the present and probable future status of instructional theory.

An Atheoretical Emphasis

In the introductory paragraphs of this chapter, I noted that inquiries about some *thing* constitute an acknowledgment that that *thing* exists—otherwise it would not make sense to inquire about it. Readers who inquire about instructional theory may not realize that some contemporary psychologists and educators contend that *no* instructional theories have been established to date.

The fact that instructional theory, as such, is of comparatively recent origin—despite the long existence of educational institutions—emerged from a systematic literature review that I started in 1967 (Snelbecker, 1974).* The initial purpose of this literature review was to identify alternative ways in which psychologists had produced new knowledge about learning processes, and to identify various attempts to use the new knowledge in practical contexts. The time period of the review was 100 years, starting in the 1870s when psychology was emerging as a science. Approximately 2000 publications were considered during the literature review.

What I found was that there had been several earlier "false starts"—that is, attempts that could have, but did not, lead to instructional theories—and that instructional theories mainly emerged since the middle of the 20th century. Dewey, James, and others around the turn of the century acknowledged that educational applications could not directly be derived from psychological research findings and theory. Instead, it was noted that some kind of *linking process* would be needed to translate potential implications, even if based on sound research and theory, so that educational practices could be appropriately modified.

In a paper about educational psychology and teacher training, Getzels (1952) commented: "Not everything in psychology or education that is of interest or even of conceivable usefulness to the prospective teacher can be included in educational psychology . . . Selection and restriction of content must be made, and this can best be done in terms of some unifying conceptual scheme or focus [p. 382]."

Unfortunately—if one agrees with Getzels about the need for some unifying conceptual scheme or focus"—at least prior to the 1950s there were few, if any, empirically tested theories established to guide educational practices. What had existed were some general views about education and a vast, diverse, and growing fund of facts that had not been systematically integrated except with regard to particular and generally isolated topics of study.

Paterson (1977) made some pertinent comments in a book entitled *Foundations for a Theory of Instruction and Educational Psychology*. He noted that "the practice of education has been a concern of society for centuries" but that even in 1977 there were few if any candidates" for inclusion in a book on *instructional theories*

---

*Editor's Note: This work greatly influenced my thinking about instructional theory, for which I will always be grateful.

[p. *x*]. Paterson contrasted the lack of instructional theories with the large number of counseling theories, and suggested that this is particularly puzzling because counseling has existed as a formal entity for only a few of the many years during which education has existed as an entity.

Part of the problem apparently stems from a pattern that has long been established with regard to educational research findings. Although descriptions differ, depending on which author's publications one reads, there has existed for several decades a tendency to focus primarily—almost exclusively—on gathering facts. There is considerable emphasis on devising improved research methodology, but virtually no interest in synthesizing resultant information into systematic statements of practical or theoretical value. The situation is illustrated by an editorial in the February, 1979, *Journal of Educational Psychology*. Editor Samuel Ball first commented on the increasing numbers of manuscripts that have been received for possible publication and expressed some regrets that the rejection rate routinely continues to be high. However, he then identified certain kinds of papers that he had found to be so infrequently submitted that he had actively requested that certain articles be written (Ball, 1979):

> A third editorial responsibility is to improve the journal's offerings to its readership. The quality of articles is heavily dependent on the quality of the submissions, and there is no problem in filling our page allotment with useful articles. But there have been virtually no theoretical, integrative articles published in years despite our announced policy that this journal publishes theoretical articles and despite the fact that our empirically dominated profession cries out for better theoretical integration. I have therefore taken the initiative to invite a number of people to write substantive, theoretical, integrative articles in their specialties [pp. 1–2].

It would appear that the lack of viable instructional theories, at least up to the 1950s, does not seem especially unusual if one considers what had been happening, during comparable time periods, in other aspects of educational research. With the exception of counseling theory and a few other areas, most topical areas in education traditionally have been investigated empirically with little or no concern about systematically integrating the information into principles and theories.

Emergence of Instructional Theory?

Paterson's comments notwithstanding, there has been some evidence that instructional theories began to emerge in the late 1950s. The presentations in this book continue a pattern that is now in its third decade. However, it is important to recognize the possibility that this so-called pattern may either be drawing to a close or that it may reflect interests of only a small segment of persons who are interested in the study of instruction.*

---

*Editor's note: This is a very important problem for the further development of instructional theory; there are presently woefully few contributors to the field. Funding agencies could have a major positive impact here.

Some versions of what would become instructional theories can be found in the literature about teaching machines and programmed instruction that began to appear in the 1950s. Many of these papers (though not all) drew heavily on Skinner's operant theory and on his practical recommendations, which subsequently became identified with the emergent behavior-modification approach. But there were other views evident in the teaching machine-programmed instruction movement, including, for example, the testing and equipment-oriented conceptualizations of Pressey (1950) and some alternative views of instruction (e.g., Crowder, 1959) which, to some extent, could be depicted as precursors of cognitive theories that would follow later. A frequently cited source that explicitly advocated a cognitive approach was Bruner's (1966) book, *Toward a Theory of Instruction.*

Influence of the ASCD

Many authors appropriately credit the Association for Supervision and Curriculum Development (National Education Association) for having popularized the term *instructional theory,* and possibly for having been the group that set the occasion for the first use of the term in a formal manner. Beatty (1965) has reported: "In April 1963, Jerome Bruner made a statement at the national ASCD Conference in St. Louis which is having important consequences. He said that we make a mistake in looking to learning theories for guidance concerning teaching. In his view, teaching practices could not be inferred from learning theories, but rather, what we need is a theory of instruction [p. 114]." Beatty explained some ways in which he disagreed with Bruner's contentions about the need for theories of instruction. Beatty (1965) then noted: "A major consequence of Bruner's speech was the selection of 'Theories of Instruction' as the focus for the ASCD Curriculum Research Institutes for 1963–1964 [p. 114]."

In the same paragraph from which this last quotation was taken, Beatty went on to explain some reservations that he—and a number of psychologists and educators—would have about the proposed reliance on theories of instruction (Beatty, 1965):

> We may learn much in this area, yet the step we are taking is more radical than we think and is fraught with pitfalls. When we move from learning theories to instructional theories, we move from science to something which is a mixture of science and of completely extra-scientific values. One can test a learning theory, any learning theory, by its accuracy of predicting outcomes. The theory is neutral and can be used to any ends, good or bad. Instructional theories are not neutral. They involve controlling behavior and controlling it to some end. In this respect the theory of instruction can range from authoritarian to democratic [p. 114].*

There are two elements in Beatty's comments that seem especially important as we now consider the current and probable future status of instructional theory. First, for knowledge producers there is the distinct possibility that instructional theory *could* (but not necessarily would) turn into a "nonscientific" venture, led

---

*Editor's note: This is a very important observation, and is true of all prescriptive sciences. For an in-depth discussion of this issue, see Herbert Simon's *The Sciences of the Artificial* (1969).

more by personal values and prejudices than by empirical evidence and objective logical syntheses. For knowledge users, there is the distinct possibility that by accepting a "theory of instruction" rather than a "theory of learning," educators and the public would, perhaps, be relinquishing controls they previously had held with regard to the methods, substance, and goals* of education.

When we consider the present and probable future status of instructional theory, it is important to keep in mind these varying degrees of support (favorable and unfavorable, perhaps even hostile!) that may exist. Moreover, it is not only the actual intentions of instructional theorists so much as it is the perception—the image—that educators and psychologists have about instructional theory that might have a major determining influence on reactions to instructional theory.

There seemed to be some receptivity among ASCD members with regard to the contributions of instructional theory. ASCD, for example, published one 118-page document entitled *Theories of Instruction* (Macdonald & Leeper, 1965) in 1965 followed in 1968 by another report entitled *Criteria for Theories of Instruction* (Gordon, 1968). But for unknown reasons, these publications typically have not been cited by many persons who subsequently became involved with either instructional theory or instructional psychology.

This particular "failure" to foster better communication with a national group of practitioners is not especially surprising, however, because of certain attitudes that have often been observed within the academic community. In brief, it is fairly common for members of the academic community not only to prize sound conceptualizations and rigorous methodology but also to tend to display reservations about topics of a *practical* nature. It is almost as though prestige within the academic community is *inversely* related to the practical value of the topic and findings of an investigation. More often than not, academicians "earn" the respect of their peers through their work on matters that have little or no apparent practical value in pursuit of "knowledge for knowledge's sake." To the extent that instructional theorists would perceive these attitudes as existing in their work environments, it would not seem surprising if the instructional theorists would set higher priorities for establishing good relationships with peers in the academic community than with educators who might find that their work has some practical value.

Consistent with the preceding descriptions is the fact that many early instructional theorists identified primarily with some academic pursuit, designating the study of instruction as a more or less incidental interest. For example, Bruner (1966) depicted himself as "a student of the cognitive processes trying to come to grips with the problems of education [p. *vii*]." Rogers is generally known as a clinical psychologist and psychotherapy theorist. Skinner's major life work has been the study of learning and of other behavioral processes. Somewhat of an exception is Gagné, although he is primarily recognized as an experimental

---

*Editor's note: As long as instructional theories prescribe models on the basis of goals (among other things), goal-setting would not be at all jeopardized.

psychologist who became involved with instructional theory largely through wartime concerns with training issues.

Influence of Curriculum-Development Projects

One other trend warrants examination. It appears that one of the major supporting conditions for the emergence of instructional theory was the existence of societal and professional interest in the development of new curricular materials, especially in the 1960s and to a lesser extent in the 1970s. It was in conjunction with the earlier-initiated teaching machine-programmed movement and the later emergent curriculum projects that many of the roots of instructional theory were established. To some extent, the "nourishment and support" necessary for the continuing development of instructional theory have seemed to depend on financial and intellectual support of various curriculum-development projects. This general interest in curriculum-development projects began to fade during the 1970s, with the concurrent emergence of an interest in *program-evaluation* activities. This general shift—among psychologists, educators, and society more generally—from curriculum development to program evaluation was accompanied by declining interest in the processes of design in general and of instructional theory in particular.

Periodically, there have been instances in which program evaluators have displayed systematic interest in the underlying rationale and theory of instruction, but they seem to be the exception rather than the rule. For example, Leinhardt's (1980) comments about the pertinence of descriptions of educational "treatments" display little recognition of the prior existence of potentially relevant *instructional* theories. The focus in this particular paper is on the extent to which intended and planned educational treatments actually were provided. The relevance of program process to program evaluation interpretations is adequately addressed. What is missing in this and countless other similar papers is an awareness about ways in which *instructional* theory could facilitate accurate descriptions of planned and implemented educational interventions, and about ways in which such evaluation research studies would also facilitate improvements in instructional theory.

It seems reasonably accurate to state that by the late 1950s and early 1960s there had been established both the recognition of a *need* for instructional theory and the initial formulations of several *versions* of instructional theory. This support came both from the academic community and from the practitioners. However, the need for instructional theory was not acknowledged without reservations. The continuing support—both within academia and within practitioner groups—cannot be assumed without question.

Relevance of "Instructional Psychology"

Instructional psychology seems to have emerged somewhat later than *instructional theory* as terms that have been formally used with consistent meanings. One curious historical and contemporary facet is the manner in which these two terms (along with their respective activities and advocates) have influenced each other. In spite of an expectation that instructional psychology might favorably influence the development and extension of instructional theory—for example, by providing data and ideas that could be incorporated in theory—at times it seems almost as though instructional psychology serves more as a competitor than a supporter of instructional theory.

Instructional psychology *generally* refers to the theory and the principles derived from the application of psychological principles in the improvement of instruction or that result when psychologists conduct research on various forms of instruction. However, if one reviews the literature during the past two decades, during times when the term instructional psychology has been used, one will find very little evidence of theory, per se. Instead, what one finds are countless facets of instruction that have been studied by psychologists and others, with data typically being interpreted almost exclusively with regard to the explicitly identified domain of study. Stated another way, the reports typically do not take into account the generalizability of findings beyond the kinds of tasks actually studied in the investigation being reported.

In part this reflects the "fact-gathering" emphasis previously noted in educational research, but it also has some other important implications for instructional theory. This tendency to delimit one's interpretations somewhat narrowly also stems from a certain amount of skepticism as to whether we can *ever* have comprehensive theories of instruction. There is at least a passive acceptance—if not an outright advocacy—of the view that we need separately identified instructional principles and explanatory systems for each kind of educational and training facet that exists. For example, there is some tendency to assume that we should study how adults learn technical material from prose in print materials without considering whether these instructional processes involve principles that can be found with other age groups, subject matter, forms of presentation or media, and so on.

Examination of various journals that either emphasize or include papers on instructional psychology, or examination of the several chapters on instructional psychology that have appeared in the *Annual Review of Psychology*, will provide ample examples of a pattern. There is a distinct tendency to compile information about an increasingly large number of areas, with little or no attempt to compress and to synthesize resultant information into coherent interpretative conceptualizations. As Ball (1979) had noted with regard to publications in the *Journal of Educational Psychology*, throughout the various instructional-psychology publication vehicles there are comparatively few theoretical, integrative articles. Moreover, in those infrequent instances in which such articles are published, there is some tendency to imply that we need a separate instructional theory for each conceivable kind of instructional context.

The instructional-psychology publications, in toto, of course provide empirical information that is desparately needed to drive and to correct instructional theories. But there is more than a little indication that these instructional-psychology journal publications could prove sufficiently satisfying that no further attempts to synthesize research reports will be forthcoming. It is as though the existence of instructional psychology as an identifiable entity is institutionalizing the restriction of interpretations at the level of a journal report. Such conditions could prove to be detrimental to the further development of instructional theory. Another possibility is that a division of labor is emerging, with some persons gathering facts and others focusing more intently on the construction of theory.

Jahoda (1981) made somewhat similar comments about relationships between empirical research and theory relevant to the substantive areas of work, employment, and unemployment: "That a gap exists between empirical research and theoretical research explanations is beyond doubt, even though the abundance of empirical studies is matched by a plethora of grand and mini theories [p. 184]." Jahoda then quoted other authors who had complained about the same problem during the past few decades. Acknowledging (Jahoda, 1981) that, too often, "empirical findings have far outstripped the development of theories capable of explaining them [p. 184]," Jahoda proposed that we should essentially accept this as a fact of life and not let it bother us.

Jahoda's comments need not involve simple resignation to the gaps between fact gathering and theory construction. Instead, one can accept this status and continue to construct theories. It does seem important, however, that this gap should not be permitted to serve as justification for stifling theory development.

Some Issues Concerning Use of Instructional Theory

The 1980s seem to be evolving into an era in which society is questioning the extent to which science can produce feasible means for coping with society's problems. This trend has been observed with regard to the physical and biological sciences as well as with the social sciences. In this contemporary extent, implications for the practical use of instructional theory are quite complex. Although it is plausible that this trend could lead to a disastrous loss of the already narrow strand of support for construction and use of instructional theory, a more likely possibility is that new ideas will be developed about ways in which we use scientific information.

The terms *knowledge use, knowledge application, technology transfer*, and *technology application* reflect a quite recent perspective about science. These terms refer to those processes by which scientific information—no matter how advanced or primitive, no matter what theory or practical application is contemplated —is to be used in some practical context. Because they serve almost as synonyms in the contemporary literature, I simply use the term *knowledge use* in this chapter.

Throughout the 20th century there has been evident an assumption that, *somehow*, research information and theory can be used. The assumption has been that the hardest part is to obtain or to produce the information, with the implication that *application* could occur readily and with ease. Consistent with this view, practically all efforts and resources have been directed towards the production or generation of new knowledge in the forms of research findings and theory. Comparatively less effort and fewer resources have been diverted towards finding systematic means by which practitioners and others might put the knowledge to practical use.

Such views have been dominant in research and theory activities relevant to educational practice throughout the past century, but some interesting changes have occurred within the past few years. These changes include the recognition that we need to devise *systematic procedures* for using information, just as we have had to devise systematic procedures for producing knowledge.* Currently, attempts are being made to learn how practitioners recognize needs for information, what kinds of information are and are not helpful, the processes by which appropriate information can be identified and made useful for the practical context, and so on. For example, one new grants program at the National Institute of Education is concerned with knowledge use and school improvement, and other federal programs are designed to aid in the distribution of information to practitioners who need assistance. Informal and formal groups are being established among persons interested in knowledge-use processes so that they can exchange ideas about means for facilitating the practical use of research information. Some long-established journals now publish articles about knowledge-use processes, and others are being started to focus primarily on knowledge-use issues and processes. For example, in 1979 a journal entitled *Knowledge: Creation, Diffusion, Utilization* was established.

When considering the current and probable future status of instructional theory, one should keep in mind these two potentially influential patterns. One involves a questioning of the *real value* of scientific information for coping with societal problems. The other consists of systematic exploration of ways by which scientific information can be made *practically useful*.

A paper by Phillips (1980) illustrates some of the skepticism that is being expressed today about the practical value of research findings and theory. Phillips (1980) suggested that both practitioners and researchers will come out best if they expect the least from each other:

> There can be no cheerful conclusion. Researchers and practitioners might follow the lead of games theorists, whose rule of rationality is codified in the so-called "mini–max" principle: Minimize the maximum loss you can suffer. If both communities do this, and also expect the loss, then anything else that happens must be a pleasant surprise. By expecting little from each other, occasionally both the researcher and the practitioner may be in for a small treat [p. 20].

---

*Editor's note: For more on this issue, see Chapter 3. Along different lines, this supports the need for *development procedures* that automatically cause an instructional theory or model to be implemented. Most of the theorists in this book have developed some procedures for using their theories.

Johnson (1980) exudes optimism, in contrast with Phillips' pessimism, and suggests that we must study the knowledge-use processes much like we have studied other problems of interest. He indicates that a closer relationship between empirical research and theory construction could aid in bridging the gap between academia and practice.

Some valuable lessons may be learned from an area that already has a few decades of experiences with practically oriented theory—namely, the theory that is relevant to counseling and psychotherapy. Goldfried (1980) points out that it has long been customary for psychologists to focus on one theory, whether in practical situations or in research settings. The pattern to which Goldfried refers is typified by Hall and Lindzey (1957) in their classic book on personality theories. Hall and Lindzey recommended that students read about different theories but then choose only one and act as though the others hardly exist. Although admittedly this may be appropriate when one is trying to conduct research on a particular theory, there is serious question as to whether choosing only one theory is appropriate for practitioners. Goldfried (1980) observed: "There is a growing discontent among therapists of varying orientations. Psychoanalytic, behavioral, and humanistically oriented clinicians are starting to raise serious questions about the limits of their respective approaches and are becoming more open to contributions from other paradigms [p. 991]." Goldfried proposed that future textbooks for practitioner psychotherapists deemphasize the unique or idiosyncratic characteristics of each theory and, instead, focus on ways by which practitioners can derive practically useful ideas from various (even "competing") theories. He especially proposed (Goldfried, 1980) that practitioners be provided "an outline of the various agreed-upon intervention principles, a specification of varying techniques for implementing each principle, and an indication of the relative effectiveness of each of these techniques together with their interaction with varying presenting problems and individual differences among patients/clients and therapists [pp. 997–998]."

There is some dynamic tension that is inherent in the contrasting views and expectations that various readers have when examining any given instructional theory. The knowledge producers—whether focusing on fact gathering or on theory construction—tend towards emphasizing the unique contributions of each theory. With this orientation, it is almost wasteful for one to invest time in a theory that does not produce ideas that are different from what previously was known. In contrast, the knowledge users—whether working as designers or as individual practitioners—routinely search for "tried and true" interventions that will prove to be reliable and helpful with practical details of providing instruction. With this orientation, it is almost wasteful to consider new ideas unless they are sufficiently powerful to warrant deviating from established, dependable procedures.

Given these different vantage points, different expectations may exist when people inquire about the status of instructional theory. The historical and contemporary patterns and perspectives, likewise, can lead people to have different needs and expectations concerning instructional theory.

OBSERVATIONS ABOUT THE
TOTAL GROUP OF THEORIES

What can be said about the status of instructional theory when one considers the present examples collectively? I identify a dozen observations, although other ideas come to mind.

First it is quite apparent that we have ideas in this volume (and elsewhere) by people who have made a *major commitment* to the study of instruction and to the development of instructional theory. This contrasts sharply with conditions in the 1950s and 1960s when most emergent instructional theorists had major commitments elsewhere. If instructional theory is to continue to evolve, it is essential that there is some identifiable critical mass of people who can and will commit themselves to the necessary research and theory-construction activities.

Second, it seems clear that the commitment is not only to gather facts but also to *synthesize information* into principles and conceptual systems. Space limitations did not permit the authors to describe relevant empirical studies sufficiently to enable readers to evaluate the extent of the support for principles described here, but there is enough information to indicate that suggestions about instruction are influenced by research findings.

Third, it seems evident that one earlier characterization of instructional theories must now be revised. On a number of occasions in the early 1960s, Bruner announced that learning theories are *descriptive* and instructional theories are *prescriptive*. This characterization has generally gone unchallenged. But the two introductory-section chapters, by Reigeluth and by Landa, respectively, explicitly support the notion that *both* instructional theories and learning theories can be *both* descriptive and prescriptive. This involves much more than a mere semantic issue. The earlier descriptive/prescriptive distinction sometimes was construed to mean that instructional theories would be much more subjective and value oriented in nature. This was one reason why Beatty (1965) and others expressed reservations about the emergence of instructional theories. What is evident in the present chapters is the position that subjectivity and values more properly should occur with regard to selecting and using instructional theories, rather than with regard to formulating instructional theories. The present chapters display systematic attempts to present *empirically tested or testable assertions* about the educational effects that can be expected to occur when one chooses various instructional arrangements. It is this body of knowledge that the present instructional theorists attempt to make available. It is then up to educators and society more generally to make decisions about "prescribing" particular methods of instruction for specific practical contexts.

Fourth, there is unanimity among these theorists that instructional theory should be comparatively *generalizable*. Thus, there is little or no support in these chapters for the view that we need to have instructional theories that are exclusively relevant to rather narrowly defined practical contexts. This matter is explicitly addressed by some of the present authors, but is implied throughout these presentations.

Fifth, there is some question as to whether any of the present candidates constitute a fully developed "theory"—however defined conventionally—but they certainly go far beyond the general maxims that were characteristic of most emergent instructional theories in the 1960s. Although critics could note that each of the present representatives addresses some issues and not others, this is not uncommon in other groups of so-called social-science theories (as well as some aspects of science more generally). The extent of detail that is provided here—frequently after extensive empirical studies and interpretative syntheses—is substantially greater than was true even 10 years ago. Thus, in spite of the appropriate critical comments that Paterson had made in 1977 about the so-called theories he reviewed, advocates of the present theories have some justification for contenting that they have been producing instructional theories.

Sixth, there is another way in which the present offerings differ from their earlier counterparts—namely, the almost uniform attempts to build instructional theory "from within" instructional psychology rather than "from without" via incidental implications of other psychology and educational-research ventures. In the 1960s, with few exceptions the emergent instructional theories routinely derived their key ideas from some aspect of psychological research and applied them to instruction. Three obvious examples were Skinner's work on learning, Bruner's studies of cognitive development, and Rogers' research on counseling and psychotherapy. Although each of the present theories has drawn from psychological research and theory in general, the major portion of the detail reflects results of *instructional research and practice*. For example, even in the 1960s, some behavior-modification enthusiasts were finding that initial ideas from operant theory had to be modified in practical instructional contexts. Such changes then were made somewhat informally without concerted attempts to formalize the ideas in principles or theories, with some occasional exceptions. In contrast, the present theories provide numerous examples in which important changes and innovations have emerged from instructional research and practice. Moreover, the present set of theories includes various ways in which these changes and innovations have led to modification or extension of the earlier theory.

Seventh, these instructional theories differ in an important way from most other contemporary theories in psychology and other social sciences—namely in their scope and focus. Although there are differences among the present offerings, there is a common theme that it is not sufficient to study components of instruction in isolation. Thus, for example, instead of interest in *only* studying attentional processes, there is also interest in understanding how instructional procedures to facilitate attentiveness interact with and relate to other instructional procedures and effects. In a sense, there is interest not only in the components of instruction but also in the *interrelationships* and *architecture* or structure of the total process of instruction. The present theories differ as to their main focus, but they all display concern with the overall process of instruction. This is not only heuristically valuable for researchers but is also of considerable importance for designers and practitioners who, thus, receive some assistance in considering their total instructional responsibilities and activities.

Eighth, in spite of the broad scope and concern of these theories, it is noteworthy that these theories suggest that instruction can be understood in terms of comparatively *few characteristics*. This contrasts with expectations one might have after considering the huge array of student differences that have been identified over the years, the various kinds of subject matter and educational objectives, the contrasting expectations about education, and so on. However, it is consistent with the theory about problem solving that Simon and colleagues (cf. Newell & Simon, 1972; Simon, 1969) studied for over a decade—a program of research that came into existence originally to aid in management decision making in practical business contexts.

Ninth, it is of interest to compare the present offerings with those instructional theories that emerged in the first decade starting in the 1950s. Most authors (cf. Hilgard & Bower, 1975, Chapter 16; Paterson, 1977; Snelbecker, 1974) typically identified these theoretical persuasions among those earlier theories: behavior modification, cognitive psychology, humanistic psychology, eclectic collections of instructional principles organized into a system, and some form of decision-oriented strategy for optimizing instructional effects. With the exception of humanistic psychology, each of these earlier-noted approaches is evident in the present array. The only present candidate that could be related to *humanistic psychology* would be Keller's motivation-oriented approach, but an important aspect of humanistic psychology has also been incorporated into the theories of Merrill and Reigeluth in the form of "learner control." The *cognitive approach* is clearly represented by Scandura, Landa, and the presentation coauthored by Collins and Stevens, and other presentations display some substantial interest in cognitive aspects of instruction. Gropper's chapter illustrates some contemporary changes in *behavior-modification theory*. The work of Aronson and Briggs (carrying on a tradition established by Gagné), of Merrill, and of Reigeluth and Stein constitute *eclectic approaches* combined with instructional-management strategies. Thus, in each instance one can detect some *continuity* from earlier versions of instructional theory along with modifications made in the intervening years. Moreover, these modifications in the theory more often than not seem to have originated from within instructional psychology rather than through some paradigmatic shift or substantive breakthrough occurring outside of instructional psychology.

Readers have probably been wondering whether the array of theories in this book is reasonably representative of contemporary instructional theories. Gropper partly addressed this point (Chapter 2) when he suggested that it could take several volumes merely to provide similar descriptions of the other instructional theories and models that have been published. Based on my own ongoing reviews, it appears that the present array is *reasonably representative* of theory-construction efforts in instructional psychology today. There are other facets being studied, but resulting papers typically do not currently lead to systematic synthesizing statements. The overall "balance" across the five "theoretical persuasions" I enumerated earlier in the present chapters seems to be consistent with the proportion of empirically based instructional-theory efforts in the field.

Tenth, one could also attempt to compare the focus of these theories on the basis of various organizational schemes. As noted in Chapter 1 of this book, Reigeluth and Merrill (1978, 1979) propose three components of a theory of instruction: methods, conditions, and outcomes. Glaser (1976] proposed four components of a psychology of instruction:

(a) analysis of the competence, the state of knowledge and skill, to be achieved; (b) description of the initial state with which learning begins; (c) conditions that can be implemented to bring about change from the initial state of the learner to the state described as competence; and (d) assessment procedures for determining the immediate and long-range outcomes of the conditions that are put into effect to implement change from the initial state of competence to further development [p. 8].

My own preference (Snelbecker, 1983) is for a scheme based on the various steps that teachers typically follow in providing instruction, recognizing that a cycle that can be identified theoretically will not simply and uniformly be implemented in actual classrooms. In this way I have reviewed literature and identified these steps: preparing students for instruction, gaining and maintaining attention, presenting information, providing for students' (overt or covert) responses, arranging feedback/reinforcement, facilitating retention and transfer, aiding understanding, encouraging creativity, and improving teacher and student management of the instructional process. Table 12.1 suggests the extent to which these instructional theories address these components, structures, and management of instruction.

Eleventh, an observation about "fragmentation" seems appropriate here. In the present chapters and elsewhere in their various publications, many of these authors have displayed some concern about the multitude of seemingly competing methods that have characterized the literature on education-relevant research. But, curiously, it would appear that they can not avoid increasing this problem to the extent that their respective theoretical statements provide new ideas. Perhaps it would be best to expect theory construction to have two reciprocal, alternating phases (aside from the empirical data-gathering aspects). Phase I would involve presentations of new principles, theories, statements about instruction. Phase II would involve comparing current ideas and trying to see how available theories compare and contrast with each other. It would appear that in instructional psychology—as well as in other sectors of social-science theory construction—we invest all of our time in Phase I and almost totally ignore Phase II. Perhaps presentations of individual theories is such a demanding task that we will have to wait for some future time when available theories can be examined, compared, contrasted, and so on.*

---

*Editor's note: A major purpose of this book is to facilitate Phase II right here and now, under the assumption that this activity is indeed very important to the development of the discipline.

TABLE 12.1
Aspects of Instruction Addressed by
the Respective Theories[a]

	Aronson & Briggs	Gropper	Scandura	Landa	Collins & Stevens	Merrill	Reigeluth & Stein	Keller
Reigeluth & Merrill								
Methods	X	X	X	X	X	X	X	X
Conditions	X	X	X	X	X	X	X	X
Outcomes	X	X	X	X	X?	X?	X?	X?
Glaser								
Analysis—Goals	X	X?	X	X	X	X	X	X
Initial state	X	X?	X	X	X	X	X	X
Implementation	X	X	X	X	X	X	X	X
Assessment	X	X	X	X	X?	?	?	X?
Snelbecker								
Preparation	X	X?	?	?	?	?	X	X?
Attention	X	?	?	?	X?	X?	?	X
Presentation	X	X?	X	X	X	X	X?	X?
Responses	X	X	X?	X?	X?	X?	X?	X?
Feedback	X	X	X?	X?	X?	X?	X?	X?
Retention and use	X	X	?	?	?	?	?	X?
Understanding	?	?	X	X	X	?	?	?
Creativity	?	?	?	X?	X?	?	?	X?
Management	?	?	?	?	?	X?	?X	X?

[a] ? = absent; X? = partially addressed; X = present.

OBSERVATIONS ABOUT
INDIVIDUAL THEORIES

A number of questions could be raised about the theories represented in this book. Of course, space limitations alone dictate that these chapters be regarded as abbreviated progress reports rather than as full descriptions and documentations of the theories. For persons who not only want to review the present chapters but also to gain more information about respective theories (for example, by pursuing references at the end of each chapter), here are some questions that might be considered for each theory:

1. To what extent is there evidence of an "instructional theory"?
2. What are the main concepts and principles of the theory?
3. To what extent is there empirical evidence relevant to the theory?
4. What implications can be derived from the theory for further research?
5. What implications can be derived for improving the extant body of theory and general knowledge about instruction?
6. What, if any, new methodologies and strategies for designing or improving instruction are provided by the theory?
7. What guidelines are available to help either practitioners or designers to use the theory?
8. What practical implications might be of value for educational administrators?
9. What practical implications might be of value for media specialists and for other educational resource specialists?
10. What are the major strengths and weaknesses of the theory with respect to the ASCD criteria (Gordon, 1968; Snelbecker, 1974, Chapter 5), Reigeluth's criteria in Chapter 1 of this book, or other criteria for evaluating theories?

These are some of the questions I had in mind as I reviewed the papers when they originally were prepared for presentation in the Symposium at the 1979 American Psychological Association Convention and when they have gone through various revised drafts to become the chapters in this book. In the course of those reviews, as I have already noted earlier, my students and I also considered some of the primary sources in which statements about the theories have been published elsewhere. However, space limitations and other practical considerations bear on the kinds of comments I can now make about these theories. Space alone does not permit me to consider each question for each theory. Thus, I select appropriate questions for respective theories. Because readers have available the chapters in this book, I primarily comment on the theories as represented in these chapters. Because some of the theories either are complementary or share certain common features, I group some of the chapters when commenting on individual theories. Otherwise, I mainly sequence my comments in accordance with the chapter sequence.

Aronson–Briggs–Gagné

Aronson and Briggs (Chapter 4) summarize key elements of a theory that is generally acknowledged as one of the early instructional theories. For brevity, I refer to this as the "Gagné theory" because Gagné provided the major initial ideas. This chapter identifies some of the work of Gagné and Briggs from which the theory in its present form has evolved. This is a comprehensive and somewhat *eclectic* theory in that it draws from many aspects of psychology learning theory, although its major knowledge base is the more traditional behavioral theories with comparatively little influence from contemporary cognitive psychology theory. It is also *comprehensive* in the sense that it deals with most of the facets of instruction indicated in Table 12.1. Though the basis for classifying educational tasks is explicitly derived from certain specified aspects of learning research and theory, this theory is oriented more towards instructional events than merely towards changes presumed to be occurring inside the student.

There are some limitations on the extent to which a designer or practitioner is aided by this theory in *managing* instruction. Thus, though certain instructional events and intended learnings are provided structure by the theory, the designer and practitioner must rely on other resources to develop an overall plan for the instruction.

Another limitation involves the kinds of instruction that readily can be planned from this theory. To get some perspective, it would be helpful if readers were already familiar with the taxonomy of educational objectives that was first publicized over two decades ago by Bloom and colleagues (Bloom, 1956). In brief, it was proposed that educational goals could be classified horizontally in terms of cognitive, affective, and psychomotor characteristics. In addition, within each of these three domains, it was proposed that hierarchical relationships could be identified with the assumption that lower-level goals should (perhaps, must) be attained before higher-level goals could profitably be attempted. The present theory includes *only a few* of the many educational goals that could be identified via Bloom's taxonomy. Moreover, there is some tendency for the Gagné theory to emphasize comparatively low-level to moderately high-level educational goals. For example, there is little emphasis on creativity and higher cognitive processes. This is not necessarily a serious limitation as long as one maintains perspective as to what aspects of the curriculum are being planned. Moreover, one can have a "good" instructional theory that deliberately was designed to address only particular kinds of educational goals. An important contribution is that Gagné's theory does identify particular educational goals and then specifies instructional means for those goals.

It should be evident from the Aronson and Briggs chapter that the Gagné theory is useful *both for designers and for practitioners*. The concepts and principles do have implications for large-scale instructional planning (e.g., organizing instructional procedures in a new curriculum project) as well as for day-to-day activities of classroom teachers and other practitioners working alone.

Space limitations here did not permit Aronson and Briggs to provide details on the extent to which various facets of the Gagné theory have been supported by research. However, from other sources (such as the references listed at the end of Chapter 4) one can find numerous areas that await and warrant empirical exploration. For example, Landa (Chapter 3 of this book) points out that different instructional arrangements could be derived from a given set of learning-theory prescriptions. Similarly, the Gagné theory stands ready for *further development* via extension and elaboration. For example, it may be possible to use the Gagné–Briggs–Aronson strategies to classify and to plan instruction for educational goals beyond those already outlined in the theory as it now stands.

Gropper and Behavior Modification

Gropper (Chapter 5) provides the only clear example of a behavior-modification theory in this book. Gropper's theory tends to be somewhat broader than earlier versions of behavior-modification theory in that it explores a wider range of instructional phenomena and it draws from a somewhat wider range of research findings and learning theory. Like the Gagné–Briggs–Aronson theory, Gropper's theory draws primarily from associationistic learning theory, to which he refers as "behavioral, reinforcement theory." However, Gropper attempts to maintain a tighter relationship with the learning-theory concepts and principles than has been the case in the Gagné–Briggs–Aronson theory. To some extent, this difference results from the fact that Gropper is drawing from ideas and empirical findings that are more homogeneous with regard to instructional concepts and principles than is true of the Gagné–Briggs–Aronson theory.

Gropper's strategy is to base conceptions and prescriptions for instruction on a systematically developed model of *learning*. For example, Gropper acknowledges that differences among students should be considered when one plans instructional activities. He also concedes that a behavioral, reinforcement conception of learning tends to deemphasize differences among students and to focus primarily on principles that are generalizable to all or most students. Then, when he outlines pertinent student differences, he resorts to the terminology of behavioral, reinforcement learning theory (e.g., different capacities to learn discriminations, generalizations, chains, etc.).

Given the foregoing descriptions, one might reasonably expect that Gropper could be either insensitive to or grossly unaware of the concerns of teachers and other practitioners. To the contrary, he not only acknowledges the day-to-day concerns of practitioners but also attempts to relate his systematically evolved views of learning and instruction to the specific *concerns of practitioners*. For example, he cautions that practitioners need explicit guidance about their subject matter and their students, because general principles of instruction (in Gropper's view) do not lend themselves readily to specific applications. Thus, Gropper, urges readers to analyze their teaching situations in terms of his theory's concepts and principles, and to identify particular ways in which conditions can be engineered to produce specific educational/behavioral changes.

Maintaining his announced reliance on behavioral, reinforcement-theory concepts and principles, Gropper carefully moves back and forth between a microscopic examination of instructional-process details and an overview of the total instructional process. For the latter, Gropper identifies as major concerns the conditions (i.e., stimulus properties, component skills, and objectives) of the teaching–learning activities, the educational interventions or treatments that can be used, and the various means by which designers or practitioners can "match" treatments and conditions.

Some readers may experience difficulties periodically when they attempt to understand the overall management of instruction that emerges from Gropper's theory because of the *extensive detail* involved in his description of instruction. This "problem" may be more an indicator of the complexities of instruction that are revealed under careful examination than an indicator that Gropper's theory is focusing on minutia. However, it is likely that some critics will prefer the latter interpretation. Moreover, it would not be surprising that at least some designers and practitioners will yearn for simpler admonitions (e.g., reinforce behaviors as they gradually resemble more closely desired learnings) as they attempt to move through Gropper's careful analyses. It is possible that such a reaction may be more likely to be expressed by a practitioner who wants help immediately on some pressing problem than would be the case with a designer who has had time allocated to analyze instruction carefully before planning procedures. However, it does seem reasonable to expect that Gropper's ideas could profitably be considered by *both designers and practitioners* who successfully maintain an understanding of their instructional contexts and of the organization embodied in Gropper's theory.

Somewhat in contrast to the reactions of knowledge users, the knowledge-producer groups (both researchers and theorists) should find a rich array of ideas to study. There is need to examine, for example, the extent to which Gropper's recommendations are similar to and different from those of the Gagné–Briggs–Aronson theory and of other instructional theorists. There are *numerous examples of testable hypotheses* displayed in the various treatments and treatment-condition matches that Gropper outlines.

Gropper's theory should be of interest to researchers and theorists. Review of his work reveals that he exercised reasonable caution in trying to relate his instructional theory to the fruits of modern learning research—at least those findings and interpretations that one can find in contemporary behavioral, reinforcement theory and research. Less obvious is the extent to which the emergent instructional principles will be supported by empirical evidence. Also known is the extent to which one could derive useful ideas from cognitive theory that might contradict, enhance, or support the instructional principles that Gropper almost exclusively derives from behavioral, reinforcement theory. Thus, the presentation of the theory in its current form provides numerous potential leads for additional research and extension of the theory.

Three Cognitive Approaches

Three chapters constitute contemporary versions of an approach to instructional theory that is quite commonly associated with Bruner's name. These three chapters were prepared by Scandura, Landa, and Collins and Stevens, respectively. As most of you are aware, Bruner (e.g., 1966) emphasized cognitive processes as the primary theoretical/conceptual basis for viewing learning and instruction. Although Bruner did *not* consider "discovery learning" as the *sole* format and technique for instruction (cf. Snelbecker, 1974, Chapter 16), discovery learning does illustrate the approach to instruction considered most appropriate for many cognition-oriented theorists.

These three chapters substantially extend views typically associated with Bruner in at least two respects. First, the *cognitive processes* that occur during learning and instruction are more elaborately described. Second, the *instructional procedures and techniques* are described in greater detail and are more explicitly linked, by the authors of these three chapters, to the underlying principles of cognitive processes.

It is of note that these three chapters have singularly unique features while sharing a common general conceptual scheme and overall approach to instruction. Collins and Stevens quite explicitly focus primarily on teaching/instructional strategies. Although both Scandura and Landa basically tend to deal with intervention techniques "after" focusing on the theorized internal processes, it is of interest that they find different methodologies and conceptualizations useful in their pursuits.

Collins and Stevens

The Collins and Stevens emphasis is evident in the title of their chapter—"A Cognitive Theory of *Inquiry Teaching*" (italics added). They report that they developed their theory through analyses of the manner in which certain teachers attempt to help their students. The types of teachers on whom they base their analyses are typically called proponents of "discovery learning," "inquiry training," and/or "Socratic method." Moreover, Collins and Stevens attempt to maintain an internally consistent theory through monitoring the goals as well as the strategies of the teachers being studied.

Collins and Stevens do not appear to permit any learning theory to constrain their exploration of teachers' goals and strategies, but pervasive throughout their research methods and their interpretations are influences of Newell and Simon's (1972) problem-solving theory. Thus, the present chapter can be viewed as (at least partly) anchored in a substantially larger body of cognitive research and theory—namely, the ventures that have been stimulated by the long-term work of Simon and Newell plus others who have followed in their tradition. This is an important observation because of the typically limited research and conceptual base from which some instructional theories are derived.

Readers who are familiar with the Newell and Simon (1972) theory know that, in studying teachers, Collins and Stevens focus on teachers' attempts to help students reach successively identified intermediate and long-term *goals*. For example, Collins and Stevens find that inquiry teachers attempt to help students to reach two types of "top-level" goals—namely, to learn particular rules or theories, and to learn how to derive (or, to discover) rules or theories. The Collins and Stevens theory attempts to articulate how students are aided in clarifying their goals and how they are aided in making progress towards their goals.

The theory that is evolving has a distinct *advantage* for practical application in that case-study-type observations constitute a central basis for the theory; thus, there are numerous practical examples that are examined in the process of evolving this theory.

A *disadvantage* tends to persist in that the methodology could cause some readers to have difficulty in recognizing the presumed patterns that cut across the respective specific examples. Perhaps more importantly, this case-rich approach may make it difficult for some practically oriented readers to discern what is *not* consistent with the present theory. Perhaps as further work is done on this theory, there may emerge a clearer designation of examples and nonexamples so that both practitioners and designers will have clear guidelines for applying this theory. The authors have demonstrated both a commitment to clarifying nonexamples and examples and have made considerable progress in this regard.

It seems likely that researchers and theorists may have slightly different reactions to the present status of the work by Collins and Stevens. For readers who are either not familiar with the Newell–Simon views or who do not accept such theory, the present efforts may be misconstrued as excessively pragmatic. This probably will not pose problems for researchers who are content to relate findings only to rather narrowly defined research questions. But it could prove to be less acceptable to instructional theorists who seek a *broader conceptualization* of instructional processes. Thus, researchers and theorists may disagree about the extent to which the Collins and Stevens chapter can be considered a "theory."

Scandura

Scandura's chapter presents different kinds of contributions and questions for readers. Of course, as Scandura cautions at the beginning of his chapter, his theory (and, for that matter, *any* theory) can*not* be depicted adequately and accurately in only a few minutes or paragraphs. However, if we keep in mind the caveats that Scandura lists (which also are appropriate caveats for *all* theories), we should gain some understanding of Scandura's approach to instructional theory, including the means and results of his efforts to construct a sound and useful theory. In brief, Scandura primarily bases his instructional theory on his conceptualization of what happens "inside" the student during instruction and learning. Scandura theorizes that we tend to organize our thinking about the world in the form of rules and rule structures.

It is as important to understand Scandura's preference for *having* a coherent and complete *conceptual framework* as it is to understand the specific features of Scandura's framework. This is a matter that I considered previously when discussing the Collins and Stevens approach. As I noted then, Collins and Stevens typify an approach with which Scandura finds some disagreement. A high priority for Scandura is to have a sound conceptualization of the internal cognitive processes when designing instruction; merely having techniques and methods is not enough.

Scandura's emphasis on "goals" can be misleading. Scandura already has cautioned readers that he is dealing with cognitive processes rather than (only?) with behavioral changes. Readers should also understand that when Scandura talks about all students' being goal oriented, he does *not necessarily* mean that they are highly motivated to reach school-based educational goals. As I note later, Landa is even more explicit in distinguishing between the goals and strategies of students versus the goals and strategies of teachers. In brief, Scandura is suggesting that a student's activities and progress and be understood in terms of that particular student's goals—no matter whether they are consciously designated—and the rules and pathways that that student believes will enable him or her to reach desired goals.

Readers could prematurely dismiss Scandura's approach as being appropriate *only* for a "logically organized" subject matter like mathematics. However, this would be unfortunate. The thrust of Scandura's approach is that virtually all subject-matter areas can be understood in terms of his structural-learning conceptualization—whether or not they traditionally have been viewed as "logically" organized.

There are various ways in which Scandura's practical recommendations seem similar to the practical guidelines of behavioral theorists, but one should be cautious in noting the differences as well as the similarities. There are similarities in that Scandura suggests that teachers should identify the student's current educational capabilities and accomplishments, and that educational prescriptions should be derived from an analysis of the present status and of the intended goals. However, in contrast with a behaviorist's emphasis on directly observable behavior, Scandura stresses the admonition that educational prescriptions should be directly derived from an analysis of the *cognitive* operations that are required to reach the educational goals.

Perhaps the key facets in Scandura's theory lie in the ways in which, according to the theory, people "use, acquire, and modify existing knowledge." This, it might be added here, is *very* closely related to certain central ideas embodied in Landa's theory. Instructional theory and practical implications, according to Scandura's and Landa's theories, are to be planned in accordance with the ways in which people evolve and change their understanding of themselves and of the world. Thus, it is neither the specific information imparted during instruction nor the behaviors that result from instruction with which we should be *primarily* concerned. Instead, both Scandura and Landa argue that knowledge producers and knowledge users should focus on the cognitive processes that occur in conjunction with instruction (before, during, after, etc.).

Landa

Landa presents an instructional theory that is quite similar to the other two cognitively oriented theories, but that has some aspects of a general systems theory orientation as well. His algo-heuristics theory is explicitly designated as a cybernetics theory (in some publications), but it is the emphasis on cognitive processes that provides its most distinctive features. Landa's theory, in comparison with Scandura's theory, differs more in terms of the *answers* that are provided than in terms of the questions that are considered or primary importance. Both theorists emphasize the cognitive processes as the major source for describing instructional processes and for designating practical educational-intervention guidelines. Whereas Scandura stresses logical operations in terms of hierarchically and horizontally organized "rules," Landa emphasizes patterned strategies.

Landa's *patterned strategies* are classified as one or more types of "algorithms" and "heuristics." Both algorithms and heuristics involve sets of strategies, systematically organized, that someone believes ("knows") will lead to particular and general outcomes. Both involve *internal* processes (i.e., not directly observable behaviors) that occur independently or in conjunction with observable behavior. Both consist of patterns of elementary cognitive operations, with "elementary" being defined relative to persons, times, and situations rather than in an absolute sense. The term *algorithm* (as used in Landa's theory) refers to comparatively regular and uniform patterns of elementary logical operations. A heuristic process may include some variations in sequences of operations or may include logical operations that are only partly clarified and understood. Thus, *comparatively*, an algorithm is theorized as having a more readily predictable course and a more likely identifiable outcome than is characteristic of a heuristic process.

Landa explicitly designates at least three types of algorithms that are relevant to instruction: an algorithm for describing the student's cognitive processes, an algorithm that a teacher could use to teach a student the proper cognitive processes, and an algorithm that someone else could use to help the teacher to learn how to teach the student.

As with Scandura's theory, it is extremely important to recognize that the theory is *not* limited to subject-matter areas like mathematics, which are frequently depicted as being "logically organized." Landa's theory, according to proponents, can be used to understand and to teach subject matter of virtually any kind. In fact, one of Landa's practical recommendations is that one can use his algo-heuristic approach (or, Landamatics) to learn how we think about instruction and about things more generally.

Summary Comments on the Three Cognitive Approaches

Knowledge producers and knowledge users should find these three approaches to be fruitful sources of ideas for their respective questions about instruction. It is likely that researchers and practitioners will be attracted to the approach presented by Collins and Stevens. For different reasons, both theorists and designers may experience some difficulties in recognizing generalizable features from their comparatively specific examples of interactive teaching. This does not mean that the conceptualizations are not present, especially given the affiliation with work typically identified with Simon and Newell. The observation is made because this approach tends to emphasize specific instances more than generalizable features.

Both Scandura and Landa—in contrast to Collins and Stevens—*strongly* emphasize the need for a generalizable conceptual scheme as a prominent feature in their work. The rules-oriented approach advocated by Scandura is related to, but different from, the algo-heuristic patterns stressed by Landa.

As a result, it seems likely that theorists and designers will be particularly pleased with the overriding conceptual scheme that can quite easily be identified in the chapters by Scandura and by Landa, respectively. However, the nature of their contributions is such that researchers should be able to detect researchable questions and that practitioners should be able to recognize practical implications for trying to understand instructional problems.

Mitchell (1980) made some observations about the use of algorithms in instructional development that seem applicable to the general popularity of cognitive theory today. He commented: "Although it appears that algorithms are being designed and applied in all phases of instructional design and development, few if any of those who have developed altogirhms . . . have made any true effort to validate their contributions [p. 14]." In fairness to the advocates of the three cognitive instructional theories discussed here, it should be noted that Mitchell is mainly aiming his critical comments at people who use algorithms in instructional theory. Advocates of the three positions described in this section consistently contend that empirical data should be obtained to test the theoretical and the practical value of the respective theories.

Complementary Components of a General Theory

Although the next three chapters (respectively by Merrill, Reigeluth and Stein, and Keller) are presented as independent approaches, I recommend that readers view them as essential complementary components of a general theory of instruction. This description is chosen carefully, with full awareness that each of the theorists whose work is represented here (and, for that matter, most theorists in general) tend to view their respective theories as general theories. For example, Scandura is quite explicit in so designating his theory, whereas the other authors provide more subtle similar indications. The reason for this suggestion is that these three chapters have a common origin (primarily associated with the Courseware, Inc., development of a large-scale computer-based instructional system called TICCIT) and involve authors who have exchanged ideas during the development of their ideas.

Merrill

Merrill's chapter on Component Display Theory (CDT) emphasizes the importance of designing instruction so that there will be consistency across designation of objectives, presentation of instruction, and evaluation of results. CDT is depicted as a "micro" theory in that it focuses on the details of specific presentations of instruction. The main thrust of CDT borrows heavily from Gagné postulate that different kinds of learner outcomes require different conditions of learning. CDT goes beyond this general position and provides explicit means for classifying types of outcomes and facets of instructional presentations.

There is a distinct "preference" in this and the other three chapters—namely, to focus more explicitly on the needs of instructional design than on the particular psychological or educational conceptualization (i.e., theory or research findings) in developing both the theory of instruction and the procedures for designing instruction. This clearly reveals a *"bias" towards knowledge users* rather than knowledge producers, at least with regard to the genesis of the theory. As the theory has evolved and has become more complex, this bias has been somewhat "neutralized," and the proponents of the Merrill et al. general theory have become engrossed in rather typical knowledge-producer pursuits (e.g., trying to identify and codify preferred concepts and principles, identifying facets in need of research, finding means for organizing newly emerged and old aspects of the growing theory, etc.). Moreover, at times the theory becomes so complex that designer *teams* are more likely to find the designated practical implications feasible than are practitioners working alone.

Perhaps because the theory mainly evolved in conjunction with written instruction, there is another "preference" that should be noted. This is the preference or the recognition that desired instructional processes and outcomes can be initiated and facilitated by the nature and organization of the instructional *materials*. Someone devising a theory of instruction from the analysis of tutorial relationships, for example, conceivably could (but not necessarily would) ascribe such responsibilities to interpersonal relationships that occur in conjunction with instruction. Whatever the reason for the origin of the emphasis, it is quite evident in each of these three chapters.

It is noteworthy that the resultant instructional theory seems to be as receptive to *cognitive* as it is to *behavioral* aspects of instruction. For example, one could conceivably relate CDT to Piagetian theory. This has been done by one of my seminar participants who was trying to use Piagetian strategies in a workshop whose purpose was to teach certain Piagetian concepts and principles. In this venture, CDT was used to inventory the desired goals and the presentation methods and to monitor the extent to which all necessary matters had been addressed. On the other hand, given the fact that CDT has drawn extensively from earlier behavior-modification concepts and principles, it also seems self-evident that CDT could be used with behaviorally oriented instances of instructional presentations.

In brief, CDT seems to be especially useful for facilitating management of instructional processes—or at least certain aspects of instruction (i.e., presentations). It seems inevitable that CDT will be of particular interest to designers and to theorists, both of whom have interests and the luxury of time to consider the general perspective and the overall characteristics of instruction. Individual practitioners may feel somewhat overwhelmed, at least when first trying to use CDT. For different reasons, researchers may find it difficult to designate specific researchable questions and/or to assess the extent to which the present form of CDT is adequately grounded in empirical findings.

Reigeluth and Stein

Whereas CDT is offered (by Merrill and colleagues) as a "micro" theory, the Reigeluth—Merrill Elaboration Theory is identified as a "macro" theory. This micro—macro distinction may pose some difficulties for readers because a case could be made for reversing these designations. That is, the management contributions of CDT are so prominent that, in some respects, the theory could be designated as macro rather than as micro. Similarly, in some respects, the Elaboration Theory could be viewed either as macro (as the authors recommend) or as micro; the potential for the micro characterization stems from the fact that Elaboration Theory can be used to deal with specific narrowly identified aspects of instruction. The authors prefer the macro designation because Elaboration Theory particularly emphasizes a broader range of phenomena than does CDT. From that view, Elaboration Theory can be depicted as dealing with four broader components of instruction—selection of topics, sequence of presentations, synthesizing of topics, and summarizing of topics. CDT only deals with presentations.

Two concepts, in my judgment, illustrate the scope and nature of Elaboration Theory: the zoom-lens analogy and the epitome. The zoom-lens analogy demonstrates the need for having *students* (i.e., not only teachers) understand relationships across major topics and relationships among facets within each topic. The zoom-lens analogy reminds us that, periodically (a "judgment decision"), the student needs assistance in understanding and reviewing these interrelationships. The epitome reminds us of the importance for students to "know where they are going" even before they begin the educational experiences; it also reminds us that such descriptions must take into account the student's level of knowledge and capabilities at that point in time and experience. Most readers will recognize the connections between these Elaboration-Theory concepts and the work of Ausubel, particularly with regard to advance organizers. Elaboration Theory extends and elaborates on certain aspects of the work on advance organizers, and has attempted to do so in such a way as to overcome the criticisms leveled against advance organizers.

Keller

Earlier it was noted that humanistic psychology is "conspicuous by its absence" in the present array of instructional theories. The Keller chapter on motivation at least partly deals with some of this missing content (as does the *learner-control* component of the Merrill and Reigeluth theories). Certainly, a strong case is made for considering motivational aspects when discussing the practical application of instructional theory. Readers quite commonly critize instructional psychologists and theorists for ignoring variations in students' motivation to learn—a matter that people in classrooms simply cannot ignore.

Readers should note carefully what kind of approach is taken in the chapter on motivation and instruction. Keller emphasizes that, rather than the currently popular (among psychologists) micro theory, he proposes that instructional theory requires a broader perspective and a more explicit consideration of variables that designers and practitioners can actually consider. Particularly, the intent is to identify major *categories* of motivational variables that seem to be relevant to individual effort and performance so that these variables can then be considered when designing instruction. As has been the case in the preceding two chapters, this chapter draws heavily from currently available research findings and theory pertinent to instruction, and a concerted attempt is made to articulate practically relevant implications for the design of instruction.

It seems inevitable that readers will react in various ways to the offerings of this chapter. Most likely to be pleased will be the theorists, because this chapter provides an array of ideas that could and should be considered when formulating instructional theories. Researchers may feel somewhat uncomfortable because researchable hypotheses are not immediately evident, and because a synthesis of this kind almost demands that one go beyond empirical facts so as to interpret the generalizable practical implications. Designers will probably find numerous ideas of a practical nature, but individual practitioners may experience some difficulty in identifying explicit, specific implications that they can actually use.

Summary Comments on Complementary Components of a General Theory

These three chapters, taken together, provide somewhat broader facets of instructional theory than do the previous chapters. That is *not* to say that they are necessarily more important! Instead, I am suggesting that this set of chapters tends to examine—and to provide practical implications relevant to—student and teacher management issues and overall issues of instructional design. Of course, each of the previous chapters also did this in varying degrees, too.

These chapters and the chapter by Aronson and Briggs have a characteristic that will variably be seen as either a strength or a weakness, depending on one's views about knowledge production and knowledge use. Specifically, these chapters make a concerted attempt to *integrate* research findings and theory from widely ranging sources. As a result they can be complimented for their synthesizing efforts because of the potential insights they provide. On the other hand, they can be faulted for "going beyond the data" and for not testing, empirically, the validity of all their assertions. This should not pose real difficulties *if* one recognizes that these are "progress reports" rather than "the final, definitive statements" for the respective topics considered.

CONCLUSIONS: STATUS OF INSTRUCTIONAL THEORY AND IMPLICATIONS FOR USERS

Over a decade and a half ago, Bruner (1966) advocated construction of instructional theories but conceded that his own efforts constituted steps towards rather than the complete attainment of a theory of instruction. Several years ago, Gerlach (1975) contended that much more work is needed on instructional theories and instructional-design procedures. Gerlach (1975) observed that "the technology of materials and methods . . . has lagged far behind the technology of goal specification and the technology of assessment [p. 1]." Given these earlier observations, one might well ask about the status of instructional theories today, and one might be concerned about their prospects for the future. When drawing conclusions about instructional theory, it seems important to keep in mind the four kinds of audiences that I described earlier in this chapter—namely, researchers, theorists, designers, and individual practitioners.

It still seems appropriate today to conclude that we are still moving "towards" instructional theory, rather than having attained some sufficiently comprehensive and adequately sound conceptualization. However, considerable progress *has* been made, and there are reasons for being optimistic about the future.

Researchers should be quite pleased not only for the growing numbers of research questions that have emerged during the past decade but also for the increasing numbers of researchers who are providing relevant empirical data.

Theorists—and persons who are seeking systematically organized bodies about instruction—similarly should be pleased about progress to date as well as about prospects for continuing future developments.

It seems likely that designers will be more comfortable with the emerging instructional theories than will individual classroom teachers and other practitioners working alone in traditional school settings. Many of the theories have reached a point of maturity at which there have become evident a rich array of features that *could* warrant consideration *if* one has sufficient time to comprehend the theory and to identify implications that are pertinent to specific local situations. Unfortunately, the theories have not yet been codified in a form that can easily be used by practitioners, and the formal preparation of practitioners typically does not provide them with sufficient skills and strategies to become good consumers of instructional-theory information.

Thus, the future of instructional theory will be influenced both by the extent of support that is provided for *producing* new knowledge (systematically organized) about instruction, and support that is provided to aid designers and practitioners in *using* such information in their work.

There are many negative features that could be described. Presently we are in the midst of an era when governmental support at all levels seems to be dwindling and there is little evidence that suggests that this pattern will become more promising for at least the next few years. The declining enrollment patterns are expected to continue for at least several years, with some predictions that birth rates—and thus, subsequently, school enrollments—may increase during the mid- to late-1980s. At least some forecasters have linked their predictions about support for instruction (and, to some extent, for instructional theory) to the changes in enrollment patterns.

However, lest one become unduly pessimistic, it is noteworthy that some quite positive features can be identified. There are several influences and patterns now emerging that could favorably influence the status of instructional theory and of strategies for designing and improving instruction. As has already been noted, the present array of chapters illustrates that, in comparison with earlier periods, today there is a growing group of *people* who have a commitment to the constructive development of instructional theory and of design strategies. With austere fiscal conditions, there is some growing public *support* for the belief that we should find ways for getting the best results from our education dollars. A convincing case can be made that instructional theory and sound design procedures can aid educators in monitoring and improving instruction. Current discussions about ways in which we could markedly improve *teacher-preparation* programs (e.g., Smith, 1980) conceivably may lead to support for aiding teachers in using instructional theories. There are numerous suggestions that efforts to improve *training in business and industry* may also lead to increased support for the development and use of instructional theory (Boutwell, 1979; Patton, 1980). But the influence that may prove to be most important is the emergence of *micro computers* as a major force in education. This deserves some exploration here.

Most readers are familiar with the fact that certain events historically have had unusual influences on our educational philosophies and methodologies. For example, the requirements for classifying military personnel during World War I is generally credited with expanding the range and quality of psychological and educational tests. The general societal concern with the negative effects of poverty, mainly being recognized in the decade of the 1960s, is generally acknowledged as having been a major influence in the improvement of our understanding about certain stages and facets of child development.

It is quite possible that, if it occurs, the emergence of widescale uses of micro computers in education may *greatly* stimulate the development and use of instructional theories and design strategies in the 1980s. For one practical reason—namely, the cost of developing educational materials for micro-computer use—it is plausible that educators will look to instructional theories and design strategies to produce effective educational courseware in a cost-effective manner. Moreover, the application of instructional theory, concepts, and principles is much more feasible with a computer-based system than with usual teacher-dominated classroom methods and techniques. Thus, computer-oriented educators can be expected to be more receptive to the use of instructional theory than has been true of many educators in the past. Finally, and perhaps most significantly, micro computers (and other kinds of computers) will quite possibly have some major impact on the views we have about education. Some (Salomon, 1979) conjecture that media capabilities influence cognitive processes. For example, Papert (1980) has emphasized that his computer language (LOGO) not only enables children and adults to interact with computers, but that it embodies revolutionary views about the fundamental nature of education. Others (e.g., Weinstein, 1981) have provided preliminary forms of what may well be some innovative instructional theories for the 1980s.

Thus, it seems that we can end this chapter with an optimistic note. Despite some limitations and frustrations both in producing and in using instructional theories, there are some sound reasons for hoping that continued improvements can be anticipated in the years ahead.

REFERENCES

Ball, S. Editorial. *Journal of Educational Psychology*, 1979, *71*, 1–2.

Beatty, W. H. Theories of instruction for what? A projection. In J. B. Macdonald & R. R. Leeper (Eds.), *Theories of instruction*. Washington, D.C.: Association for Supervision and Curriculum Development, 1965.

Bloom, B. S. (Ed.) *Taxonomy of educational objectives: The classification of educational goals. Handbook 1. Cognitive domain.* New York: McKay, 1956.

Boutwell, R. C. Instructional systems development in the next decade. *Journal of Instructional Development*, 1979, *2*, 31–35.

Bruner, J. S. *Toward a theory of instruction*. Cambridge, Mass.: Harvard University Press, 1966.

Crowder, N. A. Automatic tutoring by means of intrinsic programming. In E. H. Galanter (Ed.), *Automatic teaching: The state of the art*. New York: Wiley, 1959.

Gerlach, V. S. *Instructional design: Beyond objectives and assessment.* Paper presented at the Structural Learning Conference, Philadelphia, April 6, 1975.

Getzels, J. W. Educational psychology and teacher training. *Elementary School Journal*, 1952, *52*, 373–382.

Glaser, R. Components of a psychology of instruction: Toward a science of design. *Review of Educational Research*, 1976, *46*, 1–24.

Goldfried, M. R. Toward the delineation of therapeutic change principles. *American Psychologist*, 1980, *35*, 991–999.

Gordon, I. J. (Ed.). *Criteria for theories of instruction*. Washington, D.C.: Association for Supervision and Curiculum Development, 1968.

Hall, C. S., & Lindzey, G. *Theories of personality*. New York: Wiley, 1957.

Hilgard, E. R., & Bower, G. H. *Theories of learning* (4th ed.). Englewood Cliffs, N.J.: Prentice-Hall, 1975.

Jahoda, M. Work, employment, and unemployment: Values, theories, and approaches in social research. *American Psychologist*, 1981, *36*, 184–191.

Johnson, K. W. Stimulating evaluation use by integrating academia and practice. *Knowledge: Creation, Diffusion, Utilization*, 1980, *2*, 237–262.

Leinhardt, G. Modeling and measuring educational treatment in evaluation. *Review of Educational Research*, 1980, *50*, 393–420.

Macdonald, J. B., & Leeper, R. R. (Eds.). *Theories of instruction*. Washington, D.C.: Association for Supervision and Curriculum Development, 1965.

Mitchell, M. C., Jr. The practicality of algorithms in instructional development. *Journal of Instructional Development*, 1980, *4*, 10–16.

Newell, A., & Simon, H. A. *Human problem solving*. Englewood Cliffs, N.J.: Prentice-Hall, 1972.

Papert, S. *Mindstorms: Children, computers and powerful ideas*. New York: Basic Books, 1980.

Paterson, C. H. *Foundations for a theory of instruction and educational psychology*. New York: Harper & Row, 1977.

Patton, F. D. A third dimension: The future of educational technology in industry. *Journal of Instructional Development*, 1980, *3*, 25–27.

Phillips, D. C. What do the researcher and the practitioner have to offer each other? *Educational Researcher*, 1980, *9*, 17–20, 24.

Pressey, Sidney L. Development and appraisal of devices providing immediate automatic scoring of objective tests and concomitant self-instruction. *Journal of Psychology*, 1950, *29*, 417–447.

Reigeluth, C. M., & Merrill, M. D. A knowledge base for improving our methods of instruction. *Educational Psychologist*, 1978, *13*, , 57–70.

Reigeluth, C. M., & Merrill, M. D. Classes of instructional variables. *Educational Technology*, 1979, March, 5–24.

Salomon, G. *Interaction of media, cognition, and learning.* San Francisco: Jossey-Bass, 1979.

Simon, H. A. *The sciences of the artificial.* Cambridge, Mass.: MIT Press, 1969.

Smith, B. O. (Ed.). Pedagogical education: How about reform? (Special Section.) *Phi Delta Kappan,* October 1980, *62*(2).

Snelbecker, G. E. *Learning theory, instructional theory, and psychoeducational design.* New York: McGraw-Hill, 1974.

Snelbecker, G. E. *Introduction to educational psychology.* Book in preparation, 1983.

Weinstein, M. *LOGO's Logos—A theoretical framework for the understanding of Project LOGO work.* Unpublished manuscript, Temple University, 1981.

Concluding Remarks

There is a great need for a knowledge base to guide instructional developers and instructors (see Chapters 1 and 12). But this promising discipline is still far from being able to prescribe optimal methods for all goals and conditions. Given this situation, what is needed now?

The historical development of a discipline tends to follow a certain pattern. At its inception it is often devoted to *philosophical* concerns and orientations. These, in time, give way to *empirical* (data-based) investigations. But such observation and research tend to focus on gross, *general variables* such as discovery versus expository, lecture versus discussion, and inductive versus deductive methods. Researchers soon find that such general variables are not very useful because there is usually as much variation within each category as there is between categories. For example, two different expository methods often differ more than an expository method and a discovery method. This makes it impossible to make reliable prescriptions for the design of instruction. Hence, this phase gives way to an *analysis* phase, in which the gross variables are analyzed into relatively *elementary* components, and research is conducted on those components to identify some reliable principles (causes and effects).

The discipline of instruction has developed to about this point. In fact, the discipline has been characterized by the generation of much *piecemeal knowledge* within decidedly antagonistic camps (especially behaviorist and cognitivist) ever since the pioneering work of Skinner and Bruner (whose intellectual heritage can be traced to Thorndike and Dewey, respectively). In Chapter 2, George Gropper states:

> There is no collegial, or even competitive, building of a common knowledge base with individuals making incremental contributions to it. Instead there appear to be as many 'knowledge bases' as there are contributors to the discipline. If other disciplines

serve as a guide, this diversity does *not* argue for the maturity or sophistication of instructional theory (p. 38).

In addition, practitioners cannot easily use such piecemeal knowledge about
instruction, and it has become evident that the next phase, a *synthesis* phase, is very
much needed. Individual strategy components need to be integrated into *models* of
instruction, each of which is intended to optimize learning for a different kind of
situation, such as different goals and different conditions. And individual models
need to be integrated into a comprehensive *theory* of instruction, which in essence
is a coordinated set of criteria for prescribing which model to use when.

Different instructional theories and different theoretical perspectives should not
be thought of as competing with one another. There is some truth in all theoretical
perspectives. Each theory (or "knowledge base") provides a partial understanding
of the real world of instruction in much the same way that each window in an
unknown house provides a partial understanding of what the inside of the house is
like and therefore how to move around in that room. Some theories look at the
same room through different windows (i.e., from different theoretical perspectives),
while others look at completely different rooms (i.e., different types of objectives—
such as teaching students how to discover natural laws versus teaching them how to
apply the second law of thermodynamics). One of our greatest needs at present is
for instructional scientists to recognize that there are *different rooms* in the house
and that it is helpful, if not essential, that we look through *more than one window*
of each room in order to get a complete picture of what each room is like. Only in
this way can we proceed to build a common knowledge base for prescribing the
best way to get anywhere within the house.

Hence, of priority for all instructional scientists should be: (1) to talk in terms of
describing *individual rooms* instead of claiming to be describing the whole house;
(2) to clearly identify *which room* is being described; and (3) to use *all windows* in a
room so as to arrive at the best possible description of that room. Another of our
greatest needs is (4) to attempt to *integrate the descriptions* of the individual rooms
into a description of the whole house so that we will know how to get to more than
one "room" in the same course of instruction. It should be apparent from the
preceding chapters that the instructional theories and models described in this
book do not compete with one another. On the contrary, they complement each
other to the extent that they prescribe models for different goals and conditions,
and they overlap and thereby support each other to the extent that they prescribe
the same strategy components within models that are intended for the same goals
and conditions.

One purpose of this book is to encourage individuals in the discipline to think in
terms of contributing to a "collegial, or even competitive, building of a *common*
knowledge base" by doing the four activities mentioned above. Another purpose is
to encourage foundations and government agencies to devote more resources to
projects that contribute directly to a *common* knowledge base in *instruction.* Such

activities could include: synthesizing our existing knowledge into comprehensive models and theories of instruction; they could include extending that knowledge base where gaps are found; and they could include doing additional piecemeal work within the theoretical framework of the common knowledge base. At a time when short-term payoff is a top priority to funders, support for such integrative work holds great promise.

C. M. R.

Author Index

A

Abelson, R. P., 260, *277*
Abramson, L. Y., 417, *430*
Adams, J. S., 396, 422, *430*
Aiello, N., 252, 260, *277*
Alderman, D. L., 388, *430*
Alogic, S., 241, *243*
Alon, I., 426, *432*
Alschuler, A. S., 409, 413, *430*
Amitai, A., 425, 426, *432*
Anderson, J. R., 224, 229, *243*
Anderson, M. C., 28, *33,* 374, *379*
Anderson, R. C., 28, *33, 34,* 250, *277,*
   322, *333,* 339, 374, 375, *379*
Arbib, M. A., 241, *243*
Arter, J., 360, *380*
Atkinson, J. W., 406, 407, 408, *430, 432*
Atkinson, R. C., 28, 29, *34*
Ausubel, D. P., 27, *34,* 339, 343, 358, 359,
   373, *379,* 387, 390, 393, 404, 419, *430*

B

Baker, E. L., 30, *35,* 56, *69*
Ball, J. R., 30, *36*
Ball, S., 444, 448, *471*
Bandura, A., 394, 416, 417, *430*
Barkhudarov, L., 181, *209*

Bates, J. A., 395, 422, 423, 424, 425, 426,
   430
Beatty, W. H., 445, 452, *471*
Beauchamp, G. A., 6, *34*
Beilin, H., 204, *209*
Belopol'skaya, A. R., 208, 209, *210*
Bergan, J. R., 339, *379*
Berlyne, D. E., 394, 399, 400, *430*
Block, J. H. 29, *34*
Bloom, B. S., 5, 32, *34,* 49, *52,* 56, *68,*
   173, *209,* 332, 387, *430,* 458, *471*
Bobrow, D. G., 224, *243,* 375, 376, *380*
Boutwell, R. C., 224, 226, *244,* 284, 285,
   298, *333,* 470, *471*
Bower, G. H., 393, *431,* 454, *471*
Brainerd, C. J., 245
Brecke, F., 208, *209*
Breen, M., 257, 268, 270, *277*
Briggs, L. J., 49, *52,* 79, 80, 83, 86, 87, 88,
   89, 90, 91, 92, 93, 96, 97, *100,* 290, *332*
Brophy, J., 428, *430*
Brown, J. S., 33, *34,* 251, *277, 278*
Bruner, J. S., 27, *34,* 317, *332,* 339, 341, 343,
   361, 378, *379,* 445, 446, 460, 468, *471*
Bunderson, C. V., 21, 29, *34, 35,* 296, *333,*
   348, *381*
Bung, K., 55, *68,* 182, 208, *209*
Burnham, D. H., 410, 411, *432*
Burns, K., 208, *210, 245*

Burton, R. R., 33, *34,* 251, *277*
Bussman, H., 55, *68,* 208, *209*

C

Calder, B. J., 426, *430*
Carplay, J. A., 208, *209*
Carroll, J. B., 386, *430*
Carlsmith, J. M., 423, *431*
Chapin, M., 417, *430*
Chase, W. G., 251, *277*
Clark, R. W., 406, 408, *432*
Clauss, G., 208, *209*
Coldeway, N. S., 330, *333*
Cole, R., 360, *381*
Collins, A. M., 224, *243,* 250, 251, 252, 257, 259, 260, 262, 263, 264, 265, 266, 267, 270, 274, 275, *278,* 339, *379*
Condry, J., 393, 395, 422, 423, 425, 426, *430*
Cooley, W. W., 10, 11, *34,* 387, 388, 389, *430*
Cooper, H. M., 428, *430*
Coscarelli, W., 208, *209*
Couffignal, L., 55, *68*
Courseware, Inc., 330, *332*
Craik, F. I. M., 375, *379, 380*
Cronbach, L. J., 9, 15, 30, 31, *34,* 224, *243,* 386, 388, 391, 405, *430*
Crowder, N. A., 29, *34,* 445, *471*
Cube, F., 55, *68*

D

Dale, E. A., 96, *100*
Darwazeh, A. N., 370, 372, *381*
Davies, I. K., 29, *34, 35,* 343, *380*
Davis, R. B., 250, 261, *277*
deCharms, R., 5, *34,* 409, 416, 417, 418, 421, *430*
Deci, E. L., 393, 395, 422, 423, 426, *430*
Dewey, J., 5, *34*
Dickerson, R., *209*
Dodge, B., 389, 390, *432*
Dodson, J. D., 400, *434*
Doyle, K. D., Jr., 390, *432*
Drabman, R., 425, *433*
Dreistadt, R., 360, *380*
Dunlop, D., 55, *69*
Durnin, J. H., 208, *210,* 232, 233, 237, *243, 245*
Dweck, C. S., 417, 421, *430, 431*
Dyck, G., 417, *430*

E

Edwards, A. L., 408, *431*
Edwards, K., 208, *209*
Ephrenpreis, 208, *210,* 231, 233, 239, *243, 245*
Ellis, J. A., 303, 306, 330, *332*
Ely, D. P., 29, *34*
Estes, W. K., 227, *243,* 375, *380*
Evans, J. L., 28, *34,* 285, 310, 317, *332*

F

Fasnacht, G., 425, *432*
Faust, G. W., 9, *35,* 250, *277,* 285, 330, *333, 380*
Feather, N. T., 394, 419, 420, *431*
Feigenbaum, E. A., 58, *68*
Feldman, J., 58, *68*
Festinger, L., 423, *431*
Feurzeig, W., 257, 268, 270, *277*
Fibel, B., 419, *431*
Fisk, M., 183, *209*
Fleming, M., 27, *34*
Flesch, R., 402, *431*
Foote, T., 415, *431*
Frank, H., 55, *68*
Frase, L., 225, *245*
Frayer, D. A., 29, *35*

G

Gagne, E., 359, *380*
Gagne, R. M., 14, 23, *34,* 49, *52,* 56, *68, 69,* 79, 80, 83, 84, 86, 87, 88, 89, 90, 91, 92, 94, 95, 96, 97, *100,* 106, *161,* 173, 203, *209,* 224, 225, 226, 231, 242, *243, 245,* 284, 285, 286, 290, 297, 301, 311, *332,* 338, 341, 356, 361, 378, *380,* 387, 391, 424, *431*
Gentilhomme, I., 208, *209*
Gerlach, V. S., 29, *34,* 208, *209,* 226, 468, *471*
Getzels, J. W., 443, *471*
Ghatala, E. S., 29, *35*
Gilbert, T. F., 29, *34,* 49, *53,* 106, 140, *161*
Glaser, R., 14, 21, 28, *34, 35,* 224, *243, 244,* 285, 310, 317, *332,* 455, *471*
Goetz, T. E., 417, *431*
Goldfried, M. R., 451, *471*
Goldin, S., 251, *278*
Goldman, J. A., 417, *431*

Good, T., 428, *430*
Gordon, I. J., 24, 28, *34,* 446, 457, *471*
Gordon, W. J., 403, *431*
Grant, W. V., 5, *35*
Greene, D., 426, *431, 432*
Groen, G. J., 225, *245*
Gropper, G. L., 40, 48, 49, *53,* 106, 111, 123, 124, 140, *161,* 339, *380*
Gunter, K., 208, *209*
Gustafson, K., 8, *35*

H

Hale, W. D., 419, *431*
Hall, C. S., 451, *471*
Harlow, H. F., 423, *431*
Hartley, J., 29, *35,* 343, *380*
Haskell, R. E., 233, 241, *243*
Hebb, D. O., 24, *35*
Hilgard, E. R., 393, *431,* 454, *471*
Hiroto, D. S., *431*
Hively, W., II, 224, *243*
Homme, L. E., 28, *34,* 285, 310, 317, *332*
Horabin, I., 208, *209*
Horn, R. E., 29, *35*
Hull, C. L., 394, 406, *431*
Hunt, D. E., 391, *431*

J

Jacobson, L., 416, *433*
Jahoda, M., 449, *471*
Johnson, K. W., 451, *471*
Johnston, J. E., 388, *431*
Jones, R. A., 394, 416, 421, *431*
Joyce, B., 403, 404, 405, 421, *431, 433*

K

Kachalova, K., 181, *209*
Kaplan, A., 393, *431*
Kazdin, A. E., 425, *431*
Keislar, E., 179, *210*
Kelbert, H., 208, *209*
Kelety, J. C., 373, *380*
Keller, B. H., 390, *431*
Keller, J. M., 389, 390, 391, 393, 395, 396, 400, 405, 412, 417, 429, *431, 432*
Kelly, E. A., 389, 390, *432*
Kintsch, W., 224, *243,* 375, *380*
Klahr, D., 241, *243*

Klausmeier, H. J., 29, *35*
Klix, F., 208, *209*
Kluwin, B., 403, 405, 421, *433*
Knochel, W., 55, *68*
Kopstein, F. F., 55, 56, *68,* 208, *209*
Korelyakov, Ju. 208, *209*
Kowallis, T., 27, 30, *35,* 285, *333*
Kranzberg, M., 393, *432*
Kruglanski, A. W., 425, 426, *432*
Kuhn, T. S., 423, *432*
Kulhavy, R. W., 29, *35*

L

Lakein, A., 418, *432*
Landa, L. N., 55, 56, 57, 58, *68,* 172, 173, 176, 177, 178, 179, 182, 186, 196, 202, 205, 206, 207, 208, *209, 210,* 224, *243,* 339, *380*
Lansky, M., 208, *210*
Larkin, J., 251, *277*
Lawler, E. E., 391, 417, *433*
Lee, F., *245*
Leeper, R. R., 446, *471*
Lefcourt, H. M., 416, 420, *432*
Leinhardt, G., 11, *34,* 447, *471*
Lepper, M. R., 426, *431, 432*
Levie, W. M., 27, *34*
Levine, F. M., 425, *432*
Lewin, K., 391, 406, *432*
Lewis, B. N., 55, *68,* 208, *209, 210*
Lewis, T., 426, *432*
Lind, C. G., 5, *35*
Lindsay, P. H., *244,* 339, *380*
Lindzey, G., 451, *471*
LNR Research Group, 359, *380*
Lockhart, R. S., 375, *379*
Lohnes, P. R., 10, *34,* 387, 388, 389, *430*
Lowell, E. L., 406, 408, *432*
Lowerre, G., 217, *244*
Luger, G., 208, *210,* 233, *245*
Lumsdaine, A., 28, *35*
Lynch, M. D., 5, *35*

M

Macdonald, J. B., 446, *471*
Maehr, M. L., 391, *432*
Mager, R. F., 56, *68,* 173, *210,* 289, *332*
Mahler, W. A., 388, *430*
Malir, F., 208, *210*
Margolin, B., 425, 426, *432*

Markle, S. M., 29, *35,* 56, *68,* 135, 187, *210,* 230, 261, 324, 325, *332,* 390, 419, 424, *432*
Maslow, A. H., 394, 407, 408, 413, *432*
Maw, E. W., 399, *432*
Maw, W. H., 399, *432*
May, M. A., 91, *100*
Mayer, R. E., 137, 373, 374, *380,* 390, *432*
McClelland, D. C., 394, 406, 408, 410, 411, *432*
McConnell, J. V., 402, 415, *432*
McGaghie, W., 29, *35*
Mechner, F., 49, *53,* 106, *161*
Menges, R., 29, *35*
Menschel, H., 208, *210*
Merrill, M. D., 9, 14, 18, 21, 27, 30, 33, *35,* 49, *53,* 56, *68,* 224, 226, *244,* 283, 284, 285, 286, 296, 297, 298, 300, 303, 306, 328, 330, *332, 333,* 348, 358, 362, 363, 370, 372, 373, *380, 381,* 387, 391, 397, *432, 433,* 455, *471*
Merrill, P. F., 173, *210,* 221, 224, 226, *244,* 339, 373, 377, *380*
Merton, R. K., 416, *432*
Meyer, G., 55, *68*
Mietus, N., 183, *209*
Miller, A., *277*
Miller, G. A., *380*
Miller, M. L., 252, 260, *277*
Minsky, M. L., 224, 226, 229, 241, *244*
Mischel, W., 389, *432*
Mitchell, M. C., Jr., *210,* 465, *471*
Moen, R., 390, *432*
Montague, W. E., 28, *34,* 339, 374, 375, *379*
Montessori, M., 28, *35*
Monty, R. A., 394, *433*
Munter, P., 257, 268, 270, *277*
Murphy, F., 417, 421, *432*
Murray, H. A., 394, 406, 408, *433*

N

Neumann, J., 208, *209*
Newell, A., 173, *210,* 226, 229, 241, *244,* 251, *277,* 454, 461, *471*
Nisbett, R. E., 426, *432*
Norman, D. A., *244,* 339, 343, 359, 374, 375, 376, 378, *380*
Novak, J., 29, *35*

O

O'Leary, K. D., 425, *433*
Olsen, J. B., 330, *333*

Olson, D. R., 29, *35*
O'Neal, A. F., 330, *333*
O'Neal, H. L., 330, *333*
Ortony, A., 339, 360, 377, *380, 381*

P

Page, S., 224, *243*
Paivio, A., 377, *380*
Papert, S., 224, 229, *244,* 470, *471*
Pascual-Leone, J., *244*
Pask, G., 29, *35,* 55, *68, 69,* 224, *244*
Passafiume, J. J., 251, 275, *277*
Paterson, C. H., 443, 454, *471*
Patterson, H. L., 224, *243*
Patton, F. D., 470, *471*
Perlmuter, L. C., 394, *433*
Pescocin, A., 208, *210*
Phares, E. J., 416, 420, *433*
Phillips, D. C. 450, *471*
Plato, 257, 270, 271, *277*
Pohl, L., 208, *210*
Popham, W. J., 30, *35,* 56, *69,* 294, *333*
Porac, J., 422, *430*
Porter, L. W., 391, 394, 417, *433*
Portnoy, R. C., 208, *210, 245*
Pratt, D., 346, *380*
Pressey, S. L., 445, *471*

Q, R

Quillian, M. R., 229, *244,* 339, 359, 374, 375, *379, 381*
Raven, R. J., 360, *381*
Raynor, J. O., 407, 408, 414, *430, 433*
Reigeluth, C. M., 9, 14, 18, 21, 33, *35,* 203, *210,* 283, 285, 296, *333,* 344, 346, 348, 358, 363, 370, 372, *380, 381,* 387, 391, 397, *433,* 455, *471*
Reiser, R., 208, *209*
Reitman, W., 173, *210*
Resnick, L. B., 30, *36,* 56, *69,* 224, *243, 244,* 339, 373, *381*
Reynolds, R. E., 360, *380*
Richards, R. E., 285, 303, 306, 330, *333, 380*
Rigney, J. W., 203, *210,* 329, *333,* 361, *381*
Ringer, R. J., 418, *433*
Riter, A., 425, 426, *432*
Robin, A. L., 32, *36*
Rodgers, C. A., 370, 372, *381*
Rogers, C. R., 394, 407, 413, 421, *433*
Rogers, H. J., 242, *244*

Rokeach, M., 394, *433*
Rosenthal, R., 416, *433*
Ross, M., 426, *433*
Rothen, W., 224, *246*
Rothkopf, E. Z., 224, *244*
Rotter, J. B., 391, 394, 416, 418, 419, 420, *433*
Rudestam, K. E., 418, *433*
Rumelhart, D. E., *244,* 339, 359, 374, 375, *380, 381*

S

Salomon, G., 470, *472*
Sari, I. F., 9, *35,* 370, 372, *381*
Sassenrath, J. M., 322, *333*
Saunders, R., 250, *277*
Saville, M. R., 419, *431*
Scandura, A. M., 217, 227, 231, 233, *244*
Scandura, J. M., 32, *36,* 56, *69,* 173, 208, *210,* 217, 218, 221, 222, 223, 224, 225, 226, 227, 229, 230, 231, 232, 233, 237, 238, 239, 240, *243, 244, 245, 246,* 296, *333,* 339, *381*
Schmid, R. F., 208, *210,* 226, *245*
Schmidt, R. V., 285, 303, 306, 330, *333, 380*
Schutz, R. E., 32, *36*
Seeber, A., 208, *209*
Seligman, M. E. P., 394, 416, 417, *430, 431, 433*
Shabtai, L., 425, 426, *432*
Shulman, L., 179, *210*
Sigel, I. E., 250, *277*
Simon, D. P., 251, *277*
Simon, H. A., 15, 21, *36,* 173, *211,* 226, 229, 241, *244,* 251, *277,* 445, 454, 461, *471, 472*
Singer, D. G., 401, *433*
Singer, J., 401, *433*
Skinner, B. F., 27, *36,* 106, *161,* 387, 390, *433*
Smith, B. O., 470, *472*
Smith, K., 55, *69*
Smith, M., 55, *69*
Snelbecker, G. E., 6, 14, 21, 24, 27, 28, *36,* 173, *211,* 443, 454, 455, 457, 461, *472*
Snow, R. E., 14, 15, 24, 30, 32, *34, 36,* 224, *243,* 386, 388, 391, 394, *430, 433*
Solomij, K., 208, *211*
Spiller, R. T., 348, 370, 372, *381*
Spiro, R. J., 28, *33, 34,* 339, 374, 375, *379*
Staw, B. M., 426, *430*
Steers, R. M., 394, *433*
Steling, D., 181, *209*
Stevens, A. L., 251, 252, 257, 259, 260, 262,

264, 265, 267, 270, 274, 275, *278*
Stolurow, L. M., 55, *69,* 187, *211,* 225, *245*
Strom, R. D., 416, *433*
Suchman, J. R., 405, *433*
Sullivan, E. V., 391, *431*
Suppes, P., 30, *36,* 231, *246,* 405, *430*
Surber, J. R., 322, *333*
Sutterer, J. R., 417, *431*
Swets, J., 257, 268, 270, *277*
Sydow, H., 208, *209*

T

Teasdale, J. D., 417, *430*
Tennyson, R. D., 56, *68,* 224, *246,* 330, *333*
Tiemann, P. W., 29, *35,* 135, 230, 261, 325, *332*
Toffler, A., 5, *36*
Tolman, E. C., 406, *433*
Tosti, D. T., 30, *36,* 424, 427, *433*
Tracz, G., 55, *69*
Travers, R. M. W., 423, *433*
Tulodziecki, G., 208, *211*
Tulving, E., 375, *380*
Tyler, R. W., 5, *36*

V,W

VanLehn, K., 251, *278*
Vermersch, P., 208, *211*
Vidler, D. R., 403, *433*
Volynskaya, Z., 208, *211*
Voohries, D., *246*
Wager, W. W., 97, *100*
Walberg, H. J., 386, 388, 389, *433*
Warnock, E. H., 251, 252, 260, 275, *277*
Weil, M., 403, 404, 405, 421, *431, 433*
Weiner, B., 389, 394, 416, 417, *434*
Weinstein, M., 470, *472*
Weiser, G., 208, *211*
White, R. T., 56, *69,* 301, *332,* 373, *381*
White, R. W., 416, 417, *434*
Wilson, B. G., 27, 30, *35,* 285, *333,* 348, 370, 372, 373, *380, 381*
Wilson, H. A., 28, *34*
Winston, P., 261, *278*
Winter, D. F., 411, *434*
Wood, N. D., 285, 298, 300, 303, 306, 330, *333, 380*
Woodard, E., *245*
Wulfeck, W. H., II, 233, 237, 238, *245, 246,* 303, 306, 330, *332*

Y,Z

Yerkes, R. M., 400, *434*
Yudina, O., 208, *211*

Zaksh, D., 425, 426, *432*
Zierer, E., 208, *211*
Zock, M., 208, *211*
Zuckerman, M., 401, 403, *433, 434*

Subject Index

A

Abstract-concrete, 135, 274, 346
Adequacy of instruction, 320–327
Advance organizer, 404, 419
Algorithm, 57, 175, 178, 182, 203, 218
    general vs. particular, 203
    learning vs. performance vs. teaching, 178
Analogy, 232, 360–361, 364, 377, 403
Anecdote, 402
Assimilation (*see also* Subsumption)
Association, 107–108, 122
ATI (Aptitude-treatment interaction), 15, 31–32
Atomic component, 222 (*see also* Elementary operation)
Attitude, 83
Attribution theory, 416–417

B,C

Backward chaining (*see also* Sequencing strategy)
Causal structure, 251
Causation, 417
    personal, 417–418
Chains, 109, 196
Classification scheme, 12–13 (*see also* Concept)

Cognitive processes, 218
Cognitive processing, conscious, 328–329
Cognitive strategy, 83, 257, 405
Cognitive-strategy activator, 361–362, 365
Common knowledge base, 473–474
Concept, 12–13, 150, 167, 287–289, 296
    concrete, 84
    defined, 84
Conditions
    of instruction, 14–15, 20, 39, 43, 45, 49–50, 58, 112, 397
    of learning (*see* Learning)
Constituent skills, 125
Content categories, 287–289
Content-PPF consistency, 313–320
Context, 308
Control mechanism, 238–239
Control structure, 274
Cooperation, 412–413
Counterexample (*see* nonexample)
Criterion mode (*see* Response)
Cues, 110, 128–131, 266, 294
    interval of, 130
    number of attributes, 130
    shaping (*see* Instructional strategy)
    similarity with responses, 129
    strength, 128–131
Curiosity, 394, 399–401
Cybernetics, 56

D

Delivery strategies (*see* Methods of instruction)
Dependent variable, 252, 254–255
Design science, 15
Difficulty
   level of, 43–44, 115
   range of, 326–327
Discovery, 178–179, 195–196, 204, 258–259, 265
Discrimination, 84, 107
Divergence (*see* Instance divergence)

E

Effort, 391
Elaboration sequence (*see* Sequencing strategy)
Elaborations, 346–351, 365–366
   levels of, 346–351
Entrapment strategy, 269
Entry level, 88, 240
Epitome, 343, 346, 364, 367
   expanded epitome, 365, 367
Equivalence class, 230, 240
Events (*see* Instructional events)
Example, 191, 260, 316
Exemplar (*see* Example)
Expectancy, 395, 415–422
   concept of, 415–417
   conditions and strategies, 418–422
Expectancy-value theory, 394
Explanation (*see* Principle)
Expository, 194

F

Factor, 206, 252, 254–255
   abstract, 274
   concrete, 274
   necessary, 252–253
   irrelevant, 253
   sufficient, 252–253
Fact, 148, 287–289 (*see also* Verbal information)
Fading, 111
Feedback, 92, 264, 269, 309, 322, 409, 420–421, 426–427

G

Generality, 190–191, 305, 313–315
Generalization, 108
Goal (*see* Outcome)

H

Help, 308, 323–324
   attention-focusing, 323
   prerequisite, 323
   prompting, 324
   representation form, 323–324
Heuristic, 57, 175
Higher-order rules, 84, 231–232
   analogy rules, 232
   composition rules, 232
Hypothetical case, 264

I

Image, 167
Incrementing, 110
Independent variable (*see* Factor)
Individual differences, 123
Individual operations, 202
Influence, 411
Inquiry (*see* Methods of instruction)
Instance divergence, 261–262, 270, 295, 325
Instance, 305, 315–317
Instructional design, 7
Instructional-design theory (*see* Theory of instruction)
Instructional-development procedure, 62 (*see also* Model)
Instructional events, 89–96, 99
Instructional processes, 56, 58, 186
Instructional programs, 61, 63
Instructional psychology, 447–449
Instructional strategy (*see* Methods of instruction)
Instructional theory (*see* Theory of instruction)
Intellectual skills, 84, 86–87
Interest, 91, 395, 398–406
   concept of, 398–400
   conditions and strategies, 400–406
Instrinsic motivation (*see* reinforcement)
Isolation, 325

K

Knowledge base, 38
Knowledge producers, 440–441
Knowledge use, 449
Knowledge users, 440, 441–442

L

Learned helplessness, 394, 417, 421
Learner characteristics (*see* Student characeristics)
Learner control, 33, 327–328, 332, 362–363, 369–370
Learning
  conditions of, 82, 98
  domains of, 81
  hierarchy, 86–88, 99, 339, 356
  prerequisites, 85–91, 98, 364 (*see also* Contingent progressions)
  programs, 63
  theory (*see* Theory of learning)
Linking science, 5 (*see also* Instructional design and Instructional theory)
Locus of control, 394, 416, 418, 420

M

Macro strategy (*see* Instructional methods, organizational)
Management strategy (*see* Methods of instruction)
Matching (*see* nonexample)
Media, 93, 96, 99
Metaprogram, 62
Metatheory (*see* Theoretical framework)
Methods of instruction, 13–15, 18, 39, 43–44, 58, 128, 144–155, 186, 342–364, 397
  delivery strategies, 18–19, 284
  inquiry, 249–276, 405
  management strategies, 18–19, 284
  organizational strategies, 18–19, 283
    macro, 19, 284, 338
    micro, 19, 283, 363
  routine treatment, 144, 146
  shaping progression, 110, 128, 146
  specialized treatment, 147
  strategy component, 13
Micro strategy (*see* Instructional methods, organizational)

M

Model, 21
  instructional development, 21, 24
  instructional, 21, 48–50, 111, 187
Motivational strategy, 364, 385–430
Motor skill, 83
Multiple objectives, 155 (*see also* Macro strategy)

N

Near hits, 261
Near misses, 261
Needs, personal, 394
  for affiliation, 407, 412
  for achievement, 406–407, 408, 410
  for power, 407, 410–411
Nonalgorithmic, 58
Nonexamples, 260–261, 263, 325–326 (*see also* Practice, content)

O

Operations, 168, 171
  cognitive, 171
  demonstrations of, 191–194 (*see also* Example)
  elementary, 172–174, 185, 222, 230
  motor, 171
  prescriptions of, 191–194 (*see also* Generality)
  systems of, 176
Organization, 352
  conceptual, 355, 368, 370
  procedural, 352, 368, 370
  theoretical, 355, 368, 370
Organizational strategies (*see* Methods of instruction)
Organizing content, 344, 364
Outcomes of instruction, 15, 20, 58, 257–259, 285, 397, 422–429
  concept of, 422–424
  conditions and strategies, 424–429
  extrinsic, 422
  instrinsic, 422

P

Paradigm (*see* Theoretical framework)
Path analysis, 221, 230, 240, 373

Performance categories, 287
  find, 287–289, 304
  remember, 287–289, 302–303
  use, 287–289, 303–304
Performance-content matrix, 285–289
Performance-PPF consistency, 311–313
Personal needs, 406
Practice, 92, 137–143, 317–320
  content of, 138
    altered sequences, 140
    distortions, 139
    errors, 139, 271 (*see also* Nonexamples)
    noncriterion behaviors, 140
    cumulative series of, 143
    frequency of, 141
    transitions between, 142
    varied practice examples, 137
Prerequisite (*see* Learning prerequisite)
Presentation forms, 305–311
  primary, 305–307, 331
  secondary, 307–310, 320–325, 331
Principle, 12, 14, 16, 18, 151, 288–289
  causal, 17
  correlational, 16
  descriptive, 21–22, 351
  prescriptive, 21–22, 351
Problem domain, 227–229
Problem solving, 154
Procedural display, 310–311
Procedures, 152, 287–289
Process display, 310
Progressions
  contingent, 156–157
  learning contingencies, 157
  performance contingencies, 157
  preparatory, 125–143
Prompts (*see* cues)
Proposition, 167, 189
  empirical, 189
Pygmalian effect, 416

R

Reinforcement, 395, 423–424
  extrinsic, 423
  intrinsic, 423–424, 426
Relationships, 156–157
  horizontal, 156
  no relationship, 157
  vertical, 156

Relevance, 395, 406–415
  concept of, 406–407
  conditions and strategies, 407–415
Representation form, 309, 316
Requirements
  for learning, 39, 43, 48–49, 112, 114
  performance, 123
    recall, 123
    transfer, 123
  post-instructional, 126
Response,
  dissimilarity, 117–118
  mode, 134
    criterion, 125, 134
  number of, 120
  number of properties, 119
  properties, 116
  similarity, 117–118
Review, systematic, 92, 95, 366
Risk, 408, 412
Risk-taking, 400
Rule, 84, 187–188, 218, 229–231, 252 (*see also* algorithm)
  descriptive, 187
  higher-order, 84, 231–232, 238–239
    analogy, 232
    composition, 232
  permissive, 188
  prescriptive, 188
  procedural, 152
  solution, 238

S

Satisfaction, 395
Scoring, 409, 413
Selection strategy, 87, 274
Sequencing strategy, 88–89, 158, 198, 274–275, 341, 352–356, 364
  abstract-to-concrete, 346
  backward chaining, 158
  epitomizing, 343, 352–356
  elaborative, 343–356
  general-to-detailed, 344, 376
  integral approach, 87–88, 157, 197
  learning-prerequisite, 356, 378 (*see also* Contingent progressions)
  performance-contingent, 157
  simple-to-complex, 341, 343, 346, 354
  snowball method, 198

spiral curriculum, 378
step-by-step approach, 197
Shaping (*see* Methods of instruction)
Snowball method (*see* Sequencing strategy)
Spiral curriculum (*see* Sequencing strategy)
S-R (stimulus-response) association (*see* Association)
Standards, 408–409
Step-by-step approach (*see* Sequencing strategy)
Stimulus, 110
  control, 107
  criterion, 110
  dissimilarity, 115–117
  mode, 135
  number of, 120
  number of properties, 119
  properties, 116
  similarity, 115–117
Structural analysis (*see* Task analysis)
Structures, 348
  cognitive, 373–375
  conceptual, 348
  knowledge, 348
  learning, 356
  memory, 375–376
  procedural, 350
  supporting, 369
  theoretical, 350
Student characteristics, 15, 96, 123–124
Subsumption, 374, 376
Summarizer, 358, 365
Supporting content, 344, 364
Synectics, 403
Synthesizer, 358–360, 365
Systematic review, 366

T

Task analysis, 86, 99, 156–157, 176–177, 196, 218–221, 232–237
Taxonomy, 48–49, 144, 296, 300
Test items, 291–296
Theoretical framework, 14–20, 32, 39–50, 58, 62, 186–189, 391–395, 455
  parameters for, 43
Theory of instruction, 14, 21–23, 48–52, 59, 62–63, 189, 216, 251, 444–448, 452, 474
  construction, 30–31, 62, 65–66
  criteria for evaluationg, 24–25
  descriptive, 21–23, 51, 59, 251, 452
  history of, 27–30, 442
  prescriptive, 21–23, 52, 60, 216, 251, 452
Theory of learning, 23, 50, 62, 81
  descriptive, 63, 65
  prescriptive, 63, 65
Treatment (*see* Methods of instruction)
Trust, 412
Unit of behavior, 131–133
  amount of, 132
  integrity of, 133
  size of, 131
  standards for, 133

V,W,Z

Value, 408
  cultural, 408, 414
  instrumental, 408, 414
  personal-motive, 408
Varying cases (*see* Instance divergence)
Verbal information, 83
Web-learning, 378
Zoom lens, 340